"Half Brother, Half Son"

The Letters of Louis D. Brandeis
to Felix Frankfurter

"Half Brother, Half Son"

The Letters of Louis D. Brandeis to Felix Frankfurter

edited by Melvin I. Urofsky and
David W. Levy

University of Oklahoma Press : Norman and London

Also by Melvin I. Urofsky and David W. Levy

(eds.) *Letters of Louis D. Brandeis,* vols. 1–5 (Albany, 1971–1978)

Also by Melvin I. Urofsky

Big Steel and the Wilson Administration: A Study in Business-Government Relations
 (Columbus, Ohio, 1969)
(ed.) *Why Teachers Strike: Teachers' Rights and Community Control*
 (New York, 1970)
A Mind of One Piece: Brandeis and American Reform (New York, 1971)
(ed.) *Perspectives on Urban America* (New York, 1973)
Louis D. Brandeis and the Progressive Tradition (Boston, 1980)
Two Hundred Years of Mr. Jefferson's Idea: Religious Liberty in America (Richmond,
 Virginia, 1986)
The Supreme Court, the Bill of Rights, and the Law (Charlottesville, Virginia, 1986)
(ed., with Philip E. Urofsky) *The Douglas Papers: From the Private Files of Justice William
 O. Douglas* (Washington, D.C., 1987)
A March of Liberty: A Constitutional History of the United States (New York, 1987)
From Confederation to Constitution: Documents on the Constitution and Ratification
 (Richmond, Virginia, 1988)
Documents of American Constitutional and Legal History (New York, 1989)

Also by David W. Levy

Herbert Croly of the New Republic (Princeton, 1985)
The Debate Over Vietnam (Baltimore, 1991)

Publication of this book has been made possible in part by a grant from the National
Historical Publications and Records Commission.

Library of Congress Cataloging-in-Publication Data

Brandeis, Louis Dembitz, 1856–1941.
 "Half brother, half son" : the letters of Louis D. Brandeis to Felix Frankfurter /
 edited by Melvin I. Urofsky and David W. Levy. — 1st ed.
  p. cm.
 Includes index.
 ISBN 0-8061-2303-6 (alk. paper)
 1. Brandeis, Louis Dembitz, 1856–1941—Correspondence. 2. Frankfurter,
Felix, 1882–1965—Correspondence. 3. Judges—United States—Correspondence. I. Frankfurter, Felix, 1882–1965. II. Urofsky, Melvin I. III. Levy,
David W., 1937– .
KF8745.B67A44 1991
347.73'14'092—dc20
[347.3071 4092]   90-49279
                                                                            CIP

The paper in this book meets the guidelines for permanence and durability of the
Committee on Production Guidelines for Book Longevity of the Council on Library
Resources, Inc.∞

For Eric S. and the late Mary K. Tachau
who, in their lives and deeds,
have carried out Uncle Louis's prescription
that citizenship is the noblest profession.
In admiration, friendship, and affection

Contents

"Half Brother, Half Son"

The Letters of Louis D. Brandeis
to Felix Frankfurter

Introduction

This book contains 671 letters written by Louis D. Brandeis to Felix Frankfurter. They stretch from the first extant letter of 1910 until the last one written five weeks before Justice Brandeis's death in 1941. Of these letters, 232 have been published before, in our five-volume edition of the *Letters of Louis D. Brandeis*.[1] The great bulk of those being printed here for the first time, including virtually all of those written after 1 January 1930, were not available to us at the time of our earlier work. They had been separated out of the Frankfurter collection in the Library of Congress, and were not deposited until after the fifth volume had been published.

If these "new" letters *had* been available, we would, of course, have included them, and they would have appeared interspersed among the letters Brandeis wrote to dozens of other correspondents. That arrangement would have enjoyed certain obvious advantages, the principal one being that readers would have encountered these letters to Frankfurter within the context of Brandeis's other concerns at the moment. It would certainly have been useful to have been able to compare what he told Frankfurter with his comments to others, and to have seen how one set of his preoccupations meshed with others. Presenting the letters that way undoubtedly would have been our preference had it been possible to do so.

And yet, there is considerable (if accidental) merit in having all of the letters to Frankfurter appear together in a single volume. They form their own "context" of steadily advancing trust, confidence, and friendship, as well as steadily decreasing restraint and inhibition. Brandeis had numerous friends; with many of them he shared a wide range of social ideals, and with a few, a special intimacy. Yet outside of his family, he had no relationship quite like this one, particularly during the years when their friendship was at its height, from 1920 to 1935. Brandeis shared with Frankfurter his judgments on politicians, law, legislative programs, his brethren on the Supreme Court, mutual friends, judicial decisions, and the general state of American society that he never committed to letters sent to anyone else. Presenting these letters in isolation, therefore, will illuminate aspects of the character and opinions of both men in ways that would have been harder to see and appreciate had they been published amidst letters to others.

Another thing that will be made clearer by these letters is the extraordinary influence wielded by Brandeis and Frankfurter. It should now be possible for historians to trace back to these two men a host of congressional and judicial initiatives, political appointments in all branches of the federal government, developments in Zionist politics and Palestine policy, the hiring of particular personnel by leading American law schools, and even some specific laws and social programs. The network of their associations was enormous, far-flung, and effective, and neither man hesitated to call these elements into play. In the 1920s, days bleak for America's progressives, they helped to keep the torch of modern liberalism burning, and in fact accomplished far more in achieving their purposes than could reasonably have been expected. In the 1930s, when the progressive spirit reemerged with the tremendous energy of the New Deal, they were never shy about pressing their measures energetically or placing their disciples strategically or persuading their friends as to the right course for the nation to follow. If these letters are important, as we certainly believe them to be, it is because they reveal the intimate views of a uniquely perceptive observer of American life and illuminate an equally unique relationship between two extraordinarily gifted men. They also demonstrate how two determined and tireless fighters played their parts in shaping the course of American history for more than two decades.

The first encounter between Louis D. Brandeis and Felix Frankfurter occurred on the evening of 4 May 1905. Brandeis, forty-nine years old and already a well-known Boston lawyer with a growing reputation as a municipal reformer, came to Cambridge to deliver a talk to the Harvard Ethical Society. Frankfurter, a law student in his early twenties, sat in the audience. Brandeis's speech, "The Opportunity in the Law," argued that lawyers had an indispensable role to play in American life. But in order to play that role, he told his listeners, they would have to resist the seductive blandishments of the corporations and array themselves on the side of everyday men and women. "We hear much of the 'corporation lawyer,' and far too little of the 'people's lawyer.' The great opportunity of the American Bar is and will be to stand again as it did in the past, ready to protect also the interests of the people." [2] It would be pleasant to think that young Frankfurter remembered these words a year later. He graduated from the Law School in 1906, and after a few months in a prestigious New York law firm, took a cut in salary to work for Henry L. Stimson, the United States Attorney for the Southern District of New York. [3]

By 1910, when their correspondence began, Brandeis was a reformer of national stature. He had completed his work in connection with the reform of Boston's municipal gas system and had devised a new form of low-cost workers' insurance for the state of Massachusetts. He had argued a landmark case before the United States Supreme Court, and had just gained considerable attention for his part in the sensational Pinchot-Ballinger conservation controversy. He was in the midst of a long and ultimately successful struggle to prevent the monopolization of New England's transportation facilities, and about to enter the New York garment workers' strike, where he sought to rationalize and stabilize employer-employee relations. Before long he would be working with Robert M. La Follette and then with Woodrow Wilson and other Washington progressives on a host of national reform projects.[4]

Frankfurter stayed with Stimson in a variety of jobs and came to Washington in 1911 to work under his direction in the War Department. Between 1911 and 1914, years when Brandeis came regularly to Washington on progressive business, he was a frequent visitor at the "House of Truth," the bachelors' quarters that Frankfurter and a lively group of intellectual young civil servants maintained on Nineteenth Street. In 1914 Frankfurter accepted an offer to teach at the Harvard Law School, an offer prompted in part by Brandeis himself. For the next two years, the two men were practically neighbors, and their confidence in one another's abilities and motives grew rapidly. When Brandeis came to the Supreme Court in 1916, the special relationship that had evolved began to be reflected in their frequent letters.

Brandeis had already come to appreciate in the younger man those traits that would charm and win so many over the next thirty years: the blazing intelligence; the absolutely indefatigable energy ("Do you know what it's like," Frankfurter's wife once remarked, "to be married to a man who is never tired?"); the unparalleled talent for making friends—especially among people who counted. Felix Frankfurter knew all the gossip. And he had the most marvelous knack for hearing about what positions in the federal bureaucracy were about to come open and for knowing who among his associates, friends, or students might fill those vacancies very nicely. His bouncing gaiety, his talent for flattery, his mastery of detail, the aura he gave off as he entered a room—all made him one of the most attractive and engaging conversationalists in the country. Oliver Wendell Holmes once said of Frankfurter that he "walked deep into my heart," and Brandeis, who referred to him as "half brother, half son," might easily have echoed that sentiment.

Brandeis and Frankfurter were separated in their ages by a quarter century, but that fact may well have served to draw them together. Brandeis had always possessed a wonderful talent for collecting young lieutenants and directing them into the battle, while Frankfurter had a decided penchant for selecting and attaching himself to mentors.[5] There were other affinities as well. Both men were passionately devoted to the law, and both reposed their hopes for its better practice in the work of the Harvard Law School. Both loved facts and were suspicious of those who did not. Both knew the sting of antisemitism, having learned at an early age what it meant to be an "outsider" in Boston society. Both were relatively indifferent to getting money and suspected that there was something unclean about living too luxuriously (although Frankfurter seemed to care more than Brandeis about the amenities of life, such as good food and clothing). Both had married high-strung women who had the habit of nervous collapses; the sympathies each expressed when the other's wife had suffered "a bad week" or "a decline" were genuine and heartfelt.[6] Both men knew a lot about politics, and they loved the game.

Above all, each possessed a set of progressive social, political, economic, and judicial articles of faith very nearly identical to that of his counterpart. Brandeis tended to be more olympian and detached, better able to take the long view; it is hard to imagine him riding to the help of Tom Mooney or Bartolomeo Vanzetti. Frankfurter tended to be more excitable, more willing to put his faith in particular men rather than in social institutions; it is hard to imagine him inventing, laboriously, a new method of insuring Massachusetts workers and then guiding it painstakingly through three decades of constant nursing. But on the whole, they believed in the same principles, feared the same evils, symbolized the same tendencies in American life and thought. This identity of belief enabled them to speak knowingly and confidently to one another, in person and in their letters.[7]

The great irony in their friendship was that it came under its greatest strain at the very moment of their most impressive triumphs in national policy. With the Supreme Court's devastation of the early New Deal measures in the spring of 1935, and then with the shattering controversy over Franklin Roosevelt's Court "packing" plan in early 1937, a coolness rose between the two collaborators. In the early 1930s, Frankfurter had been able to maintain his friendship with Brandeis while at the same time cultivating Franklin Roosevelt, but now he had to make his choice. He must have been badly torn between his old loyalty to the justice and his new one to the president. It is impossible to sort out all the factors—philosophy, psychology, politics, and personal ambition—that led to the decision, but Frankfurter drifted into the orbit of the man who would later appoint him to the Supreme Court.[8] The twenty years of comradeship with Brandeis were sufficient to prevent an open and bitter break, but things were never quite the same between them. Brandeis's letters during his last four years are much less frequent;[9] they also have about them a distance, a polite caution hitherto unknown.

In March 1982, Professor Bruce Allen Murphy of Pennsylvania State University published his controversial study, *The Brandeis/Frankfurter Connection: The Secret Political Activities of Two Supreme Court Justices*. Murphy used the unpublished letters of Brandeis to Frankfurter, as well as materials from numerous other manuscript collections, to present a detailed examination of the extrajudicial involvements of both men. The Oxford University Press promoted and advertised the book with unrestrained sensationalism, the sort of publicity campaign, Edwin McDowell wrote, "usually associated with blockbuster novels."[10] *The Brandeis/Frankfurter Connection* received widespread attention, inaugurating a brief but spirited debate on the nature of judicial ethics, and the character of these two justices in particular. The *New York Times*, for example, ran a front-page story, an article of analysis, and a lead editorial;[11] other mass-circulation newspapers and magazines followed suit.

Some of the criticism levelled at Brandeis and Frankfurter on the basis of Murphy's book concerned itself with their "meddling" in politics while they were members of the judiciary. The *New York Times* editorial, in this regard, pronounced an unequivocal and not untypical verdict: "The Brandeis-Frankfurter arrangement was wrong. It serves neither history nor ethics to judge it more kindly. . . . [T]he prolonged, meddlesome Brandeis-Frankfurter arrangement violates ethical standards." According to the editorial, it was not merely that the pair refused to respect the tradition of separation of powers; rather, they pretended in various public ways that they stood aloof from "politics" while secretly playing the game. That seeming contradiction, ran the charge, lent to their conduct a note of sanctimoniousness and hypocrisy. But these condemnations, which go straight to the heart of the long American debate over judicial ethics, were not the matters that received the most attention.

Although the disclosure of the financial relationship between Brandeis and Frankfurter had been explored in print before Murphy's book (as Murphy carefully noted),[12] it was that aspect of the story that caused the most extreme expressions of surprise and outrage. Frankfurter's old friend Archibald MacLeish confessed that "reading about these activities, with their undertones of the dubious, has been one of the most disturbing experiences of my life."[13] Bob Woodward, the well-known investigative reporter of the *Washington Post*, brushed aside Murphy's suggestion of mitigating factors in Brandeis's giving money to Frankfurter: "A payoff is a payoff—secret money for secret lobbying and other efforts." It did not make any difference, Woodward said, that Frankfurter was himself committed to the work he undertook at Brandeis's suggestion. "A whore may like and believe in his or her work, but prostitution is just that, despite the passions one might bring to it."[14] And former McCarthy aide Roy Cohn (with his usual solicitude for other men's reputations) accused Brandeis and Frankfurter of "trafficking in money, trafficking in opinions, trafficking in influence." Felix Frankfurter, Cohn announced, was "a $50,000 political pimp."[15]

A group of scholars, meanwhile, has taken issue with Murphy's findings. Some have contended that he was guilty of errors of fact, some trivial in nature but others of central importance.[16] Most criticism of the book, however, centers on its tone—on Murphy's treatment of Frankfurter as "a paid lobbyist,"[17] and on the author's disposition to read into the surviving record a quality of calculation, deviousness, and covert conspiracy that distorts the truth. Even some who, like Arthur M. Schlesinger, Jr., acknowledge considerable merit in Murphy's work, regret the penchant to detect a conspiracy that sometimes seems to emerge from his pages. "In his now-it-can-be-told mood, Murphy writes something closer to a prosecutor's brief than to considered history," Schlesinger argues. Noting the "air of melodramatic exposure" that characterizes some of the book, he laments "the impression of a sinister Brandeis-Frankfurter conspiracy to run national affairs from the highest judicial bench."[18] The late Professor Robert Cover of the Yale Law School went further, calling Murphy's book "a combination of shoddy scholarship and commercial exploitation [which] has projected a scandal-mongering distortion of Brandeis's 'political' activities onto the pages of our leading newspapers." To Cover, "Professor Murphy has neither disclosed nor proven the nature of the Brandeis-Frankfurter connection; he has used and sometimes misused the evidence to argue for one extreme construction of it. . . . Murphy's poor scholarship and the press's irresponsible reporting have resulted in a spectacular conspiracy thesis about Brandeis and Frankfurter that is everywhere shaky and often demonstrably wrong." [19]

The recovery of the Frankfurter letters, the controversy over Murphy's book, and a spate of new scholarship dealing with Brandeis during these years led the two of us to take up, once again, a work that we both considered finished a dozen years ago. [20] We have, of course, our own opinions as to the issues involved in this debate; but it seems to us that our best contribution would be not to hurl our own assertions stubbornly against the assertions of others, but to present, instead, in an objective and scholarly fashion, the materials upon which the various commentators have rested some of their judgments. Many of the questions raised in this fevered discussion (although certainly not all of them) hinge upon some evaluation of the spirit in which Brandeis and Frankfurter undertook their "joint efforts." Our hope, with respect to this book, is that the letters published here will illuminate that spirit more clearly. We share the traditional faith of both democracy and scholarship that judgment will be soundest when it is based upon a careful weighing of the basic information.

The critical and scholarly response to our earlier volumes has been so generally favorable that it seemed unwise to depart very much from our former editorial practices. But some changes did seem to make sense. Rather than bracket missing letters or last names ("O[liver]. W[endell]. H[olmes]." or "Dean [Acheson]"), we have added a list of Brandeis's most commonly used abbreviations. Since all the letters in this book were written to the same correspondent, moreover, it seemed silly to call attention to that fact in 671 separate headings. But, as before, we have attempted in our annotations to make each letter more comprehensible than it would have been otherwise. We try to identify every name that Brandeis mentions (at its first appearance), to explain aspects of the problems with which he was concerned, to call attention to other letters (both in this book and the five-volume set) that might shed light on the subject, and to track down allusions and references that he used. In the interest of conserving space for more letters, we have had to severely limit bibliographic references to previous studies of the issues and personalities to which Brandeis alludes. We gratefully acknowledge our deep debt to the many scholars whose work we have drawn upon and sincerely regret our inability to mention each of them by name.

As in the previous volumes, we confine ourselves to printing only

Brandeis's side of the correspondence. In the earlier books this was done to make the task manageable. Here there is an additional reason: Frankfurter's letters to Brandeis do not survive in much quantity. (Professor Murphy, who cites hundreds of published and hitherto unpublished letters from Brandeis, cites fewer than five dozen letters written by Frankfurter to Brandeis.) It is our suspicion that Frankfurter destroyed a majority of his letters to Brandeis in the early 1940s.[21] In addition, those of Frankfurter's letters that do survive are difficult to date precisely; Frankfurter often wrote only "Tuesday" or "Friday" at the top of the page. Where it seemed accurate to do so, we have quoted from some of the surviving Frankfurter to Brandeis letters in our footnotes. We have also quoted from Frankfurter's letters to others when we thought his comments might help readers better understand a particular issue.

There is one more way in which this volume is similar to all the previous ones. It, too, has relied upon the help and support of a large number of people, and it is a great pleasure to acknowledge their assistance.

The National Endowment for the Humanities supported this project with a generous grant—just as it supported our earlier volumes. Our debt to that institution is, at this point, simply incalculable. Smaller, but timely awards were given by both the Virginia Commonwealth University Faculty Research Fund and the Research Council of the University of Oklahoma.

As always, we owe our deepest thanks to a group of dedicated and efficient librarians, archivists, and fellow historians whose patience with our inquiries can never be repaid by merely listing their names here. Nonetheless, we wish to thank Sylvia Landress and Esther Togman of the Zionist Archives and Library, New York; Jordan Schwarz of Northern Illinois University; Fannie Zelcer of the American Jewish Archives; Karen D. Drickamer of Williams College; Thomas L. Owen of the University of Louisville Archives; Erika Chadbourn and Judith W. Mellins of the Harvard Law School Library; Bernard R. Crystal of Columbia University; Frances M. Seeber and Raymond Teichman of the Franklin D. Roosevelt Library; Nelson Dawson and Nettie Watson of the Filson Club; Thelma Jaffe of the Weizmann Archives in Rehovot, Israel; Charles Donahue, Jr., of the Harvard Law School; Nathan Kaganoff of the American Jewish Historical Society; and Clarke Chambers and David Klaasen of the Social Welfare History Archives at the University of Minnesota.

The dedication of this book to Mary K. and Eric Tachau is a pitifully small return for the confidence and trust that they have reposed in us or for the friendliness and hospitality they have bestowed upon us over the long years.

Our manuscript received an extremely thorough reading from Professor Paul A. Freund of the Harvard Law School. Intimately connected with both principals of this book, the repository of incomparable knowledge of American constitutional law, probably no one else in the United States could have given us such valuable help or saved us from so many errors. We hope that he will find the final product worthy of his aid. We were also very greatly helped by the work of Philip E. Urofsky, a son of one of the editors and now associated with the firm of Shearman and Sterling of New York City. Throughout this project he served as an able and energetic research assistant and saved us countless hours by his hard and skilled work.

We received marvelous support and encouragement from a number of people at the University of Oklahoma Press, and it is a pleasure to acknowledge them here: George Bauer, John Drayton, Sarah Nestor, Sarah Morrison, and Tom Radko (now at the University of Nevada Press) deserve special mention. Linda Reese copyedited the long manuscript with a sure eye and the touch of an expert. The Press, besides doing all of the usual work in connection with a manuscript, applied for and won a grant from the National Historical Publications Commission to assist in meeting the costs of publishing a book of this size; the editors join the Press in expressing appreciation for that generosity.

We have mentioned our gratitude to our long-suffering wives, Susan and Lynne, before on these occasions—as if repeating our poor thanks could somehow even the score for all the support they have lent or all the sacrifices they have made so that we could do our work. Once again we say thanks, once again fully knowing how inadequate a meaure of our feelings this formal and public acknowledgement remains.

[1] Melvin I. Urofsky and David W. Levy, eds., *Letters of Louis D. Brandeis,* 5 vols. (Albany: State University of New York Press, 1971–78). All references in this book to letters to correspondents other than Frankfurter are to these volumes. There are approximately 1,500 letters and notes from Brandeis to Frankfurter in the Frankfurter Papers in the Library of Congress. Our criteria for selection of particular items to publish are set out in the "Editorial Foreword" of Volume I of the *Letters.*

[2] Louis D. Brandeis, "The Opportunity in the Law," *American Law Review* 39 (1905): 555, reprinted in his *Business—A Profession* (Boston: Small, Maynard, and Co., 1914), 329–43.

[3] For Frankfurter's early life and career, see Michael E. Parrish, *Felix Frankfurter and His Times: The Reform Years* (New York: Free Press, 1982), chs. 1–3, and Liva Baker, *Felix Frankfurter* (New York: Coward McCann, 1969), 1–141. Also helpful, although not always reliable, is Harlan B. Phillips, ed., *Felix Frankfurter Reminisces* (New York: Reynal, 1960).

[4] For Brandeis's early life and career, see Allon Gal, *Brandeis of Boston* (Cambridge: Harvard University Press, 1980); see also the initial chapters in Alpheus T. Mason, *Brandeis: A Free Man's Life* (New York: Viking Press, 1946), Melvin I. Urofsky, *Louis D. Brandeis and the Progressive Tradition* (Boston: Little, Brown, 1981), and Philippa Strum, *Louis D. Brandeis: Justice for the People* (Cambridge: Harvard University Press, 1984).

[5] For this trait in Frankfurter, see the psychological biography, H. N. Hirsch, *The Enigma of Felix Frankfurter* (New York: Basic Books, 1981), 27–32.

[6] For Alice G. Brandeis, see Lewis J. Paper, *Brandeis* (Englewood Cliffs: Prentice-Hall, 1983), 45, 62, 84–85, 104–105, 135, 291–93. For Marion D. Frankfurter, see Hirsch, *Enigma of Felix Frankfurter*, 50–51, 81–85.

[7] During the summer months, the Frankfurters often took a place in Chatham on Cape Cod near the Brandeis house, and the two men engaged in lengthy walks and conversations. Fragmentary notes of these conversations were made by Frankfurter, and can be found in the Louis D. Brandeis Papers in the Harvard Law School. An annotated transcription is available in Melvin I. Urofsky, "The Brandeis-Frankfurter Conversations," 1985 *Supreme Court Review* (1986): 299.

[8] See Nelson Dawson, *Louis D. Brandeis, Felix Frankfurter, and the New Deal* (Hamden, Conn.: Archon Books, 1980), 129–68, and Bruce Allen Murphy, *The Brandeis/Frankfurter Connection: The Secret Political Activities of Two Supreme Court Justices* (New York: Oxford University Press, 1982), 155–85.

[9] In part, of course, this decrease in the number of letters was due to Brandeis's advancing age—he was eighty-one in 1937, and after 1939, Frankfurter lived in Washington and could see Brandeis in person.

[10] Edwin McDowell in the *New York Times*, 12 March 1982. For other criticism of the book's promotion, see Nelson Dawson's review in *Journal of American History* 69 (December 1982): 752; Robert Cover, "The Framing of Justice Brandeis," *New Republic* 186 (5 May 1982): 17; and Thomas K. McCraw, "Louis D. Brandeis Reappraised," *American Scholar* 54 (Autumn 1985): 525. One advertisement read: "Now read it for yourself—the full story of two of history's most respected Supreme Court Justices and how they engaged in a wide range of secret political activities. *The Brandeis/Frankfurter Connection*—the book that challenges everything you ever believed about the men of the marble cloister."

[11] *New York Times*, 14, 16, and 18 February 1982.

[12] See various published letters from Brandeis to Frankfurter in the *Brandeis Letters* 4: 266–67, and 5: 43, 187–88, 290, 292–93. See also Urofsky, *Brandeis and the Progressive Tradition*, 155–56, and David W. Levy and Bruce Allen Murphy, "Preserving the Progressive Spirit in a Conservative Time: The Joint Reform Efforts of Justice Brandeis and Professor Frankfurter, 1916–1933," *Michigan Law Review* 78 (1980): 1252. This article examines some of the same ground as Murphy's first three chapters; for an analysis of the differences in tone and judgment between the 1980 article and the 1982 book, see Cover, "Framing of Justice Brandeis," 20. For other earlier mentions of the financial relations, see Dawson, *Brandeis, Frankfurter and the New Deal*, 4–5, and Hirsch, *Enigma of Felix Frankfurter*, 44.

[13] Archibald MacLeish in the *New York Times*, 21 February 1982.

[14] Woodward's review in the *Washington Post*, 11 April 1982.

[15] Quoted in the *New York Times*, 24 March 1982.

[16] See, for example, the list of unimportant errors in Arthur M. Schlesinger, Jr.'s, review in the *New York Times*, 21 March 1982. In addition, Lewis J. Paper, in *Brandeis*, 256–58, challenges Murphy's view of Brandeis and the Sacco and Vanzetti case, as well as his contention that the two men tried to keep their financial arrangements a secret. Robert Cover, in "Framing of Justice Brandeis," challenges Murphy's facts and interpretations in a number of very important matters relating to the 1930s. Leonard Baker, *Brandeis and Frankfurter: A Dual Biography* (New York: Harper and Row, 1984), 240–44, alleges errors relating to the payments Brandeis made to Frankfurter and also insists that the two men did not keep their financial dealings secret.

[17] Murphy, *Brandeis/Frankfurter Connection*, 10.

[18] Schlesinger in the *New York Times*, 21 March 1982.

[19] Cover, "Framing of Justice Brandeis," 17. For a systematic review of the charges made by Murphy, see David J. Danelski, "The Propriety of Brandeis's Extrajudicial Conduct," in Nelson L. Dawson, ed., *Brandeis and America* (Lexington: University Press of Kentucky, 1989), 11–37.

[20] Another important factor in our decision to resume the editing of Brandeis's letters, however, was the unexpected availability of a large collection of letters from Brandeis to members of his immediate family. These documents were discovered by the children of Susan Brandeis Gilbert after her death, and have since been deposited in the Brandeis University Library. A volume containing many of these letters will be published in the future.

[21] The late Pearl Von Allmen, longtime curator of the main body of Brandeis Papers at the University of Louisville Law School, told us that shortly after Brandeis's death, Justice Frankfurter came to Louisville and carried off large numbers of documents from the collection. We believe these items were letters he had written to Brandeis, and we also think it likely that he destroyed them.

Abbreviations

A.G.	Attorney General
A.S.	Alexander Sachs
B.F.	Bernard Flexner
B.N.C.	Benjamin Nathan Cardozo
B.V.C.	Benjamin V. Cohen
C.C.	Calvin Coolidge
C.C.A.	Circuit Court[s] of Appeals
C.C.B.	Charles Culp Burlingham
C.E.H.	Charles Evans Hughes
C.J.	Chief Justice
Cert.	certiorari
Comtee	Committee
D.J.	District Judge
Dean	Dean Acheson
deH.	Jacob deHaas
E. or Eliz.	Elizabeth Brandeis [Raushenbush]
E.A.F.	Edward A. Filene
F.D. or F.D.R.	Franklin Delano Roosevelt
G.W.A.	George W. Anderson
Gene or Eugene	Eugene Meyer
Harold or H.J.L.	Harold J. Laski
H.C.	Herbert Croly
H.J.F.	Henry J. Friendly
H.L.R.	*Harvard Law Review*
H.L.S.	Harvard Law School
i.a.	inter alia
I.C.C.	Interstate Commerce Commission
J. or JJ.	Judge(s)
J.M.L.	James M. Landis
J.W.D.	John W. Davis
J.W.M.	Julian W. Mack
L.H.	Learned Hand
L.S.	Law School
La F.	Robert M. La Follette
McR.	James C. McReynolds
Max	Max Lowenthal
N.D.B.	Newton D. Baker

N.R.	*New Republic*
Norman	Norman Hapgood
O.W.H.	Oliver Wendell Holmes, Jr.
op.	opinion
P.	Palestine
P.B.	Pierce Butler
P.C.	per curiam
P.D.C.	Palestine Development Corporation
P.E.C.	Palestine Economic Corporation
P.E.F.	Palestine Endowment Fund
pet.	petition
R.P.	Roscoe Pound
R.S.	Robert Szold
S.G.	Solicitor General
S.J.C.	Supreme Judicial Court
S.S.W.	Stephen S. Wise
S.V.	Sacco and Vanzetti
T.R.P.	Thomas Reed Powell
U.S.S.C.	United States Supreme Court
V.D. or Van	Willis Van Devanter
W.	Chaim Weizmann
Wick.	George W. Wickersham
W.L.	Walter Lippmann
W.Z.O.	World Zionist Organization
Z.O.	Zionist Organization
Z.O.A.	Zionist Organization of America

No. 1   June 14, 1910   Boston, Mass.[1]

MY DEAR MR. FRANKFURTER: As requested in yours of the 13th,—I am sending you under another cover a copy of our brief in the Ballinger Case.[2] If you find it good the credit is mainly due to George Rublee.[3] Thanks for congratulations on the Illinois Case.[4] You, too, have had a great victory.[5]   Yours very truly,

[1] The editors believe that this is the first letter LDB wrote to FF.

[2] The notorious Pinchot-Ballinger conservation controversy had electrified the nation during the first half of 1910; see LDB to Norman Hapgood, 8 January 1910 (references to letters by LDB are to be found in Melvin I. Urofsky and David W. Levy, eds., *Letters of Louis D. Brandeis* [5 vols., Albany: State University of New York Press, 1971–78]). LDB played a key role in the proceedings, acting as the attorney for *Collier's Magazine* in the dramatic Congressional hearings to investigate the charges against Secretary of the Interior Richard Achilles Ballinger (1858–1922). The hearings, which proved extremely embarrassing to both Ballinger and President William Howard Taft, ended in late May, and LDB, aided by George Rublee, submitted his brief to the Committee on 11 June. The brief may be found in *Investigation of the Department of the Interior*, 61st Cong., 3d sess. (Washington, D.C., 1911), 9: 5041–5182.

[3] George Rublee (1869–1957), a New York lawyer, worked with LDB on the Ballinger case and other progressive causes. President Wilson later tried to appoint him to the Federal Trade Commission, but the appointment was blocked in the Senate. He did serve Wilson, and every other president through Franklin Roosevelt, in a variety of capacities.

[4] In *Ritchie* v. *Wayman*, 244 Ill. 508 (1910), one of several cases following upon the heels of LDB's victory in *Muller* v. *Oregon*, in which he appeared on behalf of minimum-wage and maximum hours legislation passed by progressive state legislatures, LDB successfully defended Illinois' ten-hour law for women.

[5] In a case handled by FF and his superior, United States Attorney Henry L. Stimson, several officials of the nation's largest sugar companies were found guilty of tampering with scales at the port of New York.

No. 2   February 27, 1911   Boston, Mass.

MY DEAR FRANKFURTER: Thank you for yours of the 25th with the Sun editorial. Its comments are, as you say, always interesting.[1]

The Commission did, I think, quite as much as they could, and rather more than I thought they would with the efficiency argument. They accepted the fundamental principles that improvements in economy and management were possible, and that they must be made before the need would be recognized. Scientific management will follow that inevitably, as President Willard's remarks have already indicated.[2]

Very truly yours,

[1] In an editorial entitled "Mind Reading by the Interstate Commerce Commission," the *New York Sun* attacked the Commission and LDB for trying to read ulterior motives into the railroads' petitions for higher rates. The *Sun*'s charges were in connection with the I.C.C. hearings over the matter of advancing freight rates (see LDB to Robert M. La Follette, 16 September 1910, n.2). LDB appeared against the rate increases, and emphasized the need for railroads to adopt the

techniques of "scientific management," a cause close to LDB's heart during these years. If the railroads were more efficient in their operations, he argued, there would be no need for a rate increase, and he claimed that the railroads could save "a million dollars a day" by better management.

[2] Daniel Willard (1861–1942), president of the Baltimore & Ohio Railroad, had responded to the I.C.C. decision against granting the increase by declaring: "As I see it, there is only one thing for us to do—to put into effect the Brandeis greater efficiency system."

No. 3   April 9, 1912   Boston, Mass.

MY DEAR FRANKFURTER: I don't know whom to suggest for head of the Children's Bureau.[1] Indeed I do not know exactly what the function of the Executive will be. We ought to have a sociologist at the head, and Dr. Devine,[2] Dr. Samuel McCune Lindsay,[3] Prof. Felix Adler[4] or Judge Julian Mack[5] ought to be able to suggest a man.[6]

As to the Industrial Commission Board:[7] Mrs. Brandeis and I are inclined to think that Mrs. Glendower Evans[8] of Boston would prove a valuable member. She is a very active friend of labor and a strong supporter of La Follette.[9] I presume that would not bar her. She has been the most active member of our Minimum Wage Board, and has for a quarter of a century been a member of our State Board dealing with the reform institutions for boys and girls, and was also on the special Commission appointed by the Mayor to investigate our city public institutions.

You may be amused by the definition of a commission given by William Hard in his "Unemployment as a Coming Issue":[10]

"You know what a commission is. It is what it ought to be. It consists of very intelligent and thoroughly uninformed men, who together form a strong and efficient mental vacuum in which the experiment can be made whether or not the information about any given topic is yet of sufficient density to raise the wings of legislation."   Yours very truly,

[1] After a decade of agitation for a federal bureau devoted to the problems of American children, Congress had just established such an agency.

[2] Edward Thomas Devine (1867–1948), the editor of *The Survey*, was involved with a great many of the major social-welfare organizations in the country.

[3] Samuel McCune Lindsay (1869–1959), professor of social legislation at Columbia University, served as president of the Academy of Political Science from 1910 to 1930.

[4] Felix Adler (1851–1933), LDB's brother-in-law, was the founder of the New York Society for Ethical Culture and a leader of the worldwide Ethical Culture movement. See Benny Kraut, *From Reform Judaism to Ethical Culture: The Religious Evolution of Felix Adler* (Cincinnati: Hebrew Union College Press, 1979).

[5] Julian William Mack (1866–1943) was to become one of the closest and most trusted of LDB's associates. He had been appointed to the U.S. Circuit Court of Appeals in Chicago in 1911, and

afterwards was transferred to the Circuit Court in New York, where he served until 1941. While he and LDB were involved together in a few progressive crusades, they were most closely allied, together with FF, in the Zionist movement. After LDB joined the Supreme Court, it fell to Mack and others to assume various positions of public leadership within American Zionism. Mack also served as honorary president of the World Jewish Congress. See Harry Barnard, *The Forging of an American Jew: The Life and Times of Julian W. Mack* (New York: Herzl Press, 1974).

[6] President Taft named Julia Lathrop of Hull House to be the head of the Children's Bureau.

[7] In his State of the Union message, 2 February 1912, Taft asked Congress to establish a Commission on Industrial Relations to investigate American economic life. Congress complied in August 1912, but Taft's nominees were rejected by the Senate and President Wilson finally staffed the panel—with the advice of LDB.

[8] Elizabeth Glendower Evans (1856–1937) was an extremely close friend of both LDB and his wife. She had married Glendower Evans in 1882, but was widowed four years later. LDB took her under his wing and continually urged her into the battle against social evils. A member of the Massachusetts Minimum Wage Commission in 1911–1912, her work led to the establishment of the first permanent organization of the kind in the country. She was also very active in the futile fight to save Sacco and Vanzetti in the 1920s. For her evaluation of LDB, see her series of articles, "People I Have Known: Louis Dembitz Brandeis, A Tribune of the People," *Progressive* 2 (January–February 1931). For an account of the relationship between her and the Brandeis family, see Lewis J. Paper, *Brandeis* (Englewood Cliffs, N.J.: Prentice-Hall, 1983), 28–30.

[9] Robert Marion La Follette (1855–1925) was one of the towering figures of the progressive movement and perhaps its most truly representative one. In 1901, he defeated the entrenched machine and was elected to the first of three highly successful terms as governor of Wisconsin. During his tenure, La Follette pushed through a number of reform measures and secured for Wisconsin a reputation as the most progressive and enlightened state in the Union.

In 1905, he was elected to the Senate, where he soon established himself as leader of the insurgent Republicans, and by 1910, he was eyeing the presidency, with many reformers rallying to his banner. Overwork led to a breakdown in early 1911, clearing the way for Theodore Roosevelt to jump into the race (see LDB to Belle La Follette, 7 February 1912). In 1924, he finally made his run for the White House on a third-party ticket, and he received 4.8 million votes. He had exhausted his strength in this battle, however, and died the following year.

Following their first meeting, La Follette and LDB became close friends, and this intimacy extended to include both families. See Belle Case and Fola La Follette, *Robert M. La Follette*, 2 vols. (New York: Macmillan, 1953).

[10] William Hard (1878–1962), a longtime feature writer and prolific free-lance reporter, was a friend of many progressives. The quotation LDB shares with FF is from Hard's article in *American Labor Legislation Review* 2 (February 1912):93, at 98.

No. 4   July 12, 1912   Boston, Mass.

MY DEAR FRANKFURTER: I am very glad to get your letter of the 10th and that you have written me about Valentine.[1] He certainly ought to be in constructive social work if he leaves the Government service, and I am sure that there are many worthy positions waiting for such a man as he is. It is merely a matter of our knowing about them. I should think the New York School of Philanthropy, Hull House, and the Wisconsin University would be the best intelligence offices.

I am glad to know that you feel contented with the state of things politically. I have myself been much disturbed by the repeated divisions of the Progressive forces. If Clark or Harmon had been nominated substantially all Progressives might have joined in opposition to the Republican and Democratic nominees.[2] With Wilson[3] nominated, after the masterful and masterly handling of the Convention by Bryan,[4] it seemed to me that the duty of Progressives was clearly to support Wilson and practically capture the Democratic party. The insistence upon a Roosevelt-Republican party seems to me to postpone the real alignment on national, social and economic lines.[5]

I think you are entirely right in continuing in the War Department.[6] I hope to see you soon.   Most cordially,

[1] Robert Grosvenor Valentine (1872–1916), after a varied career in teaching and banking, went into government service in the Indian Bureau in 1905. In June 1909 he became Commissioner of Indian Affairs, but he resigned in September 1912. In 1913 he was named first chairman of the Massachusetts Minimum Wage Board. He was a close friend of FF's, the two having roomed together in Washington, D.C.

[2] The Democrats had just completed their hard-fought convention in Baltimore, nominating Woodrow Wilson; two days before this letter LDB publically announced his support for the nominee. Also making bids for the Democrat nomination were James Beauchamp ("Champ") Clark (1850–1921), Speaker of the House of Representatives, and Judson Harmon (1846–1927), the governor of Ohio.

[3] Few men in American history have been so much written about and yet so little understood as Thomas Woodrow Wilson (1856–1924), the twenty-eighth president of the United States. After briefly studying law, Wilson became an academic. He served as professor at Princeton after 1897, and five years later as president of the school. In 1910 he was elected governor of New Jersey. By the time of the Baltimore convention he had secured enough support to give him the nomination.

In the field of economics, Wilson viewed the business system as a means of rewarding personal morality, and he thus began to oppose the trusts because they limited the opportunity for the individual to succeed. But he did not know how to curb the trusts and frequently spoke as if they were inevitable creations of the economic system. It was LDB's proposal for regulating competition that appealed to Wilson, and the proposal brought the two men together. There is evidence that Wilson never fully understood the Brandeisian philosophy, but even so he trusted LDB and consulted with him frequently from the time of their first meeting (see LDB to Alfred Brandeis, 29 August 1912) until his death in 1924. In 1916, he rewarded LDB by nominating him to the Supreme Court.

For Wilson and LDB, see Melvin I. Urofsky, "Wilson, Brandeis and the Trust Issue, 1912–1914," *Mid-America* 49 (1967): 3, and Alpheus T. Mason, *Brandeis: A Free Man's Life* (New York: Viking Press, 1946), chs. 24–26.

[4] William Jennings Bryan (1860–1925) had been the unsuccessful Democrat nominee in 1896, 1900, and 1908, and still retained immense popularity among the rural western and southern elements of the party. He did play some part in swinging the 1912 convention behind Wilson, but LDB probably exaggerates his role in "handling" the matter.

[5] Ex-president Theodore Roosevelt (1858–1919) tried to capture the Republican nomination from his former friend and protegé, Taft. Despite clearcut victories in most of the primaries, Roosevelt found the Republican convention machinery controlled by the Taft forces. Convinced that he had been cheated out of the nomination, Roosevelt's followers walked out of the Chicago convention and, despite the reservations of most progressive leaders, called a rump convention to meet in Chicago in August. There they formed the Progressive, or Bull Moose Party, turning the election of 1912 into a three-cornered race. Although LDB supported Wilson, FF continued to

support Roosevelt. See John Milton Cooper, Jr., *The Warrior and the Priest: Woodrow Wilson and Theodore Roosevelt* (Cambridge: Harvard University, 1983).

[6] FF had come to Washington with his political mentor, Henry L. Stimson, whom Taft had appointed as Secretary of War. FF became legal advisor in the department's Bureau of Insular Affairs and remained in the Department, despite the change of political administrations, until going to Harvard in 1914. See Michael Parrish, *Felix Frankfurter and His Times: The Reform Years* (New York: Free Press, 1982), ch. 3.

No. 5   January 24, 1913   Boston, Mass.

MY DEAR FRANKFURTER: You have probably heard of the progressive law work which the Harvard Law School is undertaking, and in which Professor Pound is particularly interested.[1]

Professor Pound thinks there is an unusual opportunity to obtain what is perhaps the best criminal law library in the world, for about $5,000, and I want to help him raise that amount.

Professor Beale's[2] letter to me of the 22nd, copy of which is enclosed, will give you some idea of what the library is. I, of course, have no personal opinion, but accept without hesitation Prof. Pound's and Prof. Beale's judgment, as well as their judgment that the possession of this library is important for the advanced work which they are undertaking.

It occurred to me that you might know of some New York (or other) lawyers, who would be glad to join in making this gift.[3]

I have just returned from the West where I have been for some weeks, and have not had an opportunity of seeing Walter E. Meyers [sic][4] as I have not been in New York. I wrote him, however, on my return saying that I should be very glad to see him here. Of course I intend to see him when I am next in New York, but by reason of my prolonged absence from Boston, I am prevented from going just now.   Most cordially,

[1] Roscoe Pound (1870–1964) came to Harvard Law School from the University of Chicago in 1910, and from 1916 to 1936 headed the school as its dean. Pound greatly influenced American jurisprudence by insisting that sociological factors be taken into consideration, a direction long advocated by LDB and Holmes. See David Wigdor, *Roscoe Pound: Philosopher of Law* (Westport, Conn.: Greenwood Press, 1974), and Arthur E. Sutherland, *The Law at Harvard: A History of Ideas and Men* (Cambridge, Mass.: Harvard University Press, 1967), ch. viii. At this moment, Pound was working to introduce a course in criminal procedure and reform as part of the school's fourth-year graduate program, and the course was about to be inaugurated by Professor Joseph H. Beale.

[2] Joseph Henry Beale (1861–1943) had joined the Harvard Law faculty in 1892. Except for a brief term as dean at the University of Chicago Law School (1902–1904), he remained at Harvard until his death. In 1912 he had been named Royall Professor.

[3] On 27 January FF replied: "I have gladly written to several New York lawyers of the opportunity to ease their swollen fortunes."

[4] Probably FF's friend from Harvard days, Walter E. Meyer (1882–1957), a New York attorney who later became director of the St. Louis & Southwestern Railroad.

No. 6　　　　　**January 28, 1913**　　　　**Boston, Mass.**

MY DEAR FRANKFURTER: I did not have an opportunity until yesterday to examine the memorandum sent with yours of December 17th bearing upon the present unrest.[1]

I entirely agree with the memorandum in so far as it sets forth the difficulties which now confront the legislator, and the need of affording aid. I have, however, grave doubt whether the method suggested will be the most effective aid that could be afforded those seeking social advance.

My thought is this:—

To secure social advance we must regard the field of sociology and social legislation as a field for discovery and invention. Research is necessary as in the field of science and invention, as in the field of mechanical and other arts. In the field of mechanical invention, as in other fields of human enterprise, the successes are few and the failures are many. And the successes are rarely one man's work, or the work of a number of men consciously cooperating. The successes come very often by one man building upon another's apparent failure.

I should have little faith, therefore, in a small group of men evolving a social system or important elements of such a system. We must rely upon all America (and the rest of the world) for our social inventions and discoveries; and the value of the inventions and alleged discoveries can best be tested by current public discussion.

On the other hand, it seems to me that a small group of able, disinterested, well-equipped men, who could give their time to criticism and discussion of legislative proposals, discouraging those which appear to be unsound, and aiding those that appear to be sound, would be of great assistance in the forward movement.

I have not annotated the copy of the memorandum which you sent me as I have only the above suggestions to make. Shall I return the memorandum to the secretary?　　　Most cordially,

[1] Unfortunately, there is no copy of this memorandum, written by Eustace Percy, in either the LDB or the FF Papers. However, several newspaper clippings in the LDB MSS near a copy of this correspondence indicate that the subject involved the application of efficiency techniques to legislative drafting.

No. 7　　　　　**July 19, 1913**　　　　**Boston, Mass.**

MY DEAR FRANKFURTER: I have yours about the Philippines.[1]

I do not think that it would be wise for me to make any suggestion to

the President, unless I should see him, or he should chance to write to me on the subject.   Yours very cordially,

[1] Secretary of War Lindley M. Garrison was leaving on an inspection tour of the Philippines, and FF thought that there were some social and economic facts of which he should be made aware. He wanted LDB's advice on how to get these matters before President Wilson.

No. 8   October 24, 1913   Boston, Mass.

MY DEAR FRANKFURTER: Of course you know that Valentine is being urged as our Labor Commissioner. Mrs. Davis R. Dewey [1] is one of the members of the Board. Last evening Mrs. Brandeis met her, and Mrs. Dewey said that she personally would appoint Valentine eagerly, but that she thought some of the other members were afraid to appoint him, on account of his record in the Indian Department on Catholicism. Mrs. Dewey said that she had heard that some high Catholic potentates,—Cardinal Gibbons, [2] or some others, had said that Valentine had done the only thing he could under the circumstances, and she said that if a letter could be obtained from some distinguished Catholic, the scruples of other members of the Board might be overcome. Of course this is all confidential.

I thought that if any such thing were possible, you would not only know about it, but be able to arrange it, so I am writing you. [3]

I expect to be in Washington the latter part of next week, and look forward to seeing you.   Very cordially yours,

[1] Mary Hopkins Dewey was the wife of the well-known M.I.T. economist, Davis Rich Dewey.

[2] James Cardinal Gibbons (1834–1921), one of the most influential religious leaders of his time, was often credited with smoothing the way for the huge influx of Catholic immigration at the end of the nineteenth and beginning of the twentieth centuries.

[3] Robert G. Valentine was appointed in 1913 as the first chairman of the Massachusetts Minimum Wage Board.

No. 9   April 3, 1916   Boston, Mass.

MY DEAR FELIX: [1] *First*: I am enclosing a copy of Ernst Freund's letter to me of October 27, 1913. [2]

Second: I am enclosing a clipping from the New York Herald of today quoting the passage to which I referred:

"If this be the true interpretation (of the Interstate Commerce Commission) no reputable lawyer would have entered into such an undertaking or agreed to sustain such a relation to the Commission. I desire, however, to do the Commission the justice of saying that, while the terms of communication may be unfortunate, the real meaning cannot [be] misunderstood by fair minded men.["]

Somebody, I think it was George Rublee, said to me that Joe Cotton[3] had, a little over a year ago, made an extraordinary impression on the Court of Appeals in New York by the "new" position he had taken on frankly admitting the weaknesses of his case, and devoting himself to its strength.

If this be true, Joe Cotton might be a good man for Lippmann[4] to talk to and to have say something.   Cordially,

Look at the Central Law Journal for March 24th "The Brandeis Muddle" as to misstatement of the Harvard faculty's position.[5]

---

[1] FF had gone to Washington, D.C., to assist LDB's partner, Edward F. McClennen in the presentation of LDB's side in the bitter and protracted confimation hearings over LDB's appointment to the United States Supreme Court. President Wilson had shocked the nation by making the nomination on 28 January. The hearings began on 9 February and proceeded with some interruptions until the Judiciary Committee's favorable report on 24 May. LDB remained in Boston, but funneled reams of information and documents to Washington, mostly to McClennen (see the many letters during these months to McClennen published in *Letters* 4, 33–183). Two weeks earlier, LDB had sent FF a package of materials related to the Pinchot-Ballinger controversy (see *Letters* 4, 129–31). On the confirmation hearings, see A. L. Todd, *Justice on Trial: The Case of Louis D. Brandeis* (New York: McGraw-Hill, 1964).

[2] The subcommittee had shown considerable interest in allegations made against LDB in connection with his role in the Five Percent Advanced Rate hearings of 1913–1914. Representatives of the shippers assumed that LDB was appointed, by the Interstate Commerce Commission, to develop their side of the argument. LDB, however, contended that he was hired to advise the Commission, not on behalf of the shippers, nor on behalf of the railroads, but as a representative of the "public interest." When he argued, in April 1914, that certain freight rates were too low, just as the railroads had contended, some representatives of the shippers felt that he had betrayed their cause. See Mason, *Brandeis*, ch. xxi. To counter these charges, LDB sent FF a letter written to him by Ernst Freund applauding LDB's willingness to serve "not one side or the other of the controversy, but purely the public interest which is the interest of justice to all concerned." After Senator Albert B. Cummins attacked LDB's behavior, Freund published this letter in the *New York Times*, 6 April 1916. Freund (1864–1932), of the University of Chicago, was a highly respected teacher and writer on administrative law.

[3] Joseph Potter Cotton, Jr. (1875–1931) was a partner in a prestigious New York law firm. He had worked alongside LDB in the Pinchot-Ballinger case, and later served as undersecretary of state in the Hoover administration.

[4] Walter Lippmann (1889–1974) was one of the young, brilliant luminaries of the Progressive Era. After an outstanding career at Harvard, Lippmann was "discovered" by Lincoln Steffens and joined the staff of *Everybody's Magazine*; in 1914, he was one of the founding editors of *The New Republic*. Lippmann wrote many books and articles during a long career as one of the most influential and important social analysts in twentieth-century America. See Ronald Steel, *Walter Lippmann and the American Century* (Boston: Little, Brown, 1980). Although Cotton wrote no article for *The New Republic*, Lippmann and the other editors published many editorials and articles in support of LDB's confirmation to the Supreme Court.

[5] Alexander H. Robbins, editor of the *Central Law Journal*, had written in the editorial that the

24

Harvard faculty was hopelessly split about the nomination. In fact, nine of the eleven faculty members strongly supported LDB; one, who had recently returned from a long overseas stay, took no position; only Edward H. Warren, who had quarreled with LDB years before on Boston franchise politics, was on record as being against confirmation.

No. 10   April 6, 1916   Boston, Mass.

MY DEAR FELIX: You will remember my sending in the New Haven matter letters to Bishop Lawrence and others, endeavoring to invoke their aid in view of the moral issue involved. I enclose a copy of letter to Bishop Lawrence of May 14, 1908.[1]

You may be interested, as a contrast with the inaction of our pillars of society at that time, to look at the enclosed copy of letter from Miss Regina G. Moran of Springfield of April 4, 1916.[2]   Cordially yours,

[1] That letter (published in *Letters* 2, 148–52) was written in an attempt to arouse William Lawrence (1850–1941), the influential Episcopal bishop of Massachusetts from 1893 to 1926, to take a moral stand against the questionable dealings of the New York, New Haven & Hartford Railroad. LDB, who led the fight against what he considered a scheme to monopolize New England's transportation facilities, tried, with mixed results, to involve other leading Boston citizens in condemning the railroad on moral as well as on economic grounds. Lawrence replied that he was leaving for England and would not have an opportunity to study the matter.
[2] Miss Regina Moran, a secretary in Springfield, Massachusetts, had purchased five shares of New Haven stock in 1913 on behalf of her widowed mother, based on the railroad's optimistic claims. She now objected that the New Haven was no longer paying dividends (an outcome LDB had predicted years earlier after his study of the company's finances) and urged LDB to continue his fight against the railroad. She also praised his ideas on behalf of poor working people and hoped that he would win confirmation to the Supreme Court.

No. 11   April 6, 1916   Boston, Mass.

MY DEAR FELIX: Since talking with you on Tuesday I have examined the papers in the Warren matter[1] to see whether my recollection was correct and I find that it is.

You speak of the difficulty in the matter being that the situation is complicated. It really is not complicated and it is only by making it appear so that there can be made to appear even the excuse of criticism.

I enclose a memorandum covering the essential facts.[2]

Yours truly,

[1] The Warren will case probably claimed as much of the attention of the Senate subcommittee as any other single matter. The case involved LDB's work for the family of his first law partner, Samuel D. Warren. LDB originally acted as an "adviser" to the entire Warren family, or, as he later put it, "counsel for the situation." This arrangement worked well until the brothers and sister quarreled over the settlement, and a bitter legal controversy ensued. In the later contests, LDB acted only for

his former partner. Opponents of LDB's confirmation attempted to raise the case as an example of LDB's duplicity and double-dealing. See Mason, *Brandeis*, 238–41 and 475–77.

[2] The four-page memorandum, probably dictated by Edward McClennen (who took over the Warren litigation after LDB went to Washington for the Pinchot-Ballinger hearings), summarized the essential facts of the case and argued that LDB's conduct had been entirely proper.

No. 12   November 19, 1916   Washington, D.C.

MY DEAR FELIX: You have had considerable expense for travelling, telephoning and similar expenses in public matters undertaken at my request or following up my suggestions & will have more in the future no doubt. These expenses should, of course, be borne by me.

I am sending check for $250 on this account. Let me know when it is exhausted or if it has already been.[1]

George R. has been here this week & is becoming really interested in the new job.[2]

He had from Miller an interesting report on California, & Nicholas Murray Butler's part in the fiasco[3] which I asked him to tell Croly.[4]

The Irvings {sic}[5] are coming in this P.M.

[1] This letter marked the beginning of a long financial relationship between the new Supreme Court justice and the Harvard Law School professor. In order to defray the costs for FF's public work—work very often undertaken at the instigation of LDB himself (as succeeding letters in this volume will amply demonstrate)—LDB opened a special account for FF and made regular deposits into it. Between 1916 and 1939, when the arrangement ended with FF's own appointment to the High Court, LDB put at FF's disposal more than $50,000, a sum which, in the value of today's dollars probably approaches a third of a million dollars. For the details of the arrangement, see David W. Levy and Bruce Allen Murphy, "Preserving the Progressive Spirit in a Conservative Time: The Joint Reform Efforts of Justice Brandeis and Professor Felix Frankfurter, 1916–1933," *Michigan Law Review* 78 (1980): 1252, and Bruce Allen Murphy, *The Brandeis/Frankfurter Connection: The Secret Political Activities of Two Supreme Court Justices* (New York: Oxford University Press, 1982).

[2] George Rublee had been appointed by President Wilson to a commission investigating the operation of the Adamson eight-hour law for railroad workers on interstate roads.

[3] Probably the story related to the recent presidential campaign. California, late to report its extremely close vote, finally went to Wilson despite the handsome victory of the Republican candidate for the Senate, Hiram Johnson. Some analysts blamed the old guard Republicans for mishandling the presidential campaign of Republican Charles Evans Hughes in California. Among those who campaigned for Hughes was Nicholas Murray Butler (1862–1947), the distinguished and staunchly conservative president of Columbia University. Some felt that remarks made by Butler in California alienated progressive Republicans who voted for Johnson, but crossed over to Wilson for president.

[4] Herbert Croly (1869–1930), one of the leading political philosophers of the day, had given much thought to the problems created by the growth of big business in America. His proposed solution was to use the federal government to regulate business so it would not destroy democracy, and he articulated this argument in his well-known book, *The Promise of American Life* (New York: Macmillan, 1909). In 1914, with the help of Willard and Dorothy Straight, Herbert Croly founded *The New Republic*. When LDB was nominated for the Supreme Court, Croly wrote him: "I have not

been so pleased in a great many years over anything connected with the public welfare of the whole country." In view of *The New Republic*'s warm support, LDB replied: "I feel almost as if you and your associates must carry the responsibility." See David W. Levy, *Herbert Croly of The New Republic: The Life and Thought of an American Progressive* (Princeton: Princeton University Press, 1985).

[5] William Gage Erving (1877–1923) was a well-known Washington orthopedic surgeon. His wife, Emma Lootz Erving, was the daughter of a Norwegian diplomat and also an orthopedic surgeon. They set up a joint practice in Washington in 1904. The Ervings were close friends of the Brandeises, and the relationship with Emma continued after the death of her husband.

No. 13   November 25, 1916   Washington, D.C.

MY DEAR FELIX: Alice [1] and I talked over the matter before I sent the check and considered it again carefully on receipt of your letter. We are clearly of opinion that you ought to take the check.

In essence this is nothing different than your taking traveling and incidental expenses from the Consumers League or the New Republic—which I trust you do. You are giving your very valuable time and that is quite enough. It can make no difference that the subject matter in connection with which expense is incurred is more definite in one case than in the other.

I ought to feel free to make suggestions to you, although they involve some incidental expense. And you should feel free to incur expense in the public interest. So I am returning the check.

Several of your friends and mine have expressed to me recently the fear that you were overtaxing your strength. Be very watchful. There is much work for you ahead.

[1] By the time of this letter, LDB and Alice Goldmark Brandeis (1866–1945) had been married for a little more than a quarter century. The two were second cousins, and LDB's serious courtship of her began in the spring of 1890. They were married on 23 March 1891.

Alice Brandeis consistently encouraged LDB in his various reform efforts and, while the couple lived in Boston, she herself worked with various women's groups for a variety of reforms from suffrage to labor. After LDB went on the bench, she became more outspoken and visible in her own right—in part, no doubt, because her duties as a mother were lessened as the Brandeis daughters entered college and then married and raised families of their own. She worked on behalf of Sacco and Vanzetti, and in 1928, became vice-chair of the Progressive League for Alfred E. Smith. In Washington she labored to improve the juvenile court system and sought means for curbing juvenile delinquency.

During the years her husband sat on the Supreme Court, Alice Brandeis gained a reputation as one of Washington's most gracious hostesses. She and her husband rarely dined out, but they did not usually dine alone either. And Mrs. Brandeis's "Mondays," weekly gatherings in their apartment of distinguished Washingtonians and interesting and illustrious visitors, young and old, became a meeting place for reformers, intellectuals, civil servants, and others. The couple remained close and affectionate despite Alice's occasional illnesses and attacks of "nerves," and Alice remained interested, throughout her husband's career, in all of his causes and preoccupations. When LDB died in 1941, they had been married for several months more than fifty years.

No. 14   **December 1, 1916**   **Washington, D.C.**

DEAR FELIX: Glad to have yours of 28th.

1. Yes, I shall want a Law School man next year.[1] Magruder[2] is proving very helpful, & I have added faith in your picking.

2. I can't make out who "Newell" for Utility Board is.

3. Alice brings word from New York that Mrs. Valentine is financially unprovided for.[3] Give her enclosed chk for $1000 with Alice's & my love, unless you are planning a fund & prefer it for that.

[1] Rather than hiring a permanent secretary to aid in his Court work, LDB had FF send down to Washington each year an able Harvard Law School graduate to serve as his clerk. A complete list of the clerks can be found in Mason, *Brandeis*, 690.

[2] Calvert Magruder (1893–1968) was LDB's clerk for the 1916–1917 term. After leaving LDB, Magruder worked for a while in the wartime administration before joining the army. He returned to the Harvard Law School as a teacher and became a full professor at the age of thirty-one. FDR appointed Magruder to various New Deal agencies and named him a judge; he rose to become chief judge of the U.S. Court of Appeals for the First Circuit (Boston). President Kennedy called him out of retirement to head a panel investigating the problems of ethics in government.

[3] Both LDB and FF were hit hard by the sudden and completely unexpected death on 15 September of their friend Robert G. Valentine. Besides being a personal blow, Valentine's death left vacancies in a number of arbitration, minimum wage, and utilities boards; and LDB and FF wanted to make certain that he was replaced by able and progressive individuals.

No. 15   **May 3, 1917**   **Washington, D.C.**

MY DEAR FELIX: Miss Peabody[1] reported recently that the $1000 check sent in Valentine matter had not been cashed. I suppose that matter must await developments. I therefore suggest that you deposit that check in a special account & draw against it for your disbursements, past & future, in public matters; as the check sent you must have long since been exhausted.[2]

When the time comes for action in the Valentine matter, you must of course call upon me.

[1] Elizabeth Peabody was one of LDB's former secretaries in the Boston law office. When he went to Washington in 1916, LDB continued to use the law office staff to handle routine business and investment matters.

[2] See 19 and 25 November 1916.

No. 16   **May 16, 1919**   **Washington, D.C.**

MY DEAR FELIX: Your full report of 24th reached me last week, & somewhat earlier yours of 9th/4.[1] I had delayed from day to day writing awaiting a talk with Stanley King which came today.[2]

I realize the trying conditions in Paris & the heavy call for patience, tact and faith. Events shift so constantly that I have felt it impossible to advise in any respect and have confidence in your own good judgment aided by others who feel as we do. It seems to me still that the Zionists will get, at all events, the things essential.

I am planning still to leave with deHaas[3] for Palestine shortly after June 9, but I realize that political conditions there may make a trip at that time inadvisable and assume that through Mack and otherwise you will let me know whether it is advisable to postpone the trip.[4]

Washington, as well as Paris, has been depressed. Little has happened in things American & most of the happenings and things undone have been rather disheartening. And of occurrences abroad, so far as reported by the papers & by returning Americans, few have brought cheer. I asked Norman Hapgood[5] to report to you on conditions here and Kesselman[6] who has reported on Zionist affairs. There is a steady march forward—of course much more slowly than desired or needed. And of all our needs men are the greatest. Can't you produce a few—I long for a Sidney Hillman,[7] among others & we need badly some good business men. Eugene Meyer is a bit interested, but of course absorbed in Loan Finance problems which also move slowly.[8]

Elizabeth[9] is happy in her work, & four of your girls entertained George Bell[10] last evening & he them with glowing accounts of progress in the Garment trade.

[1] FF spent the spring and summer of 1919 at Versailles at the behest of the Zionist Organization of America. He described his position later as "holding a 'watching' brief for Zionists before the Peace Conference." See Harlan B. Phillips, ed., *Felix Frankfurter Reminisces* (New York: Reynal, 1960), ch. xvi. Although Liva Baker writes that "at the Peace Conference he was Brandeis' eyes, ears, and spokesman" (Baker, *Felix Frankfurter* [New York: Coward McCann, 1969], 83), it is clear that FF received almost no advice or instructions from LDB during this period.

[2] Stanley King (1883–1951) had attended Harvard Law School with FF. With the outbreak of war, he joined FF as a special assistant in the War Department, and, at Versailles, helped FF in his legal duties. He had just returned from Paris and consulted with LDB. From 1932 to 1946, King served as president of Amherst College.

[3] Jacob Judah Aaron deHaas (1872–1937), at one time secretary to Theodore Herzl, the founder of the Zionist movement, had been sent to the United States to help organize American Zionists. Working out of Boston, where he edited the Zionist *Boston Jewish Advocate*, he came into contact with LDB and converted him to the cause. For awakening him to the movement, LDB would remain grateful to deHaas for the rest of his life. He took deHaas with him when he visited Palestine in 1919 and personally supported him when he was under attack by other Zionists for his tactlessness and mismanagement of important affairs.

[4] LDB's plan to visit Palestine personally in the summer of 1919 was put into doubt by Mack's assessment of the political situation. After some hesitation and a cancellation of the trip, LDB decided to take FF's strong advice and make the journey. See the next few letters. For LDB's ecstatic reaction to the Holy Land, see the letters he wrote to his wife in *Letters* 4, 398–425.

[5] Norman Hapgood (1868–1937) was serving as editor of *Collier's Magazine* when he first made LDB's acquaintance; over the next dozen years, he became one of LDB's most important and effective allies in a number of reforms. *Collier's*, and later *Harper's Weekly*, also under Hapgood's editorship, carried nearly all of LDB's important articles, including the famous series "Other People's Money." When asked why he did not employ the service of other progressive journals with larger circulation, LDB replied: "I regard Mr. Hapgood as so important a factor in the American advance movement that if I have been of any service in helping *Harper's Weekly*, as his instrument, I shall feel well content with the decision made." (See LDB to J. R. Smith, 2 February 1914.) During the New Deal, Hapgood served as a courier between LDB and the White House, carrying discreet messages and advice between Franklin Roosevelt and LDB.

[6] Robert D. Kesselman (1882–1942) was controller of the Zionist Organization of America. A certified public accountant and an active Zionist, he made several trips to Palestine shortly after the World War. In 1920 he moved there permanently and established one of the first accounting firms in Palestine.

[7] Sidney Hillman (1887–1946) had first come to LDB's attention as chief clerk of the garment protocol in 1914. The following year he had been elected president of the Amalgamated Clothing Workers, a post he held until his death. An enlightened labor offical, Hillman utilized the power of his large union not only to win better pay and working conditions, but also to institute numerous welfare programs. In the 1930s, he was instrumental in leading dissident unions out of the American Federation of Labor and in establishing the Congress of Industrial Organizations.

[8] Eugene Meyer, Jr., (1875–1959) was absorbed, not by Zionism (he eventually joined the Unitarians), but by a long career in public service. In addition to his work with the War Finance Corporation and other wartime agencies, Meyer was appointed to various federal positions by every president from Wilson through Eisenhower. In 1933, he took over control of the *Washington Post*.

[9] Elizabeth Brandeis (1896–1984) was the younger of LDB's daughters. After receiving her B.A. from Radcliffe College in 1918, she served as assistant secretary, then secretary of the District of Columbia Minimum Wage Board until 1923. She then went to the University of Wisconsin from which she received a doctorate in economics in 1928; she joined the faculty of the university, and remained there until her retirement. While a graduate student she married Paul A. Raushenbush. Using her professional name of Elizabeth Brandeis, she wrote the second half of volume 3 of John R. Commons et al., *History of Labor in the United States* (New York: Macmillan, 1935), dealing with labor legislation from 1896 to 1932. In addition to her university work, she and her husband helped create the Wisconsin system of unemployment insurance, and was active in numerous civic affairs. See Paul and Elizabeth Raushenbush, *Our "U.C." Story* (Madison: privately published, 1979).

[10] George Lewis Bell (1888–1958) graduated from Harvard Law School in 1912, and had a varied career in teaching, public service, and business. In 1919–1920, he was serving as arbitrator in the New York City garment industry.

No. 17   May 19, 1919   Washington, D.C.
(Cable)

Your personal message received. I have entire confidence in your good judgment. Wrote you last week after talking with Stanley King. Please let me know soon whether in view of conditions in Palestine it would be desirable that I should postpone or cancel trip planned for June.[1] I sorrow with you and Mack over the loss of Aaron.[2]

[1] See previous letter.

[2] Aaron Aaronsohn (1876–1919) was one of the first to interest LDB in Zionism. LDB described his talk on "wild wheat" as "the most thrillingly interesting I have ever heard. . . ." (LDB to

Alfred Brandeis, 7 January 1912). Aaronsohn was killed in an airplane crash over the English Channel on 15 May.

No. 18   June 5, 1919   Washington, D.C.
(Cable)

Your cable "Agreeable" received. Cabled you through London "Upon considering Mack's detailed statement Brandeis trip indefinitely postponed." Since received your cablegram "Welcome." [1] Hesitation to go because first desire avoid London, Paris and effective transportation lacking for accomplishing direct route within time limit available for trip. Second we question wisdom of reaching Palestine before mandate is issued owing possible reactions both elements population. Trip could not be made so unostentatious as to avoid embarrassing questions. Third not having been preceded by you, Gans,[2] Flexner,[3] etc. material for rapid survey of possibility unavailable. Fourth internal American Zionists problem make[s] deHaas's remaining here desirable. Cable information or basis of judgment that would lead to conclusion favoring departure.

[1] FF's reaction to LDB's decision to cancel his trip was decisive and dramatic. He immediately inquired at the Foreign Office whether the British would consider LDB's visit to the Holy Land inappropriate, and received assurances from Secretary Balfour that His Majesty's government would welcome such a visit. FF's insistence on LDB's going to Palestine stemmed from President Wilson's decision to send an independent fact-finding mission there. FF worried that it might sway Wilson from his previous approval of a British mandate over a Jewish homeland. For Zionist maneuverings, see Melvin I. Urofsky, *American Zionism from Herzl to the Holocaust* (Garden City: Anchor Press, 1975), ch. 6, and Frank Manuel, *The Realities of American Palestine Relations* (Washington: Public Affairs Press, 1949), ch. 6.

[2] Howard Schiffer Gans (1871–1945) had served as assistant district attorney in New York before opening his own private practice in New York. During the war he was counsel to the Shipping Board and to the War Labor Policies Board, where he met and impressed FF. Although he later withdrew from the Zionist movement, during this period he was heavily involved in it.

[3] Bernard Flexner (1865–1945), a member of the distinguished family of Louisville intellectuals, was trained as a lawyer, and practiced in Kentucky and Chicago before moving to New York. Convinced in 1917 that Zionism was the only possible solution to the problems of world Jewry, Flexner joined his friends LDB and Julian Mack in active Zionist work, and was a founder of the Palestine Economic Corporation. Flexner never lost his interest in Louisville affairs and particularly in the University of Louisville. In 1946, Professor Mason dedicated his biography of LDB to the memory of Bernard Flexner.

No. 19   June 9, 1919   Washington, D.C.
(Cable)

Have received your two cables of sixth and have accordingly reconsidered decision.[1] DeHaas and I will sail as soon as possible. Now hope for reservations on Mauretania sailing next Saturday or Rotterdam sailing next Thursday.[2]

[1] FF's first cable of 6 June, dispatched at 1:00 P.M., had reiterated his view that LDB should not forego the opportunity to study Palestinian conditions on the spot. The second wire, sent at 5:00 P.M. after receipt of LDB's cable of 5 June, attempted to reassure the justice on the points he had raised. It concluded on the note that "Your failure to come may have consequences that I contemplate with utmost anxiety. Consulted Balfour who agrees with need of your coming. Weizmann concurs in this cable."

[2] The Brandeis party sailed on board the RMS *Mauretania* on the 14th.

No. 20   September 25, 1919   Washington, D.C.

MY DEAR FELIX: As to Walter L. & Zionism: He could be of greatest use by writing with a view to securing the support of the American intellectual Jews. That is

1. their support generally for the movement
2. their special aid in carrying forward our American social views in Palestine.

We shall need persistent insistence upon our idealistic program. Walter's writing and thinking should be continuous to this end, & he should keep in frequent touch with Ben Flexner.[1]

[1] Lippmann did not write for the Zionists as LDB had hoped. For his aloof attitude toward Judaism and Zionism, see the sensitive discussion in Steel, *Lippmann*, ch. 15.

No. 21   October 7, 1919   Washington, D.C.

DEAR FELIX: You will recall deHaas' & my talk with you on General Counsel for the Z.O. & eventually counsel in the several states. Please consider this & discuss it with Mack, Flexner, Gans, Szold[1] & others as occasion serves.

Meanwhile there are two matters which should receive immediate attention from the legal end.

I. To make sure that the bill for incorporation under the law of New York is in the best possible form & that steps are taken to ensure its passage as early in January as possible.[2]

II. To get ready a form or forms of bequest adequate in the several states, so that immediately after the act of incorporation is procured we may publish the forms and also prepare to utilize the occasion to get into touch with all Jewish lawyers in America, which you will recall we discussed also.[3]

In both these matters there has been unconscionable delay in the past.[4] Now we should have prepared not only the legal forms but the form of letter and the mailing list, so that we may act promptly after passage of the act.

DeHaas will send you herewith the files or part of files on each matter so that you can see what has been done. As to incorporation, I understand Louis Posner[5] has been mainly relied on. In the matter of bequests, it was taken up first with Bob Szold, then by Ben Levinson[6] in conjunction with Amram.[7]

Both matters are allied to finance, & Flexner & Gans, if not overburdened, could of course take care of these matters, but I doubt whether they will have the time.

Please let deHaas know what you think should be done about this.

[1] Robert Szold (1889–1977) had served as an assistant to Solicitor General John W. Davis before actively joining the Zionist movement at LDB's urging. In the next twenty years he would become a chief lieutenant of the Brandeis/Mack wing of the American Zionist movement. When the Brandeisists returned to power in 1930, they named Szold as head of the Z.O.A. and upon him fell the difficult task of restructuring the movement in the midst of the Depression.

[2] The Federation of American Zionists had been a voluntary association, the legal status of such an arrangement being sufficient for the needs of a small group. With the association's growth during the war years and reorganization into the Zionist Organization of America, LDB and his associates decided to secure a corporate charter from the state of New York, which would allow the Z.O.A. to benefit from certain privileges allowed incorporated nonprofit groups. The New York legislature approved the Zionist charter in its 1920 session. See LDB to Jacob deHaas, 10 July 1918.

[3] LDB was anxious to establish the Z.O.A. as a receptacle for death bequests and to alert Jewish lawyers to the possibility of having their clients designate the organization for gifts. See LDB to Jacob deHaas, 10 July 1918.

[4] See 25 July 1932.

[5] Louis Samuel Posner (1878–19[?]), a New York lawyer involved in several governmental agencies, was later to be a member of the city school board.

[6] Possibly Benno Levinson, a vice-president of the New York Law Institute and a trustee of Temple Beth El.

[7] David Werner Amram (1866–1936) was a Philadelphia lawyer and professor of jurisprudence at the University of Pennsylvania. He was active in Zionist affairs and a leader of the Philadelphia Zionist Council.

No. 22   October 13, 1919   Washington, D.C.

FF: You will recall the criticisms made by deHaas in Paris and London on Palestinian Education. The education is paid for practically by America. We have special duty in respect to it to our American contributors, as well as generally to the Cause. To discharge that duty I suggest that we create a high-class committee, composed of educators and laymen, which shall send one or more representatives to Palestine to make a thorough study so as to be able to make recommendations which will be both fundamental in character and detailed covering the system to be pursued and practical application.

The expense of the mission should be borne otherwise than by the Z.O., so that there may be no formal conflict or breach of etiquette and also for other reasons.

The creation of the Comtee & its work should be utilized as a means of developing that group interest in Palestine on behalf of the educators of which we talked.[1]

Talk this over with Laski,[2] and when opportunity serves with Abe[3] and Ben Flexner and others and when you are ready with your suggestions let deHaas have them.

[1] No such commission was created.

[2] Harold Joseph Laski (1893–1950) was one of the most important political theorists of the twentieth century. In the fall of 1916, only twenty-three years old, he came to Harvard, where he stayed until 1920, when he returned to England under heavy criticism for his support of the police in the famous Boston police strike. He then began his lengthy tenure at the London School of Economics, where he soon gained renown as a socialist theoretician, and as the chief intellectual architect of the Labour Party.

[3] Dr. Abraham Flexner (1866–1959) was a distinguished and much honored educator. Born in Louisville, the brother of LDB's friend Ben, Abraham Flexner wrote many books and articles dealing with American, Canadian, and European education—particularly medical education. Flexner was connected for many years with the Carnegie Foundation.

No. 23   December 4, 1919[1]   Washington, D.C.

DEAR FELIX: 1. The Red Clipping I have sent Graham Wallas;[2]—the several letters you enclosed have gone to Cambridge.

2. The Hoover[3] situation is pathetic.[4] It would be sad indeed, if the only use for him by the Republicans would be to kill Johnson.[5]

House's[6] hopeful possibility I heard reported by Hitz[7] as a view held also by Gregory[8]—but it seems to me beyond the possible that the Democrats would nominate him, after his rejection by the Republicans, or, indeed, that he could be elected if he won.

His coming out as a Republican applicant was a terrible blunder as I view it.

I think we might settle matters now for the Z.O. that any Conference should be in London.[9]

I hope Hillman is progressing with his bank.[10] I had a good talk with him the week before last.

[1] LDB misdated this letter as "12/4/20."

[2] Graham Wallas (1858–1932) was one of the early English Fabians and a founder and long-

34

time teacher in the London School of Economics. Perhaps the clipping that LDB was forwarding had to do with the famous "red scare" of 1919–1920, a period of fevered antiradical activities in the United States.

[3] Herbert Clark Hoover (1874–1964), after a successful career as a consulting engineer, had leaped into international prominence in 1914, when he organized relief programs for Belgium. Returning to the United States, he took over as Food Administrator during the war, and emerged in 1918 as perhaps the most capable man in the war administration. In 1921 he became Secretary of Commerce, and built up the influence and service functions of that hitherto neglected agency; and in 1928, by an overwhelming majority, the people of the United States elected him as their thirty-first president. Hoover proved too much a captive of his faith in individualism to deal adequately with the depression that engulfed America during his tenure, and he left office in 1933 scorned by many Americans.

Hoover first came to LDB's attention through Norman Hapgood, and shortly after Hoover returned to the United States, he had met with the justice. "In one hour," LDB later told Professor Mason, "I learned more from Hoover than from all the persons I had seen in connection with war matters heretofore." The two men became friends and saw each other socially as well as on political and economic matters.

[4] There had been much speculation in 1919 whether Hoover would run for the presidency in 1920, and if so, which party he would join. In the end Hoover declared himself a Republican, and reluctantly allowed his name to be broadcast as a possible candidate.

[5] Hiram Warren Johnson (1866–1945), the progressive former governor of California and now its senator, wanted the 1920 Republican presidential nomination, and he was favored by many in the party's progressive wing. But his defection to the Bull Moose party in 1912 (he had been Roosevelt's running mate) and his failure to endorse Charles Evans Hughes in 1916 had made him anathema to the conservative party leaders. LDB refers to stories that the party bosses did not want either Hoover or Johnson, but were appearing to back the former only in hopes of defeating the latter.

[6] Edward Mandel House (1859–1938) was for several years President Wilson's closest political confidant, and Wilson had deferred to his judgment when the Texan had argued that appointing LDB to the cabinet in 1913 would cause irreparable dissension within Democratic ranks. Prior to 1917 House had traveled in Europe attempting to convince the warring European powers to allow Wilson to mediate their differences. He and the president broke in 1919 over the conduct of the Paris peace talks.

[7] William Hitz (1872–1935) was a close friend of both LDB and FF. He had graduated from the Georgetown University Law School in 1900 and then practiced in Washington, D.C. In 1914 he worked for the Justice Department, and two years later he began a fifteen-year service on the Supreme Court of the District of Columbia. In 1931 he would be named a justice of the U.S. Court of Appeals for the District of Columbia.

[8] Thomas Watt Gregory (1861–1933), a Texas attorney and protégé of Colonel Edward House, had been brought to the Justice Department by Wilson as a special assistant attorney general in charge of prosecuting the New Haven Railroad for antitrust violations. In 1914 he succeeded James C. McReynolds as attorney general. What particular scheme House and Gregory had for bringing Hoover into the Democratic party is unknown.

[9] The Zionist Conference of 1920 was, in fact, held in London.

[10] Hillman had been considering developing a cooperative labor bank, one which would provide safety and credit for workers, and he would propose it at his union's convention in 1920. After much planning, the union opened a bank in Chicago in 1922 and one in New York in April 1923.

No. 24   December 4, 1919   Washington, D.C.

DEAR FELIX: 1. As to a Secretary: Are you sure that Acheson[1] would not like to stay, as Sutherland did, a second year?[2]

35

2. As to Lord Grey: [3] I hope it may be possible to see him soon.

3. I am very glad you have arranged to be in N.Y. Sunday. Many fundamental questions require decision & Mack, Wise,[4] Flexner & deHaas need your counsel.

4. I hope you will be able to jack up the Finance Comtee which sorely needs it.

5. As I said at luncheon on the 13th: We are as much in need of brains as of money. We can't do our work unless we can get men who besides having the ability will give the time to master those detailed facts, present & past, which must be considered in reaching sound decisions.

[I want you to] advise the Nat. Exec. Comtee on
- (a) on Medical Unit & malaria campaign
- (b) the educational system in Palestine
- (c) the University
- (4) the Library
- 5. the elimination of Haluka[5] through industry
- 6. the land problem in P.
- 7. Public Utilities in P.
- 8. afforestation of P.
- 9. Cooperative movement & Labor in P.
- 10. Commerce & industry in P.

I appreciate deHaas' impatience of able men who won't give the necessary time to understand & to become valuable; but we must get men who will give the time. Our few so-called leaders can't possibly do the thinking & the administrative work plus all the rest required of the office.

I hope you will take this up seriously with our associates.

---

[1] Dean Gooderham Acheson (1893–1971), after his graduation from the Harvard Law School, served as secretary to LDB from 1919 to 1921 and then entered private practice with the prestigious Washington law firm of Covington & Burling. In May 1933 he was named by Franklin Roosevelt as undersecretary of the treasury, but he resigned six months later because of differences with the president on monetary policy. In 1941 Acheson was called back into government service as assistant secretary of state. In 1945 Harry Truman named him undersecretary, and then secretary in 1949. During his four years as head of the State Department, Acheson was the architect of the Marshall Plan, the NATO alliance, and the policy of containing Russia. He also became a prime target of Senator Joseph McCarthy. Acheson's memoirs have been published in two volumes: *Morning and Noon* (Boston: Houghton Mifflin, 1965), ch. 5 of which deals with "Working with Brandeis," and *Present at the Creation* (New York: Norton, 1969), covering his years at the State Department.

[2] William Anderson Sutherland (1896–1987) had served as LDB's clerk from 1917 to 1919, after which he entered law practice in Atlanta, Georgia.

[3] Sir Edward Grey, Viscount of Fallodon (1862–1933), entered Parliament as a Liberal in 1885, and rapidly rose in the ranks. From 1905 to 1916 he headed the Foreign Office, and in 1919 came to the United States as a special ambassador to try to convince Wilson to compromise with the

Senate in order to bring the United States into the League of Nations. The president would not even see Grey, who soon returned to England, where he assumed the presidency of the League of Nations Union.

[4]Stephen Samuel Wise (1874–1949) was one of the most influential American Jews of the twentieth century. Ordained as a rabbi in 1893, Wise served briefly in New York City and in Portland, Oregon, before establishing the Free Synagogue in New York in 1907, where he served until his death over forty years later. Active in progressive politics, supporting labor and helping to found the NAACP and the ACLU, Wise had been a Zionist since the 1890s, and worked closely with LDB, Mack, and FF, helping to found the P.E.C. and playing an important part in the American reception of the Balfour Declaration in 1917. He attended the Versailles conference on behalf of Zionist programs in Palestine and followed the Brandeis faction out of the movement after the schism of 1921. Wise was one of the first American Jews to warn of the impending troubles in Germany. He later advised Franklin D. Roosevelt regularly on Jewish and Zionist affairs and was a generally accepted spokesman for a large portion of the American Jewish community. See Melvin I. Urofsky, *A Voice that Spoke for Justice: The Life and Times of Stephen S. Wise* (Albany: State University of New York Press, 1982).

[5]The organized collection of charity in the Diaspora for distribution among pious Palestinian Jews.

No. 25   January 6, 1920   Washington, D.C.

DEAR FELIX: I omitted to tell you yesterday of my talk with the Arthur Myers.[1]

I set forth to them the conditions of usefulness & when they left I understood him to say that he would take hold & would soon talk with you as to the how best.

Weizmann's[2] letter to Samuel[3] is admirable—even better than his first report from Egypt. Here is further evidence of my postulate as to character and brains.[5]

Alice & Elizabeth were enthusiastic over the luncheon. Sorry I wasn't there.

But W is all wrong about having Levin[6] come here. He would do no good, & Rosoff[7] [sic] could help only if he stayed months to become acclimated. Simon[8] could help much more & in shorter time.

[1]Arthur W. Myers (1862–1943) was a successful sugar broker with offices in Rochester and New York City.

[2]Chaim Weizmann (1874–1952) devoted his entire life to two causes, Zionism and chemistry. In 1904 he moved to England from his native Russia as a lecturer in biological chemistry at the University of Manchester, and he gradually rose to the unofficial leadership of the Zionist movement. With the fragmentation of the Zionist movement caused by the war, and with the important contacts he had made in the British government, Weizmann assumed the leadership of the world movement, and became president of the World Zionist Organization in 1919. Undoubtedly Weizmann's most important contribution to Zionism during this period was the Balfour Declaration, which he guided from conception to fruition. In 1918, the British named him head of the Zionist Commission to go to Palestine to lay the groundwork for the eventual mandatory government. Although LDB and Weizmann cooperated closely during the war, they clashed in 1920 and

1921 over the future management of the Zionist movement. LDB insisted on more practical work, while Weizmann was unsure of the political basis of the settlements in Palestine and wanted to continue developing the legal foundations for the homeland. Moreover, the two disagreed over the creation of the Keren Hayesod, a fund for the economic development of Palestine (see 6 February 1921). Weizmann challenged LDB's leadership of the American movement, and in 1921 he managed to force him out.

Weizmann's over-cautious leadership, as well as his great faith in Britain, gradually led to a weakening of his own position in the world movement, and he was ousted from the presidency in 1931. Although he was reelected in 1935, he never again enjoyed the prestige of his earlier regime. During 1947 and 1948, however, he played an important role in international negotiations over the partition of Palestine and the establishment of the State of Israel. He was the unanimous choice to be its first president.

[3] Sir Herbert Samuel, first Viscount Samuel (1870–1963), a prominent member of the Anglo-Jewish community, had played an important role in the negotiations over the Balfour Declaration, and in 1920 became the first high commissioner of Palestine, a post he held until 1925.

[4] In a lengthy letter to Samuel on 22 November 1919, Weizmann clearly analyzed not only the strengths of the Zionist work in Palestine, but its weaknesses as well, and he acutely portrayed the problems in relations among Jews, Arabs, and the British rulers.

[5] In a note to Stephen S. Wise and Julian W. Mack on this date, LDB commented: "Weizmann letter to Samuel is admirable; shows he has (at times) very sound judgment. It is character he lacks particularly."

[6] Schmarya Levin (1867–1935) was a Russian-born Jew, active in Zionism even before Theodore Herzl. He was stranded in the United States by the outbreak of World War I and was responsible for calling the 1914 meeting which led to LDB's assumption of leadership in American Zionism. Levin remained in close touch with LDB and other Zionist leaders throughout the war years.

[7] Israel Binyamin Rosov (1869–1948), a Russian oil engineer, had been a member of the early Zionist movement in that country. He settled in Palestine in 1919, and served on the Mortgage Bank and Geological Survey.

[8] Julius Simon (1875–1969) had known Herzl and was an active young Zionist leader before World War I. Throughout his life he held important and powerful positions within the Zionist executive. In 1934 he moved to Palestine and was a founder and official of the Palestine Economic Corporation, which he served as president for a quarter of a century.

No. 26   January 18, 1920   Washington, D.C.

MY DEAR FELIX: Note enclosed.

I think Holmes [1] is right. If anyone applies to the President it ought not to be the dissenters. And if anyone's sentence is reduced it (the reduction) should extend to many. [2] I hope Sayre [3] will act personally.

Julius Barnes' statement as to Hoover was fair [4] & I am convinced Hoover means it. We were together last evening & he has none of the airs of a candidate. It would be worth much to restore the old idea of "The Office Seeks the Man."

I hope you will not let Kirstein [5] rest.

[1] Oliver Wendell Holmes, Jr., (1841–1935) was undoubtedly one of the most impressive minds and fascinating characters ever produced by New England, a region famed for both. The son of a well-known litterateur, Holmes long labored in the shadow of his father, the "Autocrat of the Breakfast Table." After receiving the A.B. from Harvard in 1861, he enlisted in the Twentieth

Massachusetts Volunteers, was wounded three times, and fought for over three years before being mustered out as a captain in 1864. After the war, he took a degree in law at Harvard in 1866 and for a while practiced with the firm of Shattuck, Holmes & Munroe. But the scholarly aspects of the law attracted him more than the actual practice, and he soon was devoting more time to writing than to advocacy.

In 1880 he delivered a series of lectures at the Lowell Institute on "The Common Law," which, when published a year later, helped to modernize legal thinking in the United States. Holmes argued that the vitality of the law lay mainly in its current applications, not in its historic antecedents. The law would remain vital, he declared, only insofar as it remained contemporary to the problems it was supposed to solve; ancient origins were no guarantee of applicability. This philosophy appealed to LDB, and after the two men met, probably through Samuel Warren, they became friends.

In 1882, Holmes was appointed as associate justice of the Supreme Judicial Court of Massachusetts. In 1899, he was elevated to the chief justiceship of Massachusetts, and three years later received an appointment from Theodore Roosevelt to the Supreme Court of the United States. Holmes was to serve on the high court until 1932; in 1916 LDB joined him in his fight to transform the principles first enunciated in *The Common Law* into the law of the land.

[2] LDB is probably referring to efforts by many liberals to have a presidential pardon extended to the various persons convicted under the wartime sedition acts. It would have been highly unusual for any Supreme Court justice to have entered an appeal to the president, and thus cross fairly well-defined boundaries between executive and judicial responsibilities. Wilson did not pardon any of those convicted, although his successor, Warren G. Harding, did commute many of the sentences.

[3] Francis Bowes Sayre (1885–1972) was at that time assistant professor of law at Harvard, and would later be a full professor. From 1933 to 1939 he served as assistant secretary of state, and after the Second World War was a member of the United Nations Trusteeship Council. LDB and FF possibly hoped Sayre would act because of his close connection with Wilson; he had married the president's eldest daughter, Jessie, in 1913.

[4] Julius Howland Barnes (1873–1959) had been in charge of wheat production and supply and president of the Food Administration Grain Corporation during World War I. Barnes had declared that while Hoover was not eager to secure elected office, he would run if there was a popular demand for him.

[5] Louis Edward Kirstein (1867–1942) had worked his way up to the vice-presidency of Filene's Department Store by 1911, and he was also a director of the nationwide Federated Department Stores. He was active in both civic and Jewish agencies in Boston and was later chairman of the American Jewish Committee.

No. 27   February 11, 1920   Washington, D.C.

DEAR FELIX: Those were interesting enclosures, all of which I return.

Hoover & Mrs. dined with us quietly Saturday & we talked labor & industry. I am 100% for him. His combination of high public spirit with knowledge, ability, right mindedness, sympathy, both organizing ability & a perception of real values would do wonders in the Presidency.

I am glad you are to be in N.Y. Sunday & Monday. You are much needed. The President responded handsomely to our request.[1]

Gruesse,

[1] Negotiations in Paris on the Turkish settlement were stumbling over the fixing of boundaries for Palestine, with France pushing to expand its protectorate and influence in Syria at the expense of

the British in Palestine. LDB had written to President Wilson (see LDB to Wilson, 3 February 1920) urging him to work for enlarged boundaries. Wilson took up this suggestion and directed Secretary of State Lansing to cable our ambassador to France, instructing him to support LDB's view. (See LDB to Julian W. Mack, 9 February 1920.)

No. 28   February 17, 1920   Washington, D.C.

DEAR FELIX: When the recent Cabinet occurrences [1] are discussed, this should be brought out:

It is about as bad for a man to retire because of difference in policy & say nothing (I refer to the statement that Garrison retired on the issue of liberating the Philippines) [2] as to stay in, while disagreeing with the fundamental policies & say nothing. Of course the question when to retire depends, as Holmes would say, on a question of degree of differences.

Our general American trouble is that we make public what should be private & treat as private what is strictly a public matter, e.g. the degree & nature of the President's illness. [3]

Alice & I plan to start tomorrow for a week at Charleston (Charleston Hotel). [4] Eliz. is to join us for the weekend.

I trust the days in N.Y. were satisfactory.

[1] Due to Wilson's illness (see note 3 below), administration of the executive branch had been seriously undermined, with a number of problems receiving neither discussion nor action. Secretary of State Robert Lansing finally convened a cabinet meeting to discuss some of these problems, only to draw down Wilson's wrath upon his head. As a result, Lansing resigned from the cabinet on 14 February 1920.

[2] Lindley Miller Garrison (1864–1932), a New Jersey lawyer, served as Wilson's secretary of war from 1913 to 1916. His resignation was prompted by Wilson's unwillingness to support a strong preparedness program, as well as Congress's failure to enact a bill granting the Philippines greater autonomy and eventual independence.

[3] In the summer of 1919, after returning from his second trip to Europe, Wilson had undertaken a strenuous speaking tour to convince the American people that the United States should ratify the Paris Peace Treaty and join the League of Nations. On 25 September 1919, Wilson collapsed and was partially paralyzed by a stroke. For most of the remaining eighteen months of his administration, government officials had to deal with him through his wife and physician.

[4] Alice Brandeis had been stricken with influenza the preceding fall, and had not yet fully recuperated; LDB was taking her south for further convalescence.

No. 29   March 7, 1920   Washington, D.C.

DEAR FELIX: 1. I am asking Acheson to send you six extra copies of the Schaefer dissent so that you may attend to international needs. [1]

2. That is fine of Lord Westbury.[2] I hope you and Pound and Chafee[3] are training men who will carry out My Lord's suggestion.

3. When the record & briefs in No. 251 Twohy v. Doran, Comnr. of Internal Rev. reach your school you will find in it another instance of the injustice attending the Government's superlegal position. It was dismissed P.C.[4]

You remember "Ego sum super Grammaticum."[5]

Our greetings,

[1] In another of their notable dissents regarding civil liberties and freedom of speech, LDB and Holmes had dissented in *Schaefer* v. *United States*, 251 U.S. 466 (1920), at 482. Peter Schaefer and others published the German-language Philadelphia *Tageblatt*. They were charged with printing false news reports with the intention of furthering German success in the war. Speaking through Justice McKenna, the Court reversed the convictions of Schaefer and one of his associates on a technicality, but allowed the other convictions to stand. The gist of LDB's dissent was that the case did not present that "clear and present danger" which, Holmes had argued, was a necessary condition for abridging freedom of speech (*Abrams* v. *United States*, 249 U.S. 47, 52 [1919]). In part of his dissent, LDB wrote: "The constitutional right of free speech has been declared to be the same in peace and in war. In peace, too, men may differ widely as to what loyalty to our country demands; and an intolerant majority, swayed by passion or by fear, may be prone in the future, as it has often been in the past, to stamp as disloyal opinions with which it disagrees. Convictions such as these, besides abridging freedom of speech, threaten freedom of thought and of belief." Within one week, LDB would enter another dissent in a free speech case in *Pierce* v. *United States*, 252 U.S. 239 (1920), at 253. See Samuel J. Konefsky, *The Legacy of Holmes and Brandeis*, (New York: Macmillan, 1956), 194–201.

[2] Richard Bethel, first Baron Westbury (1800–1873), served as lord chancellor from 1861 to 1865, and was deeply involved in the reform of legal education in England. FF had evidently reported one of Westbury's ideas to LDB for contemporaneous application at Harvard.

[3] Zechariah Chafee, Jr., (1885–1957) was the son of a prosperous iron-making family from Rhode Island. In 1916 he began a forty-year career of teaching in the Harvard Law School. He was the author of numerous books on many facets of the law, his most famous work being *Freedom of Speech* (New York: Harcourt, Brace, and Howe, 1920), which attacked the Wilson administration's handling of civil liberties during World War I.

[4] *Twohy* v. *Doran* involved a tax case on appeal from the Supreme Court of Appeals for Virginia, in which George W. Twohy, the executor of an estate, sued E.J. Doran, the state's commissioner for revenue, for what he considered an unconstitutional levy of taxes upon the estate. The Supreme Court dismissed the appeal *per curiam* (by the Court) for want of jurisdiction under section 267 of the Judicial Code.

[5] "I am above grammar." Attributed to Sigismund, the Holy Roman Emperor, at the Council of Constance in 1414.

No. 30   April 5, 1920   Washington, D.C.

MY DEAR FELIX: Yours of 3rd & 4th received. Wise & Mack were here today & I understand will be with you & deHaas Friday, when present disturbing situation[1] & other general problems are to be discussed.

I. As to general international situation.

My belief is that we should show abiding faith in British & make them feel that Jews & British have an indissoluble partnership & that we expect them to live up to spirit as well as letter of the Balfour Declaration.[2]

Of course we should strengthen their good purposes by any & every communication, official & unofficial, that seems helpful, &

(a) I entirely approve of Cohen[3] conferring with Loring Christie.[4]

(b) I likewise approve of your writing Ormsby–Gore[5] & others.

(c) I am ready to send letter or cable to Mr. Balfour or Lord Robert[6] or both, if you & the others deem it advisable. If you & they think I should, please send me draft of what you think it should be.

II. Rosenblatt[7] is against Carlsbad for our conference & I rather think it may be better to show our Britishism by having the meeting in London. Talk this [over] with Simon. Continental unrest may also make this more advisable.[8]

III. I am delighted to hear that you think it will be possible to sail with us.

Yes, Hoover Republican affiliation is sad. Johnson will evident[ly] give him a hard run & also the Republican Conservatives.[9] I talked quite plainly with Stanley about ND[Baker]'s duty.[10] S[tanley] K[ing] should understand that there are realms where tact & compromise won't do.

[1] In order to exert pressure on the Allies over the disposition of Palestine, the Arabs mounted a series of attacks on Jewish settlements, culminating in riots in Jerusalem that ultimately left forty-seven Jews dead and many injured.

[2] The Balfour Declaration, issued on 2 November 1917, would remain the cornerstone and chief hope of Zionist policy until the creation of the State of Israel itself. The Declaration announced that "His Majesty's Government view with favour the establishment in Palestine of a national home for the Jewish people. . . ." The problem for the next thirty years became how to interpret the meaning and achieve the implementation of such a policy—particularly in view of another clause in it: "nothing shall be done which may prejudice the civil and religious rights of existing non-Jewish communities in Palestine,. . . ." The leading study is the splendid account by Leonard Stein, *The Balfour Declaration* (New York: Simon and Schuster, 1961). The role of LDB and of the American Zionists in getting Wilson to pressure the British to issue the Declaration is explored and debated in Selig Adler, "The Palestine Question in the Wilson Era," *Jewish Social Studies* 10 (October 1948): 303; Herbert Parzen, "Brandeis and the Balfour Declaration," *Herzl Yearbook* 5 (1963): 309; Richard Ned Lebow, "Woodrow Wilson and the Balfour Declaration," *Journal of Modern History* 40 (December 1968): 501; and Urofsky, *American Zionism*, ch. 6.

[3] Benjamin Victor Cohen (1894–1983) had been Judge Mack's clerk in 1916–1917, and in 1919 served as counsel to the Zionist delegation in London and at Paris. He returned to the United States and developed into one of the most effective and dedicated public servants of the twentieth century. A member of Franklin Roosevelt's inner circle, Cohen, together with another friend of FF's, Thomas G. Corcoran, drafted and pushed many of the most important pieces of New Deal legislation in the 1930s.

[4] Loring Cheney Christie (1885–1941), although a Canadian citizen, had served as assistant to the United States solicitor general after graduation from Harvard Law School. He would later be

legal advisor to the Canadian government and minister to the United States. Christie had been one of FF's housemates in Washington, before 1914.

[5] William George Arthur Ormsby-Gore, fourth Baron of Harlech (1885–1964), had first come into contact with Zionism during the year when he was with the Arab Bureau in Cairo. In 1918 he served as the liaison between British officials and the Zionist Commission to Palestine, winning high praise from Weizmann. In the 1930s, he was to head the Colonial Ministry during the debate over partition.

[6] Edgar Algernon Robert Cecil, Viscount Cecil of Chelwook (1864–1958), was the distinguished scion of an English family which had served the Crown since the days of Elizabeth I. Cecil was in the Foreign Office during the war, and was chairman of the Supreme Economic Council at the peace conference. An ardent supporter of the League of Nations, he received the Nobel Peace Prize in 1937.

[7] Bernard A. Rosenblatt (1886–1969), a New York lawyer, eventually became a magistrate in that city's judicial system. But his real life's work was Zionism, and he and LDB worked closely together for over three decades. After 1921, when he was elected the first American to the World Zionist executive, he and his family moved to Palestine. In 1919 he and LDB drafted the so-called Pittsburgh platform, which became the basis for American efforts to develop Palestine, and for the next fifty years he worked to put those principles into effect.

[8] The 1920 Zionist conference did take place in London.

[9] See first letter of 4 December 1919, n. 4.

[10] Newton Diehl Baker (1871–1937) had been the reform mayor of Cleveland and a leading Ohio progressive. Wilson named him to be secretary of war in 1916, and he managed the department with competence and efficiency. It is impossible to tell whether LDB had urged Stanley King to make clear Baker's "duty" with respect to the approaching election, or whether his advice had to do with Baker's role in the tense and divided cabinet at this moment while Wilson was incapacitated.

No. 31   May 2, 1920   Washington, D.C.

MY DEAR FELIX: 1. I am glad you feel contented with proceedings in Rochester.[1] The task of educating folks is no easy one. Even disaster is not a very effective instrument, & experiences are easily forgotten. One would have thought that emancipated Frenchmen might have sympathized with the struggles & errors of the Bolshevists, after their own performance in the French Revolution.

2. Mack Wise deHaas were here yesterday. I plan to spend Saturday Sunday & Monday next in N.Y.—which I can ill–afford with the Court work pressing. We can talk matters over some time on one of those days.

3. Judge Holmes was much distressed about reports on Byrne Professorship. He said he was glad to think Harvard affairs were settled, & begins to realize that freedom of speech is not a dead issue in America.[2]

4. June 12 is approaching, & I hope nothing will prevent us from sailing together.[3]

Greetings to Marian [sic].[4]

[1] Frankfurter had gone to Rochester, New York, in an effort to mediate a wildcat transit strike.

[2] Conservative lawyers on the Harvard Law School's Board of Visitors had managed to block the appointment of FF as Byrne Professor of Administrative Law because of his allegedly radical views

(see LDB to Roscoe Pound, 28 May 1919). They were particularly worried about the manner in which he would teach constitutional law. Thanks to the pressure exerted by Roscoe Pound, who threatened to resign unless the faculty's nomination of FF was confirmed, the Harvard Corporation finally named FF to the chair on 1 June 1920.

[3] To the London Zionist Conference of 1920. At that meeting LDB and Chaim Weizmann came practically to the breaking point. The Americans wanted to impose upon the world movement a greater sense of economy and purpose, to emphasize work in Palestine rather than cultural and national work in the Diaspora, and to replace many of the political and propaganda bureaus with economic programs. Weizmann evidently offered to go along with many of these proposals, but only if LDB and the Americans would take over a major role in the leadership. On point after point, he would seemingly give in to LDB; but then after conferring with his colleagues, he would back down, which led LDB to charge Weizmann with duplicity. LDB also found the endless debate of the Europeans useless and tiresome, and at one point complained that he had not come to preside over a talkfest. LDB's efforts to secure greater efficiency and emphasis on practical work in Palestine also failed, as the Weizmann faction managed to subvert his efforts to involve non-Zionist experts in the building of the homeland. For details of the conference, see Urofsky, *American Zionism*, ch. 7.

[4] Marion Denman Frankfurter (1890–1975) was the high-spirited, witty, and beautiful daughter of a Massachusetts Congregationalist minister. She graduated from Smith College and met FF in Washington in 1913. After a lengthy on-and-off courtship, and despite lukewarm feelings in both families, the two were married on 20 December 1919. Harold Laski reported to Holmes: "The boy is very happy. The girl still rather reticent and shy . . . but she makes him sing an unceasing song." Michael Parrish has written: "Their marriage fused opposites. Her cool reserve set off his ebullience. Her practical nature balanced his romanticism. His tastes ran to law, history, and politics; hers to novels and poetry. . . . It was a relationship built upon passion, friendship, and intellectual respect, but one also doomed to considerable emotional strain." (Parrish, *Felix Frankfurter*, 124.) Marion was subject to severe emotional strain and distress and to periodic nervous collapses, and she was occasionally under the care of psychiatrists. For the view that her mental and emotional difficulties stemmed from her psychic need to resist the overwhelming dominance of FF's personality, see the interpretation of H. N. Hirsch, *The Enigma of Felix Frankfurter* (New York: Basic Books, 1981), 81–85.

No. 32   September 15, 1920   Washington, D.C.

MY DEAR FELIX: Welcome home to you and Marian [sic].

I trust you will be able to spend ample time in New York for the conferences to be held and the necessary work to be done in preparing for the September 29–30 meeting.

Mack and deHaas will report to you fully on the situation. There is practically nothing I can add to what I have embodied in memoranda and letters sent deHaas and Mack [1] and my talk at the August 29 meeting of which I understand a stenographic report has been made. Please read these documents.

We have at least succeeded in keeping all matters open until Flexner's and your return. I am convinced that we can carry the Executive and ultimately the convention with our views, if adequate preparation is made and necessary work of educating individuals is done, but that we should fail without such preparation. The Chicago & Baltimore conventions should serve as warnings.[2]

It seems to me clearly wiser that I should adhere to the intention declared at the August 29 meeting that I shall not attend the September 29–30 meeting. The members ought to have the opportunity of talking matters out—in my absence; and if there is to be a controversial attitude taken or a fight, I clearly ought not to be in the meetings.

So far as Abe Tulin is concerned, it seems to me he is bound by his vote at the meeting of the delegation.[3]

I hope you bring some mitigating explanation of George Landsbury's [sic] performance with Russian gold.[4]

[1] See LDB to Mack, 1 September 1920 and to Jacob deHaas, 11 September 1920.

[2] At the Z.O.A. conventions in 1917 and 1918, numerous delegates complained about the administration's policies and methods. Once these had been explained, the convention had endorsed the administration with near unanimity. LDB believed that much of the current tension within the organization stemmed from the failure to make the administration policy clear.

[3] Abraham Tulin (1882–1973) was a Russian-born New York lawyer and Zionist leader. He would be particularly active in support of the Technion, the Palestinian technological institute. At the recent London conference Tulin had opposed LDB's plan to stay outside of the Zionist leadership.

[4] Lansbury had scandalized many people by accepting a subsidy from the Russian Communist government in support of his paper, the London *Daily Herald*.

No. 33   October 21, 1920   Washington, D.C.

MY DEAR FELIX: Re your recent letter.

1. I shall be glad to dine with the N.R. editors when I am next in N.Y., but there is no prospect of my being there soon. It seems to me advisable not to attend any Ex[ecu]tive Comtee meeting until previous controverted questions are fully disposed of, & I told deHaas yesterday that, for that reason, I deem it inadvisable to attend the Convention.

2. I shall bear Pound's birthday in mind.[1]

3. Notes from Mack, Silver,[2] Lipsky,[3] Flexner & deHaas have put me into pretty good touch with the situation. My impression is that it is improving definitely; & the discussions being had in Palestine & in London are, I think, tending to clearer vision.

4. Lipsky has ceased to be of value of [sic] the Organization. I say this entirely apart from any of the occurrences of the last two months. Definite steps should be taken to dispose of him by complete severance from office; of course in an appropriate way & generously so far as financial disposition goes, in view of earlier loyal service. But we cannot properly let him fill a job by which he retards advancement.[4]

45

Our members are sorely in need of Education. I hope the memo which I see is being published in the Jewish press will help some. In due time other lessons should be taught:

(a) what Unity means: Americans ought to be able to understand "E Pluribus Unum"
is the motto of Union & not Secession
(b) that the ideal is not the equivalent of the normal or of hot air
(c) that the idealization of American Jewish [life] is to be effective largely through Palestine realities.

6. I talked over a number of matters with deHaas about which have him talk with you when you meet.

7. I am very sorry to hear of the renewal of Mack's leg trouble. Isn't he doing too much in his several occupations? & must he not curtail?

Greetings to Marian [sic].

Thanks for the clippings from The Times & The Nation.

[1] Roscoe Pound would celebrate his fiftieth birthday on 27 October.

[2] Abba Hillel Silver (1893–1966) was in 1920 just emerging as a leader in American Zionism; he was to go on to become one of the most militant and dynamic spokesmen of Jewish nationalism in the United States. Rabbi of the prestigious Temple in Cleveland, he was among the first Reform rabbis to embrace Zionism. At Cleveland in 1921, he resigned along with the rest of the Brandeis-Mack group (see LDB to Julian Mack, 3 June 1921), but unlike some adamant followers of LDB, Silver began to work with the Lipsky administration in the late 1920s, and to some extent also made his peace with Chaim Weizmann. By the early 1940s, however, Silver renewed his criticism of Weizmann and became the acknowledged leader of the American movement.

[3] Louis Lipsky (1876–1963) devoted almost his entire life to the Zionist cause. As chairman of the executive committee of the Federation of American Zionists, Lipsky was one of a handful of men who held the young American Zionist movement together prior to 1914. From 1914 to 1920, he worked loyally for LDB but was never one of LDB's most trusted lieutenants. A brilliant journalist, Lipsky identified with the Yiddish-speaking labor Zionists and by 1920 was edging away from LDB's group (see next note). At the 1921 Cleveland convention, Lipsky led the fight against LDB, and during the 1920's he headed the Zionist Organization.

[4] Although he had long resented the secondary role he played in the Zionist organization under the Mack-Brandeis leadership, Lipsky did not emerge as an opposition leader until after the London conference, when he aligned himself with Weizmann and became his chief American aide. See LDB to Julian Mack, 17 November 1920; cf. LDB to Jacob deHaas, 25 May 1917.

No. 34   November 8, 1920   Washington, D.C.

DEAR FELIX: Thanks for the clippings.

1. My reference to Burleson's machine was to the P.O.[1]—a propos your letter being 4 days en route.

2. I have written a line to Nutter[2] which may possibly move him to call on Pound.

3. Thanks for yours re the Legal Fraternity.[3]

4. The Hamburg letter returned herewith is interesting & discerning & also encouraging. I rather think the French will subside also—soon—when they find they must foot the bills themselves.

5. I think the advice to be given serious-minded public-spirited men for the immediate future is to devote themselves to State, City, municipal & non-political affairs. If we are to attain our national ideals, it must be via the States, etc. I am convinced that the century of national expansion in governmental functions as well as in territory should now be followed by intense highminded work in the communities & for that it does not need supermen.[4]

Greetings to Marian [sic].

[1] Albert S. Burleson served as postmaster general throughout Wilson's administration.

[2] George Reed Nutter (1863–1937) had joined the firm of Warren & Brandeis upon his graduation from Harvard Law School in 1889. In 1929 he became a senior partner of Nutter, McClennen & Fish, the position he retained until his death. Nutter was active in Boston legal circles and a member of the Good Government Association executive committee from 1904 to 1934.

[3] Phi Epsilon Rho, the first national Jewish legal fraternity (soon to be called Tau Epsilon Rho) had offered its honorary presidency to LDB. LDB declined the honor (see his letter to Eugene Farber, 7 November 1920): "This form of Jewish cohesion implies exclusion of others, in activities which Jews should pursue in common with other American citizens."

[4] These remarks were occasioned, no doubt, by the sweeping victory of Warren G. Harding over the Democrat candidate James M. Cox on 2 November.

No. 35   November 25, 1920   Washington, D.C.

FF: Re yours about secretary for next year.

I leave that wholly to you. Make the choice of the man & I shall obey. If you are sure Rice [1] is the man arrange with him.

Acheson is doing much better work this year, no doubt mainly because of his greater experience; partly, perhaps, because I talked the situation over with him frankly. But for his own sake he ought to get out of this job next fall. I don't know just what his new job ought to be.[2] It should be exacting. If I consulted my own convenience I might be tempted to ask him to stay.

[1] William Gorham Rice, Jr., (b. 1892) received his S.J.D. from the Harvard Law School in 1921, and served the following year as LDB's clerk. He then went to the University of Wisconsin Law School where he remained the rest of his career, except for stints with the National Labor Relations Board and various Wisconsin labor programs in the 1930s.

[2] After finishing with LDB, Dean Acheson entered private law practice in Washington.

No. 36   November 26, 1920   Washington, D.C.

DEAR FELIX: As to the N.R.

1. I told Charles Merz[1] the other day that the N.R. ought to take up a continuous campaign against espionage & suggested to Alice Barrows Fernandez that she have Dunn[2] and Louis Howard [sic][3] use the material they gathered for Richard Cabot[4] in a pretty long series of short articles & offer them to the N.R.[5]

If Croly thinks well of this suggestion & the articles—& takes them if written—it seems to me important that the attack on espionage be not confined to industrial espionage. That is merely one bad application of a practice. The fundamental objection to espionage is (1) that espionage demoralizes every human being who participates in or uses the results of espionage; (2) that it takes sweetness & confidence out of life; (3) that it takes away the special manly qualities of honor & generosity which were marked in Americans.

It is like the tipping system an import from Continental Europe & the Near East only a thousand times worse. If Croly takes up the fight for its eradication, the immorality, the ungentlemanliness, should be made the keynote, & not the industrial wrong or infringement of liberty as in the Red Campaign.

It is unAmerican. It is nasty. It is nauseating.

2. As to labor: I think labor ought to be advised to look for a substitute for the closed shop and also for strikes. The courts and public opinion are closing in on both.

(1) For the closed shop they ought now, with the best grace possible, try to substitute the preferential union shop. That's what I tried to get Gompers[6] to do 10 years ago & not run amuck against the American idea—that the closed shop is an abridgement of liberty.[7]

(2) For strikes they ought to substitute control of credit & the cooperative movement. Let them study "Other People's Money."[8] Save & use their own aggregate savings under wise advice.

(3) They ought to be made to realize that they need

    (a) a general staff—to do thinking

    (b) a board of writers & speakers who will educate their fellow members in the significance of the policies adopted.

It is the old story of having democracy & being unwilling to pay the price.

Hopkinson's speech which I return is most interesting. Would the N.R. do well to publish the latter part of it & comment in a paragraph?

[1]Charles Merz (1893–1977) was a brilliant young journalist (he had been managing editor of *Harper's* at the age of twenty-two) presently at work on *The New Republic*. In 1921, he joined Walter Lippmann on the *New York World*; in 1931, he moved to the *New York Times*, and in 1938 became its editor.

[2]Robert Dunn, after graduating from Yale in 1918, had become an organizer for the Amalgamated Clothing Workers. Alice Barrows Fernandez worked in the Department of the Interior.

[3]Sidney Coe Howard (1891–1939), later to gain renown as a dramatist and screenwriter, was in the 1920s an investigative reporter for *Life* and *The New Republic*. In 1925 his play, *They Knew What They Wanted*, won the Pulitzer Prize.

[4]Richard Clarke Cabot (1868–1939), a wealthy Boston physician, was also lecturer in social ethics at Harvard University. He published a number of books dealing with medicine or social problems.

[5]LDB's suggestion was taken up with alacrity by Herbert Croly, and beginning in the 16 February 1921 issue, a seven-part feature entitled "Labor Spy" appeared detailing some of the abuses of commercial espionage. See *The New Republic*, 16 February-30 March 1921. An expanded version of the material, originally collected under the auspices of the Cabot Fund for Industrial Research, appeared in book form, with both Howard and Dunn listed as authors, *The Labor Spy* (New York: Republic Publishing Co., 1924).

[6]Samuel Gompers (1850–1924) was the immigrant cigar-maker who founded the American Federation of Labor in the 1880s and served as its president from 1886 until his death (except for one year in the 1890s). LDB and Gompers had debated the incorporation of unions as early as 1902 (see LDB to John Graham Brooks, 8 April 1903), and contacts between the two men were fairly regular, although never frequent or intimate, thereafter.

[7]The "closed shop" is any work situation where, by contract, only union members will be employed. In 1910, LDB developed—in connection with the New York garment workers' arbitration—what he called the "preferential union shop." It provided that "manufacturers should, in the employment of labor . . . give the preference to union men, where the union men are equal in efficiency to any non-union applicants."

[8]*Other People's Money and How the Bankers Use It* (New York: Stokes, 1914) was a compilation of LDB's *Harper's* articles which summarized and popularized the findings of the Pujo Committee (see LDB to Samuel Untermyer, 18 March 1913).

No. 37[1]   November 28, 1920   Washington, D.C.

We seem to have made a start with educating Zionists & others by the Convention proceedings.[2] It seems to me important that this work should go forward insistently. I suggest i.a. the following:

1. We must win the Yiddish press. I know its weakness & worse & the opinion heretofore held of the profitlessness of effort bestowed upon it. But difficult as the task is, it must be performed; and the situation is in several respects different from what it was.

In the first place the papers are now eager for Palestinian news. In the next, some of them have shown (like in Bubelick's [sic][3] and Idelson's[4] articles) ability & desire to understand.

This publicity work I have in mind is of a very different character from that done by Fromenson.[5] It can be done only by discreet, patient, tactful discussion & only by one who being in our inner councils, will know what is going on & will know what he can tell & what we wish to accomplish. There are reasons to believe that Alex. Sachs[6] can do this work & I think we ought to put him on it at once.

It will doubtless involve some routine on our part; but most of the work would be in educating those connected with the papers, so that they can write. The closing of the Yiddishe Volk should prove a help to us, in winning the favor of the press.

2. I hope that whatever deHaas' office, under the reorganization, may be, that he can be spared to take a series of tours throughout the country to develop his local corporation project[7] & as a bye-product [sic] of that undertake the education of the provinces. That is where our solid & profitable support must be won. And he should in the process be able to discover men competent & willing to help in our work.

[1] In addition to FF, this letter was addressed to Julian W. Mack, Stephen S. Wise, Bernard Flexner, and Jacob deHaas.

[2] The Z.O.A. convention in Buffalo seemed to provide the Mack-Brandeis administration with a full-fledged vote of confidence and for a time, at least, seemed to have silenced the opposition. Much of the debate centered around the administration proposal for economic development in Palestine, which was overwhelmingly approved. Isador Lubin, an admirer of Chaim Weizmann, wrote to him at the end of the convention warning him not to be misled by attacks in the Yiddish press; the great majority of American Zionists stood solidly behind LDB. (Lubin to Weizmann, 29 November 1920, Brandeis MSS, Z 26–2.) Actually, the Zionists rallied behind the administration at Buffalo only because they had no other choice. But when Weizmann came to the United States the following spring, the opposition would have a forceful leader as well as an able orator who could attack the Brandeis plan.

[3] The Russian-born Gedalia Bublick (1875–1948) had become editor of the Yiddisher Tagblat in 1915. He later was president of the Mizrachi Organization of America (the movement of Orthodox Jewish Zionists) and fought what he considered secularist trends in American Zionism.

[4] Abraham Zvi Idelsohn (1882–1938) was a frequent contributor to the Yiddish press as well as being a leading Jewish musicologist.

[5] Abraham H. Fromenson (1874–1935), a former writer for the New York Evening World, did publicity work for a number of Jewish organizations, writing articles in both the English and Yiddish presses. He later worked with LDB in the Palestine Economic Corporation.

[6] Alexander Sachs (1893–1973), a Russian-born economist, eventually became director of economic research for Lehman Brothers and chief economist of the National Recovery Administration. LDB had considerable confidence in his efficiency and judgment, and Sachs was then serving on the Z.O.A. reorganization committee.

[7] The scheme was to organize local corporations in many parts of the United States, each corporation making itself responsible for some small project in the upbuilding of Palestine.

No. 38   December 1, 1920   Washington, D.C.

FF: A further suggestion for the N.R.

This frequent use of the U.S. Army to quell riots in the several states is becoming a fearful abuse & danger. Look back but a few years & recall the great reluctance on the part both of State Executives to call for & of Federal to grant such use.

The N.R. should have made a thorough investigation into the facts—the records of the past & with W.Va.[1] as the modern instance come forth with a fairly long series of short meaty articles on
"Our Ireland"

It is essential

(1) that the whole facts as to past uses be ascertained

(2) that exact facts be learned [*]

(3) that the articles tell facts without comment & with the irreducible minimum of opinion

(4) that there be a series—in no other way can you make the necessary impression[2]

A. If the N.R. is to justify by its influence & results the sacrifices made for it, it must be—in the period ahead of us—more concrete in its undertakings.

B. It must be more a journal of fact—than of opinion;[3] which latter is apt to be regarded as mushy. That is, it must make its opinions tell through facts, which by their selection & method of presentation argue themselves. And in the end, facts must be presented stripped for action.

C. Its task of improving affairs must be accomplished by directing thought, & propelling influence persistently against specific evils. Remember the World's editorials on the Insurance scandal[4]—running to No. 85 & beyond.

D. It should become the educator of reforming protagonists and i.a. should get into close touch, if it does the above suggestions, with Congressmen & other publicity makers who can carry forward the fight.

[1] A rash of coal strikes broke out in West Virginia in October 1920, primarily over the problems of union recognition and a wage cut. By the end of November violence had erupted in several places, most notably Mingo County, and Governor John J. Cornwell had called out the National Guard to preserve order and protect the mines. See also 10 January 1921.

[2] *The New Republic* did not follow up on this suggestion but did print a scathing editorial attacking the reactionary attitude of the coal operators; see "Our Incorrigible Coal Industry," *New Republic* 25 (5 January 1921): 154–56.

[3] *The New Republic* has always called itself "a journal of opinion."

[4] The series of exposures, back in 1905, had alerted many to the abuses within the insurance industry, among them LDB himself, who embarked upon a long and difficult campaign to secure cheap life insurance for workers through the Massachusetts Savings Bank system. See Alpheus T. Mason, *The Brandeis Way: A Case Study in the Workings of Democracy* (Princeton: Princeton University Press, 1938).

No. 39   December 5, 1920   Washington, D.C.

DEAR FELIX: 1. I am glad you have concluded to discontinue the fortnightly trips re N.R. to N.Y. It was altogether too great a draft on time and strength.[1]

2. I shall be ready for the Mack operation any time during the next recess.[2]

3. Do exact meanwhile from Mack a temporary stay on outside work. Glad you agree with the Horning dissent.[3]

Susan has passed her bar exams.[4]

[1] FF had for a number of months played a key role in the editorial direction of the journal, and he had finally realized (despite Herbert Croly's urging) that even his enormous energy could not cope with the demands of *The New Republic*, the Harvard Law School, and the Zionist Organization of America as well as his several public service projects.

[2] Mack suffered from a circulatory ailment resulting from diabetes. Evidently this operation was postponed indefinitely, since there is no evidence that Mack was hospitalized at this time.

[3] In a case revolving around a technical point of law, Holmes wrote the majority opinion which declared that although the judge's charge to the jury, in effect ordering a conviction, may have been improper, it had not resulted in any substantive injury to the defendant, since he was manifestly guilty. LDB argued in his dissent that the judge's improper charge required a reversal, since it constituted a misuse of judicial power. *Horning* v. *District of Columbia*, 254 U.S. 135 (1920).

[4] Susan Brandeis (1893–1975) was the elder of the two Brandeis daughters. She was educated at Bryn Mawr and took her law degree at the University of Chicago. After serving four years (1921–1925) as a special assistant to the United States attorney for the southern district of New York, she opened a practice in New York with her husband, Jacob H. Gilbert. From 1935 to 1949 she served as a member of the Board of Regents of New York. She was the only member of the family to share her father's interest in Zionism and was a longtime member of the national board of Hadassah. She was also active on behalf of Brandeis University. In 1925, she became the first woman to argue before the High Court, her father, of course, disqualifying himself from hearing the case (which went against her client).

No. 40   December 10, 1920   Washington, D.C.

DEAR FELIX: *First*: I am delighted to have Marian [sic] as an ally re N.R. Sorry Sunday is too full to arrange for the dinner with Croly.

Second: If C[roly]. wants to help along specifically the labor end, he should have investigated & present clearly the following matter which I have not seen noted in the press:

The development of Strike Insurance

This is a far greater menace than mere strike breaking, which was the luxury afforded by the great. Strike insurance makes it possible to array against labor the tens of thousands of little fellows. For a premium of a few hundred dollars, indemnity against loss is secured. I understand there are three or four companies (both foreign & domestic) now operating—some of undoubted financial ability, & that these are a chief weapon of the open shop company.

Of course, they will be closely allied with the professional strike-breakers.[1]

[1] *The New Republic* did not run any articles on strike insurance.

No. 41   December 16, 1920   Washington, D.C.

FF: The Gilbert v. Minnesota opinions will go to you today. Tell me frankly whether you or Chaffee [sic] see any flaw in the reasoning in the dissent. The closing paragraph of the Court's opinion pained me most.[1]

[1] In *Gilbert* v. *Minnesota* 254 U.S. 325 (1920), the Court, speaking through Justice McKenna, upheld a 1917 Minnesota law prohibiting public speaking against enlistment and the teaching of opposition to war. In its concluding remarks, the Court declared: "It would be a travesty on the constitutional privilege [of free speech] he invokes to assign him its protection." As Samuel J. Konefsky points out, it was a strange case in which Justice Holmes voted for the limitation on free speech at the same time that LDB quoted another Holmes opinion in his dissent. In addition to pointing out that the Minnesota statute infringed upon rights and powers of the federal government, LDB objected to the fact that the law seriously impaired freedom of speech. Even the wartime powers could not be utilized to justify it, since it also applied in peacetime. The most important part of his dissent was LDB's powerful plea that freedom of speech be made part of the "liberty" guaranteed by the Fourteenth Amendment. "I cannot believe," he wrote, "that the liberty guaranteed by the Fourteenth Amendment includes only liberty to acquire and to enjoy property." See Konefsky, *Legacy of Holmes and Brandeis*, 198–201. The dissent is also noteworthy as one of the first instances in which one finds the idea that the fundamental guarantees of the Bill of Rights apply to the states through the Fourteenth Amendment. Civil liberties attorneys, most notably Walter Pollak, would elaborate on this concept until the entire Court began to accept it as true. In a little more than a decade, the Court declared, as a matter beyond dispute, that the freedoms of speech and press guaranteed in the First Amendment now applied to the states.

No. 42   December 16, 1920   Washington, D.C.

FF: This is also for JWM, SSW, BF, deH, & AS, but I want them to have with it your comments & suggestions.

Your observation that W should never be left alone for a minute, is reinforced by BVC's recent letters, & we must give close thought to producing a guardian. Lubin[1] should be induced to stay by him throughout; but another is needed. You, Mack, Wise & Flexner could not give the time if you would. DeHaas would be *persona non grata* and A.S. doubtless would be also, for different reasons.

If Lindheim is freed by that time,[2] he might meet the requirements.

It has been suggested to me that Kirstein could also if he could be induced to give up unreservedly a month or so to learning the problem & applying his acquired knowledge. He met W. in Paris & I think in London and, as I recall, the contact had favorable reactions. If K. is to be considered, we can discuss later how he should be approached. At present I merely present the problem for the consideration of yourself & others.[3]

[1] Isador Lubin (1896–1978) had done some work for the Jewish Agency and grown close to Weizmann. He would be best known, however, for his work in domestic American economic studies. Alternating between teaching and government service, and reputed to be Franklin Roosevelt's favorite economist, Lubin became the United States commissioner of labor statistics from 1933 to 1946. He was a member of the "brain trust" and even lived at the White House for a time.

[2] Norvin Rudolf Lindheim (1880–1930) had been a lawyer. He and two associates had been convicted of conspiring to conceal from the alien property custodian the fact that the *New York Evening Mail* had been purchased with German funds. He was disbarred and served a brief sentence. Afterwards he entered the fur business. He and his wife Irma were active Zionists.

[3] By the time Weizmann and his party arrived in the spring, relations between the two Zionist factions had deteriorated to such a point that it was impossible to maintain any sort of control over the Europeans.

No. 43   December 30, 1920   Washington, D.C.

DEAR FELIX: Probably a corollary of the Income Tax decision is that Congress can't prevent non-inclusion in income tax of income of State & Municipal Bonds. A resolution has been introduced for Const[itu-tional]. Amendment to change this. It will have a long, hard row of obstacles to overcome.

But there is one silver lining:—states & cities may be able to raise money cheaper than U.S.—This should make decentralization, devolution locally of governmental functions more attractive. The Croly's excessive nationalism is abating. The N.R. ought to point this out.

No. 44   January 4, 1921   Washington, D.C.

DEAR FELIX: The opinions in the Duplex Pr Co. case should go to you tomorrow.[1]

The N.R. might in view of the Senate action on passing War Finance Co. bill over veto[2]—& the special tariff bill[3]—gently touch on
"Flimflamming the Farmers"
and this need of protecting them by means of Blue Sky Laws from Congressional Gold Bricking.

I hope you saw Howard's[4] testimony about Dec. 21—on how the American farmer could, without burdening the U.S. Gov't, get if aided by the War Fin[ance]. Corp.—a first lien on the crops & income of Germany. It would, he said, only be necessary to arrange with the Allies to give us priority over the clauses for reparation.

[1] The Duplex Printing Press Company had sought an injunction against the International Association of Machinists to stop the union from waging a campaign to have printers purchase their presses from other, unionized companies. Congress, in the Clayton Act, had specifically forbidden federal courts from issuing injunctions in labor cases. By a vote of six to three, the Court, speaking through Mr. Justice Pitney, held that the Clayton Act did not apply in this case, since "Congress had in mind particular controversies, not general class war." LDB's lengthy dissent, in which he was joined by Holmes and Clarke, was a painstaking effort to educate his colleagues in the realities of industrial life, as well as to plumb the meaning of the Congress in passing the disputed section of the Clayton Act. *Duplex Printing Co.* v. *Deering*, 254 U.S. 443, 479 (1921).

[2] Agricultural interests, particularly hard hit by the postwar depression, had been agitating for relief. At the end of 1920, by a joint resolution, Congress had directed the secretary of the treasury to revive the War Finance Corporation to help farm interests. On 3 January 1921, Wilson had vetoed the measure, and argued that the major problem confronting farmers was not domestic, but the inability of European nations to pay for American farm goods, a situation that the W.F.C. would be unable to remedy. The following day both houses of Congress easily overrode Wilson's veto.

[3] Under pressure from the farm bloc, an emergency tariff had been passed in the closing weeks of the Wilson administration, only to be vetoed by the president. The Republicans moved quickly to accommodate agricultural demands, and Congress imposed prohibitive tariffs on twenty-eight agricultural items. As Wilson had predicted, the measure had practically no impact on farm income but did commit the farm state legislators to a high tariff program, and the following year Congress passed the Fordney-McCumber Tariff, imposing a general upward revision of all tariff rates.

[4] James Raley Howard (1873–1954), an Iowa farmer and president of the American Farm Bureau Federation, had testified on 24 December 1920 that all American farmers wanted was for the government to provide credits abroad on an equal basis in those areas where agricultural markets existed.

No. 45   January 6, 1921   Washington, D.C.

DEAR FELIX: Referring to my memo of 1/4, re *Farmer's Plight*:

Aside from inevitable embarrassment due to price readjustment, the fundamental trouble with the farm situation is inexcusably high prices of farm land due largely to tenant farming and rack renting.

The effective remedy is to reduce the rental. Now it is generally 1/2 of the crop. If it were made 1/3, land values would shrink, the tenants' income would grow & farmers who *own* their land would receive a fair return on its actual value.

It is good that at last Crowder's appointment to Cuba has come.[1] He considers himself sure under the new administration with Knox[2] as strong advocate.

[1] General Enoch Herbert Crowder (1859–1932) was a professional soldier who had battled Indians, served in the Philippines, and rose to provost marshal general during World War I. He performed

various services for the Cuban government during the Wilson administration, and in January 1921, Harding named him as his personal representative to the island. In 1923 he would be appointed ambassador.

[2] Perhaps Philander Chase Knox (1853–1921), an influential Republican, formerly secretary of state, and a senator from Pennsylvania. He had been a colleague of Harding's in the Senate and a rival for the presidential nomination in 1920.

No. 46[1]   January 8, 1921   Washington, D.C.

1. Re SSW's of 7. The report that Baruch[2] will give Jimmie a dinner of such proportion, and is otherwise hopeful, is most encouraging.[3]

2. I hope BF will be able to guide Jimmie's movement among the financial and business world throughout. It is important that he be kept fully in hand. Re deHaas's of 6th.

3. The Chief Justice has been ill this week—will not be in Court for some days of next.[4] This has disarranged plans of court work considerably and particularly conferences. It will not be possible for me to be in New York on 16th—and beyond that date, also, I shall be even more bound up than I anticipated. Our next recess does not come until after January 31st—i.e. we sit on that day also.

It is possible that I can arrange to give one day before February to Jimmie and it seems to me it would be better (unless you see reason to the contrary) for me to try to be in New York on 23rd rather than to entertain him at dinner here. There are no Jews here whom it would help to have him meet and while I might invite a few non-Jews to meet him at a quiet dinner in our apartment, the Cause would in no way be aided thereby, so far as I can see. Of course, if he is coming to Washington in any event, I should have him in for dinner as an act of common courtesy.

4. As to Benderly[5]—I am not convinced that we ought to try to prevent his getting subscription outside New York. We probably couldn't succeed if we tried. To try and fail would hurt us, but besides it seems to me—properly worked the competition between them and our locals ought rather to help than harm in getting money raised.

5. I feel quite sure, if what we are planning is pinning our faith on what deH calls the cream when he mentions Epstein[6] of Baltimore we shall fail egregiously. If we are to succeed it must be by stirring up new forces, who have not, in their own opinion, attained social and financial height and who see in this an opportunity.

[1] In addition to FF, this letter was also addressed to Julian W. Mack, Stephen S. Wise, Bernard Flexner, and Jacob deHaas.

[2] Bernard Mannes Baruch (1870–1965) was best known as an unusually astute expert on the stock market. Because of his intimate knowledge of the American economy, particularly with regard to raw material supply, President Wilson engaged him in public service in 1916. Baruch, as chairman of the War Industries Board, had exercised unprecedented power over the national economy. His reputation for administrative ability and judiciousness made him, thereafter, the intimate adviser of nearly every American president. Baruch was never a Zionist, and he opposed the establishment of any state on the basis of religion.

[3] Major James Armand deRothschild (1878–1957), the son of Baron Edmond deRothschild of the French branch of the family, was taken to England as a child and became a British citizen. He was active throughout his life in Zionist work and played a part in the issuance of the Balfour Declaration in 1917. He was to arrive in the United States on 18 January to raise support for an associate body to the Palestine Economic Council. There is no report of a dinner given for him by Baruch.

[4] Chief Justice Edward Douglass White (1845–1921) was to die on 19 May 1921 after a lengthy illness.

[5] Samson Benderly (1876–1944), a native-born Palestinian, had emigrated to the United States in 1898 to study medicine at Johns Hopkins. In 1910 he had been appointed director of the first Bureau of Jewish Education in the United States, and he spent the rest of his life working in various Jewish educational and social activities.

[6] Jacob Epstein (1865–1945) came to Baltimore from Lithuania as a penniless youth, and then worked his way up to operate one of the largest mail-order houses in the South. The largest contributor to Jewish charities in Baltimore, he was a recognized leader of the community.

No. 47   January 10, 1921   Washington, D.C.

FF: Who is paying expenses of U.S. troops in W. Va., there to enforce W. Va. laws? [1]

I understand that the State's Militia was merged into the U.S. Army during the war, & the State legislature concluded to establish a Constabulary instead, last year, & that this was believed not to be sufficiently organized to take care of the situation.

Also, that all the Mingo strikers are natives of W. Va.

[1] See 1 December 1920.

No. 48   January 12, 1921   Washington, D.C.

DEAR FELIX: You will remember that I called Croly's attention last year to the matter of commercial bribery & that he had a[n] article on the subject. [1]

The Trade Comm. has done some important work in this line & at my request Huston Thompson [2] had compiled the enclosed summary. This is the kind of help to better conditions which the Gov't can give through an agency & it should have all possible encouragement. If the N.R. could, with this memo as guide, look into the work here & see how it

57

could best aid by publicity, the effectiveness of the gov't might be heightened.

Will write you soon about the C Survey.[3]

[1] William Hard, "Learn from Passaic," *New Republic* 22 (14 April 1920): 213.

[2] Huston Thompson (1875–1966), a Colorado lawyer, came to Washington in 1913 as assistant attorney general, and served on the Federal Trade Commission from 1918 until the mid-1920s.

[3] A citizens' group in Cleveland, Ohio, appalled at a growing crime rate and corruption in the city courts (one municipal judge was implicated in an assassination plot), instituted an investigation of the city's criminal justice system. Working through the Cleveland Foundation, they placed direction of the survey in the hands of Roscoe Pound and FF. The final product was Pound and Frankfurter, eds., *Criminal Justice in Cleveland: Report of the Cleveland Foundation's Survey of the Administration of Criminal Justice in Cleveland, Ohio* (Cleveland: Cleveland Foundation, 1922). The report made intelligent and far-reaching recommendations, but they were beyond the political capacity of the city to implement—see Parrish, *Felix Frankfurter*, 173–74. Throughout the life of the project, LDB took a keen interest in it and consulted with FF about it regularly; see for example, 16 January 1921.

No. 49[1] January 13, 1921 Washington, D.C.

1. I enclose the Robert Szold copy of his letter to Executive December 17th and report of his interview here of December 30th.[2]

2. I think Robert Szold letter to Executive is admirable in form and matter and that National Executive should endorse it by specific vote and also authorize sending a letter setting forth clearly our views and giving Simon and deLieme[3] our full support.[4] This letter must be carefully framed and as time is short I telephoned deHaas today suggesting that he, Szold and Sachs prepare a draft if JWM approves so that definite suggestions will be ready for consideration.

3. I am, of course, of opinion, for several reasons, that no one from America should attend the London Conference.

4. I am planning to be in New York Sunday, 23rd, to confer with J[ames] deR[othschild] et al. and to attend the Elkus[5] luncheon. I will send JdeR a letter of welcome tomorrow.

5. I think we should formulate, as soon as possible, a definite statement of the proper division of functions between the World Organization and the Federations and I suggest, as the task is a difficult one requiring much concentrated thought, that Szold, DeHaas and Sachs be appointed a committee to prepare the draft. I had at first thought of doing this in a form of a personal statement or suggestion, but concluded that it had better be undertaken otherwise, i.a. because it could be well done only after much discussion with others. I enclose the rough draft

(2) pages embodying my statement which will at least suggest what I had in mind.[6]

ZIONIST UNITY
E Pluribus Unum

Unity is, of course, essential to our success. But the essentials of unity vary according to the time, the place and the subject matter of our effort. Unity does not necessarily imply uniformity. Nor does it necessarily imply concentration of power. Ends for which we unite may sometimes be attained better by diversity in means and methods than by uniformity; they may sometimes be attained better by distribution of power than by its concentration. It is important that all Zionists should consider in what respect concentration of power and uniformity in methods and means are desirable and in what respects distribution of power and diversity in methods and means will better serve our cause. We must among other things define for the World Organization and the Federations the proper spheres of initiative and of other action.

FIRST: Unity in aim is indispensable. Otherwise we shall work at cross purposes. Our aim as declared by Herzl[7] and the First Zionist Congress is to establish for the Jewish People a home in Palestine secured by public law. That, the aim for which the Zionist Organization was formed, is and must continue to be its sole aim. The legal limit of the powers of the Zionist Organization is to do those things reasonably necessary for attaining that objective. Individual Zionists have also other Jewish aims, which they, and because they are Jews, should seek to attain; but it should be done through other organizations. To attempt to attain them through the Zionist Organization would be to divert its resources and its prestige from the purpose for which it was formed; and would do so in contravention of the law of the organization. To attempt to divert the prestige of the organization and its resources in men and money is to threaten disunion. It is an essential of unity that the singleness of purpose of the organization be strictly observed.

SECOND: Although the Zionist aim is limited to the establishment of the home for the Jewish People in Palestine, it is necessary in order to attain the objective that work be done by Zionists in practically every part of the world. To what extent should that work be done exclusively by or through or under the authoritative direction or control of the World Organization? And to what extent for example shall the federations be free to initiate or conduct locally or in Palestine according to their discretion work for the common cause? The question may be answered in part categorically. In part the answer will depend largely on the character and the place in which the particular work is to be done. In part it must depend upon the conditions prevailing at the time and in the place where the work is required to be done.

(a) It is clearly the exclusive function of the World Organization and its Executive to conduct and determine all the national and foreign relations in respect to the Homeland in Palestine. In this field federations and individuals in the several countries may aid [and] should, to the best of their ability, and in every way, but only as requested by the Executive of the World Organization and always in complete obedience to its instructions. In these relations the power of the World Organization and its Executive must be not only supreme but exclusive and absolute.

[1] In addition to FF, this letter was addressed to Julian W. Mack, Stephen S. Wise, Bernard Flexner, Jacob deHaas, and Robert Szold.

[2] Although none of the manuscript collections examined contained a specific letter from Robert Szold to the Executive dated 17 December 1920, the deHaas MSS did contain an unsigned memorandum around that date with detailed plans for "the Establishment of a Jewish National Home in Palestine." In the remaining fragment, a Jewish Council is proposed that would give equal representation to the Jews of Palestine and those organizations in the Diaspora that wished to aid in rebuilding Palestine. The World Zionist Organization would deal with the mandatory power, leaving the federations more or less free to work in Palestine through whatever means they chose.

[3] Nehemiah deLieme (1882–1940), a Dutch banker and chairman of the Dutch Zionist Federation, was an important official in the Jewish National Fund. At the 1920 London Conference he had been elected to the Zionist Executive, and also appointed to the Reorganization Commission; see next notes.

[4] At the London Conference the preceding summer, the Europeans had made one effort to placate the Americans. They had agreed to appoint a Reorganization Commission to look into charges of inefficiency in the Zionist work in Palestine, and named Julius Simon and Nehemiah deLieme to head it. They convinced Robert Szold that he should join them. In the two months that the Commission functioned, it uncovered numerous instances of mismanagement, and as its discoveries began to discomfit the Weizmann leadership, the Executive maneuvered to ease Simon out and disband the Commission.

[5] Abram I. Elkus (1867–1947), a New York attorney active in Jewish affairs and Democratic politics, had been appointed ambassador to Turkey in 1916.

[6] Despite LDB's urging, a definite statement of the Z.O.A.'s position was never issued, partly because events outraced the intention. However, the ideas delineated in the following memorandum had already been explored in LDB's talk of 14 July 1920, and they would be expressed in the several documents issued after Chaim Weizmann arrived in the United States. LDB's thinking about Zionist work closely paralleled his ideas on the proper division of authority and responsibility in American governments, with the primary focus on flexibility for local and state agencies.

[7] Theodor Herzl (1860–1904), an assimilated Austrian Jew, was the founder of modern political Zionism.

No. 50   January 16, 1921   Washington, D.C.

DEAR FELIX: 1. If we are to have a sales tax, it should be a progressive one, bearing heavily on the large units. As you have often heard me insist, Bigness is the greatest curse. Steel trusts and the like are uncontrolled, and I can think of no way by which they can be curbed and ultimately broken up except through such taxation. Our futile attempts to curb them result simply in bringing the law into greater contempt. What a record of futility our Twenty Years Campaign against the Packers has been.

2. I am glad you wrote Alex. Sachs as you did.

3. I note the McElwain strike has come.[1]

4. The Cleveland Survey[2] will be interesting and instructive. It may also become an important step to better things. The chief difficulty, I fancy, will not be in discovering the cause of evil conditions or in devising legal and administrative remedies or even in getting them adopted—on paper. It will be in securing continuous, exacting application of the accepted remedy. To ensure patient, persistent and fearless application, support of a strong, earnest, stable public opinion will be necessary. To obtain that the public interest must be deep-seated. It must be fed by something more than the understanding however enriched by knowledge. Probably love of the city or at least local pride will be indispensable. Unless the citizens can be made really to care for Cleveland as an entity—to feel joy in its achievements and shame at its shortcomings—I don't see how one can expect more than mere temporary cleansing.[3]

The condition of Cleveland is particularly disheartening because it is only a few years since Tom Johnson really infused some character & civic spirit into it. I sometimes think, if he had held steadfastly to the City & resisted the temptation of a wider political field—the result might have been different.[4]

We have learned that investigations & resultant legislation, lacking the continuous support needed for real betterment, are pretty much of an illusion. We must be careful not to let surveys and research become discredited, and too much stress cannot be placed upon the futility of knowledge unless people care enough to apply it. Men must be induced to set to work to do those things public which are within their immediate grasp and within their capacities of performance. In that way possibly they may also be taught to love their community enough to make it livable.

[1] The W. H. McElwain Co. of Bridgewater, Massachusetts, had been founded by LDB's client and close friend. LDB had worked with McElwain to achieve both greater efficiency and extremely good labor relations until McElwain's death. For LDB's warm remembrance of him as one of the most progressive businessmen in the country, see LDB, *Business—A Profession* (Boston: Small, Maynard,

and Co., 1914), 5–9. LDB continued to watch the affairs of the company with interest. After the management announced a reduction in wages, the United Shoe Workers Union called a strike, and the company found its position untenable. See 20 May 1921.

[2] See 12 January 1921, n. 3

[3] On 22 January, in a short note to FF, LDB wrote: "I stick to my guess at the essential difficulty. . . . The desire for gold is not really as fundamental a source of evil as the lack of desire for that which man should live by—i.e. care for."

[4] Tom Loftin Johnson (1854–1911), after amassing a fortune in franchise operations, had gone into politics as a reformer and an advocate of Henry George's single tax. He served in Congress from 1891 to 1895, and became the reforming mayor of Cleveland in 1901. But after eight years, he ran for statewide office. See his *My Story* (New York: B. W. Huebsch, 1911).

No. 51   January 28, 1921   Washington, D.C.

DEAR FELIX: 1. You have made the position clear in your labor article [1]—I am sorry we haven't some one handy who could hammer it into A.F. of L. Or possibly you have.

2. I am glad Marion thought well of my suggestions re Cleveland.

3. Mack has doubtless reported fully on Sunday that our conference with Jimmie [de Rothschild] was encouraging. He certainly has more ability than any of us gave him credit for. Levin seemed to me pathetic in his degeneration.

4. I talked plainly to Mack in the presence of Bob Szold, deHaas & Sachs, about the need of an inflexible policy—manifested by action—on our part, & that we must be as a Stone Wall. I also told Lipsky & Schweitzer [2] later what I thought they should do or not do. Perhaps it didn't do any good, but, at all events, there can be no doubt in their minds as to what seems to me essential.

Flexner was at the luncheon with Jimmie & Dorothy (3 hours) but not at the morning session with the others.

[1] It is impossible to know which "labor article" LDB means. FF's most recent pronouncement on labor questions was a long letter, "Mr. Frankfurter Replies," in *New Republic* 25 (12 January 1921): 202. It was a discussion of conditions in the garment industry and in response to comments by a representative of the manufacturers' association.

[2] Peter J. Schweitzer (1874–1922), a Russian-born Jew, earned a fortune in the manufacture of cigarette paper, and became a leading contributor to Zionist causes. He was closely allied with Louis Lipsky.

No. 52 [1]   February 6, 1921   Washington, D.C.

1. If the London Congress is held on the 13th [2], please consider whether our best policy would not be—Absolute Silence.

We are dealing with men who do not appreciate the relation of words to acts; who distort words when spoken or written; and whose word when given cannot be relied upon. The only way to deal with such men is by acting—which includes refraining from action.[3]

2. The action we should take, in the first instance is:

1. To make sure that the Medical Unit gets $35,000 a month during 1921 and a worthy Board of Trustees.[4]

2. To do all possible to get the local corporations under way.[5]

3. To put Balfouria on the road to success.[6]

4. Do whatever BF thinks can now wisely be done for the Mortgage bank, if anything.

3. As to continuing the $25,000 a month—you know what I thought of this in the past. We may assume that what we have done was necessary.

a) If we have ample money, I have nothing additional to say except this: It was expressly agreed in London[7] that we should have monthly accounts which would show, besides disbursements

1. Amounts received from each country for shekel.[8]

2. "   "   "   "   "   " donations,
etc.

so that we could tell whether money was being contributed as proper share by others—and also whether it was being wisely expended. I have not heard that you have procured such monthly reports.

(b) If we have not ample money for the $25,000 a month *and* the $35,000 for the Medical Unit, the Medical Unit should receive the full $35,000 before anything is paid on the $25,000.

4. If we cannot give the $25,000 or other funds needed by the World Organization—our answer should always be *non-posumus* [sic].[9] I deem our policy of action—or inaction—should be supplemented by perfect formal regularity. It was partly with this in view that I insisted in London that our $80,000 should be advanced on account of shekel. There should never come from us a word indicative of separation. But of course we will not yield to their illegal or extra legal acts.

5. While I deem it important to observe absolute silence throughout the February London conference, if it is held—even to the point of refraining from answering cables—I think we should prepare with the greatest care the memo on division of powers and activities between world and local organizations—in which I hoped R.S. and deH. with A.S. would be at work and for which I sent a draft for a beginning some weeks ago.[10] I deem this of the utmost importance. After RS, deH and

AS have their draft ready, it should receive very careful revision from each of us. It should be a state paper of high order.

6. I am not in the least disturbed by the Canadian Federation's vote in favour of the Keren [Hayesod]. That, in my opinion, is exactly the kind of matter which each country (Federation) should decide for itself. If they can get most money for it by that means, let them pursue it. We who think we can't and won't pursue that course [sic]. I hope Canada will send its million.

7. Neither am I in the least disturbed by the fact that J[ames]. deR[othschild]. appears to have succeeded with non-Zionist Americans where we failed. There are Jews galore and work galore. The more people get busy and succeed in putting Jews to work, the better. That is why I strongly favour Benderly's plan [11] also yet think it should not be allowed to affect in any way our going ahead full tilt with the deHaas local corporation project. If they should collide in Palestine there will be time enough to make the necessary adjustment.

8. I cannot be in New York for the next N.E.C. meeting. I could see you here Saturday next—but if you agree in above I doubt whether it will be necessary. Felix may be here Thursday or Friday.

[1] In addition to FF, this letter was addressed to Julian W. Mack, Stephen S. Wise, Bernard Flexner, Jacob deHaas, Robert Szold, and Alexander Sachs.

[2] Chaim Weizmann wanted to hold a conference in London as a prelude to the full-scale Zionist meeting scheduled for Cleveland during the coming summer. His hope was to get the American organization to accept the Keren Hayesod, a new financial agency established in 1920 to collect money for the upbuilding of Palestine. LDB and his lieutenants were shocked at the ill-defined and inefficient outline of the proposal and of the unbusinesslike and potentially lax methods it seemed to invite. This difference was the symbolic one which led to the bitter division between the Europeans and the American followers of LDB, which culminated in the showdown in Cleveland. The American refusal to attend a London meeting in February led to cancellation.

[3] As the rift between the Z.O.A. (under the Mack-LDB leadership) and the London Executive (under Weizmann) grew wider, LDB grew more inflexible in his demand that no compromise be made with people he considered untrustworthy. Mack, by nature more conciliatory, constantly sought means of reconciliation. During the coming months, LDB would regularly urge FF to bolster Mack and to keep him firm.

[4] The American Zionist Medical Unit, started in 1918, was a team of doctors, nurses, clerks, and orderlies, to deliver health care in Palestine under the direction of Hadassah, the Zionist women's organization. The Medical Unit was always one of LDB's chief interests in Palestine.

[5] See 28 November 1920, n. 7.

[6] In order to honor Arthur J. Balfour, the Zionists planned a cooperative settlement named for him in the Jezreel Valley. It began operation in 1922.

[7] At the Zionist Conference of 1920.

[8] The *shekel* was an ancient silver coin of Palestine and also the tax paid for maintenance of the ancient Sanctuary (*Exod.* 30:13). The Zionists revived the idea of a shekel tax to support their activities and all Zionists had to purchase at least one shekel stamp each year. The sum was small, around half a dollar, but it represented a commitment to Zionism.

[9] *Non possumus* is a plea of being unable to consider or act in a given matter.

[10] See 13 January 1921.
[11] Benderly hoped to establish a system whereby local Zionist groups in America could support education in Palestine. See 8 January 1921.

No. 53 [1]   February 18, 1921   Washington, D.C.

1. I mailed JWM Special Delivery last evening a decoded cable from Palestine in which I could read only the names of U[ssischkin].[2] and W[eizmann]. Possibly that may have some bearing on the following.

2. As to AS letter to me of 17th with draft enclosed, I deem it clear that the decision (a) whether or not an answer should be made to Weizmann's letter, (b) If so—what and when, should not be made until:

I. You shall have received, and had opportunity to consider, letters under way reporting on W's Palestine activities and reasons for postponing Conference and effect of what Jimmie [deRothschild] reports and until we know whether W. et al are coming here and until

II. deHaas shall have returned so that this matter can be considered with him. W. did not mail his letter until he reached Egypt. You can, at least, be equally deliberate.

3. AS letter and memo are able documents which do him much credit;—but I think his conclusion unsound—and also some of his reasoning.

(a) He is right that we must have a definite and stable policy and that it must be maintained fearlessly and aggressively.

(b) He is right that the policy when adopted must be made known to all concerned and in the language and manner and forms of argument which those addressed will understand.

(c) He is right that we must preserve in and for the Zionist cause the democratic character of organization and not suppress the democratic spirit.

(d) He is right in his distrust of Weizmann. While I may not go as far as he or SSW in attributing to W. evil motives, I possibly go further than either in distrust; because I believe him to be incapable of keeping his word, however explicitly expressed or solemnly given. I am therefore of opinion that no arrangement made for the future should be based as a foundation upon his having "agreed."

(e) He is right in his charge of conscienceless separatism on the part of the Boris Goldberg's [3] [sic] and their like and of downright dishonesty on the part of some.

But Sachs fails to grasp, or to give due weight to, the reasons for not making a personal fight on Weizmann and also to the reasons for the program of decentralization or federation.

I. The objection to a personal fight with W. is not unwillingness to engage in personal polemics—(although they are usually inadvisable)—but that W.'s position with the British is such that we cannot pull him down publicly without toppling over, or seriously impairing, our structure. To a large part of British Officialdom and public W. embodies Zionism. We must figure with that fact just as we must figure with the fact that he is entirely untrustworthy. To attack him publicly would not only deprive us of his influence—which is great for good—but would involve a positive injury also which goes beyond the *bad* opinion of the Zionists it would foster. Furthermore, I think W. has so little control of himself that he might not be incapable of doing an act of positive injury to the cause, despite his undoubted devotion to it and inestimable service. The public fight on W. would also have serious effects within the Zionist ranks in discouraging efforts.

II. Our objection to the Keren [Hayesod] Omnibus proposition is no doubt accentuated by the quality of management which we have;—but it is far more fundamental in character and is bound up, among other things, with the fundamental reasons for objection to concentration. We object to Keren plan i.a. also because the Maaser[4] idea is wholly unsuited to America.

III. The so called Brandeis plan did involve putting under organization control by making the Executive Council (or Committee) its appointees—all Economic work and also other work undertaken by the Organization in Palestine. But it did not imply putting all, or a large part, of Palestinian economic development into the hands of that body, however able and devoted to our ideals. My thought was in line with that expressed in deHaas' letter of February 13th, 1921. The Brandeis plan contemplated leaving open to future developments—how much could or should be undertaken by the Executive Council. The amount was a matter of degree—precisely as in other governments the amount of centralization or decentralization possible—is a matter of degree. It depends, of course, largely upon men available at a particular time and upon other conditions, including existing or expected diversity of opinion, due to locality or other causes.

Under any conceivable membership of the Executive of the World Organization I should favor a very high degree of individual initiative.

My desire to reduce to its minimum the amount to be done by the Central Organization is due not only to the character of any management now available but also to the fact that the extraordinary diversity among Jews of East and West—and of the several parts of the East and the West and the Centre make it important that the task of reconciling views and methods and of assimilating the diverse be applied to as *few* functions as possible.

[1] In addition to FF, this letter was addressed to Julian W. Mack, Stephen S. Wise, Bernard Flexner, Jacob deHaas, Robert Szold, and Alexander Sachs.

[2] Menachem Ussishkin (1863–1941), an old-time Zionist, served as head of the Jewish National Fund in Palestine. He was one of the most vociferous and uncompromising of the anti-LDB group among world Zionist leaders.

[3] Boris (Dov) Goldberg (1866–1922) was a Russian industrialist and early adherent of Zionism. In 1920 he joined the staff of the Zionist Executive and settled the following year in Tel Aviv, where he died as a result of injuries incurred in the Arab riots of 1921.

[4] In order to raise money for work in Palestine, Weizmann wanted to revive the ancient Biblical practice of tithing (*ma'aser*) by which Jews gave one-tenth of their income to designated priests or to the poor. In practice the idea proved impossible to establish.

No. 54   March 2, 1921   Washington, D.C.

DEAR FELIX: 1. I am very glad to know of your Saturday in N.Y. & that you feel matters are straightened out with Mack and Flexner, deH. and Sachs. Our slogan—inter alia must be—Back up the Simon-DeLieme-Szold Reconstruction Report.[1] I hope you will be able to time your next visit to N.Y. so as to be there early in W's visit & get Mack definitely committed.

2. I am sorry Croly was bothered about supposed delay in acting on suggestions. He must not let himself be hereafter.

I hope Acheson will get himself hitched up to some job with labor folk next fall. If he does, he would be able to write some good stuff for the N.R.

Croly ought to be induced not to make the Straight life long—but distinguished by brevity i.a.[2]

3. It will be interesting to see Redlich[3]—The tragedy is becoming ever more saddening.[4]

4. We are looking forward to seeing Marian [sic] Saturday.

[1] See 13 January 1921. The report, which detailed the administrative sloppiness of the W.Z.O., bore out many of the criticisms by LDB and the Americans. Although Weizmann had promised to abide by the recommendations of the Reorganization Commission, he changed his mind and contrived to have the Executive delay formal reception of it for several months. DeLieme and Simon resigned from the Executive in protest, and Weizmann's seeming betrayal reinforced the American leadership's distrust of him and his followers.

[2] Willard Dickerman Straight (1880–1918), a young and energetic expert on China, had married the heiress, Dorothy Whitney. The couple provided Herbert Croly with the money to

establish and maintain *The New Republic*. Straight died in Paris in 1918, a victim of the influenza epidemic; and Croly agreed to write a biography. He ignored LDB's advice, however, and *Willard Straight* (New York: Macmillan, 1924) ran to 569 pages.

[3] Joseph Redlich (1869–1936) had been the last Austrian minister of finance under the Hapsburgs, and enjoyed an international reputation as an expert on law and administration. In the 1920s he became professor of comparative public law at Harvard, until he was recalled to serve once again as Austrian finance minister. Redlich was in the United States in 1921 to explain Austrian problems to American officials; see his article, "Austria: A World Problem," *New Republic* 25 (9 February 1921): 310.

[4] Austria was in a deep economic crisis, and on 11 January the government announced that it was unable to continue and that it intended to turn over the nation's affairs to the Reparations Commission. It would be several years before international loans enabled the country to establish some measure of financial stability.

No. 55   March 9, 1921   Washington, D.C.

DEAR FELIX: Judge Holmes has had a joyous birthday, and your thoughtfulness in having Haldane [1] write added much to his happiness. His only care now is getting his birthday letters answered—otherwise he seems ready for another ten years & to beat Halsbury's record. [2]

The N.R. might notice that Coolidge thought of liberty in his first address to the Senate. [3]

[1] Richard Burdon Viscount Haldane (1856–1928), the former lord chancellor of England, was considered by many to be the finest legal philosopher of his time. His tribute to Holmes's eightieth birthday was "Mr. Justice Holmes," *New Republic* 26 (9 March 1921): 34.

[2] Hardinge Stanley Giffard, first Earl of Halsbury (1823–1921), who directed the compilation of *Laws of England* (London: Butterworth and Co., 1905–1916), delivered his final decision at the age of ninety-three and lived to celebrate the seventieth anniversary of his appointment as a judge.

[3] In his inaugural address as vice president, Calvin Coolidge (1872–1933), the former governor of Massachusetts, had declared that the greatest function of the United States Senate "is the preservation of liberty, not merely the rights of the majority—they need little protection—but the rights of the minority, from whatever source they may be assailed." *The New Republic* did not comment on the address.

No. 56   March 14, 1921   Washington, D.C.

DEAR FELIX: 1. I am delighted with your letter of 11th to Mack. If anything can stiffen him—this should. His letter to me of [*] was pitiable. [1]

2. I am not surprised to hear of your N.Y. Legislative experience. It is at least a satisfaction to have issues clearly defined & have men admit themselves conservatives—flouting "foolish forward-looking policies." [2]

3. I am glad you think well of the Milwaukee Leader opinion [3] & hope Pound & Chafee will approve.

I am reading Symond's [sic] Catholic Reaction[4] & find much of contemporary interest.

[1] Although the date of Mack's letter is blotted out on the manuscript, it is difficult to understand LDB's comment in light of Mack's letter of 12 March, in which he specifically said that under no circumstances could the administration's basic principles be compromised. Moreover, Mack declared that he and the others were prepared to resign should their program be repudiated and to go to the Congress to fight the issues out there. But see next letter.

[2] The New York legislature had passed a bill abolishing the nine-member Industrial Commission, replacing it with a single commissioner of industrial affairs. Despite protests from many prolabor groups, Governor Nathan Miller had signed the bill into law on 11 March, much to the satisfaction of manufacturers. FF had gone to Albany on behalf of the Consumers' League to urge Miller to veto the bill.

[3] During the war, the Post Office Department had revoked the *Milwaukee Leader's* second-class mailing privileges on the grounds that the paper's articles were in violation of the Espionage Act. Mr. Justice Clarke, speaking for the majority, upheld the government's actions. In a lengthy dissent, LDB argued that the postmaster general had exceeded his statutory authority. As usual, he relied upon an exhaustive history of the act, seeking to demonstrate the intentions of Congress and the implied limits. Holmes filed a separate dissent, agreeing with LDB on the narrow grounds of construction, but both men also emphasized the threat to liberties in the government's action. *Milwaukee Social Democratic Publishing Co.* v. *Burleson*, 255 U.S. 407 (1921).

[4] John Addington Symonds, *The Catholic Reaction*, 2 vols. (New York: H. Holt and Co., 1887) was the fifth part of his *Renaissance in Italy*.

No. 57   March 15, 1921   Washington, D.C.

DEAR FELIX: Perhaps Ben Cohen's of Feb. 25 may stiffen Mack.

1. Sachs has doubtless sent you his full statement.[1] I enclose his personal letter of 13th. Poor Mack has gone all astray. He has been frittering away the Buffalo victory & is in danger of wrecking our organization & losing honor by an ignominious surrender.

2. The N.R. might revive: "What is the matter with Kansas?"[2] The non-partisan outrage is worse than any Southern lynching.[3] If Arthur Wood[4] is still of the American Legion, he ought to be made to "Speak Out—or Get Out." And the non-partisan victims can try an action for damages in the Federal Courts, preferably.

[1] In a memorandum to deHaas on 9 March, Sachs spelled out his belief that the European leaders coming to the United States did not want a reconciliation but a fight. He urged that Weizmann be met with an ultimatum that either he agree to a reorganization of Zionist economic policies, or that the Z.O.A. would withhold funds while it took the battle first to the convention and then to the Congress.

[2] The title of William Allen White's famous article written during the Populist heyday.

[3] The Non-Partisan League was a politically oriented farmers' group that had been organized in North Dakota in 1915. Two organizers, J. O. Stevens and O. E. Parsons, had been sent into Kansas to start a League branch there. A mob of 200 men, mostly American Legion members, had tarred and feathered them, and warned them never to come back into Benton County. The sheriff made no effort to interfere.

[4] Perhaps Arthur Wood (1870–1942), a former police commissioner of New York City, who joined the Committee on Public Information during the war and was active in veterans' affairs afterwards.

No. 58[1]   March 19, 1921   Washington, D.C.

The statement makes obvious the irreconcilable conflict.[2] Ought not the obvious be acted upon in the ZOA Government?

A coalition government is justifiable where in a great emergency party differences are sunk and their purposes postponed in the common devotion to a paramount purpose. There the divided household is temporarily united against the common enemy, and coalition is not a compromise or the vain attempt to reconcile the irreconcilable. But our differences are not as to means merely but as to ends. And the opposition differs from us in means—mainly if not wholly because they differ as to ends. Such opponents have no proper place in the Executive. Those of them allowed to survive at Buffalo remain as before an obstacle and a danger. The proper place for such opposition is among the outs.

[1] In addition to FF, this letter was addressed to Julian W. Mack, Stephen S. Wise, Bernard Flexner, Jacob deHaas, Robert Szold, and Alexander Sachs.

[2] On this day, ten members of the Z.O.A.'s National Executive Committee refused to endorse a summary statement of the Mack administration's program, and instead issued their own pronouncement. In it, they accused Mack of trying to usurp powers properly belonging to the Congess, as well as making unfounded charges against Weizmann and the other European leaders. The ten asked that Weizmann be afforded the courtesy of presenting his arguments. Among the signers were Louis Lipsky, Emanuel Neumann, Bernard G. Richards, Bernard A. Rosenblatt and Morris Rothenberg, all of whom would side against the administration at the Z.O.A. convention in June.

No. 59   March 26, 1921   Washington, D.C.

MY DEAR FELIX: We had a most interesting evening with Redlich Tuesday, at dinner with your friends the Dr. Wilmers[1]—Julia Lathrop[2] and Vernon Kellogg[3] present. I arranged to have Judge Holmes bid him come to them, & I am sure the Vernon Kelloggs have also. He had 1 hour & 40 minute talk with Hoover Tuesday & was to see Hughes[4] Wednesday.

What terrible Russian documents have come from both.[5] The newspaper men say that what Hughes wants for America isn't trade but merely the opportunity for Americans to exploit Russian natural resources untrammelled by labor laws or limitations on private property.

But the Atty. Genl. has shown he is a real thinker politically. The Debs coup[6] was worthy of L.G.

Did Marion suggest to you that Weizmann's most recent cables re Einstein[7] remind of Dr. Grierson[sic] in the "Destroying Angels?"[8]

[1] Perhaps Dr. and Mrs. William Holland Wilmer. He (1863–1936) was a Washington, D.C., ophthalmologist and professor of ophthalmology at Georgetown University.

[2] Julia Clifford Lathrop (1858–1932) was a frequent dinner guest at the Brandeises. She had long been associated with Jane Addams at Chicago's Hull House, and was a leading figure in various child welfare reforms. She was the first director of the Children's Bureau in the Department of Labor.

[3] Vernon Lyman Kellogg (1867–1937), a prominent zoologist, had been a special assistant to Herbert Hoover in the Food Administration, and after the war became permanent secretary to the National Research Council in Washington.

[4] Charles Evans Hughes (1862–1948) was one of America's great progressive statesmen, and his life paralleled LDB's at many points. As a young New York lawyer, he was swept up in the progressive movement and made a national reputation investigating gas and electric franchises and the abuses of the insurance industry in the first decade of the century. (LDB relied heavily on Hughes's insurance work to buttress his own position.) He served as a reform governor of New York between 1907 and 1910, when he received President Taft's nomination to the Supreme Court. In 1916, about a week after LDB's appointment to the Court was finally confirmed, Hughes resigned his seat to campaign against Woodrow Wilson for the presidency. From 1921 to 1924, Hughes was secretary of state under Harding and Coolidge; and after he had done considerable work in international arbitration, Hoover named him in 1930 to be chief justice of the Supreme Court, where he served until 1941. See Dexter Perkins, *Charles Evans Hughes and American Democratic Statesmanship* (Boston: Little, Brown, 1956); Merlo J. Pusey, *Charles Evans Hughes*, 2 vols. (New York: Macmillan, 1951–1952).

[5] The Harding administration was forced, in March 1921, to define its policy toward the Soviet Union, by an overture from Lenin requesting both recognition and a resumption of trade. Both Secretary of State Hughes and Secretary of Commerce Hoover issued statements rejecting the Soviet proposal. See *New York Times*, 26 March 1921.

[6] Eugene Victor Debs (1855–1926), the leader of the Socialist Party and its frequent candidate for president, had been convicted of violating the Espionage Act and sentenced to a ten-year jail term. On 24 March, in a dramatic incident staged by Attorney General Daugherty, Debs was allowed to proceed, without guards, from Atlanta to Washington, where he spent two hours with Daugherty pleading the case for his release. Debs was, in fact, pardoned later in the year. See 31 December 1921.

[7] In a major propaganda coup, Weizmann announced in late February that he would be accompanied to the United States by the legendary genius of modern physics, Albert Einstein (1879–1955), who would be seeking funds for the new Hebrew University in Jerusalem. While in this country, he visited LDB in Washington on 26 April. LDB apparently made a profound impression upon the scientist (see LDB to Alice G. Brandeis, 27 April 1921).

[8] In Louis J. Vance's *The Destroying Angel* (Boston: Little, Brown, 1912), Dr. Greyerson delivered the verdict of incurable heart disease to the novel's hero, giving him only six months to live.

No. 60   March 27, 1921   Washington, D.C.

MY DEAR FELIX: The country needs a Quo Vadis?

It will be 25 years in July, since Bryan, in a period of gloom, made his "Cross of Gold" speech.[1] We have had since then several essays at Progressivism. Have we in the quarter of a century gained or lost

71

ground—in civilization—in that which America is supposed to stand for.

In liberty and tolerance; in security to life and property; in morality; in culture. Let's have an account of stock takers. Set it down in a balance-sheet the debits and credits. Let there be an appraisal. And then the Why's and Wherefore's.

If this were carefully, artistically done by the N.R. & in a way which would provoke discussion it might make a hit—besides doing good.

What say you to this for civilization in our chief city?

Summary proceedings (divorce court)

1917–98,591	Quoted in paper	The Consolidated
1918–102,963	Marcus Braver	Gas. Co. case gives
1919–96,623	Feldman-The	498,660 as the
1920 (ten months)	N.Y Rent Law	number of the Co's
101,933	Case defended	customers, which
		must be pretty near
		the number of
		householders in
		N.Y.

[1] The famous oration praising agricultural life and the free coinage of silver which won William Jennings Bryan the nomination at the Democratic convention in 1896.

No. 61   April 10, 1921   Washington, D.C.

DEAR FELIX: 1. DeHaas reports a complete victory and fine performance on the part of yourself and others.[1] I assume you have assured yourself before leaving N.Y. that it will not be frittered away in any part by Mack's amenable qualities. We must be resolute & more vigilant than ever in defense of our autonomy. For we shall not be forgiven for winning.

2. I am doubly glad now—that in accord with our judgment—I remained here & invisible.

3. You are right about the [*] report which I am returning herewith. I am sending him a brief note of appreciation.

4. I have not read the Lansing[2] record—but you have worsted W.L. completely by your argument.[3]

5. Croly seemed to me worn & gloomy. I hope I gave him a little cheer.

[1] The Weizmann party had landed in New York on 2 April. At a two-day session of the National Executive Committee, Weizmann had temporarily surrendered to the American demands for

separation of donation and investment funds within the Keren Hayesod, and for a reorganization of the managerial methods of the World Zionist Organization. However, see next letter.

[2] Robert Lansing (1864–1928) had long been involved in foreign affairs, and when William Jennings Bryan resigned during the *Lusitania* crisis in 1915, Lansing became secretary of state in the Wilson administration. Friction between Wilson and Lansing grew over the peace negotiations, and in February 1920 the president requested his resignation.

[3] Walter Lippmann, in a long review of Lansing's book *The Big Four and Others at the Peace Conference* (Boston: Houghton Mifflin, 1921), *New Republic* 26 (30 March 1921): 137, had chided the former secretary of state for not resigning his position, given his impotence in the Wilson administration and his disagreements with the president's policies. At the very least, according to Lippmann, Lansing should have declined to go to Paris. FF, in a reply to Lippmann's review ("Mr. Lansing's Book: A Postscript," *New Republic* 26 [13 April 1921]: 198), praised Lansing who, according to FF, had made invaluable suggestions at Versailles, and had important things to say in his book about the unchecked power of the presidency in foreign affairs.

No. 62   April 19, 1921   Washington, D.C.

DEAR FELIX: 1. I am glad to know that obediently to medical advice you are letting up a bit. It is a great insurance.

2. B.F. will have reported to you on Sunday's proceedings. W's error saved us from a possible serious one.[1]

3. I do not recall anything better of Holmes J. that [sic] his D.C. Rent Law opinion & the dissent may well be compared by the reflecting student with the op[inion] of the Court in Shaefer v. U.S. & Gilbert v. Minnesota.[2]

4. The Cudahy case will also interest or amuse you.[3]

[1] After two weeks of promising negotiations, Weizmann suddenly broke off all further meetings on 17 April, and without consulting Mack, proclaimed the establishment of Keren Hayesod in the United States. Louis Lipsky, long at the center of discontent, had finally been fired by Mack on 18 April, and he, Emanuel Neumann, Bernard Richards, and other spokesmen for the Yiddish-speaking groups, organized the resistance. They bluntly told Weizmann that unless he broke off talks with Mack and promptly declared the K.H., they would desert him, and make sure that he no longer led the movement. Among the Europeans, Shmarya Levin was particularly insistent that no compromise be reached. Although LDB had been willing to go along with the talks, he appeared relieved to have further evidence of Weizmann's duplicity; with talks halted, moreover, he no longer had to worry about Mack's making too great a concession for the sake of unity.

[2] In *Block* v. *Hirsh*, 256 U.S. 135 (1921), the Court, speaking through Mr. Justice Holmes, held constitutional a District of Columbia law which placed limits upon the power of landlords to evict tenants without cause, and which protected tenants even after their leases had expired. The four dissenting minority members, McKenna, White, McReynolds, and Van Devanter, filed a sharply worded dissent which argued that the police powers of the state had to be narrowly defined, and that the rent law violated the due process clause of the Constitution. These same men, as LDB notes, were quite willing to expand the police power to limit freedom of speech when they were in a majority. For the *Shaefer* case, see 7 March 1920, and for the *Gilbert* case, 16 December 1920.

[3] *Frey & Son* v. *Cudahy Packing Co.*, 256 U.S. 208 (1921), involved a suit for damages filed against the packing company for a price-maintenance agreement that the complainants argued violated the Clayton Act. In a very short opinion, six members of the Court, including LDB and Holmes, held that there was no evidence of a conspiracy and therefore no damages could be recovered.

No. 63   April 24, 1921   Washington, D.C.

MY DEAR FELIX: 1. I trust you are "ganz hergestellt." [1]

2. About the advantages of Ben Cohen's going speedily to Europe, I don't know enough to express an opinion. I suppose much could be said to Simon & deLieme by letter; & in view of the proposal to hold our Convention about June 1, may it not be better to keep Ben Cohen here (1) to aid in the work of preparation, (2) in order to know first whether the Administration is sustained?

Until we know we can't do any effective work here or abroad. And if by any chance the Administration stand is not fully endorsed, I assume that none of us will be willing to hold executive office. We certainly can't assume or share in the responsibility of Government unless we have full support of the membership, i.e. the majority of the delegates. [2]

Had long talk with Berliner [3] yesterday who will give full support.

3. Rice impressed me very favorably. [4]

[1] "entirely recovered."

[2] See 2 June 1921.

[3] Emile Berliner (1851–1929), a German immigrant who came to the United States in 1870, was an important and wealthy inventor whom LDB wanted to involve in Zionist affairs. See 2 June 1921.

[4] William G. Rice was finishing up his term as LDB's clerk.

No. 64   April 26, 1921   Washington, D.C.

DEAR FELIX: In answer to your telegram I wired you that I think talk with W. by me inadvisable; that I think anyone's talk with him dangerous; and that, if anyone is to talk, it should be Mack in presence of Wise, deHaas [and] Ben Cohen.

As I see it we can only weaken our position by conference—weaken it for the present, but even more for the future.

Our strength within the Organization will exist & be appreciated only if it is once understood that when we take a position—we are immovable. We cannot hope to have votes enough at any Congress or Conference to overcome the Easterners—as they will practically stuff ballot-boxes as they did in effect in London last summer.

We cannot hope to convince any Congress or Conferences because the Easterners will not listen to argument & emotional oratory—subsidized to occupy the time—will prevail. They may be able eventually to appreciate facts—if they are immovable like the Rock of Gibraltar. We must therefore, by passive resistance, protect our standard. "Ich kann nicht anders etc." [1] must be our stand—politely & tactfully & sorrowfully, of course.

The abuse heaped upon Mack—no doubt with W's approval—certainly with his acquiescence, is an adminiculum [2] which should help support the same conclusions. Of course, at the bottom is the utter untrustworthiness of W. which make[s] agreement & understandings with him & even conference dangerous in the extreme. We Westerners are not, in spite of plenitude of knowledge, able to protect ourselves in any conference under such conditions.

[1] "Here I stand, I can do no other." Martin Luther's famous declaration at the Diet of Worms, 18 April 1521.
[2] A prop; in law, corroborative evidence.

No. 65   May 5, 1921   Washington, D.C.

DEAR FELIX: 1. Wired you yesterday re summer plans. [1] What have you in mind? I hope we shall spend some of the vacation together somewhere—here if not abroad.

2. Enclosed 5/3 from Mack. I assume he will send you copy of my long reply. He must be protected from a false view of duty & must, in no event, be permitted to enter the Enemy's Country without deH. as bodyguard. Our problem is so complex that there ought not be even a temptation to depart from the simple, straight & narrow path.

3. I assume deH. sent you copy of Einstein's letter to me of April 28, & of my reply, & letter to deH. suggesting that the available data be transmitted through Ben Flexner. [2]

4. I am glad you feel strongly the value of absent treatment for the WZO.

5. We must make a strong fight here during the next month.

6. Sam Rosensohn's [3] letter, returned herewith is most discerning & discriminating. [4] Would it not be good food for Mack?

7. I hope Gleason's lesson was spread.

[1] The Brandeises spent the summer of 1921 at Woods Hole, Massachusetts.
[2] See LDB to Albert Einstein, 29 April 1921. LDB directed deHaas and Flexner to send Einstein information regarding the misappropriation of funds by the World Zionist Organization. LDB believed that funds earmarked for the Hebrew University had been used for various projects in the Haifa area.
[3] Samuel Julian Rosensohn (1880–1939) had been FF's roommate at Harvard, and during the war, he had worked for Newton D. Baker (as did FF) as a labor adviser. Rosensohn would become an active Zionist, holding several positions of leadership within the movement.
[4] There is no copy of this letter in the FF Papers.

No. 66   May 20, 1921   Washington, D.C.

MY DEAR FELIX: 1. I am glad you suggested my writing Chafee.[1] I have done so and Holmes J. has been stirred to do likewise.

2. What do you know of Walter Nelles?[2] I have noted a distinction in both style & thought in his briefs—which indicates something superior.

3. The C.J.'s death arouses much speculation.[3] Like the members of the Cabinet, I am an "optimist." But I am not cheered by the important nomination noted in the morning's paper for another office.[4]

4. I have just read Judge Gary's recent encyclical.[5] It is dreadful. But it is a distinct gain to have the issue made & that we no longer pretend to be all progressives.

5. Harding's refusal to send troops to settle Mingo is a distinct gain & I note in the press (Even the N.Y. Times) a new note as to the State's obligation to police itself.[6] The Prohibition Amendment is perhaps serving in this a good purpose.

6. Zionist news is not cheering, but the continued attacks on Mack personally should tend to make him firm if you and Ben F[lexner]. will only reinforce the lesson.

7. Do you know of any good way of reaching Prest. Lewis of the United Mine Workers?[7] If it could come about in a happy way to have him call on me, I should like to tell him to go light on rate of wages & to insist upon regularity of employment. Present mine wages can't stand & should not hinder them. Coal is much too high in costs & neither mines nor RR's nor country can prosper.

I interpret the McElwain's merger as a defeat for the McE's. Probably debts overcame them.[8]

---

[1] In his important book, *Freedom of Speech*, Zechariah Chafee had critically examined the Wilson administration's restrictions on civil liberties during the war, and the Supreme Court's response to these infringements. Austen G. Fox (1849–1937), a prominent New York attorney and Harvard Law School graduate (who had led the opposition to LDB's confirmation in 1916), circulated a petition accusing Chafee of distorting facts and of holding radical views inappropriate to a professor of law. The Harvard Board of Overseers appointed a distinguished special committee to look into Fox's allegations, and on 22 May the committee heard Chafee give an eloquent speech defending both his ideas and his right to speak them. In what amounted to an acquittal, the committee completely dismissed Fox's charges. LDB's note to Chafee, on 19 May, began: "Word comes of the attack upon you for desiring to be free. . . ."

[2] Walter Ralston Nelles (1883–1937) was in 1921 a scholarly practicing lawyer in New York City. He would later become professor of law at Yale University, specializing in labor law and civil liberties. See LDB's comments about him, 31 March 1924.

[3] Edward Douglass White had died the preceding day after a lengthy illness, and Washington

was already filled with rumors about who would be his successor. On 30 June President Harding nominated William Howard Taft to lead the Supreme Court.

[4] LDB is probably referring to the appointment of James Montgomery Beck (1861–1936), a conservative New York attorney, as solicitor general. Beck served in the post from 1921 to 1925, was elected a congressman from Pennsylvania, 1929 to 1934, and became active in litigation against the New Deal.

[5] LDB may have been referring to Elbert Gary's speech on 17 May in which the head of the U.S. Steel Corporation discoursed on the need to pursue one's own economic interests in international relations. The occasion was the announcement that Gary's company would build battleships for Japan, and Gary wished the Japanese well in furthering their economic interests in the Pacific.

[6] Despite appeals from the mine owners, Harding refused to send federal troops into the troubled Mingo County, West Virginia, coal fields, declaring that there were further remedies available to state and local officials which had not yet been utilized. See 1 December 1920.

[7] John Llewellyn Lewis (1880–1969) had been the president of the United Mine Workers since 1920, and would hold that position until his retirement forty years later. The colorful and militant Lewis pioneered in social service programs for miners, was one of the founders of the C.I.O., and helped to move the American labor movement into politics.

[8] After suffering a long, damaging strike (see 16 January 1921), the McElwain Company merged with the International Shoe Company of St. Louis, a much larger firm, which announced that the McElwain plants would help meet the huge demand for its products.

No. 67   May 22, 1921   Washington, D.C.

DEAR FELIX: 1. I was glad to get your report of the Thursday joint session & that you think it was valuable as a dress rehearsal. It will, of course, be possible to extract some fangs by anticipating W's red herrings in the opening speeches at the Convention.

2. Wise and Ben Flexner were emphatic that I must not attend the Convention & expressed to me the view I had entertained. Later Bubelik [sic] urged attendance, & in a talk I had alone with deHaas last Sunday evening he also urged that I go to Cleveland for a few hours Sunday & see the stalwarts, without appearing at the Convention. This I assume, "pour encourager les autres," [1] & not to let it be inferred that I will attend no more etc.

My impression still is that it would be a mistake & that it might lead to embarrassment; for instance if there should result an attempt to have me negotiate a peace with W. etc.

We have a Court conference Sat. 4th & I must be in Court Monday, 6th. It would therefore be physically possible to attend for a few hours Sunday in all probability. But my thought is that it would be wise to leave it—that if we win at Cleveland I will come there (if desired) after adjournment to confer as to the future work. And, indeed, I am ready to meet there or elsewhere after the adjournment of the Convention to discuss our plans for the future likewise if we are defeated. But I rather feel as if more were to be lost than gained by my appearing in Cleveland until the matter is won or lost.

Let me, and New York know, whether you agree with me as to this.[2]

3. I am returning at Mack's request Einstein's letter to you & copy of your reply. It must have been a painful interview for Mack & Ben F. I am glad that W. admitted on the 19th his statement to me about the use of U. of University [sic] Funds, whatever W's view of the proprieties.[3]

4. Mohammed advised: "Ye who believe—hold fast to virtue"—I guess that's the best way for Zionists also.

Have you written anything to Eustace Percy[4] about Zionist affairs?

[1] "to encourage the others." From Voltaire's remark in *Candide* (ch. 23): "It is good from time to time to kill an admiral, in order to encourage the others."

[2] LDB did not attend the Cleveland convention; FF did attend the meeting and made a major address defending the administration and attacking the Weizmann group.

[3] See 5 May 1921, n. 2. There is no copy of FF's letters to Einstein, but they evidently dealt with the reasons Einstein had come over to America with the Weizmann party. Without fully admitting it, Einstein conceded that he did not understand all of the issues in the Zionist controversy, and would be devoting the balance of his visit to America strictly to lectures on physics.

[4] Eustace Sutherland Campbell Percy (1887–1958), later Baron Percy of Newcastle, was one of FF's oldest friends, having shared living quarters in Washington before the war. He had a long career, first in government and later in education. In addition to diplomatic work, he was a member of Parliament and an official in several cabinets.

No. 68   June 2, 1921   Washington, D.C.

MY DEAR FELIX: 1. It is good to have your letter of 1st & to know that you and DeHaas will have had full discussion of the situation last night. He is to be here tomorrow to see me after the Benderley [sic] interview[1] and will report to you.

As I see the situation now there is no reason for any change in the plans for [the] convention long agreed upon; that we must have full approval of our course & full power to carry forward our policies—or all resign and leave the power and responsibility to others.[2]

2. As to the future—whatever the Cleveland result—I postpone all suggestions until our conference which is to follow the convention. I suppose that it will be best for most that this be held in New York & I shall hold myself in readiness to meet there or elsewhere on such day and for such time as may be desired.

3. Berliner handed me check for $10,000 today which I sent to B.F. et al. in N.Y. for Medical Unit.

There are many other matters which I have deferred writing about (I got off 8 opinions yesterday & 1 more is to follow).

4. Holmes J. may have seemed somber in his letter to you after the C.J.'s death, but neither he nor she has been in better form in any June during these five years.

5. Your bout with A. G. Fox seems to have been a happy occasion. I had a full & satisfactory—and I think satisfied—letter from Chafee.[3]

6. Yes Wm. Hays has done a fine thing.[4] He had word through Ed. Lowry[5] of my trying to see him at the President's Garden Party to congratulate him & he wrote me a very nice letter.

7. Billy Hard was in last evening & has interesting things to tell of Ireland & is not without hope.

8. Sidney Hillman seems to have achieved an extraordinary victory—an amazing performance amidst the general labor gloom & stupidities.[6]

---

[1] In an interview with Samson Benderly and others, LDB tried to stress that the Zionist controversy was not over who should lead the organization, but over fundamental truths and beliefs. See LDB to Gedalia Bublick, 5 June 1921.

[2] After a long, bitter, and dramatic debate, the delegates to the Cleveland Zionist convention voted 153 to 71 at 1:30 in the morning of 6 June to establish the Keren Hayesod in the United States. Having been repudiated by the rank and file, Julian W. Mack thanked the delegates for their past support and submitted his resignation as president of the Zionist Organization of America. He then reached into his pocket and read a letter from LDB, written on 3 June, to be read just in case of this eventuality. LDB's letter affirmed support for the policies of the rejected leadership and announced his own resignation as honorary president. "Our place will then be as humble soldiers in the ranks to hasten by our struggle and policies, which we believe will be recognized as the only ones through which our great ends may be achieved" (see LDB to Mack, 3 June 1921). A string of resignations followed: among them Stephen S. Wise, Jacob deHaas, Ben Flexner, Horace Kallen, Robert Szold, Abba Hillel Silver, Nathan Straus, and FF. The delegates seemed stunned by the loss of so many of the men who had led the organization since 1914, but despite immediate calls for reconciliation, the transfer of leadership from "Americanized" Jews, led by LDB and Mack, to the Eastern Europeans, led by Louis Lipsky and other followers of Weizmann, was a genuine turning point in American Zionism. The new leadership would retain control for a full decade. See Urofsky, *American Zionism*, ch. 7, and Yonathan Shapiro, *Leadership of the American Zionist Organization, 1897–1930* (Urbana, Ill.: University of Illinois Press, 1971), ch. 6.

[3] See 20 May 1921.

[4] William Harrison Hays (1879–1954), an Indiana lawyer and an influential figure in the state's Republican party, had been named by Harding to serve as postmaster general. He would soon leave politics and enter the motion picture industry as an executive and an enforcer of "proper" screen materials. The "fine thing" he did was to restore second-class mailing privileges to the *Milwaukee Leader* (see 14 March 1921).

[5] Edward George Lowry (1876–1943), a free-lance journalist, had at one time been managing editor of the *New York Evening Post*.

[6] Thirty thousand members of the Amalgamated Clothing Workers had been on strike since 2 December 1920. Hillman had negotiated a settlement in which the workers agreed to take a fifteen

percent wage cut, but which also reestablished the impartial arbitration board in the garment industry to settle future grievances.

No. 69   June 13, 1921   Washington, D.C.

MY DEAR FELIX: Mack has doubtless reported to you on the Thursday, Friday & Saturday Conferences. The situation is promising: [1]

(1) Mack & Wise are to get together in cash before July 3, the $25,000 to cover administrative budget for twelve months.

(2) Mack, Flexner, Wise et al. are to complete before June 22 (when B.F. sails) the $50,000 required to start the Cooperative Bank—through which we are to get from J[oint]. D[istribution]. C[ommittee].—$250,000 in cash & the outstanding Palestinian small loans which may yield $100,000 more.

(3) We are to raise $250,000 for a Cooperative wholesale.

4. If & when the above shall have been accomplished deHaas may be able to resurrect & get into action the local investment companies on which he was working before the Weizmann invasion became imminent. [2]

5. Some immediate work was agreed upon which will require special attention from you: We must prepare & have ready for circulation in English, German and Hebrew, by July 15, a full and persuasive statement of our case—for circulation widely abroad in advance of the Congress. [3]

In the statement—our case for federation (or rather for dominion home rule) must be clearly & persuasively presented. Our publications have been particularly weak, disgracefully so, much below not only the English, but also far below the American sometime Opposition, eg. The New Maccabaean was far superior to the New Palestine. [4] I don't see that anyone of our crowd except you can do this. Of course several can help you. But deHaas says Ben Cohen never gets anything done and deH. (ordinarily) can't write the proper kind of statement, nor for other reasons can Sachs.

Just heard that we had accommodations on the Federal for Boston tomorrow night & at the Breakwater, Woods Hole, for Wednesday p.m.

Expect to be at 161 Devonshire St. [5] much of the morning Wednesday & will get in touch with you from there.

---

[1] After the defeat at Cleveland, LDB wrote his brother: "The result of the Cleveland convention is satisfactory to us, as it enables us to carry on our work under more favorable conditions." On 10 June the ousted forces met in New York, where LDB set out the situation: "We are from now on to free ourselves from all entanglements in order that we may sooner accomplish [our ends]. . . . We

shall, of course, remain members of the Zionist Organization of America. But we are supporters of an administration whose policies and principles have been repudiated. Those represented by the new administration we believe to be wrong. The differences between us are fundamental." (The entire talk may be found in Jacob deHaas, *Louis D. Brandeis, A Biographical Sketch* [New York: Bloch Publishing Co., 1929], 273–78.) To pursue these ends, LDB proposed the establishment of several groups that would raise investment monies for Palestine, leaving the raising of strictly donation monies to the Keren Hayesod.

[2] See 28 November 1920, n. 7.

[3] The Twelfth Zionist Congress of the World Zionist Organization was scheduled for Carlsbad in August. At that meeting, LDB's letter of resignation as honorary president of the W.Z.O. was read (see LDB to the Executive Council of the W.Z.O., written 19 June 1921).

[4] In the months preceding the convention, the administration had continued to publish as the official Z.O.A. journal *The New Palestine*, while the opposition created a new publication, *The New Maccabaean*. Most of the experienced journalists had sided with the opposition, leaving deHaas and the office workers to write pieces for *The New Palestine*. After the schism, the new Lipsky regime resumed publication of *The New Palestine*, and the name of the journal remained unchanged until the establishment of the state of Israel in 1948.

[5] The address of LDB's old law firm in Boston.

No. 70   July 6, 1921   Woods Hole, Mass.

DEAR FELIX: 1. Re Warner's letter enclosed. Couldn't you appropriately, in your survey of C[leveland].,[1] refer as one of the enduring causes of crime to crime in high places, i.e. such lawlessness as the American Legion & Ku Klux Klan?

"If gold rusteth, what should iron do?"[2]

2. I have written Mack [and] deH urging all kinds of preparedness so as to enable us to get off the Congress statement etc. immediately after our July 16–17 conference.

3. Mack feels quite deeply about B. Flexner's not making good on things undertaken. Did he talk with you about it?

And shouldn't he be definitely communicated with? I wrote JWM & DeH. to send BF immediately a report on our doings.

Hope you found Marion in good form.

Emma Erving & Selma[3] have motored over for yesterday & today.

[1] See 12 January 1921, n. 3.

[2] Geoffrey Chaucer, *The Canterbury Tales*, "Prologue," 1:496.

[3] Selma was the daughter of the Brandeises's friends, William and Emma Erving.

No. 71   [August 1921]   [Woods Hole, Mass.]

"Thus the class war plunged Greek society into every kind of moral evil. And honesty which is the chief constituent of idealism, was laughed out of existence in the prevailing atmosphere of hostility and suspicion."

Thucydides III. 83

81

DEAR FELIX: 1. This came to me through Toynbee's [1] "The Tragedy of Greeks," a brilliant and illuminating lecture (1921) which Alex. Sachs has in pamphlet form and which you and Marion should read when Cleveland survey and the Fourteenth Amendment permit.

2. I am delighted that you secured Lewis Straus, [sic] [2]—delighted for him & for us.

3. Loring C's letter & the papers are most interesting. [3] Having seen S. I shouldn't be sorry if he fell never to rise again, despite his knowledge his cleverness & his having written the "Hapsburg Monarchy." [4] He really is un-British like [*] who spoke French too well.

4. The Republican trials over taxes & tariff are refreshing & I think Lasker will be sorry soon of his Shipping Board honors. [5]

We plan to leave here on Tuesday the thirtieth for Washington.

We have seen Mrs. Straight twice since I wrote you. [6]

[1] Arnold Joseph Toynbee (1889–1975) was just embarking on his career as a historian. His reputation would reach its peak with *A Study of History*, a twelve-volume *magnum opus* published intermittently between 1934 and 1961.

[2] Lewis Lichtenstein Strauss (1896–1974) had served as Herbert Hoover's secretary until the end of the war when he joined the powerful brokerage house, Kuhn, Loeb & Co., becoming a full partner in 1929. He served on the Atomic Energy Commission under President Truman and as its chairman under President Eisenhower, and was secretary of commerce in 1958–1959. Strauss was exactly the sort of bright, young Americanized Jew that LDB was exceedingly anxious to involve in Zionist work.

[3] Loring Christie's letter to FF dealt in part with the activities of Henry Wickham Steed (see next note).

[4] Henry Wickham Steed (1871–1956) was currently serving as editor of *The Times* of London. The book LDB mentions here, *The Hapsburg Monarchy* (London: Constable, 1913) was written while Steed was a *Times* reporter in Austria.

[5] Albert Davis Lasker (1880–1952) was a pioneer in the American advertising industry and prominent in Jewish affairs. On 21 June, Lasker had been appointed chairman of the U.S. Shipping Board and served until June, 1923.

[6] Dorothy Whitney Straight (1887–1968), the widow of Willard Straight, devoted her life to philanthropic works, including the founding of *The New Republic*, and the establishment of the New School for Social Research. In 1925, she would marry Leonard Elmhirst, an English educational reformer.

No. 72   August 25, 1921   Woods Hole, Mass.

DEAR FELIX: 1. We have seen Croly twice & are to lunch there today. The family & Mrs. Evans are enthusiastic over Mrs. Straight.

2. Thanks for Harold A's [1] interesting letter—also for the interesting Labor article from the London Nation, [2] which I have given Croly.

3. Yes Miss Lathrop is the best politician going. I think the administration is in need of such talent.

4. Very glad the [Cleveland] Survey work is progressing so well. I suppose the talk of Oral Exposition will begin in September. But for that I should congratulate Marion.

5. Miss Follett is here.[3] She expresses great regret that [s]he has not had more time with you. She is among our few thinkers.

6. I have read the whole of Well's Outline[4]—without skipping—& think he has really made an important contribution by way of tool. It should stay the white man's arrogance.

[1] There is no copy of any letter from a "Harold A." in the FF MSS.

[2] LDB is probably referring to "Labor and the Cost of Living," *Nation & Athenaeum* 29 (13 August 1921): 706. A parliamentary committee had just reported against the government's proposed cut in wages, because of significant advances in the standard of living. LDB no doubt wanted Croly to pursue this type of reasoning in regard to current claims about the high cost of labor in relation to the cost of living.

[3] Mary Parker Follett (1869–1933) was a well respected writer on social psychology, public administration, and management. Probably her best known book was *The New State; Group Organization and the Solution of Popular Government* (New York: Longmans, Green, 1918).

[4] Herbert George Wells (1866–1946) was the immensely popular and prolific English novelist, social reformer, socialist, and historian. LDB was reading one of his most popular books, *The Outline of History* (New York: Macmillan, 1920).

No. 73   August 25, 1921   Woods Hole, Mass.

F.F. Some industrial researchers should determine and make clear to consumers how much of the high cost of some necessaries e.g. clothing and shoes is due to mere change of styles.

The wasteful cost of such change appears at every stage in the processes of manufacture and distribution. It is an important factor in irregularity of employment, since it prevents production & storing of articles otherwise staple. It introduces an undesirable speculative element into both production and merchandising, resulting i.a. in demoralizing bargain sales.

The long period of enforced economy ahead of us offers an opportunity of enabling those who desire this stability to resume in a measure their sometime freedom of purchasing what they had come to desire, thus saving money & effort, and escaping the flightiness of fashion which is inconsistent with the dignity of man.[1]

And be it remembered, the changes in style deprive us also of that best, the most beautiful or most useful, with which chance or labor sometime blesses us.

In a reactionary world it should be possible to get some converts to the doctrine that change is not necessarily improvement. Let those who want to buy it pay the price.

[1] See also LDB to Alice Goldmark, 26 February 1891.

No. 74[1]   **August 26, 1921**   **Woods Hole, Mass.**

Re JWM's of 24, 23 and 25:

1. I am strongly of the opinion that Miss Szold should stay in Palestine and should not return to America in any eventuality or for any purpose, even for a short visit.[2]

Our supreme task is the moral regeneration of the Palestinians, new and old. That task and not the Medical Unit was the reason why Miss Szold's going there was significant. Miss Kallen's[3] letter to her brother has shown that we did not exaggerate the seriousness of the evils or the difficulties which confront us. Our meagre forces on the firing line should be strengthened by other women of the right calibre as soon and so far as this is possible. But under no circumstances should we weaken our position there, and Miss Szold's return, even for a brief visit, would be a serious weakening.

Leading [sic] for the Hadassah forces in America should be found in the governing Seven or some new leader for America should be found by them who will rise to the responsibilities.[4] If the Seven cannot hold the 16,000 they must hold as many as they can. But surely the summons to support Miss Szold on the firing line should be a mighty weapon or rallying cry.

"When could they say, till now, that talked of Rome,

That her wide walls encompassed but one man?"[5]

2. The decision as to Mrs. Danziger[6] can await the receipt of report on the Congress.

As to S.S.W.—Aug. 19

3. I think it would be wiser not to send any greeting to the Congress.[7] America is represented by the delegates. We are represented by the Statement and our Resignation.

4. I can arrange to be in New York on September 11 or probably any other time in September. But would it not be wiser to fix some later day so that we could have (a) fuller reports of the Congress before us, and (b) Ben Flexner present, and (c) Rosenbloom[8] of course. And should we not arrange for a session, not of one, but of two or three days, of uninterrupted consideration of the Simon's matter to be passed upon.

84

If and so far as we are certain of the men we want and can get for the Palestine Development Council trustees we should begin their education by having them present at some of our sittings.

5. Has the money subscribed at Pittsburgh been collected.

6. Are the two concerns incorporated.

[1] In addition to FF, this letter was addressed to Julian W. Mack, Jacob deHaas, Stephen S. Wise, and Abba Hillel Silver, and is to be found in the Julian William Mack Papers, Zionist Archives and Library, New York City.

[2] Henrietta Szold (1860–1945), the daughter of a prominent Baltimore rabbi, early became interested in Zionism, and in 1909 founded Hadassah, the Women's Zionist Organization of America, which has administered a comprehensive program of health services in Palestine and then Israel for decades. When the Nazis came to power she organized the Youth Aliyah, which brought thousands of German children to Palestine, thereby saving their lives. Upon the urging of LDB, Miss Szold agreed to remain in Palestine.

[3] Deborah Kallen (1889–1957), the sister of Horace M. Kallen, moved to Jerusalem in 1921 and spent the remainder of her life there as a teacher.

[4] With Miss Szold's removal to Palestine, her close friend and associate, Alice Seligsberg, assumed the presidency of Hadassah, supported by a strong executive board dominated by pro-Brandeis women, including Irma Lindheim, Zip Szold, and Rose Jacobs.

[5] William Shakespeare, *Julius Caesar*, act 1, sc. 2, lines 154–55.

[6] Ida S. Danziger, a Hadassah leader.

[7] The Twelfth Zionist Congress in Carlsbad; see 13 June 1921, n. 3.

[8] Solomon Rosenbloom (1866–1925), a Pittsburgh banker active in Jewish communal affairs, was taking an important part in the newly formed Palestine Development Committee.

No. 75   August 29, 1921   Woods Hole, Mass.

DEAR FELIX: 1. The C.J. has written me twice about his plans for relieving Court congestion & I hope to talk with him when he returns to W[ashington]. end of September.[1]

2. No I haven't seen Pound's Indiana speech.[2]

3. The discussion of the Ohio Packing Case I will look for when I return to W.[3]

4. Manly Hudson has written me (& presumably you) contentedly about the International Court.[4]

We leave for Washington tomorrow.

[1] President Harding appointed former president William Howard Taft (1857–1930) to succeed Edward D. White as chief justice of the United States—thereby fulfilling a lifelong wish of this distinguished public servant. There had been a history of conflict between LDB and Taft, of course, stretching back to the days of the Pinchot-Ballinger conservation controversy. Taft had been a bitter and public opponent of LDB's confirmation to the Supreme Court in 1916 (see LDB to Norman Hapgood, 14 March 1916). Time had slowly healed the animosities of the progressive era, however, even if the philosophies of the two men were not much changed (see the charming account of LDB's chance encounter with Taft in his letter to Alice G. Brandeis, 4 December 1918). When word came of the appointment, LDB wrote Taft a note of congratulation, urging him to give thought to means

for streamlining the federal court system. Taft answered with a friendly note of his own, and the way was paved for good, even cordial, relations between the two men despite divergences of view on key judicial questions. For Taft's service in his last public office, see Alpheus T. Mason, *William Howard Taft, Chief Justice* (New York: Simon and Schuster, 1965).

[2] Pound's speech, given as part of the Indiana University centennial celebration, defended the basic tenets of sociological jurisprudence. Law still relied primarily upon logic, but a logic devoid of any reference to facts was unsuited to the needs of the nation. In the future, he predicted, legal education would incorporate more of the new knowledge of the social sciences. "The Future of Legal Education," in *Indiana University, Centennial Memorial Volume* (Bloomington: Indiana University Press, 1921), 259–72.

[3] See 19 April 1921, n. 3.

[4] Manley Ottmer Hudson (1886–1960) was a teacher of international law at Harvard and a consultant to the State Department, the International Court, and the United Nations.

No. 76   September 6, 1921   Washington, D.C.

DEAR FELIX: 1. Re yours of 3rd concerning Pound, whose letter is returned herewith. I talked to Norman. He will write nothing now, will confer with you before writing anything. Had planned to say something about Pound & you when your Cleveland Survey [1] is published. He had letters from Pound & from Chafee recently.

He apparently know[s] nothing of the real developments (of course I said nothing to him), but he remarked, the other day, that the enemy is gunning primarily at Pound, think they can brush you & Chafee away when P. shall have been disposed of. [2]

It will be wise later, after you see Pound, to consider whether fighting publicly may not be a necessary course. [3] Norman leaves for Petersham tomorrow.

2. I am much relieved that operation on Mack does not appear to be imminent. If he could be frightened into careful diet, that might serve. [4]

3. I am interested in John Walker's plan to study, but hope he will be very careful not to lose full touch with his labor friends. Roger Baldwin [5] suggested recently that there was danger of his doing so, & this was before his proposed study period.

4. After Dean's visit I am sure I can add nothing to your & Marion's knowledge of Washington affairs. But I may add, that I have not discovered that any progress has been made since June. My father would have said: "Nichts Erfreuliches." [6]

5. I note we are being much discussed at Carlsbad. [7]

6. Villard's [8] article on the Times is admirable. I did not think he could do anything as good. [9]

[1] See 12 January 1921.

[2] Although conservatives opposed to the liberal philosophy of the Harvard Law School faculty

had been defeated in their attack on Zechariah Chafee (see 20 May 1921), they still hoped to force the resignation of Pound. Staunch support from President A. Lawrence Lowell as well as some of the more prominent law school alumni thwarted the conservatives' plans.

[3] Hapgood did not write anything about the difficulties at Harvard.

[4] Mack had been troubled for several years by diabetes and complications arising from the condition, including phlebitis; he did not undergo surgery at this time.

[5] Roger Nash Baldwin (1884–1981), after several years' work with juvenile courts, had been a founder of the American Civil Liberties Union in 1917, and was its director from 1917 to 1950. During his long life Baldwin was a constant crusader for numerous causes involving civil rights and liberties.

[6] "Not very pleasant."

[7] At the Twelfth Zionist Congress. See 13 June 1921, n. 3.

[8] Oswald Garrison Villard (1872–1949) had been editor and publisher of the *New York Evening Post* from 1897 to 1918, and afterwards was editor and owner of *The Nation*. Villard wrote widely on a number of liberal causes.

[9] In "Adolph S. Ochs and His Times," *Nation* 113 (31 August 1921): 221, Villard had praised Ochs for transforming the paper in twenty-five years into the country's most reliable purveyor of news. However, he attacked Ochs for ignoring news that did not support his own narrow-minded opinions, and for fostering much race hatred. Ochs, according to Villard, also ignored the needy. "For not even the Jews, Mr. Ochs's race, has [the paper] pleaded as ardently as have others, apparently for fear lest it be further decried and criticized as a Jew paper; how else can one explain its refusal to print the British report on the Polish pogroms save as paid advertising?"

No. 77   September 12, 1921   Washington, D.C.

FF: Our merchant marine presents, perhaps, the most difficult of our purely economic problems. At the moment, attention is being directed to Shipping Board deficits.[1] These can end only when all the vessels have been disposed of. But if disposed of to be used by Americans in foreign commerce, a most serious expenditure is threatened. They cannot be operated in competition with foreign bottoms, British, Dutch, Norwegian, Greek, Japanese, without a subsidy. And the tonnage is so large that the subsidy, aside from other objections, would be burdensome in amount. The demand for a subsidy of those vessels [which] are held privately will doubtless be irresistible.

We ought to have a large ocean tonnage, e.g. as a protection in case of war. But we could utilize a large ocean tonnage in coast-wise trade, protected by our shipping monopoly. If we did this wholeheartedly in connection with our inland water navigation and short land hauls, we could provide for that great increase in transportation facilities which will be required in the near future without much new development of our railroad facilities. As to railroads the law of diminishing returns is largely applicable. Speaking generally, any large increase of their traffic will tend not to lower but to higher costs on railroad operation.

Would it not be worthwhile to have some good man look into this for the N.R.; and if upon enquiry this view seems sound, put forth the suggestion in a commanding article.[2]

[1] The United States Shipping Board had been established by Congress in September 1916 in order to purchase, build, and then maintain large numbers of merchant ships. During the war there had been no question about the vast amounts of money required, but by 1921 the crisis was over, and the Board still operated at a deficit in excess of $5,000,000 monthly. There were increasing demands that it curtail its operations, and the directors promised to end activity sometime in 1922.

[2] See E. J. Clapp, "The American Transportation System," *New Republic* 30 (15 March 1922): 72.

No. 78   September 29, 1921   Washington, D.C.

MY DEAR FELIX: I have just finished Parts I and II of the Survey.[1] The work is done ably and thoroughly, with dignity and discrimination. It is well-planned & effectively edited. And the conclusions are sound. With increased insistence, however, comes the question: "What will he do with it?"

What should be done is made clear. But can the forces be aroused to the kind of persistent, unostentatious detailed effort which is essential to the attainment of results worthwhile? They are obviously possible, if only the community will care, or even a small part of it will care enough.

There is little more that outsiders can do, unless it be this: Have the [Cleveland] Foundation arrange now that through the same investigators and directors, it will have annually, say for ten years, a survey of the progress made during the preceding year. That would give notice both that it is in earnest & that the job is one in which time is a necessary element & continuity of effort indispensable.[2]

[1] See 12 January 1921, n. 3.

[2] There was no formal follow-up on the Cleveland Crime Survey.

No. 79   November 3, 1921   Washington, D.C.

MY DEAR FELIX: 1. As to deH. I have yours—also, today, one from Mack of which you have the carbon. He doubtless will send you also copy of my answer of today.[1]

2. As to Kallen.[2] I enclose his letter just recd. Ought not he also work out his future in Palestinian realities? Will these temporary providings here by Mack ever lead to anything worthwhile for Kallen? And if we are to have an influence on Palestinian development, must it not be through Americans who will settle there—"for richer for poorer" "in health & in disease?"[3]

3. At Mack's request I have also written Ben V. Cohen. Is not Palestine the future for him? Perhaps he may find happiness, & not merely Surcease of Sorrow, there.[4]

4. At Mack's request I also wrote Ben Flexner expressing the hope that he would be in Washington soon & that we might talk things over.

5. I enclose letter from Harold. It is the bluest I know of his & I fear his turning to America is not destined to be justified by results. Certainly in our own affairs conditions are not promising.

6. I have written Pound.

7. You doubtless heard that George Rublee has come here as partner for Covington, Burling, & Rublee.

8. Yes, it is fine that Susan is to have the experience of special Asst. in the Building Construction Cases. She is very happy to work under Podell[5] for whom as a trial lawyer she has great admiration. I don't know how P. happened to make the offer. He went to Louis Posner to get her.

Susan has liberty to continue her private practice & thanks to Mack & Learned Hand,[6] she has considerable private work in the receiverships. She is having a joyous time with an endless succession of professional thrills. Mack did her an exceptionally good service in starting her receiverships last summer.

9. We are to dine with Wells[7] at Norman's next Wednesday.

Our greetings to Marion.

10. I have heard things about Tom Lamont's recent financial dealings[8] which accord with what you say of the [*].

[1] With the displacement of the LDB-Mack leadership in June, Jacob deHaas wielded considerably less power than he had commanded from 1914 to 1921. Moreover, many members of the Central Committee of the Palestine Development Council were unwilling to put up any longer with deHaas's abrasive personality. As a result, he began to talk about moving to Palestine. LDB offered to contribute generously to a fund to be established for the purpose of settling deHaas there; but deHaas decided not to make the move and he remained in the United States until his death. See LDB to Julian W. Mack, 3 November 1921.

[2] Horace Meyer Kallen (1882–1974) was a well-known social critic, philosopher, and sociologist. He is probably best remembered for his work on "cultural pluralism." Kallen was always a committed Zionist and a part of the LDB-Mack wing of the movement. In 1919 he had left the University of Wisconsin to begin his long teaching career at the New School for Social Research in New York City.

[3] Kallen did not settle in Palestine either.

[4] Ben Cohen also decided to remain in the United States.

[5] Susan Brandeis had been appointed a special assistant to David Louis Podell (1884–1947), a distinguished New York trial lawyer, who had just become assistant attorney general in the southern district of New York in charge of antitrust cases. Susan Brandeis had the responsibility for investigating building trade monopolies.

[6] Learned Hand (1872–1961), after practicing law in Albany and New York City, had been appointed U.S. District Court judge in 1909; in 1924 he was elevated to the circuit court of

appeals, where he remained until his retirement in 1951. An extremely passionate yet intellectual approach marked his handling of cases, and his commitment to civil liberties won him the love and respect of liberals during the 1920s. Many considered him worthy of appointment to the Supreme Court, and when Holmes retired in 1931, there was a futile effort made to have Hoover appoint Hand as Holmes's successor.

[7] H. G. Wells was in the United States in the fall of 1921 for the Washington Naval Conference (see next letter).

[8] Thomas William Lamont (1870–1948) had an extraordinary double career as a journalist and a banker. In 1911 he joined the J. P. Morgan organization, and his financial dealings with the British and French before World War I led to some criticism that he was one of those bankers who lured the United States into the war. At this time he was also the owner of the *New York Evening Post*. In 1943 he became chairman of the board of J. P. Morgan and Company.

No. 80   November 13, 1921   Washington, D.C.

MY DEAR FELIX: It is good to have your and Marion's greeting. [1]

Hughes has done an admirable job. His persuasive business-like, determined manner was appropriate to the proposal, which almost took on the character of a command without its form. Of course, this part is relatively easy. But the elan of initial success may carry him far. [2]

My own belief is that we westerners might as well recognize that we have established that we lack the character & intelligence which alone would justify our controlling Asia and that we should begin an orderly retreat. When we shall have evacuated, it will be China and India, not Japan, that dominates.

My real concern is about America. Will there develop here a worthy civilization? Success in this international situation, where all the nations are anxious to have us help them "let go" may turn our heads further & divert us again from a consideration of our own shortcomings.

We have seen the [Loring] Christies, the Zimmerns [3] and [H. G.] Wells, and Regina.

My greetings to Marion,

[1] This date marked LDB's sixty-fifth birthday.

[2] In recognition of the growing naval armaments race between Japan and the United States, Senator William Borah had amended the 1921 Naval Appropriations Act to request the president to invite Great Britain and Japan to discuss naval disarmament. Secretary of State Charles Evans Hughes opened the conference in Washington on 12 November 1921, and boldly proposed that the large powers agree to a ten-year "holiday" in the construction of battleships, as well as scrapping some of their existing ships. Hughes secured a number of treaties, but the most important provisions established a ratio of parity of capital ships at five each for the United States and Great Britain and three for Japan, and recognized Japan's "special interests" in the Pacific.

[3] Alfred Zimmern (1879–1957) was a well-known British intellectual and writer. Although he spent his life studying and writing on foreign relations, his best known work was probably *The Greek Commonwealth* (Oxford: Clarendon Press, 1911), which was one of LDB's favorite books. See

the perceptive treatment of this in Philippa Strum, *Louis D. Brandeis: Justice for the People* (Cambridge, Mass.: Harvard University Press, 1984), 237–42.

No. 81   December 2, 1921   Washington, D.C.

DEAR FELIX: 1. As to Hillman's Russian plan.[1] As President Wilson used to say: "It is an interesting suggestion." Subject to obvious risks, it seems also politically & economically sound. But I thought it wise to make two suggestions to H.

    1. That W. O. Thompson[2] do [sic] not see State Dept.—until Hillman has talked with Raymond Robbins [sic][3] & through him won William Boyce Thompson,[4] Tom Thatcher,[sic][5] & men of that stamp.

    2. That in view of Hillman's American situation it is unwise, at the present time, for him to be too prominent & to give his opponents the Soviet Club; that when he appears before the public in this matter, it should be as labor consorting & cooperating with the capitalists.

    H. seems to think that he has so deflated war wages that they are now only 50% above prewar & that he has no struggles ahead. I can't take that cheerful view of the situation. To me it seems there is a long lane of lowering prices which we must travel & then there will be few upgrades relatively.

    2. I am glad you are poking Mack (and I hope Wise & Silver) on collections. We have only 30 days more.

    I wish our organization were as effective & efficient as the Hadassah.

    3. [Manley] Hudson has just been in. I am glad he is so active & eager.

    4. Don't let Chafee waste himself on practice or Scott.[6] The salaries will go further in the era of lowering prices ahead & with it will come some living perhaps. If need be, salaries must be raised.

[1] Sidney Hillman, who had been born in Russia, wanted to establish a Russian-American Industrial Corporation, a cooperative venture to produce clothing by modern factory methods in the Soviet Union. After raising money and negotiating with the Russians, Hillman and his supporters established several factories which produced clothing during the mid-1920s. Soviet officials ended the arrangement before 1928, as Lenin's New Economic Policy was supplanted by Stalin's Five-Year Plan.

[2] William Ormonde Thompson (1870–1942) was an experienced labor lawyer and a close personal friend of Hillman. He served as counsel to the International Ladies Garment Workers' Union and accompanied Hillman on his second trip to the Soviet Union in 1922.

[3] Raymond Robins (1873–1954) was a noted social reformer and settlement house activist and a leading authority on the Soviet Union. He knew both Lenin and Trotsky and was a tireless advocate of better relations and eventual recognition.

[4] William Boyce Thompson (1860–1930) had served with Robins on the Red Cross mission to

Russia in 1917. He was a businessman in New York banking and insurance circles, and he undertook several diplomatic missions for the United States government.

[5] Thomas Day Thacher (1881–1950) was a graduate of the Yale Law School and a New York lawyer, close to both FF and LDB. He was appointed a federal district judge by President Coolidge in 1925 and became solicitor general in the Hoover administration. Like Robins and William Boyce Thompson, Thacher had also served on the Red Cross mission to Russia in 1917.

[6] In view of low salaries at Harvard, both Zechariah Chafee and Austin Wakeman Scott (1884–1981) were thinking about entering private practice. Scott was a specialist in the law of trusts. Both men stayed at Harvard for the rest of their careers.

No. 82   December 31, 1921   Washington, D.C.

MY DEAR FELIX: Thank you for the interesting enclosed returned herewith.

1. Your letter to Freund[1] is admirably put and absolutely sound. I am glad Farrand[2] is so comprehensive in his assent. But I think the memo. of conference with Freund & Stone indicates a purpose of taking up far more subjects than can possibly be well done at one time.[3]

Couldn't they limit themselves to a single state. Perhaps Illinois, where Freund is, would be the most convenient. It surely would present problems galore. After that has been fully explored there would be time to go elsewhere with the light gained by that experience in research.

2. I am enclosing letter from Will Hays' secretary.[4] He is apparently not doing what I talked over with you & suggested to him. Won't you talk this over with Chafee & let me have his formulated suggestions to send to Hays?

3. The A.G.'s[5] & President's actions re Debs has been inexpressibly bad.[6]

4. I am glad you like the Lumber dissent. I was waiting for a chance to say some of those things. There is a touch of humor in the guides of the two other dissenters in my last paragraph.[7]

5. About Pitney's virtues I will tell you more when we meet.[8]

6. Yes, we shall have now the test of American International Statesmanship.[9] My grave concern is on the National. As I said to you, prosperity of the status quo ante will not go far toward satisfying any of us; and we are not likely to have even that for a long time to come. We really have problems ahead that can't be lied away by "loyal optimism."

7. Was glad to see Magruder yesterday.

Every good wish to you and Marion for the New Year.

[1] Ernst Freund (1864–1932) was a well-known and highly influential professor of law at the University of Chicago.

[2] Max Farrand (1869–1945), a well known historian at Yale, would become director of the

Huntington Library in 1927. He was also an adviser in educational research to the Commonwealth Fund.

[3] Freund had proposed a study on administrative law and practice which he hoped would be financed by the Commonwealth Fund; FF was serving as an adviser to both Freund and Farrand, but the project did not receive financial support.

[4] George Walbridge Perkins, Jr. (1895–1960), son of the Morgan partner and financial angel of the Roosevelt Bull Moose campaign, was serving in 1921 as executive secretary to the postmaster general, William H. Hays. He later served as an American representative to NATO. The matter under discussion here probably involved the restoration of mailing privileges to radical groups that had been suspended during the war and in the Red Scare that followed the Armistice.

[5] Harry Micajah Daugherty (1860–1941), a Columbus, Ohio, attorney and a close friend of Warren Harding, had been named attorney general in the Republican administration. He was forced to resign that office on 28 March 1924, and he was later indicted, but acquitted, of charges to defraud the government.

[6] On 23 December 1921, Warren Harding had commuted Eugene V. Debs's prison sentence, and Debs had been released from the Atlanta penitentiary on Christmas Day. In the memorandum prepared by Daugherty (reprinted in full in *New York Times*, 31 December 1921), Debs was considered undeniably guilty of sedition, and his commutation was seen as an act of charity. Because Harding merely commuted the sentence, and did not pardon Debs, the Socialist leader did not regain his citizenship.

[7] LDB had written a strong dissent in an antitrust case brought against an association of hardwood manufacturers. The majority of the Court held that the agency was in violation of the law, but LDB argued that the dealers were legitimately trying to impose some rationality upon a chaotic industry that had been ravaged by cutthroat competition. His jibe at the majority consisted of reminding his brethren that in the steel case, where U.S. Steel controlled fifty percent of the market, and in the shoe machinery case, where the accused controlled nearly all of the market, the Court had found against the government. Why, then, did they find the lumber dealers, who controlled between them about one-third of the market, in violation of the law? LDB was joined by McKenna and Holmes. See *American Column & Lumber Co. et al.* v. *United States*, 257 U.S. 377 (1921). LDB's dissent is at 413.

[8] Mahlon Pitney (1858–1924), a New Jersey political leader and judge, had been appointed to the Supreme Court by Taft in February 1912. LDB's praise for Pitney came in connection with his views in *Truax* v. *Corrigan*, 257 U.S. 312 (1921). A restaurant owner in Arizona, being picketed as a result of a labor dispute, applied for an injunction; but Arizona law, restricting the use of the labor injunction, denied him that remedy. He contended that he had thus been deprived of property without due process and denied equal protection of the law. Chief Justice Taft, for the majority, struck down the Arizona anti-injunction law. As historian Paul Murphy has written: "The ruling left no doubt that to Taft business was property and any infringement upon the way it was conducted was a potential infringement of property rights." Pitney, whose lower court rulings had been antilabor, was more tolerant of the legislation: "I can find no ground for declaring that the State's action is so arbitrary and devoid of reasonable basis that it can be called a deprivation of liberty or property without due process of law. . . ." LDB filed a massive dissent holding that the Constitution should not be interpreted so as to stifle social experimentation, and FF was so angered by the chief justice's opinion that he attacked it in *The New Republic* ("The Same Mr. Taft").

[9] LDB refers to the Washington Naval Conference (see 13 November 1921, n. 2) which was ending.

No. 83   January 15, 1922   Washington, D.C.

DEAR FELIX: 1. I had intended to talk with Gerry [1] about his future, and on receipt of your letter asked him to come in.

He is decided that he does not want to teach. He wants to write, but to write as an incident to practical work and to that end wants to continue in practice in New York. He is interested in Cooperation and in the labor problems and would like to get into practice in those connections. I warned him against being absorbed by the financial interests.

2. I will write Kallen that I hope for a talk with him when I am next in N.Y.

3. Garment workers appear to be on top at present—for the moment.[2]

4. We are hoping to have Crowder in Wednesday.

5. Why is the N.Y. crowd—Survey folk et al so down on Zimmern?

And what is the matter with Z's style? Compare his paper on the "Legacy of Greece" with The Greek Commonwealth.

Our best to Marion.

[1]Gerard Carl Henderson (1891–1927) was a brilliant young lawyer, journalist, and public servant in whom LDB took a special interest—occasioned, at least in part, by the fact that Henderson married Frank W. Taussig's daughter Edith and was, therefore, distantly related to him. Henderson was also one of FF's favorite students, and after graduating from Harvard Law School in 1916, alternated between private practice and federal jobs. In 1921 he had become general counsel to the War Finance Board. He died at the age of thirty-six, a victim of a sudden infection of the eye. He wrote two books on administrative law.

[2]A strike of the Ladies' Garment Workers' Union had begun in November 1921, over the manufacturers' determination to restore the "piecework" system and the Union's bitter opposition to it. The Union had won an injunction on 12 January enjoining the manufacturers from conspiring to violate the old contract; and on 14 January, the owners reopened the shops. The strike was declared over on 18 January.

No. 84   January 21, 1922   Washington, D.C.

DEAR FELIX: 1. We [were] much interested by the FF. numbers of the N.R.[1] The Mooney case[2] bids fair to have historical significance not unlike the Calas and the Dreyfus.[3] And Beck is doing his part to make it an enduring sore.

2. Do tell us the particulars about Lamont's $2,000,000 loss. How much of it was the original purchase price & how distributed in the less than 3 years?

And who are the foolish 31[sic]?[4]

3. I am glad to hear of H. L. Shattuck's activity.[5] We should get some public service from Henry Lee's grandson.

4. The Arthur Woods dined with us Wednesday. It is very difficult to escape all the contamination incident to great wealth.

5. W. O. Thompson was here. He seems sound on Hillmann's [sic] problems & means to go ahead hard on the Cooperative Bank.[6]

Our Greetings to Marion.

[1] The only signed piece by FF in *The New Republic* during these weeks was a letter on the Mooney case (see next note). Several other articles, appearing anonymously, however, were on topics of interest to FF and might have been written by him. One was "The Political Function of the Supreme Court," in the 25 January issue (which would have been available by this date); another was on corruption in Boston politics, "What's the Matter with Boston," in the issue of 11 January.

[2] On "Preparedness Day," 1916 (22 July), a bomb exploded in San Fancisco killing nine persons and wounding forty. Several radicals, including Thomas J. Mooney, were arrested and charged with murder. Although Mooney was convicted, evidence emerged after the trial of perjury oh the part of key witnesses against him. FF enlisted himself in the cause of a new trial for Mooney with great energy and determination, but Mooney remained in prison until 1939. The lengthy exchange, "The Mooney Case," *New Republic* 29 (18 January 1922):212, contained a letter from Solicitor General James M. Beck and a reply from FF, which summarized the case for Mooney.

[3] In 1762, after a trial sullied by religious overtones, the French Protestant merchant, Jean Calas (1698–1762) was convicted of murdering his own son, who, it was alleged, had converted to Catholicism. Calas was tortured, broken on the wheel, and burned. The philosopher and social critic Voltaire was outraged at the trial and led a vigorous press campaign which finally overturned the verdict, thereby vindicating Calas's name. The infamous Dreyfus affair also occurred in France. In 1894, Alfred Dreyfus (1859–1935), a Jewish captain on the French general staff, was convicted of selling secrets to Germany. His trial was also highly questionable and resulted in a sentence of life imprisonment on Devil's Island. Only in 1906, after monumental efforts by the French novelist Emile Zola and thousands of others, was Dreyfus finally pronounced innocent.

[4] Thomas Lamont had sold the *New York Evening Post* to a combination of thirty-four purchasers.

[5] Henry Lee Shattuck (1879–1971) was the grandson of the prominent Bostonian Henry Lee (1817–1898). He served in the Massachusetts State legislature and was for many years a trustee and treasurer of Harvard College.

[6] See 2 December 1921, n. 1.

No. 85   February 3, 1922   Washington, D.C.

DEAR FELIX: 1. It would be a great mistake not to make a wholly new index covering 1–35 HLR. The new index would give new opportunity for selling whole sets, & it would greatly widen & deepen the influence of the review for the future.[1]

If the H.L.R. trustees' funds will not permit, friends of the School should be called on for contributions. I shall be glad to contribute. Give the Law School Assn. something to do. Let them raise money.[2]

2. The matter of accuracy & thoroughness should be definitely taken up by the faculty. Next to knowing how to think legally, they are the most important requirements of lawyers. The graduates' actual knowledge is necessarily limited. But they ought to be guaranteed intellectually trustworthy. High ability, resourcefulness, imagination, the essentially legal mind, come, like kissing, by favor of the gods (although

there is much in the way of development that training may do in them). But accuracy & thoroughness is [sic] possible for everybody who is worthy of being graduated by the H.L.S. It means banishing indolence & carelessness & teaching that being occupied—called working—is not taking pains.

3. I am glad that my next secretary looks promising & interesting.[3]

4. Your Dr. Metz and Aaron Sapiro[4] were both in. The latter is a most engaging person, with all the hopefulness & exhilaration of the days when the world was young. I approve of his going ahead regardless; but I think he is underestimating

(a) the danger which inheres in not having also cooperative credit institutions to supply the needed money,

(b) the danger of the cooperative producers squeezing the consumers.

5. You have doubtless heard from Wise of our Balfour visit,[5] & from deHaas of his visit Wednesday. Mrs. Fels[6] was here today, Mendel Berlis yesterday, & from Mack daily communications; so there is no danger of forgetting Jerusalem.[7]   My greetings to Marion,

[1] A comprehensive index of the *Harvard Law Review* was not published until 1927, and it covered the first fifty volumes; there had been earlier indexes for volumes I–X and I–XXV. See 25 March 1922.

[2] See 23 April 1922.

[3] William Edward McCurdy (1893–1967) served as LDB's secretary during the 1922–23 term, and he then returned to a lengthy teaching career at Harvard. After World War II, McCurdy was associate director of Allied legal units in occupied Germany.

[4] In 1922 Aaron Sapiro (1884–1959) was one of the country's leading experts on cooperative marketing. He was to become best known, however, as the man who stopped Henry Ford's anti-Semitic campaign in the 1920s. In the 1930s, Sapiro's name was often linked with Al Capone and other mobsters, and although he was acquitted of charges of racketeering, Sapiro was eventually disbarred.

[5] Arthur Balfour was in the United States as a British delegate to the Washington Naval Conference. He had met with a group of American Zionists on 12 January, reaffirming his faith in the Zionist movement. He repeated this pledge privately to several of LDB's associates.

[6] Mary Fels (1863–1953) was the widow of Joseph Fels (1854–1914), a soap magnate and former client of LDB's. The couple had become interested in the theories of Henry George and worked to apply single tax methods both in America and Palestine.

[7] *Psalms*, 137:5.

No. 86   February 15, 1922   Washington, D.C.

FF: Mr. W was remarkably improved.[1] His voice was natural, his face also, & he seemed mentally as well as physically invigorated. He is following much more keenly current events.

[1] On this date, LDB had gone to see former President Wilson.

No. 87 **March 9, 1922** **Washington, D.C.**

DEAR FELIX: 1. Holmes J. was in fine form yesterday. Never better.

2. We are delighted to know that you & Marion are planning to be here by April 16. It has been a long wait.

3. The report on the Law Club is fine. In this connection & others I shall want to talk with you of tutors. The papers were returned today.

4. I am glad you spoke so strongly to Mack re Jabo[1] et al.

5. I am strongly of opinion that you should not permit your name to appear as Contributing Editor of the N.R. It would not help H.C. & would harm otherwise.

Very sorry H.C. thought it wise to take Bob Littell[2] from here & to put him on book reviews.

6. The Redlichs were in Monday, in good form. I encouraged J[osef].R[edlich]. to write on the importance of decentralization in USA which he feels strongly.

7. The Ambergs were in also.[3] She seems very wise. I wonder whether he has developed as finely as he should have. This is only a doubt, not the expression of an opinion.

8. Let me tell you of a talk with Prof. John H. Gray[4] when we meet.

[1] Vladimir Yevgenievich Jabotinsky (1880–1940) was a Russian Jew who became a Zionist as a result of the pogroms at the turn of the century. He had organized the Jewish legion during World War I, and in the early 1930s he broke with the world organization to set up a rival Revisionist Zionist group. Jabotinsky had no love for Great Britain and generally took extreme positions in asserting Jewish rights.

[2] Robert Littell (1896–1963), whose father had been one of the original editors of *The New Republic*, came onto the journal in 1922 and remained until 1927. Then he joined the *Reader's Digest* and, in 1942, became its senior editor.

[3] Julius Houseman Amberg (1890–1951), a Harvard Law graduate and a Michigan attorney, served as FF's special assistant during World War I, and as Henry Stimson's assistant in World War II. He had married Callie Sutherland Smith in 1916.

[4] John Henry Gray (1859–1946) was an economist and a professor of political science at several universities. He also worked for the Interstate Commerce Commission.

No. 88 **March 25, 1922** **Washington, D.C.**

MY DEAR FELIX: 1. Re H.L.R. Index (Barclay letter returned herewith).[1]

Monte Lemann,[2] Dean Acheson & I think that the list of cases should be omitted. They are of little value to the practitioner.

Also that it would be most regrettable to issue a supplementary volume covering the 10 years. At the Harvard Law School there should be no such thing as second best. Noblesse Oblige. Let us have an Index covering the 35 volumes, as soon as may be.

2. We have seen something of Mark Potter[3] of late & think well of him. We'll ask them to come in at the Monday P.M. to meet you & Marion.

3. Your report re Legislature & on School are cheering.

4. I am glad you & Marion liked my Bruere letter.[4] I want to talk with you also on this subject.

[1] See 3 February 1922.

[2] Monte M. Lemann (1884–1959) had been a classmate of FF's at Harvard Law School, and both LDB and FF took an active interest in his career. He was a leading attorney in New Orleans, a professor at Tulane, and a contributor to legal periodicals. In 1929, LDB and FF secured his appointment to the Wickersham Commission for the study of criminal justice in the United States.

[3] Mark Winslow Potter (1866–1942), a New York attorney, had been a member of the Interstate Commerce Commission since June 1920.

[4] See LDB to Robert W. Bruere, 25 February 1922. Bruere (1876–[?]), an experienced social worker, expert on industrial relations, and editor of *The Survey*, invited LDB to speak informally to a group connected with the Department of Research and Education of the Federal Council of Churches. LDB feared he had been unclear, and summarized his remarks in a famous letter on democracy, social reform, and personal responsibility. Professor Alpheus T. Mason calls the letter "his creed in essence" (*Brandeis*, 584–85).

No. 89   April 2, 1922   Washington, D.C.

FF: Why does the Law School discriminate so against Federal Law? Doubtless many rich federal nuggets lie concealed beneath the many general titles in the Programme of Instruction. But no aggregate of uncoordinated parts can supply the needed treatment.

Is this seeming neglect a survival of the days when the School was provincial, the federal functions few and the Military rules received more discussion than the Constitution?

What we need is comprehensive consideration of the respective fields of federal and state law, civil and criminal, and not merely jurisdiction, procedure and the so-called federal common law.

And the course should be one for undergraduates.[1]

[1] In 1924–1925, FF introduced a course in "Jurisdiction and Procedure of the Federal Courts," which soon became a standard part of the undergraduate law curriculum at Harvard. Contrast this letter with LDB's advice of 1889, LDB to Christopher C. Langdell, 30 December 1889.

No. 90   April 8, 1922   Washington, D.C.

DEAR FELIX: I was immersed in Court work which delayed correspondence & now find so much to say about interesting enclosures returned herewith, that I think it best to await our discussion orally next week. Holmes J. was beset with a cold & did not attend the Conference.[1] He is merely housed, not abed. He is enthusiastic over Walter's Public Opinion.[2]

The Conference seemed dreary without him.

[1] The weekly Saturday conference of the Court for the discussion and assignment of pending opinions.

[2] Walter Lippmann had just published *Public Opinion* (New York: Harcourt, Brace, and Co., 1922), an analysis of the forces that molded public attitudes on various questions, as well as the obstacles to wide dissemination of knowledge.

No. 91   April 9, 1922   Washington, D.C.

DEAR FELIX: Happy to say Holmes J. is ganz herzgestellt.[1]

He was out today (a) for luncheon, (b) for a drive, & (c) plans to dine at the hotel as usual, Sunday evening.

[1] "entirely recovered."

No. 92   April 14, 1922   Washington, D.C.

MY DEAR FELIX: 1. I am very sorry to learn through Dean that you have not been well. Hope you are ganz herzgestellt.[1]

2. I was particularly interested in A. G. Barrett's letter.[2] He has been closely associated with the monied element.

3. The poor position of labor should be commented on

(a) Anti Trust Co—
    Farmers exempted by Marketing Bill[3]
    Exporters by Edge Bill[4]
    Railroads by Transportation Act[5]
    Capitalistic Organizations by ———
Only labor & the small traders are trammeled.

(b) War burdens & relief
    Farmers have War Finance[6] & Farm Board Aid[7]
    Large concerns, Excess Profits Tax Repealed etc.
    Railroad Investors, Transportation Act etc.
    Capitalists, Reduced Surtaxes
Labor has instantaneous dismissal from Navy yards et al.

Your Dr. Johnston was in & at Monday's at home [also] Darling and his mother.

[1] "entirely recovered."

[2] Perhaps Alexander Galt Barret (1870–1931), a Louisville lawyer and a Harvard Law graduate.

[3] The Cooperative Marketing Association Act (February 18, 1922), ch. 57, 42 *Stat.* 388, permitted farmers to act in associations for purposes of marketing without being in violation of the antitrust laws.

[4] The Edge Act (December 24, 1919), ch. 18, 41 *Stat.* 378, amended the Federal Reserve Act in order to permit American banking corporations to do foreign banking business.

[5] The Transportation Act of 1920 (February 28, 1920), ch. 19, 41 *Stat.* 456, ended federal wartime control over the railroads.

[6] The War Finance Corporation Act (August 24, 1921), ch. 80, 42 *Stat.* 181, amending the 1918 act establishing the Corporation, provided aid to farmers.

[7] A series of Federal Farm Loan Acts (1916, 1920, 1921) facilitated the loaning of money to the nation's farmers.

No. 93   April 23, 1922   Washington, D.C.

MY DEAR FELIX: I trust you understand that I shall be glad to contribute to any or all of the small Law School funds which we discussed.

I consider these current needs a distinct asset of the School which may be made to serve an important purpose. They may be used to bind successful graduates and others to the School, by keeping them alive to its growth and problems, and it may serve also to awaken and develop, through them, the bar, by acquainting them with the growth of legal education. For the present it would be undesirable to have the needs met either (a) from income of a general endowment, or (b) from gifts of the whole amount from single individuals, or (c) from funds derived through increasing tuition fees. That is, the recurrent need must be preserved, for it is desirable that the School should have to call on its graduates, justifying itself from year to year; and it is likewise desirable for the graduates that they should be called on for support.

It was good to have you & Marion here.

No. 94   May 16, 1922,   Washington, D.C.

MY DEAR FELIX: The longer letter to be written after my return from Kentucky must be further deferred. But in view of yesterday's decisions, I stop amidst pressing matters to send this:

The N.R., The Survey & like periodicals should not be permitted to misunderstand yesterday's decision on The Child Labor[1] and Board of Trade[2] cases, & should be made to see that holding these Acts void is wholly unlike holding invalid the ordinary welfare legislation.

That is—that we here deal

    (1) With distribution of functions between State & Federal Governments

(2) With the attempt at dishonest use of the taxing powers.

I think you will also like McR's[3] opinion cutting down referee's fees in N.Y. Gas Cases.[4]

[1] In 1918, the Supreme Court had struck down the first federal Child Labor Act as unconstitutionally exceeding the power to regulate interstate commerce (*Hammer* v. *Dagenhart*, 247 U.S. 251). Congress then passed a second Child Labor Act, relying on the taxing power rather than the interstate commerce clause. Once again the Court struck the statute down, declaring that Congress had abused its power. Speaking for all but Justice Clarke, Chief Justice Taft differentiated between a tax and a penalty, in that the latter was used merely to disguise the real purpose of regulating labor in plants that the Court had already held were local in nature. See *Bailey* v. *Drexel Furniture Company*, 259 U.S. 20 (1922). It was to be almost two decades before the Court finally—and unanimously—upheld a federal child labor law, under the commerce power, in *United States* v. *Darby*, 312 U.S. 100 (1941). For FF's treatment, see his "Child Labor and the Court," *New Republic* 31 (26 July 1922): 248.

[2] In *Hill* v. *Wallace*, 259 U.S. 44 (1922), the Court declared invalid a section of the Future Trading Act (August 24, 1921), ch. 86, 42 *Stat.* 187. That Act was designed by Congress to stop the gambling in grain futures on the Chicago Board of Trade. The Act provided a heavy tax on such trading. But, as in the child labor case, the Court—again speaking through Chief Justice Taft, but this time with LDB rendering a concurring opinion—ruled that this was an improper use of the federal taxing power and that futures trading in Chicago was not interstate commerce and, therefore, not liable to regulation by the federal government.

[3] James Clark McReynolds (1862–1946) had been Wilson's first attorney general, and LDB worked closely with him in drafting a new antitrust law and in prosecuting the New Haven Railroad. Aside from his passion against monopoly, McReynolds was extremely conservative, and to ease him out of the cabinet, Wilson named him an associate justice of the United States Supreme Court in 1914, an appointment that Wilson frequently regretted. McReynolds was antisemitic, and he practically never spoke to LDB after the latter joined the Court. When LDB resigned in 1939, McReynolds's name was conspicuously absent from the usual letter sent by the remaining justices to a departing member.

[4] In eight cases, argued and decided together (see *Newton* v. *Consolidated Gas Co.*, 259 U.S. 101 [1922]), McReynolds ruled, for a unanimous Court, that the fees awarded to a master are subject to judicial review, that they should be liberal but not exorbitant, and that, in these particular instances, the compensation awarded was excessive.

No. 95   May 31, 1922   Washington, D.C.

FF: For our talk—when we meet:

1. Cleveland Survey[1]
2. Criminal Law Course[2]
3. State & Nat'l Action (& in this connection U.S.S.C.)
4. W.L.'s Public Opinion[3]
5. P.D.C.
6. Ben Avon Case[4]
7. N.R.—particularly George Soule[5]
8. Coal—Bradley, Hoover et al[6]
9. Russia (Mrs. Harriman)[7]

I had an enjoyable call from Kerr, also from Freund.

I think you will be interested in several of last Monday's decisions—i.a.

NY Chinese Case [8]

NY ICC Courts case. [9]

We have been doing a "land office business."

[1] See 12 January 1921. Probably the two wanted to discuss the continuing struggle to implement the recommendations of the final report.

[2] See 2 April 1922.

[3] See 8 April 1922, n. 2.

[4] *Ohio Valley Water Co.* v. *Ben Avon Borough*, 253 U.S. 287 (1920). McReynolds had spoken for a six-man majority in holding that due process was violated by a statute establishing an administrative rate system which did not permit judicial review of the rates. LDB dissented at 292, joined by Holmes and Clarke, and argued that the state's procedures were fair, in that a limited but appropriate scope of judicial review was provided.

[5] George Henry Soule (1887–1970) had been one of the bright young men associated with *The New Republic* since 1914; he went on to be an editor of the journal from 1924 to 1947. Soule had a distinguished career as a social investigator and writer on economic topics.

[6] The coal strike which spread across the entire country in April had grown extremely bitter. Secretary of Commerce Hoover had taken an active part by securing an agreement from operators still in production to refrain from raising their prices. Joseph Gardner Bradley (1881–1971), son-in-law of LDB's old law partner Samuel D. Warren, was one of West Virginia'a leading coal operators. See 4 September 1922.

[7] Possibly Florence Jaffray (Mrs. J. Borden) Harriman (1870–1967), a prominent reformer and Democratic party official, whom President Roosevelt would name as ambassador to Norway in 1937.

[8] Although LDB writes that this is a New York case, he probably means *Ng Fung Ho* v. *White*, 259 U.S. 276 (1922), a California case which was decided on 29 May. LDB spoke for a unanimous Court in this case involving the deportation of four Chinese. He ruled that the deportation orders for two of them were valid; but, as the other two had claimed and partially established citizenship, on that basic issue they were entitled to an independent judicial proceeding.

[9] *Industrial Commission of New York* v. *Nordenholt Co.*, 259 U.S. 263 (1922) was also decided on 29 May. This case involved a complicated question of jurisdiction. A stevedore was killed while unloading a ship, and his mother claimed compensation from the New York State Industrial Commission under the Workmen's Compensation Law. The Commission awarded compensation. The company overturned the award in the appellate court, arguing that it was not local law, but maritime law that should determine the matter. Justice McReynolds, for a unanimous Court, reversed the appellate decision.

No. 96　　　　　　　June 12, 1922　　　　　　　Chatham, Mass.

MY DEAR FELIX: It is lovely here. [1]

We shall be ready for you and Marion on the 19th or as soon thereafter as you are able to come.

It is possible that I shall have to leave (for a day in New York) on the 20th, as I promised deH to be there on the 21st if he gathers about 20 pecunious men. But there is this "if"—and besides, you and Marion will be no less welcome, in any event.

I tried in vain to reach you Saturday;—and Thursday, Anderson [2] and I assaulted Langdell Hall [3] in the hope of finding you, Chafee, Sayre and Magruder. My greetings to the 8 hour men.

[1] The Brandeises were quite captivated by Chatham and eventually purchased a summer cottage there. They spent virtually every summer after this one on Cape Cod. For a description of the place, see Mason, *Brandeis*, 582.

[2] George Weston Anderson (1861–1938) was one of LDB's oldest comrades. Their association began in the days of the Public Franchise League, one of LDB's earliest public activities back in Boston at the turn of the century. LDB always remembered him as the one person with whom he had seriously disagreed, but who had nonetheless vigorously supported his confirmation in 1916. Anderson served on the Interstate Commerce Commission during World War I, and in 1918 was appointed judge of the U.S. Circuit Court of Appeals in Boston.

[3] The Harvard Law School.

No. 97   June 16, 1922   Chatham, Mass.

MY DEAR FELIX: 1. We look forward to the 23rd. Our telephone is Chatham 13 Ring 2 (the W. T. Sears house). I assume you and Marion will prefer an afternoon train. I think there are two now (since the change on June 12).

2. The examination papers are interesting. [1] Perhaps it is fortunate that we JJ. don't have to pass annual exams.

3. I wish someone would produce something effective, for constant quotation, on the cowardly pretence of rejecting able men, on the ground that their judgment is unsound.

4. Pound hasn't overcome all his anti-Bolshevism yet.

5. Charles Warren's USSC. in History of US. interests me intensely. [2] It seems to me better than Beveridge's Marshall. [3] And it suggests to me this re Child Labor decision: [4]

About every really important decision (at least in the early days), gave rise to some proposal of the disappointed class to amend the Constitution.

If one of your young men would gather the data (Warren furnishes much) an interesting article might be written, as bearing on recent proposals, including LaFollette's & Mrs. Kelley's. [5]

6. I hope Marion has written Elizabeth about California.

[1] FF had sent the final examination papers from one of his classes.

[2] Charles Warren (1868–1954), a Boston lawyer and legal historian, was a former assistant attorney general of the United States. He also wrote and lectured extensively on legal history. His most famous work and the one LDB was reading this summer, was *The Supreme Court in United States History*, 3 vols. (Boston: Little, Brown, 1922).

[3] Albert J. Beveridge, *The Life of John Marshall*, 4 vols. (Boston: Houghton Mifflin, 1916–19).

[4] See 16 May 1922.

[5] In the light of such cases as *Bailey* and the antilabor attitude evinced by the Court in other cases (see next letter), a number of progressives urged revision of the Constitution to limit the Court's power to nullify laws. Addressing the American Federation of Labor convention in Cincinnati, Senator Robert M. La Follette on 14 June 1922 had proposed a constitutional amendment that would have prohibited lower federal courts from invalidating legislation and would have allowed the Congress to override a Court decree regarding specific legislation simply by repassing the measure. On the same platform and also endorsing the proposal was Florence Kelley (1859–1932), the tireless labor expert and social reformer. LDB had been closely associated with her in preparation of his landmark brief in *Muller* v. *Oregon*, 208 U.S. 412 (1908).

Whether or not FF himself took up LDB's suggestion, Charles Warren did so in an address to the Massachusetts Bar Association on 14 October 1922 entitled "The Early History of the Supreme Court of the United States in Connection with Modern Attacks on the Judiciary."

No. 98   August 31, 1922   Chatham, Mass.

FF: I think you have let off [*] too gently. I think he is wrong almost in every respect (except that the op[inion]. should have been so clear that he couldn't have [*]). His "legal logic" with which you say you "agree" is faulty:

Every entity, unless it enjoys immunity, is liable for its wrongs. A natural person, a firm, an association, a corporation, in some states even the sovereign, is so liable. The unions, in effect, claimed for themselves immunity. The court denied the immunity. [1]

But even where no immunity exists, liability for an alleged wrong can be enforced, only if:

1. The defendent is properly before the court. This involves

(a) going before a court with jurisdiction over subject matter and party

(b) joining proper necessary parties

(c) adequate error

2. The plaintiff is proven to have suffered a legal wrong.

3. The defendant is proven to have committed a legal wrong.

4. The pleadings are appropriate to recovery for the wrong proven.

The courts having held the Unions do not enjoy (as a matter of substantive law) immunity for wrongs committed, had to decide (as a matter of procedure) whether the unions had been legally brought into court. And it properly decided this (namely 1. above) before taking up any other question. If it had decided that unions have an immunity as a matter of substantive law, like the sovereign ordinarily, or if it had decided that the unions were not legally before the Court, it would have gone no further. But holding that the unions were not immune and that they were legally before the Court, it necessarily proceeded to the determination of the other three questions. It found, then, that the plaintiffs

104

had suffered legal wrongs; that the International Union had committed no wrong whatsoever; that the District and local union had committed wrongs; but that these wrongs proved were not those sued on; that is, were not violations of the federal law.

To have proceeded first to the determination of questions 2, 3 or 4 supra would have been, at least, bad judicial practice; for the Court should not have enquired into them, unless it had decided that unions were not immune as matter of substantive law and were, as matter of procedure, properly before the Court.

The liability sought to be enforced was not the joint and several liability of the members of the union. It was the liability of the unions as entities. If the judgment below had been affirmed, no person would have been liable *qua* member. Only the property of the entity, present and thereafter to be acquired could have been reached to satisfy that judgment. There were joined as defendants 66 natural persons, but not *qua* members. As to these only questions 2, 3 and 4 actually arose.

If the judgment had been affirmed and had not been satisfied by, or out of property of the Union, a question might have arisen whether by any proceeding the individual members could be made to satisfy the judgment. That is, whether there is a members' liability akin to a stockholders' liability; and also whether there is, otherwise, an individual liability for the wrongs proven. But no such question could arise or was discussed in that case.

It is not true that a union can be liable only if every member authorized or ratified the alleged wrong deed or that a union cannot be liable unless every member is liable. Entities are often liable for acts which were neither actually authorized nor ratified, as a railroad for the conductor's negligence or wanton act. And, of course, a person who is a member may be liable, although the union is not. To hold that a union could be liable only if every member authorized or ratified the act would involve treating the union not as entity but merely as the joint agent of the several members. That a labor union is an entity was certainly not new law.

---

[1] The first *Coronado* case, which the Court had decided on 5 June 1922, stirred up a great deal of controversy, and much of the debate centered on what the decision actually meant for the rights of unions. In an effort to break the local mineworkers' union, some coal operators had locked out union workers in western Arkansas. Violence inevitably followed, leading to destruction of several mines. The operators sued the union for treble damages under the Sherman Antitrust Act; and in the original jury trial, the local judge directed the jurors to find for the owners. The decision, for $600,000 plus costs, was affirmed by the circuit court of appeals, and then it was appealed to the Supreme Court in October 1920, where Charles Evans Hughes argued the case for the union. The

Court divided in conference, five to four, against the union; but before a decision could be handed down, Chief Justice White died, and the case was rescheduled for new argument after Taft took his seat.

LDB in the meantime had prepared a dissent against the original majority decision, in which he argued that the Court had to be consistent on the limits of federal law. In earlier cases, notably *Hammer* v. *Dagenhart*, the Court had placed a narrow interpretation on what constituted interstate commerce; certainly the effect upon interstate commerce of the output of these Arkansas mines was no greater than the merchandise in the *Hammer* case. Although Taft originally had favored finding against the union, according to Professor Alexander Bickel, LDB managed to win him away from that position. Instead, the Court's decision, delivered by Taft, overturned the award, holding that the Sherman Act was inapplicable here; instead, a new trial was ordered, and the Court declared, much to LDB's satisfaction, that unions could be sued under common law for damages.

It was this part of the decision that confused many people, since it appeared to open the door to all sorts of actions against unions. But while there would undoubtedly be harassments, the real question was not whether unions could be sued, but for what they could be sued. This not only imposed some social responsibility upon the unions but also gave them a new status before the courts, and it was this issue which LDB had recognized. Taft's having delivered the opinion for a unanimous Court elicited a later comment from LDB to FF: "They [the conservatives] will take it from Taft but wouldn't take it from me. If it is good enough for Taft, it is good enough for us, they say—and a natural sentiment."

See *United Mine Workers* v. *Coronado Coal Company*, 259 U.S. 344 (1922). For a discussion of the case and of the content of LDB's undelivered dissent, see Bickel, *The Unpublished Opinions of Mr. Justice Brandeis* (Cambridge: Harvard University Press, 1957), ch. 5; see also FF, "The Coronado Case," *New Republic* 31 (16 August 1922): 328.

No. 99   September 4, 1922   Washington, D.C.

For FF:

What to Do

When the coal and rail strikes are ended,[1] a rational people should begin to think how a recurrence of like situations can be prevented. Clearly it is not by prohibiting strikes by compulsory arbitration or by crippling trade unions. It is not by physical force or by legal coercions. As long as these industries are privately owned or operated strikes in them must be permitted; and, even if publicly owned and operated, their employees must be free to join the unions. The promise of better conditions lies in industrial sanitation, not dosing.

First: Trade unionism should be frankly accepted and all war upon it, direct and indirect, by employers must cease. Unions should be free, at all times and under all circumstances, to use any form of persuasion (as distinguished from coercion) upon other workers to join their unions. Non-union workers should be protected against coercion; but never by or through the employer, or by any act or proceeding brought or done in his interest. Protection may be afforded unto the non-union man only by action or proceeding instigated and conducted by himself or on his behalf by the state.

Second: The employment by the employer of the private detectives and of the private armed guards, and the employers [sic] resort to the injunction must be discontinued. It should be recognized that such remedies can lead only to more war. Civil redress by the employer should be had only through action for damages; and violations of the criminal law should be vigorously prosecuted. Even on behalf of the State (or Nation) the injunction should never be used as a remedy for or for the prevention of acts which are criminal. Like most "easier ways" the use of the injunction in this connection is fraught with evil. The resources of the State are ample in the criminal law if it be made effective. There may, however, conceivably be instances where the non-union man should have protection by injunction for his personal rights against trade-union oppression; but the occasions for intervention by injunction would certainly be few.

Third: Such enlargement of the rights of unions and discontinuance of the use of armed guards, detectives and injunctions would appear to involve great damages to property and great loss and inconvenience to the public. In fact the loss would probably be at once much less than it is now. For the withdrawal of the present delusive protection against labor union excesses and this enlargement of their rights would tend:

(1) To remove the all pervading, irritating causes of discontent; the general conviction that the powers of the government are perverted by and in aid of the employers; and the deep sense of injustice suffered even in the Courts. It is of the essence that the curb upon trade union action should be administered by Court only by proceedings in which disputed facts are determined by juries. If trade unions are convicted of wrongful acts—by laymen—the belief in the impartiality of courts may be restored.

(2) To effect on the part of the employer to ascertain and to remove, or minimize, the substantive causes of discontent. The existence of the present delusive protection operates as a strong incentive to arbitrariness and inconsiderateness and as a discourager of constructive thought. Nine-tenths of the injustices of which workers complain in the country could be removed by persistent application of the inventive mind to the situations involved in the relation of Employer & Employee. But for the delusive "easier way," necessity would again prove itself the mother of social-industrial invention.

(3) To the creation of conditions which would leave the employer and the community less exposed to serious loss by arbitrariness on the part of the unions. The delusive present protections leads [sic] employers and

the community to expose themselves without insurance to such arbitrariness, and thereby encourages it.

(4) Ordinarily we insure ourselves against every conceivable bodily accident, error, or the wrongdoing of others. We provide not merely for money indemnity, but for insurance in kind, the spare part or tire, the factor of safety in bicycle or bridge, the safety-deposit box and the registered bond. But we fail to store adequate commodities, duly distributed, of coal and pig iron as to keep in adequate repair an ample supply of cars and locomotives, so that a relatively short interruption of work prove [sic] embarrassing.

(5) Investors of ordinary prudence have learned to insure against accident, error and wrongdoing by not putting all their eggs into one basket. But our unreasoned passion for bigness and for integration has led us to disregard in social-industrial life that wise warning. Safety lies in diversity, in decentralization, financial and territorial, with protective federations, in maintaining independent supplies of substitutes. Some restrictions against arbitrariness on the part of coal barons or miners may be found in hydro-electric power light and heat and oil or natural gas. Some protection against arbitrariness of railworkers, in water transportation, the trolley, the auto and the air service. And the existence of such ways is a mighty curb on arbitrariness.

Fourth: If the all pervading, irritating causes of discontent and the specific unnecessary injustices due to inconsiderateness and want of thought on the employer's part are removed as above indicated, the field of necessary conflicts of interest between employers and employees will be narrowed to relatively small and hence manageable proportions, and the temper of the parties will be such that reasonable adjustment will ordinarily be possible. If, in the exceptional case, adjustment as a result of negotiation proves not to be attainable, the remedy lies not in force, physical or legal, but in passive resistance. The remedy for the arbitrary demand of an excessive price for an article or service is doing without. Employers and consumers must have courage and must exhibit their powers of endurance when emergencies arise. Walls, mercenaries and laws have never succeeded in affording for long protection to a fear-ridden, comfort-loving people. Employer and consumer must show that they love justice and independence more than they do goods or ease. In the exercise of these qualities, the true preparedness indicated above, and vigorous enforcement of the criminal law if need be, lies the democratic way out.[2]

[1] Both strikes were over within a matter of days. The anthracite coal strike ended with the miners winning their fight to avert a wage reduction, after President Harding, Secretary of Commerce Hoover, and both Pennsylvania senators brought all of their influence to bear on the operators. On 13 September the national strike by railroad shop workers collapsed in the face of a court injunction. The shop workers had originally walked out in protest against a U.S. Railroad Labor Board decision that reduced their wages; at the end of the strike they finally accepted the original proposals of the Board.

[2] The substance of this letter appeared as an unsigned article, "What To Do," *New Republic* 32 (4 October 1922): 136.

No. 100   September 6, 1922   Washington, D.C.

FF: To saddened Americans seeking the light which shall lead them from the slough of despond, the N.R.'s advertisement of the "three special numbers"—Sept. 27, "The teaching of English Literature"; Oct. 25, "Educational number"; Nov. 22, "Fall Literary Number" must bring disheartenment. It sounds like a comfortable, bourgeois, self-supporting, Mid-Victorian "Home and Fireside." Mrs. Straight's enlightened beneficence should give us a clarion call; and its essentials are:

1. Distinction—in thought and form. Thought bears on knowledge, the fruit of research. Quality as distinguished from quantity. Articles one cannot afford to miss.

2. Direction. The pathfinder must possess and exercise insight, judgment, decision. There must be neither deviation nor dissipation, no pleasing "abstecher" [1] to explore interesting ruins, to gather rare flowers, or even to kill a noxious animal, however large the variety. Every article must follow the same general direction. And the direction must be pursued without change.

3. Movement—unbroken movement. That is an essential of holding both interest and confidence. There must be no stop for meditation or consideration, and no thinking aloud. The thinking of leaders must be done at midnight in the cave, while the followers, without, sleep; and doubts must be suppressed.

4. Militancy—Courage, resourcefulness, aggressiveness, dash. Man—and woman too loves the fighter. They turn from the querulous and even from the wise critic. The gallant and the bold seem brilliant; and they are always interesting.

The editor must seek to hold the readers' interest, not by diversions, but by skillful presentation of the varieties of experience of the pilgrims plodding the weary way. To the knowing, every rock and every grain of sand, the trees and the flowers mark the watershed. So each day's wisdom sustains and the memories of a richly-stored past may be used as indicating that the trail followed is the right one. And while all roads lead to Rome, the greatest joy of the traveller is in the unexpected glimpse of the Holy City far away. And the Journal of distinction, direction, movement & militancy will never be mistaken for propaganda.

[1] "diverting excursion."

No. 101   September 14, 1922   Chatham, Mass.

FF: 1. The household is desolé that you and Marion can't come. We shall hope to see you at the Bellevue tomorrow evening & will telephone on arrival.

2. I have looked at all the Fed. Ry. Cases on the 1913 Act, creating the crime of stealing from interstate R.R. cars. A more unjustifiable invasion of State functions can't be found.

No. 102   September 19, 1922   Washington, D.C.

F.F. Enclosed article of Buell[1] is much saner than all the La Follette-Gompers talk,[2] but it shows the urgent need of Scott's article on dicta, the Constitution & the USSC.[3]

The remedy for the prevailing discontent with USSC must be sought:

1. In refraining from all constitutional dicta.

2. In refusing to consider a constitutional question except in "cases" or "controversies"—"initiated according to the regular course of judicial procedure"

3. In refusing to pass on constitutional questions if the case can be disposed of on any other

4. In refusing to hold an act void unless it clearly exceeds powers conferred etc.[4]

[1] Raymond Leslie Buell (1896–1946) was in 1922 an instructor in government at Harvard. He later gained renown as a writer and lecturer on foreign affairs. In "Reforming the Supreme Court," *Nation* 114 (14 June 1922):714, he had listed some of what he considered the Supreme Court's recent abuses of the power of judicial review; and after discounting such drastic methods as impeachment of justices or constitutional amendment, he suggested that all cases invalidating state or federal laws require at least a two-thirds majority of the Court.

[2] See 16 June 1922, n. 5.

[3] Austin W. Scott did not publish any articles on this subject either in the popular press or in any legal periodical.

[4] For a discussion of LDB's policy of "judicial restraint," see Konefsky, *Legacy of Holmes and*

Brandeis, passim. Compare LDB's elaboration of these points fourteen years later, in his concurring opinion in *Ashwander* v. *TVA*, 297 U.S. 288, 341 (1936).

No. 103   September 20, 1922   Washington, D.C.

FF: As bearing on waste in distribution as distinguished from production, note these figures—shown in record of The Andrew Jergens Co. v. Woodbury, 273 Fed 952 (now before us on pet. for cert.).[1]

Sales in 1919	$2,147,925
Advertising expenses in 1919	668,149

This is the concern which sells Woodbury's Facial Soap & it has been in business since 1901.

I don't know what the mark up of retailers is; but note advertising is that of the producer. The retailer presumably has a 100 per cent mark up.

And advertising is only a part of the producer's distributing expense.

[1] The Jergens Company claimed an unlimited right to use the name "Woodbury" or "Woodbury's" on their product, having entered into a contract with John H. Woodbury. But the Delaware District Court held that the right was not unlimited and that Woodbury could use his name on his own products. The Supreme Court denied certiorari; see 260 U.S. 728 (1922).

No. 104   September 23, 1922   Washington, D.C.

FF: Toledo Newspaper Co v. U.S. 247 U.S. 402[1] is bearing rich fruit.

See U.S. v Craig 266 F. 230; 279 F. 900. Ex parte Craig 274 F. 177. Recently, May 22/22, reaffirmed (Hough[2] & Rogers[3] jjs—L.H. dissenting.) Pet. for Cert. pending in USSC.[4]

Also Fleming v. U.S. 279 F. 613. Pet for Cert pending in USSC.[5]

In all these the judge contemned hears & decides his own case. Certainly in U.S.A. with the 24 new Fed. Judges[6] this cannot be necessary in cases of constructive contempt, at least, & it seriously endangers respect for law.

Doesn't this fall within Chafee's province?

[1] This case, involving the recurrent problem of contempt by publication, was decided by the Supreme Court in June 1918. In the midst of a Toledo traction dispute, the *Toledo News-Bee* published a derogatory cartoon picturing the judge in the case offensively. The judge, feeling that his authority was contemned, reviewed the paper's coverage after the traction trial was over. The paper was charged with contempt, the case was tried summarily without a jury, the defendent found guilty, and a substantial fine imposed. A federal statute, in force since 1831, limited summary contempt procedure to misbehavior in court "or so near thereto as to obstruct the administration of justice." The majority of the Supreme Court declared that the judge had not

exceeded his authority. Justice Holmes wrote a dissent, arguing that nothing the paper did interfered with the conduct of the trial, and that therefore, summary proceedings were not justified. LDB joined in Holmes's dissent. The decision was overruled in 1941—*Nye* v. *U.S.*, 313 U.S. 3.

[2] Charles Merrill Hough (1858–1927), after ten years on the federal district court, had been elevated by Wilson to the U. S. Circuit Court of Appeals in New York. Both FF and LDB had high regard for Hough's abilities and thought him to be among the best of the federal judges.

[3] Henry Wade Rogers (1853–1926), after teaching law at the University of Michigan and serving as president of Northwestern University, was appointed a circuit court judge in 1913.

[4] The *Craig* case, decided in the Southern District of New York in February 1921, also involved a contempt proceeding and a utilities dispute. In this case, the utility was in receivership and various matters were coming before the New York court for decision. The comptroller of the city of New York wrote and published a letter to the Public Service Commission. This letter was highly critical of the judge, who found the writer in contempt of court. The case came to the Supreme Court as *Craig* v. *Hecht*, 263 U.S. 255 (1923). Justice McReynolds, in the majority opinion, declared that the means sought for relief was not proper and dismissed the suit. Holmes, joined by LDB, dissented, charging that not only was the relief sought proper, but that the lower court judge had abused his power.

[5] *Flemming* v. *U.S.* was heard in the Ninth Circuit Court of Appeals and decided in March 1922. This case involved a proceeding in the United States Court for China, a court created in 1906. During the trial the defendant demanded a change of venue on the grounds of extreme prejudice on the part of the judge. In this connection, he read in open court a statement accusing the judge of embezzlement and conspiracy. The judge held him in contempt, and the circuit court of appeals upheld the ruling. The case would be disposed of without hearing by the Supreme Court (260 U.S. 752), ten days after this letter was written.

[6] In September 1922, Congress authorized the creation of twenty-four new judgeships; see Chap. 306, 42 *Stat.* 837.

No. 105   September 24, 1922   Washington, D.C.

DEAR FELIX: Enclosed memo on transportation is not for publication. But I should like you to study it. The N.R. should declare soon a definite policy on transportation.[1]

And it should make its readers understand (what most Americans fail to realize) that to social-political reform there are three essentials:

1. Ascertaining what it is best to do
2. Getting the consent of the community to doing it
3. Actually doing it, after consent is given

We have developed only 2. We have become, in many fields, masters of "selling" ideas as well as material things. Any old idea will do. And the poorer the idea, the greater the skill of the salesman & hence his emoluments.

A conference is a coming together to determine the means by which, or to develop the motive power for, putting things over. Of course, only to get consent, and then "what ought to be done will be considered as done."

We plan to go to N.Y. Tuesday & to be there (Alice in Scarsdale) at City Club, Wednesday, Thursday, Friday.

[1] See 4 and 30 September 1922.

No. 106   September 25, 1922   Washington, D.C.

F.F.: Re Prohibition

Among the questions on which the N.R. should take promptly a clear & virile stand, to be pursued persistently, is that of *concentrating* all Federal effort on performing the essentially federal function of excluding smuggling of liquor from foreign countries or interstate, and *leaving* to the States all intra-state violations of the law.[1]

Certainly this would tax to the utmost federal capacity for achievement.

There should be no attempt to change the Volstead Act. If there is any change of legislation needed, it should be limited to the appropriation, i.e. confining the appropriation to use in the essentially federal field.

I have not overlooked the recent article[2] in the N.R. taking, on the whole, this view. But it was egregiously what a N.R. article on the subject should *not* be.

It was weak, wooly, apologetic, ineffective.

[1] See 24 October 1923.
[2] "The Enforcement of Prohibition," *New Republic* 32 (13 September 1922): 59.

No. 107   September 29, 1922   New York. N.Y.

MY DEAR FELIX: 1. The Sept 27 issue of N.R. is fine.[1] The brisk North West Wind sweeps through it, and the 3 articles dealing with law are all vigorous and straightforward.[2] You did a fine job.

2. It seemed on the whole, wiser not to arrange to meet the N.R. editorial board, but to leave matters on our Chatham talk with H. C[roly]. & such suggestions as I make through you. I shall send you from Washington, before I reenter the judicial monastery, some further suggestions for N.R. policies.

3. Mack has doubtless reported fully on our Conference. The tragedy pursues us—in health disabilities. I suppose we shall not see Rosenbloom here before next summer, and B.F. was to leave Thursday for

Baltimore, for an operation—which, however, he deems slight. He spoke of 10 days absence—then of seeing me with Dr. Alfred Kohn(?)[3] about Palestine. His report is favorable & he is enthusiastic about P. Ben seems in fine form, so far as disposition to help goes.

4. We talked hard to Dr. Wise. I think he realizes fully the futility of the Congress plan & promised to work hard on our lines.

5. I also had a heart to heart talk with Lewis Straus [sic]. He too has made definite promises, but I am not sure they will be fulfilled.

6. Mayono Abrahams was in today—talk of establishing a teahouse in Jerusalem & she tells me Jesse Sampter[4] is returning to P. Oct 10. Deborah Kallen's going back shows fine spirit.

Our best to Marion.

[1] LDB refers to the body of the issue, not to the attached "Fall Literary Supplement," which he so vehemently denounced in his letter of 6 September 1922.

[2] The issue contained two anonymous editorials, "Labor Injunctions Must Go," possibly written by FF himself, and "Criminal Justice," a comment on both the Mooney case and the Sacco and Vanzetti case (see 8 November 1925, n. 12). In addition, the issue carried an article by Zechariah Chafee, "The Rand School Case," which examined the attack on the Socialist party's school in New York City.

[3] LDB probably refers here to Dr. Alfred Einstein Cohn (1879–1957), a distinguished heart specialist attached to the Rockefeller Foundation from 1911 until his death, and one of FF's closest friends.

[4] Jessie Sampter (1883–1938), after an assimilationist childhood, had become attracted to Jewish life. A prolific author, she wrote widely on Jewish and Zionist subjects, and in 1919 took up residence in Palestine, where she was a close associate of Henrietta Szold.

No. 108   September 30, 1922   Washington, D.C.

F.F.: Re N.R. policies I am enclosing as my last will & testament before opening of term memo as follows—of course not for publication—but for your study or consideration:

(1) On Prohibition
(2) On Capitalism
(3) On the spread
(4) On Fear
(5) On transportation (supplemental)
(6) Labor Saving devices[1]

What to do about Capitalism

We recognize the evils and abuses of Capitalism. But we do not believe in Communism; we do not believe in State Socialism; and we do not believe in Guild Socialism. We do believe in consumer cooperation. But we also believe that private capital has now and at least for a long time to come must have an important part to play in the best development of America and its ideals. We believe that the part of private capital may be a beneficent one and should be confined in a sphere which is desirable or necessary. What shall be the limitations? To curb its power; and to remove the abuses lest the popular wrath against private capital [————].[2]

First: Consumer cooperation should be encouraged in every field of commerce, industry, finance or service, where it is or may hereafter become feasible. So far as it can, from time to time, supersede privately owned businesses, it should be encouraged to do so. It is essentially democratic. It gives the consumer the ultimate control of what is actually his, but. . . . It puts upon the consumer the ultimate responsibility for its proper conduct; and in so doing develops the consumer. If properly conducted, consumer cooperatives [————]. will eliminate wastes & particularly the excessive spread between cost of production and the price to the consumer.

Second: Producers' cooperatives should be encouraged. They limit the power of the capitalists and of the middle man, and lessen the abuses common in the use of private capital. They do this by enabling small private capitalists, like the consumers, to help themselves. The producers' cooperatives are also democratic. They distribute the responsibility, as well as the right to the profits, among those directly interested as producers. Hence, they develop the producer. Ultimately, the producers' cooperatives to a large extent, merge into consumers' cooperatives, that is, the consumers through their cooperatives should become also producers, as they already are to a considerable extent.

Third: Cooperative banks & credit unions should be encouraged. Like producing cooperatives, the credit unions lessen the menacing power of the finance, high and low, by [————]. And like consumers' and producers' cooperatives, credit unions are essentially democratic. The direct gains from the capital go to those whose capital is used. The owners of the capital have the ultimate responsibility for its proper use. And the responsibility develops those upon whom it rests.

Fourth: The sphere of private capitalistic control is now and will necessarily be, from time to time, further narrowed, through the assumption by the nation, state or municipality of functions which the public or community concludes cannot properly be performed by or be entrusted to private ownership or management. Such are now the municipally owned water, gas, electric light and power services, and tramways, motor buses, ferrys and wharves—and the gradual substitution of the modern state highway for the privately owned toll-pike.

Fifth: In order that such extension of the government functions may really limit capitalistic control it is essential that the government—national, state and municipal—should free themselves from the need of banker intervention in securing the necessary capital (see "Other Peoples Money"—"Where the Banker is Superfluous").

Sixth: The further limitations upon capitalistic power must be sought through tax legislation which will limit the rate, or amount, of income or accumulation of the individual, and the size of the financial or individual units through which business is done, i.e.

(a) Super—that is, graduated—income taxes, state and national (Here is the best field for curtailing accumulation)

(b) Graduated inheritance taxes—state & national

(c) Super corporation taxes—national—that is making the larger corporation pay a higher prorate on capital or profits, in recognition of bigness as a curse, because of the menace, social and economic, which inheres in size by reason of its dominant position and its power of endurance.

The failure of the anti-trust laws is due largely to

(a) To its failure to recognize size as the danger and aiming only at combinations.

(b) To its adoption of prohibition & the criminal penalty. Illegal combination was inherently difficult to prove. Furthermore, it was not deemed by the community a wrong. Size should not be prohibited, should not be treated as criminal, but should be discouraged by super-taxes & by being thus made less profitable. The equalitarian argument will appeal to many as requiring the handicap, so as to produce a square deal.

Seventh: The special danger of tax exempt capital should be met wherever it exists, by national super-inheritance (estate) taxes.

Eighth: Whether the business be private capitalistic, cooperative or public, the labor union is the essential. Employees must have that protection. On the other hand, consumer cooperation is the best curb on trade union as on capitalistic employer excesses.

Ninth: When the principle of unsolicited life insurance (as promoted by Savings Bank Ins.) becomes widely accepted, but not before, life insurance will be the simplest and most appropriate sphere for governmental (preferably state) activity. If the state does the life insurance business—

116

(a) the large accumulation of liquid capital now represented by life insurance investment will be (in part) ended.

(b) the huge requirements of the governments (which do the insurance) can be met without the issue of bonds, i.e. the insurance reserves will consist of direct obligations of the govt to pay the insurance, instead of indirect obligations to pay the bond which secures payment through the proceeds when sold or paid.

(For working of life insurance in this respect see Business a Profession insurance articles.)

The impoverishing spread

This subject is pre-eminently one for the N.R. because

(1) To treat it properly, it is essential that there be much careful, and some strictly pioneer, investigation.

(2) It will be necessary to attack advertising as practiced, of which that in magazines (see clipping annexed)[3] is only a small part.

Investigation will, I think, confirm that for say 3/4 of a century prior to 1900, invention & development in the fields of production and transportation resulted (with temporary interruptions) in a fairly steady trend toward lower costs of production and lower costs to the consumer.

It was a period in which lessening of the cost of production and of transportation was engaging the best minds and offering the largest rewards. And the advances in production and transportation, being directed to the field of the necessaries of life, the standard of living could rise without the cost of living rising.

Since say 1900 the cost of production of transportation has tended to rise. The progress in reducing specific costs in these arts has been small. It has been mainly (a) in reducing costs of production through the elimination of skilled labor, a process socially injurious & tending to a great increase of the contribution of capital clamoring for a return, or (2) in lessened cost in new articles (like the auto) which are largely luxuries. Such reduction in costs on early stages [————] Ford is a genius & a "sport," the exception which tends to prove the rule.

Thus, in general, the cheapening the costs to the consumer of the necessaries of life has not only ceased, but was followed by a tendency to a fairly steady rise, and both the inventive mind and the emoluments of business have gone to the distributor, including in this term the selling department of the manufacturer who, to a greater and greater degree, has assumed the functions of distributor.

Distribution, in its development, should have been attended by reduction in costs & expense similar to the earlier lessening of the cost of production.

Unlike the progress in manufacturing methods which resulted in lower costs, the progress in distributive methods have resulted mainly in greater & wider distribution of particular brands. This expense rate (when all distribution costs are reckoned) has tended to rise. The greater profits are made, not in the main by a larger profit per unit, but by largely increasing the number of units sold by the particular concern.

Essentially the only elements in distribution in which costs have been apparently lessened are

A. By the parcel post. And this has been due, in part

(1) At the expense of the railroads, who were, for a considerable time, and perhaps still are underpaid, and

(2) At the expense of the taxpayer, parcel post being run at a loss by the P[ost]. O[ffice]. Department.

B. By the Cash & Carry stores, where, in fact, it is the service which has been lessened:

1. No credit—hence no loss on credit & no bookkeeping

2. No delivery costs &

3. Practically no returns & no exchanges.

From the consumer's standpoint, the legitimate sphere of advertising (in any form) is limited

(a) To creating a volume of demand sufficiently large to secure the lowest costs of production & distribution.

(b) To introducing a new—useful or enjoyable—article.

(c) to ensuring sale of that which is of deserved quality.

The selling methods pursued, in so far as they entail greater costs, are not only anti-social, but tend [to] ever increasing extortion from the consumer (in that they fail to give value) & tend to ever greater mechanization of industrial life. The nationally advertised branded goods make the retailer practically an automatic machine, instead of an expert to whom the consumer pays, in profits, compensation for expert service & trustworthiness. Every brand becomes, in effect, a profit making "fighting brand," & the great selling expense is, as to the consumer, mere waste. Some chain stores, notably A & P, are eliminating this waste by establishing their own brands. If they give to the public the saving [———] attempt toward proper distribution.

In a large part of the field there is no social justification for the national widespread market for very many of the trademarked articles. The distribution costs, notably unnecessary transportation & advertising, should be discouraged.

In this investigation of the wastes, much data may be found in the recent

(a) "Report of Joint comtee of Agricultural Enquiry"
67 Cong. 1st session, Rep. 408

(b) In Federal Commn Reports & Cases

(c) & in Fed. Court Trademark & Unfair Competition Cases, but there *must be much original* investigation in order that the facts may be properly ascertained & presented.

The merits of labor saving devices

The funds available to N.R. for research should be applied in part to an attempt to ascertaining [sic] whether prevailing tendency toward labor saving is really cost saving. The tendency toward substitution of machine-tenders for skilled operatives etc. is certainly anti-social. I doubt whether (except in factories like Ford's) it is not, in large measure, also uneconomic. That is, whether the limit of machinery & organization efficiency in substitutions for human labor may not have been exceeded, just as the limit in size of greatest efficiency has been, involving as it does

(1) A greatly increased plant charge, of
    (a) interest
    (b) repairs
    (c) depreciation
        obsolescence and often
    (d) failure of continuous use
(2) Increased organization, supervision expense

And isn't the capitalist and white collar man thus silently exploiting & undermining the overall producer?

[1] Of the six memoranda referred to, copies were found in the FF collections only of the ones dealing with "Capitalism," "On the Spread," and "Labor Saving devices." For LDB's suggestions on "Prohibition," see 25 September 1922, and for "Transportation," 24 September 1922.

[2] Unfortunately, the only copy of this lengthy memorandum is a poor photocopy of the original draft, with many crossed-out lines, and several completely illegible passages, indicated in this letter by [————].

[3] Attached to this memorandum was an article from *The New York Times* of 27 September 1922 dealing with the distribution of more than $95 million in advertising in 1921, placed in seventy-two magazines. Although this figure represented a drop from the $132 million spent in 1920, it was still well above the 1915 figure of nearly $39 million.

No. 109   October 2, 1922   Washington, D.C.

FF: I have just re-read Pound's admirable "Project for a Professorship of Criminal Law."

This seems a most appropriate time for launching the Project. And should it not be done on the lines which I suggested to you last spring with a view to ensuring widespread and continuing interest of the bar in the School and its work? [1]

[1] See 23 April 1922.

No. 110   October 2, 1922   Washington, D.C.

FF: 1. Re N.R. & yours of 30th.

A heavy term begins today and I must jettison all thoughts on N.R. & its policies. It was with this in view that I sent you the various memoranda. [1] My purpose was not to have them submitted to H.C. & the board, but to clarify my own mind as to what was desirable, & to have you take over to yourself the thoughts if, and so far as, they seemed to you sound. I should, therefore, think it inadvisable to send the transportation, or any other of the memoranda, to H.C. in their present form. If, and so far as, you may deem the views expressed valuable and you have the opportunity to present them personally at any meeting of the N.R. board which you may at any time attend, I have of course no objection to your doing whatever your judgment dictates.

2. I have no doubt that H.C. wishes to fight. Possibly he has the will to do so. But I think he would suffer from inhibitions like those to which JWM is subject; and that he lacks the fighting force. He really doesn't know how. He is essentially the philosopher, and as indicated in "America as the Promised Land," [2] it is the crying need of a national policy with which he is filled. He does not see, or feel, the greater all pervading problems which Raymond Fosdick [3] presents so forcibly in his Wellesley address, [4] nor does H.C. really feel that the national problems must be tackled by dealing with the myriad of single problems which our so-called civilization has cast upon us.

3. I think the proposed letter to Davis [5] re injunctions is a bit of evidence of H.C. not knowing how. The letter proposed re W. Z. Foster [6] presented a clear case of lawlessness, the Chicago injunction, [7] confirmed by W. after long hearing & about [to be] appealed would furnish J.W.D. the best possible material for a step back.

4. Re J. H. Clarke's [8] letter, I am reminded of "Wenn ich ein Künstler war ich mahlte traun nur hübsche mädchen interessante Frauen" [9] Holmes J. would have a different opinion of the "unimportant cases."

5. The Ormsby-Gore letter presents unfortunate truths which we must not permit to stay in our Palestinian activities.

6. No, I have not seen E. B. Whitney's brief in the Debs case. [10]

[1] See 24, 25, and 30 September 1922.

[2] LDB probably meant Croly's *The Promise of American Life* (New York: Macmillan, 1909).

[3] Raymond Blaine Fosdick (1883–1972) was a New York laywer and public official who undertook many governmental assignments during his life. See 8 November 1925.

[4] See "Our Machine Civilization," *Current Opinion* 73 (September 1922): 362.

[5] John William Davis (1873–1955), a lawyer and congressman from West Virginia, served as solicitor general from 1913 until 1918 and then as ambassador to England. Currently, Davis was president of the American Bar Association, and in 1924 would be the Democratic candidate for the presidency.

[6] William Z. Foster (1881–1961) had been a labor organizer for the American Federation of Labor, and had come to national prominence in the steel strike of 1919. In 1921 he joined the Communist party of the United States, which he later headed as national chairman from 1932 to 1957.

[7] Attorney General Daugherty had just secured a highly questionable injunction in Chicago against the railroad unions. The injunction, which was sweeping and severely antiunion, was issued by Judge J. H. Wilkerson.

[8] John Hessin Clarke (1857–1945) was a liberal Ohio lawyer and judge whom Wilson had appointed to the High Court only a few weeks after LDB's confirmation in 1916. He had just announced his resignation from the Court in order to devote himself to the cause of the League of Nations.

[9] "If I were an artist, I would paint only pretty girls and interesting women." Perhaps LDB's criticism referred to Clarke's decision to leave the Court and, particularly, the retiring justice's contention that too much effort was wasted on "unimportant cases." Clarke's letter was reprinted in 260 U.S. vii.

[10] The reference is to *In re Debs*, 158 U.S. 564 (1895), the notorious case in connection with the Pullman strike, in which President Cleveland secured an injunction against the union. The *Debs* case was being compared to the case presently being debated (see n. 7). Critics of Daugherty and the Harding administration contended that the Debs injunction was not nearly so inclusive or restrictive as the one obtained in Chicago. Edward Baldwin Whitney (1857–1911) had been the assistant attorney general in 1895 and argued the *Debs* case for the government.

No. 111   October 10, 1922   Washington, D.C.

FF: Much of the best and original legal thinking in America during the last generation is to be found in the law journals, and it is, in the main, inaccessible to the bench and the bar. Now that the law journals have become an incident of the law schools of the Universities, the number of valuable contributions should increase rapidly. Would it not be desirable that the Law Schools should cooperate in publishing an Index covering all valuable articles, which have appeared during the last 35 years, (like

Poole's Index) and arrange for supplements to be published annually thereafter? The fact that articles would be thus made accessible should tend to encourage production. It ought to be possible to secure from graduates the necessary funds. I should be glad to contribute to the fund.

No. 112   October 19, 1922   Washington, D.C.

FF: 1. I delayed writing you about Holmes J. because I wanted to make up my mind. I now think he is in good form & able to carry the load. He looks well, has attended throughout all sessions & conferences and has written opinions with customary speed. He has been often tired physically & at times mentally; but I think this has been due mainly to the unfortunate fact that he has not been able to work as usual in his study because the repairs incident to elevator construction at 1720[1] are not yet completed. The annoyance of living at the Powhatan & travelling to & from, necessarily per carriage, has put much strain upon him. He should work easily when he gets back to 1720, & has the rest which the next recess will make possible.

2. I humbly withdraw my suggestion for a law periodical index,[2] and suggest instead a society for instructing judges & practitioners in tools of the trade. I had not known of the quarterly index, in existence for 15 years. It is not just what I had in mind; but it is clearly adequate to meet our needs. Of Jones' book I had known, indeed, had bought it a quarter century ago. It had slipped my mind; but, as I now recall, it seemed to me rather poor, perhaps because of the then paucity of material.

3. Rosenbloom's letter of Sept. 28 saying that he would be here for the proposed Thanksgiving conference is the most encouraging event in recent Palestinian affairs.[3]

4. JWM may have sent you copy of my letter about Fohs.[4] He was here Sunday & I am trying to get him to take a continuous part in P.D.C. councils.

5. Our greetings to Marion & best wishes for 37 River St.

[1] Holmes lived in Washington at 1720 I Street. Throughout the 1920s there were frequent expressions of concern from both FF and LDB over Holmes's physical ability to continue the heavy workload of the Court. Holmes, now eighty-one years old, continued on the Court for another decade before he finally bowed to old age.

[2] Evidently FF had advised LDB that such an index already existed. Leonard A. Jones had published *An Index to Legal Periodical Literature* (Boston: C.C. Soule, 1888), covering the years up to 1886, and in 1899 produced a second volume covering 1887–1899. Frank E. Chipman then continued the series, and ultimately, five additional volumes appeared irregularly until 1938. In

1928, however, a more comprehensive index began to appear on a yearly basis published by the American Association of Law Librarians and entitled *Index to Legal Periodicals*.

[3] Solomon Rosenbloom had completed a mission for the Brandeis group to explore conditions in Palestine.

[4] Ferdinand Julius Fohs (1884–1965) was an oil geologist from Kentucky, active in investigating Palestine's natural resources on behalf of the Zionists. Fohs's work led to the establishment of several of the most productive industries in Palestine, including the great potash and bromine plant on the Dead Sea.

No. 113   October 23, 1922   Washington, D.C.

F. 1. It is fine to have your cases under the I.C.C. Act with a gracious inscription.[1] A furtherwise contribution is made in today's decision in the Waste Merchants Case. The decision of the Court of App. of the district (Robb)[2]—and the C.J. dissenting was monstrous.[3]

2. McCurdy will send you extra copy of my ops. as requested. I have not tried him out fully, but think he will measure up to your expectations.

3. As to next year's secretary,[4] I shall leave your discretion to act untrammelled. Wealth, ancestry, and marriage, of course, create presumptions; but they may be overcome.

4. Enclosed by Senator Walsh of Mont.[5] you may not have seen. I am confirmed in the belief:

(a) that the only effective remedy for U.S.S.C. actions in holding statutes unconstitutional is to change the attitude of judges in approaching the allowed function. Statute-Killers when confronted with an objectionable law say: How can I manage to hold it void? Constitutionalists say—How can I manage to sustain it?

(b) That it was a great mistake to hold that corporations were citizens entitled to sue in Federal Courts on the grounds of citizenship.

5. I wrote E. O. Poole as suggested.[6]

6. I wrote Ben F[lexner]. some time ago and had acknowledgement from him, which indicated that the operation was a serious matter.[7]

7. Had not heard of Deedes' resignation.[8] That is, indeed, serious, and I suppose changes at home may bring other difficulties.

8. That's a very interesting letter of Harold A.[9]

9. [*] are pretty disappointing.

10. Glad Phillips found Louis W.[10] helpful.

11. Your talk to the women must have been impressive.

12. I am not surprised at Fosdick's and Manly [Hudson's] report on [*].

13. Yes, Hoover is tired & disappointed. He is doing neither country or himself much good by the talk. He will be happier when he goes West in Nov. to his River problems.[11]   Our greetings to Marion,

[1] FF had sent the new edition of his *A Selection of Cases Under the Interstate Commerce Act* (Cambridge, Mass.: Harvard University Press, 1922). The work was originally published in 1915.

[2] Charles Henry Robb (1867–1939) had been a justice of the Court of Appeals for the District of Columbia since 1906.

[3] A suit had been brought against the Interstate Commerce Commission by New York waste paper dealers to force a change in the rate schedule through the New York harbor. The I.C.C. had held investigative hearings before turning down the request, and the Supreme Court of the District of Columbia had dismissed the merchants' suit. The court of appeals, however, had reversed the Commission. In a short opinion for a unanimous Court, LDB reversed the appellate court, holding that the I.C.C. had proper jurisdiction, it had investigated, and its findings were not subject to court review. *Interstate Commerce Commission* v. *United States ex rel. Members of the Waste Merchants Association of New York*, 260 U.S. 32 (1922).

[4] See 17 June 1923.

[5] Thomas James Walsh (1859–1933) was the crusading liberal from Montana, who served in the Senate from 1912 until his death. A steadfast progressive, Walsh had taken a leading part in the subcommittee hearing LDB's nomination in 1916. He and LDB became friendly, and Walsh was a frequent visitor. His most notable public service was about to unfold: his well-publicized investigation into the Teapot Dome scandal in 1922–1923. Franklin Roosevelt named him to be his first attorney general, but Walsh died two days before the inauguration of the new administration.

[6] Perhaps Ernest Poole (1880–1950), a prolific reporter, correspondent, and writer of fiction. Poole had contributed an introductory essay, "Brandeis," to LDB's book, *Business—A Profession*.

[7] See 29 September 1922.

[8] Sir Wyndham Henry Deedes (1883–1956) was a soldier and a British colonial official who had become an expert on Turkish affairs. In 1920, he began service in Palestine as a civil secretary under Herbert Samuel. He had won the praise of both Jews and Arabs for his fairness. But he had just announced his resignation, frustrated by what he regarded as insurmountable problems. For the rest of his life he was an ardent supporter of Zionism.

[9] Harold Courtenay Armstrong (b. 1891) was a traveler and writer who specialized in topics relating to the Middle East.

[10] Louis Brandeis Wehle (1880–1959) was LDB's nephew, the son of Otto Wehle and LDB's sister, Amy. Like his uncle, Wehle entered the law and was active in public service. During the 1920s and 1930s he handled a large part of LDB's private legal work related to the republication of LDB's writings.

[11] Hoover convened the Colorado River Commission on 9 November at Sante Fe. The difficult negotiations paved the way for what later became Hoover Dam.

No. 114   November 14, 1922   Washington, D.C.

FF: 1. It was good to have your and Marion's greeting.[1] It seems very long since your all-too-brief visit.

2. Emma Erving, Dean and Alice, George R[ublee] and many others were in yesterday, our first Monday afternoon. We missed much Norman [Hapgood] & his Elizabeth.

124

3. Mrs. Upton[2] was among the callers. She had campaigned 6 weeks in Ohio & Indiana. Says Beveridge felt sure of election the evening before election day.[3] Pomerene seems to be, on the whole, the most distinctly beaten man personally, by women, by labor & the Drys.[4] On the whole the result is cheering. And but for the Anti-Dry vote Mass. did very well.[5]

Clarence (Judge) Goodwin[6] was also in. He & wife had been much at the McAdoo's[7] this summer. It is a bit painful to find him (doubtless as representing the general feeling) thinking only of getting in—not of doing those things to make staying in a possibility. Gere H[enderson] says Brookhart[8] talk is of cleaning out the whole Reserve Board personnel. It's evident that there will be something doing at all events—if not the right thing.

3. [sic] Yes I have, thanks to you, read the Coronado note in the Nov. Yale L.J.[9] A worthy discussion.

4. I think you will be interested in my two R.R. (I.C.C.) cases delivered yesterday[10] as fodder for the classroom—and also as to manner of disposing, in the Zucht case.[11] I wish it might be taken as a precedent for other Fourteenth Amendment cases, but it wont.

5. See Bacon Bros Case,[12] Cert. denied yesterday—for terrible [*] performance.

6. We were almost without a quorum yesterday. Day[13] (for some reason) didn't come. Van Devanter[14] was out the first two hours at the oculists (a contagious eye trouble which is almost over) & McR. has had gout in his foot!!! which housed him much of the last 3 weeks. But OWH. is back in 1720 I & much happier.[15]

The World did a good job on C.E.H.[16]

Did you hear of Dr. Lowenstein's[17] bizarre suggestion that Magnum W. Alexander,[18] F. P. Fish[19] or O. D. Young[20] be invited to make opening addresses at the Palestine Conference?[21]

[1] The day before had been LDB's sixty-sixth birthday.

[2] Harriet Taylor Upton (1855–1945) was a pioneer in the women's rights movement, a member of the Republican National Committee, and an effective campaigner.

[3] Beveridge was defeated in the Indiana senatorial campaign by Samuel M. Ralston, a former governor of the state.

[4] Atlee Pomerene (1863–1937) had been in the Senate representing Ohio since 1911. A moderate progressive, Pomerene had nevertheless opposed both the Eighteenth and the Nineteenth Amendments and the combined forces of women and prohibitionist voters defeated his reelection in 1922.

[5] Although the Republicans narrowly won both the senatorial and gubernatorial races, Massachusetts Democrats swept back into power after a dismal showing in the 1920 election, recapturing

many seats in the state legislature. In a referendum, the voters turned down a bill which would have provided for state enforcement of prohibition.

[6] Clarence Norton Goodwin (1871–1956), a Chicago lawyer, had been a justice on the Illinois Appellate Court from 1915 to 1917. He then resumed private practice and was not, despite his wishes, reappointed to the bench.

[7] William Gibbs McAdoo (1863–1941), a lawyer and Democratic politician, had been one of the ablest men in the Wilson administration, serving as secretary of the treasury, administrator of the nation's railroads during the war, and one of the president's closest advisers—as well as being the president's son-in-law since his marriage to Wilson's daughter Eleanor in 1914. After the war he moved to California and opened a private practice there.

[8] Smith W. Brookhart (1869–1944) was a colorful and controversial Republican progressive from Iowa. He had just been elected to the Senate.

[9] "The Coronado Coal Case," *Yale Law Journal* 32 (November 1922): 59. The anonymous author called the decision "an excellent example of judicial courage."

[10] The two cases were *Keogh* v. *Chicago & Northwestern Railway Co.* et al., 260 U.S. 156, and *Baltimore & Ohio Southwestern Railroad Co.* v. *Settle et al.*, 260 U.S. 166. Keogh sued eight railroad companies which had joined in the Western Trunk Line Committee, alleging that the combination violated the Sherman Antitrust Act and prevented a lowering of his freight rates. The railroads replied that the freight rates had, after extensive hearings, been approved by the Interstate Commerce Commission as being reasonable. LDB for a unanimous Court ruled that under the Sherman Act, no damages could be calculated on the basis of some hypothetical lower rate, since the lower rate would benefit all competitive shippers in Keogh's business to an equal extent. In the second case, the railroad sued a lumber dealer, Settle, who instead of shipping lumber from the South direct to his place of business (Madisonville, Ohio) at the published interstate rates, had shipped it to another depot and then, without unloading the cars, to his place of business by the cheaper intrastate rates. LDB (with McReynolds dissenting) ruled that these shipments partook of the nature of interstate commerce and that the interstate rates should therefore be paid.

[11] In *Zucht* v. *King*, 260 U.S. 174, Rosalyn Zucht had refused to be vaccinated, and therefore had been excluded from the public schools of San Antonio, Texas, by the terms of a city ordinance. She charged, under the Fourteenth Amendment, that the requirement for vaccination deprived her of her liberty. LDB, for a unanimous Court, ruled that, in view of a long line of precedents, the attack on the ordinance did not present a substantive federal question; and her charge of discriminatory enforcement could not be brought to the Court by a mandatory writ of error, but only by a discretionary writ of certiorari. The opinion reflects LDB's strict construction of the Court's jurisdiction.

[12] *Bacon Brothers Co.* v. *E. Frank Graber*, 260 U.S. 735.

[13] William Rufus Day (1849–1923) of Ohio had been appointed to the Supreme Court by Theodore Roosevelt in 1903. Day had already announced, two weeks earlier, his resignation from the Court.

[14] Willis Van Devanter (1859–1941) had served in the Wyoming territorial legislature, and as chief justice of the new state's supreme court. From 1897 to 1903 he was an assistant attorney general of the United States, and then went on to the court of appeals; in 1910 Taft had elevated him to the United States Supreme Court. Although a member of the conservative bloc, he and LDB maintained cordial relations.

[15] See 19 October 1922.

[16] No article or editorial criticizing Charles Evans Hughes appeared in the New York *World* at this time.

[17] Perhaps Solomon Lowenstein (1877–1942), a New York City social worker and rabbi. He had been in Palestine during 1918–1919 with the Red Cross and was active in numerous Jewish charities.

[18] Magnum Washington Alexander (1870–1932) was a well known industrial engineer connected with Westinghouse and General Electric, and since 1916, president of the National Industrial Conference Board.

126

[19] Frederic Perry Fish (1855–1930) was president of the American Telephone & Telegraph Company.
[20] Owen D. Young (1874–1962) was chairman of the board for General Electric and honorary chairman for the Radio Corporation of America. He was probably best known for the "Young plan" of 1929, reducing German reparation payments.
[21] Probably the conference being planned for early March, 1923, by supporters of the Keren Hayesod to launch a major fund-raising drive. Major addresses would be made by Chaim Weizmann, Louis Marshall, and Samuel Untermyer.

No. 115 December 14, 1922 Washington, D.C.

MY DEAR FELIX: Re yours of 7th & 12th

1. You and Pound know from my letter of last term[1] how, in my opinion, Law School needs should be financed, and why. There are special reasons why funds for Criminal Law & Legislation chair should be raised by a fairly wide appeal to the successful & influential alumni and friends of legal education. If the School adopts a plan on those general lines for raising the money, I shall, of course, be glad to contribute, and should be disposed to subscribe such sum as you and Pound think would be most helpful in inducing a fairly wide participation.[2] If, however, the School concludes to pursue the "easier way" and appeal to Foundations for the whole or part of the funds needed, my disposition would be to do nothing but regret the lost opportunity.

2. I think it would be better for you *not* to write the C.J. about the report of your action re P.B.[3] Your letter to his son[4] ought to have done all that can properly be done to set matters right.

3. Opinions in the Cave-in Case[5] have gone to you today (also copy of the record & briefs which please return). I shall be glad to hear what you & Pound think of this.

4. Enclosed copy of War Department letter of 5th (which came after opinions were delivered) may interest you and show that adherence to Ct Claims procedure has practical value.

5. I see (through driving home via Charles) more of H[olmes] than heretofore, but there is nothing I can say on the subject you suggest & have in mind.

6. When C.J. is in minority, the senior associate who is not is supposed to assign case, but, in fact, the C.J. is apt to do so.

7. I had not known of offer to Miller. I am told our Clerk's office says M.C.J. will be nominated.[6]

8. I fear little is to be hoped from Governors' Conference.[7]

9. Ernst Freund will be disappointed about Ill. Constitution vote, but I am not.[8]

127

10. Vernon Kellogg says W. A. White[9] is to write on some economic subject

Tell him to postpone that & write on Free Speech.

11. Those Mass. Child Labor figures are pretty bad.

Enclosed Shipping Board articles, cowritten by Dean, seem to me very clever. Could you get him to write on Pitney. It might educate the bench & it would be an act of Justice to Pit. [10]

[1] See 23 April 1922.

[2] See second letter of 19 December 1922.

[3] Undoubtedly Pierce Butler (1866–1939), a Minnesota lawyer nominated to the Supreme Court by President Harding and currently undergoing a strenuous and bitter confirmation hearing in the Senate. Butler would eventually be confirmed and would promptly align himself with the Court's conservative faction. For a meticulous study of this appointment, see David J. Danelski, *A Supreme Court Justice is Appointed* (New York: Random House, 1964). FF's name was mentioned as one of those actively opposing Butler's confirmation, a charge he denied.

[4] Robert Alphonso Taft (1889–1953), son of the chief justice, was in 1922 practicing law in Cincinnati and beginning his political career, which culminated in his fifteen-year tenure in the United States Senate, where he became the acknowledged leader of the conservative wing of the Republican party.

[5] A Pennsylvania state law requiring a certain percentage of coal deposits to be left in place so as to avoid mine cave-ins had been challenged as violating a contract that predated the passage of the law, a contract that allowed full exploitation of the mineral resources. Holmes, speaking for the Court, said that the state had exceeded the limits of its police power in voiding the contract. LDB dissented and argued that "coal in place is land; and the right of the owner to use his land is not absolute." See *Pennsylvania Coal Company* v. *Mahon*, 260 U.S. 393 (1922); LDB's dissent is at 416. See also LDB to FF, 28 December 1922.

[6] Perhaps speculation on a replacement for Justice Mahlon Pitney.

[7] On this day a special Governors' Conference on Law Enforcement opened in White Sulphur Springs, West Virginia. Despite numerous speeches against prohibition by individual participants, the conference ultimately issued a mild statement promising support to the federal government in enforcing prohibition.

[8] A special constitutional convention had been called in Illinois in 1920 to revise the existing document, which dated from 1870. The revision, in which Ernst Freund had a hand, would have done much to streamline the administration of the state government and courts, but it included two controversial provisions: one opening the way for state income tax and the other reducing the influence of Cook County (Chicago) in the state legislature. On these issues the proposed constitution was defeated by more than 700,000 votes on 12 December.

[9] William Allen White (1868–1944) had purchased the Emporia (Kansas) *Daily and Weekly Gazette* in 1895 and had made it into one of the most widely read and quoted country papers in the nation. He was a leading progressive and a prolific contributor to liberal periodicals.

[10] No articles signed by Acheson were published on the shipping situation, nor did he write on retiring Justice Pitney.

No. 116   December 19, 1922   Washington, D.C.

MY DEAR FELIX: 1. Re Law School Fund: letter goes to you under another cover.[1]

2. The Pitney article—It will be much better to have you write the N.R. article if you have the time. I suggested to Dean that he should write one for the [Harvard] Law Review. He said he would be glad to do so & to read all P's opinions—to which I added "including those in N.J." If he also writes one appropriate for a weekly, it may well go to the Nation or elsewhere.

I hope when you write it will be over your own name.

3. As to P.B. I have copy your message & return [*]'s letter. The N.R. has not lacked in the militant quality in its latest number.[2]

4. I note Pound has approved Hugh Willis'[3] draft of Procedure Act. I fancy courts will have to change their attitude on social-industrial questions etc. before the people will knowingly repose more power in their hands. The vote on the Illinois Constitution[4] was significant. And our S.C. jurisdiction bill is effectively hung up.

5. Ramsay McDonald's[sic][5] article[6] which you sent is most encouraging. That labor should plod the weary way upward willingly is a great tribute to the English.

[1] See next letter.
[2] LDB doubtless refers to "Pierce Butler and the Rule of Reason," *New Republic* 32 (20 December 1922):81. The anonymous editorial begins: "President Harding is not himself a stupid man, but in appointing Mr. Pierce Butler an associate justice of the Supreme Court, he has perpetrated from his own conservative point of view an extraordinarily stupid mistake." The editorial further argued that Butler would twist the Constitution to prevent social and economic experimentation.
[3] Hugh Evander Willis (1875–19[?]) was professor of law at the Indiana University Law School and an authority on constitutional law.
[4] See preceding letter, n. 8.
[5] James Ramsay MacDonald (1866–1937), the leader of the British Labour party, would become the first Labour prime minister of Great Britain in 1923; and would serve a second time beginning in 1929. LDB and MacDonald would meet in 1929 to discuss Palestine (see 10 October 1929).
[6] Perhaps "The Coming Elections in Great Britain," *Nation* 115 (18 October 1922):408.

No. 117   December 19, 1922   Washington, D.C.

MY DEAR FELIX: Re yours of 17th

I understand that you and Pound have under consideration the plan of raising for the Law School, a fund of twenty thousand (20,000) dollars a year for ten years, of which $10,000 yearly shall be for a chair in Criminal Law and $10,000 for a chair in Legislation; and that all shall be raised by contributions from members of the bench and the bar.

If this fund is so raised, I shall be glad to contribute, of that amount, one thousand (1000) dollars a year for the period of ten years, that is, annually five hundred (500) dollars for the chair in Criminal Law and five hundred (500) dollars for the chair in Legislation.[1]

[1] In his report for the academic year 1923–1924, Roscoe Pound called for the establishment of professorships at the Harvard Law School in criminal law and legislation, but he was evidently successful only in his bid for the former.

No. 118   December 28, 1922   Washington, D.C.

MY DEAR FELIX: 1. Enclosed is the Willis leaflet.[1]

2. I don't think there were any special facts in the Sutherland[2] Election of Remedies case,[3] which account for it, but there may, of course, have been early experiences.

3. In the Cave-in Case,[4] that phrase "paramount rights" to which you refer might have been made less liable to misinterpretation.[5] The suggestion as to "evidence"[6] was to meet (a) a clause in H[olmes]'s op. which he dropped out, and (b) a local Pa. practice. I will tell you more when we meet;—also about some other shots, where the miss-fire [sic] is not disclosed to the public.

See 5 below.

4. Met Charles Warren recently. He shares our views as to proper jurisdiction of Federal District Courts. I have urged him to be General Staff for like-minded bar & Statesman. Had written him on the subject earlier; and he is pursuing his studies. I think a general invitation from the Harv. Law Review (without mentioning the specific subject) might lead to his sending later something valuable on proper scope of federal jurisdiction.[7]

5. The fortnight's recess for Holmes J.—without other work to do than to read Frazer's "Golden Bough"[8] has had a wonderful restorative effect. He was much fresher at the Conference yesterday than at any time this term—joyous in spirit & active physically as well as mentally.

6. As to Pound's enquiry about McCurdy—I think very well of him. A steady, intelligent, reliable worker with a legal mind, he should develop steadily. He has not disclosed any touch of genius. But it may be hidden beneath his impassive exterior. And it is possible that the class may awaken it & him.[9]

7. That was a fine letter of Hallowell's[10] & I am glad to know they are all taking so seriously the needs of the N.R. There is visible considerable more punch in it of late.

8. I am glad the door is wide open for McCurdy at the P.O.

9. Your letter to Guthrie [11] is informing. He ought to say something worthwhile.

10. Gus Hand [12] was in Xmas—thought there was some chance of Hough or C. Pound [13] being appointed to P[itney]'s place. Yesterday's appointments of N.Y. Dist. Judges for So Dist. won't make Hand very happy. [14]

11. Holmes J. speaks disrespectfully of the Mt. Hope Case. [15]

12. Isadore Levin [16] was in yesterday & spoke lovingly of you.

Our best to you & Marion for 1923.

[1] See first letter of 19 December 1922.

[2] George Sutherland (1862–1942), a two-term senator from Utah, had recently been named to the Supreme Court, where he established himself as the most articulate spokesman for the conservative bloc. While he frequently voted on the opposite side from LDB, the two men shared a quiet respect and liking for each other.

[3] The case was *United States* v. *Oregon Lumber Co.*, 260 U.S. 290, decided on 27 November 1922. The United States government sued the lumber company for fraudulently acquiring lands valued at $65,000, and sought to recover that sum. However, earlier, the government had brought a case not for the damages, but to recover the lands. Both "remedies," the majority of the Court ruled, were appropriate to the facts of the case; but having selected one remedy (recovery of the land), the government could not afterward maintain an action at law to recover the damages. LDB wrote a dissenting opinion and was joined by Chief Justice Taft and by Justice Holmes. LDB argued that "the doctrine of election of remedies is not a rule of substantive law. It is merely a rule of procedure or judicial administration."

[4] See 14 December 1922, n. 5.

[5] In his dissent, at 417, LDB had written: "Every restriction upon the use of property imposed in the exercise of the police power deprives the owner of some right theretofore enjoyed, and is, in that sense, an abridgement by the State of rights in property without making compensation. But restriction imposed to protect the public health, safety or morals from dangers threatened is not a taking. The restriction here in question is merely the prohibition of a noxious use. . . . The State merely prevents the owner from making a use which interferes with paramount rights of the public."

[6] LDB, at 419–20, argued that the defendant in this case had failed to "adduce any evidence from which it appears that to restrict its mining operations was an unreasonable exercise of the police power."

[7] This suggestion probably resulted in Charles Warren, "Federal Criminal Laws and the State Courts," *Harvard Law Review* 38 (1925): 545.

[8] Holmes was probably reading the new condensed version of *The Golden Bough, A Study in Comparative Religion* (New York: Macmillan, 1922) by Sir James G. Frazer. The classic study had appeared in two volumes in 1890.

[9] Pound was about to offer William McCurdy a teaching position at Harvard Law School. McCurdy accepted and began his teaching career there in September 1923.

[10] Robert Hallowell (1886–1939) had been one of the founding editors of *The New Republic* in 1914, serving as business manager and treasurer. In 1925, he abandoned journalism, moved to Paris, and began a second career as an artist.

[11] William Dameron Guthrie (1859–1935), after a distinguished career as a leader of the bar, had become professor of law at Columbia in 1909. He had just retired from that position.

[12] Augustus Noble Hand (1869–1954) had been named by Wilson to the United States District Court in 1914, and in 1927, Coolidge would elevate him to the court of appeals where he served until 1953. Augustus and Learned Hand were cousins.

[13] Cuthbert Winfred Pound (1864–1935) was another judge admired by LDB and FF. In 1915 he was appointed to the New York Court of Appeals, and when Cardozo was elevated to the Supreme Court, Pound succeeded him as chief judge of the New York court.

[14] Harding had named two new judges to Augustus Hand's court: Henry Warren Goddard (1876–1955), a Wall Street lawyer active in Republican politics, and Francis Asbury Winslow (1866–1932), the district attorney of Westchester County.

[15] There is no Supreme Court case by this title, but Holmes may have been referring to a fairly well-known Illinois decision, *Mount Hope Cemetery Association* v. *New Mount Hope Cemetery Association*, 246 Ill. 416 (1910), dealing with trademark and property infringement. The new cemetery cut down a hedge to connect its driveways to that of the old cemetery, deliberately took a similar name, and advertised as if it were the older and better known operation. The Illinois Supreme Court enjoined the new cemetery from continuing all of these activities.

[16] Isadore Levin (1894–1976) was a recent graduate of Harvard Law School, practicing in Michigan. See 16 March 1928.

No. 119   January 3, 1923   Washington, D.C.

F.F.: 1. The letter to Cobb [1] is most effective. I wish he would ask leave to publish it.

Possibly Norman H. could make him see the need of attaching a good lawyer to the World. As you know, H. and I spoke of Dean for the job. Dean could act specifically on Supreme Court decisions.

2. Holmes J. felt so perky yesterday that he insisted on getting out of the carriage yesterday to walk with me from 12th & H home. And he said today that he felt better for the walk.

3. As to Cave-in etc. there are indications that Benjamin is accentuating the tendency of age to conservatism. [2]

4. Isn't Baker really something of a Toto [*]? What does Marion say?

5. At the Chief's dinner of the Circuit Judges Friday, I was surprised to find (a) that Gilbert, [3] the old gent, reads the Nation, is keen against suppression of free speech and for amnesty. (b) that Baker J. [4] is really a polite reactionary, the kind that reads Puck, and thinks he is progressive.

6. That clipping about Wheeler [5] gives me great joy. I return it, so that you can use it when you introduce him to a Boston audience.

7. Talk with the Circuit Judges far more than confirms the guess that, with the exception of N.Y. & one or two other states, the appointment of new judges was wholly unjustifiable & that some of the prospective appointments are mere pork.

8. Pierce Butler makes a good impression.

9. The Bulletin of A.A.U.P. goes to you under another cover. It is a fearful story which, I hope, will be written up not only for the American people but in some English magazine. [6] I think Butler and his ilk would

appreciate their crime better if it were discussed in England than through any American comment.

[1] Frank Irving Cobb (1869–1923), for many years an insider in progressive circles, was the editor of the New York *World*. FF had written to Cobb on 1 December 1922 taking exception to some editorials on Supreme Court decisions, and explaining that one had to report not specific cases alone, but general principles and judicial procedures. Sometimes these would lead to regrettable results in particular cases, but served the higher duty of creating a general pattern of sound decisions. Cobb thanked him fulsomely, and indicated that he would try to take this into account in the future.

[2] For Holmes's decision in the Cave-in case, see 14 December 1922, n. 5. Robert Morris Benjamin (1896–1966) was serving as Holmes's clerk during this term; he would later enter private practice in New York.

[3] William Ball Gilbert (1847–1931) had practiced law in Portland, Oregon, before becoming a federal district judge in 1892; in 1912 Taft had elevated him to the circuit court of appeals.

[4] Frank Elisha Baker (1860–1924) had been a judge on the Indiana Supreme Court when he was named to the court of appeals in 1902.

[5] Burton Kendall Wheeler (1882–1975) was a Montana lawyer and politician who had been elected to the United States Senate in 1922; a great favorite of LDB's and FF's during the 1920s, Wheeler served in the Senate until 1947. In 1924, he was Robert M. La Follette's running mate in the Progressive party's attempt to capture the White House; but he was best known for leading the isolationist bloc in Congress against Franklin Roosevelt's efforts to involve the United States in fighting fascism.

[6] "Columbia University vs. Professor Cattell," *AAUP Bulletin* 7 (November 1922):433, provided documents relating to the wartime dismissal of Professor James M. Cattell. President Nicholas Murray Butler and the Columbia trustees had fired Cattell in 1917 for "treason," "sedition," and "opposition to the enforcement of the laws of the United States." The celebrated case, in which the AAUP issued a severe censure of Columbia, resulted in Charles Beard's resignation from the university and the AAUP's publication of *Academic Freedom in War Time* (in the February-March *Bulletin* for 1918). The documents reprinted here dealt with Professor Cattell's attempt to secure his pension after twenty-six years of continuous service at Columbia. See Richard Hofstadter and Walter P. Metzger, *The Development of Academic Freedom in the United States* (New York: Columbia University Press, 1955), 499–502.

No. 120   January 4, 1923   Washington, D.C.

F.F.: *First*: Here is my answer to Big Business & High Finance with their Stock Dividends and Anti-trust decisions & their repeal of Excess Profits & Reduction of Super income tax laws.

Put on all corporations (except utilities including railroads) a super-corporation tax, progressive in rate

(1) Base it on all values over $1,000,000

(2) Include in values bonds as well as stocks & surplus & undivided profits

(3) Make the rate very low at $1,000,000, but in the higher stages quite accute [sic].

(4) Life insurance should be included, but have more favored treatment. The argument:

The only justification to the big unit is supposed greater efficiency. If they have it, they can afford to pay the greater tax, making it a sort of excess profits tax. (See every prospectus of proposed or effected consolidations.) If they are not earning more, than [sic] they have no justification for existence.

This tax would eliminate the judicial factor of the Sherman Law Cases, the constitutional quibbles, the accountants' juggling, the [Justice] department's shortcomings. It is for all practical purposes, certain in amount.

Second: My answer to the State & Municipal Tax Exempt Bonds (really resulting, so far as Federal taxation goes, from Evans v. Gore [1]) is not the propose[d] amendment [2] (which would in large part paralyze development through State, as distinguished from federal control) but a super inheritance tax, progressive in rate, on tax exempt securities, held at or within 5 years of death. See Watson case, 254 U.S. 122. [3]

---

[1] In *Evans* v. *Gore* 253 U.S. 245 (1920), a district judge had claimed that the federal income tax violated the provision of the Constitution prohibiting the reduction of judges' compensation while in office (Art. III, Sec. 1). In the majority opinion, Justice Van Devanter concluded that since the tax was enacted after the judge had taken office, it could not apply to his salary. Both Holmes and LDB dissented, and Holmes argued (at 264) that the constitutional clause did not apply, since the tax did not single out the judiciary or have any threatening purpose.

[2] State and municipal bonds were normally exempt from federal income taxes. As a result, many wealthy people avoided taxation by investing their capital in such bonds. See next letter.

[3] New York law distinguished between property in an inheritance that had been taxed during the owner's lifetime and property that had not yet borne such taxation, and the state levied a heavier inheritance tax on the latter. In *Watson et al.* v. *State Comptroller of New York*, 254 U.S. 122 (1920), LDB had delivered the Court's decision in a three-page opinion that held the law to be a legitimate classification.

No. 121   January 29, 1923   Washington, D.C.

FF: 1. Very glad you and Marion consent to the expense fund. [1]

2. Sorry it was not possible to assent to Bob Patterson's [2] request to talk to the HLS A[ssociation]. of NY.

3. Pound's letter was presented by Gerry. [3] Of course, I didn't say anything to him about the professorship. But I did have a chance to ask him what he proposed to do. He said he expected to be here until Fall, mainly on the Trade Com[missio]n work and then return to practice in N.Y. He must have had Pound's letter some days before.

4. N.R. was right in rejecting W. Hard's.

5. I was interested in Ames competition briefs etc. I wish you and Pound would consider whether it would not be better to substitute for the made-up cases in the moot courts, real ones. Take, for instance, some appropriate cases from our Court. Put the record & briefs in hands of counsel (preferably when the record is short & the briefs poor) & let them go at it. The men would then spend their time in thinking & formulating results in writing & speech & not lose themselves in search for cases. And there would be a better opportunity for comparing performances. I think a worthy supplement to the Case System could thus be worked out.

6. William Allen White was here (He, the Victor Murdocks[4] & Frank H. Simondses[5] dined with us Saturday). I talked to him re "The Fruits of Fear" & he seemed much interested. The Whites & the Murdocks plan to sail for the Mediterranean in a week.

7. I am told A. N. Hand is strong in condemnation of the Sanford appointment.[6]

8. Am not surprised at your report on J.H.C. address.[7]

9. I think there are good reasons—largely psychological—why large super estate tax on state & municipal bonds would not largely affect their saleability.[8]

If the rich investor were an actuarial (politico-economic) man, he would have calculated on mortality tables his own expectancy of life etc. & buy accordingly. But he too is human. (a) Death seems far off. (b) He expects to live longer than his expectancy. (c) He may sell his bonds before he dies. (d) The Estate tax law may be changed. (e) He doesn't really care very much whether his heirs receive less net—

But he does care mightily that his own income shall not be abridged (1) Partly because he may wish to spend it (2) Partly because it hurts to give up so large a proportion of it.

Furthermore there is always a large market for tax exempts that would be practically unaffected by the super estate tax—i.e. Those not rich, and corporations.

10. We met Holmes J. walking alone on K. St. yesterday PM. Blooming and buoyant, having practically written the last opinion in his hands.

11. We reached No. 300 Friday on General docket—i.e. case entered about Mch 15/22. The bar has been caught napping & there were many passed.

---

[1]On 16 January LDB had written: "I have had some concern lest your most commendable public services in many causes may involve you quite unconsciously in incidental expenses which in the

aggregate are pretty large. And unless you and Marion object, I want to send you on Feb 1 check for $1000. on this account. I know there can be no better use of the funds."

[2] Robert Porter Patterson (1891–1952) graduated from Harvard Law School in 1915 and began practice in New York City where he was active in the Harvard Law School Association (from 1937 to 1949 he would be president of the Association). He became a district judge in 1930 and was appointed to the circuit court of appeals in 1939, but resigned to join the War Department, and in 1945 was named secretary of war.

[3] Gerry Henderson was being considered for the new chair in legislative law at the Harvard Law School, but neither FF nor Pound knew if Henderson was interested. LDB had agreed to talk to Henderson, but had suggested that Pound explain what was involved in a letter to Henderson.

[4] Victor Murdock (1871–1945), like his longtime friend William Allen White, was a Kansas editor and progressive politician. He had served in Congress for more than a decade, and in 1917 was appointed to the Federal Trade Commission. Currently he was serving as Chairman of the FTC.

[5] Frank Herbert Simonds (1878–1936) was a reporter, associate editor of the *New York Tribune* from 1915 to 1918, and an author of several works including a five volume history of World War I.

[6] On 25 January, President Harding had announced the nomination of Edward Terry Sanford (1865–1930) to replace Justice Pitney. Sanford had graduated from Harvard law in 1889, and later became a federal judge in Tennessee.

[7] Probably an address by recently retired Justice John H. Clarke.

[8] See preceding letter.

No. 122 February 19, 1923 Washington, D.C.

DEAR FELIX: One of the most important cases set for the 28th was reassigned today. The list is so uncertain that I think you had better have the Clerk wire you Friday, and perhaps again on Saturday.[1]

Holmes' Arkansas Case today is a satisfaction.[2]

I am enclosing the galley of the New England Divisions Case[3] which you may care to see speedily.

[1] On 14 March, FF would argue the landmark case, *Adkins* v. *Children's Hospital*, 261 U.S. 525. In 1918 Congress had authorized the Minimum Wage Board in the District of Columbia to establish wage minimums sufficient "to women workers to maintain them in good health and to protect their morals." That statute was attacked as a denial of due process, and FF was asked by the National Consumers' League to defend it. Since his daughter Elizabeth served on the Minimum Wage Board, LDB naturally disqualified himself from the case—although his sentiments on such legislation were no secret. On 9 April, the Court handed down a five to three ruling invalidating the statute. Justice Sutherland dismissed the voluminous data adduced by FF in support of such laws, claiming that such evidence had no relevance to the legal issues. Holmes wrote a forceful dissent, and even Chief Justice Taft could not support Sutherland's "Spencerian edict." The brief was published as Felix Frankfurter and Francis H. Stephens, *District of Columbia Minimum Wage Cases. Briefs . . .*, (New York: Steinberg Press, 1923). For a brilliant contemporary exposition of the case see Thomas Reed Powell, "The Judiciality of Minimum Wage Legislation," *Harvard Law Review* 37 (1924): 545. Not until 1937, did the Court uphold wage legislation—in *West Coast Hotel* v. *Parish*, 300 U.S. 379 (1937), and then Chief Justice Hughes relied heavily upon the reasoning in Holmes's 1923 dissent.

[2] The case was *Moore* v. *Dempsey*, 261 U.S. 86, announced on this date. In September 1919, a group of Negroes were gathered in their church when some whites attacked and fired upon them. In the ensuing disturbance a white man was killed, and five Negroes were charged with the crime. Both before and during the trial mob pressure was intense, and the court-appointed counsel did not

move for a change of venue; neither did he consult with his clients, call any witnesses, nor put the defendants on the stand. The "trial" lasted about forty-five minutes, and the all-white jury found the men guilty of murder. Holmes, for the majority of the Court, declared that these proceedings constituted a violation of due process, thus vindicating his earlier dissent in the Leo Frank appeal, *Frank* v. *Mangun*, 237 U.S 309 (1915). McReynolds and Sutherland dissented.

[3] The Transportation Act of 1920 gave the Interstate Commerce Commission power to establish rate zones, to consider the needs of particular carriers in setting rates, and to divide returns in different ratios among joint carriers. LDB delivered the unanimous opinion of the Court upholding the law and the I.C.C. powers, declaring that the rate division was not in violation of the due process clause. See *New England Divisions Case*, 261 U.S. 184 (1923).

No. 123   March 5, 1923   Washington, D.C.

DEAR FELIX: It is good to know that Marion & you think well of Chatham for the summer.

Elizabeth fears she must miss your Minimum wage argument. Friday she was operated on—appendicitis—after 36 painful hours. She is doing finely & is comfortable at the Emergency Hospital. We were fortunate in having her here, with Dr. Mitchell & Dr. Parker at hand. Six days earlier she was in the snow-covered Mountains of Maryland & Pennsylvania.

It is a relief to have Congress adjourn, & the President away. Of him I hear even worse things.[1]

[1] The administration of Warren G. Harding was beginning to crumble. The president himself left the capital for a vacation in Florida—within five months he would be dead. Although no major scandals had broken yet, Washington was rife with rumors of corruption in high offices, including the cabinet itself. These rumors would ultimately coalesce in the notorious Teapot Dome Scandal, one of the worst instances of executive misbehavior since the administration of President Ulysses Grant. Before it was over several members of the administration would be indicted for attempted bribery in connection with the leasing of oil rich government lands to private companies, and a cloud of suspicion would hang over other officials. See the excellent study by Burl Noggle, *Teapot Dome: Oil and Politics in the 1920s* (Baton Rouge: Louisiana State University Press, 1962).

No. 124   March 21, 1923   Washington, D.C.

DEAR FELIX: 1. Tell Marion to prepare for a long summer at Chatham. We have taken for the season the Hyde House (the house with the blue blinds & the five cottonwood trees to which we walked Harold A.) and there is an annex for the Frankfurters. Auntie B. is to find us a cook. I shall have my law books & the library can be augmented to satisfy your needs.

2. Glad you had so satisfactory a talk with deH. I have written Wise as you suggested.

137

3. Donald Richberg[1] was in Sunday. He is very promising. I suggested he apply to you for young men.

4. Homer Hoyt[2] was in Saturday. I think him a hopeful economist.

It was good to see you.

Alice had a very bad time end of last week, but is well along on the mend. Eliz. is home & getting her strength back.

[1] Donald Randall Richberg (1881–1960) was an important liberal lawyer in Chicago, specializing in public utilities and labor matters. He had helped to organize the Bull Moose party in 1912, and would follow his law partner, Harold L. Ickes, to Washington and become a high level figure in the New Deal—counsel for the National Recovery Administration and then executive director of the National Emergency Council.

[2] Homer Hoyt (1895–1984) taught economics at various colleges and universities. He served as an economist for the War Trade Board during World War I, and in the New Deal, as principal housing economist for the Federal Housing Authority. Currently he was teaching at the University of North Carolina.

No. 125   April 6, 1923   Washington, D.C.

F.F.: 1. I had a good talk with Mack whom you will be seeing these days. Yes, deHaas is doing good thinking. I assume he is sending you carbons of his letters to me.

2. I hope, in the readjustment of courses, you may be able to shift "Restraints of Trade" to one who would enjoy it more, & yourself get on to state & federal jurisdictions. There is [a] fair bit of work to be done there and great need. Some of the reworking of state jurisdiction which our western Courts of Appeal have been guilty of I will talk to you of later.

3. I should be surprised if the business boom does not break in time to help the Democrats in the 1924 campaign. The RR program proclaimed by the Executives is positive evidence of their folly.[1] The equipment is undoubtedly needed. But they should have ordered it 1–2 1/2 years ago when prices were low & business slack. It is just 50 years this spring since I witnessed the Vienna Bankrott[2] which preceded the crash of '73.

4. Mrs. Evans writes that Marion wants to know whether there are cooking possibilities in the Annex [in Chatham]. As I understand, No. It is strictly a "Season sale," bedrooms, garage or woodshed, etc. There may be possibilities of leasing for her mother & sisters nearby. But I guess nothing can be done about that till we are on the spot.

5. I hope you will let Marion compare, as manifestation of culture, the Harvard Club 25th Annual Meeting leaflet with the Amalgamated 1923 Almanac.

6. Alice is, I think, gaining, but still slowly. Eliz. is gradually regaining her strength.

I thought Marion might like to preserve this in her strong box.[3]

Marion will find, in the Webb's[sic] "Decay of Capitalistic Civilization"[4] much support for her views on advertising.

[1] The railroads had recently announced that they would spend over $700 million during 1923 for new equipment and improvements, an increase of more than $200 million over their normal expenditures.

[2] "Bankruptcy." LDB refers here to a tour of Europe he and his family made when he was fifteen years old in 1872. He carried through the rest of his life a vivid memory of that time and would frequently remind his brother Alfred of the anniversaries of their seeing various sights.

[3] LDB enclosed a clipping which reported that a number of Republicans had urged President Harding to hire a press agent so he could better "sell himself" to the people.

[4] Sidney and Beatrice Webb, *The Decay of Capitalist Civilization* (New York: Harcourt, Brace, and Co., 1923).

No. 126   April 26, 1923   Washington, D.C.

MY DEAR FELIX: 1. As you assume—I did not say, or dream, the views re Muller v. Oregon brief attributed to me.[1]

The only thing I ever said, on which anyone could have built the story, was my suggestion to Josephine[2] in 1908 as to the title for the popular edition of the brief. I suggested when asked: "What any Fool Knows." They thought "Women in Industry" more appropriate.[3]

2. The Lion Bonding & Surety Opinion[4] disclosed the worst conduct of CCA I have run across. It shows what convictions of "Divine Right" & "Manifest Destiny" will lead men to.

3. In Pusey & Jones,[5] there is a passage which may lead those whole [sic] feel like GWA to refuse to appoint receivers a la Metropolitan.[6]

4. Alice is making good progress this week & we hope to take the Federal Saturday. I will plan to call you up from Miss Roscoe's & shall hope to lunch with you Sunday.

4. Poor N.D.B. is incorrigible.   Greetings to Marion.

DeHaas was here Monday & records many failures but has courage.

[1] It is unknown what remarks were attributed to LDB or in what quarters, but the matter doubtless came up in connection with the Supreme Court's rejection of FF's "Brandeis brief" in the minimum wage case (announced one week before).

[2] Josephine Clara Goldmark (1877–1950) was LDB's sister-in-law and collaborator with LDB in the famous brief for the *Muller* v. *Oregon* case back in 1908 (see LDB to Louis B. Wehle 10 February 1908). After graduating from Bryn Mawr in 1898, she had joined Florence Kelley in the National Consumers' League, and as director of research profoundly influenced labor legislation in the early twentieth century. She was closely associated with Alfred E. Smith, Robert Wagner, and Frances Perkins in the attempt to legislate greater safety in industrial settings. During the New

Deal, her association with FF and Perkins made her an influential figure in the drawing of national labor laws.

[3] The Brandeis brief in *Muller* v. *Oregon* was published as *Women in Industry* . . . (New York: National Consumers' League, 1908).

[4] *Lion Bonding & Surety Co.* v. *Karatz*, 260 U.S. 77. This case was tried jointly with another one, *Department of Trade & Commerce of Nebraska* v. *Hertz*. Both involved the actions of the Eighth Circuit Court of Appeals in regard to the insolvency of Lion Bonding, a Nebraska insurance corporation, following a conflict between the Nebraska state courts and the Minnesota federal district court concerning the administration of the company's property. The court of appeals upheld the Minnesota receivers and overrode the Nebraska proceedings. LDB, for a unanimous Supreme Court on 23 April, reversed the court of appeals in both cases. The federal court was without jurisdiction, he argued, and he defended the prerogatives of the state courts. The last line of his decision was: "Lower federal courts are not superior to state courts."

[5] *Pusey & Jones Co.* v. *Hanssen*, 261 U.S. 491, was decided on the same day as FF's minimum wage case, 9 April. Again the case involved questions of jurisdiction in receivership cases, and again LDB delivered the Court's opinion, with McKenna and Sutherland dissenting. Both the federal district court and the Circuit Court of Appeals for the Third Circuit approved the petition of a creditor to have a receiver appointed. LDB reversed the lower court rulings, however, on the ground that the Delaware statute did not confer upon creditors the right to a receiver and that the federal court could not, as a matter of equity, do so upon the petition of a simple contract creditor.

[6] In his opinion in *Pusey & Jones*, LDB took special pains (at 500) to distinguish that case from *In re Metropolitan Railway Receivership*, 208 U.S. 90 (1908) where the company expressly agreed to the appointment of a receiver, admitted to its insolvency, and waived the matter of jurisdiction in the federal court.

No. 127   May 14, 1923   Washington, D.C.

F.F.: 1. I hope Guthrie has favored you with his book of addresses & that you have read the one on the Lusk Laws. [1]

In this connection read:

    (a) Editorial Comm. & Fin. Chronicle, May 12/23, p. 2049 [2]

    (b) Mahaffy, Greek Life & Thought, pp. 143 [3]

2. Glad to see the Harv. Law Review performing in May issue its function of enlightened public opinion on U.S.S.C. [4] With 20 such organs, & the service continued throughout 10 years, we may hope to see some impression made. There must be persistence.

Who wrote the article on Portsmouth Case? [5] It is very well done.

3. I will bring full set U.S.S.C. reports to C[hatham].   Do you want anything else?

4. When you have Mahaffy in hand read also:

    (a) On old men in government pp. 3–5

    (b) On courage p. 55 [6]

5. Hope Pound is really out of Filene foundation.

                        5/15

6. What you say of Alfred Cohen & Rockefeller Foundation is very interesting.

7. A pretty sad note of Massingham.[7]

8. I shall be glad to see E. Angell.[8]

9. Yes. Minn. tax case is good. Will tell you about that & others some day, with some reflections on the ultimate.

Greetings to Marion,

[1] Guthrie had just published *The League of Nations and Miscellaneous Addresses* (New York: Columbia University Press, 1923), which contained two essays on the red-hunting Lusk Committee of the New York legislature, both of them justifying the expulsion from the assembly of five Socialist members.

[2] The *Commercial and Financial Chronicle* had commended several new organizations that had been established to foster greater respect in the United States for law, order, and the Constitution. Among these were the Liberal League, founded by Nicholas Murray Butler, Bishop Manning, and others, and the Minute Men of the Constitution, headed by Charles G. Dawes, former director of the budget.

[3] Sir John Pentland Mahaffy, *Greek Life and Thought from the Age of Alexander to the Roman Conquest* (London and New York: Macmillan, 1887). On page 143 Mahaffy described the attempt of the ancient Greeks to control thought by prohibiting the keeping of any philosophic school without permission. There followed "a great exodus of philosophers," and the law was repealed within a year.

[4] Manley O. Hudson, "The Turntable Cases in the Federal Courts," *Harvard Law Review* 36 (1923):826, criticized two recent Supreme Court decisions, *United Zinc & Chemical Co.* v. *Britt*, 258 U.S. 268 (1922), and *New York, New Haven & Hartford R.R. Co.* v. *Fruchter*, 260 U.S. 141 (1922). Hudson argued that the decisions weakened liabilities of land occupiers for injuries to small children who inadvertently came onto the land. Holmes wrote the majority opinion in the first case, in which he was joined by LDB, though the latter deplored the willingness of the Court to review such cases.

[5] In the same issue appeared an anonymous student note on *Portsmouth Harbor Land & Hotel Co.* v. *United States*, 250 U.S. 1 (1919), which had been reargued at 260 U.S. 326 (1922). In both instances the Court, speaking through Holmes, held that firing artillery on government ranges did not constitute compensable damage to neighboring property interests. LDB dissented, arguing that the noise and discomfort did constitute damages.

[6] Mahaffy described the sad state of Greek politics at the death of Alexander as having been due to the rule of elderly men in nearly all of the city-states. "If the laws were not obsolete, the politicians were so." The reference to courage dealt with Demetrius Polioketes (337–281 B.C.), who aroused the valor of his men by his own personal example.

[7] Henry William Massingham (1860–1924) was a progressive English journalist with Liberal and then Labour party leanings. From 1907 to 1923 he was the editor of *The Nation*.

[8] Ernest Angell (1889–1973), a Harvard Law School graduate, was currently working as a New York lawyer. During the 1930s he joined the Securities and Exchange Commission, and he was later a leading figure in the American Civil Liberties Union.

No. 128   May 20, 1923   Washington, D.C.

DEAR FELIX: 1. Let me know what records & brief[s] of this term you want, so that they may be segregated before the shipment goes to the University of Chicago.[1]

2. I am glad of your letter in the Nation. M.O.H. deserved a jog.[2]

3. The Challenge to Hoover in the latest N.R. is admirable.[3] It

has all the qualities I plead [sic] for last September,—i.a. notable distinction.[4]

The writer should collect material from Hoover's occasional addresses, May 1922 to May 1924, for an article to appear May 1924 entitled
"But the World's Wise are not Wise"
& make him swallow then his voluminous prophecies.[5]

The article on China is also very good.[6]

4. I expect to send you by parcel post tomorrow some Oregon Case brief & other material for use at Harvard & other law schools, as you deem best.

5. Recent numbers raise N.R. to a higher level. If Bruce Bliven[7] has done this, he has accomplished much in very short time.

Alice was looking forward to a visit from Marion & you yesterday.

[1] Beginning in October 1916, his first term on the Court, LDB sent his personal set of records and briefs of Supreme Court cases to the University of Chicago Law School.

[2] In "The Liberals and the League," *Nation* 116 (4 April 1923): 383, Manley O. Hudson had criticized American liberals for failing to support the League of Nations. In his answer (published in the 16 May 1923 issue), FF argued that the question was not so simple. The idea of the League was certainly good, but no one had yet determined the conditions, the responsibilities, or the rights involved in membership.

[3] In what the anonymous author called "a friendly challenge" to Hoover, the article urged that the secretary of commerce turn his attention to ironing out the fluctuations in the business cycle. See "An Open Letter to Mr. Hoover," *New Republic* 34 (23 May 1923): 334.

[4] See 6 September 1922.

[5] 1 *Corinthians*, 3:18–19. No such article appeared in *The New Republic*.

[6] In "China and the Powers" (also in the 23 May issue), the editorialist analyzed Chinese politics and urged that other powers not interfere in internal Chinese matters.

[7] Bruce Bliven (1889–1977) had been a newspaperman before joining *The New Republic* in 1923; he directed its editorial policy until his retirement in 1955.

No. 129 June 9, 1923 Washington, D.C.

DEAR FELIX: Would Gary's[1] 12 hour day[2] give a good occasion for launching the campaign for a tax on bigness[3]—the real curse.

See Norman in June Hearsts.[4]

Hope to see you Tuesday.

Monday's ops will interest you.

Since writing the above I have read your review of Jones book,[5] and am glad you [wrote] there on size etc.

[1] Elbert Henry Gary (1846–1927) and LDB had been foes for years. Gary had left his Chicago law practice to organize the Federal Steel Company, and when that company joined others in forming the United States Steel Corporation, J. P. Morgan chose Gary to be the giant firm's chief executive.

[2] LDB had been a critic of the harsh working conditions at U.S. Steel at least since 1912 (see

LDB to Charles H. Jones, 13 February 1912). Beginning in the last week of May 1923, a renewed flurry of condemnation, led by social workers and religious leaders, denounced Gary's labor policies, and especially the twelve hour day he imposed upon his nonunionized work force.

³ See 4 January 1923.

⁴ Hapgood's editorial, "The Ku Klux Klan and the Louisiana Outrage," *Hearst's International* 43 (June 1923): 56, detailed the extraordinary political power the Klan had amassed in that state. It was part of a continuing series on the organization

⁵ FF had reviewed Franklin D. Jones, *Trade Association Activities and the Law* (New York: McGraw-Hill, 1922), in *Columbia Law Review* 23 (1923): 601. In his review he disagreed with the author that the antitrust laws had effectively barred the growth of large corporate entities.

No. 130   June 17, 1923   Chatham, Mass.

DEAR FELIX: 1. As to Maslon.[1] I told McCurdy I should want him some time in Sept., probably from the middle to the time he must go to Harvard,[2] & that I want him to have, at the end of that period, time to show Maslon the ropes. Except for this I do not think I shall need Maslon before Oct. 1. He had better keep in touch with McCurdy. Of course, McC. could give him this instruction at any time, so far as I am concerned.

2. As to super-power. W. Va. case[3] was evidently decided largely on ground that natural gas had been made an article of interstate com[merce], inviting large investment & reliance upon its continued supply. What would happen in the absence of these elements—quare.[4]

I do not see how a State e.g. N[ew]. H[ampshire]. could let its power enter into interstate com. without danger of robbery unless it got federal protection, either:

(a) through a fed. interstate com. law & Com[mission]., or

(b) through an application of the doctrine of the Webb-Kenyon law (Clark Dist. Co. case)[5]

Of course you will recall the limitations therein stated, which might prevent extension of the doctrine, as well as the criticism of the doctrine (see Minnesota Law Rev. articles)[6] and nothing would be safe.

My own opinion has been that it was wise (1) to treat the constitutional power of interstate Com. as very broad & (2) to treat acts of Congress as not invading State power unless it clearly appeared that the federal power was intended to be exercised exclusively (3) to rectify the tendency to hold federal power exclusive by applying the Webb-Kenyon doctrine.

Shall talk over Ben Avon[7] when you come here. Things are going well here. Alice seems to be gaining pretty steadily. We have canoed some and walked considerably.

[1] Samuel Henry Maslon (b. 1901) had immigrated to the United States as a small child. He clerked for LDB during the 1923–1924 term and then settled in Minneapolis to practice law.

[2] See 28 December 1922, n. 9.

[3] *Pennsylvania* v. *West Virgina*, 262 U.S. 553 had been decided by a divided Court on 11 June. A 1919 West Virginia law prohibited the sale of natural gas to other states until West Virginia's needs had been fully met. Pennsylvania, suing in the Supreme Court, alleged that the law imposed an undue burden on interstate commerce; and the Court upheld Pennsylvania. LDB and McReynolds (who, in the end, filed separate but similar dissents) argued that the Court had no jurisdiction since the real parties in interest were companies in the two states, who were not parties to the suit. Justice Holmes dissented on the issue of whether the untapped gas being controlled was actually in interstate commerce. See also 20 November 1923.

[4] [and] for what reasons.

[5] The Webb-Kenyon Act of 1913 (37 *U.S. Statutes* ch. 90: 699), passed over Taft's veto, provided cooperative federal support for state laws regulating intoxicating liquors and, exempting liquor from normal immunities of interstate commerce, controlled the traffic between "wet" and "dry" states. This law was upheld in *Clark Distilling Co.* v. *Western Maryland R.R. Co.*, 242 U.S. 311 (1917).

[6] Noel T. Dowling, "Concurrent Power Under the Eighteenth Amendment," *Minnesota Law Review* 6 (1922): 447.

[7] See 31 May 1922, n. 4.

No. 131   June 19, 1923   Chatham, Mass.

FF: You doubtless noticed that we denied Certiorari to CCA in the Mennen Case,[1] which set aside the Federal Trade Com[missio]n order prohibiting the Mennen Co. from giving to jobbers more favorable terms than to the so called Cooperative purchasing Co of the retailers.

The N.R. might well point the moral—that the way for the cooperatives etc. is to refuse to carry Mennens & have their own brand—nonadvertised.[2]

[1] *Federal Trade Commission* v. *Mennen Co.*, 262 U.S. 759. By denying certiorari, the Supreme Court sustained a circuit court of appeals ruling and left standing the pricing policy of the Mennen Co. that discriminated between ordinary retailers and cooperatives.

[2] *The New Republic* ran no such article.

No. 132   September 16, 1923   Washington, D.C.

F.F.: My greetings to you & Marion on the homecoming. Es war ein schones Zusammensein.[1]

1. Potter Com[missione]r dined with me Thursday. Says Richberg's argument in the recent valuation motion (as to original costs) was a beautiful piece of advocacy, as fine in tack and method as in substance.[2]

2. John R. Commons[3] dined with me Friday. He was very enthusiastic over Bill Rice, says he did an extraordinarily good job in connection

with the drafting of unemployment bill & considers him a distinct gain for Wisconsin.

Commons talked himself out on present-day economic & social-industrial problems. He has a fine spirit, an open mind & a happy freedom from classic economic theories. But his vision is narrow & his thinking not deep.

3. I think Van Vleck should include in his immigration survey[4] a thorough study of the cancellation of naturalization cases.

4. Maslon is here & I have set him to work.

5. The Palestine days in N.Y. were busy ones. deH. and B.F. (in his field) have done thinking. I have arranged in divers ways to take care of deH. Administration Fund requirements.[5]

Walton Hamilton[6] is to dine with us today.

[1] "It was a nice get-together."

[2] In 1914, Robert La Follette had sponsored legislation authorizing the Interstate Commerce Commission to evaluate all railroad property as the basis for determining rates. When the I.C.C. findings pleased neither consumer groups nor the railroads, La Follette helped establish the National Conference on Valuation of American Railroads (Donald Richberg was its general counsel) which attacked the estimate of $20 billion as the value of all railroad properties. The Conference, using the "original cost" method, estimated the value at $12 billion; the railroads, relying upon the cost of "reproduction" declared the value to be more than $40 billion. Richberg had unsuccessfully argued before Mark W. Potter and the other I.C.C. commissioners that all valuation matters be returned to the Bureau of Valuation for recomputation according to the "original cost" method.

[3] John Rogers Commons (1862–1944) was professor of economics at the University of Wisconsin and one of the outstanding authorities on labor law and economics. He directed numerous studies that provided factual information useful for social reformers throughout the country. Undoubtedly his most enduring work was *The History of Labour in the United States*, 4 vols. (New York: Macmillan, 1918–1935), of which LDB's daughter Elizabeth wrote part.

[4] William Cabell Van Vleck (1885–1956) taught law and served as dean of the George Washington University Law School for forty years. His special field was the law relating to aliens, and he labored for many years, under prodding from both LDB and FF, on his *The Administrative Control of Aliens* (New York: Commonwealth Fund, 1932).

[5] On 6 September LDB had met with members of the Palestine Development Council in New York to chart the future work of the group. At the urging of Jacob deHaas, the P.D.C. agreed to establish local leagues to recruit members and raise money for work in Palestine.

[6] Walton Hale Hamilton (1881–1958), long a favorite of both LDB and FF, was an economist and lawyer currently teaching at the Brookings Graduate School. In 1928 he began a lengthy tenure at the Yale Law School. He wrote several treatises on both legal and economic subjects.

No. 133   October 24, 1923   Washington, D.C.

F.F.: 1. Holmes J. closed our first 3 weeks sitting in fine shape physically & mentally. He walked with me from the John Paul Jones statue to 1720. His mind is in much better condition than at any time during the 1922 term & quite as good as at any time during the 1921 term.

2. Have you seen R.P.'s endorsement of the Community Trust?

3. The Amidon[1] letter is fine. I have written him.

4. The President (C.C.) seems to be quite in harmony with your paper on liquor.[2] The answer to Stimson[3] should be:

Do not change the Volstead Law in any respect. Leave the percentage of alcohol where it is. Merely provide in the annual appropriation bills that the prohibition money shall be used for protection against smuggling from abroad & from one state or territory into another, and the suppression in the District of Columbia & any government reservation, etc.

5. I had a good talk with Mack Saturday. In answer to enclosed letter, I have written him that I do not think the C.J. believes he is shirking etc.[4]

7[sic]. I think Alice is gradually regaining what she had lost since the early days of August in Chatham.

9[sic]. There is one bit of Palestine work which I should like to have you undertake if you see no objection. You know that for years I have believed that an appropriate letter should go to a select body of Jewish lawyers calling attention to the possiblity (now through the P.D.C. or P.E.F.) of bequests for Palestine.[5] There were 5 years of delay before anything was done. Then it was left to deHaas to send out some letters. I don't know how much he has done of this. But whatever it was, it was nothing. The letter should have gone from our distinguished lawyers in distinguished form. I think one signed by you as chairman etc or something would be most effective.

You will know what to say, to whom to send it, who else should sign, etc. But this idea, which may win us much money & open the way to other support, should be appropriately followed up.

Glad Marion finds the Blunt so interesting.

[1] Charles Fremont Amidon (1856–1937) was one of the federal judges whom LDB and FF admired greatly. He served as judge of the District Court for North Dakota from 1896 to 1928.

[2] In an address before the American Academy of Political Science, FF had argued against a call from Henry L. Stimson (see next note) for full national enforcement of prohibition. FF noted that although he personally disagreed with prohibition, the policy had been adopted as the law of the land, and there were now three courses open: repeal, nullification (by making believe the law did not exist), or enforcement. The first two options were dangerous, and only the third was honest. But, he maintained, the best method would be to have the states enforce local laws, with the federal government concentrating on fighting smuggling, both from outside the country and from one state to another. See FF, "A National Policy for Enforcement of Prohibition," *Annals of the American Academy of Political Science* 109 (September 1923): 193. See also 25 September 1922.

[3] Henry Lewis Stimson (1867–1950) had been FF's first guide and mentor, the man who

snatched him from private practice and introduced him to public service. FF had worked for Stimson when the latter had been a United States attorney, and then had moved to Washington when Taft named Stimson secretary of war. Hoover would name him secretary of state in 1929, and Franklin Roosevelt reappointed him as secretary of war when World War II began. He was a man of unquestioned ability and integrity, as well as of impressive social connections.

[4] Mack's Zionist work, together with his activities in numerous non-Zionist causes, led him to fear that others might think he was not fulfilling his responsibilities on the Court of Appeals.

[5] See 7 October 1919.

No. 134   November 4, 1923   Washington, D.C.

FF: Bliven's article on the farming situation[1] is sensible, forceful and clear. If Secy Wallace[2] or Eugene[3] can deny any statement of fact, or question the conclusions, they should be made to do so now. And neither lies nor bunk should be tolerated.

[1] Bruce Bliven, "Why the Farmer Sees Red," *New Republic* 36 (7 November 1923): 273. The article explored the sources of farmers' anger and attempted to dispel some of the myths about farming that were held in the East.

[2] Henry Cantwell Wallace (1866–1924), secretary of agriculture under both Harding and Coolidge, had been a farmer himself, and for many years was manager and editor of the famous agricultural magazine, *Wallace's Farmer*.

[3] Eugene Meyer was attempting to deal with the farm crisis through the War Finance Corporation; he had just returned from the West and made a report on farming conditions to President Coolidge.

No. 135   November 20, 1923   Washington, D.C.

F.F.: 1. In connection with the Japanese Alien Land Cases,[1] following matter arising incidentally should receive separate appropriate comment—

The Jap. get 1/2 the crop—only;

The owners get 1/2 for furnishing, practically, only the land (paying taxes thereon)

I think throughout history you probably could not find such rack-renting as we have made common in America.

The church took 1/10th. (I think even of its [*] lands)

The Attica tenants thought 5 per cent to the landlord was high.

2. In connection with the Craig Contempt case,[2] this point arising incidentally should receive separate treatment.

The absurdity of the running of a municipal utility being committed for years to a Federal Court, in a state which is the financial center of America & where probably nearly all the utility's securities are held.

3. I suppose you have noticed the interesting fight by N. Dak. etc. to insure its supply of Lignite coal.[3]

4. The W. Va. natural gas cases[4] were argued, if possible, more badly than ever before. The questions of substantive constitutional law and of procedural constitutional law involved are as important as any now conceivable. Neither the bar, the public or the interests great or small indicated in any way that they cared in the least. Charles Warren, who was present, could tell a strange tale of the lack of interest as compared with that which he described as having been taken on similar occasions a century & less ago. The court room was empty, even the lawyers awaiting later assigned cases not being in attendance. One might have supposed that a default judgment was being entered in a police court on the promissory note of an insolvent. No Atty. Genl or other person appeared as amicus. No member of the S.C. peeped.

5. Replying to your enquiry re Mellon tax reduction plan.[5] I am wholly contra.

(a) I don't think there will be any appreciable surplus in 1925, unless there are heavy cuts in War & Navy appropriations, which is not to be expected.

(b) The classes & individuals who are now suffering from the tax burden would not benefit appreciably. Those who would benefit are the rich & big business. They have been the beneficiaries of the excess war profits tax removal.

And of course, I am agin taking from the States their tax exemption on bonds.

I am deep again in early Italian history, now in the thirteenth century from which much modern wisdom may be deduced.

[1] On 19 November 1923, the Supreme Court handed down two decisions relating to the California Alien Land Law of 1920, which forbade aliens who were ineligible for citizenship (namely Japanese) to own land or enter into any contracts, such as sharecropping, which would give them the benefit of the land. The legal question was whether the California law could go further in limiting the rights of aliens than the 1911 treaty between the United States and Japan. Mr. Justice Butler delivered the opinion of the Court, which upheld the statute. LDB and McReynolds believed there were no justiciable questions involved and that the cases should have been dismissed. See *Webb* v. *O'Brien*, 263 U.S. 313 and *Frick* v. *Webb*, 263 U.S. 326.

[2] See 23 September 1922, n. 4.

[3] North Dakota was protesting new rail rates that increased freight costs of native lignite coal by 40 to 60 percent. The state's governor blamed the increase on eastern rail and coal interests, which had long battled against use of the cheaper lignite fuel.

[4] See 17 June 1923, n. 3.

[5] Pittsburgh industrialist and multi-millionaire Andrew William Mellon (1855–1937) served as secretary of the treasury until 1932. On 11 November, he had proposed a $323 million tax reduction, the major cuts being from upper bracket incomes, with the surtax on incomes over $100,000 being reduced from 42 to 25 percent.

No. 136   November 24, 1923   Washington, D.C.

FF: 1. Re yours of 22. I am entirely content to have you switch my $1000 conditional subscription to the youthful tutorial experiment if you desire.[1]

2. Marion must have been pleased by the N.D.B. election as Director.[2]

3. B. Hand[3] is here to see the C.J. I had some light talk with him last evening at Dean's & expect to see him again this afternoon.

4. I am glad to know the bankers are scared re Willett. The degree of their robber rapacity was a great surprise to me even as late as 20 years ago.

[1] In addition to supplying money to defray FF's public work, LDB also began to channel funds to aid in FF's efforts at the Harvard Law School. Starting in 1924, LDB provided the funds for a graduate fellowship to work under FF. See James M. Landis, "Mr. Justice Brandeis and the Harvard Law School," *Harvard Law Review* 55 (1941): 184.

[2] Baker had been appointed four days before as a director of the Baltimore & Ohio Railroad.

[3] B. Hand is [Billings] Learned Hand.

No. 137   December 3, 1923   Washington, D.C.

FF: (1) I wish you would have N.R. give its data in support of its statement in Dec 5 issue that tax exempt securities exceed $28,000,000,000.[1]

2. Arthur Fisher[2] was in—returned from the Ruhr with plans to stampede the presidential candidates, via the farmer vote, to support of Britain vs. France.[3] I think he was much disappointed at my attitude.

3. Cal. must find the Craig case quite embarrassing.[4]

4. Did you know that until recently Lincoln Steffens had been denied by the British authorities entry into England.[5] That was going some for lovers of free speech.

5. The W.Va. gas case are [sic] decided by vote of McKenna J.[6]

[1] *New Republic* 37 (5 December 1923): 28. The editorial commented on a proposal for increasing the estate tax on tax-exempt securities. *The New Republic* returned to the subject, giving greater statistical substantiation, in "Overworking the Tax Exempts," in the issue of 23 January 1924 (pp. 220–21); but in this discussion the magazine used Secretary Mellon's own estimate of $11 billion dollars in such securities.

[2] Arthur Fisher (1894–1960), after graduating from the Harvard Law School in 1920, served as counsel to various agricultural cooperative marketing organizations.

[3] The wartime alliance between England and France was very near the breaking point over the French invasion of the Ruhr in January 1923. The British refused to take part in the occupation (undertaken because of the German default in reparations payments) regarding the action as an invitation to anarchy. The occupation lasted until 1925 and was eventually terminated on the recommendation of the Dawes commission.

[4] For details of the Craig contempt case, see 23 September 1922, n. 4. Immense pressure came upon Coolidge to pardon Craig or to commute the sentence. On 4 December, acting on a recommendation from Attorney General Daugherty, President Coolidge found the charges against Craig to be valid, but set aside the prison sentence.

[5] Joseph Lincoln Steffens (1866–1936) was one of America's leading publicists and social reformers, winning national recognition for his *The Shame of the Cities* (New York: McClure, Phillips, and Co., 1904), a series of exposures on corruption in leading municipalities. Steffens, who had known LDB for almost two decades, grew ever more radical after the war. In 1919, he went with the Bullitt mission into Bolshevik Russia, interviewed Lenin, and made his famous statement: "I have seen the future and it works." The English relented and gave Steffens, now living in Paris as an expatriate and practically an American exile, a visa in October 1923.

[6] For the details of the case, see 17 June 1923, n. 3. The matter was re-argued (see 20 November 1923) on 20 November (*Pennsylvania* v. *West Virginia* and *Ohio* v. *West Virginia*, 263 U.S. 350). As LDB points out, the Court was badly divided. Taft did not participate in the rehearing, and Holmes, McReynolds, and LDB dissented from the majority of five. The deciding vote, therefore, was cast by Justice Joseph McKenna (1843–1926), a California congressman who served as McKinley's attorney general and had been appointed to the Supreme Court in 1898.

No. 138   December 10, 1923   Washington, D.C.

FF: 1. The Mayer N.R. *is* distinguished.[1]

2. Very interesting correspondence with Walter [Lippmann] & L.H. The latter's place should be in the Appellate Court & preferably here.

3. It will be interesting to watch the Labor Party in England now.[2]

4. I saw Hopkins[3] for a few minutes at Ned Lowry's Friday & am more patient about him. I think he is really struggling manfully for light; is deeply harried by the world's perplexing problems—particularly those of his job; and like most mortals who have a job, finds its requirements beyond him.

5. Hoover was also there—He looked sad. There was no light in his eyes.

6. Meddill McCormick was also at the Lowry's, the same as heretofore with considerable doubt whether he can get a renomination & election.[4]

[1] LDB refers to the article, "Lese Majeste Mayer," *New Republic* 37 (12 December 1923): 57. The piece, perhaps written by FF himself, was a thorough and scathing denunciation of the decision in the Craig contempt case (see 23 September 1922, n. 4). Quoting liberally from Holmes's dissent (in which LDB had joined), the article examined the whole matter of contempt—whether it should be applied when there is no effect on the judge's ability to do his job, and whether the case should not automatically go before another judge. Julius M. Mayer (1865–1925) was the New York judge who heard the original case, was denounced by Controller Craig, and sentenced him for contempt of court.

[2] In the general election—called by Prime Minister Baldwin, perhaps prematurely, to pass upon his scheme to relieve unemployment by means of a protective tariff—the Conservatives suffered heavy losses and Labour made very significant gains.

[3] It is uncertain which "Hopkins" LDB refers to here, but it might have been William Rowland Hopkins (1869–1961) who, three days before, had been appointed city manager of Cleveland,

Ohio—a city in which FF was keenly interested since his study of crime and criminal procedures there.

[4] Joseph Medill McCormick (1877–1925) was an Illinois progressive, and publisher of the *Chicago Tribune*. He had served one term in the Senate, and his current doubts were well founded: in 1924 he would be defeated in the Illinois Republican primary by ex-governor Charles S. Deneen.

No. 139   January 3, 1924   Washington, D.C.

FF: a) I entirely agree with you that Mack must not be allowed to "abdicate" his judgment.[1] Moreover, I don't understand in whose favor he is abdicating. I fear he is suffering i.a. from the perils of propinquity. The poor fellow is suffering in heart and body. I was not surprised to have his telegram saying that a sore throat would prevent his leaving *before* today—which I assume means that it may be after.

2. I think you have rather got Alvin Johnson[2] re taxes.

3. The N.R. article on the passing of the frontier—presumably his—is admirable.[3]

4. Prof. Ludwig Stein[4] called on me. He is a very good Redlichlike sample of what European civilization produces, & has the tact which Germans lack. I think you & Marion will find him good company.

5. I am venturing to send again Check for $1000 toward defraying your disbursements re public affairs.

[1] See also 11 January 1924.
[2] Alvin Saunders Johnson (1874–1971) left teaching to work for *The New Republic* in 1917. He stayed with the journal until 1923, when he became director of the New School for Social Research in New York City, a position he held until 1945. Johnson was also the coeditor of the important *Encyclopedia of the Social Sciences* in the late 1920s and early 1930s. He specialized in economic topics, but wrote on politics and cultural matters as well.
[3] The anonymous article, "Exit Frontier Morality," *New Republic* 37 (2 January 1924): 137, speculated (after the manner of Frederick Jackson Turner, thirty years before) on the effect upon the American character of the passing away of the frontier.
[4] Ludwig Stein (1859–1930) was born in Hungary, and trained in Berlin (where he served for a while as a rabbi). He became a professor of sociology and philosophy and was a prolific writer in these topics and on the history of Jewish thought.

No. 140   January 6, 1924   Washington, D.C.

F.F.: I had an interesting, harmonious and surprisingly intimate hour's talk with Morawetz.[1] It may well lead to his making important contributions, intellectual and financial, to legal education & specifically to Harvard L.S.

The immediate manifestation is a promise that he will ask you to call on him when you are next in New York. He, like Guthrie, has confidence in you. He, more in you than in Pound, whom, he fears, may be a bit "metaphysical."

It came about in this way: You know we were together at C[ambridge]. 2 years. When he entered, I said: "Now before we talk about our business, tell me about yourself." With astounding directness he said, as he sat down, and started giving an account of himself: "I haven't made as good use of my life as you have." Then, he recounted the vapidness of his achievements re Acheson [sic] & Norfolk & Western,[2] & his mistake in paying no heed "to the human" until it was too late; said he had tried to do something in foreign affairs, & economics, & legal education, but without much success.

Then he took up German reparations, told of his futile attempt to influence Hughes etc. In all his views on this subject we were in accord. Then, he took up the Institute,[3] told of early plans he had had, went into detail on the matter I had heard from Guthrie,[4] & asked me whether I could recommend the needed young men. He still believes the task is a possible one, but he knows now the difficulties & I think sees my reasons for apprehensions. As to the manner & means by which alone, the task could possibly be performed, we agreed fully.

Finally, I told him that he ought to eschew all other things, & devote his mind & special talents & rich experience solely to legal education, pictured to him what he might accomplish, & laid before him my old idea of drafting for the Law School the young men, 10 at a time, etc. He was enthusiastic, said he had had just such a thought about legal & economic research work; & had, some years ago, told Dr. Pritchett[5] that he would himself finance three.

Finally I clinched the situation by advising he talk matters over with you. He promised he would ask you to come. He has, of course, some heretical views:-

Is eager for Foundation aid (Abe Flexner) & clings to American Institute ideas. But he is in fine mood & good health; & far finer than he was 40 years ago.

I really enjoyed the hour; & think you may be able to lead him where he can be of great service. His mind is of rare clarity, & I think he wants to do. In all he said he was merely dissecting himself. There was not even a suggestion of the morbid.[6]

[1] Victor Morawetz (1859–1938) had been two years behind LDB at the Harvard Law School. He went on to a career which included both legal work and practical business experience. He wrote textbooks on commercial law, and LDB was so impressed with his ability and potential (calling him "the controlling intellect of the great Atchison Railroad system") that he had used Morawetz

as an example of how legal training could prepare men for important roles in society in his 1905 address, "Opportunity in the Law."

[2] Morawetz was counsel in the reorganizations of both railroads.

[3] Morawetz, together with Elihu Root and George W. Wickersham, had founded the American Law Institute in February 1923, to clarify, improve, and reform the American legal system.

[4] On 18 December 1923, LDB reported to FF that he had heard, from William Guthrie and another donor, that there was disillusionment about the American Law Institute.

[5] Henry Smith Pritchett (1857–1939) had been named president of the Carnegie Foundation for the Advancement of Teaching in 1906 and continued there until 1930.

[6] See 14 January 1924.

No. 141   January 11, 1924   Washington, D.C.

DEAR FELIX: (1) I am glad you found it possible to consent to help deHaas at Buffalo.[1]

(2) Mack seems to have recovered his balance & some of his cheer.[2] I suspect that what contributed most to his collapse was discovering that he had been led into a disloyalty of secrecy as against deHaas.

(3) Prof. Heinrich Loewe[3] of Berlin, here on National Palestine Library, will doubtless call on you soon. I found him an engaging party.

(4) Re Amidon's letter. I guess from what N.D. told me, Baker was formerly no other than he is.

(5) You gave Walter L. much good advice. I begin to believe again (as I did in my younger days) that no man without legal training is to be trusted in American public affairs.

(6) I saw Hoover at White House yesterday. He was downcast. Thinks defeat of Cummins on Interst[ate]. Com[merce]. Comtee[4] destroys his (Hoover's) plan for consolidating RRs on which he has been hard at work for 6 months; that his plan would otherwise have gone through; & that it would have solved the RR problem within 5 years; also that it was 5 RR presidents who did the killing.[5]

Marvellous credulity.

[1] Jacob deHaas had been on a speaking tour for the Palestine Development Council.

[2] See 3 January 1924.

[3] Heinrich Loewe (1867–1950) was a professor and librarian at the University of Berlin. He was a pioneering German Zionist and an authority on Jewish folklore. For years he labored to establish a Jewish national library in Jerusalem.

[4] On 9 January, Senator Robert M. La Follette and five of his supporters sided with the Democrats to defeat Albert Cummins's bid for reelection as chairman of the important Senate Committee on Interstate Commerce, thus demonstrating that he and his independents controlled the swing vote in the Senate.

[5] In his annual report for 1921, Hoover had called for consolidating America's railroads into larger systems, in order to gain the benefits recognized during the government's operation of the entire rail network during the war. Hoover, however, wanted the new groupings to be privately

153

owned. He would have received strong support from Cummins, who was coauthor of the 1920 Transportation Act, which did encourage the consolidation of competing lines. Among the railroad operators, the larger and more profitable roads opposed Hoover's scheme, while the smaller ones showed a greater receptivity to the idea.

No. 142   January 14, 1924   Washington, D.C.

DEAR FELIX: Re your letter, & later enclosure of Morawetz of 9th:[1] I think you will do better by feeling your way & relying on your own great tact.

What I felt had been done with M. was this:

1) To make him feel that there is an opportunity to make memorable use of his ability, experience, leisure & financial opportunity, by legal & educational work in connection with the H.L.S.

2) Also, that if he wants to see anything worthy accomplished re restatement of the law,

  (a) that he must do it himself not per alias, but with the aid of others

  (b) that the others must be young men of exceptional ability & inclination

  (c) that they must be trained for the work & tried

  (d) that this could be done by the process of annual experimentation through my plan & selection

  (e) that nothing worthy could be done except by work extending over a long series of years (I mentioned 10, which I thought was what the Germans used in preparing, with much help, their Commercial Code.)

M. says he "pegged" his age at 55 1/2[2] & I made him feel there was time enough ahead for him.

3) Also, I said to him that in the broader work of legal education, he could & of right should have an important influence, through close cooperation with the H.L.S. & being in its Councils.[3]

M's letter returned herewith.

[1] See 6 January 1924. FF had sent LDB Morawetz's letter of 9 January asking FF to see him the next time he was in New York ("I am writing this as the result of a conversation which I had last week with Judge Brandeis in Washington"). At the bottom of Morawetz's letter, FF told LDB that he was making a special trip to see Morawetz: "Will you please indicate (1) What you think I ought to put up to him & (2) how."

[2] Actually Morawetz was four months away from sixty-five years of age.

[3] On 20 January LDB wrote: "Your M[orawetz] interview is good as a starter. With your nursing, training & pruning, there should come some fruit."

154

No. 143   January 31, 1924   Washington, D.C.

DEAR FELIX: 1) This of Coolidge deserves honorable mention.[1]

2) Sutherland's branch bank opinion[2] almost makes me excuse his minimum wage doings.[3]

3. I suppose you will show Couzens[4] that the progressive estate tax on tax exempts may begin, for all in excess of his frugal $60,000 man. It's an interesting manifestation: "Wenn Gott nur mich gesund erhalt."[5]

4. I am very glad of your success in Buffalo.[6] It will help a lot all around.

5. I trust N.R. will realize that Denby, as a Ballinger Committee man, ought to have shown more discretion,[7] & will remind C.C. how the G.O.P. suffered from trying to whitewash Newberry.[8]

[1] LDB had enclosed the *Washington Post's* account of Coolidge's speech to the governmental budget organization, delivered on 21 January. He had marked the portion of the address where the president spoke in opposition to increased state subsidies. Such subsidies, he argued, were improper from a budgetary point of view, and also, by broadening the field of government activities, impaired the efficiency of both the federal and the state governments.

[2] *First National Bank in St. Louis* v. *Missouri*, 263 U.S. 640. A national bank in St. Louis opened a branch office and proposed to open several more; the bank thus violated Missouri state law, which prohibited branch banking. The question was whether state law could control a federal institution within its boundaries. Sutherland, in the majority opinion, ruled that state law should apply so long as it did not impair the function for which the federal institution was created and that, in this case, Missouri law must be upheld.

[3] Sutherland had delivered the opinion striking down the District of Columbia minimum wage law in 1923. See 19 February 1923, n. 1.

[4] Senator James Couzens (1872–1936) made a huge fortune in the automobile business, and then entered politics, serving in the Senate from Michigan from 1922 until 1931. Although a Republican, he was a sharp critic of Secretary Mellon's tax proposals and a spirited, even bitter, exchange of letters between the two filled the newspapers in January 1924. Among the issues debated were the role of tax exempt securities in national revenue, and the point at which large tax-exempt holdings in inherited estates might be subject to the estate tax.

[5] "If God will only keep me healthy."

[6] See 11 January 1924, n. 1.

[7] Edwin Denby (1870–1929) had represented Michigan in the House of Representatives between 1905 and 1911. Harding named him secretary of the navy, and he was currently caught up in the exploding scandal involving the leasing of federal oil reserves (see 5 March 1923, n. 1). He resigned under immense pressue on 18 February; but he resigned effective 10 March, defying the Senate to bring impeachment charges against him.

[8] Truman Handy Newberry (1864–1945), a former secretary of the navy, had been the Republican candidate for the Michigan senatorial seat in 1918, and in a vicious campaign against Henry Ford, Newberry won election narrowly. Ford, however, inspired a thorough investigation into Newberry's campaign expenditures. A case was brought against him which ultimately reached the Supreme Court (*Newberry* v. *U.S.*, 256 U.S. 232 [1921]) where, by a five to four vote his conviction for violating the Corrupt Practices Act was overturned. In January 1922, the Senate voted forty-six to forty-one to seat him. But when some Senators threatened to reopen the investigation into his election, he resigned in November 1922. A new Corrupt Practices Act of 1925 was a consequence of the Newberry case.

No. 144   February 3, 1924   Washington, D.C.

FF: 1. Death came to one of noble striving.[1] Perhaps we shall witness again: "but if it die, it bringeth forth much fruit."[2]

2. The oil retainers come as a bad blow to McAdoo's prospects.[3] The eternal curse of easy money.

3. The admiralty rule case[4] shows what poor bill drafters the USSC, aided by L.H. et al are. Of course no one (OWH, J. McR & the C.J. were on the Comtee) ever thought about the rules enough to know anything. It makes one more fearful of T. W. Shelton's cure all.

5. [sic] That's a nice letter from Wingert.[5] I showed it to Maslon, who, perhaps, still longs for practice in Boston. Would Elizabeth care to know Wingert?[6] And would it be wise to remind Nielson[7] of Eliz's desire for a position in Economics? She is keen now for a job.

[1] On this date ex-President Woodrow Wilson died in Washington, D.C.

[2] John 12:24.

[3] McAdoo, running hard for the Democratic nomination, had been dragged into the Harding scandals when testimony revealed (1 February) that upon resigning from Wilson's cabinet he represented one of the oil companies for retainers totalling $250,000. McAdoo replied that his work had nothing to do with American leases, only with Mexican properties; but many of his friends felt that the revelation badly damaged his campaign for the presidency.

[4] *Washington-Southern Navigation Company* v. *Baltimore & Philadelphia Steamboat Company*, 263 U.S. 629, a suit for libel in admiralty, turned upon an interpretation of Rule No. 50, which had recently been revised (6 December 1920) upon the recommendation of a Supreme Court committee. The new rule, LDB declared for a unanimous Court, did not empower the district court to stay proceedings in this case; it was intended merely to formulate practice already settled and not to give the district court an additional power.

[5] Emmert Laurson Wingert (1899–1971) had graduated from Harvard Law in 1923 and moved to Wisconsin. After a year on the attorney general's staff in Madison, he went into private practice. In the late 1950s Wingert was a member of Wisconsin's Supreme Court.

[6] Ironically, after Elizabeth Brandeis moved to Wisconsin, she and Wingert cooperated closely on matters related to Wisconsin social legislation.

[7] William Allan Neilson (1869–1946), a scholar of English literature, had assumed the presidency of Smith College in 1917 and held it until 1939. Throughout his life Neilson was engaged in numerous liberal and civil rights causes.

No. 145   February 9, 1924   Washington, D.C.

FF: 1. Morawetz letter enclosed. He & his new wife[1] were in for tea. For the few words which I had with him, he said his talk with you was very satisfactory; that he was convinced that his idea of continuing Am Law Institute work with the teaching work was wrong; that what he called my idea was right; & that if he could get the man, he would be disposed to stake the man himself for a progressive teaching & "it would be fun to watch him." I told him you could doubtless get him the man; that you got me my secretaries etc. Keep at him.

2. Nicely talked with me the other day (seeking advice) about the offer you made him for the next year. I advised him to accept.[2]

3. The House correspondence is interesting.

4. Did Farrand doubt Gerry [Henderson]'s work's value?

5. Gerry is West again for the War Farm Corp.

6. Holmes J. has not been so well. Not serious at all, but he talks considerably about adjusting himself to age etc. And there arise questions of judgment something like last year.

[1] Morawetz had just married Marjorie Nott, his second wife.

[2] James Mount Niceley (1899–1964) had graduated from Harvard Law School in 1923. FF placed him as Justice Holmes's secretary for this year and hoped to lure him away from private practice and into academic life. See, however, 8 March 1924.

No. 146   February 21, 1924   Washington, D.C.

FF: 1. Recent issues of the World disclose unexpectedly (to me) rich fruit of your correspondence with Walter L. re receiverships.[1]

2. Mellon has happily gotten "his"—an immensely important thing of wider significance even than the tax defeat is the basting of official propaganda—Truth may yet prevail.[2]

3. Please let me know by return mail what you know of Frank Fetter[3] (Princeton) and of Cornwall[4] (Vt.)—who are suggested (privately) for the Trade Commission by good friends of ours.

4. You will find the U.S. ex re Tisi (No. 132)[5] & No. 184,[6] of this week's [decisions] quite interesting on Admin[istrative] Law.

[1] Beginning on 17 February, the *World* published a series of articles to ascertain "the extent to which the Federal Courts have been engaging in business through receiverships." Researched by Frank Hopkins and Henry F. Pringle, the series charged that creditors usually lost out while lawyers cleaned up on fees.

[2] After a long and sometimes bitter debate over the tax plan of Secretary Mellon (see 20 November 1923), the House voted for the Democratic substitute, proposed by Texas representative John Nance Garner. The Garner plan extended the proposed tax reduction to farmers and small merchants—despite Republican claims that such a move would result in a serious deficit in the coming years.

[3] Frank Albert Fetter (1863–1949) was a professor of economics at Princeton University from 1911 to 1931. He wrote a number of textbooks and monographs on economic topics.

[4] Ellsworth B. Cornwall, the son of another Princeton professor, had practiced law in New York City and then settled on a farm in Vermont. He was currently president of the Vermont Farm Bureau. Neither he nor Fetter was appointed to the Federal Trade Commission.

[5] *U.S ex rel. Tisi* v. *Tod*, 264 U.S. 131, was decided on 18 February, LDB delivering the Court's

unanimous opinion. An immigrant named Tisi had been arrested for having some leaflets advocating the overthrow of the government, and had subsequently been ordered deported. Tisi argued that he did not read English, did not understand the pamphlets, and that he had also been denied due process by the authorities. LDB reviewed the steps in Tisi's hearing, and concluded that no violation of due process had occurred. "The denial of a fair hearing is not established by proving that the decision was wrong," unless, of course, the error of an administrative tribunal was "so flagrant as to convince a court that the hearing had was not a fair one." In this case, that degree of unfairness was not shown, and the order for deportation should stand.

   [6] In *Mahler* v. *Eby*, 264 U.S. 32, Herbert Mahler (and four other aliens) violated the Selective Service Act and the Espionage Act of 1917, and by a law of 1920, aliens who disobeyed either of those wartime laws were liable to be deported. Mahler and the others argued that the deportation order was void because the Espionage Act and the Selective Service Act had been repealed; that the law of 1920 was an *ex post facto* law; and that it was unconstitutional because it lodged legislative authority in an executive officer, whose criterion for deportation under the law (that the alien be "an undesirable resident") was vague and uncertain. Chief Justice Taft, for a unanimous Court, ruled on 18 February that the *ex post facto* rule applied only to criminal laws; that the right to expel undesirables is a sovereign right of any nation; that the delegation of authority to the officer was proper; and the fact that they had broken the laws was sufficient to place them in the category of "undesirable citizens." On the basis of a technicality, however, the Court ordered a rehearing of the case.

No. 147   February 25, 1924   Washington, D.C.

DEAR FELIX: 1. J.W.M. & deH. will report to you on the Thursday conference. I think it was helpful.[1]

   2. Pepper[2] is showing the same lack of political sense which characterized his Ballinger performance—[3]

   i.a. I am informed by high authority that he is gunning for the Presidency.

   3. Hamilton brought Meickeljohn[4] in last Wednesday & this Wednesday they (and Prof. Dodge)[5] are coming in to dine.

   4. I am glad you & Scott thought the admiralty opinion worthwhile.[6] It involved [*] more work than appears. There seemed to be nowhere available the data needed & the search was a long one. It is that kind of thing that Scott ought to do, I felt many times while the task was in hand.

   5. Today's dissent re Jensen case will interest you. I thought this a good occasion to let the law journal contributors know that they are helping.[7]

   6. C.C. wanted Charles Choate[8] to prosecute[9] and & [sic] he would have done so, had not his partners had in the past 2 retainers from Sinclair.[10]

   7. Have had long talk with Elwood Mead.[11] He confirms all & even more about the possibilities economically of Palestine. It's all up to the Jews who go there.

158

¹ Ever since the fight at Cleveland in 1921, Chaim Weizmann had been attempting to create an organization that would bring wealthy non-Zionists to support restoration work in Palestine, and thus fill the gap left by the departure of the Brandeis group. After nearly three years of negotiations with Louis Marshall and Felix Warburg, Weizmann had worked out the tentative structure of what would ultimately be called the Jewish Agency. At Louis Marshall's behest, a preliminary conference composed primarily of non-Zionists had been called for 17 February 1924 in New York. Over 150 prominent American Jews not directly affiliated with the Z.O.A., including LDB and Julian Mack, were invited; Weizmann alone represented the Zionist Executive. Despite an auspicious start, it would take more than five years of further negotiation between the Zionist Executive and the non-Zionists before the so-called "pact of glory" established the Agency at Geneva in 1929.

For details of the negotiations, the Agency's accomplishments and its ultimate transformation into a completely Zionist organ, see Urofsky, *American Zionism from Herzl to the Holocaust*, ch. 8, and Selig Z. Chinitz, "The Jewish Agency and the Jewish Community in the United States" (M.A. essay, Columbia University, 1959).

² George Wharton Pepper (1867–1961), a prestigious Philadelphia lawyer, had represented his friend Gifford Pinchot in the Pinchot-Ballinger hearings of 1910. In 1922 he was appointed to fill a vacancy in the Senate, and ran successfully for election for a full term thereafter.

³ During the 1910 hearings, Pinchot had been frustrated by Pepper's inability to understand that Pinchot wanted not to be defended, but that the whole affair be publicized as much as possible. Here LDB refers probably to Pepper's statement in the *New York Times* for 24 February seemingly placing the blame for the unfolding oil scandal not on the men involved, but on the post-war situation which had engendered corruption throughout the country.

⁴ Alexander Meiklejohn (1872–1964), the renowned educational philosopher and reformer, was currently president of Amherst College, but two years later he would found the famous Experimental College at the University of Wisconsin.

⁵ Professor Robert Elkin Neil Dodge (1867–1935) taught English at the University of Wisconsin and was chairman of the department.

⁶ *Red Cross Line* v. *Atlantic Fruit Co.*, 264 U.S. 109, issued the week before, involved a 1920 New York law requiring that arbitration actually take place if contracts provided for it; prior to that law, arbitration could not be enforced. The question before the Supreme Court was whether disputes arising out of maritime contracts were within the scope of the New York statute. The Atlantic Fruit Co. argued that maritime contracts were under the exclusive jurisdiction of the admiralty courts, and that the suit should be dismissed because of a lack of federal question. LDB declared that a state may, in fact, confer upon its courts jurisdiction to cause an arbitration to take place.

⁷ On this date the Court handed down its decision in another maritime case, *Washington* v. *Dawson* (combined with *California* v. *Rolph*, 264 U.S. 213) in which workmen's compensation laws were held to be inapplicable to longshoremen since those workers were covered by the interstate and foreign maritime laws. LDB, however, filed an elaborate dissent (at 228) in which he traced various aspects of both admiralty and state compensation laws; he saw no reason why state laws were not valid. In the process, he attacked the doctrine in *Southern Pacific* v. *Jensen*, 244 U.S. 205 (1916) upon which McReynolds's majority opinion rested and which found a New York compensation law infringing upon the domain of maritime law. LDB argued that *Jensen* was wrong to begin with, and he buttressed his dissent with copious citations of recent articles in various law journals.

⁸ Charles Francis Choate, Jr. (1866–1927), one of the leaders of the Boston bar, had crossed swords with LDB over the merger of the New York, New Haven & Hartford with the Boston & Maine Railroad. Choate had been the New Haven's counsel.

⁹ The government decided to appoint a special prosecutor to deal with the Teapot Dome scandals. Eventually, Harlan Fiske Stone and Owen J. Roberts assumed the task, and both men would eventually sit with LDB on the Supreme Court.

¹⁰ Harry Ford Sinclair (1876–1956) was president of the Sinclair Consolidated Oil Corporation. Since it was his company that had secured the controversial leases for the Teapot Dome oil reserves, Sinclair was catapulted into the center of the great scandal.

[11]Elwood Mead (1858–1936), an agricultural engineer, pioneered in irrigation work. He undertook a number of Palestinian projects and became an authority on that country.

No. 148   March 8, 1924   Washington, D.C.

F.F.: 1. OWH seemed happy on his birthday & was thoroughly alert at the Conference.[1]

2. Beware of V.—High authority who has seen him recently says he is mentally unbalanced.

3. I should think Jos. Cotton might feel a bit uncomfortable at the disclosures.

4. To my mind, as you know, the most disreputable & blameworthy part of the Harding Administration was the association with, & influence of McLean.[2] That was worse than occasional grafting even in high places, because it expresses decadence. I think to make the country realize how leaders have fallen, it should know what McLean is, which now only those familiar with Washington life do. It is proper that all who have touched that pitch should be shown up as defiled. B. Baruch's endearing telegram is not to his credit.[3]

5. I am sorry for Nicely's decision.[4] He is so good a fellow that the regret is apt to come "twenty years after."

6. The fall of the franc is encouraging.[5]

[1] Holmes became eighty-three on this date.

[2] Edward Beale McLean (1886–1941), the publisher of the *Washington Post*, had lent Albert B. Fall $100,000, allegedly to permit Fall to enlarge his ranch holdings in New Mexico. During the Harding administration McLean was in close contact with many of the figures later touched by the scandal.

[3] The Senate committee investigating Teapot Dome had uncovered a number of telegrams sent in code by McLean. One of them referred to Bernard Baruch and implied that Baruch, who thought highly of McLean, was going to put in a good word for the publisher with Senator Thomas J. Walsh.

[4] See 9 February 1924, n. 2. Nicely had decided to go into private practice in New York City.

[5] The long depreciation of the French franc had by this time threatened the economic stability of France and the continued existence of the Poincare government. At the beginning of the year the franc had been worth 5 cents; on this day it slipped to 3.42 cents. The French government finally stabilized the franc at 5.1 cents with the help of an American loan, an action that trapped many speculators.

No. 149   March 15, 1924   Washington, D.C.

FF: If Croly is really prepared to fight for his country:

Let him utilize this extraordinarily favorable opportunity to enter upon the struggle to uproot the detective system root and branch—in government and in industry. And

Let him vow to strive without ceasing until the system is driven out or his own death release him.

If the detective system lives, our ideals cannot survive. If I were dictator, I should abolish the system today without reserve, in every department of life and take all chances.[1]

My letter to Pres Eliot[2] was: "Luigi Cornaro[3] taught how to attain long life. You teach how to use it."

I enclose letter just received from Mack. Please tell him that I think it better for me not to talk to the C.J.—partly because I should not feel clear what to ask of him without talking first to Mack. Therefore I suggest your talking the matter over fully with Mack, which, in any event, he would wish.

My own thought is that Mack is better off acting as a District Judge. He is freer there & can deal there not only with law but with men.

You will recall what Webb[4] D.J. (of Maine), New England's greatest D.J. in half a century, said when practically tendered the office of Circuit Judge: "There is not much difference between little great men."

[1] See also 26 November 1920.

[2] Charles William Eliot (1834–1926), the illustrious former president of Harvard, would turn ninety in the next week. LDB had known Eliot since his law school days and although the two men disagreed on important topics (such as the advisability of labor unions), they professed deep respect for one another. At a crucial moment in LDB's confirmation hearings in 1916, Eliot had written a warm letter to the committee advocating LDB's appointment.

[3] Luigi Cornaro (1467–1566) was a Venetian nobleman known for his treatises on a temperate life. His *The Sure and Certain Method of Attaining a Long and Healthy Life* was written when Cornaro was in his eighties.

[4] Nathan Webb (1825–1902) was appointed district judge for Maine in 1882.

No. 150   March 17, 1924   Washington, D.C.

1. I think the public has a pretty general conception of the impropriety of ex-officials practicing promptly before the Departments; & will know more when the returns come in in response to the Norris[1] Resolution.[2] An article from you would, of course, be illuminating. But I think at the moment what is more needed is an article on the text of your letter to C.C.B.[3]—re dereliction of Amer. Bar Ass. J. W. Davis and C. E. Hughes, as ex Presidents should be particularly addressed.

If there hadn't been in the Dept. of Justice during Palmer's[4] and Daugherty's Administration a single criminal act, the obvious demoralization of the Dept. would have aroused any fearless body of lawyers capable of indignation & with a sense of professional duty. The decadence was so obvious as not to escape detection even by the blind. They were bent on suppression of knowledge. Among the elect in high places there is now no indignation except at the exposure. It is only over Kerby speaking[5] that vested interests rise in denunciation.

Bob Woolley,[6] Ned Lowery [sic] & Frank Lyons [sic][7] are talking Carter Glass[8] for Pres[ident].

[1] George William Norris (1861–1944) had represented Nebraska in Congress since 1903, and continued to do so until 1942. A crusading liberal throughout his career (being one of three Republicans to break party ranks and vote for LDB's confirmation in 1916), Norris was a leading expert on both farm policy and water power development. His expertise in the latter field was demonstrated in the effort to save Muscle Shoals and to establish the TVA.

[2] On 26 February the Senate had unanimously adopted resolutions introduced by Norris calling on various governmental departments to supply the names of any congressman or cabinet official who, within two years of leaving government service, appeared in connection with any claim against the government, or who belonged to any law firm making such appearances.

[3] Charles Culp Burlingham (1858–1959) was one of the leading figures of the New York bar during his long lifetime. His friendship with FF and with Franklin D. Roosevelt, and his contacts with other important political and legal figures made him one of the best informed men in the nation for over five decades.

[4] Alexander Mitchell Palmer (1872–1936), a Pennsylvania attorney, served in the House of Representatives from 1909 to 1915. During the war he was alien property custodian, and in 1919 Wilson named him attorney general. It was during Palmer's tenure that the United States underwent the "red scare" and the questionable "Palmer raids" that rounded up radicals and, in some cases, deported them.

[5] Frederick M. Kerby had been a humble stenographer for Richard Ballinger during the conservation controversy. Troubled by his conscience, Kerby eventually came forward with information crucial to LDB's case against the Taft administration. For the details see LDB to Knute Nelson, 21 March 1910.

[6] Robert Wickliffe Woolley (1871–1958) had worked for a number of newspapers before becoming chief investigator for the Stanley Committee investigating U.S. Steel in 1911. An insider in Democratic party affairs, he held several positions within the party and in Democrat administrations, including a stint on the Interstate Commerce Commission from 1917 until 1921.

[7] Frank Lyon, now a Washington, D.C., lawyer, had joined the Interstate Commerce Commission in 1887, the year of the agency's founding, and was periodically associated with it in later years. In 1916, he testified on LDB's behalf at the confirmation hearings.

[8] Carter Glass (1858–1946) of Virginia had been a member of the House of Representatives where, as chairman of the Banking and Currency Committee, he was one of the chief architects of the Federal Reserve Act. After short service as Wilson's secretary of the treasury, he went to the Senate and stayed there for the rest of his life.

No. 151   March 31, 1924   Washington, D.C.

FF: 1. I am arranging with Maslon to hold himself available for my work until Oct. 1 so that there will be no need of my seeing Ege[1] before that date. Maslon will write him.

2. In Walter Nelles I am much disappointed. He has been before us

much in deportation & anarchist cases. Shows mental acuteness and sincerity, but an extraordinary lack of judgment. He suggests that when Count Johanness sued in slander for charging him with "the contagious disease" of insanity, there was some basis in medical science for the claim. Nelles has really behaved like some of his unbalanced clients.

3. Is the A.G.'s broadly announced support of C.C. a subtle oriental revenge?[2]

Bruce Bliven may have told you that I talked earnestly to him.

[1]Warren Stilson Ege (1900–1979) graduated from Harvard Law School in 1924, clerked for LDB for a year, and settled into private practice in St. Paul, Minnesota.

[2]Harry M. Daugherty, the disgraced attorney general, had been named a delegate-at-large to the approaching Republican National Convention. He announced his support for Calvin Coolidge in late February and continued to assert it thereafter.

No. 152   April 6, 1924   Washington, D.C.

1. Marion is dead right about J. W. Davis—in every word she says. J.W.D.'s acts & omissions during the last 3 years have been thoroughly in harmony with the judgment she expresses.[1]

2. Your review of the St. Louis Administrative Law volume is admirable in every respect.[2] I am eager, as Powell[3] is, to have your Due Process of Law book appear in due time & to have it followed by one specifically on Administrative Law.[4] But I cannot regret that you have devoted to other tasks a part of your time during the last 5 years. The sum total of good to the community—pre-eminently through your teaching [and] inspiring writing—has been fully as great as it could have been through the book. And the book will be, as the country as well[,] all the better for what you have so generously done in stimulating & aiding the efforts of others.

3. C.N.'s[5] appreciation of a kind word—since his war & postwar experiences—is almost pathetic.

4. I will try to get hold of VanVleck & see how he has grown qua Dean [of George Washington University Law School].

5. Daugherty's answer to Pepper is a ripper.[6] P. has about as much political sense as Hoover, and is as little of a statesman.

6. I am glad you think well of Stone. I am sure some would like to make a vacancy for him on the Court. But, even if one came, it is question[able] whether he, as a Morgan man, could get the votes before Nov[.], or after if CC is beaten.[7]

7. Powell's article in Mch. issue should open eyes & cannot fail to help.[8] Such shots continued a few years may revolutionize attitudes. He

talks English, & you may see in Monday's journal entries some reflex. Some might say, "He talks turkey."

8. I think Wheeler (despite Eastern newspaper yapping) is doing an uncommonly good job.[9] I hope his uncoverings will make Stone & others realize

"Quid latet apparebit
Nil in ultum remanebit." [10]

9. Walter L. will need a lot of education before he will be competent to guide opinion on American affairs.

10. Of course I shall be glad to see Amberg. I should have better hopes—if it were his wife.

11. Can't E. P. Costigan [11] be lured away from his worse than useless job to some law school. His labors are a monumental exhibition of "Time elaborately thrown away."

---

[1] John W. Davis, who was now being prominently mentioned as the Democrats' presidential candidate, had resigned as ambassador to England in April 1921, and promptly became the head of a prestigious Wall Street law firm, whose clients included J. P. Morgan & Company, Standard Oil, and United States Steel. LDB, who had thought highly of Davis as solicitor general, told him in 1919 that he hoped someday to see him on the Supreme Court. In 1923 Davis had been sounded out to see if he would accept the appointment that ultimately went to Sanford, but Davis turned it down. See William H. Harbaugh, *Lawyer's Lawyer: The Life of John W. Davis* (New York: Oxford University Press, 1973), chs. 12–13.

[2] FF had reviewed (in *Harvard Law Review* 37 [1924]: 638) *The Growth of American Administrative Law* (St. Louis, 1923), a collection of essays by six distinguished authorities.

[3] Thomas Reed Powell (1880–1955) was professor of law at Columbia and an authority on constitutional law. The next year he would move to Harvard, where he remained until his retirement.

[4] FF never got around to publishing a book on due process, and there would be a long delay before his book on administrative law appeared, but FF and J. Forrester Davison, *Cases and Materials on Administrative Law* (New York: Corporation Trust Co., 1932) became a standard text on the subject.

[5] Charles Nagel (1849–1940), a prominent St. Louis attorney, had married LDB's sister, Fannie, in August 1876. With Fannie's suicide in 1890, contact between LDB and Nagel became infrequent. Nagel rose in Republican politics and became a cabinet officer in the Taft administration. Nagel had dropped FF a note of appreciation for the enthusiastic review, especially of his own chapter detailing his interpretation of administrative law while secretary of commerce.

[6] On 3 April 1924, Senator George Wharton Pepper had told a Portland, Maine, political convention that the appointment of Daugherty as attorney general had been "a grave error in judgment." Daugherty attacked the speech (which most people assumed had Coolidge's endorsement), and by implication, hit at those Republicans who had convinced Coolidge to oust him from the cabinet.

[7] On 4 April 1924, President Coolidge had named Harlan Fiske Stone (1872–1946) as attorney general. Stone, who was then dean of the Columbia Law School, was also a member of the firm of Sullivan & Cromwell, which handled a number of large business clients including, on occasion, J. P. Morgan & Company. As it turned out, a vacancy on the Court did occur with the resignation of Joseph McKenna on 4 January 1925, and Coolidge within a few weeks named Stone to the Court.

164

In June 1941, President Roosevelt elevated Stone to the chief justice's chair. Despite Stone's connections with Wall Street and business, he became a close ally of LDB's while on the bench, and during the 1930s especially he could be counted among the liberals on the Court.

[8] Thomas Reed Powell, "The Judiciality of Minimum-Wage Legislation," *Harvard Law Review* 37 (1924): 545 was a devastating critique of the majority reasoning in the Washington minimum wage case.

[9] Burton K. Wheeler was taking a leading part in the investigation of the administration of Harry Daugherty, Harding's former attorney general. The "yapping" LDB mentions was probably the attempt of some to connect Wheeler's old Montana law firm with oil dealings (see 25 May 1924).

[10] "What is hidden will be apparent; nothing will remain unpunished." From the hymn "Dies Irae," attributed to Thomas A. Celano, lines 17–18.

[11] Edward Prentiss Costigan (1874–1939), a Denver attorney involved in numerous progressive causes, had been named to the United States Tariff Commission in 1917. Costigan resigned in 1928 and three years later was elected for a single term as senator from Colorado.

No. 153   April 16, 1924   Washington, D.C.

1. The N.R. has painted J.W.D. so well [1] that he who reads will have no excuse for letting him run. [2]

2. Enclosed No. 94. will interest you. [3] It is good to have the 4 appointees desired by the Yale Reviewer lined up on the same side.

3. Isn't Hughes' keynote grand? [4] It reminds of 1916.

[1] "Why Mr. Davis Shouldn't Run," *New Republic* 38 (16 April 1924): 193. The anonymous editorial, which quoted LDB and Pound on the social function of a lawyer, denounced Davis's recent professional activities and associations.

[2] A play on words from Habakkuk, 2:2—"write the vision and make it plain upon the tables, that he may run that readeth it."

[3] No. 94 was *Burns Baking Co.* v. *Bryan*, 264 U.S. 504. Nebraska had passed a law regulating not only the minimum size of bread loaves, but the maximum as well; and the Court, speaking through Mr. Justice Butler, held the statute, insofar as it concerned maximum size, to be unreasonable. LDB, joined by Holmes, entered an extensive dissent in which he described the entire history of such regulatory legislation to justify its reasonableness. He consulted numerous trade journals and wrote: "Much evidence referred to by me is not in the record. Nor could it have been included. It is the history of the experience gained under similar legislation, and the result of scientific experiments made, since the entry of the judgment below. Of such events in our history . . . the Court should acquire knowledge, and must, in my opinion, take judicial notice, whenever required to perform the delicate judicial task here involved."

[4] On 15 April, Secretary of State Hughes delivered the keynote address at the New York State Republican Convention. He promised that the guilty would be punished within the Republican party and insisted, to the cheers of the delegates, that "the best assurance of the future is in the character of Calvin Coolidge." The text of his address may be found in the 16 April *New York Times*.

No. 154   April 21, 1924   Washington, D.C.

1. Since writing you yesterday have yours enclosing the Burlingham correspondence. I hope Croly understands B, a charming companion but

a pretty poor adviser in these days when righteous indignation is our greatest need. B. should consort with Perkins & Sedgwick. The N.R. is standing up valiantly for continuance of the investigation & should not yield a hair's breadth in its vigorous demand.[1] The apologetic is our worst enemy now.

2. Have just read your plain talk on Bruce. It should do good.

3. Malcolm Sharp[2] was in today. He bears the Meiklejohn spirit.

4. I was sorry that I had to dissent on Holmes J. today.[3] But there was another incident a la Scranton.[4]

[1] See for examples, "The Republicans' Defence: Bluff or Apology," *New Republic* 38 (16 April 1924): 192; and "President Coolidge Gives Himself Away," *ibid.* (23 April 1924): 217.

[2] Malcolm Pitney Sharp (1897–1980) had graduated from Harvard Law School in 1923 and, after a brief period in private practice, returned to Harvard for graduate work. He first joined the faculty at the University of Wisconsin, and in 1933 he began his long service as a professor of law at the University of Chicago.

[3] Technically, LDB did not "dissent" on Holmes, he "concurred in part" in *Chastleton Corporation* v. *Sinclair*, 264 U.S. 543. The Washington, D.C., Rent Commission had been created during the war to control rents in the face of the influx of government workers flocking into the capital. When the Commission ordered a reduction in the rent of apartments owned by the Chastleton Corporation, the corporation charged that an "emergency" no longer existed and that the law was therefore invalid. Holmes reversed the lower courts which had upheld the Commission and ruled that an investigation of the actual conditions was proper. LDB agreed that the Commission's order should be reversed, but argued that the Supreme Court was not required to pass upon the constitutionality of the District Rent Acts.

[4] See 14 December 1922, n. 5.

No. 155   May 6, 1924   Washington, D.C.

FF. 1. B.F. made an admirable statement Sunday (4 hours to 8 auditors). He has done a prodigious amount of work of a high order, with some brilliant conceptions. He is, indeed, thrilled; has grown largely in understanding and sympathy in this connection; and has exhibited good ability. Of course, all this is merely planning & laying the foundation. If he has the stick-to-it-iveness, I have no doubt he can succeed & do a work worthy of the Flexners. But it will require that he devote himself to this work practically to the exclusion of all else.[1]

2. Walton Hamilton told recently of Abe F[lexner]'s sayings and doings which are most creditable to his sense of what is really worthwhile in educational & research effort—above all of freedom in its pursuits. It supported what Meiklejohn had told me.

3. I hope you wont let Cardozo[2] publish his lectures unless it will clearly conduce to his reputation—which is not only excellent, but

widespread. That is, unless you think this is not only good, but the best he can do, let him try at it some more.[3]

4. I am glad Bob Herrick[4] has not had an all to[o] pleasant winter.

[1] Flexner's renewed enthusiasm for the Zionist cause would make itself felt as a founder of the Palestine Economic Corporation in 1925–1926, and as its president until 1931.

[2] Benjamin Nathan Cardozo (1870–1938), after a boyhood in New York City, an education at Columbia, and a legal practice that won him the respect of fellow lawyers and the New York bench, became a judge—eventually the chief judge of the New York Court of Appeals. His thoughtful and articulate decisions made the court, according to FF, "the second most distinguished judicial tribunal in the land." When Justice Holmes resigned from the United States Supreme Court in 1932, President Hoover, ignoring the fact that there were already two New Yorkers (Hughes and Stone) and one Jew (LDB) on the Court, appointed Cardozo to take the seat. Universally acknowledged as one of the greatest judges in American history, Cardozo served on the Supreme Court until his death. See FF's affectionate sketch in *The Dictionary of American Biography*, supplement 2.

[3] Cardozo delivered a series of lectures at Yale University in December 1923; they were published as *The Growth of the Law* (New Haven: Yale University Press, 1924).

[4] Robert Herrick (1868–1938) was a professor of English at the University of Chicago for thirty years, and a novelist of some reputation in this period.

No. 156   May 11, 1924   Washington, D.C.

DEAR FELIX: 1. This is very good. I doubt that I have any suggestions unless it be to make more pointed our practices—(a) to hold acts unconstitutional "as applied"—and (b) to let them stand, except at the instance of a party who can show that the Act hurts him.

That M[anley]. O. H[udson]. should be willing to support advisory opinions, so obviously bad in American affairs, to help his international striving, discloses a new danger in these foreign missionaries.[1]

2. I suppose you have seen Haine's [sic] article in Apr/24 Texas Law Review, a very creditable piece of work.[2]

3. The McAdoo article in this week's N. R. is fine.[3]

4. C.C. will be up against vetoing or acquiescing this week & later which will test his mettle & judgment.[4]

[1] In an article in the *Harvard Law Review*, Hudson had presented a generally favorable view of the practice of courts providing advisory opinions to legislatures and to contesting parties prior to adjudication. See "Advisory Opinions of National and International Courts," *Harvard Law Review* 37 (June 1924):970. In a "Note" appended at 1002, FF had added a caveat in which he held it "dangerous to encourage extension of the device of advisory opinion to constitutional controversies."

[2] Charles Grove Haines, "Judicial Reviews of Legislation in the United States and the Doctrines of Vested Rights and of Implied Limitations on Legislatures," *Texas Law Review* 2 (1924): 257, 387.

[3] "Money and Government," *New Republic* 38 (14 May 1924): 299. The unsigned editorial was a denunciation of William G. McAdoo for allowing personal materialism to interfere with public service.

No. 157   May 25, 1924   Washington, D.C.

FF.: 1. It's good to know that the year's teaching has been so satisfactory. In American law, the next 25 years belong to the teachers.

2. You will find George Anderson as hot as you on C.E.H. A. considers him the most malign influence now in public life in America.

3. I [am] glad of the lesson you are trying to spread by E. E. Hunt [1] & Prof F.W.T.[2]

4. The Stone-Wheeler letters are fine. I am told authoritatively (a) that Vanderlip[3] knew 2 weeks or more before the Wheeler indictment came, that it was to be.[4] (b) that recently when he talked to the A.G. about it, Stone said that the "large fee" was an incriminating fact. Think of that for a New Yorker with S's connections.

5. I guess the Anti-Spy campaign would secure many recruits now.

6. Holmes J. had some bad days last week—pain in abdomen. But he seemed pretty well mended today & hopes he would be allowed by his M.D. to attend Court tomorrow. I warned him that the day would be a long one.

[1] Edward Eyre Hunt (1882–1938) had worked with Hoover in Belgian relief, and was afterward associated with the Red Cross and other social agencies as an investigator and organizer.

[2] Frank William Taussig (1859–1940), one of the best known economists in the country, was also the brother of LDB's sister-in-law, Jennie Brandeis. Taussig, connected with Harvard University through his entire academic career, was best known for his work on the tariff; in 1916, President Wilson had named him chairman of the newly created Tariff Commission.

[3] Frank Arthur Vanderlip (1864–1937), a prominent business leader and president of the National City Bank of New York, had been making speeches deploring the extent of corruption in business and politics. He had organized the Citizens Federal Research Bureau to investigate such matters, and had personally resigned from a number of directorships.

[4] On 8 April, Burton K. Wheeler had been indicted by a grand jury in Montana on charges of accepting retainers to use his influence to get gas and oil permits from the Interior Department. A special Senate committee, headed by William E. Borah, reported on 20 May that the entire episode looked like a frame-up, and that there was no hard evidence to support the charges. Wheeler had been head of the committee that uncovered evidence leading to Attorney General Daugherty's ouster from the cabinet, and it later emerged that Daugherty had sent the Federal Bureau of Investigation to discover "evidence" against him. The Wheeler indictment proceeded up to the Supreme Court of Washington, D.C., which exonerated him, and in January 1926, the Justice Department announced that it would not pursue the matter.

No. 158   May 28, 1924   Washington, D.C.

1. We had Senator & Mrs. Wheeler in Sunday. He has been terribly hard hit by the indictment, & that the A.G. won't order it dismissed despite the Borah [1] report. The long strain of continuous hard work, immeasurably increased by the criminal proceedings, has worn on his strength & he needs all the cheering up which can come through appreciation. A personal word from you, in addition to your fine "piece" in the N. R. (which he had not then seen) will help. [2] And I hope you can gently suggest to Pound & to Z. Chafee that a letter (promptly sent) would be in order.

2. Ben Dinard [sic] [3] (Minneapolis) was in yesterday. He seemed quite depressed (a) by the difficulty of getting a living through practice (b) by the very engrossing work necessary to do it, which compels exclusion of contemplation & all things otherwise appealing. I suspect his brother's blindness adds much to the burden, & that his salary is a bit meagre. He did not complain of that however; rather of the exhausting quantity of the grind. There ought to be a place at some law school for as attractive a fellow as he appeared to me.

[1] The chair of the Senate committee investigating the charges against Burton K. Wheeler was Senator William Edgar Borah (1865–1940), a progressive Republican who represented Idaho in the Senate for six terms. Borah, who had voted against LDB's confirmation to the Supreme Court in 1916, is best remembered as a determined isolationist working to keep the United States out of the Legue of Ntions and removed from involvement in international affairs during the troubled 1930s.

[2] "Hands Off the Investigation," *New Republic* 38 (21 May 1924): 329. The article was a summary of the achievements of Thomas J. Walsh and Burton K. Wheeler in investigating the Washington scandals, and an appeal to resist mounting efforts to cripple such investigations.

[3] Benedict Spinoza Deinard was the son of a Minneapolis rabbi. He had done postgraduate work at Harvard in 1922 and returned to Minneapolis where he continued to practice law.

No. 159   June 3, 1924   Washington, D.C.

FF.: 1. Sen. Ashurst [1] told me with much satisfaction of inserting your article in the Congr. Record. [2]

2. You cornered the A.G., and I don't think he helped himself by attempting what Hough J. call[s] a hurdle. He hasn't stood the acid test.

3. The Child Labor resolution brings new dangers. [3] I guess we'll have to remember that our first instalments from women suffrage are this & the prohibition amendment. One would think that the Hull Housers would occasionally think of Chicago conditions. Mrs. Medill McC[ormick]. is eloquent on the almost unbelievable corruption (political) there. Interesting as coming from Mark Hannah's [sic] daughter.

4. In the Frank tragedy it is, at least, a mercy that the victim was a Jew.[4]

5. Read the House Immigration Report. Whatsoever one may think of the policy, all must recognize that it is a very weak legislative presentation. The N. R. might appropriately say this about July 1.[5]

6. You will find some things of interest in yesterday's opinions.[6]

7. Holmes J. is in fine form again, and seems to have had the joy of a child in yesterday's honors.[7]

8. La Follette has again exhibited his political skill.[8]

There will be much to talk over at Chatham.

The Hamiltons were in Sunday in fine form & very happy over the developments at the Brookings School here.

[1] Henry Fountain Ashurst (1874–1962) had been a member of Arizona's territorial assembly and then served as the first senator from that state from 1912 to 1941.

[2] See preceding letter, n. 1. FF's article may be found in *Congressional Record*, 69th Cong., 1st Sess. (Washington, 1924): 9080–82.

[3] On 2 June 1924, the Senate passed the proposed child labor amendment and sent it to the states for ratification. Foes of the proposal gained some satisfaction in that the Senate did not allow for the special ratifying conventions in the states, but instead left the matter to the more conservative legislatures.

[4] A reference to the notorious murder of Bobby Franks; see 10 September 1924, n. 1.

[5] During 1924 Congress had again dealt with the explosive issue of immigration, and both houses had come up with measures severely limiting immigration. The conference committee report on the Johnson bill proposed national-origin quotas and excluding the Japanese completely. The report and bill were adopted on 15 May, and President Coolidge signed the measure into law on 26 May 1924. For the *New Republic's* comments, see "Corollaries of the Immigration Law," *New Republic* 39 (11 June 1924): 61.

[6] On 2 June the Court handed down seven opinions. LDB wrote one majority opinion in *United States* v. *American Railway Express Co.*, 265 U.S. 403, upholding the power of the Interstate Commerce Commission to set certain routes. He also entered one dissent, in which he was joined by Holmes, in *Pacific Gas & Electric Co.* v. *San Francisco*, 265 U.S. 393, differing from the Court's interpretation of how public utility rates should be set. Here LDB was following the line he had set out in the *Southwestern Bell* case. (See 18 July 1927, n. 4).

[7] The day before, President Coolidge had presented Mr. Justice Holmes with the Roosevelt Memorial Association medal. In part the citation read: "In peace and in war, as a soldier and as a jurist, you have won the gratitude of a nation by your uniformly gracious and patriotic devotion of great talent to its service."

[8] Senator La Follette had just announced his intention to form a third party for the approaching presidential election if the two major parties refused to accede to the demands of American progressives. On 4 July the new Progressive party, meeting in Cleveland, nominated him and, as his running mate, Burton K. Wheeler. There were persistent reports that La Follette wanted LDB to resign from the Supreme Court and be his running mate, and as early as March the rumors reached the press (see the *New York Times*, 18 March 1924). Throughout the summer the speculation continued (see *New York Times*, 3, 14, and 19 July). La Follette never discussed the matter directly with LDB, but he did send an intermediary to Chatham to explore the possibility. To his brother, LDB wrote on 19 July: "The Senator will have (if he keeps his health) a grand fight. If I had several watertight compartment lives, I should have liked to be in it. The enemies are vulnerable & the times ripe." For the results of the campaign, see 7 November 1924.

No. 160   September 6, 1924   Chatham, Mass.

FF.: Since our talk on conspiracy, I have looked at the cases in U.S.S.C. & at those in the Fed. Rep. since 196. We have over half a century of experience with J.C. §37 (R.S. 5480).[1] There are available data on which the careful and sagacious might determine the usefulness of this form of prosecution & eliminate the abuses.

The enquiry shows, among other things, to what extent

(1) The field of state function has been invaded.

2. The proceeding has been used to secure trial at a jurisdiction deemed more favorable to the Govt.

3. The conspiracy count has been joined to those for the substantive offence (as the indictments have been consolidated) in order to secure admission of evidence which would have otherwise been excluded wholly or as against certain defendants.

4. Injustice has been done by including in a single proceeding many issues in part distinct & involving many defendants.

5. The discretion of the trial court has been abused by admitting evidence of declarations as against alleged coconspirators before the fact of conspiracy has been clearly established.

The survey has been painful & has confirmed my conviction of the need of a fundamental enquiry into the causes of prevalence of crime in America. I don't think we can get far in cures until the diagnosis shall have been made.

[1] Chapter 37 of the Judicial Code dealt with questions of jurisdiction, and specifically with the matter of removing a case from state to federal court. Section 5480 of the *Revised Statutes* dealt with conspiracy to commit mail fraud. LDB had often contended that mail fraud cases within the federal jurisdiction were one of the chief causes for the clogged condition of the federal judiciary.

No. 161   September 10, 1924   Washington, D.C.

FF.: 1. Yours of Labor Day has come with Amidon's worthy & touching appreciation, which I return.

2. Shortly after Leopold and Loeb[1] are sentenced, the appropriate person or persons ought to see their respective fathers & induce them to give (as an expiation or a memorial) say to the Law Schools of U. of C[hicago]. and Harvard the fortunes which the sons would presumably have inherited—these to be used for the study of the causes & remedies for crime in America.

My distrust of Endowments is not lessened, but they are a presence.

And these fortunes, if given now, would help stimulate and direct pursuit of the enquiry so urgently needed.

3. Leonard Blumgart (Nation Sept 10)[2] should have made clear that, while diagnosis, strategy & treatment of crime, sin, disease are in rudimentary stages, moral standards—attained through thousands of years of experience—are not: "The law that abideth & changes not ages long."

We are expecting Justice & Mrs. Higgins[3] tomorrow evening.

[1] Richard Loeb (1905–1936) and Nathan Freudenthal Leopold (1904–1971) were both from well-established Jewish families in Chicago. In 1924 they tried to commit the "perfect crime" in kidnapping and murdering young Bobby Franks. After a sensational trial (the two teenagers were defended by Clarence Darrow), they were sentenced to life imprisonment plus 99 years. Loeb was murdered by a fellow inmate in 1936, and Leopold was paroled in 1958.

[2] Leonard Blumgart, "The New Psychology and the Franks Case," *Nation* 119 (10 September 1924): 261. Blumgart tried to apply his science to the Loeb-Leopold case: "I do not indict the parents; I indict all society. . . . I would make of every law-breaker a patient whose whole personality, including his heredity, his social, physical, and mental history from birth would be taken into account, and who would be treated on the basis of that complete understanding and not solely on the basis of his crime."

[3] Henry Bourne Higgins (1851–1929), a distinguished judge of Australia's High Court and chief judge of the Federal Court of Conciliation, was a good friend of FF.

No. 162   September 29, 1924   Washington, D.C.

That Oct. 1 article is a rip-snorter.[1] Of course C.C. won't understand. But J.W.D. can and will; and some others high in authority may get an inkling. I hope it will receive its due of comment;—approval or attack, it matters not which. What will Mr. George Rublee say?

Would it not be possible to get some one to write (say for the Atlantic, i.e.) a comparison of the actual security of life & property in U.S.—and on the other hand in Britain, Canada, Australia, New Zealand, South Africa? Could Harold Armstrong do it, or Loring Christie or Phil Kerr[2] or Lionel Curtis?[3]

The Higgins[sic] are coming in this evening, & we have asked Father Ryan[4] to meet them.

[1] An unsigned editorial (obviously by FF), "The Red Terror of Judicial Reform," *New Republic* 40 (1 October 1924): 110, attacked both Coolidge and Davis for their stands on judicial reform. Both men, in speeches delivered only hours apart, defended the Supreme Court's majority in nearly identical terms. FF listed areas in which that majority might have been guilty of the "slaughtering of social legislation on the altar of the dogma of 'liberty of contract.'"

[2] Philip Henry Kerr, eleventh Marquess of Lothian (1882–1940) was a well known English journalist and public official. He specialized in imperial politics and in 1939 was appointed ambassador to the United States, where his speeches did much to elicit American support for the British war effort.

[3] Lionel George Curtis (1872–1955) was another British author, adviser on colonial affairs, and an associate of Kerr's (later editing Kerr's speeches). None of these writers produced an article along

the lines suggested by LDB. The suggestion was provoked by FF's assertion (see n. 1, above) that life, liberty, and property are not less protected by other constitutional arrangements in the English speaking world.

[4]John Augustine Ryan, S.J. (1869–1945) was a professor of moral theology and industrial ethics at Catholic University and a leader in the Catholic social justice movement.

No. 163   October 3, 1924   Washington, D.C.

1. It is significant that, while Wig. et al., (Aug. 24 Journal of C.L.) can distinguish between industrial regulations crimes & other mala in se,[1] they ignore the difference between political & other crimes, despite Italian guidance.[2]

2. I asked McK how he learned English. His answer was, in substance, that like Topsy, he grew. I guess that he had (45 to 50 years ago) what good things were going & current in the Victorian Age. He thinks a schoolmaster out West helped him. The engraving gave him great joy. The poor fellow has had a dreary summer with his wife desperately ill, probably dying now.[3]

3. Saw the C.J. today. He is about as his letter to me indicated.

4. Sandford [sic] is much pleased with his trip, although it took him 2 months to get over his tiring speaking engagements. Sutherland likewise needed 2 months to rest up from term & post term labors.

5. Talked yesterday with one conspicuous in the Wilson Administration who said he talked earnestly to J.W.D. in 1921—urging his opting to W.Va, instead of N.Y., & that he reject offer of a Cravath partnership. In the latter, he thinks, it was his advice which was followed. He said he put up to J.W.D.—N.Y. *or* President then & again, via Polk, in July/24.[4]

6. The director of the Louisville Community Chest was in today. I asked him what they are doing for the Consumers' League. He answered $3400, & that he is in Washington to try to get the Treas[ury]. to remit taxes on the Chest's income which he says is being imposed because of this allowance to the League!!

7. Have you ever gotten anything from Victor M[orawetz] in money or otherwise.

8. At the Circuit Judges' dinner yesterday Woods[5] said to me, as I sat down by him after C.J. left: "I have just been saying to the C.J. that I am much alarmed by the judicial function of setting aside rate decisions of Utility Commissions. It would have been much better to have left the whole matter to the legislatures." I referred him to N. R. Oct 1st.

9. At the dinner I had also a brief talk with the A.G. on detectives.

Evidently he had done far less, in the way of reform, than we supposed.[6] He had lopped off abuses, but has left the t[h]reat practically intact. Says about 120 have been taken off, about 60 new added (most men of legal training) & has now between 500 & 600 in the Bureau of Investigation. He promised to call on me soon to talk the matter over.

10. Rogers C.J. said he had been asked to run as Gov. in Conn., but, although he was entitled to retire as judge, he didn't care to do so.

11. Your introduction to Cooke's volume just recd reads well.[7]

McAdoo must be examined by M.D.'s which will probably *prevent* his campaigning.[8]

[1] An evil by itself.

[2] John Henry Wigmore (1863–1943) was the dean of Northwestern Law School and a noted expert on evidence. The August 1924 edition of *The Journal of the Institute of Criminal Law and Criminology* began with an editorial written by John. H. Wigmore and his associates—"The Progress of Penal Law in the United States of America, 1874–1924," which was a hymn of praise to the Italian pioneers in the field of criminal law.

[3] Mrs. McKenna died about one week after this letter was written.

[4] Upon his return from England, Davis had to decide between joining the firm of Craveth and Leffingwell, or that of Stetson, Jennings and Russell. He chose the latter, partly upon the urging of his close friend Frank Lyon Polk (1871–1943), a high ranking State Department official who was entertaining an offer from the same firm. For the decision, see Harbaugh, *Lawyer's Lawyer*, 181–85. LDB probably meant to write "July/20."

[5] Charles Albert Woods (1852–1925) had been judge of the Fourth Circuit Court since 1913.

[6] Upon entering office, the new attorney general, Harlan F. Stone, announced that he was going to dismantle the Federal Bureau of Investigation by dismissing all of the dollar-a-year men from their investigatory roles.

[7] FF contributed a short introduction to Morris Llewellyn Cooke, *Public Utility Regulation* (New York: Ronald Press Co., 1924), 1–8. Cooke (1872–1960), a leading consulting engineer and efficiency expert, had been linked with LDB in the scientific management movement. He later administered the Rural Electrification Agency in the New Deal.

[8] McAdoo underwent minor bladder surgery on 6 October and was effectively kept out of the campaign for Davis's election.

No. 164   October 6, 1924   Washington, D.C.

1. I think Jean F.[1] is right about the "New Bigelow Papers."[2] Yours to B[en Flexner]. seems almost the best. That such a man as he can't see, explains much in history, as well as in biography.

2. Hough and G.W.A. are both so illuminating on Contempt, & so scornful of judicial proprieties, that they might be willing to put into the shape of a contribution for the H.L.R. their views on this subject. A dignified legal symposium might be helpful.[3]

3. I hope the N. R. Oct 1, will lead to such a discussion in the Am. Bar Assn Journal.[4]

4. The Hobsons[5] were in to dine Saturday & he enquired, at once,

about you. We had Judge Wood[s], Grace Abbot[6] & Ernest Gruening[7] to meet him.

5. The last has done an admirable piece on Journalism in the Sept. Century.[8] I still think there will be no escape from the miserable state of our press & periodicals until we break the back of advertising.

6. Ege is a pleasant fellow & gives promise of helpfulness.

7. Your last two envelopes brought many things for thoughts of deep interest.

8. O.W.H. was in fine form yesterday, save as to back.

9. Had 2 1/2 hours with J.W.M. He is fine & lovable, with much cause for sorrow.

[1] Jean Atherton Flexner was the niece of Bernard and the daughter of Abraham Flexner.

[2] The *Bigelow Papers*, by James Russell Lowell, were a series of nine letters by "Hosea Bigelow" published in the 1840s to protest the Mexican War.

[3] No such symposium appeared in the *Harvard Law Review*.

[4] See 29 September, n. 1. In the December issue, Robert L. Hale called attention to *The New Republic*'s article and discussed the issues raised by it. See Hale, "Judicial Review Versus Doctrinaire Democracy," *American Bar Association Journal* 10 (December 1924): 882.

[5] John Atkinson Hobson (1856–1940) was an English economist whose work anticipated some of John Maynard Keynes's general theory. He was probably best known, however, for his pioneering work, *Imperialism: A Study* (London: James Nisbet and Co., 1902).

[6] Grace Abbott (1878–1939) had been trained as a social worker by Jane Addams at Hull House. In 1921 she had succeeded Julia Lathrop as chief of the Children's Bureau, and retained that position until 1934.

[7] Ernest Gruening (1887–1974) was at the height of his journalistic career in 1924, serving as managing editor of *The Nation* and also as La Follette's publicity director for the presidential campaign. A distinguished second career was still before him. In the 1930s he moved to Alaska and served as the territorial governor from 1939 to 1953. He then represented Alaska in the Senate from 1956 to 1969.

[8] In "Can Journalism Be a Profession?," *Century* 108 (September 1924): 687, Gruening lamented the consolidation and disappearance of many American newspapers, and argued that "two tendencies more or less antagonistic are molding the destinies of our press. In the conflict of the *profession of journalism versus the newspaper business*, the latter is romping to victory."

No. 165   October 9, 1924   Washington, D.C.

1. Pound has doubtless told you of his letter to me of 10/6 about the L.S. building plans,[1] and of my reply which was:

"Thank you for letting me know about the plans under consideration.

Do let me talk with you when you are next here. I have grave apprehensions and want to suggest an alternative."

Entre nous, the alternative is roughly this:

Make frank recognition of the fact that numbers in excess of 1000, and the proposed 350 seats lecture halls & lectures, are irreconcilable with H.L.S. traditions & aims. Instead, make frank avowal of a purpose to aid in building up the lesser schools. Then aid in placing H.L.S. resources at their disposal so far as possible, i.a., create a new kind of exchange-professorships—i.e., H.L.S. professors who go out, as legates, temporarily to aid in developing lesser schools & there teach and take in exchange the local professors who shall come for a year or so to H.L.S. to *learn*.

Also arrange that picked students from such lesser schools may enter, not only postgraduate H.L.S. classes, but the higher undergraduate classes. Of course, I see the difficulties of putting such an alternative scheme into operation. But it is "constructive—not destructive." Be the mother church for the new & worthy legal education & legislation.

2. It is fine to hear of Marion on the stump.[2]

3. " " " " " " Herman A. in perfect health again.

4. Guthrie's partner H. was not happy when I last saw him.

5. Who wrote the World editorial?

6. S. Adele Shaw[3] is able enough to understand even if she doesn't heed.

---

[1] As the popularity and prestige of the Harvard Law School increased, its physical facilities, dating back to the nineteenth century, became strained. Dean Pound advocated a large scale expansion of the school's physical plant, faculty, and student body. On 21 October he named a committee, chaired by E. H. Warren and including FF, to consider plans for a new building, but the committee—probably under FF's prodding—recommended that the school be more selective in its admissions rather than less, and that it seek $4.2 million in additional endowment funds for program purposes. Eventually, Pound announced a drive to raise $5.4 million for building and endowment, but the effort yielded only slightly more than $2.3 million. See Sutherland, *Law at Harvard*, 262–70.

[2] On behalf of La Follette's independent presidential bid.

[3] S. Adele Shaw had been the youngest member of the famed Pittsburgh Survey, and then joined Survey Associates. She was active in Pittsburgh civic affairs.

No. 166   October 25, 1924   Washington, D.C.

FF.: Re yours 21.

1. I talked with S.[1] about H. L. S. as suggested. He knew nothing of conditions, did not know there was a problem, &, of course, had not thought on the subject. His reaction was wholly toward our view, thought larger numbers irreconcilable with proper teaching of the case-system to which he is wedded. He realized that he had not thought on the subject; later suggested it was a matter which ought to be thoroughly discussed by and in the faculty; & said he would think further himself. He asked about Williston[2] and Beale, would be much influenced probably by Williston's views, possibly by B.'s. I should doubt whether he

would stand adamant against P[ound]'s insistence & it would be desirable to arrange an interview. I suppose you have reason to think that S.['s] opinion would carry large weight with P. I don't see why.

2. As to use of my alternative suggestion.[3] Do with it what you please. Disclose or withhold authorship—appropriate it; modify it; or any other treatment you deem helpful. I should think you, with Williston, would be more potent in argument than anyone else could be with P.

3. As to method of limitation: I think there should be strong insistence that in consideration of the subject, the questions should be definitely segregated:

(a) whether limitation to, say, 1000 is desirable.

(b) if so, the mind of man may be then put solely upon devising or selecting the best, or least objectionable means.

(c) if not, the mind should proceed to devise the means which will make numbers least harmful.

S. began by asking for means & method of limitation, before expressing an opinion. But I convinced him of the wisdom of rejecting that method of approach, & he then agreed that we must limit, & having determined on that, find the best method of applying the limitation.

I have no definite views as to methods of selection. A field for wide research & inventive thought is open. A few things seem clear:

(a) Limitations must *not* be effected by raising tuition fees.

(b) The methods must ensure national representation, geographically & in respect to colleges.

(c) Provision must be made for star men (undergraduates) of other law schools.

(d) Provision must be made for teachers of or those definitely preparing for teaching at other law schools.

[1] Perhaps LDB's colleague, Justice Edward T. Sanford, who had graduated from Harvard Law School in 1889.

[2] Samuel Williston (1861–1963) had taught at the Harvard Law School since 1890. He was an authority on contracts, and served as reporter and chief author of the influential *Restatement of Contracts*. In 1929 he received the first gold medal of the American Bar Association for "conspicuous service to American jurisprudence."

[3] See 9 October 1924.

No. 167 October 31, 1924 Washington, D.C.

FF.: 1. A Biddle[1] for La Follette is certainly astounding.

2. It's sad about P[ound].

3. C.C.B. is interesting.

4. Of course J. H. W[igmore]. will fume over both the Wan and Arndstein opinion.[2] It will be fine to see his performance.

5. I am sorry H. C. has more deoges.[3] N. R. appeal for subscribers seems to me finely frank. People ought to be able to appreciate the effort although they vote against the measures. But most subscribers are as unreasoning as L[aw]. S[chool]. faculty members.

6. Let me know what you hear about Julia Lathrop's Massachusetts campaign.[4]

7. If J.W.D. & his Democrats are as badly beaten as the British Liberals seem to be at this writing it will be a healthy performance.[5]

8. We shall look for Marion's piece.

9. Holmes J. has finished all his ops. (3)—only "adorable leisure" awaits him.

[1] Probably Francis Biddle (1886–1968). Biddle had clerked for Justice Holmes in 1911–1912, and despite his aristocratic background, went on to serve a number of progressive causes. Especially active in New Deal years, Biddle was appointed solicitor general in 1940, and between 1941 and 1945 was attorney general of the United States.

[2] Both *Wan* v. *United States*, 266 U.S. 1, and *McCarthy* v. *Arndstein*, ibid. at 34, were decided in October 1924, and in both cases LDB delivered the opinion for a unanimous Court. After the murder of three Chinese in Washington, D.C., the police went to New York and brought Wan back to Washington where, despite his serious illness and intense pain, they subjected him to merciless and constant questioning, day and night, for weeks. The lower court had accepted his confession as admissible because no "threat" or "promise" had been used to obtain it. LDB, in an opinion which meticulously and dramatically recounted the "torture" of Wan's interrogation, ruled that the confession was made under compulsion and, therefore, was neither voluntary nor admissible as evidence.

The *Arndstein* case had dragged through the courts for nearly five years, and had twice before come to the Supreme Court. Arndstein was a voluntary bankrupt, and in 1920 was brought before a New York commission to ascertain the extent of his property. He answered some questions, but refused to answer others, claiming the constitutional right against self-incrimination. The government argued that in such cases, the right did not exist; but LDB ruled that a bankrupt's books and papers could not be withheld from scrutiny, but he had all of the normal protections when testifying in person.

[3] "troubles." By 1924, Croly and *The New Republic* were facing serious difficulties: internal quarreling, falling subscriptions (down from the wartime high of 35,000 to around 14,000), and an ever increasing debt to Dorothy Straight (by 1924, the magazine owed its benefactress more than three-quarters of a million dollars). Finally, in what was essentially a bookkeeping trick, the magazine declared bankruptcy and was reorganized.

[4] To secure passage in that state of the proposed constitutional amendment giving Congress the right to regulate child labor. Although Massachusetts itself had adequate protection in state law against abuses of child labor, a referendum was held on the question. Other state legislatures were said to be watching the Massachusetts canvass with interest. The battle had heated up when high officials in the Catholic Church came out against the proposal. The measure was defeated by more than 400,000 votes.

[5] After a defeat in Commons, Ramsay MacDonald called for a general election on 29 October. The Liberals suffered a debacle at every level, and Stanley Baldwin's Conservative party swept into power.

No. 168   November 3, 1924   Washington, D.C.

F.F.: 1. I suppose you have seen the straw vote in the Nov. 1 New Student.[1] That is the most discouraging feature in our life. It means that youth has its eye on the main chance, almost to the exclusion of other things. It is just what we of Public Franchise League experienced nearly a quarter of a century ago.

2. Alice bids me say, as to Marion's article, that quite apart from the merits of the argument, there is in it undeniably literary quality, that it has atmosphere & style.

3. I guess the British labor defeat will hurt us considerably.

[1] Upon surveying more than 120 American colleges and universities, *The New Student* reported the following results: Coolidge, 30,141; Davis, 13,825; and La Follette, 7,491. Coolidge's triumph was general except for a few places in the South where Davis was able to maintain a lead.

No. 169   November 7, 1924   Washington, D.C.

F.F.: 1. As to Austin W,—Ask Nutter and McClennen[1] who know much more of his work than I do. My impression is that he has the intellectual quality & some acuteness of mind, but is not an A-1 man. Moreover, he seems to be doing good work where he is and should be left in C.

2. Tuesday's events constitute a dismal deluge of surprises.[2] But there are some rays of sunshine peeping through the clouds:

(a) It looks as if extension of federal functions had rec'd an important check. Billy Hard says C.C. is strong against it (with the education bill a strange exception) & that Sen. Wadsworth[3] & Ogden Mills[4] who are against extension of federal functions will be his chief advisors legislatively. Hard says also that J. W. Davis's own strong feeling (largely suppressed) was against federal assumption of state powers.

(b) It looks as if we should have practically no federal legislation (except appropriations bills at the short session) before 1926. That closed season, with Washington free of legislators, would be something to be thankful for. Meanwhile the community might be induced to think.

(c) Davis & the like are, I suppose, not likely to reappear as Democratic nominees for another generation.

3. However bad the Tuesday showing is, I think we may say that it reflects truly the American attitude. I can't imagine a fairer election. Every party was amply heard orally & in the press, without more than

179

the inevitable fallacious or unwise misrepresentation in argument. It was a time of calm, economically—neither boom nor depression. There was no undue excitement political or otherwise for any cause; no hysteria; nothing abnormal or unusual to deflect the judgment. The vote is a representative precipitate of American life, with its virtues and its shortcomings. It should lead one to think. I don't believe in "the slush fund" theory.[5]

4. Alice thinks your conversion of J.W.M. is a notable achievement.

5. We are to have the Wheelers, the Costigans & Laura Thompson[6] in to dine tomorrow.

6. That's a good memo of yours re dormitories [at Harvard].

7. Poor N.D.B.

8. Enclosed re Zinovief letter[7] would afford a good text for a sermon on detectives, or a dime novel, "The Biter Bitten."

9. What do you know of the qualities & antecedents of Mark Sonnheim?

I suppose Dave Walsh will try again—for Lodge's place.[8]

Send the explanation of the Mass[achusetts] Child Labor Amendment vote.[9]

England with Birkenhead in and Winston[10] has dangers ahead,—But it's good to see Eustace Percy get a chance.[11]

[1] Like George Nutter, Edward Francis McClennen (1874–1948) had been a partner in LDB's Boston law firm. McClennen came to the firm in 1895 after graduating from Harvard, and stayed until his death, becoming a full partner in 1916. LDB had considerable respect for "Ned's" ability, and chose him to play the crucial role of managing LDB's Supreme Court nomination hearings in 1916. For McClennen's warm feelings toward LDB, see his reminiscence, "Louis D. Brandeis as a Lawyer," *Massachusetts Law Quarterly* 33 (1948): 1.

[2] On 4 November, Calvin Coolidge buried both John W. Davis and Robert M. La Follette under an avalanche of 15.7 million votes, and the Republicans captured complete control of both houses of Congress. La Follette's Progressive party garnered only about one-sixth of the popular vote.

[3] James Wolcott Wadsworth, Jr. (1877–1952), a New York Republican, had served in the Senate since 1915. In 1933, he began an eighteen year service in the House.

[4] Ogden Livingston Mills (1884–1937), another Republican, served in the House from 1921 until his defeat in the New York gubernatorial contest of 1926. Coolidge then named him under secretary of the treasury, and Hoover made him his treasury secretary in the latter part of his administration.

[5] The allegation, made in the closing weeks of the campaign, charged that the Republicans had accumulated a huge slush fund and had virtually "bought" the election.

[6] Laura A. Thompson (1877–1949) worked for the Children's Bureau; she later became librarian for the Department of Labor.

[7] One of the factors in the recent English election was the so-called Zinoviev letter. Allegedly written by Grigori Evseevich Zinoviev (1883–1936), the leading Bolshevik and chairman of the Executive Committee of the International, the letter instructed the British Communist party on subversive activity. Its publication caused widespread comment and a reaction against the Labour party. Zinoviev, who was later executed in Stalin's Great Purge, denied having written the letter.

[8] David Ignatius Walsh (1872–1947) had been an old ally of LDB's in Massachusetts reform activities, and was a major figure in the state's Democratic party. He served as governor in 1914–1915, and then as senator after 1919. Although Walsh was defeated in a reelection bid, Henry Cabot Lodge (1850–1924), the influential and conservative Republican who had held the other Senate seat from Massachusetts since 1893, died soon after the election. Walsh was promptly elected to fill the vacancy and served there until 1946 when, ironically, he was defeated by Henry Cabot Lodge, Jr.

[9] See 31 October 1924, n. 4.

[10] Winston Leonard Spencer Churchill (1874–1965), later to be one of England's greatest prime ministers, had just reentered the government as chancellor of the exchequer. During the 1930s he was a constant critic of the policy of appeasing Hitler, and in 1940, took over leadership of the government. He also wrote history and won the Nobel Prize for literature in 1953.

[11] Frederick Edwin Smith, first Earl of Birkenhead (1872–1930), reconciled his differences with the Conservatives and accepted the position of secretary of state for India. Eustace Percy, an old friend of LDB and FF, was named president of the Board of Education. See 10 January 1926.

No. 170   November 14, 1924   Washington, D.C.

FF.: 1. George Rublee, who lunched with Gerry [Henderson] yesterday reports that G. voted for Coolidge.

2. It was a relief to find that George and our other birthday guests [1] (Billy Hitz, Emma E[rving]. & the Achesons) were as ignorant of Lord Courtney as Alice & I.

3. Enclosed from Norman [Hapgood] and from Gruening may interest you.

4. Senator (Theodore) Burton [2] says, the Coolidge victory was due, above all, to the faith of the people in him—as able, clean & one of the plain people. The[y] were not interested in Teapot Dome. Next (sed longo intervallo [3]), conservatism as against radicalism; & inter alia the Supreme Court issue. [4]

Arthur Bullard [5] says: The first cause of the Coolidge victory was that neither LaF. nor Davis had anything to offer—(like things which stirred the younger men 20 years ago)—that next comes the Klan as a factor [6]—then the Supreme Court—And that Dawes [7] was effective in bringing into the Coolidge fold, a large part of the biederer [8] Germans.

Frank Lyon says LaF. had nothing to offer the farmers; & that conservative Democrats voted in large numbers for Coolidge—radicals for LaF., hence Davis' poor showing.

Billy Hitz says Gregory said, late in Sept., that Davis would be lucky if he got the solid South. [9]

George Rublee admits that Davis could not make his hearers believe that he really cared.

Bullard says the Klan beat Davis in W. Va.

[1] The day before had been LDB's sixty-eighth birthday.

[2] Theodore Elijah Burton (1851–1929), an Ohio Republican, had represented that state in the House and then the Senate for many years.

[3] "But with a long interval between."

[4] In September, La Follette had proposed that Congress be empowered to repass legislation declared unconstitutional by the Supreme Court. The idea provoked a widespread debate over the powers of the Court during the campaign.

[5] Arthur Bullard (1879–1929) was a prolific magazine journalist and author. He specialized in international relations, especially on Russian affairs.

[6] The revived Ku Klux Klan, which exploded into American politics with tremendous force during the early 1920s and greatly influenced political life in numerous states, had been an important issue during the campaign. The question badly disrupted the Democratic convention in July. During the summer and fall, both La Follette and Davis issued forthright condemnations of the Klan, but President Coolidge refused to comment on the issue and maintained his silence right up to the election.

[7] Charles Gates Dawes (1865–1951) was the author of the famous "Dawes Plan" for relieving the German reparation burden through private loans. He had just been elected as vice president, and at the end of his term was named ambassador to England.

[8] "respectable."

[9] Davis carried every state in the South, but not a single state outside the South.

No. 171   November 20, 1924   Washington, D.C.

F.F.: 1. Your article on Injunctions & the S. C. is in every way admirable.[1]

2. Glad you had so satisfactory a talk with C[harles]. W[illiam]. E[liot]. Isn't he extraordinary? But Holmes J. gives promise of doing likewise. He has not been in better form these 8 years.

3. T. W. Gregory was in to dine yesterday with Dodd and the Hamiltons.

4. T. W. Gregory was in Sunday. Most enthusiastic over Manley Hudson's performance at Geneva,[2] and heartsick over moral decadence in Texas where he is now living. (Houston)

5. I don't see that there is anything I can suggest for the N. R. that you & I haven't talked over.

6. The Dept. of Justice says the A. G. is slated for the S. C.;[3] Dick for England (unless it be Hoover); & Hoover for Secretary of State (if not to England).[4]

[1] In an unsigned article, "Injunctions and Contempt of Court," *New Republic* 40 (19 November 1924): 40, FF had written approvingly of the Supreme Court's sustaining the right of trial by jury in criminal contempt cases.

[2] Hudson had attended the recent Geneva meetings of the League of Nations and had participated in a number of committee sessions as a representative of the Non-Partisan Association for the League, headed by former Justice John H. Clarke.

[3] See 1 January 1925.

[4] Frank Billings Kellogg had been recalled from the Court of St. James to replace Charles Evans Hughes, who had resigned as secretary of state following the 1924 election. To replace Kellogg,

Coolidge nominated Alanson Bigelow Houghton (1863–1941) on 13 January 1925. Herbert Hoover remained as secretary of commerce.

No. 172   December 7, 1924   Washington, D.C.

FF.: 1. I approve of your answers to F.K. and C.W.E.[1] That such letters could have been written shows that not only freedom of speech, but freedom of thought, are far from guaranteed in America.

2. Whoever writes on "Fear in America" should bear in mind that once it was the "Land of the Free and the Home of the Brave." Americans must be taught to be ashamed of being afraid of anyone but the Lord.

3. I authorize you to relinquish my inchoate rights in Landis if you deem it for the public good.[2]

4. The new requirement for H.L.S. will doubtless operate more effectively in terrorism than by direct screening.[3]

5. The H.L.S. financial desires leave me stone cold.[4]

6. J. B. Reynolds' article in the Feb 23 Yale L. J., "Proposed Reform of Amer. Criminal law," which came to me recently (was it from you?) gives me a better opinion of his value than I had had. I wish he might have begun with his criticism of the A.B.A.'s performance.

7. Did you see the Aug 22 number of the World Tomorrow? Spencer Miller[5] wrote an introductory article which showed real insight into our lacks re Crime & Criminals.

8. Grace Abbot, who was in last evening, thinks there is little chance for the Child Labor Amendment this year.[6]

9. John M. Nelson[7] & Edw. Keating[8] were also in. I talked to them i.a. of the need of political thinkers for the Progressives—a la the Webbs etc.[9] A General Staff. They are quite agreed & would welcome aid.[10]

10. Both, I think, feel as we do about the misfortune that R.M.LaF. talked.

11. W.L. doubtless got his push re law editor from George Rublee. I put it up to George to tackle W.L., some time ago. W.L. was here recently but didn't "pay his respects."

12. Nelson thinks that the feeling against Socialism is so strong that the Progressives lost more than they gained by the alliance.[11]

13. Enclosed from Miss Emmerich may interest you.

14. I don't think R. P. Reeder has made good.

15. Auntie B. seems much relieved by what you did re W. G. Thompson.[12] But the size of the fee is a bit like Julius Henry C.[13]

16. Morawetz said your man seemed happy at Cravath & H. & he (M) didn't think it would be proper to mar his chances.

[1] It is unsure who "F.K." was, but Charles W. Eliot wrote on 26 November to thank FF for sending him some material on Palestine. Then Eliot wrote: "Many Harvard men are worried because they think you are a Socialist. I observe that educated Jews easily entertain socialistic views. In what sense are you a Socialist? Marxian, pink, parlor, or red?" FF replied three days later, denying that he was a socialist, and offering to meet with the former Harvard president to discuss his views. FF did not deal with Eliot's anti-Semitic slur, but did note that "socialist" had become an epithet for any sort of views disliked by the conservative establishment.

[2] James McCauley Landis (1899–1964), still a student at Harvard Law School, would become one of the leading figures in American legal education. FF had arranged for Landis to clerk for LDB during the 1925 term—but in view of the important articles Landis and FF had been working on, LDB here offers to give up those services. In the end, Landis did in fact clerk for LDB during the 1925–1926 term, after which he returned to teach at Harvard until 1933. Franklin Roosevelt appointed him to the Federal Trade Commission, and later to the Securities and Exchange Commission, where he was named chairman. In 1937 he went back to Harvard as dean of the Law School, a position he held until he resigned in 1946 to pursue a variety of assignments both in governmental work and in private practice.

[3] In 1924, Harvard Law established a new admissions requirement. Applicants from "first-list colleges" had to stand in the upper three quarters of their classes and applicants from "second-list colleges" in the upper quarter.

[4] See 9 and 25 October 1924.

[5] Spencer Miller, Jr. (1891–1968), a publicist, wrote on prison, labor, crime, and educational topics.

[6] See 31 October 1924, n. 4.

[7] John Mandt Nelson (1870–1955) was a La Follette Republican from Madison, Wisconsin. He served in the House of Representatives from 1906 to 1919, lost the 1918 election, and then returned for the period 1921 to 1933.

[8] Edward Keating (1875–1965), a Democrat from Colorado, served in the House from 1913 to 1919. Upon his defeat, he stayed in Washington and edited *Labor*, the magazine of the railroad brotherhoods.

[9] Sidney (1859–1947) and Beatrice Potter Webb (1858–1943) were illustrious British members of the Fabian Society, the group of English evolutionary socialists that exerted so much influence on radical politics. In 1930, LDB and FF would cross swords with Sidney Webb, by then Lord Passfield, over the question of Palestine; see 22 October 1930, n. 1.

[10] For the substance of their discussion, see 1 January 1925.

[11] The Socialists had endorsed La Follette and refused to run a candidate against him in the recent election.

[12] William Goodrich Thompson (1864–1935), a Harvard Law School graduate (1891), was about to take over the Sacco and Vanzetti defense (see 8 November 1925, n. 12). The case had been made even more complicated by conflicts between lawyers defending the two Italians, and it was thought that Thompson (who took an early interest in the case, but who had been shunted aside by those then serving as defense attorneys) would add prestige to the cause. He asked for a $25,000 advance.

[13] Julius Henry Cohen (1873–1950) was a well known New York attorney. LDB had encountered him in the protracted garment workers strike and protocol negotiations in 1910, when Cohen appeared as the lawyer for the manufacturers.

No. 173   December 13, 1924   Washington, D.C.

1. Pursuant to recommendation I have written RP: "The alternative which I have thought out is so far reaching that exploration of it must await our meeting for a long talk." [1]

2. George Rublee reports that he was requested (by Dwight Morrow[2] I think) to take a hand in reorganizing the Federal Trade Comn. There is a vacancy. He offered it to Gerry H{enderson} who refused. Eugene M Jr. told George—finding the salary is only $10,000, that Gerry cant live on that.

3. The A. G. called the other today [sic]—(1) to renew [*]'s request (2) to talk detectives etc.[3] I told him generally my views on that & other phases of federal criminal practice. I am not sure he will "go through."

4. Some day read the Secy of Agriculture's Annual Report just issued i.a. the first 25 pp.[4] It is a sane well written document, wholly at variance with official propaganda of the last 2 1/2 years.

5. The [New York] World, under your guidance has done well.

6. Very sorry to hear what you report of R.P. What wrought the changes?

7. Pitney's character deserves the proposed Memorial. I was glad to be able to say a few words to his Jr. at the funeral[5] & to express my approval of his practicing in N.Y.

8. Re proposed extension of U.S. liability for torts etc.

Observation of cases under the War Act & Tucker Act[6] etc. convince me that the new legislation should contain fees unless

(a) prohibiting taking of cases on contingent fees unless permission so to do for cause [**] by the Court prior to the bringing of the suit.

(b) making such prosecution on contingent fee pleadable in abatement;[7] and

(c) limiting the amount of the fee in any event.

The abuse is very serious. To prohibit assignments of claims vs. U.S. & then permit what is in effect the worst form of assignment is indeed stupid. While America was a poor country, contingent fees were often justifiable. Now they rarely are except in case of the poor.

9. Please send me your article on duty etc. of Congress to investigate.[8]

---

[1] See 9 and 25 October 1924.

[2] Dwight Whitney Morrow (1873–1931) was a New York attorney. After a decade with J. P. Morgan & Co., and a distinguished wartime service in shipping and supply, Morrow became ambassador to Mexico in 1927. Despite his business connections, Morrow had the confidence of many progressives.

[3] See 3 October 1924.

[4] *Report of the Secretary of Agriculture—1924* (Washington, D.C., 1924). The *Report* acknowledged that "it would be a mistake to conclude that the American farmer is done with the troubles of the depression period," and that the improvements in harvest and in profits would be unequally distributed among the farming population.

[5] LDB's former colleague on the Court, Mahlon Pitney, had died on 9 December.

[6] The Tucker Act, approved on 3 March 1887, provided for the bringing of suits against the United States government; see 24 *U.S. Statutes* 505. It is unclear precisely which "War Act" LDB is referring to here.

[7] A plea in abatement is one which raises an objection to a claim (in this case, the matter of the contingent fee) and permits the plaintiff to renew his suit stripped of the objectionable feature.

[8] See 28 May 1924, n. 1.

No. 174   December 17, 1924   Washington, D.C.

1. Yes. I think a pamphlet giving the existing legislation well grouped & well analyzed (re Fed. Jur.) would be valuable, of course omitting the tare.

2. I think if some fellow would write for the H.L.R. an article on Dismissal for Want of Jurisdiction on ground that question involved—(e.g. Zucht v King [1]) it would be of help to the Court (if it were read), & doubtless to the Bar. We are pestered with cases which we would have dismissed before argument if D[e]f[enda]nt's counsel had known enough to move to dismiss.

3. Prof. Pretham is an engaging person.

4. Prest. Angell [2] asked me to give the Dodge Lectures. Of course I won't but it indicates that they are not very afraid.

[1] See 14 November 1922, n. 11. No one wrote on this topic for the *Harvard Law Review* during this period.

[2] James Rowland Angell (1869–1949) was a well known psychologist and educator. He had been the president of Yale University since 1921 and would continue in that capacity until 1937.

No. 175   January 1, 1925   Washington, D.C.

Our best wishes for 1925 to you & Mrs.

1. A. N. Hand called Sunday, was evidently anxious to talk H.L.S. for he called twice, I having been out when he came first. Beale had visited him, & set forth his plans to H. & to Hough (whom H. invited for the evening). H. set forth his views. He is entirely of our way of thinking. When he got through I told him in detail why I concurred with him. [1]

You were not mentioned by either of us in this connection. He said Beale said that (practically?) everybody except Williston was for the plan, which contemplated doubling the faculty in numbers, etc.

H. is to be in Cambridge on the 16th.

2. Had you thought of making an attempt now to start Malcolm

Sharp at teaching law somewhere? I understand that he is disappointed at not having any work with L & S in labor controversies. He might now be more ready to go at teaching.

3. You will recall our asking John M. Nelson (with E. Keating) to dine to talk over election results.[2] I set forth to him my views (a) the need of a general staff of thinkers, who shall be divorced from office & the political task of putting things over. (b) the need of developing a body of doers, by setting men to the accomplishment of local tasks within their capacities.

He stated as to (a) at this time his favorable inclination, as he had himself thought vainly about what he ought to put through if, by chance, the Progressives succeeded. Last week he telephoned for a[n] appointment, said he was wholly convinced of (a), that he had been talking over the whole situation with two men of high character & public spirit in the House. One a good Republican, the other a good Democrat. That he was pretty sure that they could form, in the next Congress, a coalition which could control the House & that they (the three) wanted to develop the (a) project etc., Nelson putting himself & associates in the background. He wanted me to pick out men for the general staff whom he could call on etc. after March 4. I told him of you (of course confidentially) & that I would ask you to think up men to ask. It seems to me that we ought to be able to find a group of men willing to be the politico-economic thinkers, who would, in privacy, think out what it is wise to do, why & how.

4. A. N. Hand told me of Charles Howland's[3] reaction to Meichel-john [sic] which is very unpromising & may, I fear, stand in the way of any help from the N.Y. source. If you start H. on C.H. you will doubt-less hear the same story.

5. The Willett verdict[4] is indeed a strong argument for juries.

6. A. N. Hand said that Beale & others at the H.L. School admit that the quality of the graduates is worsening. H. is quite convinced that the School is already too large & is prepared to see evidence like this in support.

7. Mack was in today. We talked H.L.S. a little. Told him I wanted not a bigger H.L.S., but 20 Harvard Law Schools & told him what Hand had said. I did not develop my ideas either to him or to A.N.H.

8. Hermann [sic] Blumgart[5] was in. A fine fellow & a terrible tragedy. He told us of your wonderful reception at the Union.

9. I am glad to hear what you write about Landis.

10. Mack will tell you of our talk as to his own future.

11. The talk now is that the A.G. will be the next choice for the U.S.S.C.[6]

12. Tell your mother that Estelle[7] is looking well.

13. I am venturing to increase the amount of the check enclosed, so as to more nearly defray the disbursements of our joint adventure.

[1] See 9 October 1924.

[2] See 7 December 1924.

[3] Charles Prentice Howland (1869–1932), a graduate of Harvard Law School, was active in a number of educational programs, including the Rockefeller Foundation and the General Education Board.

[4] The Willett-Sears felt manufacturing company had been unmercifully denied credit and squeezed for outstanding loans by a conspiracy of Boston bankers and financiers, who ultimately took over the profitable business at a bargain price. This long and laborious case (187 days of testimony and 170 volumes of evidence) resulted in the jury's awarding the plaintiff more than $10 million. The details are in FF and James M. Landis, "Bankers and the Conspiracy Law," *New Republic* 41 (21 January 1925): 218.

[5] Herrman Ludwig Blumgart (1895–1977) was a Boston physician and longtime professor of medicine at the Harvard Medical School. He was a close friend of FF and his personal physician.

[6] Four days later, President Coolidge did nominate Attorney General Harlan Fiske Stone to fill the vacancy created by the resignation of Mr. Justice McKenna. Stone was confirmed by the Senate on 5 February and took his seat on 2 March.

[7] Estelle Frankfurter (b. 1895), FF's sister, was a trained social worker, who served in several governmental and social agencies in Massachusetts, Washington, D.C., and after World War Two, in Berlin and Israel.

No. 176   January 7, 1925   Washington, D.C.

1. Your report of Chicago doings is most interesting. The doings should prove fruitful.

2. Has Walter Pollack [sic] been considered a Law School possibility?[1] I have no opinion. But his contemporaries seem generally enthusiastic, & A. N. Hand said he deemed him by all odds, the best equipped of any man suggested for B's place.[2]

P. has no show for that. Wheat[3] was turned down by the pol[itician]s. Chas. H. Tuttle[4] and Tom Thatcher [sic] are now the nominees before the pols. for selection.[5]

You will know whether P's success at the bar is sufficient to tie him to that.

3. There is an inside view which conforms to Wick's re the A.G. What he will be on the Court "only the event will teach us in its hour."

4. Holmes J. was laid up by lumbago—i.e. housed under M.D.'s order, but is otherwise O.K. & expects to get to Court today.

5. You had better have sent you (if not already received) the Report

of Hearing of Jud[iciary] Com[mittee] on "Jurisdiction of C.C.A. & S.C.U.S." in H.R. 3206, Serial 45. Dec 18/24 confirms testimony of V.D. et al.—if not already in hand.

[1] Walter Heilprin Pollak (1887–1940) was a Harvard Law School graduate who practiced in New York, and was one of the decade's leading civil liberties attorneys. He never taught at Harvard.

[2] "B" is (Billings) Learned Hand, Augustus Hand's cousin, who had just been appointed to the circuit court of appeals.

[3] Alfred Adams Wheat (1867–1943) had extensive experience in arguing cases before the Supreme Court as a member of the Department of Justice. President Hoover would appoint him to the Supreme Court of the District of Columbia in 1929 and he became chief justice of that court in 1930.

[4] Charles Henry Tuttle (1879–1971) was a New York City attorney active in public causes.

[5] The appointment, in fact, went to Thomas D. Thacher.

No. 177   January 7, 1925   Washington, D.C.

FF.: Let the Business School authorities verify these figures of total corp stock [1]—and furnish also the corresponding figures for corporate, state & municipal and federal bonds of all kinds.

If these are correct figures, they provide the worst of all conceivable indictments of our financial-industrial system.

The rich are ceasing to be partners. They are taking the safer place of creditors. The poorer are to hold the bag without control. $61 billions in property value in 1900, means about $31 billion in 1923.

I suppose in that period the corporate assets in dollars have much more than trebled.

The total cap. stock figures seem incredible. [2]

[1] LDB sent FF, with this letter, a *Washington Post* editorial of this date, entitled "The Rise of the Small Investor." The editorial contained figures to show the rapid increase in the value of corporate stock and in the number of stockholders in United States corporations since 1900.

[2] According to the editorial, the total capital stock of all American corporations was $71.4 billion in 1923 (the 1924 figures were not yet available).

No. 178   January 15, 1925   Washington, D.C.

1. I am glad to join your "Supplement." The Bibliography should prove very helpful.

2. O.W.H. is not in the least disturbed about the newspaper items re his retirement. [1] He believes them to be inspired. And as Fuller C.J. [2] said: "I don't propose to allow myself to be paragraphed out of my job."

3. Wouldn't it be well to urge Auntie B. to make now the quick trip to England of which she talked last summer. Of course she must be back

by June 1—for Chatham's sake. It won't be quite as cheerful among Labor folk there as it might have been.[3] But I fancy there will be hopefulness enough to permeate her.

4. Frank Symonds[4] says it was George Harvey[5] and Borah who displaced Hughes.[6] F.S., I am told, thinks Harvey is gunning for another member of the Cabinet who will succumb within a few months, & I think the man F.S. has in mind (name withheld) is Hoover.[7] I have no further data & no personal opinion.

5. Alvin's excuse is a pretty poor one.

6. Senator Tom Walsh (who was in last evening) thinks (fears) the Child Labor Amendment will be beaten. It is in danger even in Montana.

7. Hope you noticed "Mr. Morgenthau" in the Jan 9. New Palestine. Why couldn't our crowd write as well?

[1] See for example *New York Times*, 10 January 1925. These rumors of Holmes's imminent retirement continued through the winter and spring; but Holmes would not leave the Court until 1932.

[2] Melville Weston Fuller (1833–1910), the eighth chief justice of the United States, served from 1888 until his death twenty-two years later. He once called LDB the ablest man who ever appeared before the Supreme Court and one who was "also absolutely fearless in the discharge of his duties."

[3] See 31 October 1924, n. 5.

[4] LDB probably meant Frank H. Simonds, the journalist (see 29 January 1923, n. 5).

[5] George Brinton McClellan Harvey (1864–1928), a powerful businessman and publisher, was editor of the *North American Review*. For many years an "insider" in Republican politics, his was the "smoke-filled room" where Harding was selected to be the Republican standard bearer at the 1920 convention.

[6] See 20 November 1924, n. 4.

[7] Hoover served through the Coolidge administration.

No. 179   January 23, 1925   Washington, D.C.

1. The Willet-Sears article[1] should serve as a mene, mene tekel.[2] At all events "pain has been given to my brothers." The episode is merely an expansion of the C. Morench & Sons Co. experience, which I related to you, & which made me realize, in my forties, what's what in High Finance.

2. Hillquit and Hunt presented creditably the Penn RR. Labor Adjustment Cases.[3]

3. I think C.E.H. will find the C.J. quite as unwilling to yield as is O.W.H. If the C.J. takes care of himself, he may last a decade.[4]

4. Walter Lippmann was in Sunday. We had a very sympathetic talk. I gave him views & facts re centralization & prepared the way for a later talk on Crime.

5. Bruce Bliven was in for an hour & had to listen to some views on the U.S.A.—child labor & the like with which you are familiar.

6. I like your answer to H.F.S.[5] He told me a few days before he made the appointment what he had in mind. I told him that I had heard crit[ic]isms. He said he knew they were unfounded.

7. What you write about R.P. is amazing.[6] And now comes George R[ublee]. and tells me that this morning's N.Y. Times reports that R.P. has accepted.

The world will correlate Baker and Pound. And Loustavy to A.L.L[owell]. will say: "Thou art the man."[7]

[1] See 1 January 1925, n. 4.

[2] From *Daniel*, 5:25—the "handwriting on the wall."

[3] *Pennsylvania Railroad Federation* v. *Pennsylvania Railroad Co.*, 267 U.S. 203 and *Pennsylvania Brotherhood* v. *Pennsylvania Railroad* Co., 267 U.S. 219, both argued on 13 January. The Transportation Act of 1920 set up a Railroad Labor Board in order to adjust labor disputes. The Pennsylvania Railroad refused to bargain with a delegation chosen by the workers, claiming it did not represent the majority of the workers. The company sent out an alternative ballot with no union representative on the list. Taft, for the Court, ruled that the Board relied only on moral sanction, carriers were not bound by Board rulings, and could establish their own systems of choosing employee representatives. Representing the appellants were Morris Hillquit (1869–1933), one of the country's best known Socialists, and Henry Thomas Hunt (1878–1956), a reform lawyer from Cincinnati (and former mayor of that city) and later general counsel to the New Deal's Public Works Administration.

[4] Chief Justice Taft lasted only another half decade, dying in 1930. But Charles Evans Hughes did, in fact, succeed him as chief justice.

[5] Attorney General Stone was considering establishing an advisory board on the federal prisons, and he had written asking about one of FF's recent graduate students as a possible staff member, as well as suggestions for the board itself. FF replied on 22 January with a strong recommendation for Sam B. Warner, currently teaching at the University of Oregon Law School. He also urged Stone to consider Herman Adler and Ben Flexner as members of the board.

[6] Rumors had reached the press that Roscoe Pound had been offered and had accepted the presidency of the University of Wisconsin. Pound stayed at Harvard.

[7] Nathan to King David, 2 *Samuel*, 12:7.

No. 180   February 6, 1925   Washington, D.C.

Our jurisdiction bill will doubtless become a law within a few days.[1]
When it does, this story, with a moral, may well be written:
U.S.S.C.—venerated throughout the land.
Despite the growth of population, wealth and
governmental functions, & development particularly
of federal activities[,] the duties of the Court have,
by successive acts passed from time to time throughout a generation,
been kept within such narrow limits that
the nine men, each with one helper, can do the work as
well as can be done by men of their calibre, i.e. the
official coat has been cut according to the human cloth.

Congress, Executive Depts., Commissions & lower federal
courts.—All subject to criticism or execration.
Regardless of human limitations, increasing work has been piled upon
them at nearly every session. The high incumbents,
in many cases, perform in name only. They
are administrators, without time to know what they are
doing or to think how to do it. They are human machines.[2]

[1] The Jurisdictional Act was passed by Congress on 13 February and became effective on 13 May 1925. A copy of it can be found at 260 U.S. 687.

[2] This letter was incorporated into a *New Republic* editorial, 25 February 1925, pp. 3–4.

No. 181   February 7, 1925   Washington, D.C.

1. As to Emory Buckner[1] & Prohibition Cases, I agree. But he does not need any legislation of any kind, if he will formulate this plan & keep his mouth, & that of his underlings, resolutely shut.

A. Examine all prohibition cases now in & coming in. Divide them into two classes: (a) those involving smuggling from abroad or bringing in from other states; (b) those involving violations wholly intra-state.

B. Then, give the preference in trials (without saying so) to cases in class (a). That will take up all the ability of the office; all the capacity of available judges; and all the appropriation available for prohibition. If & when there is any surplus capacity, etc., he can take up (b). Parallel lines are said to meet in infinity.

2. I wrote J.W.M., suggesting, as a means of tackling crime in America & his individual problem, that he secure his assignment for a long period in the Criminal Sessions in N.Y. He says that he agrees fully & had talked with Gus Hand & will again about this.

3. That letter from Edison[2] is fine. It gives me a different opinion of him than I have ever had. And E.A.'s[3] service (unintended) in getting it is the best of his achievements in a decade.

4. Do you think the naive Solicitor Gen will appreciate [T.]R.P.'s skit?[4]

5. Norman H., the Keatings & the Donald Richbergs are coming in tomorrow for dinner to discuss the state of Progressivism.

[1] Emory Roy Buckner (1877–1941) was a leader of the New York bar, and for a time associated with Elihu Root's firm. Coolidge had just nominated him to be U.S. attorney for the Southern District of New York. The Senate quickly confirmed him, and he began serving on 2 March. Both LDB and FF took a great interest in Buckner's handling of the prohibition cases.

[2] Thomas Alva Edison (1847–1931) was the renowned inventor and businessman. There is no copy of a letter from Edison in the FF Papers.

3 Edward Albert Filene (1860–1937) had once been among LDB's closest associates and friends as well as one of his most appreciative clients. He and his brother had built one of Boston's leading retail establishments and, at LDB's urging and with his constant advice, embarked upon a pioneering program of employee relations. Filene was also active in a large number of philanthropic organizations. In later years, the two men fell out over philosophic issues, principally questions related to the dangers of "bigness" in American economic life.

4 No doubt LDB was referring to Thomas Reed Powell's sarcastic review of Solicitor General James M. Beck's new book in the current issue of *The New Republic*: "You can read it without thinking. . . . you will be glad of the nice restful book that Mr. Beck has written."

No. 182   February 14, 1925   Washington, D.C.

1. Who is Ashby Williams, who was on the War Dept. Board of Contract Adjustment? See my U.S. Bedding Co v. U.S. Jan 5/25. He wrote a very good opinion.[1]

2. Our jurisdiction bill was signed yesterday.[2] It got through by making some changes insisted upon by T. J. Walsh, the C.J. tells me. I have not seen what these changes are, but think, from what he remembered & particularly from the fact that VanD approved, that they should be satisfactory. I still think that (except as to Ct of Claims), the bill doesn't touch the most serious unnecessary burdens incident to the prior jurisdictional acts as construed. I hope that we may make a rule allowing 10 minute oral arguments on Certiorari. We certainly need that aid. Wheat says there is already considerable dissatisfaction.

3. Nellis [sic][3] was in yesterday & the talk was promising. I put on him the job of exploration, reports, etc.

4. I guess the function in selecting Thatcher [sic][4] is not very different from that in selecting Buck[ner]. I am credibly informed that Washington settled on Wheat for D.J. The N.Y. pol[itician]s. vetoed this. Then the A.G. wanted Tuttle. The H. W. Taft[5] forces were strong for T. & Tuttle was dropped.

5. I am glad about C. Warren's paper.[6] Saw him since he heard from the Review. He is well satisfied.

6. My talk with Ege, in the effort to divert him from N.Y., led to R. D. Williams (the C.J.'s Secy—last year's Editor in Chief of Yale L.J.) coming in to talk of his future. He is now booked for John Davis' firm. If he is as good as he looks, he ought to be in law-teaching.[7] It might be worthwhile to make some enquiries about him from the Yale Faculty. Perhaps that would induce them to give him a try there & save his soul. (He is a progressive & seemed largely on that account, to hesitate at the threshhold of the N.Y. firm.)

7. I hope you saw Silas H. Strawn's "A Few Fundamentals" in the Feb. Cornell L.Q.—particularly p. 205.[8]

8. Wetting's review there of the Wan Case revived my regret at Z.C[hafee].'s treatment of it in the N.R.[9]

9. I am glad W.L. is so apt a pupil. He tried to get Dick Boekel[10] for the paper, on an exclusive N.Y. job, also David Friday.[11]

10. We have had both Friday and Walter Stewart[12] in to dine.

11. I think Marion may enjoy the lofty exhortation of Silas H. Strawn's "Whither our leaders lead."

[1] *U.S. Bedding Co.* v. *United States*, 266 U.S. 491, was decided on 5 January, LDB reading the Court's unanimous opinion. The company had sued to recover losses allegedly caused by dealings with the War Industries Board. LDB, in upholding the government, cited favorably the opinion by Ashby Williams, *In re Claims of the United States Bedding Co.* et al. 4 *Decisions of War Department Board of Contract Adjustment* 325.

[2] See 6 February 1925.

[3] Probably Walter R. Nelles.

[4] See 7 January 1925, for the appointment of Thacher.

[5] Henry Waters Taft (1859–1945) was the chief justice's brother and a prominent New York City attorney in his own right.

[6] LDB, always interested in seeing that lower courts received greater attention, was pleased to see the appearance of Charles Warren, "Federal Criminal Law and the State Courts," *Harvard Law Review* 38 (1925): 545.

[7] Charles Dickerman Williams (b. 1900) had graduated from Yale Law School in 1924. After clerking with Chief Justice Taft, he entered government service until 1931, when he did join a New York law firm. Williams never taught law.

[8] Silas H. Strawn, "A Few Fundamentals," *Cornell Law Quarterly* 10 (1925): 201. The article purported to be a point by point rebuttal of the Progressive party's position which Strawn characterized as radical, Soviet, and Socialist. On page 205, Strawn recited a list of statistics designed to show the marvelous prosperity of the United States.

[9] Frank B. Wetting in "Notes and Comments," *Cornell Law Quarterly* 10 (1925): 225. For the *Wan* case, see 31 October 1924, n. 2; and for Zechariah Chafee's comment, see "Compulsory Confessions," *New Republic* 40 (12 November 1924): 266.

[10] Richard Martin Boeckel (1892–1975) was an experienced Washington correspondent who had worked for a number of newspapers and magazines. In 1923 he founded and was editorial director of *Editorial Research Reports*, a news service to dozens of newspapers around the country.

[11] David Friday (1876–1945), a liberal economist and writer on economic topics, was currently teaching at the New School for Social Research in New York City.

[12] Walter W. Stewart (1885–1958), another economist, was director of research for the Federal Reserve Board. In 1938 he joined the Princeton Institute for Advanced Study and remained there until his retirement.

No. 183   February 21, 1925   Washington, D.C.

1. It would be fine to have you & Marion here for a week. When may it be?

2. I think if you would write (& have Pound as well as yourself sign) a request to the C.J. to have (a) our Reporter include annually in the

reports the judicial statistics, & (b) to lay the matter before his Council of Judges at his Sept. meeting for similar action by the Cir. & Dist. courts—for publication in the Federal Report—he would be disposed to comply.[1]

I suppose you could get the Deans etc. of Yale & other law schools to join in the request. That would help. Also indirectly, it would tend to make the Fed. judges realize a bit more that they are being watched throughout the country & that there is being developed an enlightened public opinion which will judge the judges.

3. What you report about Buck[ner] is fine. If he can be induced to be steadfast at his job 4 full years so as to show real results, for which at least that period is essential, he can create by his conspicuous position an example that will be potent through the country.

4. I told J. M. Nelson that you would be ready to see him after March 4 & he will write you for an appointment.[2]

5. I am glad you talked with Croly about Child Labor. I assume you will now put it up to Julia Lathrop et al. to get to work in the States. By the way, what does her Illinois do—on paper & otherwise. What Miss Kelley's N.Y.? What Grace Abbot's [sic] Nebraska? etc.

I note yesterday's note in Mass. It should arouse the Mass folk to work at home.

6. The Am. Woolen Report of $6 million deficit should teach folk again that Southern competition is not the trouble with the textile industry.[3] I suppose the woolen mills in the South are an obviously negligible quantity.

But to see textile wages go down 10% & living costs go up nearing 10% should make Dorothy Brown & the like give themselves up to thinking.

7. Is Croly getting any data on that Verona, Miss. schoolmaster story from Collier's?[4]

8. Louis Levine has done a fine job on the Int. Garment Workers Union history.[5]

[1] FF was beginning to collect judicial statistics preparatory to the major project he undertook with James M. Landis, culminating in *The Business of the Supreme Court* (New York: Macmillan, 1927). Beginning in the October 1930 term, the Court expanded slightly its own statistical reporting, indicating for the previous three years the nature of its cases (original or appellate jurisdiction) and the number of cases disposed of. No information for lower courts was included.

[2] See 1 January 1925.

[3] For the company's report, see *New York Times*, 19 February 1925.

[4] LDB had come across a story about a Verona, Mississippi, school teacher who had trained a large number of distinguished pupils—civic, political, and economic leaders. *The New Republic* never ran such a story, but *Collier's* did.

⁵Louis Levine, *The Women's Garment Workers* (New York: B. W. Huebsch, 1924). Levine (1883–1970) changed his name to Lewis Levitski Lorwin, and became a prolific economist and author; he was about to enter a seven-year stint as an economist for the Brookings Institution.

No. 184   March 6, 1925   Washington, D.C.

FF.: 1. Not even an Edgar Allan Poe could have imagined how terrible would be Dawes' V.P. address.[1]

2. I hope the humorists wont overlook this in C.C.'s Inaugural:

"Mindful of these limitations, the one great duty that stands out requires us to use our enormous powers to trim the balance of the world."[2]

3. Yes, the C.J., like the Steel Corporation, is attaining old time production records. He has no intention of yielding to CEH (who told me that he will take six months vacation.)

Miss Grady[3] reports that your Sunday address at Ford Hall was "Superb!"[4]

[1] Vice President Dawes shocked the Senate in his inaugural address by ignoring the normal pleasantries and launching a vigorous attack on the body and its antiquated rules. The *New York Times* wrote: "Some Senators looked aghast. Others leaned forward, amazement in their faces. Others took it humorously, and a few put their hands over their mouths as if to stifle laughter." The text of the address can be found in the *Times* for 5 March.

[2] The quotation, which is accurate, appears near the end of Coolidge's address. LDB is amused at the word "trim," which can also mean to cheat. The text of the President's remarks are also in the *Times* for 5 March.

[3] Alice Harriet Grady (1873–1934) began working for LDB as a secretary when she was a young girl, worked her way up to manager of the office staff of the law firm, and enjoyed LDB's confidence and trust throughout her life. She developed a special interest in LDB's Savings Bank Insurance reform and in 1920 became deputy commissioner of the system and then headed it up until her death. She kept her former employer closely informed of the details and progress of the system he had invented.

[4] FF had spoken the previous Sunday on "The Meaning of the Progressive Movement," and spoken in terms of moral and economic regeneration.

No. 185   March 6, 1925   Washington, D.C

FF.: 1. The Court (V.D.) is inspiring a bar educational campaign on the new jurisdiction act. The S.C. and Federal Reporters will carry the act in full[1] & their house organ will have an article by Bunn—which will be reprinted in the Minnesota L. R.[2] The C.J. will stir up Am. Bar Ass. I suggested to V.D. that Stone have the Columbia get an article[3] & that Williams have done [sic] Yale.[4] Others will doubtless follow.

It occurs to me that Landis might care to write an article for the Oct. H.L.R. which would overtop them all;—taking up not only the obvious changes etc., but things more occult & problems which will develop, doing something which might mark the primacy of H.L.R.[5] There will probably be a pretty comprehensive revision of the L.C. Rules also.

2. On the political education of the people (the true democratic process which we practiced with such success in Mass. & which our impatient friends shun), the history of Kentucky affords a striking example of which the memory should, at an appropriate time, be revived. The fight between the Old Court party and the New Court party. See Kentucky in the Nation's History p. 395 (By R. McNutt McElroy.)[6]

3. I met your some time chief, ex-Secretary Wilson,[7] today. He looked so well, & so much younger than when I last saw him—in 1918, when he lunched with me—that I hardly recognized him. We resumed our conversation on irregularity of employment and the coal mining business. He has learned nothing since.

4. Stone's satisfaction in his appointment of Buckner has not abated.

5. Have you seen George Anderson of late. Since September I have had nothing from him except occasional dissenting opinions. I fear he is as much in need of a trip abroad as Auntie B.

6. Walter Meyer was in—the first time for 5 years. Wall Street liberty has not removed the Hamlet disability.

7. B. F. with Mim[8] & Jean were in—full of cheer—on the way to Louisville. Jean is an attractive maid.

8. Eugene Meyer was also in. I guess he feels that Republicans as well as republics are ungrateful & smarts a bit under unfounded attacks.

9. McAdoo was in for a long talk—puzzled. No chg.

10. Buckner has "done splendid."

11. H.C.'s estimate of "6 to 10" years for Republican rule is pretty liberal.

12. It is fine to know that Pound will take a section on Criminal Law and that young Thayer[9] is to have a chance at Comparative Law.

[1] 266 U.S. 687. The act does not appear to have been published in the *Federal Reporter*.

[2] Charles W. Bunn, "The New Appellate Jurisdiction in Federal Courts," *Minnesota Law Review* 9 (1925): 309.

[3] Paxton Blair, "Federal Appellate Procedure as Affected by the Act of February 13, 1925," *Columbia Law Review* 25 (April 1925): 383.

[4] See 5 October 1925.

[5] In November 1928, FF and Landis published "The Supreme Court under the Judiciary Act of 1925," *Harvard Law Review* 42: 1.

[6] Robert McNutt McElroy, *Kentucky in the Nation's History* (New York: Moffat, Yard, and Co.,

1909). The passage tells of the struggle in the election of 1825, when "the leaders of the Old Court party wisely decided to make the campaign . . . a campaign of education." The dispute centered around the role of the judiciary and the attempt of the legislature to subvert its independence.

[7] William Bauchop Wilson (1862–1934), a Scottish immigrant and former miner, rose through Congress to become Wilson's secretary of labor. FF had been associated with him when he headed the War Labor Policies Board.

[8] Mim was Mary Flexner (1873–1947), the sister of the famous Flexner brothers and for many years a companion of her brother, Bernard.

[9] James Bradley Thayer (1899–1976) was a son of a dean of the Harvard Law School and the grandson of a professor there who had been one of LDB's own teachers. Young Thayer joined the faculty in 1925 and remained there for two decades.

No. 186   March 12, 1925   Washington, D.C.

1. Do you know Herman H. Phleger [1] of San Francisco? He made an uncommonly good argument for Employers in the Building Strike-Anti-Trust Case (American Plan) [2]—a young fellow.

2. Will centralizing progressives stop to think of the manifestations of federal power [in] (a) The Wheeler prosecution. (b) Consumer's income taxes?

3. Houston (?), your mulatto, called today. An engaging fellow. I talked to him of the danger of his sacrificing quality by his spread between practice & teaching. How able is he, & how old? & what is his quality otherwise? [3]

4. The Costigans were in, she reporting on Chicago Conference. Alice thinks your Ford Hall talk might aid Mrs. C. in her puzzle. Have you a copy which we can send her?

5. William Allen White is urging Costigan to return to the West & there is a chance that he may shake off the Washington paralysis. I am to talk to him soon.

6. Leo Rowe [4] was in—reported on Latin America. He is enthusiastic over Hughes' dealings with Latin American relations—says their representatives revered him & that even Hayti can be explained away. Says Hughes had no interest in Europe, because he had no faith in the powers. Did not believe there was any way to help them at present. Alice thinks R. should know this.

7. My Republican friends seem well content with the Warren rejection. But it's quite a slap for C.C. & the Journal of Commerce says that it portends difficulties hereafter for the Administration. A resubmission should develop a good fight, perhaps. [5]

8. Charles Warren, [6] who is much concerned by drugs (He had the

narcotic cases under him while in the Dept.), thinks the Act has been practically futile; and that conditions have grown infinitely worse since. Cannot someone be found who will really enquire into the results of the Federal police legislation (other than liquor) & exhibit the balance sheet? I am disposed to think that it does grave harm to a great degree otherwise than in centralization. i.a. in misleading the community into the belief that the fed. Govt (or any government) can help, instead of turning folk back to themselves for the remedy in self-mastery. I dont feel as unhappy as many of my friends at the international refusal to stop opium production in the East. Such action would doubtless result, if taken, in bootleg production in America by methods hitherto unthought of. Whenever the[re] must be federal legislation, as a defense measure, the Webb Kenyon Act, with the Reed Amendment (when appropriate) should probably be the type to be followed.[7]

March 13,

Yours of 12th just rec'd. Delighted to know you & Marion are coming.

[1] Herman H. Phleger (1890–1984), a California lawyer, had done some postgraduate work at Harvard Law. In time he became an expert on American foreign relations and served on many public bodies concerned with foreign affairs.

[2] *Industrial Association of San Francisco* v. *United States*, 268 U.S. 64. Sutherland, speaking for a unanimous Court on 13 April, upheld a San Francisco association of contractors and building supply dealers, which had been charged under the Sherman Antitrust Act of conspiracy to restrain trade. The association required permits to obtain building materials and denied such permits to those who did not support their "open shop" plan. The Court held that this did not violate the Sherman Act because the arrangement applied entirely to local, and not to interstate, commerce.

[3] On 20 March LDB wrote to FF: "That of Houston's is interesting. It suggests that his father is a West Indian. He told me that one of his grandmothers was a runaway Kentucky slave."

[4] Leo S. Rowe (1871–1946), a professor of political science and a leading expert on Latin America, had served since 1920 as director of the Pan-American Union.

[5] Charles Beecher Warren (1870–1936), a Michigan lawyer, had served as ambassador to both Japan and Mexico. President Coolidge had nominated him to replace Harlan Fiske Stone as attorney general. But the Senate, reacting to persistent reports concerning his business dealings in sugar, rejected the nomination on 11 March, the first rejection of a cabinet nomination since 1868. Coolidge did resubmit the nomination, and the Senate once again rejected it on 16 March.

[6] Charles Warren, the legal scholar, not to be confused with the rejected nominee described in the above note.

[7] See 17 June 1923, n. 5.

No. 187   March 17, 1925   Washington, D.C.

1. I shall be glad to contribute toward your second Research Fellow.
2. J. M. Nelson was in Sunday. I told him of your coming & he has

doubtless written you to arrange for appointment. He is slow of movement, & you must allow for time.

3. There will be much for us to discuss when you come, so we shall not invite folk to meet you & Marion unless there are some whom you wish specially to see.

4. Was it C.C.'s Christian spirit that induced him to turn the other cheek for another slap re Warren? [1]

5. When you come a word about "Gene and Agnes."

6. O.W.H. was kept home yesterday by Mrs. because of his throat. It's all the result of his Birthday Excesses. [2] Besides seeing folk, he insisted on writing 14 letters & an opinion. Result—didn't sleep much the night after; then the throat weakness commenced itself & prevented good nights thereafter. And finally Saturday, he & others stupidly persisted in Conference to 5 PM. OWH was in perfect shape on the morning of the birthday.

[1] See preceding letter.
[2] Holmes's eighty-fourth birthday had been 8 March.

No. 188   April 2, 1925   Washington, D.C.

FF: Your and Marion's visit was all too short. There is much more to talk over.

1. Re curtailing jurisdiction on ground of diversity of citizenship. [1] Why should a plaintiff ever be permitted to sue in a federal court of the District of which he is a citizen & resident? Why should he be entitled to sue an alien in a federal court? Why should a consolidated & domesticated corporation ever have a right (under the diversity of citizenship provision) to enter or removed [sic] to the federal court?

2. The N.R. editorial treatment of the Colorado treaty is plumb silly. [2] Opponents of the Child Labor amendment are not proposing dissolution of the union or abrogation of federal powers. Those who cherish the promise of American life [3] should remember that time & patience are indispensable factors in its realization. And as to speed in federal action, they should not forget Muscle Shoals. [4]

3. Have you heard from Max L. & Sharp? [5]

4. Do you recall Shiras J. in DeArnaud, No. 151 U.S. 488, 493:

"We are relieved from considering whether the newfangled term "military expert" is only old "spy"writ large." [6]

[1] The phrase "diversity of citizenship" refers to questions of federal court jurisdiction. The Constitution provides that citizens of different states, engaged in litigation, may enter the federal court system. LDB, believing this privilege much abused, wanted to limit access to federal courts as much as possible.

[2] In "An Interstate Compact Fails," *New Republic* 42 (1 April 1925): 144, the editor denounced the futile attempt of seven western states to arrive at a sensible agreement on the use of the waters of the Colorado River. The negotiations over the Boulder Dam project, he said, provided ample evidence that state control was unworkable. Narrow local interests were not able to settle the difficult technical questions of irrigation versus power; only the federal government could provide the expertise and objectivity required.

[3] A reference to *The New Republic* editor Herbert Croly's book of that title.

[4] During World War I, the federal government had constructed a dam and two nitrate plants on the Tennessee River at Muscle Shoals, Alabama. During the 1920s, Senator George W. Norris led a battle to expand the facilities to serve as a yardstick for the measurement of private power company performance. Although Norris twice secured congressional approval, the idea was vetoed first by Coolidge and then by Hoover. During the 1930s, Muscle Shoals became the pilot plant of the enormous Tennessee Valley Authority.

[5] LDB and FF were urging Max Lowenthal and Malcolm P. Sharp to write an article on the problem of contempt of court.

[6] Charles de Arnaud had claimed that the federal government owed him $100,000 for his services as a "military expert" employed by John C. Fremont. The Supreme Court dismissed his claim and in the opinion, Justice George Shiras, Jr. (1832–1924) supplied the phrase quoted by LDB. *de Arnaud* v. *United States*, 151 U.S. 483 (1894).

No. 189   May 5, 1925   Washington, D.C.

FF: 1. The menace of the A.L.I. is being manifest in this proposed Crim. Proc. Code.[1] I talked earnestly to George R. Nutter & to Learned Hand. They agreed & intended to make a fight, but apparently didn't. Ask Nutter to tell you about the situation.

2. Alice suggests that if Hermann A. wants to accomplish something through his Committee, he had better win Mrs. Hodder[2] first.

3. I suppose you saw the May World Tomorrow. Why Prisons?[3]

4. Some one (like a Samuel Roundley) ought to attack the long sentences in our federal courts. They remind much of the 200 capital offences of 1800, & are, in a way, worse. They are the [sic] not merely paper penalties—see e.g. Orsatti v. U.S.[4] (a Bledsoe[5] outrage) as to which our Court denied petition for Certiorari (1015) last Monday. Here we are dealing with something other than war hysteria.

5. The Shaffer [sic] Case (North Dakota farm Act—Van Devanter)[6] and the Alpha Cement Case (Mass. Foreign Corp Tax) McReynolds,[7] show that relief can be had only through application of the Webb-Kenyon Act theory (Clark Dist. Co. Case).[8] Wouldn't it be well to start that idea? It might take in these days of revulsion against federal control.

6. The C.J. is about—I think fully—as well as at any time these 18

months. He ought to be more careful about over exertion than he is. But he has done much less need than Judicial Statistics.

7. The May 5 N.R. brings helpful matter.

[1] The American Law Institute, meeting in Washington, D.C., announced plans to draft a model code for criminal procedure. See *New York Times*, 17 May 1925, for a discussion of the code.

[2] Jessie Donaldson Hodder (1867–1931), a Boston social worker and active in prison reform, was associated with Elizabeth Glendower Evans in Boston reform circles and well known to Mrs. Brandeis.

[3] The entire May 1925 issue of *The World Tomorrow* was devoted to the question "Why Prisons?" It included articles by George W. Kirchwey, Harry E. Barnes, Winthrop D. Lane and others.

[4] 268 U.S. 694. The Supreme Court denied certiorari on 4 May. Orsatti and others were indicted and convicted for bribing a prohibition officer. The evidence showed that the idea originated with the defendants, but that the officer subsequently planned, induced, and procured repeated violations. Orsatti claimed that this constituted entrapment, but the court held that since the idea originated with the defendants, the rule of entrapment did not apply.

[5] Benjamin Franklin Bledsoe (1874–1938) was a California lawyer appointed by President Wilson as a district judge for southern California. He had resigned in March 1925 to go into private practice.

[6] *Shafer* v. *Farmers Grain* Co., 268 U.S. 189, decided on 4 May. The North Dakota Grain Trading Act assumed control over wheat buying in the state, applying standards and regulations in an attempt to eliminate fraudulent practices. Van Devanter argued in his majority opinion that the commerce clause denied regulation of interstate trade to states and that since this trade was largely interstate, the act could not be supported. LDB dissented without opinion.

[7] In another decision on 4 May, again with LDB in dissent, the Court, this time speaking through McReynolds, declared illegal a Massachusetts tax on a "foreign" corporation dealing exclusively in interstate commerce. *Alpha Portland Cement Co.* v. *Massachusetts*, 268 U.S. 203.

[8] *Clark Distilling Co.* v. *American Express Co.*, 242 U.S. 311 (1917). The case involved a West Virginia law (enacted before national prohibition) which would have forbidden the importation of liquor into the state for personal use. This would obviously have been state interference with interstate trade, except for the fact that the Webb-Kenyon Act of 1913 (see 17 June 1923, n. 5) withdrew interstate immunity from such shipments.

No. 190   May 13, 1925   Washington, D.C.

FF: 1. With old Boston vital on Free Speech & arrayed, would it not be well to try to start the move for abolishing speaking licenses for the [Boston] Common?

2. With Mass. excited about the Alpha Cement decision, could not H. L. Shattuck (aided by ex asst Atty Genl Hitchcock, who is learned on taxes) start the Webb Kenyon idea [1] as to Foreign Corp[oration]s? La. with the Texas Transport, [2] Mo. with the Oil Pipe Line decisions, & many more communities dismayed at amendment of their license fee taxation, would surely be glad to join & with the Back to the State Movement on the rise, Congress might do some work on these lines.

3. I am returning [to] you Jim Wilson letter & enclose one from a very different Texas District Judge—please return it.

4. Will you kindly send Alice a list of any persons (and addresses) here or abroad, whom you or Marion think we might be likely to forget in making up our list for Elizabeth's wedding announcement.[3]

[1] See 17 June 1923, n. 5. William Harold Hitchcock (1874–1953), a Boston lawyer, served as assistant attorney general of Massachusetts from 1915 to 1920. He then became chairman of the Massachusetts Board of Bar Examiners.

[2] *Texas Transport & Terminal Co., Inc.* v. *New Orleans*, 264 U.S. 150 (1924). The Court, with LDB and Holmes dissenting, once again restricted the power of the state to tax, through licensing fees, a corporation engaged exclusively in interstate commerce.

[3] On 20 April 1925, LDB's younger daughter Elizabeth announced her engagement to Paul Arthur Raushenbush (1898–1980), her colleague in the economics department of the University of Wisconsin. He was the son of the illustrious social gospel minister and theologian, Walter Rauschenbusch, and would later play a major role in developing unemployment compensation plans for Wisconsin and the country.

No. 191   June 2, 1925   Washington, D.C.

1. Your and Landis' papers go back today. Receipt herewith. This is a most promising piece of work.[1] Thank you.

2. I guess Powell is right about your Yale L.J. article.[2]

3. Your questions re B. v. R.[3] are in order: (1) Case heard early in '23 term, assigned to V. Recently reassigned to me to equalize burdens. (2) Court may not know as well at time of considering pet. for cert, whether question involved is a state question, as it does later. (Sometimes it doesn't know later, the Salem Trust Co. & Mfrs Finance Co, 264 US 152).[4] (3) In Hooker and Esteve cases,[5] the question dealt with was a federal question. Hence it was permissible to use the appropriate language discarding old terms. Here question was a state question; the inappropriate language was hallowed by state use; and, in laying down the state law, it seemed obligatory to use "the language of the country."

4. That's a fine report you are making to Nelson.[6]

5. C.C. is doing good work for us on state functions. Note the enclosed by Rogers. What poor statesmanship & politics the Democrats have been guilty of, omitting to grasp this issue.

6. George Soule was in last week & I talked to him on this subject & particularly on cutting public jobs to fit the human cloth available.

7. We gave Fred Delano a deserved tribute yesterday in closing the Texas-Okl. receivership.[7]

8. The U.S.S.C. is probably 100 cases worse off than last year at terms end. We have disposed of the usual number of cases & certs, but the inflow seems very large now.

9. Magnes probably told you of his talk with me, I hope accurately. It was an entirely harmonious talk.[8]

10. The Hough book has not come yet.[9]

11. O.W.H. in resplendent form.

12. Your telegram re Peelis came dramatically while I was talking with Ford & Miller. I have made it clear to both that you are the Supreme Adviser, & that Miller comes through you.[10] M. will doubtless go to Louisville within a fortnight for the first conference with Alex Humphrey,[11] Helm Bruce[12] et al. More of this when we meet.

13. I think you will find Stone's Trade Assn. ops. his best work.[13]

[1] FF and James M. Landis were about to publish the first instalment of what later became *The Business of the Supreme Court*. See "The Business of the Supreme Court—A Study in the Federal Judicial System, Part I: The Period Prior to the Civil War," *Harvard Law Review* 38 (1925): 1005. For LDB's evaluation of the completed project, see his letter to FF, 1 August 1927. After seeing the final version of this instalment, LDB wrote on 11 July 1925: "You and Landis have made a fine beginning. . . . The foundation is solidly laid. And already there is provided a ferment for thought & a rich quarry for arguments. It is thrilling."

[2] Again collaborating with Landis, FF published "The Compact Clause of the Constitution: A Study in Interstate Adjustments," *Yale Law Journal* 34 (1925): 685.

[3] *Benedict* v. *Ratner*, 268 U.S. 353, had been decided the previous week, with LDB speaking for a unanimous Court. The case involved a complex question of New York bankruptcy law. The circuit court of appeals (with LDB's friend, Learned Hand) upheld Ratner, but the High Court reversed the judgment. LDB wrote to Hand: "With trepidation, I send you the opinion in Benedict v. Ratner in which we are boldly reversing you. . . . " And to FF he wrote: "Enclosed will interest you—at least for its boldness. We are reversing L.H. . . . on a question of N.Y. law."

[4] The Salem Trust case had been in and out of federal courts for several years; the sticking point was which courts had jurisdiction in establishing bankruptcy rules and procedures. For final disposition, see 280 Fed. Rep. 803 (1925).

[5] *Boston & Maine R.R.* v. *Hooker*, 233 U.S. 97 (1914), ruled that railroads could not unilaterally change their liability schedules without the permission of the Interstate Commerce Commission. *Western Union Telegraph Co.* v. *Esteve Bros. & Co.*, 256 U.S. 566 (1921), held, with LDB speaking for the Court, that when a utility offered two types of service, with one carrying a greater liability for error, a customer could not sue for the greater liability if he had used the other service.

[6] See 1 January and 21 February 1925.

[7] Frederic Adrian Delano (1863–1953), a railroad executive, had served as the court appointed receiver in *Oklahoma* v. *Texas*, 268 U.S. 472. The Court approved his final report of the receiver and wrote: "In terminating the receivership the Court expresses its high appreciation of the admirable service of the receiver in satisfactorily managing a large estate in novel and difficult circumstances."

[8] Judah Leon Magnes (1877–1948) was a Reform rabbi who had earlier crossed swords with LDB over Zionist matters. In 1921 he had moved to Palestine to work for the Hebrew University in Jerusalem. He had just been appointed chancellor and in 1935, would be named to its presidency. Magnes and LDB had discussed the underlying philosophy behind the Hebrew University (see LDB to Julian W. Mack, 13 June 1925, for his account of their conversation).

[9] Charles M. Hough, ed., *Report of Cases in the Vice-Admiralty of the Province of New York* (New Haven: Yale University Press, 1925).

[10] Beginning in 1924, LDB interested himself in the improvement of the University of Louisville. Operating through university officials and members of his family still residing in Louisville, LDB attempted to supervise the establishment of a first class educational institution in the city of

204

his birth. The story of that attempt can be traced in Volume V of *The Letters of Louis D. Brandeis*, starting with his letter to Adele Brandeis, his niece, on 24 September 1924; see also Bernard Flexner, *Mr. Justice Brandeis and the University of Louisville* (Louisville: University of Louisville, 1938). LDB sought advice from FF on ways in which the university's law school might be improved. Arthur Younger Ford (1861–1926), a Kentucky journalist and businessman, had become president of the University of Louisville in 1922. Robert Netherland Miller (1879–1968) was a tax lawyer who had offices in both Louisville and Washington, and who agreed to serve, under FF's direction, in the upbuilding of the law school. Miller, who was born in Louisville and who taught there, had been a classmate of FF's at Harvard.

[11] Alexander Pope Humphrey (1848–1928) was a Louisville attorney and a leading Republican conservative.

[12] Helm Bruce (1860–1927) was another prominent Louisville attorney.

[13] The day before, the Supreme Court had decided two important antitrust cases: *Maple Flooring Manufacturers Association* v. *United States* 268 U.S. 563; and *Cement Manufacturers Protective Association* v. *United States*, 268 U.S. 588. Harlan Fiske Stone had written the opinions in both cases, which were decided by six to three votes. The government had attacked both trade associations as being in violation of the Sherman and Clayton acts. Both groups collected and disseminated information, and while no overt price fixing took place, the government argued that the statistical services led to an informal price maintenance. Stone, echoing arguments that LDB had used over a decade earlier, took pains to draw a distinction between illegal acts that restrained trade and legal but cooperative endeavors that supported free trade.

No. 192   June 20, 1925   Chatham, Mass.

FF: 1. That is fine news about M[arion]'s progress.

2. The Cleveland Survey & Soule correspondence, Mohl & Holmes letters returned herewith.

3. Yes, La Follette died fittingly.[1] He had put all there was in him into the great fight, never sparing himself. And he knew not fear.

4. That's a fine promise of Herbert Samuel's.[2] It will make a different Palestine to have him at the head. I hope that this hope will keep Mohl there.

5. From B.F. comes a note & DeSenectute. Marvelous that like Rose's books on Renaissance Art, this translation should come from benighted Arkansas.[3]

6. I am glad to hear that War books have gone to 809.

7. Susan sent me T. R. Powell's editorial in N.Y. World on U.S.S.C.[4] Yours in the N.R. was illuminating.[5]

8. The N.Y. Times begins to talk plainly on the crime of keeping China poor through the tariff bar.[6]

9. I will send Al the H.L. Library list of Kentucky material.[7]

10. We are beginning to reap a fine harvest in Federal Judges. Perhaps it may help in the "back to the states" movement—however illogically.

11. Your Research boys evident[ly] are doing well.

I am sending under two other covers the October Term 1924 Survey, which you & Landis may wish to see now.

[1] Senator La Follette had died on 18 June.

[2] Herbert Samuel, the British high commissioner in Palestine, had just resigned his post and was returning to England.

[3] Flexner had sent LDB a new translation of Cicero's *De Senectute* (New York: G. P. Putnam's Sons, 1923). The translator was William Armistad Falconer (1869–1927), an Arkansas lawyer and judge and a professor of law at the University of Arkansas. George Basil Rose (1860–1943) was a Little Rock attorney and an authority on Renaissance art. His principal contribution was *Renaissance Masters* (New York: G. P. Putnam's Sons, 1898).

[4] On 21 June the *World* had an editorial on the tax exemption extended to federal judges, and questioned whether, despite the Supreme Court's 1920 ruling in Evans v. Gore, a tax really diminished judicial salaries in such a way as to be unconstitutional.

[5] FF's comments related to the Gitlow case (see next letter). See *New Republic* 43 (24 June 1925): 110.

[6] See the editorial, "The Powers and China," *New York Times*, 20 June 1925.

[7] For building up a Kentuckiana collection at the University of Louisville library.

No. 193   [n.d., July 1925]   Chatham, Mass.

FF: 1. Goethe (Italienische Reise,[1] March 5, 1787) speaks with great enthusiasm of a Neopolitan law-reformer "Ritter Filangieri"[2] & quotes F. as placing Baptista Vico,[3] an older Neopolitan law-writer, even higher than Montesquieu.[4] Do you know anything about Vico?

2. I am delighted with this reading of his "Italienische Reise." It gives me a wholy new impression of Goethe, and a very loveable one. There is nothing of the super-man, nothing of his arrogance or inconsiderateness of [*]. It exhibits him as an earnest seeker after truth, forever and endlessly striving to develop himself, to aid others, or at least to share the results with us. And there is throughout a rarely generous spirit and much real humility. One forgets entirely that this is literature & thinks only of the uncommonly fine, serious minded, lofty spirited man.

3. This would interest Morrison [sic].[5] Goethe mentions (March 26, 1787) that the Corvette (apparently a liner) on which he is to sail from Naples to Palermo was built in America. She was apparently a Neopolitan vessel.

4. Your "Compact" article[6] is setting many thinking. [*]'s letter is interesting. If you have Victor Duruy's History of Rome[7] at hand you & Marion will find some interesting statements concerning conflicts between the City States under the Roman Emperor, i.a. Vol VI p. 49 (in C.F. Jewett Pub. Co. Ed.) and much on the reluctance of the good

Emperor to interfere except where there were controversies between the cities or danger from the barbarians.

5. That's a promising letter from Botts.

6. Enclosed from Burlingham exhibits Manton C.J.[8] as jurisdiction & law reformer.

7. The Syracuse ad. & some other things suggest "Dass es noch nicht alles Tage abend ist."[9]

8. There is some intrinsic evidence & some circumstantial which tends to confirm your information re Gitlow Case.[10]

9. Alice bids me tell you that Auntie B. has made great strides towards par, & that, if we can keep her from yielding to some calls which might take her away for awhile, we hope to see her quite herself again this summer.

I hope the reports from Marion continue good.

We had a fine visit from Hermann [sic] B[lumgart].

[1] Goethe (1749–1832), the great German intellectual and writer, was certainly one of LDB's favorite authors. His *Italienische Reise (Italian Journey)* recounts a trip through Italy during the years 1786 to 1788. Probably LDB was reading the new Alfred Kuhn edition of the work (Munich: F. Bruckmann, 1925).

[2] Gaetano Filangieri (1752–1788) was an Italian Enlightenment figure, a gifted lawyer and legal reformer. He was best known for his multivolume *La Scienza della Legislazione*.

[3] Giambattista Vico (1668–1744), the noted Italian philosopher, legal theorist, and historian, was extremely influential among eighteenth-century intellectuals.

[4] Montesquieu (1689–1755) was one of the founders of modern political science, and his *Spirit of the Laws* (1748) exerted great influence in both Europe and America. Montesquieu himself acknowledged the influence upon his own work of Vico.

[5] Samuel Eliot Morison (1887–1976) was one of FF's Harvard colleagues, a member of the history department there from 1915 to 1955, and one of the country's greatest historians. LDB thought highly of Morison and took an interest in his attempt, with others, to gather material for the study of early American history.

[6] See 2 June 1925, n. 2.

[7] (Boston, 1883). See 1 September 1925.

[8] Martin Thomas Manton (1880–1946) had been appointed to the bench by President Wilson in 1916. Two years later he was elevated from district court to the Circuit Court of Appeals for the Second Circuit, and soon became the senior judge. After 1929, however, his financial situation became precarious and he began accepting bribes from various litigants. Finally, in 1939, he was convicted and sent to prison for one year.

[9] "Don't count your chickens before they are hatched."

[10] *Gitlow* v. *New York*, 268 U.S. 652, had been argued in November 1923, but was not decided until 8 June 1925. Gitlow had been convicted under the New York criminal anarchy law for advocating the violent overthrow of the government. Although the majority of the Court upheld the conviction, it also ruled for the first time that the protections of free speech guaranteed through the First Amendment applied to the states through the due process clause of the Fourteenth Amendment. This idea had first been proposed by LDB in his dissent in *Gilbert* v. *Minnesota* (1920). Justice Holmes, joined by LDB, entered a dissent attempting to apply the "clear and present danger" test from the *Schenk* case. "Whatever may be thought of the redundant discourse before us," Holmes wrote, "it had no chance of starting a present conflagration."

No. 194   **July 29, 1925**   **Chatham, Mass.**

FF: 1. Alice's & my gratulations to you & Marion on returning to Cape Cod waters. We are sorry it cannot be Chatham. When things get settled at Chilmark & you have time, we hope to have you with us at least for a few days.

2. Our congratulations also on the Cambridge house.[1] It will mean much to the students as well as to Marion.

3. J.W.M. doubtless reported to you on his & Hermann's visit Sunday. We talked things Palestinian. It was fine to see them, but I don't suppose we did much to advance the cause. DeHaas had asked to come here, I invited him for today & expected him this AM. Have heard nothing. Doubtless he will turn up this evening. I hardly expect this visit to do much for the cause either.

J.W.M. was motored here & back by Berenson.[2] Es hat ein Galgen gesicht.[3]

4. Bryan died finely & dramatically.[4]

5. The Bob Brueres[5] were here two days. He has a fine spirit.

[1] In the summer of 1925, after teaching at Cornell, FF and his wife moved from Boston to Cambridge.

[2] Lawrence Berenson (1891–1970) graduated from Harvard Law School and then clerked for one year for Julian Mack. He opened a law practice in New York City and also became an active Zionist.

[3] "He had a hang-dog look."

[4] William Jennings Bryan had been in Dayton, Tennessee, aiding in the prosecution of John T. Scopes. A few days after he had been savagely crossexamined by Clarence Darrow at the close of the trial, Bryan died in his sleep at Dayton.

[5] Robert Walter Bruere (1876–19[?]) was a prolific writer on social topics, specializing in labor and industrial relations. During the 1920s he was an editor of *The Survey*.

No. 195   **August 12, 1925**   **Chatham, Mass.**

FF: 1) Re the Spy system. I think (if not already covered by your instructions) it would be well to impose on one of Hamilton's men, the duty of getting together the history in U.S.A. not only of the practice of employing spies, but also of the "views of the Fathers" etc. on them. In those early days, when there was real thought on what they already termed "Political Service"—some things must have been said which would be very effective in debate.

2. R.P. does not seem to have been calmed by the vacation period.

3. Had not heard of the Intern. Shoe-McElwain decision.

4. R.W.C., as one of the props of virtue for the "Christian prince" Gary![1]

5. I see no objection to your writing the C.J. for the report of the proceedings at Judicial Conference. His address is Pointe-a-Pic, Prov. of Quebec.

6. Eastman[2] has had reorganization fees actively in mind for some time.

7. Paul & Elizabeth came back joyously & in fine shape. The[y] hope to see you some time some where before starting West about Labor Day. Perhaps via N.Y.C.

8. What has Croly done re that Verona, Miss., Collier clipping?[3]

[1] Richard Washburn Child (1881–1935) was the son of Walter Child, one of LDB's earliest clients and oldest friends. A prolific and popular writer, he was also a lawyer and a friend of Warren G. Harding, who appointed him ambassador to Italy. In 1925, Child joined with Elbert H. Gary in establishing the National Crime Commission, an organization intended to awaken public interest in the treatment and prevention of crime. LDB's sly reference here is to *Richard the Third*, III, 7 : 6: "Two props of virtue for a Christian prince."

[2] Joseph Bartlett Eastman (1882–1942) had been one of LDB's chief lieutenants in Boston franchise politics at the turn of the century, and developed into one of the nation's most astute and dedicated public officials. He served for many years on the Interstate Commerce Commission and was named federal coordinator of transportation during both the New Deal and the first year of World War II. "Joe Eastman," LDB once commented, "has more interest in the public service and less in his own career than any man I have ever known."

[3] See 21 February 1925, n. 4.

No. 196   August 15, 1925   Chatham, Mass.

FF: 1. That's a grand report which O.W.H. gives of himself, & it carries much of promise for the 1925 Term. He may be interested to be reminded that one B. Franklin read Port Royal's "Art of Thinking"—at the age of 16.[1] Despite the obvious differences, the new portrait of Goethe which his "Italienische Reise" brought me,[2] led me to think oftener of OWH. than of any other person—in some of the finest intellectual qualities.

2. The ABA is obviously one of the carefully planned acts.[3] You will find evidence of another in the enclosed letter which please return.

3. That's a cheering report of R.P.'s.

4. I guess Hillman must feel hard hit by the Injunction, & to be otherwise a bit worried.[4]

5. It looks as if real disaster were impending for the Coal Union—disaster more nearly attributable to obvious unwisdom than most which affect humans.[5]

6. I hope there will be some chance of you & Paul [Raushenbush] getting better acquainted before he & E go West about Labor Day. He seems a rare find.

[1] Antoine Arnauld and Pierre Nicole, of [the Jansenist community at] Port Royal, *Logic: or The Art of Thinking* (English translation, London, 1687). Benjamin Franklin mentions reading the book, along with John Locke's work, in the first section of his *Autobiography*.

[2] See undated letter, July 1925.

[3] The American Bar Association meetings were to open in Detroit on 3 September.

[4] On 13 August the New York Supreme Court granted an injunction prohibiting picketing of the International Tailoring Company by members of Sidney Hillman's Amalgamated Clothing Workers Union. Hillman called the decision "an open invitation to employers to start sweat shops in the city under the protection of the courts."

[5] Talks had been under way since early July in an attempt to avert a threatened nationwide coal strike. In August the discussions were deadlocked, despite deep public concern and official offers to mediate. Then on 31 August, John L. Lewis issued the strike order, and over 150,000 workers at more than 800 mines walked off their jobs.

No. 197   August 25, 1925   Chatham, Mass.

FF: 1. We are extremely sorry to hear that the knee incident is so serious, & hope Marion will make you take very good care of yourself.

2. Please tell Harold [Laski], when you write, that Alice & Elizabeth are very sorry that the official notice [1] duly mailed did not reach him & Frieda.

3. The Hamiltons were here for three nights & we enjoyed them much. They are distinctly of the right sort.

I have about finished my review—or rather survey of Roman history. I know more than I did when Buckland [2] & I met. But he would still think my views in the main, "tosh."

This history furnishes many additional arguments or illustrations for our views on national functions.

[1] Of the wedding.

[2] Probably William Warwick Buckland (1859–1946), the British authority on Roman law. See next letter.

No. 198   September 1, 1925   Chatham, Mass.

F.F.: 1. I think you should pay Alice royalty for the Curio-book reading. It was she, as I recall, who brought it to Hermann's attention.

2. Not much light can be gained from our action on the orders in Bankruptcy enquired about. [1] It was agreed, at the outset, that our Comtee should act merely as a comtee on third readings. The subject has been much threshed out by a special comtee of the Judicial Council in conjunction with representatives of several associations of credit men & lawyers, & the C.J. had participated in these earlier functions. Still,

210

considerable time was spent by Sanford on this job (time he could ill afford) & quite a little by the C.J. I spent only a few hours.

3. In the Roman survey, Duruy (English translation presided over by J. P. Mahaffy) was my piece de resistance, Ferrero (Zimmern's translation) was my entree.[2] I plan to read Cicero's letters & some Tacitus, but I guess it is pretty clear that Toynbee put an appropriate estimate upon the Roman contribution and that Wells is,[3] in substance, not far wrong. The Romans had the great advantage of controlling the publicity agents, and of having their writings survive. The value of these writings as a means was undoubtedly great; & as their influence much greater than their value. On the whole I should put the Romans first as a quarry for warnings. Of course, they serve also as a base base [sic] for precious metals. They shine most in their performances in the period prior to the Punic War. The decline began at the end of the first Punic War.

4. I have not seen the Keynes statement on centralization.[4]

5. I think Mrs. La Follette[5] (who will continue the La Follette's Magazine) would like to publish this note of Christie's on Furuseth[6] and that there could be no objection on L.C.'s part if his identity were concealed. She would, besides, appreciate it much as evidence of your interest in the continued publication.

5[sic]. Paul & Elizabeth have no very good impression of [*]. Eliz. sampled his course on Const. Law & then fled to the Law School course. Both say he is "terribly conservative" & "popular."

6. P. & E. leave probably next Saturday, possibly not until Labor Day. We are to leave possibly as early as Friday Sept. 10 & not later than Monday the 14th; & plan to spend a day (possibly two) at the Bellevue. We hope that your obstinate knee will not prevent our seeing you before we leave Mass. for Washington.

The household's greeting to Marion.

P. & E. think highly of Mason.[7]

[1] A special committee of the American Bar Association had met with LDB, Chief Justice Taft, and Justice Sanford to draw up a model bankruptcy bill, which they hoped Congress would adopt to replace the antiquated statute then on the books.

[2] Jean Victor Duruy, *History of Rome, and of the Roman People, from Its Origins to the Invasion of the Barbarians*, 8 vols. (Boston: C.F Jewett, 1883), trans. by M. M. Ripley and W. J. Clarke, ed. by J. P. Mahaffy; Guglielmo Ferrero, *The Greatness and Decline of Rome*, 5 vols. (New York: G. P. Putnam's Sons, 1907–1909), trans. by Alfred E. Zimmern and H. J. Chaytor.

[3] H. G. Wells, *The Outline of History*, 2 vols. (London: Macmillan, 1919–1920), provided a rather critical view of Roman society.

[4] The noted English economist, John Maynard Keynes, later First Baron of Tilton, (1883–1946), had issued a number of statements, mainly in connection with his attack on the

fiscal policies of the British government (see 8 November 1925). Only a few days before this letter he had again called for central control of the currency.

[5] Belle Case La Follette (1859–1931) was the first woman to graduate from the University of Wisconsin Law School. She married Robert M. La Follette in 1881, and until his death was his partner in all his ventures and crusades. After her husband's death, she undertook much of the research and wrote the first third of the two-volume biography, which was finished after her own death by her daughter Fola. (The Brandeis family made financial contributions to help her finish the book.)

[6] Andrew Furuseth (1854–1938), one of LDB's favorites, was a Norwegian immigrant seaman who rose to the presidency of the International Seamen's Union. The Loring Christie article referred to here is "Andy Has Undertaken a Big Job," *La Follette's Magazine* 17 (June 1925): 83. The letter recounts Furuseth's plans to go to Europe to persuade governments to undertake reforms similar to those he and La Follette had accomplished in the La Follette Seamen's Act of 1915.

[7] In 1925 Alpheus Thomas Mason (1899–1989) was at the beginning of his teaching career at Princeton, from which he retired in 1968 as McCormick Professor of Jurisprudence. According to Professor Mason, at the time of this letter LDB may have been aware of his book, *Organized Labor and the Law, with Especial Reference to the Sherman and Clayton Acts* (Durham, N.C.: Duke University Press, 1925), a topic that would certainly have been of interest to LDB. Within a few years Mason began a lengthy study of LDB's career, with books on savings bank insurance, the New Haven struggle, judicial philosophy, and finally a semiauthorized biography, *Brandeis—A Free Man's Life* (New York: Viking, 1946). See 21 February 1940.

No. 199   September 24, 1925   Washington, D.C.

F.F.: 1. I am glad you wrote me about the personal needs and I'll send the $1500 now or in installments as you may prefer. Your public service must not be abridged. Marion knows that Alice and I look upon you as half brother, half son.

2. R.P.'s university address is a masterpiece.[1] Abe F[lexner]. and Fosdick are right about the pusillanimous ending. This ending, like his acceptance of the arbitration duty, discloses his weaknesses. I guess he knew what advice he would have gotten from his associates had he asked for advice.

3. I am sending the address to Alfred[2], with the suggestion that he give it to [Arthur Y.] Ford, for daily reading.

4. You doubtless include Glenn Frank's[3] editorials in your daily reading.

"Ach Gott, Ach Gott, Ach Gotte
Ich Scham mich vor der Lotte"[4]

5. Alice & I want much to see & hear Alfred Cohen if he & wife come to Washington, but hardly feel justified in asking him to come solely for our education.

6. Robert Miller has doubtless told you (or will) about his engagement to Judge Frederic Dodge's[5] daughter. I think he, too, should have R.P.'s University address.

7. You packed much good advice in the letter to Fosdick. But I guess serving God and Mammon remains as difficult as of yore.[6]

[1] Pound had delivered the commencement address at Indiana University on 8 June, published as "The Prospects of the American University," *Indiana University News-Letter* 13 (August 1925): 3. Pound drew a parallel between modern universities and medieval churches, and not unlike the medieval monasteries, modern universities were departing rapidly from what once passed as the standard education. While Pound found much to lament about this, he ended on an upbeat note, finding much worthwhile in modern academic life.

[2] Alfred Brandeis (1854–1928) was LDB's brother, and throughout his life, probably his closest friend. Alfred had remained in Louisville to go into business with his father, and he had become one of the leading merchants and most influential citizens of the city. During World War I, Alfred worked under Herbert Hoover in the Food Administration as a dollar-a-year man, handling the problems of wheat production and distribution. The two brothers were extremely faithful correspondents and hundreds of surviving letters between them demonstrate the lifelong affection they felt toward one another. LDB had enlisted Alfred and various members of Alfred's family in his attempt to help improve the University of Louisville.

[3] Glenn Frank (1877–1940) had worked for E. A. Filene, and in 1925 was called to the presidency of the University of Wisconsin. He was forced out of office by the La Follettes in 1937, and he died three years later in an automobile accident while campaigning for the Republican nomination to the United States Senate.

[4] "Oh God, Oh God, oh God
   I am ashamed in front of Lotte."

[5] Frederic Dodge (1847–1927) was the United States circuit judge for the first circuit from 1912 to 1918. His daughter, Elinor, married Robert N. Miller on 25 October 1925.

[6] Fosdick had written to FF on 18 September, and noted that Pound in his Indiana speech had called for more creative experiments by the schools. Fosdick said that the General Education Fund had the money, but needed the academics to provide them with fundable ideas. FF replied on 20 September, suggesting that more research was needed into the causes of crime.

No. 200   October 3, 1925   Washington, D.C.

FF: 1. Alice thinks you may not have seen the enclosed on "The Grammar."

2. Alice wants to know who Croly's "Elizabeth," protector of Gates, is.

3. Alice also wants to know what, if anything, you & Marion propose to do about the Higgins-sent periodical.

4. As to Landis' name being appended to the articles on U.S.S.C. production:[1] You will know whether there is to be anything in them which would make it undesirable. I am content with any decision you make as to this.

5. I assume you wrote Croly that I would not attend the Toynbee dinner. When you see A.J.T. give him my warm greetings.[2]

6. Rennie Smith[3] is to dine with us & the Hamiltons & Basil Manlys this evening.

7. That's an interesting clipping on the Crime Wave of 1852.

8. Caillaux's[4] going home "[**]," with his being so shown up, as true to his Gallic form, may bring his downfall. Tis great to see the Great "hoist with his own petard."

9. Ought not B.F. have selected Oct 12th for his discovery and Nov 5 for the explosion?[5] DeHaas et al will have schadenfreude.[6] Oct 10 is the day of the Red-Peasants International.

10. The Gary Comte & R.W.C. should paste the R.P. letter into their hats.[7]

11. The N.R. in the Advertising Editorial[8] (& elsewhere) should not neglect the duty of the Consumer. "Lass Dich nicht Beschummelnt"[9] should be a fundamental teaching in a democracy. Slaves & subjects should be protected; Free men afforded an opportunity of protecting themselves. And of course of going to h————, if they prefer that to other resorts. Also, of course, for the consumer, protecting oneself implies having a choice. But in America, the margin is usually so large that one can easily "go without."

12. Following your suggestions: I will ask Miss Malloch to deposit in a special account for you, in B of L Engineers Bk Boston $1500 & send you a check book. You should receive notification from her some time next week.

13. Yes O.W.H. is in fine shape.

14. J.M.L. is taking hold finely.

---

[1] With James M. Landis now clerking for LDB, FF wondered if there would be any objection to having his name continue as coauthor of the "Business of the Supreme Court" series in the *Harvard Law Review*. Landis's name disappeared from the articles in November 1925, and reappeared in January 1927.

[2] The eminent historian had arrived in the United States in July for a series of speeches.

[3] Rennie Smith (1888–1962) had entered government service in England as parliamentary secretary, and was later appointed undersecretary for foreign affairs.

[4] Joseph Marie Auguste Caillaux (1863–1944) was a colorful and controversial French statesman. As finance minister, he had just completed a visit to America to negotiate war debts. Upon his return to France there was a debate over his financial policies, and many calls for and rumors of his resignation; but he managed to weather the storm.

[5] A joke on Guy Fawkes Day (November 5) and Columbus Day (October 12).

[6] "malicious pleasure; gloating."

[7] See 12 August 1925, n. 1. Pound's letter was a brief analysis of the weakness of the criminal justice system. It was sent to the *New York Law Review* and republished in *New Republic* 44 (30 September 1925): 135.

[8] "The Wastefulness of Advertising," *New Republic* 44 (30 September 1925): 139, was extremely critical of the value of advertising: "To determine technical merit on the basis of who can shout loudest and longest is a neanderthalic survival which civilized society will some day outgrow."

[9] "Don't let yourself be swindled."

No. 201   October 5, 1925   Washington, D.C.

F.F.: 1. Apropos "The Strategy of the Progressives" & much else in the N.R.[1] I think the fundamental error in the political science of the philosophic editor is that he fails to realize that in government, as in other spheres of human activity, happiness is usually attained, if at all, as a bi-product [sic]; and that, because of our finite wisdom, and the infinite possibility of error in judgment, we are more likely to be right in turning our thoughts primarily to the simpler problem of means than directly to hoped for ends. He talks of enacting progressive legislation. What? As Holmes used to say: "State your proposition and I'll deny it." Lindsay Rogers[2] has made a very practical suggestion. It would take a very few Wisconsins to make anything hopeful, possible in politics.

2. The C.J. has written upon Swan's insistence an article on the new stat. and the rules for the Yale L.J.![3] It will doubtless appear in the Oct. issue. He is apparently in the same relatively good condition that he was last term.

3. I suppose we shall begin the term with 800 cases on the list, of course most of the recent ones pets for certs.

4. I shall send for the Demosthenes Private Orations to which Max R. refers. Lionel Curtis was in for an hour today. I found some points of complete agreement, to which the talk was confined.[4]

Bureau of Labor Statistics et al give recent prices (cost of living) at 173 + as compared with 1913. Irving Fisher[5] et al. give wholesale prices at 153 + as compared with 1913.

Is the 20 point difference due to relatively increased retail distribution costs? And how much has been the increase of wholesale distribution costs? Ask your N.R. economists & others.

Dr. Leon Reich[6] (whom you will recall from Paris) was in & talked i.a. of your "Uncle Henry."

[1] "The Strategy of Progressive Politics," *New Republic* 44 (7 October 1925): 163. The long editorial was an attack upon the contention of Lindsay Rogers whose article "Progressive Half-Preparedness," appeared in the same issue (pp. 169–72). Rogers argued that progressives must give up the attempt to elect presidents and concentrate instead upon consolidating local pockets of progressive sentiment.

[2] Lindsay Rogers (1891–1970) was a professor of political science at Harvard until 1929, when he moved to Columbia.

[3] Thomas Walter Swan (1877–1975) was in 1925 dean and professor of law at Yale. In 1927 he was named judge for the second circuit court. Taft's article is "The Jurisdiction of the Supreme Court under the Act of February 13, 1925," *Yale Law Journal* 35 (1925): 1.

[4] Curtis, who believed in the "federation" of former British colonies, was visiting in the United States at the Institute of Politics at Williams College.

[5] Irving Fisher (1867–1947) taught economics and statistics at Yale for nearly half a century and was for many years considered one of America's premier authorities on economics.

[6] Leon Reich (1879–1929) was a Polish Zionist leader.

No. 202   October 17, 1925   Washington, D.C.

FF: 1. I think Federal Receiverships an admirable subject. The reports and court records in libraries plus the financial journals should afford rich material, particularly in supplement of an investigation of the court records in S[outhern].D[istrict]. of N.Y.

2. Let Marion consider this alternative explanation: The N.Y. masters may think that they do well to have your courses studied *in loco* by students who they will later win by their wiles. There will again be the question whether as Edmund Benedikt[1] said of his uncle: "Ganz Innspruch Manschelt."

3. Carl Wheat,[2] who is here, will doubtless talk with you about soon about [sic] the proposed interstate commerce motor vehicle bill. He should be shown how not to do it.

4. The Wisconsin action taking the $9,000,000 state tax off the small fellows is the most intelligent use of the taxing power for social ends that came in many a year.[3]

5. Re C.C. Tolerance Speech, Alice sends this clipping from Time.[4]

6. Langdon Davies' "New Age of Faith" wont be liked by American Patriots.[5]

[1] Edmund Benedikt (1851–1929) was an Austrian jurist, editor and publisher of the influential *Juristiche Blatter*. Benedikt and LDB had a boyhood friendship in 1872–1873, when the Brandeis family lived in Europe. Their acquaintanceship began because LDB's mother and Benedikt's mother were best friends.

[2] Carl Irving Wheat (1892–1966) was a prominent California attorney and expert on utility law.

[3] By a law of 1925, Wisconsin shifted more of the tax burden upon industry by cancelling the personal property tax write-off against the income tax. See W. Elliot Brownlee, Jr., *Progressivism and Economic Growth: The Wisconsin Income Tax, 1911–1929* (Port Washington: Kennikat Press, 1974).

[4] *Time Magazine* of 19 October (an issue, incidentally, which featured LDB's picture on the cover) reviewed President Coolidge's address to the American Legion in Omaha. Sometimes interpreted as a rebuke to the Ku Klux Klan, the speech lamented the growth of wartime intolerance and made a plea for brotherhood in America.

[5] John Langdon-Davies, *The New Age of Faith* (New York: Viking, 1925), speculated on the impact of new findings in science, particularly in evolution and heredity, upon human society.

No. 203   **October 20, 1925**   **Washington, D.C.**

F.F.: 1. Since writing you yesterday of W.L.'s book[1] I have your letter. With the specific things which you say I agree entirely. But I think it is a remarkable book with the classic quality in thought and expression. The defects are the inevitable ones due to his qualities and lacks which we have often discussed. "Denn der Sonne Busen ist liebeleer."[2] Still, I think his book will be distinctly helpful to those who try to think on political science; & that this helpfulness will more than outweigh the misuse which the Industrial Conference et al. will make of his statements. Walter's criticisms should compel others who feel and care as we do, to come to grips with the difficulties instead of closing their eyes and "just grabbing" as Mr. Starts suggested.

W.L. has a definite art as a mind, and a pen. For the rest we must look elsewhere.

2. Those are good letters from & on Gottlieb[3] & the Research Fellowships.

3. Alice asks whether you have seen Toynbee. If he is coming here we want, of course, to see him.[4]

[1] Lippmann had just published *The Phantom Public* (New York: Harcourt, Brace, and Co., 1925), which was a sequel to his *Public Opinion* (New York: Harcourt, Brace, and Co., 1922). In his new work Lippmann questioned the very idea of whether a "public" exists. In fact, he argued, there is no such thing, but rather a number of competing factions, with only a handful truly informed about the great questions of the times.

[2] "For the sun's bosom is without love."

[3] Leo Gottlieb (b. 1896) was a young attorney assisting Emory Buckner. His application for membership in the American Bar Association was in jeopardy ostensibly because of the methods he had used in gathering evidence against violators of the prohibition law. The attempt to block Gottlieb was interpreted generally, by LDB and other friends of Gottlieb, as being inspired by corrupt lawyers and others resentful of Buckner's crackdown. Judge A. N. Hand issued a statement saying that Gottlieb's methods were perfectly legal and proper.

[4] See 3 October 1925, n. 2.

No. 204   **November 8, 1925**   **Washington, D.C.**

1. Your compact clause proposition is doing effective work.[1]

2. It would be fine to have Ray Stevens landed in Siam.[2]

3. Keynes may or may not be right in his "Economic Consequences of Mr. Churchill."[3] But a country which can produce men who think as vigorously, write as effectively, and speak out as fearlessly, as he does, has a good chance of winning out against all comers.

4. Our Courts project should receive hearty support from all opponents of U.S. entering the League [of Nations].

5. Alice & I called on the R.P.s. He was not in but she was. She has developed much since they dined with us at Otis Place. Alice took her Friday to make the Ambassadorial calls.

6. The customary P.C. is, in most cases, inadequate. I suggested that instead, brief ops. be written like my Davis v. Henderson, 266 U.S. 92, a form that seems to me better than the N.Y. C[ourt]. of A[ppeals]. memos.[4] The suggestion didn't prevail. But there is other ineffectual grumbling at the defects of the P.C. The Whitney P.C. was intentionally blind.[5] The reasons, later.

7. J.W.M. reported for 2 hours on international and national Jewish matters. "Nichts Erfreuhliches"[6] as my father used to say.

8. Have just rec'd Raymond Fosdick's Colgate address.[7] He is one of the most disappointing of men. He sees, but he doesn't do. If instead of putting up the job vaguely to the "young," he would, having arrived, strike out boldly from his pinnacle, some things would be started—and at least the "young" inspired to action. He is teaching them the charms of hot air.

9. Ripley's remedy isn't very promising. But it's something to have a man speak out.[8] Could not others be induced to think? And then have men who want to think together, but not in public, come together in a small group to consider the economic state of the nation. It's clear, I think, that the gentle enslavement of our people is proceeding apace—politically, economically, socially—& that the only remedy is via the individual. To make him care to be a free man & willing to pay the price. There is, of course, [no] mechanism possible to promote the desire & when existing to make it effective. But we need now a diagnosis i.a.

10. Morris Cohen[9] is weekending with Jerome Michael[10] & they are coming in this afternoon.

11. It will be interesting to see H.J.L.

12. You will soon see L.D.'s individual portrait in the press.

13. Keynes Point III is very fine.

14. The Judd Welliver incident was an example of our most dangerous enslavement—the intellectual.[11] The interests have made great strides in this line.

15. The Sacco-Vanzetti expense a/c is a terrible indictment of our criminal justice.[12]

[1] See 2 June 1925, n. 2.

[2] Raymond Bartlett Stevens (1874–1942), an old friend and progressive ally of LDB's, served as special adviser to Siam (now Thailand) from 1926 to 1935. On 27 October, LDB had written to

FF: "As you are dispersing offices Warwick-like, can't you find something for Ray Stephens [sic]. I am told he is in several ways, hard-up."

³(London: L. and V. Woolf, 1925); the American edition of this thirty-two-page pamphlet was entitled *The Economic Consequences of Sterling Parity* (New York: Harcourt, Brace, and Co., 1925). In it Keynes attacked the policy of the chancellor of the exchequer, Winston Churchill, in forcing the resumption of the gold standard which Britain had deserted after World War I. Keynes blamed the inflation and high unemployment of the 1920s on the government policy and called for a centralized currency control which could avoid both inflation and depression.

⁴A majority of cases appealed to the Supreme Court were and are dismissed "per curiam," literally "by the court" with no explanation. In the *Davis* case, LDB had written a very brief statement summarizing the major issues and the reasons why the Court had chosen not to act. The New York method, mentioned here by LDB, failed to provide the litigants with sufficient information.

⁵On 19 October, the Court had dismissed the appeal in *Whitney* v. *California*, 269 U.S. 530, for want of jurisdiction. It was later restored to the docket; see 21 May 1927, n. 4.

⁶"nothing very pleasant."

⁷Fosdick, a League of Nations undersecretary, advocated American entry into the League; Colgate University had just awarded him an honorary degree.

⁸William Zebina Ripley (1867–1941) taught political economy at Harvard for a third of a century, 1901–1933. He had just issued a warning against the control of big business by bankers because of the diffusion of stock ownership. See *New York Times*, 29 October 1925.

⁹Morris Raphael Cohen (1880–1947), one of the country's best known and most influential intellectuals, taught at the City College of New York.

¹⁰Jerome Michael (1890–1953) was a special assistant to the attorney general. In 1927 he began a long tenure as a professor of criminal law at Columbia University.

¹¹Judson Churchill Welliver (1870–1943) had risen through Iowa journalism to an editorship of *Hampton's*. During the 1920 campaign he directed Harding's publicity, and from 1920 to 1925 he advised Harding and Coolidge. Welliver had just resigned from his position as chief clerk at the White House to accept a public relations job for the American Petroleum Institute.

¹²In 1920 a murder and payroll robbery in South Braintree, Massachusetts, led to the arrest and trial of two Italian immigrants and radicals, Nicola Sacco and Bartolomeo Vanzetti. Their conviction and death sentence led to a tremendous outcry and to unceasing efforts to win them a new trial. The case received unprecedented attention throughout the world. FF enlisted himself directly in the effort to secure justice for the two men, and his important book, *The Case of Sacco and Vanzetti* (Boston: Little, Brown, and Co., 1927), a scathing indictment of the judicial proceedings, had wide popularity and influence. LDB sympathized with the two men, but disqualified himself from acting on their last-minute appeal to the Supreme Court because members of his family, Mrs. Evans, and his friend FF were so deeply engaged in their behalf. After all the heroic efforts failed, the two men were executed on 24 August 1927. The reference in this letter was to the report issued by the defense committee, stating that over $282,000 had already been spent on legal and related costs and that only $4,500 was left on hand.

No. 205   November 15, 1925   Washington, D.C.

FF: 1. It is fine to have your and Marion's greetings to the birthday. The Adams-Jefferson Correspondence has a special appeal to me—these days.¹

2. I am glad to know of the fight in the faculty.² Strange to have R.P. away at such times. And stranger still that he, Anderson and Bliven should waste their time on E.A.'s alleged Foundation.³ He says he is

entrusting to these gentlemen the spending of $100,000 a year. "Wer's glaubt bekommt einem silbernen halben thaler."[4]

3. You spoke wisely to Lovett.[5]

4. DeHaas was in, yesterday, & left me saddened. N.Y. et al have left their mark, and not only on the heel.

5. Our friends seem to be having a good deal of dining. The stomach is next to the heart no doubt, sed longe inter vallo.[6]

[1] On 13 November, LDB became sixty-nine years old. FF and his wife had sent him Paul Wilsatch, ed., *The Correspondence of John Adams and Thomas Jefferson (1812–1826)* (Indianapolis: Bobbs-Merrill Co., 1925).

[2] In the fall of 1925, Dean Pound had added, as part of his plan to enlarge Harvard Law School, three new men to the faculty. FF and some others opposed these additions on the grounds that the three were unimpressive and their subject areas marginal to the purposes of the school.

[3] In 1922, Edward A. Filene had established The Twentieth Century Fund to aid economic, industrial, civic, and educational improvements.

[4] "Anyone who believes it gets a silver half-dollar."

[5] Probably Robert Morss Lovett (1870–1956), an English professor from the University of Chicago and a prolific writer, who joined the staff of *The New Republic* during the 1920s.

[6] "but with a long interval between"

No. 206   November 29, 1925   Washington, D.C.

FF: 1. We are relieved by what you write and others tell us of the operation.[1] Take very good care of yourself. There is much work that only you can do—until your disciples have taken their proper places.

2. What you write about the [Harvard Law School] Faculty, Ray Stevens and Page[2] is, indeed, cheering. (By the way, it was Alice who started the thought which places Ray at Siam.[3])

3. Mack reports BF & himself happy over the P.E.C. adjustment, and himself & others happy over the [*] adjustment & harmony at Baltimore.[4] For me, the outcome is saddening. Of course Palestine will get some needed material aid. But spiritually, it will suffer by the depreciation of Zionist activity into charity-drive materialism. And for America it is a defeat or submergence, of what I had hoped from the Zionist movement. My Carnegie Hall address of Sept. 1914 and the democratic idealism of [the] 1915 Zionist Convention & meetings are indeed out of date.

4. I know [*]. "He comes from Sheffield."

5. We are asking the [*] for Wednesday evening for a quiet talk, & shall get the Carl Beckers[5] to join us.

[1] FF decided to undergo surgery on his knee, which had been bothering him for several months.

[2] Perhaps FF had written to LDB about Robert Guthrie Page (1901–1970), a Harvard Law

School student who would serve as LDB's clerk for the 1926–1927 term. Despite LDB's urging that Page return to teach at Harvard, he went into private practice in New York City. In 1947, he became president of the Phelps Dodge Corporation. See 13 October 1929.

[3] See 8 November 1925, n. 2.

[4] It had become painfully obvious that the Palestine Economic Corporation did not possess the resources necessary to accomplish the investments it hoped to make in Palestine. With Bernard Flexner serving as the negotiator, arrangements had been concluded with the Jewish Agency to absorb an enlarged P.E.C. The Jewish Agency, still in the process of formation, was Chaim Weizmann's attempt to fashion an organization that would enlist the support of wealthy non-Zionists in the upbuilding of Palestine. LDB, while personally opposed to the absorbtion of the P.E.C., realized that he could do little to stop it.

[5] FF had made the acquaintance of the noted historian Carl Lotus Becker (1873–1945) the previous summer when he had taught at Cornell.

No. 207 December 11, 1925 Washington, D.C.

FF: 1. It is grand to have had three letters from you—the best evidence in itself that all goes well.[1] And that just received tells of your homegoing today. Take very good care not to overdo.

2. What you write of the Faculty discussions & attitude is most encouraging. I guess RP will have to fall into line. It's fatal for a man who has kinks to go away & let his associates coagulate.

3. Susan is making an unambitious marriage upon which we look hopefully.[2] She is very sure of herself. And the year of their acquaintance has been unquestionably the year of her best development.[3]

4. George Rublee was in yesterday in great happiness over Ray [Stevens]'s appointment.[4]

5. Carl Becker said apropos R.P. & the Wisconsin presidency:[5] "When a man writes a good book, they want to make him keep books." Our congratulations to Marion.

[1] See preceding letter, n. 1.

[2] LDB's daughter was engaged to Jacob H. Gilbert (1883–1966), a lawyer whom she had met in New York when the two were on opposite sides of a minor litigation. They were married at the end of December.

[3] During the year Susan Brandeis had argued a case before the United States Supreme Court (her father, naturally, absenting himself from the bench and from any deliberation regarding the case); she thus became the first woman in American history to accomplish this feat.

[4] See 8 November 1925, n. 2.

[5] See 23 January 1925, n. 6.

No. 208 December 27, 1925 Washington, D.C.

FF: 1. I am very sorry for Wise and for the Cause that he should have precipi[ta]ted the Jesus incident at this time upon a "united" Jewry.[1]

Three months later, after a successful campaign, it might have served a valuable purpose i.a. in advertising the fact of Klausner's book[2] & that through it that already something is going to [*] from the Palestine Renaissance.

2. That was a characteristically generous and gallant act of Nathan Straus.[3]

3. In my talk with Wise (and wife) Dec. 15 (which went off I think very satisfactorily) I made clear to him as I had to Mack the day before my personal sadness over the Zionist situation & which [sic] I couldn't take part in the Campaign in any way.

4. Do you know anything of Waldo Frank's operations? I think he married one of my (Naumburg) relations.[4]

5. My talk with B.F. was short & pleasant. I said nothing to him of matters I had talked with Mack & Wise.

6. That memo on "trial trips" of young men at H.L.S. to which JWM. referred was (as I recall) in the form of a letter to Judge Loring,[5] as Chairman of the Visting Comtee of which I was a member. I haven't a copy here—may pick one up when I am again in Boston. The date was probably somewhere in the late nineties.

6. I have heard nothing from R.P. since he called on Alice's Monday & rather hope I shall not. I know we should not agree; & he would probably say something that would compel dissent on my part.

7. I will ask Miss Malloch to deposit in your special account on Jan 1st or 2d Two thousand (2000) as heretofore & to advise you.

8. Eugene Meyer was in Xmas day—cheerful & not, I fancy, very busy. I rather think, from what he said, that he was instrumental in placing Gerry at Miller & Otis. He certainly recommended G. to accept & M. & O. to take him.[6]

Our best to you & Marion for the New Year.

[1] On 20 December 1925, Stephen S. Wise delivered a sermon entitled "A Jew's View of Jesus." In it, Wise acknowledged that Jesus was a real figure, not a myth—although denying his divinity and emphasizing his "Jewishness." The angry outcry from elements of the Jewish community was tremendous (the Yiddish newspaper *Tageblatt* accused him of leading "the younger generation to the baptismal font"), and a lengthy debate ensued.

[2] Wise's sermon was based on Joseph Klausner's *Jesus of Nazareth: His Life, Times and Teaching.* The book had been published in 1922, but not translated into English until 1925. Joseph Gedaliah Klausner (1874–1958) had moved to Palestine after the Russian Revolution and taught literature, literary criticism, and history at the Hebrew University.

[3] One of the aftermaths of Wise's sermon was a demand for his resignation from the chair of the United Palestine Appeal. Straus wrote Wise urging him not to resign and donating $150,000 for social work in Palestine in addition to the $500,000 he had previously pledged. Wise sent in his resignation to the UPA; but on 3 January 1926, after an outpouring of support from many nonorthodox Jews, the organization refused to accept it.

[4] Waldo David Frank (1889–1967), a well-known writer and man of letters, was a contributing editor to *The New Republic*. In 1916 he had married Margaret Naumburg, a pioneering New York City educator. The couple later divorced. There were numerous Naumburgs in LDB's family tree, most of them stemming from the marriage of his great aunt, Bertha Wehle to a Naumburg.

[5] William Caleb Loring (1851–1930) was a Boston lawyer and minor public official. He served as associate justice of the Supreme Judicial Court of Massachusetts from 1899 to 1919, and during the 1920s lectured at Harvard on legal practice.

[6] Gerard Henderson had worked for Eugene Meyer at the War Finance Corporation. He resigned in 1925 to join the New York law firm of Miller & Otis.

No. 209   January 6, 1926   Washington, D.C.

0. I found nothing worthy in Hale's article except the reference to Philip P. Wells'[1] article.

1. The recent interstate commerce cases lead me to suggest again that a state bloc in Congress be educated to the necessity of a quasi Wilmot Proviso[2] on all legislation involving the debatable ground between state & federal powers.

2. Your Economist friends should comment on:

   A. Hoover's solicitude to protect auto manufacturers & users from excessive rubber costs[3]—of material necessarily imported. Although in 1913, rubber per pound cost 57 cents per pound in 1926[4] rubber per pound cost only 38 1/2 cents while

   B. He makes no comment on the increased cost of other articles also used.

(a) steel billet in	Nov 1913	$23.50 per gross ton
(open hearth [*])	Oct '26	35.00
(b) oil (Kans. Okla)	Oct '13	$1.03 per barrell[sic]
	Oct '26	2.37

Articles produced in this country; also

(c) coal (Bitum.)	Oct '13	$1.40 per ton
	Oct '26	2.25

3. Our materialistic friends have expanded the greeting of wishes for a happy new year, to "Happy & Prosperous New Year."

We are giving ever new evidence that

"Nichts ist schwerer zu ertragen
Als ein Reihe von schonen Tagen."[5]

[1] Philip Patterson Wells (1868–1929), a former student, librarian, and instructor at the Yale Law School, was an expert in the law of forestry and conservation. LDB had worked with him briefly in the Pinchot-Ballinger conservation controversy.

[2] The Wilmot Proviso of 1846 was intended to prohibit slavery in all newly acquired U.S. territory. It never became law.

[3] Hoover entered into a long campaign of criticism against the price of imported rubber and, particularly, the control of the supply by the British. See, for example, his testimony before the House Committee on Interstate and Foreign Commerce, summarized in the *New York Times*, 7 January 1926.

[4] LDB apparently meant "1925" here and throughout the letter.

[5] "Nothing is harder to endure than a series of beautiful days."

No. 210   January 10, 1926   Washington, D.C.

FF: 1. Alice hopes you have seen something of Auntie B. She was hard hit by her sister Eugenia's death—although to Eugenia the passing was a great mercy.

2. Alice sends enclosed about Eustace Percy. The lot of those who practice economy in government is not an easy one.[1]

3. The most important advice one can give Buckner is to persist—not only in the course taken, but in office. He should take (internally) the vow not to quit before the end of the four years. Time is the great factor in real achievement.

4. Gus Hand should be led to have gathered the statistic—of time spent by his Court, say in the last 5 years, on cases under #215 (Postal frauds). He spoke to me of this burden—especially great because of the length of the trials. If & when his data is worked up, he, or someone, ought to get them from the other districts. The law is bad as criminal legislation. If we can get rid of the postal fraud cases, we shall get rid also of one of the largest & most pestilential body of detectives, masquerading under the title of inspectors.

5. Hoover's talk on foreign monopolies (rubber et al) is more mischievous even, and less justified, than his anti-bolshevist scare. His statistics would do honor to a Nordau.[2]

Note in this connection clipping on Philippine hemp monopoly enclosed.[3]

6. When Powell gives us his annual reflections on the performances of USSC, he will doubtless have something to say of recent developments re stare decisis[4] re hearings & dissents.

7. Wont Landis be able to do some of the things you hoped for in their vacation times[?][5]

[1] Eustace Percy was serving as president of the National Board of Education in England. In response to the retrenchment efforts of the Baldwin government, he issued a circular restricting funds for local educational development. The resulting outcry was intense and bitter, and it came both from radicals and conservatives. Percy withdrew the circular as a result of this two-sided pressure.

[2] Max Nordau (1849–1923), a philosopher and social analyst, had been one of the elder

statesmen of the Zionist movement. Nordau refused the presidency of the Zionist Organization after Herzl's death and maintained a middle ground between various factions.

[3] General Leonard Wood, governor of the islands, had just approved a law prohibiting the export of abaca seeds from the Philippines, thereby attempting to secure a monopoly there on hemp. See *New York Times*, 6 January 1926.

[4] *Stare decisis* is the legal doctrine that demands adherence to precedent in the resolution of a present case.

[5] James M. Landis accepted a position at Harvard Law School upon the completion of his duties as LDB's secretary. On 1 January LDB had written FF: "My congratulations on securing Landis already next year. I think it wiser for him not to wait. He is so mature that he has less need than the ordinary teacher for a preliminary bout at the bar."

No. 211   January 24, 1926   Washington, D.C.

FF: 1. The coincidence of dropping the Wheeler prosecution & the shame of Daugherty ought not to pass without scathing rebuke of C.C & the Department of Justice.[1]

2. As to Wheeler. He ought to be induced to vow that he will devote himself unreservedly to stamping out the spy system in the federal government. That, with due aid, should be his task. It would be potent as ladder & pedestal; and it will, if accomplished, be a worthy movement.

3. The N.R. & the [New York] World should not let pass the farmers' surplus agitation without uncovering a fundamental cause of the farmers' plight—the gross overvaluation of the land. It is not only the most wide-spread of all causes, but is far reaching in its consequences. I think the farm economists would have to admit that (excluding the war years) farms in the last 25 yrs have not earned anything like a fair return on their selling price in the rich territory of the midwest. Iowa lands today could easily earn a fair return on say $75 to $100 an acre. The cry is that it doesn't on $300 to $400. Many owners (of the equity) have paid that much. Many others have leased on that basis. Carl Vrooman[2] admitted to us that on his Iowa or Illinois lands he is getting 50% of the crop & furnishing only the land with improvements tax free. That means, of course, that every tenant must support, in effect, two families. The overvaluation has promoted the evil of tenancy.[3]

The indirect effects of the overvaluation are i.a. the heavy burdens incurred for taxation & other things, which never would have been dreamed of, but for the land inflation.

The common answer is that farmers have gotten their pay for a generation largely in the increment of value. That is—in plain English—that the farms have produced a very small income & hence are not worth anything like the selling values. There is little probability that any real & permanent improvement can come without rectifying the fundamental situation. Of course, it is very, very difficult. But there ought to be at least a peep hole into the truth.

4. The other fundamental need is integrating agriculture, thus letting people move to the producing territory instead of expecting miracles in cheap transportation. Manufactures etc. should move to the raw material.

5. You certainly have done much effective work through the World.

6. I am not surprised at what you say of R.P.

7. I hope your Social Science Research Council wont "formulate" anything until after a long period of secret conference a la Fed[eral] Const[itutional] Convention.

8. *Who* are the Milton Research Fund? I should think Mass. a peculiarly fit place for such a survey[4]—because the difficulties inherent in getting at causes would probably be less there than in any large community in the U.S. But I guess that only a very small part of the causes are technical or professional; and that one will have constantly to bear in mind

"Sie sprechen eine Sprache, die ist so lieb [sic], so schon, Doch keine der Philologen kann diese Sprache verstehen."[5]

9. The proposal to publish R.P. papers would now meet with greater favor with [*]—in view of [*] new trend.

10. That is a fine letter from the Boston Carmen's Union & does them great credit.

11. I hope C. W. Pound will realize how much work is required of him if the judicial statistics are to be of much value. Some of his opinions indicate that he does not realize the value of hard work in that field.

12. You did well to bring to the [New York] Herald Gus Hand's views on Registration.

13. OWH enters his 4th week of the sitting in quite as good shape as he did any. His work in Court & in Conference has never been better.

14. I am glad to see your article in the latest HLR.[6]

15. Some political science man with a historical sense & style should use the interesting parallel afforded by the recent Mass[achusetts] movement to protect by state action the small cities from financial irregularities of officials and the limitation of local expenditures—with the con-

trol gradually assumed by the Imperial Prussian Govt (in the time of the good Emperor) on account of the dishonesties & extravagancies over the finances of the many city states—and the gradual emasculation of the local civic & political life, and thereby the destruction of the great training ground for political etc. leaders.

Duruy's "Rome" has many interesting passages on this.[7]

[1] There were two developments in the ongoing political scandal investigations within the same week: the Department of Justice announced that it would not appeal the decision of the Washington, D.C., Supreme Court, which voided the indictment against Burton K. Wheeler (see 25 May 1924, n. 4); and former Attorney General Daugherty was cited for contempt of court for refusing to answer questions before the federal grand jury. The "scathing rebuke" LDB wanted came from Wheeler himself in a Senate speech on 4 February. In that speech he denounced the Department of Justice and the attitude of Coolidge who, Wheeler said, seemed more interested in shielding the department than in seeing justice done.

[2] Carl Schurz Vrooman (1872–1966), a publicist and writer specializing in farming problems, had been assistant secretary of agriculture in the Wilson administration.

[3] See next letter and also 1 February 1926.

[4] FF was about to embark upon another crime survey, modeled in part on the work he and Roscoe Pound had done at Cleveland. This one was to examine Boston, and it was designed to explore the "effect of legal control on the restraining of crime and the efficacy of the law's treatment of criminals." LDB would make numerous suggestions to FF regarding the work. The Boston crime survey never was completed, but three volumes appeared in 1934.

[5] "They [the stars] speak a language so majestic, so beautiful, and yet no linguist can understand this speech." LDB misquoted, substituting "lieb" (lovely) for "reich" in the original. The quotation is from Heine's *Buch der Lieder* of 1851.

[6] The article was another instalment in the series, "The Business of the Supreme Court of the United States: A Study in the Federal Judicial System," *Harvard Law Review* 39 (1926): 325.

[7] See 1 September 1925, n. 2.

No. 212   January 26, 1926   Washington, D.C.

FF: Enclosed from Ripley and Harrigan requires your attention. I wrote Ripley that I don't remember.[1] Please write Harrigan also.

If your agricultural economist is historical minded,[2] I hope he will tell us whether history records any dirt farmer who has rendered unto the landlord as much as 50% of the gross product. And note the Iowa tenant referred to supplied really a part of the plant—i.e. the agricultural implements as well as supplies to run them & the seed. My impression is that the temple slaves of Asia, the Prussian tenants, the tenants of the monastery lands & even the French peasants before the Revolution—though worse off in fact—did not yield to their landlords any such part of the product of the land.[3]

[1] William Z. Ripley, who was writing about both railroads and banks during these months, wanted the source for a quotation by LDB.

No. 213   January 28, 1926   Washington, D.C.

1. L & N. RR Co. v. Rice, 247 U.S. 201 (see 1914 removal provision) suggests opportunity for nibbling at needless Federal jurisdiction. [1]

2. Our N.Y. friends are not very sympathetic on plans for reducing federal receiverships.

3. I hope Wheeler will direct his efforts to eliminating the spy from the federal service, & not tackle also the labor spy which this week's Christian Century talks of his doing. [2]

4. Thatcher [sic] talks well. H.F.S. is very proud of having appointed him.

5. I am daily more impressed with the judicial murder being committed by incompetent & careless [*] lawyers, particularly those for labor unions and public bodies. Something emphatic and comprehensive should be said on this, and that many times.

Couldn't Richberg lead other unions to select some good lawyers like himself.

6. Your tale of [*] is almost surprising, but Francis Peabody (at least a good fellow) explains much. I don't wonder Williston is ashamed of his fellows.

7. Susan's office will remain for the immediate future at Woolworth Building. They are living, for the present at Hotel Astor until an apartment in that neighborhood shall have been secured & made habitable.

8. The clipping is from Susan's Jack. [3] He has had much experience at the criminal bar, is a good lawyer, & thinks it would be well for you to talk over Criminal Administration with him some day.

Is Bond C.J. a son of Hugh Bond who was General Counsel of the B & O a generation ago—a very good lawyer who worked himself to death? [4]

---

[1] *Louisville & Nashville Railroad* v. *Rice*, 247 U.S. 201, decided on 20 May 1918. The railroad sued Rice for $145 (the cost of disinfecting livestock cars). The district court decided it lacked jurisdiction in the case, citing Section Twenty-eight of the Judicial Code, that removal from a state to a federal court had to involve a sum of more than $3000. The Supreme Court, speaking through Justice McReynolds, reversed, and ruled that the lower court had jurisdiction because it had to interpret the Interstate Commerce Act. LDB was intrigued by the possibility of limiting federal jurisdiction by setting a higher dollar limit on such cases.

[2] See 24 January 1926. "Congress Asked to Investigate Labor Spy System," *Christian Century* 43 (28 January 1926): 101.

³Jack Gilbert had sent LDB a clipping from the *New York Times* giving New York State's police statistics for 1925. The state constabulary made 25,734 arrests and obtained 23,364 convictions.

⁴Carroll Taney Bond (1873–1943) had been a judge since 1911 and chief judge of the Maryland Court of Appeals since 1924. He was not the son of Hugh Lennox Bond (1858–1922), the railroad attorney whom LDB describes.

No. 214   February 1, 1926   Washington, D.C.

FF: 1. Butler's priority opinions Jan 11—will add another discourager to friendly receiverships.[1] (This was written before receiving B. Hand's letter on the subject.)

2. With the rising tide against overloading federal courts, would it not be well to make some preparatory moves toward reducing the civil jurisdiction. I suppose diversity of citizenship can't be wholly gotten rid of in ordinary cases, but some nibbling might be done. How would it do to try to increase the limit from $3000 to $6000—or even higher? To take away the jurisdiction established in Lee v. C & O Ry Co. 260 U.S. 653 & even as to original jurisdiction?[2] To take away removal in suits of shippers under interstate Com. laws. (So. Pacific v. Stewart, 245 U.S. 359, 562[3]) similar to provision in Employer's Liability Act? Or even to go further & take away original jurisdiction? To reduce the jurisdiction re National Banks? Nibbling would do a lot of good, if persisted in.

3. A passage in Feb 5 N.R. which I attribute to you suggests:

"Du bist am Ende was du bist.
Setz dir Perucken auf von millionen Locken,
Setz deiner Feuss auf ellen hohen Socken,
Du bleibtst am Ende was du bist."[4]

4. Alice fears that my reference to Carl Vrooman's leases on shares may lead you to think he is a rack-renter.[5] Of course, he is among the best of landlords. You doubtless recall the report of the U.S. Commissioner on Industrial Relations of 1915 on this subject.

5. Walter Meyer was in Sunday. There is evidently considerable disgruntlement in the P.E.C. with B.F.'s procrastination. Walter thinks it was he who saved the trick. I hope B.F. will not delay now.[6] He should be in Palestine by early March.

6. There is much talk here of Coolidge steamroller on World Court[7]—that the Senators (backed by constituents) were opposed in numbers sufficient to defeat the measure, but that they didn't dare to

229

oppose the administration. The feeling raised by the cloture is very intense. Your excellent letter to the Herald[8] should go to those who you think would be strengthened by it. The tendency to repress Congress to which you call attention is as serious and stupid as anything that could be imagined in the political field.

7. We had the Shepards in last week. I hope you are getting something re Spies. We are to see the Hamiltons tomorrow & I will try to poke him up.

8. Indiana is waking up—with your aid.

9. Very sorry to hear Cardozo has been so unwell.

10. Did you find the reference to my statement quoted by Ripley?[9] & what is it?

11. There are certainly dangers ahead re P[ublic] U[tility]. Valuations.

12. H.F.S. talked to Norman with great pride of what he did as A.G.—including in its results—Buck[ner]—Daugherty exposure etc.

[1] On 11 January, Justice Butler handed down four cases involving the Priority Act for distributing the assets of bankrupts. 269 U.S. 483, 492, 503, and 504. Perhaps the most important was *Price* v. *U.S.* (492) where Butler ruled that taxes due to the United States are "debts" within the meaning of the Act.

[2] In *Lee* v. *Chesapeake & Ohio Railway Co.*, decided in January 1923, Van Devanter expanded the "diversity of citizenship" prerogatives of defendants. Lee, a citizen of Texas, sued for an injury sustained in Kentucky while boarding a train of the Chesapeake & Ohio Railway, a "citizen" of Virginia. Lee brought suit in the Kentucky state court, but the company successfully petitioned for removal to federal district court. Lee wanted the case remanded to the state court, but the Supreme Court denied his challenge.

[3] In this 1917 case, Stewart charged that his cattle had been injured and several had died while being shipped by the railroad. The company petitioned to remove the case to district court which found in favor of Stewart as did the circuit court of appeals. Thereupon the railroad appealed to the Supreme Court on a writ of error and eventually the Court scheduled the case for rehearing.

[4] Probably the unsigned editorial (*New Republic* 45 [3 February 1926]: 279) criticizing Justice Stone for voting with the majority rather than dissenting with LDB and Holmes on the matter of upholding an Oklahoma law. "Apparently Mr. Justice Stone does not find it congenial to shiver with Holmes and Brandeis; he prefers the warmth of the solid majority." The German poem reads:

"You are in the end what you are
Put on wigs of millions of locks
Put on your feet very high socks
You remain in the end what you are."

[5] See 24 January 1926.

[6] Walter Meyer was treasurer of the Palestine Economic Corporation. The organization was attempting to define its program in Palestine, and had announced its intention to develop hydro-electric power projects and build some low-cost workers' housing.

[7] The Permanent Court of International Justice had been established in the League of Nations Covenant and was declared open in May 1922. The United States, though not part of the League itself, was eligible to participate in the court, and a debate raged over whether or not to join. The

Senate isolationists, men who had done so much to defeat the Treaty of Versailles, were dead against American participation despite President Coolidge's warm endorsement. They resorted to delaying tactics and the addition of "reservations"—the same tactics that had defeated the treaty. The isolationists had mounted a filibuster in the Senate on 15 January; but on 25 January, cloture was voted 68–26. The opponents responded by offering new reservations and the debate dragged on for years. The United States never joined the World Court although several Americans served as judges.

[8] No letter from FF appeared in the *Herald* at this time, nor is there any copy of an unpublished letter on this subject in the FF Papers.

[9] See 26 January 1926, n. 1.

No. 215   February 12, 1926   Washington, D.C.

FF: Isn't there among your economists some one who could make clear to the country that the greatest of social-economic troubles arise from the fact [that] the consumer has failed absolutely to perform his function? He lies not only supine, but paralyzed & deserves to suffer like others who take their lickings "lying down."

He gets no worse than his deserts. But the trouble is that the parallelogram of social forces is disrupted thereby. It destroys absolutely the balance of power & lets producers and distributors "trim the balance of the world" as CC would say.[1]

Ripley showed cleverness & courage as well as discernment in his recent essay.[2] But no real good can come from it. The curse of bigness rests upon such endeavor.

But consumers—if they did their duty—could be as effective continuously as they were momentarily in 1920 by the Buyers' Strike.[3]

As for the Consumers' League—lucus a non lucendo[4]—usurping functions not theirs.

[1] See 6 March 1925.

[2] See 8 November 1925.

[3] Beginning in the late spring of 1920, a nationwide nonbuying movement had been deemed successful in lowering prices on selected commodities.

[4] "A grove [lucus] is so called because it excludes the light [lux]"—that is, a ridiculous appellation, a misnomer.

No. 216   February 15, 1926   Washington, D.C.

FF: 1. Holmes J. had, I think, merely one of the customary colds, which rack him 2 or 3 times a term. He was housed a week, beginning a fortnight ago; has since been out driving every day for about a week; and he attended Conference Saturday in pretty good shape. I see no occasion for anxiety.

2. The C.J. is off for a week in Atlanta, and H.F.S. said at Saturday's Conference that he expects to take some days off in Florida with Hoover on the latter's (I suppose USA's) "boat."

3. What the Spy system needs is not investigation, but limitation, and gradual extirpation, by means of the appropriation bills.[1]

4. Your correspondence with John Hay[n]es Holmes[2] is good enough for publication. His own paper is abler than I had thought him capable of. Of course you laid him out. Senator Walsh was in for a dinner last Thursday in his best form. In the course of his talk, he furnished a fine example to point your tale. I talked to him of the terrible action of the Senate Democrats on the Revenue Bill.[3] He said that he had given it no attention in the Comtee, being absorbed in the World Court, & relying on the Senator from N.C.[4]

Mack was in on route to Florida, in a happy mood. I suppose talking Palestine is nearly as good fun as dancing. Van Vriesland was also in. He has grown much since 1919.

[1] See next letter and 23 June 1926.

[2] John Haynes Holmes (1869–1964), pastor of the Community Church in New York from 1907 to 1949, was a close friend and ally of Stephen Wise's in numerous liberal causes, and a leading Christian ally of Zionism. He published *Unity*, a journal of liberal political and Christian thought.

[3] The Revenue Act of 1926, which reduced taxes on the wealthy, had just been passed by the Senate. The Democrats, instead of providing opposition, fully supported the measure, and it passed by a vote of fifty-eight to nine.

[4] Furnifold McLendel Simmons (1854–1940) represented North Carolina in the Senate for thirty years. The ranking Democrat on the Finance Committee, he had voted for the tax reduction, and defended his fellow Democrats for joining his lead; see his statement in the *New York Times*, 12 February 1926.

No. 217 February 23, 1926 Washington, D.C.

FF: 1. I enclose letter for Auntie B. which please read, and hand to her in due time. I prefer that it be not read at the dinner.[1] But if you think that it will add materially to her joy, you are at liberty to read it.

2. The quotation from a letter to Powell which you sent, I note. As Herbert White says: "I see."

3. The Wheelers were in yesterday & I talked to both about the campaign against spying, mentioning the Appropriations bill as the field for attack. He will need much education from you to become effective in this. Of course, he ought to master the specific facts as to each item of spy-appropriation in each bill; & with thorough knowledge, make a speech on each on the proper occasion.[2]

[1] FF was organizing a public dinner to celebrate Elizabeth Glendower Evans's seventieth birthday on 28 February 1926.

[2] See preceding letter, and 23 June 1926.

No. 218   February 26, 1926   Washington, D.C.

FF: 1. Glad of your letter to Cummings.[1] Did I mention to you that I had suggested to Walsh, when he was in to dine, the desirability of cutting down jurisdiction of D.Cts? He said he would come in some day to talk about it.

2. What Beveridge says as to the gagged Senators is common talk here. It would be a healthy thing if Borah and Jim Reed[2] succeeded in defeating a few aspirants for re-election.

3. If it won't unduly re-open the correspondence with John Haynes Holmes, the New Leader clipping might well go to him.

4. I learned today from Miss Comstock[3] of Radcliffe's buildings scheme, & told her my views.

5. What would B. Hand like to accomplish?

6. If my history isn't wrong, we are now passing through the first experience in 50 years of actual retreat in social, political, economic progress as evidenced by legislation. Heretofore we had times of unrest, and reactionary administrations or reactionary public opinion, but never actual retreat. If this is true historically the N.R. or others ought to say so.

9. [sic] The N.R.'s "Confession of a Shirt Stuffer" is clever.[4]

10. Alice bids me refresh your memory as to this from Ruskin's Inaugural.[5]

"It is necessary for the English people to be reminded that the object of instruction here is not primarily attainment, but discipline, & that a youth is sent to our universities, not (hitherto at least) to be apprenticed into trade, nor even always to be advanced in a profession, but always to be made a gentleman and a scholar. But they must first understand that education, in its deepest sense, is not the equalizer, but the discoverer of men; and that, so far from being the instruments for the collection of riches, the first lesson of wisdom is to disdain them, and of gentleness, to diffuse."

11. We hope your dinner went off well.[6]

[1] Perhaps Homer Stille Cummings (1870–1956), a Connecticut attorney and activist in the Democratic party. An early supporter of Franklin D. Roosevelt, he was appointed attorney general and

served in that position until 1939. He was a leading figure in the president's plan to "pack" the United States Supreme Court in 1937.

[2] James Alexander Reed (1861–1944) had come up through Missouri Democratic politics to serve a long senatorial career, 1911–1929. For the story of how he was finally, and after much struggle, won over to support LDB for confirmation in 1916, see A. L. Todd, *Justice on Trial: The Case of Louis D. Brandeis* (New York: McGraw-Hill, 1964), 221–23.

[3] Ada Louise Comstock (1876–1973) had been a dean at Smith when she was called to the presidency of Radcliffe in 1923. In 1943, she left Radcliffe to marry Professor Wallace Notestein.

[4] *New Republic* 46 (3 March 1926): 35. The anonymous piece was a satirical examination of "Crackum Q. Bunkus," a businessman, and how he became prominent and well known.

[5] John Ruskin (1819–1900) was one of the best known art and architecture critics of his age. The Inaugural Lecture was delivered at Oxford in 1870, as Ruskin began, as Slade Professor, his course on "Lectures on Art."

[6] For Mrs. Evans; see preceding letter.

No. 219   March 8, 1926   Washington, D.C.

FF: 1. O.W.H. has approached the day in fine form, physically & mentally, & in excellent spirits.[1]

2. We are very sorry to have missed the Sunday with you. But of course, you had to stand by R.P's side—He needs more than that.

3. Since reading Pres. Comstock's Annual Report, I am confirmed in my attack on her Brick & Mortar policy.[2]

4. You did well in writing Herman. Sometime, when you can do so innocently, ask Alfred Bettman, who probably has a copy of Newt. Baker's oral argument in the Village of Euclid Zoning Case before our Court, to let you see it. And note the closing paragraphs on giving "industry a free hand."[3]

5. Kirchwey has written a very unworthy article on the Crime Wave in the latest Survey.[4]

6. I called Wambaugh's[5] attention to the N.R. article on "Confession of a Shirt Stuffer,"[6] & recd an appreciative, characteristic reply.

7. Alice sends special thanks for your letter on Auntie B's birthday party.[7]

8. No, T. J. Norton did not argue 417—J. W. Terry appeared for the Santa Fe.[8]

9. I guess 315 gave most pain.[9]

[1] On this date, Justice Holmes celebrated his eighty-fifth birthday. See next two letters.

[2] See preceding letter.

[3] The landmark case, *Euclid* v. *Ambler Realty Co.*, 272 U.S. 359, was argued on 27 January, reargued on 12 October, and finally decided on 22 November 1926. Newton D. Baker represented the owner of a tract of land in the Cleveland suburb. The village had passed a comprehensive zoning

ordinance prohibiting all industrial uses in certain areas, and the landowner charged that this ordinance deprived him of liberty and property without due process of law. The lower court found the ordinance unconstitutional. But the Supreme Court, speaking through Justice Sutherland (and with Van Devanter, McReynolds, and Butler dissenting), argued that zoning ordinances were a necessary part of the modern world of urbanization, that, while the "meaning" of constitutional guarantees does not change, their "application" has to be modified in view of changing conditions, and that, in this case, the Euclid ordinance was within the police powers of the village. Baker couched his argument in terms of free enterprise: "That our cities should be made beautiful and orderly is, of course, in the highest degree desirable, but it is even more important that our people should remain free. . . ." (379).

[4] George W. Kirchwey, "Crime Waves and Crime Remedies," *Survey* 55 (1 March 1926): 593; the article was a chatty introduction to an issue devoted to the crime problem. George Washington Kirchwey (1885–1942) had been one of the Columbia Law School and Kent Professor of Law at Columbia. He was particularly interested in criminology and served on many investigating commissions on the problems of crime and criminals.

[5] Eugene Wambaugh (1856–1940) had been at Harvard Law School with LDB in the late 1870s. After practicing in Ohio and teaching at the University of Iowa, he joined the Harvard faculty in 1892. He remained there until 1925, interspersing his professorial duties with various governmental assignments.

[6] See preceding letter, n. 4.

[7] See 23 February 1926.

[8] No. 417 was *Texas & Pacific Railway Co.* v. *Gulf, Colorado & Santa Fe Railway Co.*, 270 U.S. 266. John Wharton Terry (1860–1936), a Texas lawyer, argued for the Santa Fe, assisted by Thomas J. Norton.

[9] No. 315 was *Marion & Rye Valley Railway* v. *U.S.*, 270 U.S. 280; LDB handed down the decision for a unanimous Court on 1 March. The railroad sued to recover a $14,000 loss suffered while it was, technically, under the control of the United States, by provision of the wartime Federal Control Act of 1918. The Court denied the claim because the government, in reality, had exercised no control whatsoever over the railroad during the period in question.

No. 220   March 14, 1926   Washington, D.C.

FF: 1. OWH bore his birthday week in the pink of condition physically & mentally and in the most joyous spirits—despite heavy court work and nearly 100 letters answered. Your beautiful piece in the NR will add to his happiness. [1]

2. Newton Baker made an admirable argument in Wisconsin v. Illinois & the Chicago Sanitary District. [2] It was not only good in advocacy, it revealed grasp, vision and intellectual power of a high order. OWH & I agreed entirely on this. Pity B. has not the supporting character. He might, if he had, do great things.

3. That lack of character, of this strength, is our greatest weakness, impressed me more & more. I thought of it again last evening when a telegram from George C. Lee [3] advised me of Storrow's death. [4] S. might have been the first citizen of Boston—even of the old grand manner. He had ample ability & in station, means and perception of a changing

world would have been competent to deal with almost any situation. But whenever the supreme test came—he wasn't there.

4. A newspaper item says Mass. has gained in farm population about 30,000 since 1920—a very large percentage compared with a total of 150,000; also that the new farmers are individual owners of the farms, presumably small farms and cheap land. If the item is true, it may have great significance. Isn't there some economist who can think as well as plod, who will look into the matter & interpret it?

5. As bearing on my enquiry of some months ago, of our Western and Southern rapacious farm rack-renting,[5] I suppose you noticed in Hirst's Jefferson[6] p. 217, that in France the rents of the agricultural laborers were "about half" of the produce and "English rents about a third." But neither English or French tenants provided expensive plant like the modern agricultural machinery.

6. Who wrote "Governors as State Bosses" in N.R.? The concluding paragraph is particularly wise.[7] I fear this is another reform of "the easier way" kind. In this article it is always the last steps "that cost." The first are easy & seemingly bear good fruit.

7. The "Nickel Plate Decision" is also discerning.[8]

8. Buckner's talk on "Light Wines & Beer" is being much criticised by some of his one time ardent friends.[9]

9. The McCamant episode, of which the N.R. brought me the first detail, must be disturbing to Canny Cal, particularly after the Woodlock turn down.[10] Ad interim appointments to such offices are indefensible.

10. J. H. Holmes dies hard. But he learns a bit while protesting.

11. Elizabeth & Paul had Meiklejohn in with the Phil La Follettes[11] for supper & the talk did not break up until midnight. Phil & wife were tremendously impressed. Eliz. who heard M's first session with 70 students says he is a wonder.

12. Yes the U.S. Daily is a bright, valuable publication.[12] I have had the U. of Louisville subscribe & preserve the file.

13. Your report of Friendly & others of your students is cheering.[13]

14. The Boston Criminal survey[14] should bear rich fruit. I should think it perhaps the most promising of all fields for such an enquiry.

15. I wish to record my doubt as to the wisdom of AS's housing plan.[15]

[1] See preceding letter. FF's tribute was an unsigned editorial, "Mr. Justice Holmes," *New Republic* 46 (17 March 1926): 88. "The fruit of his wisdom has become part of the common stock of civilization. Wherever law is known, he is known."

[2] 270 U.S. 634. Baker, representing the state of Ohio, made his argument on a motion to

dismiss, on 10 March 1926. The dispute was referred on 22 March to a special master, Charles Evans Hughes.

[3] George Cabot Lee (1871–1950) was a Boston banker associated with James J. Storrow (see next note) in the Lee, Higginson Company.

[4] James Jackson Storrow (1864–1926) had died on 13 March. He was trained as a lawyer, but was ultimately more important as a banker. Storrow was always active in civic undertakings in Boston.

[5] See 24 and 26 January 1926.

[6] Francis W. Hirst, *The Life and Letters of Thomas Jefferson* (New York: Macmillan, 1926).

[7] The unsigned editorial, *New Republic* 46 (17 March 1926): 85, examined the report of the Hughes Commission on the reorganization of the New York state government. While generally favorable, the writer raised questions about centralizing power in the hands of the governor.

[8] *Ibid.*: 87–88. The editorial discussed the refusal of the Interstate Commerce Commission to approve the Nickel Plate Railroad merger. The disapproval came, not on the grounds of economic feasibility, nor of public desirability, but on the basis of the questionable way the deal had been promoted.

[9] Buckner's speech before the Economic Club of New York on 3 March advocated experimentation with the prohibition on light wines and beer.

[10] Raymond Clapper, "Portrait of a Federal Judge," *New Republic* 46 (17 March 1926): 96, was a slashing attack on Wallace F. McCamant (1867–1944), who had nominated Coolidge for the vice-presidency in 1920, and was given an interim appointment as judge of the Circuit Court of Appeals for the Ninth Circuit. When the time arrived for his confirmation by the Senate, Hiram Johnson revealed that McCamant held some unusually bizarre opinions. He had once called LDB an "avaricious mountebank," and labelled Theodore Roosevelt "un-American" for favoring recall of judicial decisions. The nomination was referred back to the Judiciary Committee and it failed of confirmation. Thomas Francis Woodlock (1866–1945) was an Irish immigrant associated for many years with *The Wall Street Journal*. Because he was a specialist in railroad affairs, Coolidge nominated him for the Interstate Commerce Commission. Woodlock's nomination was confirmed, but only after an adverse committee recommendation, a protracted Senate debate, and rumors of a "deal" with President Coolidge.

[11] Philip Fox La Follette (1897–1965) had been trained to politics by his father, the Senator, from an early age. He eventually served as governor of Wisconsin in 1931–1933 and again in 1935–1939.

[12] The new newspaper had begun publication on 4 March, under the editorship of David Lawrence.

[13] FF's praise of Henry Jacob Friendly (1903–1986) was well founded. After serving as LDB's clerk, 1927–1928, Friendly went on to a distinguished career as a lawyer and, after 1959, as a circuit court judge and chief judge. In 1926, he was in the process of planning his career, and he and his parents appealed to LDB and FF for their advice; see 28 October and 9 November, 1926.

[14] See 24 January 1926, n. 4.

[15] Alfred Emanuel Smith (1873–1944) was one of the genuinely colorful and influential politicians of his generation. A poor boy from New York's lower East Side, he had risen through machine politics to the speakership of the state assembly. He became associated with an important group of New York social workers and championed liberal causes. With wide public support he won the governorship in 1918, but was defeated in the Republican landside of 1920. He swept back into power in 1922, and was reelected in 1924 and 1926. As governor he compiled a solid progressive record, and in 1924 made his first attempt to secure the Democratic presidential nomination. In 1928 Smith became the first Catholic nominated by any major party, but Herbert Hoover easily defeated him by more than six million votes.

Governor Smith had transmitted a comprehensive housing plan to the state legislature in late February, involving, among other proposals, destroying outmoded tenements and replacing them with model housing. See *New York Times*, 23 February 1926, and next letter.

237

No. 221   ~March 21, 1926   Washington, D.C.

FF: 1. I think I have never seen O.W.H. so joyously playful as now. He said yesterday at luncheon that the last 15 years—"his old age"—had been unquestionably the happiest period of his life.

2. Enclosed editorial from J of C (which appeared since I wrote you) touches on the objections to Smith's housing plan which I had in mind.[1] I stated the objection to Alfred Bettman who (with wife) were [sic] with us Friday evening. I think both in this matter & in his state reorganization [Smith] shows the qualities of a social minded, enlightened, efficient administrator—but not of a far-seeing statesman.

3. No. 10. was argued by Walter Pollock [sic]. Noscitur a sociis.[2]

4. A trustworthy lawyer from the South who was in yesterday said his rich clients had said in 1924—"we hope Coolidge will be elected, but, of course, we cant vote for him." I think there may be more dangerous reactions from rich southerners, who have gotten so without much effort, than has attended the more laborious process in the North.

5. Anti-Court and Anti League Senators are having some "schadenfreude."[3]

6. The Journal of Commerce has data from Milan confirming N.R. Italian debt views & suggesting that the "balanced budget" is faked.[4]

7. I wonder who is carrying the French, Belgian & Italian loans to stabilize the currency, which J. P. Morgan & Co. made.

[1] The *Journal of Commerce* editorial of 16 March, entitled "Congestion and Housing," raised questions about the concentration of workers' housing in a central, overcrowded, congested area.

[2] "He is recognizable by his associates." No. 10 was an early stage of the landmark case of *Whitney* v. *California*. For this stage of the proceedings, see 269 U.S. 530, 538. For a fuller description and the outcome, see 21 May 1927, n. 4). Walter Pollak's "associates" for this part of the Whitney case were Walter Nelles and John F. Neylan.

[3] "malicious pleasure." For the background of the dispute over the World Court, see 1 February 1926, n. 7. The League of Nations debate was opened again by the irreconcilables in the Senate over a quite minor incident. Ambassador Alanson Houghton was reported to have returned from England with damning and pessimistic reports on the League and on European politics generally; when word of his alleged report was leaked to the press, a furious European reaction ensued. See *New York Times*, 22 and 23 March 1926.

[4] "The Dishonest Italian Settlement," *New Republic* 46 (24 March 1926): 132.

No. 222   April 8, 1926   Washington, D.C.

1. 263 U.S. 353 was written within a few weeks of the time—date—when it was taken over from another Justice. Quite a number of "long times" are due to the same cause. Many are due to the intentions of a minority to write a dissent. It not infrequently happens that the

dissent is never written. And sometimes the expected dissenter "shuts up" altogether. Delays of this nature extend sometimes over months. There are instances in which, in this manner, cases are carried over to another term & yet no dissent is written.[1]

2. Harold [Laski] has been in Monday, Tuesday, & Wednesday, & we have had much talk. It is cheering to find him substantially in agreement with you & me on American problems. "In unserer Bunde des Dritte."[2] A pretty small society these days. For the present, we have not Norman, who [h]as added to the League of Nations Faith, the Religion of Mass Production. E.A.F. should rejoice.

3. To the C.J.'s more judges—add Kocurek's [sic][3] Referendary. He seems to believe in all experts—expect[4] expert judges. Another Essay in the "easier way."

4. Sidney Hillman happened to come in while Harold was with me, & we three had an hour together, of which I shall have much to tell you. HJL. & S. are in agreement as to this also. Bob Bruere is to bring in Nash tomorrow.

[1]LDB might have made an erroneous citation here. There was no case beginning on p. 353. 263 U.S. 351 was *Hightower* v. *American National Bank*, a case involving the relationship between two banks, one of them in financial difficulty. It was argued on 25 January 1923 and decided on 3 December of that year—a longer than average delay, but not so strikingly long, perhaps, as to have attracted FF's attention. The opinion was written by Justice Van Devanter.

[2]"Our band of three."

[3]On 28 March, LDB had written that "the C.J. is clean mad on 'more judges.'" Albert Kocourek (1875–1952) was a Northwestern University law professor and writer on jurisprudence.

[4]LDB may have meant to write "except."

No. 223   April 29, 1926   Washington, D.C.

FF: 1. Alice bids me send you enclosed from George D. Pratt, Jr.[1] & asks you to let her know what you think of the project & specifically whether she should send some money.

2. The new Gospel of Service through mass production & instalment sales, suggests: "From God and Mammon to God via Mammon."—an Easier Way for the Ascent of Man.

3. G's letter to you indicates another Jos. Cotton. "And when he grew up, He was lost totally."[2]

[1]George Dwight Pratt, Jr. (1864–19[?]) was a Springfield, Massachusetts, insurance executive who resigned in 1901 to devote himself to various philanthropic, civic, educational, and charitable enterprises.

[2]Gilbert and Sullivan, *Patience*, Act 2.

No. 224   May 2, 1926   Washington, D.C.

I am inclined to think that the most copious & futile of the single wastes of our Court's efforts have been in the Federal Liability Cases both (a) before the Sept. 6, 1916 Act, on writ of error and (b) since, in granting certioraris [1]. It might be worthwhile to put one of your jurisdiction sharps on that enquiry.

[1] Section Two of that law permitted the Supreme Court to reexamine and reverse decisions from the highest state courts, just as if the cases had risen through the federal system. The same section also permitted the Court, by certiorari, to require reviews of such decisions in the state court systems. See 39 *U.S. Statutes* 448 (1916).

No. 225   May 13, 1926   Washington, D.C.

FF: 1. That is indeed a most encouraging performance by the British & should raise the world's estimate of their worth & value to civilization. And I am very glad of the part Herbert Samuel has played. [1]

2. The Polish performance is also characteristic. [2] Will Clarence Dillon [3] surrender his Order, & cry "give me back my legions?" I guess it will be "widows & orphans" who do the crying.

3. I am glad you have put up to Croly the Foundations. Their evil influence seems ever-more pervasive. [4]

4. As to Morawetz. You will recall Decker's Dutchess [sic]: [5]

"One who might indifferently be made
The Courting Stick for all to practice on"

5. Harlan still lisps not among his fellows on the N.Y. performance. But you still note his activity as purveyor of the fine arts.

6. That is good what you say of the Dean of Calif. L.S.'s [6] aims, & the Cornell letter is most encouraging.

7. The Passaic clippings are good. [7]

8. O.W.H. has finished the last of his assigned opinions & I hope he will take some rest now. He has talked much of being tired & rushed. No conference until May 27, & then nothing of importance for him in the way of work.

[1] Sir Herbert Samuel was taking a leading part in attempting to settle the British coal strike. On the basis of a formula of his devising, the coal workers' union had agreed to abandon its call for a general strike and to resume negotiations with the mine owners. Despite this encouraging sign of progress, however, the coal strike dragged on until November.

[2] Bloody street fighting had broken out in Warsaw during the week, leaving more than two hundred dead. The colorful and controversial war hero and nationalist, Joseph Pilsudski, emerged from retirement and eventually assumed dictatorial powers.

[3] Clarence Dillon (1882–1979) was a Texas-born financier, speculator, and international banker. In addition to unprecedentedly large dealings on Wall Street, Dillon arranged for financing for half a dozen European governments, and in 1925 was officially recognized for his services by the Polish government.

[4] Eventually Croly published "Foundations and Private Enterprise," *New Republic* 47 (14 July 1926): 216, an anonymous editorial pointing out the internal contradictions, wastefulness, and potential dangers of charitable foundations.

[5] Thomas Decker, or Dekker (1570–1641), was a popular and prolific English dramatist.

[6] The dean of the University of California Law School was Orrin Kip McMurray.

[7] Clippings doubtless related to the violent and bitter textile workers' strike centering in Passaic, New Jersey.

No. 226　　　　May 23, 1926　　　　Washington, D.C.

FF: 1. I concur as to Pepper. My high Republican friends, although they may regret Vare, have no tears for P.[1]

2. I had not heard of Morawetz's action. It may have been a flush of sentiment. He is a native of Baltimore, where his father was a physician.

3. I hadn't heard that the U.S.S.C. building project has been killed.[2] I hope so. But those who think otherwise have not mentioned the alleged death.

4. Senator Walsh has doubtless written you that there is again danger that the Sheldon bill[3] will be reported. The Sen. Judiciary [Committee] appears to be a terrible body.

5. The Sir Alfred Frederick Whites were in Thursday, & Rennie Smith on Tuesday.

6. The killing of the Haugen bill[4] is good legislative action, but may make trouble for C.C.

7. There will be much to talk over at Chatham.

[1] George Wharton Pepper had just been defeated in Pennsylvania's Republican primary for reelection to the Senate, in spite of huge financial contributions and vocal campaign support from Secretary of the Treasury Andrew Mellon. The defeat was followed by allegations, on both sides, of financial wrongdoing and excessive campaign spending; and in 1930, the Senate denied William Scott Vare (1867–1934), the man who had beaten Pepper, his seat on account of campaign excesses.

[2] For three quarters of a century the Supreme Court had met in the old Senate chamber of the Capitol building. There had been, from time to time, proposals to establish a building for the exclusive use of the Court, one that would symbolize the Court's role as one of the three coequal branches of the federal government. These proposals had always been lost and ignored—much to the satisfaction of LDB, who preferred the modest and Spartan quarters in the Capitol. At William Howard Taft's insistence, however, a palatial new building was planned and erected for the nine justices, and it was occupied and used for the first time at the opening of the October 1935 term. LDB, though, refused to occupy the suite of offices allotted to him in the new building, and until his retirement continued to work out of his home.

[3] There is no one by this name in the Congress at this time; perhaps LDB knew of a private bill submitted by or for a "Sheldon."

[4] The McNary-Haugen Bill was designed to meet the problem of agricultural surplus and

thereby to help relieve the farm crisis of the 1920s. It stipulated that the government buy surplus crops at a relatively high price and sell them abroad at the world price; farmers would pay an "equalization fee" to compensate the government's loss. The bill had a long, complex, and difficult history. It was first introduced in January 1924. It was rejected several times by the House (including a defeat during the week this letter was written—a defeat which had the full approval of President Coolidge). Eventually the bill was passed in early 1927, but Coolidge vetoed it on 25 February.

No. 227   June 22, 1926   Chatham, Mass.

FF: Thanks for the British works which shall go to Louisville. I have been re-reading Chafee's Freedom of Speech with ever growing admiration of his head, his heart and his character.[1]

What has become of McCurdy's enquiry into the P.A.[2] & Van Vleck's into the Immigration Dept?[3]

Couldn't you get started through your men a series for the HLR covering the danger of arbitrariness etc. in the several federal Depts & Bureaus? The impending change re naturalization & deportation suggests thought & may suggest preventive remedies.[4]

In 1819, Jefferson wrote in acknowledging a copy of the No Amer Review: "I see with pride that we are ahead of Europe in Political Science."[5]

And in the same year this: "And if Caesar had been as virtuous as he was daring and sagacious, what could he, even in the plenitude of his usurped powers have done to lead his fellow citizens into good government? I do not say to *restore it*, because they never had it from the rape of the Sabines to the ravages of the Caesars."[6]

[1] Zechariah Chafee, *Freedom of Speech* (New York: Harcourt, Brace, and Howe, 1920).
[2] McCurdy, LDB's former clerk, now teaching at Harvard, published nothing on public administration.
[3] See 16 September 1923, n. 4.
[4] Both houses of Congress were considering modifications in deportation rules (increasing the number of those deported and the reasons for deportation) and naturalization (with an eye to speeding the process).
[5] Jefferson to John Adams, 19 January 1819.
[6] Jefferson to John Adams, 10 December 1819.

No. 228   June 23, 1926   Chatham, Mass.

FF: I omitted to ask you what progress is being made in the effort to reduce the appropriations for spies in the public service.[1] It may take a generation to rid our country of this pest, but I think it probably can be done, if the effort is persistent and we are prepared for action when, in the course of time, "the day" comes. The temper of the public at some

242

time in conjunction with some conspicuous occurrence will afford an opportunity & we should be prepared to take advantage of it. Knowledge—detailed & put into effective usable forms is the foundation onto which to build. The machinery for collecting the data must be perfected.

For the process of nibbling at appropriations, the next years may afford promise—on the one hand, the wets indignant at prohibition practices; on the part of anti-administration forces, the policy of pin-pricks; and on that of the administration the policy of Economy.

The subject is so closely allied to evidence that possibly you could interest Maguire[2] or Morgan,[3] if they are likeminded with us. And, if so, some among their students could be enlisted, who could, i.a. make the work undertaken, at the Brookings School a bit effective. Or possibly you might stir up some one in the Political Science deparment at Harvard to work with the HLS. And/or this subject could (locally) be appropriately pursued in connection with the Milton enquiry into Criminal Administration in Boston.[4]

[1] See 15 and 23 February 1926.
[2] John MacArthur Maguire (1888–1978) taught at Harvard from 1923 to 1957. He had served in the Justice Department during the war.
[3] Edmund Morris Morgan (1878–1966) had come from Yale's law school in 1925, and he remained at Harvard until 1950. Like Maguire, he was a specialist in the law of evidence. In 1948, together with G. Louis Joughin, he wrote *The Legacy of Sacco and Vanzetti*.
[4] See 24 January 1926, n. 4.

No. 229   June 25, 1926   Chatham, Mass.

FF: 1. Would it not be desirable to let follow, after your article on overruled etc. cases of USSC,[1] one on cases reversed, in effect, by Congressional action—distinguishing between (a) cases where Congress apparently undertook to correct what it deemed our erroneous construction, from (b) those where its presumed actual intent was not made effective either because (1) of a casus omissus[2], or (2) other inadvertence or want of precision in drafting the statute.

You will recall that I dealt with this matter somewhat in the Weitzel case[3] & later.

The recent Washington Quarantine case & legislation is in point.[4]

2. Wouldn't it be possible to interest Bohlen[5] and Dickinson[6] directly & through them students, to make the necessary investigation & present in the [Harvard] Law Review articles bearing on the redress for the invasion of civil and political rights through arbitrary etc. governmental action, by means of civil suits?

243

I think the failure to attempt such redress as against government officials for the multitude of invasions during the war and post-war period is also as disgraceful as the illegal acts of the government and the pusilanimous action of our people in enacting the statutes which the states and the nation put on the books.[7] Americans should be reminded of the duty to litigate. Dickinson, at least, ought to have a hereditary concern about liberty.

I hope the NR will pay its respects to "Pepper, the Consistent" and "Mellon, the Honorable."[8]

[1] See "The Business of the Supreme Court of the United States," *Harvard Law Review* 39 (1926): 1046.

[2] A case not provided for, in this instance by a particular statute.

[3] *United States* v. *Weitzel*, 246 U.S. 533 (1918). Weitzel, appointed receiver of a Kentucky bank, had been charged with embezzlement under a law that mentioned "every president, director, cashier, teller, clerk, or agent," but did not mention "receivers." LDB, for a unanimous Court, ruled that "statutes creating and defining crimes are not to be extended by intendment because the court thinks the legislature should have made them more comprehensive."

[4] The state of Washington, plagued by a dangerous alfalfa weevil, promulgated a quarantine order which prohibited transporting alfalfa into Washington. The Oregon-Washington Railroad shipped some alfalfa anyway, contending that states cannot impose quarantines when Congress has acted in the matter, and a 1912 law gave the secretary of agriculture responsibility for preventing the spread of infectious plants and animals. The Supreme Court, speaking through Chief Justice Taft, agreed with the railroad (Sutherland and McReynolds dissenting), and overturned the Supreme Court of Washington, which had allowed the quarantine. Congress, in response, immediately reviewed the federal law with an eye to permitting states to issue such protective quarantines. *Oregon-Washington Railroad & Navigation Co.* v. *State of Washington* 270 U.S. 87 (1926). The case was decided on 1 March.

[5] Francis Herman Bohlen (1869–1942) taught law at the University of Pennsylvania Law School from 1898 to 1938; from 1925 to 1928, however, he was Langdell Professor at Harvard.

[6] John Dickinson (1894–1952) had come to Harvard Law School in 1925 from a partnership with William G. McAdoo. Dickinson, a descendant of the revolutionary publicist of the same name, left Harvard in 1927 for Princeton and the University of Pennsylvania. He held a number of important governmental positions, and in the mid-1930s was assistant attorney general.

[7] See 16 July 1926.

[8] A reference to the disputed Pennsylvania Republican primary (see 23 May 1926, n. 1) and Andrew Mellon's role in it. See "The Pennsylvania Idea," *New Republic* 47 (30 June 1926): 154.

No. 230   July 2, 1926   Chatham, Mass.

1. Cobbett (Cole's Life of C[1] p. 208) said (1816): "A reformed Parliament would . . . want no secret service money"; it would sweep away the hosts of "horrid scoundrels" and informers; there would be none of this "disgraceful spy-work."

2. I am glad to see that the announcement of your criminal survey is out.[2]

I suggest that, as an incident of the current survey, special care be taken to ascertain and record:

(a) The character (ethical) of the evidence through which it is sought to obtain a conviction—e.g. to what extent it is of the character held legal in Burdeau v McDowell 256 U.S. 465,[3] & the many cases where fed crimes were prosecuted in U.S. courts with evidence illegally procured by state officials.

(b) The instruments through which the evidence [is] introduced—e.g. by policemen & (1) to what extent detectives & undercover men & (2) ordinary policemen, inspectors etc.

(c) The extent to which there are convictions due to transactions which involve participation of police or detectives, even where they fall short of entrapment.

(4) [sic] The attitude, demeanor & conduct of the representatives of the government: policemen, jail officials, court officials, prosecuting officers & judges—all engaged in the function of enforcing & administering the law.

I have grave doubt whether we shall ever be able to effect more than superficial betterment unless we undertake to deal fundamentally with the intangibles; and succeed in infusing a sense (A) of the dignity of the law among a free, self-governing people and (B) of the solemnity of the function of administering justice. Among the essentials is that the government must, in its methods, & means, & instruments, be ever the gentleman. Also we must recognize the fallacy of the [***] that the main function of Courts is to settle controversies. This view seems to me a bit of that finite 19th century wisdom of the Militarians which has brought so much evil as well as good. There are times of ease & prosperity when the pressing danger is somnolence rather than litigiousness.

I think that, in respect to evidence as in other respects, there is a limit to what can be accomplished by the mercenary alone. There must be some point at which the ability of the citizen to shift the burdens of government upon the paid expert—be he policeman or executive— ends.

Your survey should note particularly the limits of the mala prohibited, as distinguished from the mala in se.[4] It seems to me we were rather presumptuous in brushing away the distinction—another bit of really shallow rationalization; that there is, moreover, an essential difference between a crime and a delict;[5] & that there are few acts or omissions which ought to be treated as crimes which do not arouse righteous indignation. For these some other solution should be found than existing penalties.

[1] G. D. H. Cole, *The Life of William Cobbett* . . . (London: W. Collins Sons and Co., 1924).

[2] See 24 January 1926, n. 4.

[3] McDowell was dismissed from his job for fraud; his company dispatched another employee to Pittsburgh who took over McDowell's office, blasted open two safes containing private papers, and turned over the evidence he found there to company officials. Justice William R. Day, for the majority, ruled that McDowell's later conviction was legal because the government itself did not do an illegal act in obtaining the evidence. LDB and Holmes dissented.

[4] The distinction between an act prohibited by law and an act morally wrong.

[5] A "delict" is an act by which a person causes damage to another.

No. 231   July 10, 1926   Chatham, Mass.

FF: 1. In Cole's Cobbett you will find in England of 100 to 125 years ago, many replicas of our governmental spy activities, and you will be particularly interested in the example on pp. 403–4, of the pro[vo]cative spy in the Trade Union (1833) followed by action of Special Parliamentary Comtee & dismissal from the position in the P[olice]. D[epartment]. to which the spy had been promoted.

2. Couldn't Sen. Walsh be induced, a propos the Wan Case,[1] to have ordered an investigation into Third Degree practices by federal officers? That would naturally extend into the spy system.

3. The N.R. financial man might well enquire, in connection with increase of Savings Deposits, what has been the decrease (since 1919) in amount and in the number of holders of War Savings Certificates outstanding—and what has been the decrease in the numbers of holders of U.S. War bonds. I understand that there has been a decrease in the number of holders, altogether out of proportion to the decrease in the amount of War bonds outstanding.[2]

4. Re criminal survey: I suggest that a very careful debit account be made for Suffolk County,[3] from all available sources (i.a. newspapers, police records etc. including burglary & surety ins. cos.) for the 12 months preceding say July, 1926, and the credit against that debit, for each subsequent year, of the (a) arrests, (b) convictions, for these particular crimes. I guess it will be found that a ridiculously small percentage even of the reported crimes of magnitude are ever prosecuted.

5. This by J. R. Lowell[4] may remind you of some L of N friends:

"Transcendentalism—the maid of all work for those who could (or would) not think"

6. Please have copy of the June HLR. sent me—also of the last preceding number containing your article.[5] My copies are at the binders.

7. I will bear J.W.M.'s July 19 in mind.[6]

8. The Andrew Winslows are coming this evening for 2 nights.

[1] See 31 October 1924, n. 2. LDB's remark was occasioned by a review of the case in *The New Republic* for 7 July 1926. Wan had just been given his freedom, seven years after his arrest.

[2] *The New Republic* did not follow up this suggestion.

[3] See 24 January 1926, n. 4. Suffolk County includes Boston and most of its suburbs.

[4] James Russell Lowell (1819–1891) was one of the leading essayists, poets, and literary critics of his time.

[5] FF had installments of "The Business of the Supreme Court" in both the March and June issues of the *Harvard Law Review*; 39 *HLR* at 587 and 1046.

[6] 19 July 1926 would be Julian Mack's sixtieth birthday.

No. 232   July 16, 1926   Chatham, Mass.

FF: 1. Wouldn't it be possible to have some one in Congress move for a Claims Commission to make reparations to American citizens for the outrages incident to the Jan 20 Palmer raids?[1] An article on the Sedition law reparations would prepare the way. And the move for appointment of the Commission might lead to diplomatic representations by foreign nations who have settled their debts & by Russia, when it is recognized. Americans ought not to be allowed to forget their Sicilian Vespers.[2] We need a John Quincy Adams to persistently press forward the right to free speech.[3]

2. It is fine that Nicely appreciates his association with Holmes J. & that he wants something other than he has. Couldn't he be "saved from the burning?"[4]

3. Every N.Y. lawyer I meet speaks highly of Thatcher [sic].[5]

4. The C[hesapeake] & O[hio] and the Illinois Central, to whom my brother wrote about the RR library, have promised hearty cooperation.[6]

5. I should think young Walter Fisher would like that job.[7]

[1] See 25 June 1926. During raids authorized by Attorney General A. Mitchell Palmer in 1920, the government rounded up over four thousand suspected radicals and eventually deported 556 of them.

[2] "Sicilian Vespers" refers to a popular uprising in 1282 by Sicilians against their French rulers, during which many Frenchmen were murdered. The signal for the revolt was the ringing of the vesper bell in Palermo.

[3] A reference to the effort of former President John Quincy Adams who, despite the House of Representatives' "gag rule," insisted on debating the issue of slavery in the 1830s.

[4] Holmes's former clerk, James M. Nicely, remained in private practice until 1929, when he became vice-president of the Guaranty Trust Co. in New York.

[5] Judge Thomas Day Thacher.

[6] One of LDB's proposals for building up the University of Louisville was to improve its library by adding a collection of materials related to American railroading.

[7] Walter Taylor Fisher (b. 1892) was the son of Walter Lowrie Fisher, former secretary of the

interior. The son was a Chicago lawyer who did serve in some public offices, but not during the mid-twenties.

No. 233   July 25, 1926   Chatham, Mass.

1. This, from Arthur Young's [1] "Thoughts on the Establishment of a Chamber of Manufacturers" pp. 452–3 ed. 1785, may interest friends of "The Chambers" & of the Hoover boom: "Now the union of all sorts of manufacturers, not for the improvement of their fabricks, but for the conversion of themselves into politicians to watch with kindling jealousy the motions of the legislature; . . . ; to quicken, alarm, and give alacrity to apprehensions; to array private feeling in the garb of public needs; . . . to give facility to discontent, and vigour to resistance—an institution that does all this, is wonderfully different from the combination of talents for the purpose of improvement which might have done honour to the projector; it may become, instead of a society of arts, a den of politicians."

2. Re yours of 23rd about Landis. I had heard nothing of this cheering event—from him or otherwise [2]—and, of course, know nothing of the facts, on which to form an opinion as to whether it would be wise for him to borrow. If it is wise for him to incur an indebtedness, I much prefer that the loan should be made by me than by someone else. If upon talking the matter over with him, you and he conclude that it is desirable for him to borrow, I shall be glad to lend the two thousand ($2000) which you name. [3]

3. This, attributed by Murray to Sir John Fortescue's [4] "On the Governance of England" (1471), is interesting in connection with present French finances: "he contrasts the readiness with which the taxes are paid in England with the "grudging" they call forth in France."

4. We expect Elizabeth & Paul on Tuesday via Rochester.

[1] Arthur Young (1741–1820) was an English writer on agriculture, economics, and politics.
[2] Landis had announced his engagement to Stella G. McGehee, and the two were married on 28 August.
[3] See next letter.
[4] Sir John Fortesque (1394–1476) was an eminent English lawyer and, after 1443, chief justice of the King's Bench.

No. 234   July 31, 1926   Chatham, Mass.

FF: 1. Your & Corcoran's [1] "Petty Federal Offenses" [2] is admirable. Interesting and important; important in itself & as pointing the way that others should go.

(a) Did you examine the Plymouth Colony law & practice? I didn't recognize or notice references to that.

(b) What do you plan shall be done for the other of the 13 States? If you have no such investigation in mind, what would you think of suggesting it to some Southern Law School Review—say No. Carolina?

2. I have also read now your March & June instalments of "The Business of the Supreme Court." They is [sic] very informing & enlightening. When this series becomes known to the Bar and the federal judges, high appreciation of the service is sure. Its general educational campaign will go far, like Warren's History,[3] in removing the areas of dense ignorance.

What would you think of taking up, when this series is finished, The Business of the Fed District Courts" & then that of the C.C. of Appeals? You are better fitted, with your preparation & aids, than any other person could possibly be for the task; a considerable part of the work must have been done—however much remains—through the work on the present series and for other articles in H.L.R. etc; and, with Friendly & Landis at your side, you could, at least, stake out your claim during the present year without unduly interfering with the work you have planned for the sabbatical. There is no need of early completion.

3. You have rendered a distinct service to the profession & to history, in laying bare so fully, in a business-like way, the performance of the despicable Cummings [sic]. "Quidquid latet apparebit."[4]

4. I have a note from Landis, telling of his engagement. He does not mention the loan. So, I shall write him a word of congra[tula]tion, without mentioning the loan, & leave you to say to him whatever further may be necessary on that subject.[5]

His Index has not yet arrived.

5. Mack's success in the [*] case & Buck[ner]'s appreciation must make easier the task of keeping him on the Criminal Calendar.[6]

6. Alice sends her best to you & Marion & we hope the rest of the summer will go as well with you both. The Columbia experience will prove to have increased appreciably your influence.[7] Of course, we count on seeing you here or elsewhere before we return to Washington about Sept 10.

[1] Thomas Gardiner Corcoran (1900–1981), one of FF's "boys" at Harvard, clerked for Holmes and then practiced law in New York City. During the New Deal, the gregarious Corcoran became one of the most influential of all the protégés of FF and LDB to work with Franklin Roosevelt. Together with Benjamin Cohen, Corcoran helped draft the Securities Act of 1933, the Federal Housing Act of the same year, the Securities and Exchange Act of 1934, the Public Utilities Holding Company Act of 1935, and the Fair Labor Standards Act of 1938.

[2] FF and Thomas G. Corcoran, "Petty Federal Offenses and the Constitutional Guaranty of Trial by Jury," *Harvard Law Review* 39 (1926): 917. The article dealt with the extent to which the Constitution compels Congress to provide a jury trial in enforcement of federal penal laws, and the extent to which Congress may adopt English common law summary procedure by judges without juries in so-called petty or minor offenses. The writers examined English and American colonial history to show an unbroken practice extending two centuries before the Constitution of such summary procedures. The question had special relevance to the enforcement of prohibition.

[3] See 16 June 1922, n. 2.

[4] "Whatever is hidden will appear" (from the hymn "Dies Irae," attributed to Thomas A. Celano). This appears to be a remark directed against Albert Baird Cummins, the Iowa politician who rose as a progressive and became increasingly conservative with the passing years. In the end, he was a Coolidge regular. Cummins, who had voted against LDB's confirmation in 1916, had died the day before at the age of seventy-six.

[5] See preceding letter.

[6] On 21 July, LDB had written to FF: "I am glad to know Buckner thinks so well of JWM as trial judge. Others have said the like to me. Mack likes Nisi Prius much better than opinion writing. Why doesn't he concentrate on Jury trial work—preferably criminal in New York? He couldn't render a better public service, or do more for his reputation & happiness." A *Nisi prius* court normally consists of a single judge and jury hearing a case at first impression, as distinguished from an appellate court.

[7] During July and August, FF and Thomas R. Powell taught Constitutional Law at Columbia.

No. 235   August 11, 1926   Chatham, Mass.

1. Would it not be useful to have the Commonwealth or other Foundation undertake a comprehensive study of lawyers fees—with special regard to contingent fees, ambulance, tax return and other chasing, and what court rules and/or legislation should be adopted to stay the evils? Among the subjects for special consideration would be what the fee provisions should be where the claim is against the Federal or a State government; also what should be the special protections if any, where payments are made from other people's money.

2. Norman talked too much at Williamstown yesterday. [1]

3. We are looking forward to seeing you two and the Cohens on Monday.

[1] Norman Hapgood was a participant in the sessions of the Institute of Politics at Williams College.

No. 236   August 15, 1926   Chatham, Mass.

FF: 1. In your investigation into the business & practices of the Federal Courts, I hope the importance of putting an end to the abuse, in contempt cases, of judges deciding on alleged contempts of their own authority, where the act complained of was not in their presence & could not, therefore, have directly interfered with the orderly conduct of the proceeding, will be steadily borne in mind. Some day, with appropriate

Judiciary Committee, the legislation necessary can be secured, if the proper foundation has been laid.

2. It is fine to have R.P. on record in appreciation of what you are doing in & for H.L.R.

3. The judicial estimate & diagnosis re E.A.F. must be very annoying to the gent. Some day a Jewish American Plutarch will contrast his generosity & public spirit with J.R.'s.[1]

3. [sic] Ned McClennen reports you & Marion at Saturday's hearing before Mack.[2] It would have been better for JWM if he could have kept hands off; but A[nderson]. needed a substitute. He was pretty near the breaking point when last seen.

4. Glad you are getting the foundation for Crime Survey laid satisfactorily. The result of N.Y.'s recent legislation should make some Crime reformer debutantes pause.[3]

5. Also the N.Y. jurors' action re Third Degree etc. stay police atrocities.[4]

6. The C.J. writes that the Doctor says he is getting better.

Our best to Marion.

[1] Julius Rosenwald (1862–1932) had been vice-president and treasurer of Sears, Roebuck & Co., from 1895 to 1910, when he became president of the organization. During World War I, President Wilson named him to head the committee on supplies of the Council of National Defense. An extremely wealthy man, Rosenwald supported a variety of philanthropic interests, including Hebrew colonization, the Y.M.C.A., and Negro education.

[2] Julian Mack had just become the presiding judge in a bizarre and sensational trial involving Harding's attorney general, Harry M. Daugherty, and the alien property custodian, Thomas Woodnut Miller. The matter involved the speedy and suspicious return of war confiscated property to its owner ($7 million worth) and the subsequent "payment" by the German owner of part of the proceeds to the two men. The case dragged on through two trials, but ended inconclusively because Daugherty had destroyed the financial records. See the lucid account of the matter in Martin Mayer, *Emory Buckner* (New York: Harper and Row, 1968), ch. 9.

[3] In April and May of 1926, the state of New York passed almost two dozen unusually tough laws designed to combat the "crime wave" sweeping the state and the nation. The so-called Baumes Laws, after the assemblyman most closely associated with them, touched everything from possession of weapons to refusal to testify to the sentences for first-time offenders.

[4] Probably LDB is referring to a sensational incident which took place in the Bronx County Court on 10 August. In a trial of the Oberst gang, one of the defendants, Philip Oberst, was on the stand. He was testifying in detail about the brutal treatment he had received at the hands of the police upon his arrest. In the midst of his description of a beating he had received, one of the jurors leaped to his feet, obviously shaken, and begged to be relieved from the torture of such testimony. A mistrial was immediately declared.

No. 237   August 17, 1926   Chatham, Mass.

FF: In going over certioraris I am again impressed with the terrible waste of federal courts' time by prosecution under Section 215. When one considers how small a part of the means of practicing fraud the mail now is,[1] this invasion of state police powers is especially unjustifiable. I hope your papers[2] will give us full data on this. Some day, a favorable Congress may be found disposed to modify, if not wholly repeal, the Section, if the adequate foundation is laid.

A vigilant, militant state might keep its citizens as free from the fraudulent raids as from the ravages of typhoid. The fraud animal would learn to avoid such a community.

High finance would doubtless support the present measure (as it does enactment of a national Blue Sky law[3]) as helping them to a monopoly of the investments field. But someday, there will be a chance of slipping in, despite their barriers.

It is fine to hear the admirable performance of Mack in the Oil Case. Marion's estimate is confirmed by what comes from others concerning his judicial activities. But "Ich mochte gerne alles thun" is even more dangerous than the "Alles wissen"[4] desire.

[1] See 6 September 1924.

[2] The "Business of the Supreme Court" series.

[3] A law regulating the sale of stocks and bonds for the protection of the public.

[4] But "I am prepared to do everything" is even more dangerous than the desire "to know everything."

No. 238   August 23, 1926   Chatham, Mass.

FF: 1. The deep interest of the historians & pol. science men in your papers[1] may encourage them to imitate your example of cooperation with research students. Couldn't you, through them, get some of the surveys into American fields of political experience in which we are specifically interested, entered upon?

2. Notestein's[2] studies into Parliamentary history[3] would give him a great foundation for research into our own Constitution, institutions & procedures which might vitally affect decisions of U.S.S.C.

3. Is your Boston Crime Survey to be limited to violations of State law, or will it include the federal field?

4. The death of Judge Rogers[4] yields the usual crop of untruthful estimates of the services of the decedent. William Cobbett never failed to avail himself of a like opportunity to make a frank balancing of accounts. There may be good reason for silence as to the living, but of the dead—nil nisi Verum(?).[5]

5. The fight for Blaine against Lenroot in the primaries is proving a

hard one, I guess.[6] Bob La F. is devoting to it his whole time apparently. If that is successfully disposed of, I should think you might find him, as well as Jim Reed, ready to look into the Mass[achusetts]. situation.

6. Notestein's Raleigh Address[7] contains much that should be pondered over by political scientists & those of their students who aspire to public life.

7. Have you considered including in your "Business of USSC" Series a survey of moot cases? The enquiry would disclose some instances of bad straining besides Ohio v. W. Va.,[8] as well as Artful Dodges.

8. Via B.F.'s friend Insull[9]: the Jew has behaved pretty badly in Illinois. So has S.I. abjured the connection?

9. We hope you & Marion will keep Thursday, Sept. 9, free for dinner at the Bellevue. We plan to reach Boston that evening.

10. Since writing you re contempt legislation I have stumbled across "Lese Majeste" in the Aug 18 Nation,[10] which indicates that the proposed reform could receive widespread newspaper support.

11. President Eliot ended finely a fine life.[11]

[1] The "Business of the Supreme Court" series.

[2] Wallace Notestein (1878–1969) was a distinguished English historian, presently at Cornell, but soon to begin his long tenure at Yale University.

[3] Notestein's recent works included *The Journal of Sir Simmonds O'Ewes* (New Haven: Yale University Press, 1923), and *The Winning of the Initiative by the House of Commons* (Oxford: Oxford University Press, 1924).

[4] Judge Henry Wade Rogers had died on 16 August.

[5] "Nothing but the truth."

[6] Wisconsin was experiencing an unusually strenuous Republican senatorial primary race. The incumbent, Irvine Luther Lenroot (1869–1949), had been an ally of the late Senator Robert M. La Follette, and they had cooperated closely with LDB in drafting antitrust legislation fifteen years earlier. But Lenroot had grown increasingly conservative, and his reelection was felt to be an important gauge of President Coolidge's popularity and policies. Former governor John James Blaine (1875–1934), another old La Follette ally, had retained the good will and support of the late Senator's family. In September, Blaine defeated Lenroot and served one term in the Senate.

[7] Notestein's study of the parliamentary initiative (see n. 3 above) had originated as an address in Raleigh on 2 October 1924.

[8] The case was argued and decided along with *Pennsylvania* v. *West Virginia*, 262 U.S. 553 (1923). For details, see 17 June 1923, n. 3.

[9] Samuel Insull (1859–1938) had risen from being Thomas A. Edison's private secretary to one of the most powerful businessmen in the country. As president of Chicago Edison, he masterminded the economics of delivering electrical power, and eventually built and/or managed the public utilities in 5,000 communities in thirty-two states, mainly through pyramided holding companies. In 1929 he was wiped out by the crash, and fled to Greece to avoid prosecution for his business practices. Eventually he was cleared of all charges.

[10] "Lese Majeste," *Nation* 123 (18 August 1926): 142. Focussing on a particularly outrageous Indiana case (where the state Supreme Court ruled that the truth of an editor's charges about a judge did not matter if his remarks brought the judge into public contempt), the anonymous article condemned the "tyranny" of recent contempt of court rulings.

[11] The former president of Harvard died on 22 August at the age of ninety-two.

No. 239   September 21, 1926   Washington, D.C.

FF: I should like to stimulate the U. of Louisville to strive to collect (preferably through present Senators, Congressmen, their predecessors, & the families of those deceased) for the Railroad Library:

(a) The Comtee reports & reports of hearings, in both House & Senate which led to the enactment of the Interstate Commerce Act.

(b) The Committee reports & reports of such hearings which led to each amendment.

(c) (if possible) Such Comtee reports & reports of hearings on proposed amendments, not adopted.

I suppose the Harvard Law School Library contains a large part of this material, or, in any event, that you have data which will cover a list of, at least, (a) and (b).

Could you have made for me (in duplicate) a list of these documents to be striven for; and also, have noted thereon the Kentuckians, if any, who were members of the House and/or the Senate Comtees on Interstate Commerce at the times of the several hearings etc.?

The Hamiltons were in Sunday—report Graham Wallas as coming Mch 1. H. says he had a 3 hour talk with Abe Flexner who is much pleased with what the Brookings School is doing & with the prospects of Meiklejohn's College.

No. 240   October 7, 1926   Washington, D.C.

1. Thanks for your wishes for the Oct. 1926 Term. The Court starts in well. The C.J. appears to be in as good form as at the beginning of the 1925 Term. O.W.H. is even better than last year—bright, light-hearted, without any weakening of powers discernible; Sutherland happy over his summer's gain; & the rest in their usual health.

2. The C.J. did his best for you re statistics—told me he had carried out your suggestions & given to the cause the best Comtee possible. He is a great admirer of Hough & told how he & others put him over with T[heodore]. R[oosevelt]., who wanted Geo. W. Alger.[1]

3. As to the S.G.'s son—I should not wish either to grant or deny his "faculty scholarship" without talking with him personal[ly]. His father's son should better be able to show good cause or to know why his request is not granted. He may not understand the considerations which determine.[2]

254

4. We are not surprised at Marion's view of Fred Cabot.[3]

5. Tom Corcoran is coming in to dine this PM. with the Ed. Keatings, Father Ryan and Eva Kean.

[1] George William Alger (1872–1967) was a New York City lawyer who was active in numerous civic concerns—especially labor legislation, prison and parole policy, and the regulation of the movie industry.

[2] FF had been inquiring about the possibility of a scholarship for William Mitchell, a student at the Harvard Law School, and the son of the solicitor general, William DeWitt Mitchell (1874–1955). The father had been appointed by Coolidge in 1925 to his post, and served as attorney general through Hoover's administration, and LDB had a very high opinion of his abilities and his character (see 1 March 1929). Mitchell was later appointed counsel to the congressional committee investigating the Japanese attack on Pearl Harbor. The son (b. 1903) graduated magna cum laude from Harvard Law School in 1928. He practiced in St. Paul and then moved to Washington, D.C. Between 1953 and 1957 he was the general counsel for the Atomic Energy Commission.

[3] Probably Frederick Pickering Cabot (1868–1932) a Boston lawyer and scion of the aristocratic Cabot family, who was married, moreover, to a Higginson. Cabot was president of the trustees of the Boston Symphony.

No. 241   October 15, 1926   Washington, D.C.

1. Do you hear anything under-ground about Daugherty-Miller disagreement?[1]

2. Jack Gilbert says that Mack's charge was the fairest charge he has ever heard in a criminal case.[2] Altogether JWM seems to have given further evidence that his service & reputation can best be furthered by sticking to the Criminal Session, and with Criminal law the chief centre of interest at the moment, he could hardly do better, for many reasons.[3]

3. The HLR should not miss, or fail to treat adequately No. 230, Industrial Comn v. Terry & Tench Co., in which we reversed N.Y. C.A. (Cardozo) in a P.C.—!![4] The significance of the decision, in connection with some other recent ones on the same general subject might be made clear.

The Amer Hebrew is properly forgetful.

[1] The jury had reported hopeless disagreement after sixty-five hours of deliberation in the government's conspiracy case (see 15 August 1926, n. 2).

[2] Judge Mack's charge in the Daugherty case came on 9 October and required an hour and forty-five minutes to deliver. See New York Times, 9 October 1926.

[3] See 31 July 1926, n. 6.

[4] State Industrial Board of the State of New York v. Terry & Tench Co., Inc. and United States Fidelity & Guaranty Co., 273 U.S. 639 (1926), decided on 11 October. It involved a worker injured while employed on a floating raft, repairing a pier. Cardozo (for a unanimous New York Court of Appeals) reversed an original award on the ground that maritime law should apply and that the state law (the New York Workmen's Compensation Act) should not interfere. The outrage here expressed, and

also expressed in *Harvard Law Review* 40 (1926): 485, was not due so much to the ultimate decision as to the fact that the Supreme Court would reverse so distinguished a state court *per curiam*, without even delivering an opinion.

No. 242   October 27, 1926   Washington, D.C.

FF: Under another cover the Myers Ops [1] go to you by first class mail. Senate resentment & plans should take the form:

(1) Of extending classified Civil Service to take in most of the now exempt offices.

(2) To transfer to heads of Dep. many offices now in President's class.

There is much on this & other matters which I hope to write about soon.   In haste

I am also sending Landis a copy of the Myers Op.

[1] *Myers* v. *U.S.*, 272 U.S. 52 (1926). This important case centered on Woodrow Wilson's removal of Frank Myers, a postmaster. Wilson discharged Myers without requesting the Senate's consent (as required by a statute of 1876), thereby reopening a question of removal power as old as the republic itself. Myers sued and in this case the Supreme Court confirmed the removal. Chief Justice Taft (speaking with the authority of an ex-President) delivered a seventy-one page opinion supporting a president's power to remove not only cabinet officers but lower federal officials as well. Such power, he contended, was a necessary tool in the exercise of executive responsibilities. LDB, Holmes, and McReynolds dissented separately, and Taft exploded in anger, calling the dissenters men "that have no loyalty to the Court and sacrifice almost everything to the gratification of their own publicity. . . ." Instead of creating the precedent that many feared, including the destruction of the Civil Service system, the decision had little impact and was qualified in *Humphrey's Executor* v. *U.S.*, 295 U.S. 602 (1935), when the Court struck at Roosevelt's growing power by denying the right to discharge a Federal Trade Commissioner on grounds outside those specified by Congress.

No. 243   October 28, 1926   Washington, D.C.

FF: 1. Telegram recd. I mailed you yesterday (first class) the Myers op and also under separate cover the Dorchy [1] & a letter. This incident should help awaken interest in political science. Some of the majority are not happy.

2. The N.R. editorial on the N.Y. candidates was a fine bit of work. [2]

3. I am glad of the temporary arrangement W.L. has made. [3]

4. The N.R. & the [New York] World should not fail to face Hoover with his inconsistencies. The attack on the British. Rubber restriction policy etc. [4] vs. the encouragement of the cotton restriction policy. H. said to a friend of mine that he thought he could not only withdraw the 4,000,000 bales now, but could reduce acreage 25%; because 80 percent

of the crop is raised on borrowed money & the U.S., by means of Fed[eral].Res[erve].B[oar]d & banks could compel compliance with conditions next year.

5. Mass. with its Butler-Coolidge campaign is the centre of national interest.[5] It would be grand if Walsh should win. I have been hearing inside about Coolidge administration and am inclined to think that it is in some ways worse than Harding's. There are exceptionally well advised folk here who are glad of the Daugherty disagreement,[6] because worse sinners are still high in office in the odor of sanctity. Among other things, the prohibition end is said to be more corrupt, and all with CC's connivance.

6. Mr. & Mrs. Friendly were in for an hour. Their misapprehensions as to facts & relative values of Practicing Lawyer v. Professor of Law, are many.[7] Most of the time, after their recital, was spent in disabusing their minds.

(a) The only definite advice I gave them was to leave their son alone; to let him make up his own mind & not merely to say so, but let him see & know that they will be happy in whatever decision he makes. I put this as strongly as I could; & I think they understood me.

(b) I definitely refused to transmit through them any advice to the son. They wanted specifically to know whether I advised him to take a post graduate year at C[ambridge]. I said I would not advise on that unless I talked with the son etc. And I agreed that I would see him, if he comes here Christmas week.[8]

7. Thanks for I.C.C. memo.[9]

8. You may care, during the Crime survey, to carry in the back of your mind, Tolstoi's views on Crime & Punishment. The father of E. A. Goldenweiser wrote an essay on "Resurrection" under the title "Crime a Punishment and Punishment a Crime" which was translated & published by the son in Washington in 1909.[10]

9. Holmes J. was downed by a head cold, caught from Butler J. & absent from Ct yesterday on that account.

[1] *Dorchy* v. *Kansas*, 272 U.S. 306 (1926). Dorchy, vice-president of the mine workers' union, called a strike in violation of Kansas law, and was convicted in Kansas courts. The purpose of the strike was to force payment of back wages to an aggrieved worker. LDB, for a unanimous Court, upheld the conviction: "But a strike may be illegal because of its purpose, however orderly the manner in which it is conducted. To collect a stale claim due to a fellow member of the union . . . is not a permissible purpose."

[2] *New Republic* 48 (27 October 1926): 256. The editorial pointed out that the issues being raised by Republican candidates were irrelevant and that New Yorkers would cast their votes on the

basis of two questions—prohibition and whether the presidential ambitions of Governor Smith ought to be furthered.

[3] Lippmann had been paying a retainer of sorts to Thomas Reed Powell for occasional analyses of legal matters, which the *World* used as a basis for news stories or editorials. On 6 October, Lippmann had written to FF that since Powell consulted with FF prior to sending these analyses, FF was doing the work and should receive a retainer. FF declined the offer, and for the while Lippmann continued to send the money to Powell.

[4] See 6 January 1926.

[5] The Massachusetts senatorial campaign saw LDB's old friend, David I. Walsh, pitted against Republican William Morgan Butler (1861–1937), who was running with the strongest possible support from Coolidge, Hoover, and Charles Evans Hughes. His campaign was being taken as a measurement of support for the administration, especially as he was serving as the national chairman of the Republican party at the same time. On 2 November, Walsh defeated Butler by a substantial margin.

[6] See 15 October 1926.

[7] See 14 March 1926, n. 13.

[8] See 9 November 1926.

[9] See 21 September 1926.

[10] Emanuel Alexandrovich Goldenweiser (1883–1953) was an ecomonist and statistician who specialized in monetary questions. His father's book was Aleksandr Solomonovich Gol'denveizer, *Crime a Punishment and Punishment a Crime: Leading Thoughts of Tolstoi's "Resurrection"* (Washington: n.p., 1909).

No. 244   October 29, 1926   Washington, D.C.

FF: 1) You have done an extraordinary thing in educating the Herald to its stand on S.V.[1]; the World also.

2) I am wondering whether the S.V. decision[2] won't make some anti Republican votes in Mass. on Tuesday.

3. It looks as if the Herald would be heard from again on the Myers decision.[3]

4. The supplemental J.W.M.—H[arlan]. F[iske]. S[tone]. correspondence is interesting.

5. O.W.H. was in Court again today in good form.

6. The Frank Tannenbaums[4] were in last evening. He after 18 months in Mexico (where he had been 3 times before). He is writing his book for the Inst. of Economics & is to use it for his PhD thesis at Brookings.[5]

The story is a fine & promising one for the present Mexican govt, & he told me things of Sheffield[6] which make him take rank with the worst of our representatives in Mexico.

7. I hope Marion read at least part of her President's address on advertising.[7]

[1] On 26 October, the Boston *Herald* had carried a powerful editorial declaring that Sacco and Vanzetti should not be executed. The paper claimed that it did not know whether the two men

were guilty or not, but so many inconsistencies surrounded the case that only a complete rehearing would allow justice to be done in the case.

[2] On 23 October, Judge Webster Thayer denied a defense motion for a new trial for the condemned men.

[3] See 27 October 1926.

[4] Frank Tannenbaum (1893–1969) had been jailed in 1914 for leading a labor revolt. At Sing Sing prison he was befriended by the warden who eventually got him into Columbia University. Tannenbaum earned a doctorate in economics at the Brookings Institution and became an expert on Latin America and on social and labor conditions in the United States. From 1935 until 1961, he taught at Columbia.

[5] Tannenbaum's dissertation was published as *The Mexican Agrarian Revolution* (New York: Macmillan, 1929).

[6] James Rockwell Sheffield (1864–1938), a Harvard Law graduate, went into New York politics. In 1924, Coolidge appointed him ambassador to Mexico and he served until 1927. In 1930, Hoover would name him special ambassador to Venezuela.

[7] On 27 October, Coolidge addressed the American Association of Advertising Agencies. He told them that advertising helped to stimulate and maintain American prosperity, a view with which LDB and Marion Frankfurter were entirely out of sympathy. The president's remarks can be found in the *New York Times* for 28 October.

No. 245   November 1, 1926   Washington, D.C.

1. H. J. Friendly has asked me to see him Nov. 21, which I have agreed to do.[1]

2. Page has not mentioned the offer.[2] He is doing good work here.

3. The Herald's reprint of the World editorial is another bold step. It must be giving our brothers pain.

4. If Mass. beats Butler handsomely I shall, indeed, "Have Faith in Massachusetts."[3]

I haven't felt such interest in political prospects for many a day. Basil Manly [sic],[4] who was in yesterday, seems full of hope. Thinks the Old Guard is sure to lose control of the Senate & that Progressives will be able to raise their heads. He thinks that there can be a working arrangement between Democratic & Republican Progressives.

5. The N.R. editorial on Why Voters don't Vote has in it much truth. But I don't think that the lack of race homogeneousness has much to do with it.[5]

6. R.P.'s Pittsburg address leaves us with an uncomfortable feeling. Of course there are some good passages.[6]

7. O.W.H. is OK again.

[1] See 28 October and 9 November 1926.

[2] Despite an offer to return to Harvard Law School, LDB's clerk, Robert Page, decided to enter private practice in New York City. See 9 November and 30 November 1926.

[3] See 28 October 1926, n. 5.

[4] Basil Manley (1886–1950), an economist, worked as a technical adviser to the Bureau of Labor Statistics, the Federal Trade Commission, the War Industries Board and numerous other federal and New York state agencies.

[5] "Why Voters Don't Vote," *New Republic* 48 (3 November 1926): 284. The anonymous editorial was a thoughtful analysis of the growing lethargy and indifference among American voters. It was the result "chiefly of the gradual disintegration of the social democracy whose vitality accounted for the former American success in the art of self-government."

[6] Pound had delivered the commencement address at the University of Pittsburgh on 9 June 1926, later published as "Culture and Population," *University of Pittsburgh Bulletin* 3 (October 1926). LDB would have disliked much of the talk, since Pound argued that size by itself was not bad, and many good things could only be achieved in large mass. Culture, for example, relied upon large populations, and many of the finest universities were also large.

No. 246   November 4, 1926   Washington, D.C.

FF: 1. Tuesday's election will lift a great weight from many a depressed American.[1] It is fine to think that C.C. "lost on errors." That's how most games, in war and in peace, are lost. I think from all one reads & hears in W[ashington] that there is many a Republican who feels malicious joy & will begin to talk that C.C. is a liability instead of an asset. Basil Manly [sic] says, he hasn't a friend in the Senate, now that Butler is out.[2]

2. It will, indeed, be fine if you can get Charles P. Howland to devote himself to the [Crime] Survey. He couldn't make better use of his time, and I am sure he would feel immense satisfaction in the work.

3. Stoughton Bell's[3] list on Administrative Law is a fine tribute to your course.

I suppose you and Marion have heard from Auntie B. that Susan's son is a strapping fellow & that all goes well with them.[4]

It's a great thing to have Morton Prince & his ilk take a hand in S.V.[5]

[1] The elections were a victory for the antiadministration forces. The Republican majority was cut in both houses of Congress: the House had 237 Republicans to 195 Democrats, with two Farmer-Laborites and a Socialist; and the Senate was extremely close with forty-eight Republicans to forty-seven Democrats, and one Farmer-Laborite, Henrik Shipstead. But since the Republican majority included such anti-Coolidge senators as Blaine, Norris, Borah and La Follette, Jr., it was clear that the Senate could be controlled by a union of Democrats and progressive Republicans.

[2] See 28 October 1926, n. 5.

[3] Stoughton Bell (1874–1967) had graduated from the Harvard Law School in 1899, after which he entered private practice in the Boston area.

[4] The Brandeis's first grandchild, Louis Brandeis Gilbert, was born on 2 November 1926.

[5] Morton Prince (1854–1929) was a well-known physician and psychiatrist in Boston. He had been a mayor of the city and one of LDB's chief allies in the Public Franchise League at the turn of the century. On 30 October, he announced his support for a new trial for Sacco and Vanzetti in a letter to the *Herald*, and took his place beside FF as an activist on behalf of the condemned anarchists.

260

No. 247   November 9, 1926   Washington, D.C.

1. The C.J. is incorrigible re Certioraris. But I guess we are over the worst of it for this season. He stands alone in his irresistible appetite.

2. That's fine about C. P. Howland. I hope you will arrange to keep him fully employed.

3. I suppose you will have someone to present the Community's responsibility. You will recall my tale of the surprise of the Kentucky giant that his young son used less words. We must remember "The wages of sin is death." I doubt whether any system of criminal administration can grapple successfully with our crime problem, unless the American can be made to modify his tests of success—of the worthwhile. That vice infects means and ends alike. And I think probably the most fruitful result of your work will be to make that appear. As I ponder over the problem, this admonition came ever ominously like the motif in the Wagner opera.

4. John Mason seems to be experiencing religion.

5. I think it clear that I had better not broach the subject of HLS to Page.[1] But rather let him come to me if he wants to. If you plan coming here to ask him, couldn't you arrange for some day after Nov. 14 & before Nov 22, when Court reconvenes. I suppose you might not think it wise to be here on Nov. 21 when Friendly is to be & possibly not to be here at all until after his visit. His father seemed to think the son was being subjected by you and J.W.M. to "undue influence."

I am glad the parents understood me.[2]

6. I judge that the [Boston] Globe has followed the Hermes suit,[3] from what I read in A.F. of L. news bulletin.

7. Landis did notable work on the Myers case.[4]

8. I'll send you tomorrow an address of J. B. Eastman's on relative expenditure for regulation etc., which you may care to see & the N.R. may find of value in some connections.[5]

[1] See 1 November and 30 November 1926.

[2] See 14 March and 28 October 1926; see also, 13 October 1929.

[3] The steamship *Hermes* had collided with another steamer in New York's East River, and its owners claimed that the other ship had failed to heed correct signals. In July 1927, the circuit court awarded damages to the *Hermes*'s owners, 21 F.2d 314; the Supreme Court shortly afterwards denied certiorari, 275 U.S. 569.

[4] For the case, see 27 October 1926. James M. Landis had done the prodigious research on LDB's forty page dissent in the case. He combed the Senate journals through the decades in order to determine what the practice was in presidential dismissals.

[5] Eastman's address before the National Association of Railway and Utilities Commissioners was summarized and praised in detail in "Public Economy—an Inside View," *New Republic* 49 (19 January 1927): 237.

No. 248   November 15, 1926   Washington, D.C.

FF: For your letter and Marion's greeting warm thanks, and also for the Rostovtzeff.[1] As you knew, it deals with a subject of intense interest to me; and I am glad to have this access to the fruits of later studies and discoveries.

Tell me what you know about R.[2]

The day went off well, and it brought from O.W.H. a few beautiful lines.[3]

That was a beautiful thought of my friends to which Mack gave expression in announcing to me the gift to HLS.[4]

[1]LDB became seventy years old on 13 November; and FF and his wife had sent him Mikhail Ivanovich Rostovtsev, *The Social and Economic History of the Roman Empire* (Oxford: Oxford University Press, 1926).

[2]Rostovtsev (1870–1952) had been born in Russia but migrated to the United States during the 1917 revolution. He taught ancient history at Wisconsin until 1925, and then moved to Yale, where he taught for twenty years. He is recognized as a pioneer social historian of the ancient world.

[3]In honor of LDB's birthday, Holmes had written: "You turn the third corner tomorrow. You have done big things with high motives—have swept over great hedges and across wide ditches, always with the same courage, the same keen eye, the same steady hand. As you take the home stretch the onlookers begin to realize how you have ridden and what you have achieved. I am glad that I am still here to say: Nobly done."

[4]To mark the seventieth birthday, a group of LDB's friends presented a gift of $50,000 to the Harvard Law School to establish the Brandeis Research Fellowship.

No. 249   November 30, 1926   Washington, D.C.

1. When your "Business of lower federal courts" is developed, it would be well to have made clear to the states, how they could avoid in tax cases the enjoining of their tax collections through suits in federal court—by removing the possibility of the claim there is no adequate remedy in the state courts, if the tax is paid etc. There ought to be a whole article devoted to this subject, so that even those who need the Kindergarten course could understand. And copies of the Review should go to the high state taxing officials & the Attys General etc.

2. I think there ought to be worked out also an article showing how, by appropriate changes in state criminal administration, the excuse for going into federal Equity courts for injunction because of claim of ir-reparable damage, due to multiplicity of suits & oppressive penalties, before the final adjudication of validity, could be obviated.

3. By careful work on these & cognate lines, with state cooperation which seems now procurable, the whole illegitimate brood of such re-sorts to equity & the federal courts could be stamped out.

4. In 87 etc. I have endeavored to make clear, as a matter of statutory construction, the "occupying the field" doctrine.[1] I think the states could be taught, by a similar ABC article that, if they wish to preserve their police power, they should, through the "state block" in Congress, see to it in every class of Congressional legislation that the state rights which they desire to preserve be expressly provided for in the acts.

5. Page has not referred to the Professorship matter again—although he has had chances to do so.[2]

6. I hope you will have recd before this last week's ops.

7. As to Harlan's liberalism—wait.

8. Miss Grady quotes you as saying that I am to be asked for suggestions for subjects re. Research Fund.[3] If I am, I shall submit them to you for consideration before sending anything in.

9. Could the [New York] World be stimulated to enter upon a persistent attack upon Mellon tax plans & prophecies—to be conducted throughout the session, to avert further Democratic blunders? E.g. urge "Debt Payment the best Preparedness."

Hardy's book on the surtaxes would doubtless help.[4]

10. I was glad to see the Lefkowitz editorial in N.R.[5] That is a vital subject which the World should also campaign for & the recent Fries incident in Washington in which Genl Fries was downed should afford lovers of free speech & thought some encouragement.[6]

11. I am glad there are prospects for Wells.

12. The Brewster Gould incident should help.[7]

13. There was meat in N.R.'s "Inertia" editorial.[8]

---

[1] *Napier* v. *Atlantic Coast Line Rd Co.*, 272 U.S. 605 (1926). For a unanimous Court, LDB struck down a state law requiring automatic doors on locomotive fire boxes as a safety device. The grounds given were that the Boiler Inspection Act had "occupied the field" of regulating locomotive equipment in interstate commerce and that the states were precluded from such activity.

[2] See 3 December 1926.

[3] See 15 November 1926, n. 4.

[4] Charles Oscar Hardy, *Tax-Exempt Securities and the Surtax* (New York: Macmillan, 1926).

[5] Abraham Lefkowitz was a New York teacher who had been denied a promotion because of his radical opinions and activities outside the classroom. The editorial "Are School Teachers Citizens?" *New Republic* 49 (1 December 1926): 28, was a ringing denunciation of such attempts to coerce mindless conformity and stifle true education.

[6] Brigadier General Alfred Amos Fries, head of the Chemical Warfare Service of the Army, defended the use of poison gas in the next war. He was vigorously attacked by the National Council for the Prevention of War (Alice Brandeis was an officer of the group) and by other antiwar and women's organizations. In response, Fries and others in the War Department tried to link the pacifists with the Bolshevik menace. The response to the militarists' attacks was strenuous and, after a meeting between representatives of various liberal groups and Secretary of War John W. Weeks, the latter warned his officers against unjustified remarks.

[7] Arthur Robinson Gould (1857–1946) had just been elected to the United States Senate as a

Republican from Maine. It emerged, however, that in 1911 he had paid a $100,000 bribe to the premier of New Brunswick for railroad favors. The governor of Maine, Ralph Owen Brewster (1888–1961), had assailed Gould for excessive campaign expenditure, which evoked a counter-charge from Gould, namely that Brewster was in league against him with the Ku Klux Klan. After investigation by the Senate, Gould was allowed to take his seat.

8 "Inertia as a Patriotic Ideal," *New Republic* 49 (24 November 1926): 4. Taking the occasion of the U.S. retreat, once again, from joining the World Court, the editorial contended that the prevailing mood in American politics was to equate inertia and true patriotism. This accounted for the steady abandonment of genuine progressivism. The editorial was probably written by Herbert Croly.

No. 250   December 2, 1926   Washington, D.C.

FF: Yesterday PM. my secretary had telephone enquiring whether Dr. Weizmann could see me that evening.[1] He answered for me impossible. W. asked whether he could come this AM, and 10 AM. was fixed for his call. He stayed 50 minutes. On entering the room he offered his birthday congratulations "though late." I immediately asked him when he had last been in Palestine & of conditions there. He reported fully. Then I asked him about the Pritchett incident.[2] This we discussed fully. He reported that he would answer further on Sunday at Carnegie Hall. I advised that he do not answer in form, or refer, in any way to Pritchett, but that he make a clear and comprehensive statement of facts, empha-sizing i.a. the Surplus Govt revenues, the small army & police as well as economic development.

Then he reported fully on political conditions, his talks with Briand[3] Amery[4] etc; and, finally, as to his project for a comprehensive survey to be undertaken by Elwood Mead (with the assent of our Govt) with non-Jewish aids who shall remain a year in Palestine. I asked whether he had talked this over with [Bernard] Flexner. He said no—not to anyone yet, except Mead. I asked whether any reason why he should [not] talk it over with F. He answered emphatically no reason; & said he would do so. He thinks that with the kind of report which he expects would come from the American experts, it would be possible to raise $10,000,000 a year for 10 years; & thus during these 10 years to settle 25,000 persons a year in Palestine. His statements throughout were conservative & I told him I thought that his project was sound & should be capable of achievement, provided provisions were made for proper spending, as well as raising of the money.[5]

The talk was calm & friendly throughout; no mention by me what-soever of our past relations; and none by him except in a parenthetical

264

clause, to the effect that he was aware of our differences but I must admit he had stuck to the job.

He said as he was leaving that he thought it would be advisable to spend a few days here to get into touch with some of those high in authority here[6] & that he planned to come back before or after Christmas for this purpose. I agreed that it would be & that Elwood Mead would be an advisable avenue. Nothing was said definitely by me or by him about his seeing me when he came again, or about my aiding him.

I had told him that Flexner et al. could, if they approved, doubtless help both in securing assent that Mead make the survey & also in financing.

[1] Weizmann had arrived in America in late October in order to raise funds for the United Palestine Appeal.

[2] Henry S. Pritchett had just returned from a trip to the Middle East. He presented a report to the Carnegie Foundation contending that Zionism was bound to fail. The movement was "unfortunate and visionary," Pritchett said, because of the poverty of the land and the brooding hostility of the native Arab population. The full text of the report can be found in the *New York Times* 29 November 1926. Naturally, Pritchett's views sparked angry replies from many Zionists, including Weizmann.

[3] Aristide Briand (1862–1932), the distinguished French statesman, was currently his country's minister for foreign affairs.

[4] Leopold Charles Maurice Stennett Amery (1873–1955) was serving as England's secretary of state for the colonies; he was a longtime student of British colonial affairs.

[5] See 15 February 1927.

[6] Weizmann had been received by President Coolidge on 2 November, a few days after his arrival; on 2 December he conferred with Vice-President Dawes and Secretary of State Kellogg.

No. 251   December 3, 1926   Washington, D.C.

FF: 1. Page told me this morning (without having specifically discussed the subject with me) that he had decided to decline the Law School offer[1] and go in with the Taft boys at Cincinnati. He said he had no logical reason for so doing; but that he felt he could not trust himself to go to Cambridge, as he wouldn't work there. Bob Taft has been elected Prosecuting Atty for Hamilton Co., which I understand means 2 years & may mean four for him out of the Taft firm work. P. said, of course, he could have gotten more money in N.Y.

I am sorry P. isn't going to Cambridge. But I have considerable sympathy otherwise with his choice. It is a good connection; a city that surely needs regeneration; & is small enough for those 3 fellows to accomplish something towards that end, if they persist. He had not mentioned the Cincinnati possibility to me before. Page is an Ohioan by birth which is a further justification.[2]

2. I enclose memo re Weizmann visit. Please send me 2 typewritten copies of this.

[1] See 1, 9, and 30 November 1926.

[2] In the end, Page did not go to Cincinnati, but to New York; see 4 February 1927.

No. 252   December 5, 1926   Washington, D.C.

1. In connection with the new threat of a McNary Haugen bill,[1] Francis Parkman's dramatic story of the first attempt to deal with surplus production in America—the tale of the beaver skin crop (told, I think, in his "Old Regime in Canada") should be revived.[2]

2. Ask Auntie B. about Fries. She has or had all the clippings & should be able to give you the full story. The most encouraging event re free speech for many a year.[3]

3. I am glad you corrected Basil Manly's [sic] step.

4. Allyn Young[4] uses the term "speculation" in a very narrow sense. What is occurring is a wholly new kind of speculation—the boom is not in prices, because it is in production capacity coupled with credit to consumers. It is true that there is nothing "mathematical" in the cycles. But I am inclined to think they are "inevitable" because they are result of the lack of self-control & of foresight in Man; as well as other qualities. I think your Rostovtzeff[5] would be a good course for economists.

5. Others, I know, agree with your judgment as B. Hand's comments on me.

5. [sic] As to Rostovtzeff—he is very illuminating on futile attempts of the Roman Emperors to deal [with] the problem of farm surpluses despite their power to legislate for the whole of their world.

6. Newt Baker is his charming clever self.

Tell Allyn Young that when he comes here next I should be glad to see him.

[1] See 23 May 1926, n. 4.

[2] Parkman described the disastrous French attempts in Canada, around 1700, to control the surplus of beaver skins being trapped and traded. A government guaranteed price, regardless of the demand, sent large numbers of trappers and traders into the wilderness and resulted in an intolerable surplus of pelts. See Francis Parkman, *The Old Regime in Canada*, 2 vols., (Boston: Little, Brown, 1897 edition) 2: 104–08.

[3] See 30 November 1926, n. 6.

[4] Allyn Abbott Young (1876–1929) was a leading economist; he had been a professor of economics at Harvard since 1920.

[5] See 15 November 1926, n. 1.

FF: 1. Will you kindly send me a list of the cases (so far as you have collected them) in which our Court has overruled—earlier cases—on the relative powers of State and U.S. dealing with the Commerce Clause.

2. I hope the Virgi[ni]an Ry Case [1] may (with the aid of comment in the Reviews) do much toward breaking up the pernicious practice of the C.C.A.—more particularly of the District Courts in deciding cases without opinion.

3. Hough has done a very good job re statistics; and your answer will help in important particulars.

4. I am eagerly awaiting the Verdict in your letter to R.P. re Margold. [2] You certainly presented a strong case & presented it with great skill.

5. C. P. Howland was in 1/2 hour last week. I put up hard to him responsibility of bar & community & I think he assented.

6. The R.P. Crimson incident [3] was characteristic. Is there any next act? I was glad to see Friendly in it.

7. Has the Herald accepted R. W. C[hild]'s tender?

8. B.F., Julius Simon & Paul Singer were in for a long conference Sunday. There seems to be a heavy Jewish revival.

9. Do you know anything about Harlan's this year's secretary? Of course a Columbia man & I suppose of the Law Review. I think his name is Handler. [4] H. brought him in Monday to Alice's tea; he struck me very favorably—e.g. in his desire to teach law. He will have a course on Trade Relations at the Columbia Summer Session of 1927.

10. The Brookings folk say Carl Becker made a talk on 1776, at their recent commencement exercises, so remarkably fine, that even Dodd's high reputation has been completely distanced. [5]

11. Abe Flexner was in with Jean last Thursday—in fine condition & very jolly. I suppose Ben [Flexner] has reported to you the inside of the Pritchett matter. [6]

12. O.W.H. is in fine form. He has made a remarkable discovery. If he goes to bed an hour earlier and sleeps an hour longer at night, he isn't so apt to fall asleep the next day.

13. How is Van Vleck progressing with his Immigration-Deportation Report. [7] There should be careful consideration of methods & rules of verbal examination of immigration as to right to enter, & the keeping of him incommunicado. It ought either to be justified, or be abolished.

[1] *Virginian Railway Co.* v. *U.S.*, 272 U.S. 658, had been decided two days before, LDB giving the Court's opinion. The Interstate Commerce Commission had issued an order to the railroad respect-

ing rates on coal. The railroad got a stay from the district court pending its appeal, and the I.C.C. appealed. LDB admitted that the district court had the power to issue such a stay, but it needed cause to do so, and since there was no opinion, the high court could not determine any justification for the stay. LDB then launched into a two page scolding of the lower court for not stating its reason in an opinion. The Supreme Court upheld the I.C.C.

[2] Nathan Ross Margold (1899–1947) was a Rumanian immigrant and a Jew, who had come to FF's attention as a student at Harvard. From 1925 to 1928 he was an instructor at the Law School (and no doubt the letter to Pound was to secure his reappointment). But in 1928 the proposal to award him a professorship divided the faculty and the administration bitterly. President Lowell refused to appoint another Jew and another social liberal; and the faculty (which had voted for Margold with but two dissenting votes) followed Pound's recommendation that they not fight Lowell on this matter. FF, of course, was furious. Margold himself left teaching to undertake a wide variety of professional and governmental responsibilities until his early death.

[3] There is no article in the *Harvard Crimson* at this time of an "incident" concerning Roscoe Pound. Possibly the incident occured at a *Crimson* dinner.

[4] Milton Handler (b. 1903) was, as LDB suspected, a graduate of Columbia Law School (1926) and on the *Law Review*. After his year with Stone, he combined a distinguished career of private practice with teaching at Columbia and governmental service. He was a specialist in antitrust and trademark law. During the Roosevelt administration he worked in a number of New Deal and wartime agencies.

[5] Carl L. Becker delivered his famous lecture, "The Spirit of '76," at the Brookings Institution on 19 November 1926. The occasion was a celebration of the 150th anniversary of the year of the Declaration of Independence and Adam Smith's *Wealth of Nations*. Also on the program, speaking on "Virginia Takes the Road to Revolution," was the well known American historian, William Edward Dodd (1869–1940), a friend of Becker's and a professor at the University of Chicago. In the 1930s, Dodd served as America's ambassador to Hitler's Germany. He also edited, with Ray Stannard Baker, some of the papers of Woodrow Wilson, but is best remembered for his work in southern history.

[6] See 2 December 1926, n. 2.

[7] See 16 September 1923, n. 4.

No. 254   December 19, 1926   Washington, D.C.

FF: Haven't you an economist who can utilize these two modern instances re Morgan trusts to teach a moral?

Steel Trust—$235,000,000 Melon. [1]

Shipping Trust—Failure. Evidenced by selling out to English of White Star Lines & others contemplated.

Is Gary abler than P.A.S. Franklin? [2]

No. Steel controlled the market prices. I.M.M. [3] holding no control, couldn't.

[1] A "melon" is a division of profits amongst stockholders. The U. S. Steel Corporation had just announced a 40 percent stock dividend.

[2] Philip Albright Small Franklin (1871–1939) was one of the country's leading shipping magnates.

[3] Franklin had been the president of the International Mercantile Marine Co. since 1921.

No. 255   December 21, 1926   Washington, D.C.

FF: 1. Roberts [1] made an uncommonly good impression on our Court. In case of doubt, I should accept his judgment as to advisability of trial of a case.

2. Thanks for references to your articles. Are you able to give me the data as to our overruling ourselves in cases under the Commerce Clause? [2]

3. If you have some economist & government men, willing to look a little ahead, have them get some coming PhD [to] write on the danger of tax exemption of education, philanthropic, religious etc. institutions, e.g. foundations. That will prove a much greater point before long than tax exempt state securities. The latter is largely a question of wise or unwise state financing, particularly with the decline of federal taxation.

[1] Owen Josephus Roberts (1875–1955), a former professor of law at the University of Pennsylvania, had been appointed by President Coolidge as one of the special prosecutors in the Teapot Dome investigation in 1924. In 1930, Hoover named him to the Supreme Court, where he served until 1945. During the court tests of New Deal measures in the mid-1930s, Roberts proved to be the swing vote in an evenly divided court. From 1948 to 1951, he returned to the University of Pennsylvania as dean of its law school.

[2] See 15 December 1926.

No. 256   January 1, 1927   Washington, D.C.

Our best to you and Marion.

1. I hope you will protect Cardozo from all this Jewish pressure [1]—local, national & international. He will serve the Jewish people best by conserving his health and calmness of spirit in order to do his judicial job as well as he can do it. With his frail health and unfamiliarity with tribal warfare, this course seems imperative. You can make this clear to him.

2. Weiz[mann] is welcome to Marshall. [2] But he wont get me for his new Commission. [3] And I shall refrain from giving him any money for this undertaking lest he represent that it is (in part) my Commission. I understand that he has already done some tall talking of that nature to the Jewish Press.

3. Alice bids me tell you that Dick Child is so forsaken that he sent us a Xmas card. [4]

4. We are glad to hear that the S.V. article is so far advanced. [5]

5. Who is David Cecil?

6. Ellery Sedgwick's approach is interesting. [6]

7. Have Redlich let us know when he is to be here so that we can arrange a dinner for him.

OWH is in good form. I called on him today as he didn't go to the White House.

¹To become active in Jewish and Zionist affairs.

²Louis Marshall (1856–1929), the influential leader of the aristocratic American Jewish Committee, had crossed swords with LDB over the Jewish Congress movement in 1915–1916. At first an open anti-Zionist, Marshall eventually moderated his stand without ever joining the movement. Relations between Marshall and LDB always remained formal and courteous, but also somewhat uneasy. Besides his Jewish activities, Marshall worked in the NAACP and was a lawyer in many civil liberties and civil rights cases.

³One of Weizmann's purposes in visiting the United States was to make peace between Zionists and wealthy non-Zionists like Marshall. He courted Marshall openly, offering a tribute to the American leader at a dinner honoring his seventieth birthday (12 December 1926). The "Commission" referred to was originally designed to serve as a successor to the defunct Zionist Commission, but it never got that far. Instead, it initiated the long negotiations that led, with Marshall's support, to the establishment of the Jewish Agency.

⁴Richard Washburn Child was going through a much publicized divorce case at the moment.

⁵This was FF's sensational article, "The Case of Sacco and Vanzetti," *Atlantic Monthly* 139 (March 1927): 409. The article, which soon became an influential book, dissected the case against the two Italians with meticulous and devastating attention to detail, and roundly attacked the trial and subsequent hearings for their unfairness. The publication of the article and the book brought FF much criticism—some alleging that it was improper to comment on a case still being adjudicated, others suggesting that FF's work on behalf of the radicals (so reminiscent of his work for Tom Mooney) was unbecoming for a Harvard professor. Nevertheless, FF's writing on the case quickly gained high marks for its accuracy and argument, and constituted an important landmark in the case, bringing publicity to the effort on behalf of the two men. For the story of FF's involvement and of how he came to write the article and book, see Phillips, ed., *Felix Frankfurter Reminisces*, ch. 20. For LDB's views, see 9 March 1927.

⁶Ellery Sedgwick (1872–1960) had been editor of the prestigious *Atlantic Monthly* since 1909. Perhaps FF had explained to LDB how Sedgwick was trying to secure the article for the *Atlantic*—despite the fact that FF had promised it to Herbert Croly for *The New Republic*.

No. 257   January 7, 1927   Washington, D.C.

FF: Pursuant to request, I mailed you complete file, 1916–1925 Terms of synopses, first class mail spec. delivery. I think there is nothing in the synopses which you cant use (you will know if there is). But, of course, the source of the synopses should not be mentioned publicly.

Lorwin (Louis Levine) mentioned last evening, as if it were an encouraging sign, that there was a heavy trend among Columbia students to study of philosophy & that Will Durant's book was a "Best Seller." ¹ I think some one should make clear to the public that this is a very bad sign.

Philosophy is rather the cyclone cellar for finer souls. As it was in the declining days of Greece, and as the monastery was in the so called Dark Ages.

In our Democracy, the hopeful sign would be recognition of politics & government as the first of the sciences & of the arts.

[1] Will Durant, *The Story of Philosophy: The Lives and Opinions of the Greater Philosophers* (New York: Simon and Schuster, 1926).

No. 258   January 10, 1927   Washington, D.C.

FF: 1. The Steel Melon (and Gary's 80 years),[1] should not be allowed to pass without recalling the near 25 years record of the Trust's long hours. (Since writing this Alice calls my attention to the Jan 1 Survey, p. 465.)[2]

2. Ellery Sedgwick made a hit with "Things in the Saddle." He should try "Life, leisure and the pursuit of pleasure"—with special reference to the decay of interest in politics & political science.

3. Elizabeth & Paul will be ready for jobs in the fall. Let them know if you hear of anything promising. Their address is 4006 Pine St., Phila. 1/13/27

4. Since writing the above, I have yours of 11. The S.V. development amazes me as much as it does Bliven. It is an extraordinary achievement.

5. The report on Lowell at the Faculty Meeting is also extraordinarily good.

6. Couldn't you get the Herald to come out like the World & the Boston Globe on Nicaragua & Mexico? This bids to be the most shameful episode in our history. Miss Grady sent me the Globe editorial. We showed it to Senator Bob & he said eagerly that he would put it into the Congr. Record.[3]

[1] On the steel "melon," see 19 December 1926. Elbert Gary had celebrated his eightieth birthday amid national recognition on 8 October 1926.

[2] "Havoc Wrought by the Shorter Work Day in Steel," *Survey* 57 (1 January 1927): 465, was a series of chronological quotations relating to the twelve-hour workdays in the corporation. Both LDB and Paul U. Kellogg, editor of *The Survey*, had been longtime critics of U.S. Steel's labor policies. LDB had spoken against labor conditions in the company's plants before the Stanley Committee in 1912, and Kellogg had published an entire volume (by John Fitch) in his *Pittsburgh Survey* (1910) relating to steel workers and their laboring conditions.

[3] Coolidge had withdrawn the Marines from Nicaragua in 1925 and within months the country was torn by a civil war that pitted a liberal, anti-American rebel force against the conservative Diaz regime, friendly to the United States. In 1926, Coolidge returned the Marines to Nicaragua, justifying his action in terms of the protection of American property—including an interest in a potential canal. As 1927 began, Coolidge's policies came under heavy attack, especially by Senate Democrats and isolationists. Three days before, LDB had written to FF that Coolidge and the State Department "are behaving as badly as man could conceive—it is amazing to me that Congress lets them."

As far as Mexico was concerned, the problem centered around oil properties and whether or not the Mexican government would honor a pledge that guaranteed American owners their property rights. When Mexico seemed to waver, some urged intervention; and Coolidge and Secretary of State Kellogg talked tough. The Senate, however, urged nonintervention and arbitration in the strongest terms, and Coolidge backed away from the threatened interference in Mexican affairs. The *Boston Globe* editorial of 10 January, criticizing both American actions in Nicaragua and the government's refusal to explain its objectives honestly to the public, was entered into the *Congressional Record* on 12 January by Senator La Follette; 69th Cong., 2d Sess., 1470.

No. 259   February 4, 1927   Washington, D.C.

FF: 1. Alice sends you the enclosed re R.P. etc.

2. It has occurred to me that the best start for the needed investigation of the government prostitutes—sometimes called spies, and euphemistically known as detectives, inspectors, special agents & intelligence officers, would be:

—to have Richard Boekel's [sic] Editorial Research Bureau write up the subject for his clients. Couldn't you get the Boston Herald and/or the New York World and/or the N.R. and/or The Nation [to] make the request of Boekel? He is apt to do a good job.

3. We saw much of Salvemini[1] for dinner Wed. & had the Senator Shipsteads, the Gifford Pinchots[2], & after dinner other folk in to meet him, including i.a. Charles Ross,[3] the head of the Post Dispatch Washington Bureau, which did such a good job in exposing the [*] incident & that of Flurry. Eliz. & Paul were also here, happening in for the day.

4. We are asking the Chinese minister[4] for tomorrow. That's a grand awakening of theirs.[5]

5. I suppose you noted John Haynes Holmes' article in the Feb. Survey Graphic[6]—repeating things of his correspondence with you. I have asked him to see me when he is next here. "Ich habe ihm etwas zu sagen."[7]

6. I guess S.S.W. is not happy over the Jewish "unification."[8] Have heard nothing from J.W.M.

7. Yours of yesterday has just come. I haven't read "The Fat Boys"[9] yet, but Eliz. spoke most enthusiastically of it to Alice; & Alice thinks also it is Marion's best.

8. I was surprised to learn from Page the other day that he had not settled on Cincinnati & that he was still in doubt. He has gone to N.Y. for 2 days to view the scene.[10]

9. Walter Child told me some time ago of Robert Dodge's vision.

10. We had Sen. David Walsh in the other evening with the John A. Nelsons & the Lowell Mellets,[11] trying to make them take advantage of what I think is the best time for fighting these six years.

272

11. G. W. Anderson is in today. Enroute to Florida. He thinks E.A. [Filene] is going a bit crazy. Anderson was a long time reaching that insight.

12. The [*] letter, returned herewith, is interesting; also what is said about The World.

13. I suppose you have told Bruce Bliven what I think of his article on Kellogg. [12]

14. Will R.P. write the Foreword? [13]

[1] Gaetano Salvemini (1873–1957) was a well-known Italian historian and one of the earliest and most vocal critics of Mussolini. He had arrived in the United States on 6 January and embarked upon an anti-Fascist speaking campaign. In 1932, he left Italy and became a naturalized American citizen in 1940. From 1933 to 1948 he taught Italian history at Harvard.

[2] Gifford Pinchot (1865–1946) was the first American professional forester, a leader in the conservation movement, and a longtime friend and ally of LDB, dating back to their work together in the conservation battles during the Taft administration. He served as governor of Pennsylvania from 1923 to 1927, and again from 1931 to 1935.

[3] Charles Griffith Ross (1885–1950), the chief Washington correspondent of the St. Louis *Post-Dispatch* since 1918, would become an editor in 1934, after having won a Pulitzer Prize in 1932. During Harry S. Truman's presidency, Ross served as his press secretary.

[4] Sao-Ke Alfred Sze was envoy extraordinary and minister plenipotentiary from China.

[5] LDB refers to a series of spirited and violent antiforeign demonstrations that were then occurring in China; see next letter.

[6] John Haynes Holmes, "What is Worth Fighting for in American Life," *Survey* 57 (1 February 1927): 549. The article was a rambling and semiautobiographical discussion of ideals.

[7] "I have something to tell him."

[8] See 1 January 1927.

[9] "The Fat Boys," *New Republic* 49 (2 February 1927): 300. The unsigned piece recounted a scholarly meeting, attended and dominated by a group of sleek and officious "fat boys" from the leading foundations.

[10] See 3 December 1926.

[11] Lowell Mellett (1884–1960), an editor for the Scripps-Howard chain, later went into government service. Between 1940 and 1944, he served as an administrative assistant to President Roosevelt.

[12] Bruce Bliven may have written the anonymous "Two Years of Mr. Kellogg," *New Republic* 49 (26 January 1927): 262, a scathing survey of the secretary of state's record of blunders in his first two years in office. For LDB's view of Kellogg, see next letter.

[13] FF published three important books during 1927: *The Business of the Supreme Court* (with Landis); *The Case of Sacco and Vanzetti*; and *Mr. Justice Holmes and the Constitution*. Pound did not contribute a foreword to any of them.

No. 260   February 8, 1927   Washington, D.C.

1. I am convinced that ineptitudes & worse of our State Dep. are such that there is great danger, with Mexico, Nicaragua & China active, [1] in going 8 months with[out] a Congress sitting. I think the [New York] World ought to use all its influence to force an extra session.

2. I heard the inside of K[ellogg]'s China doing—they show a shiftiness equal to his otherwise inadequacy.[2] Moreover, I heard of action by the Navy Dep. (in an entirely different connection) which reminds of the worst in the Dreyfus Affair. My information comes from a very reliable source.

3. This of Norris' is good, but is wholly inadequate.[3] Moreover, request should be directed also to Commerce Dep & to Federal Reserve Bd who have less occasions for "incompatible with the public interest."[4] We ought to know how many people, how much property & specifically what large U.S. interests are being "protected."

4. There ought to be a general onslaught of the long established practice of State Dep not to publish annual or other reports.

5. Would the Herald join the World in #4?

[1] See 10 January 1927, and preceding letter.

[2] Frank Billings Kellogg (1856–1937), a Republican senator from Minnesota, became Coolidge's secretary of state in 1925. In the face of antiforeign demonstrations in China, Kellogg had tried to enunciate an American policy on 27 January. He insisted on maintaining an "open door," but was willing to make tariff concessions to the Chinese. There was much talk during these months of possible intervention by force to protect American nationals in China; see also 29 March 1927.

[3] LDB had enclosed a clipping reporting the Senate's unanimous passage of a resolution sponsored by George W. Norris calling upon Kellogg for information concerning American held oil concessions in Mexico.

[4] The Norris resolution contained the usual proviso, "if not incompatible with public interest."

No. 261   February 15, 1927   Washington, D.C.

1. Too bad R.P. is so.

2. I think you had better do the suggesting to J.W.M. of abstention during the oil trial; & perhaps write him before to prevent his burdening himself.

3. I shall have considerable to say to him re Zionist affairs. I presume you have had through him & deH, theirs & my interchange of letters.[1]

4. Pritchett correspondence returned herewith.[2] I guess he will subside.

5. Weizmann impressed me more than ever with his ability, resourcefulness & Mephistophelian quality. I rather think M[ephistopheles] "was ein Hund dagegen."[3] When with him, I felt like the good Christians who grasped at the Cross for protection.

6. What does not appear by correspondence sent you is that his operations here are greatly disturbing the British.

7. He has completely transformed the character of the proposed sur-

vey[4]—so that it is now pre-eminently a political instrument, besides being propaganda to win the American bankers.[5]

[1] The letters dealt with a quarrel between Mack and deHaas over Weizmann's Jewish Agency plan. Mack was willing to let the proposal go forward; deHaas wanted to attack it openly.
[2] See 2 December 1926, n. 2.
[3] "a dog by comparison"
[4] See 2 December 1926.
[5] See 1 January 1927.

No. 262   February 26, 1927   Washington, D.C.

1. There are rumors of a S.V. article in the forth-coming March Atlantic to which we are looking forward.[1]

2. So far as I can recall, there are now no questions pending on the construction of the 1925 Jurisdiction [Act]; that under 238 and 266 as amended having been disposed of by my recent opinion & that of Stone putting the limitation of the right to appeal where it should be.[2]

3. Hughes argued the Los Angeles case poorly.[3] Other recent arguments of his show likewise (as do [John W.] Davis') the evil of understanding too much.

The RR brief in the Los Angeles case was, however, a very good one. Find out when you have occasion, who did it. The I.C.C. didn't challenge the jurisdiction. I have not heard just why. I guess they foolishly wanted our Court to decide all their difficulties for them.

4. You cannot conceive how painful, distressful & depressing it was to listen (officially) to Cal's Washington's Birthday address.[4] I think the purpose of those behind (who must have prepared the address) was to confiscate the whole of G[eorge]. W[ashington]'s good will for Big Business, by showing that we owe everything we value to the qualities of business efficiency, commercial courage & vision & thrift & that these were G.W.'s dominating qualities fitting him for the greatest of the World's achievements. Even his religion was of the efficient business type, as described. I have been told from all high that the purpose of the talk being made now was to set the "key note for the next five years of talk." There is no man in [the] U.S [who] could have so perfectly—by looks, voice & action—have [sic] deprived G.W. of every idealistic aim or emotion.

When I tried to recall the next most depressing & distressful experience of a lifetime, I had to go back to 1894, when in preparing for the Public Institutions Hearings,[5] I went to Long Island (Boston Harbor)

Poor-House hospital & passed through the syphilitic ward. I had a like sense of uncleaness. Alice administered music as a restorative. And happily Bob Bruere came in to dine with us alone.

5. I saw much of Wise & of Mack Saturday & Sunday, but it will take all of the six weeks (of the Boston oil case) for you to wipe out of Mack's mind his deep reverence for the magnificent potency of money in Jewish affairs. He seemed surprised & stunned when I urged upon him that there were two things Jews needed more than money in their great problems:

1. Thought
2. Compelling high conduct in carrying out their plans & projects.

6. I learn from Kohler[6] via Wise that Cardozo's physician has prohibited his making any more speeches.

7. I am glad to hear of Roger Foster's[7] going to H.L.S.

8. [*] Robert Fritz was in yesterday. Spoke with enthusiasm of your course at Columbia.

9. About the Ky declaratory judgment case,[8] more when we meet.

10. It was news to me that [John] Hay had as Secy of State made an annual report.[9]

Holmes J. is in superb form.

[1] See 1 January 1927, n. 5.

[2] Actually, both cases involving these sections of the 1925 Jurisdiction Act had opinions written by Stone. In *Waggoner Estate* v. *Wichita County*, 273 U.S. 113 (1927), the Court upheld Section 238 which provided for appeals of substantive constitutional questions directly from the district courts to the Supreme Court. In *Smith* v. *Wilson*, 273 U.S. 388, the Court approved Section 266, which allowed that a final hearing on preliminary injunctions did not require a full three-judge court if the plaintiff did not press the issue. In both cases, the Court established rules that limited the right to appeal on procedural issues.

[3] *United States* v. *Los Angeles & Salt Lake Railroad Co.*, 273 U.S. 299 (1927), involved a suit challenging the power of the Interstate Commerce Commission to value property for rate decisions under the 1922 act. Hughes acted as counsel for the railroad, and put forward an interpretation of the commerce clause that even a conservative court had rejected years earlier. LDB spoke for a unanimous Court in upholding the Commission.

[4] On 23 February LDB had written his brother: "The President's address yesterday, which I attended reluctantly (in robes) was one of the most painful experiences of a lifetime." For the text of the message, which was also broadcast widely by radio, see *New York Times*, 23 February 1927.

[5] At the urging of his friend Alice N. Lincoln, LDB had enlisted in the effort to reform the laws and practices of poorhouses, mental asylums, and other public institutions for orphans and the mentally or physically afflicted wards of the state. See LDB to Amy Brandeis Wehle, 1 February 1895, n. 1.

[6] Perhaps Max James Kohler (1871–1934), a New York lawyer and Jewish activist. He was the son of the theologian, Kaufmann Kohler, and wrote several books on Jewish topics and Jewish history.

[7] Roger Sherman Foster (b. 1900) taught law at Harvard until 1929, when he moved to Yale. He became an attorney for the Securities and Exchange Commission in 1935.

[8] *American Railway Express Co.* v. *Kentucky*, 273 U.S. 269 (1927). A declaratory judgment merely confirms the rights of the parties without ordering anything to be done. In this case the Court affirmed that the American Express Company was responsible for the debts, in Kentucky, of its predecessor firm, the Adams Express Company.

[9] See 8 February 1927.

No. 263   March 6, 1927   Washington, D.C.

1. O.W.H. approaches the birthday[1] in as good form as, and in a more joyous spirit than, at any time these ten years.

2. Mr. & Mrs. John Graham Brooks[2] have been here for a fortnight, & are kicking up their heels more gaily than even the OWH's at their ages.

3. Graham Wallas seems quite as young as in 1919.[3]

Altogether, it seems a time of age having its fling.

4. When is the S.V. book to appear. The Atlantic article[4] is receiving some mention here (not from members of U.S.S.C.)

5. Buckner has had a fine victory. 11 to 1 vs. Daugherty is almost as good as a conviction.[5]

I am sorry that B. has concluded to resign; a[nd] particularly that he should have given the reason therefor that he did.[6]

6. I guess Sapiro didn't do a good job.[7] Some extrinsic evidence has come to me. He certainly proved himself a poor advocate in U.S.S.C. in a case involving the Ky Coop. law.[8]

"Schuster bleib bei deinem Leisten."[9]

7. David Reed has proved himself as poor a politician as Pepper.[10]

"Schuster etc,." could be said also of them.

8. Tell Marion that Newton D. Baker (who came in recently to make some enquiries) mentioned, in talking about bar matters (quite incidentally & with undoubted sincerity) your correspondence with you [sic] re Crime Comn. & said he had become convinced you were entirely right & that nothing could be accomplished except through local (state) action.

[1] Holmes would be eighty-six on 8 March; see next letter.

[2] John Graham Brooks (1846–1938) had left the Unitarian ministry in 1891 to work for labor and reform, and served as a federal investigator of strikes, a lecturer, and an organizer of many workingmen's and consumers' organizations.

[3] Wallas was sixty-nine.

[4] See 1 January 1927, n. 5.

[5] The second Miller-Daugherty trial (see 15 August 1926, n. 2) ended on 4 March with the conviction of Miller and the discharge of Daugherty after an eleven to one vote by the jury in favor of his conviction.

[6] On 25 February, Buckner announced that he would be leaving his position as United States attorney after having served two years in the office. Among the reasons he offered was that he had to educate his three daughters and could no longer afford to live on his savings.

[7] Aaron Sapiro had defended Colonel Thomas W. Miller in the second Miller-Daugherty trial.

[8] *Liberty Warehouse* v. *Grannis*, 273 U.S. 70 was decided in January. The question was whether or not a federal court could rule on a state law under the Kentucky Declaratory Judgment Law. The matter arose over the regulation of tobacco sales at public auctions. The Court found for the company; Sapiro defended the state's attorney, Grannis.

[9] "Cobbler remain at your last."

[10] David Aiken Reed (1880–1953), the Republican senator from Pennsylvania from 1922 to 1935, had become embroiled in the bitter Vare-Pepper contest for the Senate and supported Vare (see 23 May 1926, n. 1). Reed had just ended a long filibuster designed to prevent the Senate's investigating committee from opening ballots in certain Pennsylvania districts, thereby appearing to oppose a full and free investigation of the charges against Vare.

No. 264   March 9, 1927   Washington, D.C.

1. OWH's birthday went off most happily. He circulated in the morning an excellent opinion—in [a] case which was assigned to him Saturday evening, & which he wrote Sunday AM. Sunday PM he spent in rollicking laughter at "The Black Pirate" (Douglas Fairbanks). Monday he delivered with much joy the Negro primary opinion.[1] He was never more eager in pursuing the early spring flowers & birds—and carried me off to the Duncan Phillips Gallery the other day, after Court, to see an Egyptian head for which we both care much.

2. I wrote you Sunday asking for the S.V. book. Monday it came.[2] It will prove an event of importance with bench & bar; perhaps a turning point.

3. Do you know Wachtell,[3] a young Jewish lawyer from N.Y., who argued the Wiener bank case[4] the other day against C. E. Hughes? W. made a strong impression on the Court—in every way a fine presentation—much better than his distinguished opponent.

4. I am glad Brewster is so intelligently active,[5] and

5. Also of Reynold's [sic][6] letter. Where did he get his Webb-Kenyon suggestion?

6. Kallen report etc. enclosed at Mack's request.

7. J.W.M. seems ever more eager to support Ch. W.[7]

[1] Holmes, speaking for a unanimous Court, struck down a Texas law providing for an all-white primary for the Democratic party; *Nixon* v. *Herndon*, 273 U.S. 536.

[2] *The Case of Sacco and Vanzetti: A Critical Analysis for Lawyers and Laymen* (Boston: Little,

Brown, 1927). The book was an outgrowth of the *Atlantic Monthly* article (see 1 January 1927, n. 5).

[3] Samuel Robert Wachtell (1886–1943), an immigrant born in Austria-Hungary, practiced law in New York for thirty years, specializing in international finance. In the 1930s, he devoted nearly all his efforts to rescuing Jewish refugees from Europe. See also 22 February 1928.

[4] The property of the Austrian Wiener Bank-Verein had been seized during the war, and some of its Austrian creditors had sued, to enforce their claims against the Alien Property Office. The court held in favor of the bank, ruling that under Austrian law, where the debts were payable, the claims had been satisfied by a deposit in court by the bank. *Zimmerman* v. *Sutherland*, 274 U.S. 253 (1927).

[5] Perhaps Maine governor Ralph Owen Brewster, in the Sacco and Vanzetti case.

[6] Probably James Burton Reynolds (1870–1946), an ally from LDB's Boston years when Reynolds had been vice president of the People's Lobby, who had gone on to hold influential positions in the Republican party organization.

[7] See 15 February 1927. Mack also favored Weizmann's proposed "survey" (see 2 December 1926), while LDB had his suspicions about it.

No. 265   March 21, 1927   Washington, D.C.

1. O.W.H. made last week the important biological discovery that if he put in too much steam, he does not sleep so well at night. But he entered upon 3 week recess with (a) all birthday letters disposed of (b) his opinions all written (that assigned Saturday comes back from the printers at 5 PM today). He is eager for drives & flowers & interesting visitors.

2. Enclosed from Jerome Michael will show you that Anti-Semitism doesn't govern there. [1] Stone J. is entitled to credit as urging M's appointment. M. had talked with me, was determined not to return to the kind of work he had been doing before he came here; & rejected a tender in a large office with prospects good for court work. He wanted to be U.S. D.J.

3. J.W.M. has doubtless reported on his 2 hrs with us. He found a telegram for B.F. saying he agreed with me & seemed quite discomfitted. I talked plainly to him—whether he will remember, I don't know. I found that he had assumed (and no doubt repeated to others) that I had advised Miss Szold & Mrs. Lindheim [2] to have the Hadassah withdraw from Z.O. What I advised them was not to enter next year into the U[nited]. P[alestine]. A[ppeal]. And *they* could not conceivably have misunderstood, as many things as to their future in Z.O. were discussed. Of course, JWM had his thoughts elsewhere when talking with Miss Szold.

4. I am glad you put it strong to JWM about sticking to his judicial work in B[oston]. I told him he must cancel his speaking engagements also for the evening *preceding* the hearings.

5. Drinker's³ guess on Certs is not sound. There is far more agreement on Certs. than on argued & submitted cases. I don't recall his cases.

6. You will find among the P.C.'s quite a number of cases recently which would doubtless have been honored with opinions, if work were not pressing hard on some of the members.

7. It is an interesting reflexion that McR's Jensen aberration⁴ has led through this alleged State rights judge to federal compensation for longshoremen—a most irrational federal function.

8. I had so strongly your view of H.M.K. that I didn't read his screed.⁵

9. It's good to know that the Phila. bar responded so well.

10. George W. Anderson is here on way home in fine health & much improved spirits.

11. R. Walton Moore (to whom you have doubtless sent the [*] article (as I suggested to C.) had not even heard of it. You doubtless saw his paper in the March 12 Congr. Rec.⁶

¹ Michael had just been hired at Columbia Law School.

² Irma Levy Lindheim (1886–1978) succeeded Henrietta Szold as president of Hadassah, the Women's Zionist Organization, and served in that office until 1928. In 1933, five years after the death of her husband, Norvin, she moved to a kibbutz in Palestine where she did agricultural labor and some autobiographical writing.

³ Probably Henry Sandwich Drinker (1880–1953), a Philadelphia lawyer who had studied at Harvard, but then graduated from the University of Pennsylvania.

⁴ See 25 February 1924, n. 7.

⁵ Perhaps Horace M. Kallen's article, "Fascism: for the Italians," *New Republic* 49 (12 January 1927): 211, a defense of fascism and of Mussolini.

⁶ This must be an error for there was no *Congressional Record* for 12 March.

No. 266   March 29, 1927   Washington, D.C.

1. That's a fine lot of letters, & the [Boston] Herald has done well re SV. The Rudolph Albrocchi letters ought to be reproduced somewhere.

2. I am not surprised at either the Union Club, the Back Bay or the Boston bar.¹ If C[harles]. N[agel]. writes for the American Bar Assn-Journal, let me know.²

3. As to the 3 U.S.S.C. Justices on H.L.S. [fund-raising] Drive: OWH talked with me about the constant requests, which the mail brings, a month or two ago, and was much relieved when he heard my views. I doubt whether he would wish to give, even if the objections which I have to the scheme did not exist.³

Sanford also talked with me. He also was relieved on hearing my views, largely because he has calls from his Tennessee Educational Institutions (which he was & in part still is connected) & which are making drives.

But, I think, both O. W. H. and Sanford feel as I do that the School is going all wrong in its bigness. I should be glad, at the proper time, to aid further in research work under your direction. But I should think it unwise to give until the Drive is well in the background. I don't want any inference drawn, from anything I do, that I favor it. Of course I remain silent, unless asked.

3. [sic] That's a fine quotation from Spinoza. And I was delighted with Morris Cohen's paper on S. in the N. R.[4]

4. R. Walton Moore, who is wholly of our view re Mexico & Nicaragua,[5] tells me confidentially that Dwight Morrow is very much troubled about Mexico & the possibilities of our intervening; also that C.C. would like to get rid of K[ellogg]., but doesn't know how to do it or whom to substitute.[6] Of course, C.C. hasn't the courage. He is showing up his nothingness.

5. As to China, I am less troubled. Of course, we are doing terrible things.[7] But the 400 millions there & the distance make it pretty certain that all occidentals will be wiped out soon, as they deserve to be. And it would not be surprising if that were the beginning of the end of the whites in Asia.

6. We had a fine evening with Abe Flexner.

[1] The debate over the Sacco and Vanzetti case raged through the spring and summer of 1927, and it arrayed the traditional forces of American conservatism against radicals, liberals, intellectuals and labor.

[2] Charles Nagel did not write for the *ABA Journal*, but he had his say on Sacco and Vanzetti in a laudatory review of FF's book in *Harvard Law Review* 40 (1927): 1031.

[3] See 25 May 1927.

[4] Morris R. Cohen, "Spinoza: Prophet of Liberalism," *New Republic* 50 (30 March 1927): 164. "It is because he so well exemplifies the faith that the way to human salvation is through reason and enlightenment that Spinoza may well be considered the philosopher-prophet of liberalism."

[5] See 10 January and 8 February 1927.

[6] Kellogg remained as secretary of state until the end of the Coolidge administration.

[7] See 8 February 1927.

No. 267   April 6, 1927   Washington, D.C.

1. The S.V. decision came quick & of course was not unexpected by you.[1] It will perhaps heighten the already great impression your book has made.

2. Gooch, who was in this afternoon for tea, says Lowell[2] told him

that "its publication stopped dead the Law School drive." I hope it is so. At all events the arrest is a fortunate thing for the School.

3. Please say to Prof. Whitehead[3] that we shall be very glad to have him, Mrs. Whitehead and Prof. Woods[4] (& the others if any) take a cup of tea with us on Sunday April 17th at say 5 P.M. at Florence Court.

4. We are awaiting Al Smith's declaration with eagerness.[5] You have given him (via Belle[6]) good advice.

5. Glad to see the spirit of Ky even in a banker.

6. It's good to hear that young Amram is doing worthy things.

7. Alice was particularly interested in Hans Zinsser article.[7] His grandfather was a revolutionary associate of Dr. Goldmark.[8]

[1] On 5 April, the Supreme Judicial Court of Massachusetts denied a motion for a new trial for Sacco and Vanzetti. The motion had been made after a confession by a professional criminal, Celestino Madeiros, who had admitted committing the crime, and stating that Sacco and Vanzetti had taken no part in it. Judge Webster Thayer had ruled against a new trial on the basis of the Madeiros confession in October 1926, and with the state's high court sustaining his decision, the way was now open for the formal sentencing. The death sentence was pronounced upon both men on 9 April.

[2] Abbott Lawrence Lowell (1856–1943) had succeeded Charles W. Eliot as president of Harvard in 1909, and remained as the university's head until 1933. A member of an illustrious New England family, Lowell had graduated from the Harvard Law School three months after LDB. After two decades of practice, he began teaching at Harvard in 1897, and had vigorously opposed LDB's confirmation in 1916. FF and Lowell were constantly at odds, and FF came to feel that Lowell was a narrow-minded conservative and an anti-Semite to boot. On 1 June 1927, Governor Alvan T. Fuller appointed Lowell and two other men to serve as an Advisory Committee with regard to the possibility of clemency for Sacco and Vanzetti. The committee made its secret report to the governor on 27 July, and a week later Fuller denied clemency.

[3] Alfred North Whitehead (1861–1947), the renowned British philosopher and mathematician, joined the Harvard faculty in 1924; he remained in Cambridge until his retirement in 1937.

[4] Probably James Haughton Woods (1864–1935), Whitehead's colleague in the philosophy department, who had taught at Harvard since 1891.

[5] For all practical purposes, Al Smith had announced his presidential candidacy at his inaugural as governor on 1 January 1927. The "declaration" LDB refers to here is undoubtedly Smith's famous reply to C. C. Marshall. In April 1927 Marshall, an Episcopalian, raised the issue of the suitability of a Roman Catholic for president through a letter to the *Atlantic Monthly*. Smith decided to meet the issue directly, and he published, in the May issue, a reply which defined his views and asserted the absolute separation of church and state.

[6] Belle Linder Moskowitz (1877–1933) was part of that circle of New York social workers and political activists that included LDB's Goldmark relations, as well as the crowd gathered around *The Survey*. She and her husband, Henry (who had been closely associated with LDB in the garment workers arbitration in 1910), were strong supporters of Al Smith.

[7] Hans Zinsser (1878–1940) was a leading bacteriologist who later achieved a kind of popularity with his *Rats, Lice and History* (Boston: Little, Brown, 1935). The article referred to may have been "The Perils of Magnanimity," *Atlantic Monthy* 139 (February 1927): 246.

[8] Dr. Joseph Goldmark (1819–1881), a Viennese scientist, had fled to the United States because of his participation in the abortive revolt of 1848. LDB married one of his daughters, and worked with another to attain protective legislation for women workers.

282

No. 268   April 9, 1927   Washington, D.C.

Re yours of 7.

1. Frank Taussig pleases me even more than Moors.[1] And may give more pain in high quarters.

2. Enclosed from Adele Shaw will show you that the disease is endemic elsewhere. Her protest, & that of the Pa. school boys on Nicaragua, shows that all is not lost.

3. I wrote Alfred Cohn last week & shall try to rekindle the fires in him. He has promised to spend an evening with us.

4. Stoughton Bell does not surprise me.

5. As I wrote you, your protest on S.V. may, in the long run, prove the more fruitful because of the action of the S.J.C.[2]

6. Tell Holdsworth[3] we shall hope to see him.

7. Tell Beard[4] to let me know when he is next in Washington. His paper (which I shall return to you in a few days) is illuminating. But while College Presidents & Trustees are properly blamed, the would be political scientists cannot be exculpated for their barrenness.

Some of the greatest works in political science, in other countries, were published anonymously. This is true of Montesquieu's work i.a. And in other fields, for instance history, America had its rich who labored diligently in silence to produce notable works—Prescott, Motley, Parkman.[5]

[1] John Farwell Moors (1861–1953), a lawyer and broker with impeccable New England credentials (and the law partner of a Cabot) and Frank W. Taussig had both come out on behalf of Sacco and Vanzetti. Moors was active in the effort to persuade Governor Fuller to appoint an Advisory Committee.

[2] See preceding letter, n. 1.

[3] Probably Sir William Searle Holdsworth (1871–1944), an accomplished and prolific historian of English law at Oxford University. He was in the United States to lecture at Northwestern and to receive the Ames medal from the Harvard Law School.

[4] Charles Austin Beard (1874–1948) was one of America's most influential and productive historians. He taught at Columbia University from 1907 until 1917, when he resigned in a dispute over academic freedom in wartime. A progressive in politics and engaged in reform activities himself, his most famous work was the controversial *An Economic Interpretation of the Constitution* (New York: Macmillan, 1913).

[5] William Hickling Prescott (1796–1859), John Lothrop Motley (1814–1877), and Francis Parkman (1823–1893) were leading American historians of the nineteenth century.

No. 269   April 11, 1927   Washington, D.C.

Opinion in No. 412 herewith.[1]

If anything can awaken Trade Unionists from their lethargy, this should.

And perhaps it needs a jolt of this kind to arouse them in this era of friendly cooperation.

[1] *Bedford Cut Stone Co.* v. *Journeymen Stone Cutters' Assoc.*, 274 U.S. 37, was decided on this date. The case involved a group of peaceful stonecutters who refused, in accord with their constitution, to "finish" limestone cut by nonunion cutters. The company sought an injunction; and although it was refused by two lower courts, the Supreme Court granted its request. Paul Murphy calls the ruling "the high point in the trend toward utilizing the antitrust structure to curb labor activity." Holmes joined LDB in a strong dissent. The decision infuriated organized labor and occasioned much comment in the liberal press. For FF's comment, see 26 April 1927, n. 3.

No. 270   April 14, 1927   Washington, D.C.

Copies of opinion enclosed. Bishop Lawrence's assent should help deepen the rift.[1]

1. The S.V. correspondence & newspaper reaction is fine. The action of the S.J.C. damns it pretty effectively; but it will help the holy cause. Another instance of "the Blood of the Martyrs becoming the seed of the Church." Your own press is doing fine work.

2. I am in hope that our new Dred Scott decision will help another cause in a Sumter way.[2]

3. Sir Wyndham Deedes was in yesterday. He is a fine fellow, & happily a long talk passed off without any reference by either to Dr. W, or any performance of the Z.O.

4. I don't remember whether I told you that I had 2 invitations to dine with Kerensky,[3] which must have been initiated by him. I declined as usual but sent him word I should be glad to see him at Florence Court.[4] Was relieved (as in London) that he was "prevented" from coming.

5. The N.R.'s "Mr. Moore's Private War" hit the Times a hard blow.[5] Has The Times made any attempt to justify?

6. I thought Borchard's article[6] also well worthwhile.

6. [sic] I shall be glad to see Patrick Dorff Monday at 9:15 AM & if Alice can arrange it, will ask him in to dine with us Wednesday evening.

7. Stoughton Bell is true to form.

8. Wasn't it pretty bad form for Waite [sic] J. to justify himself.[7]

9. Re water power, I suppose you are watching the Wisconsin situation. The Fox River Co. case was argued this week.[8]

[1] Episcopal Bishop William Lawrence had headed a list of five distinguished Massachusetts citizens who petitioned the governor for a commission to review the Sacco and Vanzetti case.

[2] See preceding letter. The reference is to the notorious pre-Civil War slavery case, *Dred Scott* v.

Sanford, 19 How. 393 (1857), a case which markedly quickened the pace of disunion and led inexorably to Fort Sumter.

[3] Alexander Feodorovich Kerensky (1881–1970) had risen to power in the turmoil of wartime Russia after the February 1917 revolution. In November he was overturned by Lenin and the Bolsheviks and forced to flee. He lived in London and Paris, but in 1927 was visiting the United States. He moved to this country permanently in 1940.

[4] The Brandeis apartment.

[5] The anonymous article in the 13 April issue was a scathing attack upon Frederick Moore, the reporter sent by the *New York Times* to cover China. Quoting from his dispatches, *The New Republic* showed that he was ignorant of Chinese affairs, hostile to the Nationalist movement, and consistently proforeigner. His "news" stories, the article charged, were only thinly veiled propaganda designed to encourage foreign intervention to put down an imagined bolshevik threat.

[6] Edwin M. Borchard, "How Far Must We Protect Our Citizens Abroad?" *New Republic* 50 (13 April 1927): 214. The article argued against the practice of a state being obliged to come to the aid of one of its citizens abroad, and argued instead for an international court where individuals could bring suit without involving their countries.

[7] LDB probably refers to Judge William Cushing Wait (1860–1935), a member of the Supreme Judicial Court of Massachusetts since 1923, and the author of the opinion denying a new trial to Sacco and Vanzetti on the basis of the Madeiros confession. See 6 April 1927, n. 1.

[8] *Fox River Paper Co.* v. *Railroad Commission of Wisconsin*, 274 U.S. 651, was argued on 11 and 12 April and decided on 31 May. The company built a dam on the Fox River in 1878; but laws stretching back to 1841 and territorial days forbade building and maintaining a dam without legal consent. The state's railroad commission refused to permit the company to maintain the dam and the company sued under the due process clause of the Fourteenth Amendment. In his opinion, Justice Stone ruled that the Supreme Court did have jurisdiction because a federal right was asserted, but that the "property" of the company was defined by the rulings of the state court, which did not violate the due-process guarantee.

No. 271   April 20, 1927   Washington, D.C.

We liked your Whiteheads & Patrick Dorff very much.

Philip Guedalla [1] was in yesterday at Wise's suggestion. We shall try to reach the McNeils.

1. Glad to see No. VII. Business of the S.C. [2]

2. When I see you, let me talk with you, re "Business" etc. of
   (a) claiming federal question below.
   (b) affirming decrees on Prelim[inary]. Inj[unction]. as in Humboldt Cattle Co. & Hawaii School Law Cases. [3]
   c. Allowing Certiorari's e.g. in Fed. Empl[oyer's] Liability Cases.
   d. P.C.'s.

3. In June or Nov. issue there should be an expansive note, or an article a propos P.C. in Pinkerton Case. [4]

4. Op. in No. 1. [5] More of this when we meet.

5. O.W.H. had a stomach upset Monday & was at home Monday, but in Court Tuesday—a remarkable recovery. He has never been more keen to enjoy the beauties of returning Spring. [6]

6. Sutherland is in poor shape. Was back again Monday & Tuesday, but should not have been.

7. Your correspondence & other data indicate an ever rising, widening, deepening movement in S.V. Estelle,[7] who was in yesterday, has doubtless reported on the volume coming in to the Prest. & Secy. of State. Roland Boyden & C. P. Curtis Jr. are a great addition to your forces.[8] Prest. Lowell can't be altogether unfriendly.

[1] Philip Guedalla (1889–1944), a British biographer and historian, was currently serving as president of the British Zionist Federation.

[2] FF and James M. Landis, "The Business of the Supreme Court—A Study in the Federal Judicial System: VII. The Judicial Act of 1925," *Harvard Law Review* 40 (April 1927): 834.

[3] In *Humboldt Land & Cattle Co.* v. *Allen*, 274 U.S. 711, the Court affirmed, per curiam, the decree of the Nevada District Court. *Farrington* v. *Tokishige*, 273 U.S. 284 (1927), involved the constitutionality of an act of the Hawaiian territorial legislature regulating foreign language schools. The high court ruled that the district court had not abused its discretion in issuing an interlocutory injunction against the enforcement of the act.

[4] *Pinkerton* v. *Wengert*, 274 U.S. 712. There was no notice of the case in the *Harvard Law Review*.

[5] Case No. 1 was *Federal Trade Commission* v. *Claire Furnace Co.*, 274 U.S. 160. It had been argued in December 1923, reargued in November 1925, and decided on 18 April 1927, with Chief Justice Taft giving the opinion. Twenty-two companies in coal, steel, and related industries contended that the Commission had exceeded its powers by requiring them to submit monthly reports. The Supreme Court ruled that since the Commission's order was enforceable only by requesting the attorney general to institute mandamus proceedings, such proceedings offered sufficient legal remedy to corporations who wished to challenge the constitutionality of the order. Therefore, this particular suit against the Commission could not be entertained.

[6] On 2 April, LDB had written: "O.W.H. seemed the youngest man at yesterday's conference."

[7] Estelle S. Frankfurter, FF's sister.

[8] In addition to Bishop Lawrence, two other members of the five-man delegation to Governor Fuller (see preceding letter, n. 1) were Roland William Boyden (1863–1931), a Brahmin lawyer with the prestigious firm of Ropes, Gray, Boyden & Perkins; and Charles Pelham Curtis, Jr. (1891–1959), another extremely well connected and well respected Boston attorney and author.

No. 272   April 26, 1927   Washington, D.C.

1. All of the Court, I think, realize how great a loss is suffered in Hough's death.[1]

2. The batch of letters & clippings returned herewith show how much more valuable to Massachusetts & the country the S.J.C. has made your work by its denying relief.[2]

3. The widespread upswing is a tribute to the American people as well as to the quality of your publications. This is the first event (other than the war) for many years which has made a deep rift in Boston's upper ten, & seems really to have stirred those with the faculty for being right, in many parts of the country. Coming after the protest against Kellogg's Latin American policies it is indeed heartening.

4. Your "Reminds of Involuntary Servitude" is a stirring document.[3] It looks as if the A.F. of L. were really alive to the danger.

5. The poverty of the British Labor Party in lawyers, reminds of the old time difficulties of Whig Chancellors in finding men fit to be judges.

6. Poor R.P. I guess he will dissolve through sheer lack of vertebrae.[4]

7. That the Epicurean C. C. Burlingham should have become a S.V. protagonist[5] is a remarkable manifestation of the power in your story & the deep down possibilities for Americans. Ellery Sedgwick's rising to the opportunity & Burr's support of the Bishop[6] in his tilt are also very significant.

8. Alice bids me ask you for the Rev. Gordon's "impudence" letter.[7] It is truly great to have smoked him out.

9. Will Charles Nagel write the Amer Bar Asso'n Journal?[8]

10. Auntie B. must have great joy in Harry Taber's fire.

11. When we meet, remind me of "law review criticisms of the courts."

We were glad to see the McNeils [sic] and Calvert.[9]

[1] Judge Charles M. Hough had died on 23 April.

[2] See 6 April 1927, n. 1.

[3] "'Reminds of Involuntary Servitude,'" *New Republic* 50 (27 April 1927): 262. This anonymous article, obviously written by FF, denounced the Supreme Court's decision in the Bedford stonecutters' case (see 11 April 1927). The title is a quotation from LDB's dissent. Referring to that dissent, FF wrote: "The only consolation about the Bedford Cut Stone case is that the moral judgment upon the decision has already been authoritatively uttered as part of the decision."

[4] By the end of the 1920s, FF and his dean, Roscoe Pound, had become enemies. Pound thought that FF's constant crusading on behalf of radical causes was costing the law school dearly; FF thought that Pound lacked moral courage. See Parrish, *Felix Frankfurter*, ch. 9, for the story of growing animosity between these two one-time friends.

[5] Burlingham spoke out in a letter to the *New York Times*, 20 April 1927.

[6] See 14 April 1927, n. 1.

[7] Rev. George Angier Gordon (1853–1929), the longtime minister of Boston's Old South Church, denounced Bishop Lawrence's letter (see 14 April 1927, n. 1) as "impudent." Massachusetts judicial officials, Gordon argued, were perfectly capable of handling the matter without interference from outside authorities.

[8] See 29 March 1927, n. 2.

[9] Probably Sayre Macneil (1886–1961) and former law clerk, Calvert Magruder, both on the Harvard Law faculty.

No. 273   April 27, 1927   Washington, D.C.

Your telegram reached me at Court. Your letter with the Wigmore blast & your answer did not come to me until late this afternoon.[1] I talked personally to Holmes J., & he is fully prepared for any rabid attack by Wigmore on any one, through W's attacks on him.[2]

W's attack on the Senate in the April Illinois Law Review[3] & other performances are evidence of an unbalanced mind.

The enclosed from Graham Wallas to Alice will be good evidence for Marion as to how W's ploy strikes the intelligent layman.

I agree with you, W's performance, however sad & unpleasant, will not affect the results—indeed, it should help, however painful[ly], to the ultimate end sought. S.V. is only an incident in a long battle line.

I will return the other clippings later.

[1] On 26 April the *Boston Transcript* ran an explosive, front page article under the headline "Wigmore Attacks Frankfurter." Dean John H. Wigmore had accused FF of gross inaccuracies and bias in his work on the Sacco and Vanzetti case. FF responded immediately and at length in the next morning's *Boston Herald* (the editor, Frank Buxton, holding publication until the reply from FF arrived). For FF's exciting version of the incident, see Phillips, ed., *Felix Frankfurter Reminisces*, 215–17. The telegram from FF to LDB read: "Holmes may hear at second hand about Wigmore attack and be troubled by it. Please assure him not slightest reason for concern. Quite contrary have had nothing but commendation from important lawyers and others on my reply. Nothing but condemnation and pity expressed for Wigmore."

[2] See Wigmore, "Abrams v. U.S.: Freedom of Speech and Freedom of Thuggery in Wartime and Peacetime," *Illinois Law Review* 21 (1920): 539.

[3] Wigmore had written an editorial, "Every Senator a Legislative Dictator," *Illinois Law Review* 21 (1927): 804; it was an intemperate attack on the way any one irresponsible Senator could obstruct legislation.

No. 274   April 28, 1927   Washington, D.C.

The morning papers & mail from Miss Grady bring good news. The respite given Maderos [sic],[1] and the request of Pound[2] et al for the Review, coming after the Wigmore article,[3] appear at the most effective time conceivable.

With your crushing reply to Wigmore, those responsible for his intercession should feel humiliated—if their prejudices have not made them proof against emotions as well as ideas.

Your copies of Wigmore & the reply returned herewith.

Beveridge's death is sad.[4] I had not realized that he was so old.

[1] Madeiros (see 6 April 1927, n. 1), who stood convicted of murder and was due to be executed, received a stay of execution on 28 April. In the end, Madeiros would be executed on the same night as Sacco and Vanzetti.

[2] Roscoe Pound had joined others in petitioning Governor Fuller for a complete review of the Sacco-Vanzetti case. See *New York Times*, 27 April 1927.

[3] See preceding letter.

[4] Albert J. Beveridge had died the day before at the age of sixty-four.

No. 275   May 2, 1927   Washington, D.C.

1. O.W.H. closed yesterday's sitting (our last argued case) in fine form & eager spirit—with all his cases written. (Save such as the C.J. may give him to help out other jjs.)

2. The award of the Pulitzer prize for "We Submit" comes at an opportune time.[1]

3. One of the important by-products of your S.V. stunt is the assertion by Law School professors of the Law Schools' prerogative as guardians of law & justice. The performance of Yale's Dean & Associates is a notable event.[2] I had hoped (and still hope) that C.C.B. will stir Columbia & the other N.Y. Schools to similar action. Is there not hope of something similar from the Cornell men? Wigmore's sad performance[3] should really help much in this connection, and [it] is almost a noblesse oblige for others who disagree with him. A rare opportunity is afforded the Law Schools to amplify their jurisdiction. F.W.T.[4] gave, I think, poor advice to C.C.B.

4. It was natural that the Transcript should resurrect the Roosevelt letter. I had been thinking of the Mooney case & wondering whether your S.V. action might not lead some able, courageous man who cares, to write up the terrible Mooney story.[5] It is all of a piece with what I see of the California judiciary & bar.

[1] "We Submit" was the 26 October 1926 editorial in the Boston *Herald*, written by F. Lauriston Bullard, and urging a new trial for Sacco and Vanzetti. Bullard's editorial had just been awarded the Pulitzer Prize for the best editorial of 1926.
[2] Yale's acting dean, Robert M. Hutchins, spoke along with FF at a mass meeting of the Yale Liberal Club on behalf of Sacco and Vanzetti.
[3] See 27 April 1927.
[4] Perhaps Frank W. Taussig.
[5] For the *Mooney* case, see 21 January 1922, n. 2. The "Roosevelt letter" was the ex-President's rebuke to FF, 19 December 1917, for FF's reports on the Mooney case and on the Bisbee, Arizona, deportations. Roosevelt's letter is an hysterical denunciation of such "Bolsheviki of America" as La Follette and Amos Pinchot. For the text, see E. E. Morison et al., eds., *The Letters of Theodore Roosevelt* (Cambridge: Harvard University Press, 1951–1954), 8: 1262–65. See next letter, n. 4.

No. 276   May 6, 1927   Washington, D.C.

1. Your S.V. should yield also this important by-product: Students may realize now that a Law School professorship affords an admirable pedastle [sic] for participating in the practical affairs.

2. Ernest Hocking's letter to the Herald (Apr. 27)[1] is the most valuable contribution to the subject which has come to my notice.

3. Fabian Franklin's debut is significant.[2]

5. [sic] And the N.Y. Ev. Post editorial surprising.[3]

6. If the Transcript's public can still "sit & read" your answer to the Colonel[4] should add to their education.

7. Your S.V. as the second best seller[5] helps to answer the question I meant to put: "How many copies have been sold?"

8. You have made things clear for MacDonald et al. I feel rather grieved that he didn't stay in England & spend his time preparing for the fight.[6]

9. C. Nagel would render better service if he reviewed the book for the American Bar Assn. Journal.[7]

10. George W. Crocker, in his courageous controversies preserves some of the old puritan spirit.[8]

11. Your letter to Shattuck[9] should have set at rest the Governor's doubts; but the malicious censurers will not be silenced.

12. When we have some quiet days in Chatham remind me to speak to you of the P.C.'s.

---

[1] William Ernest Hocking (1873–1966) taught philosophy at Harvard from 1914 until his retirement in 1943. His letter to the Boston *Herald* appeared on 30 April, and discussed the Sacco-Vanzetti case in light of changes which had been made in the criminal appeals process in Massachusetts in the last decade. Where superior courts had previously been able to examine appeals *de novo*, they were now bound to look at only certain procedural matters, which, if not violated, prevented the overturning of a decision even if it were wrong.

[2] Fabian Franklin (1853–1939) was an author, editor, and man of letters who wrote on current affairs. His "debut" was a letter to the *New York Times* (27 April) in support of FF's book on the Sacco and Vanzetti case. See also his thoughtful article, "The Logic of the Sacco-Vanzetti Case," published in the obscure *McNaughts' Monthly Magazine*.

[3] In an editorial on 29 April, the *Evening Post* predicted that in postponing the execution of Celestino Madeiros, who had confessed to the crime for which Sacco and Vanzetti were under sentence of death, Governor Fuller had given "virtual assurance that these two men will not be sent to the chair without full reconsideration of the case."

[4] In response to Theodore Roosevelt's attack on him for his defense of Mooney, FF had written to the ex-president on 7 January 1918. In the five-page letter, FF attempted to correct a number of factual misstatements, but he also insisted that wartime hysteria could not be allowed to get in the way of justice.

[5] FF's book sold widely, but neither *Publishers' Weekly* nor Alice P. Hackett and James H. Burke, *80 Years of Best Sellers, 1895–1975* (New York: R.R. Bowker Co., 1977), list the work as a "best seller."

[6] Liberal party leader Ramsay MacDonald spent most of April and May 1927 visiting the United States.

[7] See 29 March 1927, n. 2.

[8] LDB undoubtedly meant George Uriel Crocker (1863–1929) a civic leader of Boston and former city treasurer. Crocker had come forward to testify that he had heard trial judge Webster Thayer express bias against Sacco and Vanzetti on many occasions.

[9] In response to rumors that FF had "a financial interest" in the Sacco-Vanzetti case, FF wrote a

lengthy letter to Shattuck on 28 April setting forth the facts of his involvement in the case, and denying any financial interests at all. The following day, Shattuck sent on FF's letter to Governor Fuller.

No. 277   May 9, 1927   Washington, D.C.

1. It's fine to know that the Law Schools are availing of the opportunity you have given them.[1] I hope their participation will have due publicity.

2. Your [Boston] Herald friends showed in their Life editorial: "In der Beschrankung zeigt sich erst des Meister."[2]

3. They, the N.R. & W.L. may find in the New Statesman, April 16 article "Trade Unions & the Courts of Justice,"[3] a discourse on the limitation of the judicial horizon which may be useful in other connections.

4. R.P. and other "Drivers" should bear in mind the principles laid down by Innocent III[4] for almsgiving:

The motive should be love; the purpose to attain
Heaven; the manner cheerful; and the method
"according to rules."

Where does Poison Ivy come in?

5. When did Prof. Whitehead say that about the lack of moral courage in America? It was this thesis on which I began my talk with him.

6. We expect the Holdworth's [sic] Thursday for tea—and Alfred Cohn for dinner.

7. Prof. Wigmore has presented legal evidence which precludes the necessity among the knowing of a [*].

[1] In the late spring and summer of 1927, a number of leading law school faculties made public pleas for a new trial for Sacco and Vanzetti.

[2] "Show yourself first the master of details." Goethe. The Boston *Herald* editorial of 4 May, entitled "Life Slanders Us," complained of a *Life* cartoon depicting Massachusetts as intolerant and prejudiced because of its treatment of Sacco and Vanzetti. Justice had not been perverted, the paper claimed; the two men had been fairly tried, and convicted of a heinous crime.

[3] The anonymous editorial attacked the Trade Union Bill pending in Parliament. In the first place, the editorial argued, the bill aroused old class antagonisms that should have been left alone. Moreover, the bill was so vague and uncertainly worded that everything would depend upon how it was interpreted in the courts.

[4] Innocent III (1160–1216), one of the ablest, most active, and influential of the medieval popes, served in the office between 1198 and 1216.

No. 278   May 11, 1927   Washington, D.C.

Saw O.W.H. today. He was in great shape.

1. The explanation of Bently [sic] Warren[1] is doubtless Williams-town.

2. S.V. will ensure due attention to your Crime Survey.

3. Now that "Business of the U.S.S.C." is on the homestretch, Landis and Friendly may want to begin biting on "Business of the Lower Federal Courts." Enclosed copy of letter of April 14/27 to the C.J. (which please return) indicates that an effective beginning may possibly be made in reducing the jurisdiction of the District Courts.

I think there are serious objections to creating minor federal courts for petty crimes. But curtailment might be effected

    A. In Civil Cases, i.a.

        (1) By largely restricting the Diversity of Citizenship jurisdiction.[2]

        (2) By largely restricting suits in which jurisdiction is dependent on federal questions

        (3) By confining to the state courts all suits to enforce federal employers liability law—all under seamens law not in Admiralty

    B. In Criminal Cases, i.a.

    By opening state court to punishment of federal crimes (as suggested by Charles Warren). The States would probably bite, if they got a contribution for doing the federal work.

Articles in Nov–Dec/25 [sic] & Jan/28 Law Review might educate Norris' Comtee[3] & Congress.

[1] Bentley Wirt Warren (1864–1947) was a prominent Boston attorney, active in civic affairs and a former member of the Massachusetts House of Representatives. He wintered in Williamstown.

[2] See 2 April 1925, n. 1.

[3] George W. Norris was the chairman of the Senate Judiciary Committee.

No. 279   May 21, 1927   Washington, D.C.

1. It's good to see the U. of P[ennsylvania]. fall into line.[1] I trust the contagion is spreading among the Law Schools.

2. My congratulations to you and Patterson on No. 1. of Harvard Studies in Administrative Law. It is fitting that No. 1. should be "The Insurance Commission [sic]"—& fortunate that it should be written by a professor of a university other than Harvard.[2]

3. When will No. 2. appear?[3]

4. I had sent copies of the Whitney opinion[4] to Laski, Learned Hand, [*], Villard & Morris Cohen; & after your letter sent copies to Chafee and Justice Higgins.

5. Enclosed from Borah is, I suppose, to make amends for 1916.[5]

6. Alvin Johnson was in yesterday. That is a terrific job which he is undertaking with Seligman.[6]

7. Lowell Mellett (editor, Scripps-Howard newpapers 1322 N.Y. Ave, Washington) undertook the Espionage campaign at my suggestion & finally put it into the hands of Ruth Furness,[7] a very competent young woman who produced a series of 11 articles of value. I think it would encourage Mellett, if you write him & ask for a copy of the articles.

[1] In the effort to get a new trial for Sacco and Vanzetti.

[2] Edwin Wilhite Patterson, *The Insurance Commissioner in the United States* (Cambridge: Harvard University Press, 1927). Patterson (1889–1965) taught law at Columbia.

[3] The second volume was John Dickinson, *Administrative Justice and the Supremacy of Law in the United States* (Cambridge: Harvard University Press, 1927).

[4] *Whitney* v. *California*, 274 U.S. 357 (1927). Anita Whitney was convicted under California's Criminal Syndicalism Act of 1919 while helping to organize the Communist Labor party in that state. The Supreme Court, speaking through Justice Sanford, upheld the conviction. Sanford argued that the California legislature had determined that certain activities constituted the necessary "clear and present danger" which permitted the limitation of speech. LDB, with Holmes joining, wrote a long concurring opinion arguing that the Court could decide upon different criteria in different cases on "clear and present danger" and that it was not obliged to accept California's definition. LDB made clear that his personal definition (particularly on the ground of the "imminence" of the danger in Anita Whitney's speech) would have resulted in overturning the conviction. LDB concurred in the opinion, apparently, because there was not opportunity to "inquire into errors now alleged," and also because the Court had never clearly fixed the meaning of the "clear and present danger" formula. Samuel Konefsky writes of LDB's opinion: "But even if Brandeis had not essayed so searching an examination of the meaning of 'clear and present danger,' his opinion would have been notable for another reason. In it is to be found one of the most moving expositions of America's heritage of freedom. The passages in which he states his libertarian creed do indeed reveal him to be, in Professor Chafee's phrase, one of the 'strongest conservators of Americanism.' " For Konefsky's illuminating discussion of the Whitney case, see *The Legacy of Holmes and Brandeis*, 209–23. See also 26 June 1927, n. 10.

[5] The enclosure is unknown; the reference is to Borah's opposition to LDB's confirmation in 1916.

[6] Alvin Johnson and E. R. A. Seligman began work in 1927 on the monumental *Encyclopedia of the Social Sciences*. The preparation stretched from 1927 to 1933, and publication of the volumes extended from 1930 to 1935.

[7] LDB undoubtedly meant Ruth Finney (1898–1979), and he uses the correct spelling in the next letter. Finney was a California journalist who moved to the Washington Bureau of the Scripps-Howard chain in 1923.

No. 280   May 25, 1927   Washington, D.C.

1. I note Gov. Fuller's[1] "Italia fara da se."[2]

2. Before Lindbergh[3] gets off the front page, the N.R. should draw

the lesson of his heritage. His father—farmer-labor insurgent. The dignity & sense for the worthwhile of his mother.[4] His Scandinavian ancestry—which gave us also Andrew Furuseth. Moral courage—self-reliance—individuality.

Enclosed from "Labor" on these lines.

3. After you have seen Ruth Finney's stuff, it would be fruitful probably to advise Mellett to have her go to N.Y. to go over thoroughly the material of the Amer. Civil Liberties League.[5]

4. Has Ellery Sedgwick made any progress with "Life, Leisure & Pleasure?" He might follow such an article with "The Midas Touch—Our Curse?"

5. Saw OWH today. He is in fine shape. He confessed to me that, importuned by Cochran, he had sent the HLS fund $100. (One hundred).

6. Things are in a pretty bad way in England.

7. We are expecting to see Morris Cohen Sunday.

[1] Alvan Tufts Fuller (1878–1958), a former Massachusetts congressman, was serving as governor of the state.

[2] "Italy will take care of herself." Fuller was under heavy pressure to appoint a high-level commission, preferably composed of outsiders, to investigate the Sacco and Vanzetti trial. On 25 May, however, he announced that he intended to keep the investigation in his own hands. Within a week he changed course and appointed an "advisory committee" to help inform his decision on whether or not to grant clemency. See 2 June 1927.

[3] On 21 May, Charles Augustus Lindbergh, Jr. (1902–1974) became, by any standard, the transcendent hero of the hour, by completing the first solo transatlantic flight in *The Spirit of St. Louis*. For the attempt to read a symbolic meaning into his flight and to "draw lessons" (as LDB does here) from his personality, see John W. Ward, "The Meaning of Lindbergh's Flight," *American Quarterly* 10 (1958): 3.

[4] Charles Augustus Lindbergh (1859–1924) was a liberal congressman from Minnesota between 1906 and 1916. He is credited with having introduced the resolution which led to the establishment, in 1913, of the Pujo Committee to investigate the "money trust"—a phrase that Lindbergh used as freely in those days as LDB did. In 1902 he married Evangeline Lodge Land.

[5] See preceding letter.

No. 281   May 31, 1927   Washington, D.C.

1. Very glad to hear Minnesota was so hospitable to S.V. & that others' activities continue. It has been a great campaign of education & we never needed it so much.

2. I chance[d] to pick up the Saturday Evening Post (latest) at the barbershop, & read an editorial[1] which would not have been possible even for the National Conference Board 10 years ago.

3. Did you notice this in Siegfried's "America Comes of Age"[2] p. 69: "But what are we to think of a country of British origin where liberalism

has to seek its champions among foreigners & Catholics? The reason is clear enough. In its pursuit of wealth and power, America has abandoned the ideal of liberty to follow that of property."

4. No 894[3] and 549[4] enclosed if duly impressed upon bench & bar may have an important effect (in connection with Virginian Ry Case)[5]—in

 A. Severely curbing proneness of district court, in issuing restraining orders, interlocutory and final injunctions—both in cases under §266,[6] and in those relating to I.C.C. orders.

 B. In limiting the labors of our court (in connection with Buder case,[7] Moore v. Fidelity[8] & Smith v. Wilson[)].[9]

Haven't you some effective student who could make a survey of the action of the 3 judge courts in these connections & enforce the lessons we are attempting to teach.

The States, with this encouragement, ought also to attempt to protect themselves by proceedings under the provision added to 266.

5. Morris Cohen agrees that O.W.H. is distinctly younger than he has been for years.

[1] Perhaps "Wastebasket Government," *Saturday Evening Post* 199 (28 May 1927): 30, a plea for reorganizing and streamlining the Department of Interior in the name of greater governmental efficiency.

[2] Andre Siegfried (1875–1959), the noted French traveler and man of letters, had just published *America Comes of Age, A French Analysis* (New York: Harcourt, Brace, and Co., 1927).

[3] No. 894, *Lawrence et al.* v. *St. Louis—San Francisco Railway Co.*, 274 U.S. 588, was decided on this date, and LDB gave the Court's opinion. Oklahoma law prohibited a railroad from moving its shops or division points without permission of the state's Corporation Commission. In 1917 the company wanted to move some shops and a division point, but the Commission refused to grant permission and issued a temporary restraining order which was still in effect in 1927. Finally the company decided to make the move without notifying or seeking permission, and then brought suit before a three-judge district court under Section 266 of the Judicial Code (see below, n. 6), charging that Oklahoma was violating the commerce clause, the due process clause, and the equal protection clause. The district court, without opinion, gave the company even more than it asked and enjoined the Commission from even hearing the case. But LDB, for the Supreme Court, ruled that the court's decree was contrary to the law because it did not define the injury making such a decree necessary nor state why the injury would be irreparable. This did not automatically make the decree void, but evidence of the danger of irreparable injury was necessary to justify its issuance, and without an opinion, there was simply no such evidence in the record.

[4] Number 549, *Arkansas Railroad Commission* et al. v. *Chicago, Rock Island & Pacific Railroad Co.*, 274 U.S. 597, was decided on this date and also written by LDB. The Interstate Commerce Commission issued an order that interstate rates not be higher than comparable intrastate rates. Accordingly the railroad raised its intrastate rates and sued when the Arkansas Commission suspended the new rates for examination. The district court agreed with the company and set aside the State Commission's order and, as in the case above, did so without an opinion. LDB ruled that "where there is a serious doubt whether an order of the Interstate Commerce Commission extends to intrastate rates, the doubt should be resolved in favor of the state power." And, in the final paragraph of his opinion, he hammered home the moral: "In *Virginian Ry. Co.* v. *United States* . . . and in *Lawrence* v. *St. Louis-San Francisco Ry. Co., supra*, we called attention to the importance to

the parties, to the public and to this Court of supporting the decree, in cases of this character, by an opinion which shall state fully the reasons for setting aside a commission's order."

[5] See 15 December 1926, n. l.

[6] Section 266 of the *Judicial Code* set down the requirements for the issuing of injunctions based upon the alleged unconstitutionality of state statutes. On 13 February 1925 an amendment to this section required that requests for such injunctions be heard by three-judge courts rather than by single judges.

[7] *Ex parte Buder*, 271 U.S. 461 (1926). A dispute arose in St. Louis when a bank sought to restrain enforcement of a tax levied upon its stockholders. Buder, a tax officer, requested a writ of mandamus against the district court, appealing directly to the Supreme Court under Section 266. LDB, for a unanimous Court, denied the request because the law involved was not alleged to be unconstitutional (as 266 required), but merely not in force. Any hearing of the case, therefore, would have to come through the circuit court of appeals.

[8] *Moore* v. *Fidelity & Deposit Co.*, 272 U.S. 317 (1926). Three insurance companies applied for an injunction against the state's insurance commissioner after he had cancelled their authorization to sell a certain kind of automobile insurance. LDB delivered the unanimous opinion in this Oregon case dismissing the suit since the requirements under Section 266 had not been met.

[9] *Smith* v. *Wilson*, 273 U.S. 388 (1927). Justice Stone delivered the opinion in this Texas case. Some citizens sought an injunction against county commissioners and other officials who wished to levy an assessment on them for improvements on the Brazos River. Again, the provisions of Section 266 had not been met and the case was dismissed for lack of jurisdiction.

No. 282   June 2, 1927   Washington, D.C.

1. Yours of 31st just received. I am deeply chagrined at my oversight in not having Miss Malloch make the deposit of $2000 on Jan 1st/27. I am writing her by this mail & asking her to advise you immediately on making the deposit. Until further notice, it is my intention that $1500 shall be deposited Oct 1, and $2000, Jan 1 during each year for our joint endeavors through you.[1] If by any chance, the deposit is not regularly made please enquire of Miss Malloch or let me know.

I have realized that S.V., inter alia, must have made heavy demands for incidental expense, as well as time, & meant to ask you when we meet whether an additional sum might not be appropriate this year. Let me know.

2. Fuller's advisory board is not as good as the one you intimate as possible.[2]

3. We are doing some heavy reversing of 8th Circuit & 2d. Some note should be made how the Circuits fare.

I am asking Landis & his Mrs. to join us Tuesday evening.

[1] See 19 and 25 November 1916.

[2] See 25 May 1927, n. 2. On 1 June, Governor Fuller announced that his advisory committee on the Sacco and Vanzetti case would consist of three distinguished Massachusetts citizens: A. Lawrence Lowell, president of Harvard and a frequent opponent of FF; Judge Robert Grant (1852–1940), for many years a probate judge but best known as a novelist; and Samuel Wesley Stratton (1861–1931), physicist, former director of the National Bureau of Standards, and since

1923, president of the Massachusetts Institute of Technology. The advisory committee held hearings in the second week of July, and on 27 July reported its opinion to the governor. On 3 August Fuller announced his decision, denying clemency to the two condemned men.

No. 283   June 5, 1927   Washington, D.C.

1. I trust you have received 'ere this word from Miss Malloch that the check has been deposited.[1]

2. There should be in "Business of USSC" or elsewhere, a full exposition of the methods & practices of our Court, which have been large factors in its relatively good performance as compared by the Supreme Courts of the States, i.a.

A. Encouragement of oral argument. Discouragement of oratory. Socratic method at argument applied through the judges. We have almost no cases submitted in briefs, and those few are either a first for us or a surrender.

B. Assignment of cases to the Js by the C.J. after discussion and vote at conference.

C. Distribution of opinions in print, and consideration at subsequent conference. Ample time thereafter for writing dissents & at conference for suggestion & then recirculation of revised opinion.

D. Consideration of every case, certiorari & motion by every judge before the conference & action thereon at the conference.

E. Limiting, by means of certiorari, the number of cases by the human limitation of 9 judges' working time.

F. Discouraging rehearings.

G. Importance of length of service, as distinguished from method of selection of judges.

H. Team play, encouraging individual enquiry (and dissent) as distinguished from subservient ignorant unanimity.

I. Tradition.

J. The play of public opinion upon the Court's performance.

These factors play probably a larger part than elevation of status, high responsibilty & greater ability incident to wider selection.[2]

K. And the extraordinary service through longevity & loyalty in the Clerks & Marshal's offices are also to be considered.

The above elements & others which will occur to you, should be made the basis of a campaign in the several states through the Law Schools & the Law Reviews for bettering the state tribunals. In the main, their product is shocking. And their methods are perhaps more so.

3. Your memo on graduate students embodies much wisdom persuasively presented.

[1] See preceding letter.

[2] FF took up this suggestion and paraphrased this section of LDB's letter in the "Preface" of *The Business of the Supreme Court*, vii–viii.

No. 284   June 16, 1927   Chatham, Mass.

1. Alice & I hope that in planning your busy summer you will leave some break for idle days at Chatham.

2. Your Governor seems to be very diligent.[1] Let us hope that knowledge may be accompanied by wisdom.

3. If the Va Law Register is at hand, look at Major A.S. Lanier's strange performance. He publishes his rejected brief in the Coast Guard Case.[2] Perhaps in search of fame as great as has attended "Rejected Addresses."

4. I am reading The Federalist with amazement that such lofty, closely reasoned arguments should have been vote-getters in 1787–1788.

5. Hope you will have satisfactory dinner tomorrow, & that after it you will have a talk with deH. on Zionist affairs. He is very sad over the dashing of his hopes.[3]

[1] Governor Fuller spent much of June investigating the Sacco and Vanzetti case. On 15 June, for example, he interviewed members of the jury that had convicted Vanzetti of another crime prior to the South Braintree highjacking.

[2] Alexander Sidney Lanier published his brief in *Virginia Law Register* 12 (1927): 747. Lanier had been on the losing side in *Maul* v. *United States*, 274 U.S. 501 (1927), a complicated case involving a Coast Guard seizure of a ship beyond the twelve-mile limit.

[3] The year 1927 marked the beginning of the expulsion of the Lipsky regime from Zionist affairs. Everywhere one looked chaos seemed to reign in American Zionism. Membership fell and fundraising—which had become almost the only function of the American organization—dropped off to such an extent that important commitments in Palestine were left without support. Allegations of mismanagement tore the fabric of the movement. Under these circumstances even Zionists who had supported Lipsky and Weizmann were ready for a return of the LDB-Mack wing of the Zionist organization. It would not be until 1931, however, that the actual transfer of power would be accomplished. The hopes of deHaas may have been "dashed" by LDB's letter to him of 5 June. LDB told deHaas that judicial duties and increasing age would prevent him from resuming his old position of leadership in the movement; his role would be to give advice when asked for it, to help financially, and to study Palestinean problems during the summers. No doubt deHaas had hoped that if LDB returned to active management, he would elevate the controversial deHaas to his former position of power and influence.

No. 285   June 20, 1927   Chatham, Mass.

1. It's good to know that the blue books are so promising.

2. The June 15 H.L.S. Endowment Fund Statement corrects the implied misstatement. Did J.W.M. intervene?

3. Did Alfred Cook [1] answer you? And what has Wells done?

4. Ramsay's [*] paper on the Trade Unions Bill is admirably done. [2] It has made some things much clearer to me.

5. Someday, I hope, one of your disciples will write an article for H.L.R.(?) showing what & how the States might prevent federal encroachment & neutralize the decisions on "occupying the field" [3] & assumed exclusive powers. In that connection, the false prophecy (for the last two generalities) of Madison in Federalist XLVI is of interest:

> "But ambitious encroachments of the federal government, on the authority of State governments, would not excite the opposition of a single State, or of a few States only. They would be signals of general alarm. Every State would espouse the common cause, etc."

See also, a truer prophecy: (ibid)

> "If, therefore, as has been elsewhere remarked, the people should in future become more partial to the federal than to the State governments, the change can only result from such manifest & irresistible proofs of a better administration, as will overcome all their antecedent propensities."

6. As bearing upon the quality of our legislation & the quantity, these passages of the Federalist (Hamilton) LXII are interesting:
    1. "the facility & excess of law making seem to be the diseases to which our governments are most liable."
    2. "What indeed are the repealing, explaining, and amending laws, which disgrace our voluminous codes, but so many monuments of deficient wisdom; so many impreachments exhibited by each succeeding against each preceding session;"
    "A good government implies two things: first fidelity to the object of government, which is the happiness of the people; secondly, a knowledge of means by which that object can best be attained. Some governments are deficient in both of these qualities, most governments are deficient in the first. I scruple not to assert that in American governments too little attention has been paid to the last."

7. Federalist LXXXIII refers to practice in Mass. N.H. Conn. & R.I.

of allowing a party a chance of 2 out of 3 jury trials. I think Chief Justice Bradley[4] told me that in R.I. the practice prevailed in his day. In connection with S.V., it would be interesting to know when & how the practice came to be abolished in Mass. & whether there was a comparable practice in criminal cases.

8. Carroll [sic] Wight[5] appeared yesterday to say goodbye before sailing for Greece today (and Italy, on the way back) & to tell us of his appointment as Associate Professor of Greek at Johns Hopkins. He had in one class 26, in another 48 in Greek, & besides a proseminar course. He sent special greetings to you. His son is having good success as a portrait painter & is in much better health.

[1] Perhaps Alfred Arthur Cook (1873–1950), a New York City attorney.

[2] See 9 May 1927, n. 3. The bibliography in Benjamin Sacks, *J. Ramsay MacDonald in Thought and Action* (Albuquerque: University of New Mexico Press, 1952) lists no published paper by MacDonald on the Trade Unions Bill.

[3] The doctrine that the states were prohibited from legislating in particular areas where federal authority was said to "occupy the field."

[4] Charles Smith Bradley (1819–1888) was a former Rhode Island state senator and chief justice of that state's supreme court. In 1876 he returned to his alma mater to teach and LDB knew him as a Harvard Law School student.

[5] Carol Van Buren Wight was a summer neighbor of LDB's at Chatham. Besides teaching Greek at Johns Hopkins, he wrote several volumes of original poetry.

No. 286   June 26, 1927   Chatham, Mass.

1. My thanks to you and Landis for the H.L.R's with Business of S.C. & my congratulations on finishing this part of a very important job.[1]

2. Your Progress Report in the Crime Survey has also come. You have laid out the work in the grand manner & wisely. It should prove an important contribution all along the line.

From the "Why Crime?" I assume there will emerge articulately also a discussion in some form of crime by the unquestionably normal. I have a feeling that the very proper study of the large percentage of crime among the abnormal involves a danger of dwarfing the responsibility for crime of our social & economic institutions, our values & aspirations. I don't know whether there is anything in Branson's "Does Crime Increase with Tenancy?" referred to in the June/27 La Follettes[2], but it suggests one of the many possible causes of that nature which require consideration. What Laski says p. 8 in his Inaugural[3] on the relation of psychology to political science expresses in another field something of the thought I have as to necessary enquiries.

3. I hope you approved of my emphatic "No" to J.W.M's suggestion that you go on the Zionist Interim Comtee[4] in some capacity.

4. S.V. seems to go well. I suppose you saw the Report in Richard Boekel's [sic] Editorial Research issue of June 21.[5]

5. His issue of June 14 on patronage & the presidential nominations will, I hope, lead Croly et al. to starting a movement to put the 1st, 2d, 3d class post offices etc. into the classified service & to secure abrogation of Frank Hitchcock's[6] atrocious rule of 1912, abrogating the Roosevelt rule of taking the highest & substituting the choice from the first three.

6. The World's "A father & his Son"[7] is a worthy piece. I am surprised the N.R. didn't make more of this subject.

7. Moorfield Storey was true to form.[8]

10. [sic] The pardon of Anita Whitney was a fine job.[9]

11. JWM's lead at the polls is heartening. Liberals must have been an important factor.

12. If S.V. goes right, is Franklin Hichborn the man to move in the Mooney case?[10]

13. You made a wise disposition in Tchernowitz's matter.[11]

14. That quotation of Maitland's[12] will, I hope, find a place sometime in an article on our P.C's.

[1]The final two instalments of the project were "The Judiciary Act of 1925," *Harvard Law Review* 40 (April 1927): 834; and "The Future of Supreme Court Litigation," *ibid.*, (June 1927): 1110.

[2]Winifred B. Cossette, "Does Crime Increase with Tenancy?" *La Follette's Magazine* 19 (June 1927): 92, reported on a study by Eugene Cunningham Branson (1861–1933), a teacher of rural sociology at Alabama Polytechnic Institute. In his survey of Crenshaw County crime, Branson found a far higher percentage of tenant farmers involved in crime than freeholders, and he attacked the tenancy system for degrading men and driving them to illegal activities in order to support their families.

[3]Harold J. Laski delivered his Inaugural lecture, "On the Study of Politics," on 22 October 1926 at the London School of Economics; it is reprinted in his collection of essays, *The Danger of Being a Gentleman* (New York: Viking, 1940), 33–60.

[4]A tentative peace proposal by disenchanted former Lipsky supporters called for an interim committee to manage the ZOA, composed of representatives from all factions.

[5]The issue was given over entirely to J. M. Landis, "The Case of Sacco and Vanzetti."

[6]Frank Harris Hitchcock (1867–1935) was a Washington, D.C., lawyer who undertook numerous public jobs. He was Taft's campaign manager in 1908, and then his postmaster general.

[7]*New York World*, June 1927. The piece was about Charles A. Lindbergh and his father. See 25 May 1927.

[8]Moorfield Storey (1845–1929) was a prominent Boston attorney of aristocratic bent who had been a foe of LDB's for many years. Storey had recently taken the occasion to state that he regarded Sacco and Vanzetti's trial as a fair one and that he thought the two men were guilty.

[9]For the Whitney case, see 21 May 1927, n. 4. Anita Whitney was saved from a fourteen-year term at San Quentin by the pardon, on 20 June, from California Governor C. C. Young.

[10]For the Mooney case, see 21 January 1922. Franklin Hichborn (1869–1963) was a former California newspaperman, now a publicist and lecturer extremely active in California social and political causes.

[11] Chaim Tchernowitz (1871–1949) was a Talmudic scholar and author teaching at the Jewish Institute of Religion. He wanted to raise $100,000 for his Talmud project and LDB had urged Julian Mack to help secure the money from Jewish lawyers (see LDB to Mack, 11 December 1926).

[12] Frederic William Maitland (1850–1906), the well known historian of English law, had taught at Cambridge.

No. 287   July 9, 1927   Chatham, Mass.

1. Cardozo has done an uncommonly good job in Campbell vs City of N.Y. by showing how Connally v Gen. Const. Co. can be avoided & its poison delimited.[1]

2. Have any of the city planners proposed a special municipal excise tax, a progressive super tax, based (a) upon percentage of area covered (b) upon height of building, over the standard. Thus, fixing as standard, say 1/2 of the area and as height say 60 feet & 15 feet cellar?

Such a law, plus division of railroad freight charges into terminal & line haul—with terminal representing not less than actual cost of service—would go far toward solving the excessive growth of cities & congestion of traffic.

3. Sam Morrison [sic] will be good at anything. But I rather wish he had limited himself to a narrower subject.[2] e.g.

   (a) To a history of the departures in practice from the American ideals of liberty & equality, or

   (b) To non-Anglo Saxon contributions to American ideals of civilization.

   (c) To American intolerances to ideas later embraced with avidity.

   He is particularly fitted to do such a job for freedom.

4. Henry Ford made a handsome retraction.[3]

5. I hope the Hamiltons found you & Marion yesterday.

6. That's good about Nutson.

7. We shall bear Parrington[4] in mind.

[1] Both Oklahoma and New York had statutes which stipulated that workers hired to do public work had to be paid at the "prevailing rate" by the state. In *Connally* v. *General Construction Co.*, 269 U.S. 385 (1926), the Supreme Court held that the Oklahoma law was unconstitutionally vague and obscure—insufficient, in short, to sustain a criminal prosecution. But in *Campbell* v. *City of New York*, 244 N.Y. 317 (1927), Cardozo deftly upheld the "prevailing rate" stipulation and showed why the Connally case did not apply to the New York situation.

[2] Morison had just published *The Oxford History of the United States, 1783–1917* (New York: Oxford University Press, 1927).

[3] Henry Ford (1863–1947), the eccentric and brilliant car inventor and manufacturer, publicly apologized on 8 July for his long campaign of anti-Semitism. He issued orders to the *Dearborn Independent* to end its attacks on Jews and moved to settle, out of court, a libel suit brought against him by Aaron Sapiro. The formal apology came in a letter to Louis Marshall, after a series of meetings between Marshall and Ford's representatives.

[4] Perhaps Vernon Louis Parrington (1871–1929), the University of Washington literary historian, whose *Main Currents in American Thought* would win the Pulitzer Prize for 1927.

No. 288   July 18, 1927   Chatham, Mass.

1. Your VIII Business of S.C. of U.S. is admirable.[1] I.a., it is an appropriate foundation for two series of articles:

(a) The annual review of the business of preceding term.[2]

(b) The discussion of the several classes of cases of which the inflow can be appropriately stopped at the source; treated each in a separate article.

2. I omitted to ask you about the proposed article for the English Law Quarterly.[3] Will you have time for that this Summer? I hope you will leave yourself some time for a real rest this Summer. Your 1927–28 Term will be a strenuous one, as the last has been.

3. If the writer of requisite qualities can be found, a volume in your administrative series on the Mass. Commission (R.R., Gas & E[lectric]. & P[ublic].U[tilities].) with special reference to application of the prudent investment rule; its effect upon the investment & return of capital, i.e. the property of the corporations; its influence upon the community in securing generous & wise actions, when confronted with unexpected conditions (as in State Guarranty [sic] of Boston Elev.—its action re Mass. Eastern St. Ry. Co.—Bay State) would be very instructive & might have influence elsewhere.[4]

It was fine to have Marion & you & to feel you are now so near.

[1] See 26 June 1927, n. 1. Part VIII was the final instalment.

[2] *The Harvard Law Review* has continued to run annual reviews of the Supreme Court's business. In the 1920s and 1930s these reviews (which became biennial in the 1930s) were written by FF and one of his students, or, later, by one of his students working alone. In recent decades, they appear annually as a joint project of the *Law Review* staff, with an overview introduction by a noted constitutional scholar.

[3] The *Law Quarterly Review*, published in London, would run a three part series by FF and Nathan Greene, entitled "The Use of the Injunction in American Labor Controversies." The first instalment appeared in April 1928 (44:164). See also 44:353, and 45:19 (1929).

[4] No such volume appeared in the Harvard Studies in Administrative Law. The question LDB raises is how to determine a fair rate of return for public utilities. Most of the country followed a system, sanctioned by the Supreme Court in *Smyth* v. *Ames*, 169 U.S. 466 (1898), which based the rate of return on an estimated present reproduction cost of the utility's property. This was a far from simple formula, and it involved many intricacies and the exercise of much judgment. The state of Massachusetts used another method, advocated by LDB in his laboriously detailed dissent (with Holmes) in *Southwestern Bell Telephone Co.* v. *Public Service Commission*, 262 U.S. 276 (1923), called the "prudent investment rule." The rate base was determined, not by the present value of the company's assets, but by the amount of money actually paid into the company by original investors in the company's securities. Since it was practically impossible to determine this figure for the majority of public utilities, a complex system was devised which measured the value of property at

its purchase or installation, allowed for depreciation, and so on. This evaluation, once determined, would be fixed and, in general, unchanged for the future. See the clear and helpful discussion in Irston R. Barnes, *Public Utility Control in Massachusetts: A Study in the Commission Regulation of Security Issues and Rates* (New Haven: Yale University Press, 1930).

No. 289   July 22, 1927   Chatham, Mass.

Re yours of 20th.

1. The enclosures returned herewith are interesting. I was particularly glad of your reply to [*].

2. As to your going before the Commission or the Governor.[1] If by their wholly spontaneous action you are called, you must of course go—But I think it would be unfortunate to have (a) anyone interested in S.V. stimulate a call from either the Gov. or the Comm., or (b) to have you go before either under such circumstances.

3. Auntie B. came back Tuesday evening physically fatigued,[2] but in joyous spirits, which have perdured since.

4. I have found since our talk on Communism a passage once quoted by me from Achad Ha-Am[3] which indicates that the remarkable quality of living for the future salvation of the class—as distinguished from the individual—is a Jewish trait.

[1] See 25 May and 2 June 1927.

[2] Elizabeth Glendower Evans was very active on behalf of Sacco and Vanzetti—indeed FF credited her with awakening his own interest in the case. See 5 August 1927.

[3] Ahad Ha-Am (literally, "a man of the people") was the pseudonym for the great Jewish editor and essayist, Asher Zvi Ginsburg (1856–1927).

No. 290   July 28, 1927   Chatham, Mass.

1. We are glad to know that you & Marion plan to be here again before Aug. 15. Elizabeth and Paul are due here August 1st & I am sure E. will be eager to talk with you about the course on Labor Legislation which, to her joy, Commons has asked her to give, as well as other things.

2. Was J.R.'s S.V. chk spontaneous?[1] Or did J.W.M. promote it?

3. Syracuse L.S. was thinking of W. G. Rice Jr. a few months ago. Do you know whether they asked him?[2]

4. That['s] good of Lippmann on S.V.

5. Has any adequate study been made of the exercise of the Pardoning Power in the United States? Could the Commonwealth Fund be induced to put the appropriate man on an intensive study of its exercise by the President—with special reference to the grounds; i.a. miscarriage in

court proceedings? If that were done, it might be easier to get like studies started for each of the states, which should follow.

6. Some one, with the competence, ought to be put also into the job of collecting American causes celebres—miscarriages of justice as evidenced by pardons or otherwise. Such a collection would make much easier the S.V. struggles of the future.

7. Elizabeth writes that Prof. Commons says he remembers my having used in some writing something like the phrase, "Reasonable value is welfare economics." Did I, & if so, where? Commons wants to use it as a motto for his new book.[3]

---

[1] Perhaps a contribution to the defense fund by Mack's friend, the Chicago philanthropist, Julius Rosenwald.

[2] LDB's former clerk remained at the University of Wisconsin.

[3] Professor Commons published only one book in 1927, a revision of his earlier work with John B. Andrews, *Principles of Labor Legislation* (New York: Harper and Brothers, 1927). It appeared without a motto from LDB.

No. 291   August 1, 1927   Chatham, Mass.

Upon reading your & Landis' Business,[1] the sense of its significance is deepened. The appearance of the book with an adequate index will be an event of importance in American law. The story is so interestingly told that it will be read. It brings together, for the first time, the facts necessary to an understanding of what is; and it is fertile in suggestion of what should be. The disclosure of sources consulted carries proof of imagination as well as thoroughness. The influence of the book, direct & indirect will be widespread. It must induce many to try and do likewise. And it sets the pace. When it is supplemented by the further studies which it suggests we shall really begin to know how the administration of our law can be bettered.

I assume No. 100 39 HLR. pp 57–8 has been modified by Holmes J. sitting in Boston & the C.J. in Norfolk a few years ago.

Do you recall Abbe [*]'s definition of eloquence—"The art of saying Everything without going to the Bastille."

---

[1] The articles by FF and Landis would soon be published as a book, *The Business of the Supreme Court: A Study in the Federal Judicial System* (New York: Macmillan, 1927); see 13 November 1927.

No. 292   August 5, 1927   Chatham, Mass.

Wednesday's action came as a complete surprise to all of us except Jack [Gilbert], who had felt sure, from his experiences, that the decision would be what it has proved.[1] Auntie B. telephones that she will not be here again before Monday Aug. 15th—I assume you also will be bound up with S.V. for the immediate future & must postpone Marion & your visit to Chatham. But we shall hope that there will be merely a short postponement. Let us know.

You & Auntie B. have played noble parts.[2]

Samuel Rubin's address is 111 No. Charles St. Baltimore.

[1] On 4 August Governor Alvan Fuller announced his findings in the Sacco and Vanzetti case. His view was that the two men had received a fair trial, and that their execution must be carried out.
[2] See next letter.

No. 293   August 24, 1927   Chatham, Mass.

1. To the end, you have done all that was possible for you.[1] And that all was more than would have [been] possible for any other person I know. But the end of S.V. is only the beginning. "They know not what they do."

2. When you and Marion shall have read deHaas' "Herzl"—let me know whether I am wrong in thinking that it is a great biography.[2] I had no conception that he could do it.

3. When we meet, remind me to tell you of my talk with Nicely about his future.[3]

4. Re Criminal Survey: I forget whether I wrote you: the testimony of State's evidence accomplices should go into the discard with the twin abominations—spies and third degree.

5. Be sure now to take all the rest you can before Term begins.

6. If we do not see you & Marion here before then (and in any event) bear in mind that we plan to leave here on Sept. 8. And shall hope you two can dine with us at the Bellevue that evening. Our plan is to leave Boston for Washington the next evening (Friday).

7. All your enclosures have gone to the Law School with a "Please do not forward."

[1] Shortly after midnight on 22 August, Sacco and Vanzetti were executed. Hours before, the defense lawyers appeared in Chatham to ask LDB to issue a stay. He met them on the porch of his summer home and told them that, for personal reasons, he could not agree to have any part of the case. Probably he was led to this conclusion by the fact that both his wife and his daughter Susan were active in the controversy as were two of his closest friends, FF and Mrs. Evans—and all were arrayed on the side of the defense. Such intimate connection with one side of the case precluded any sort of judicial participation. For the story of the lawyers' visit to Chatham, see the front page of the *New York Times*, 22 August 1927.
[2] Jacob deHaas, *Theodor Herzl*, 2 vols. (Chicago: Leonard, 1927). The day before, LDB had

written directly to deHaas: "You have told a great story in the grand manner. It has dignity and self-restraint—the majesty of truth."

³ See 9 February and 8 March 1924.

No. 294   September 17, 1927   Washington, D.C.

1. Current Certioraris suggest that when the investigation is made into cases under Crim. Code §215,¹ note be made (a) how many of the crimes are clearly intra-state and (b) in how many the mailing is merely an insignificant incident of a fraud actually perpetrated, by word of mouth or other writing etc.

2. The Certs. also enforce importance of the enquiry into P[ost].O[ffice] Fraud orders etc.

3. It looks now as if we might have more than 200 certs. presented Oct 3.²

4. You have given Older good advice. The right sort of book would be a distinct contribution.³

5. My conviction deepens re. importance of publishing (a) full record in S.V. plus (b) supplemental record of all Fuller's & Lowell Com'tee's notes of testimony, and getting Dep. of Justice papers, however meager. Despite the lapse of 7 years, it may well be possible to get affirmative proof of evidence as a result of adequate thinking—and the full report will furnish starting points & raw material for thought.⁴

6. I guess O'Brien agrees fully with Villard as to his own action & inaction.⁵

7. Lowell Mellett was in yesterday. I think he can be relied upon, when the Scripps-Howard help is needed.

8. Re Mack's of Sept 1 on "Herzl—deHaas dinner." Of course, "no" means "no." More of this & of other things when we meet at dinner Thursday evening.

9. Hildegarde⁶ read me her father's letter in the Springfield Republican and showed me the Fabian Franklin ad. in the Herald of the Springfield Republican Editorials, which she & Ellen Thayer carried with them. Ellen T. is the daughter of my class-mate A.S. Thayer,⁷ a Powwow man⁸—father was of an old Worcester family. There was no suggestion of relationship to Webster Thayer, but I didn't ask. They came here after a visit in Worcester.

It's good to hear that Holmes J. is again in good form. It would have been better had Corcoran spent July & Aug. with him, also.⁹

I am looking forward to the "Historical Trials."¹⁰

[1] The section covering mail fraud. See 17 August 1926.

[2] The October 1927 term was to begin on 3 October.

[3] Perhaps FF was trying to encourage Fremont Older (as he would try to encourage other writers) to tell the story of the Sacco and Vanzetti case. Older (1856–1935) was a California journalist and writer. Neither he nor anyone else named Older published a book on the case.

[4] Bernard Flexner and Charles C. Burlingham edited a six volume edition of the transcript of the trial (New York, 1928–1929). For a full bibliography of the record of the case, both published and unpublished, see G. Louis Joughin and Edmund M. Morgan, *The Legacy of Sacco and Vanzetti* (New York: Harcourt, Brace, 1948), 557–58.

[5] Robert Lincoln O'Brien (1865–1955) was a powerful Boston journalist, the owner and publisher of the *Boston Herald* and the *Boston Traveller*. O'Brien described, about a year later, his own feelings and doubts in a privately circulated piece, *My Personal Relations to the Sacco Vanzetti Case as a Chapter in Massachusetts History*. O'Brien had come to feel that the two men were, in fact, guilty. Villard, editor of *The Nation*, worked for the cause; he was a founding member of the Citizens National Committee for Sacco and Vanzetti, and made personal appeals to both Governor Fuller and President Lowell on behalf of the two men.

[6] Hildegarde Nagel (1890–1985) was LDB's niece, the daughter of his sister, Fannie, and Charles Nagel.

[7] Albert Smith Thayer (1854–1925) had received his LL.B. in 1877. He practiced in New York, and published several articles on property law.

[8] LDB's moot court club at Harvard Law School.

[9] Tom Corcoran had finished his term as Holmes's secretary during the summer.

[10] Sir John Macdonell (1846–1921), *Historical Trials* (Oxford: Oxford University Press, 1927), describes various famous trials, including those of Socrates, Joan of Arc, and Sir Walter Raleigh, among others.

No. 295   September 26, 1927   Washington, D.C.

These Chinese cases [1] present food for Civil Liberties Assn activity. Some steps should be taken, through Chinese minister, consuls or otherwise, to help Chinese to better counsel.

Some way should be pursued to make the Federal official suffer for such illegal acts. And to make sure, through Congress or otherwise that illegalities such as here condemned do not go unnoticed.

Re Lawrence Brooks. [2] G.W.A. should talk to him.

[1] There were a number of cases involving Chinese, many of them centering on questions of admission into the United States (275 U.S. 475 [1927]) or the rights of naturalized citizens of Chinese descent (275 U.S. 78 [1927]). Unfortunately it is impossible to know to which cases LDB refers, or even whether they were cases before the Supreme Court.

[2] Perhaps Lawrence Graham Brooks (1881–19[?]), the son of John Graham Brooks. Lawrence Brooks was a Massachusetts attorney; in 1928 he accepted appointment as a special justice of the First District Court of Eastern Middlesex County.

No. 296   September 28, 1927   Washington, D.C.

1. The Macdonnell [sic] interests me deeply. [1] It and certioraris renew and strengthen my conviction that few tasks in connection with the Criminal Law are so important as a thorough enquiry into, & exposition

of, the practices of the police in connection not only with 3rd degree, but generally re the interrogation of persons arrested. And this is true also of the interrogations by the Govt. of aliens or alleged aliens in deportations & like proceedings.

It needs such enquiry & exposition to revive our appreciation of the horrors of official inquisitorial methods.

Is there some good man who can be put to this?

2. I suppose you saw in yesterday's U.S. Daily, McCarl's ruling (p. 1) on expenses incurred by undercover men.[2]

3. Hale's correspondence with Lowell may be another urge to publish the "Testimony."[3] If he does, it will doubtless lead him into new troubles. Francis Hackett's letter is fine.[4]

4. Norman is evidently much stirred.[5]

5. Whom have you recommended for Phila?

6. Couldn't the Literary Guild or some similar organization be led to take up deHaas' "Herzl."[6]

7. Friendly has arrived & Page is installing him.[7]

8. Prof. Lyon[8] of Brookings, who lectured at Chicago U. this summer, says "They talked of nothing but S.V. at table."

[1] See 17 September 1927, n. 10.

[2] John Raymond McCarl (1879–1940), a Nebraska lawyer and former secretary to George Norris, was Controller General of the United States from 1921 to 1936. He had recently ruled that federal funds could not be used to operate a speakeasy for the purpose of apprehending violators of the Volstead Act. The issue had arisen over payment to undercover agents.

[3] See 17 September 1927.

[4] Francis Hackett (1883–1962), a brilliant and fiery Irishman who came to the United States in 1901, was one of the original editors of *The New Republic*. He eventually settled in Denmark with his wife. He had written to FF on 6 September praising him for his work on behalf of Sacco and Vanzetti, and denouncing the officials for their "hard-heartedness."

[5] Probably about Sacco and Vanzetti; see next letter.

[6] See 24 August 1927.

[7] Henry J. Friendly replaced Robert G. Page as LDB's clerk for the October 1927 term.

[8] Leverett Samuel Lyon (1885–1959) was an economist at the Brookings Institution from 1925 until 1939, when he returned to Chicago as head of the Association of Commerce and Industry.

No. 297   November 13, 1927   Washington, D.C.

1. My thanks to you & Landis for "Business"—an impressive volume, which came on the birthday eve;[1] and to you & Marion for the greeting which came this morning.

2. Upton Sinclair, who was here Friday & Norman, who was here a week earlier, will both help to keep S.V. alive.[2]

3. The Burns-Sinclair incident[3] should make it easier to induce Sen.

Tom Walsh and Sen. Wheeler to take up the detective abuse and for the [New York] World to push it. I suppose Hitz told you about Burns['s] attempt to get at the file at Dep. of Justice during Gregory's administration & the disappearance of the papers incriminating B. in the Oregon matter, during the Daugherty regime.[4]

4. As to Certiorari in Goodman et al. Holmes J. is incorrigible when there is an opportunity of curbing the power & province of a jury.[5] And the worst is yet to come.

5. I have asked Friendly to send to [you] from time to time instances of P.C.'s & of Certs. granted or denied that deserve study.

6. OWH is in his best form. Yesterday (& it was after a 4 1/2 hour conference i.e. until 5 PM): "I found some years ago that I began to puff on walking, but I have not observed yet that I get more fatigued in work or using my mind." He was never more fresh in conference.

7. Sutherland is reported better,[6] but the Chief thinks he should make up his mind not to come back to work before spring. His wife is sicker than he is now. And Van Devanter has had a stroke which bears heavily upon him. But his work in conference is unimpaired.

8. Weiz[mann]. got up a grand dinner to Lord Balfour, which has some advantages to the cause. But the Jewish multitude is beginning to catch on.

[1] See 1 August 1927; 13 November marked LDB's seventy-first birthday.

[2] Upton Beall Sinclair (1878–1968), the famous muckraking novelist whose *The Jungle* (New York: Grosset and Dunlap, 1906) won him enduring fame, continued to turn out topical novels. His book on the Sacco and Vanzetti case was *Boston, A Novel* (New York: A. and C. Boni, 1928).

[3] The newspapers were suddenly full of a new scandal in the aftermath of the Teapot Dome frauds. It was revealed on 2 November that the notorious W. J. Burns Detective Agency had been employed by Harry F. Sinclair to tamper with the jury in his trial. The judge immediately declared a mistrial, and a grand jury began examining the jury tampering charges.

[4] In 1909, William John Burns (1861–1932), founder and president of the detective agency, had probably tampered with another jury in Oregon in connection with a land fraud case. The man thereby convicted, one Willard N. Jones, of Portland, was pardoned after an investigation of Burns's activities by Attorney General Wickersham in 1911. Under Daugherty, in the Harding administration, Burns was appointed head of the secret service.

[5] The Goodman case involved the death of a man who had driven a truck across a railroad crossing and been struck by a speeding train. The jury had awarded damages to the widow, and the railroad had appealed on the ground that the man had been negligent. Holmes, speaking for the Court, reversed the jury decision, finding for the railroad. *Baltimore & Ohio* v. *Goodman* 275 U.S. 66 (1927).

[6] Justice Sutherland had fallen ill at the start of the October 1927 term; he did not return to the Court nor participate in any cases until 3 January 1928.

No. 298   November 21, 1927   Washington, D.C.

1. 67 & 68 enclosed will interest you & Landis.[1]

2. The N.R. has properly taken Al Smith to task in his attitude toward Estate tax.[2] It is strangely doctrinaire. How did it happen.

3. Lovett has not done the Herzl credit.[3] I hope Norman will do better in the Nation.[4]

4. I am glad to see N.R. paying its respects to Burns.[5]

5. We clean up today all certs. presented prior to day [sic]. Some have been denied which should not have been. Some expansions in the orders will interest you.

6. John Dewey[6] on the Lowell report[7] reminds of Ben Butler's[8] interjection when a Harvard Medical School Prof. was being qualified as an expert in a will case: "So you are a professor at the Harvard Medical School. We hung one of those for murder not long ago."

7. Louis Glavis,[9] who was in today, says there is a lot of stuff on Burns in N.Y. where there was an effort 7–8 years ago to take away his state license.

8. It's fine to hear of Thompson's expedition & the happy results.

9. We had Gardner Jackson's[10] sister[11] in to dine yesterday.

10. Harlan F. S. says that the incriminating report was in the Dep. of Justice in his day, was read by him, that thereupon he fired Burns and 30 of his henchmen who had "criminal records"—which I understand means, had been sentenced for some cause.

Tell Marion that Elizabeth is now a PhD. There is much enthusiasm at Madison about her thesis.[12]

---

[1] No. 67 was *City of Hammond* v. *Schappi Bus Line, Inc.*, 275 U.S. 164 (1927), and No. 68 was *City of Hammond* v. *Farina Bus Line & Transportation Co.*, 275 U.S. 173 (1927). The two bus companies contended that a Hammond, Indiana ordinance discriminated against them. But, for a unanimous Court, LDB returned the case to a lower court for further proceedings on the grounds that the matter was "not yet ripe for decision" by the Supreme Court.

[2] The editors condemned Smith for joining those who were trying to repeal the federal estate tax. Smith argued that such a tax was properly within the sphere of state power, but the editors contended that such reasoning only helped millionaires avoid taxes in inheritance-tax-free states, like Florida. *New Republic* 53 (23 November 1927): 3.

[3] For Robert Morss Lovett's review of deHaas's biography of Theodor Herzl, see "A Leader of Zion," *New Republic* 53 (23 November 1927): 21.

[4] Norman Hapgood, "A Hero of the Jews," *Nation* 125 (7 December 1927): 645.

[5] See *New Republic* 53 (23 November 1927): 1: "If the latest charges against him are upheld, Mr. William J. Burns . . . will have forfeited all claim to the respect of honest Americans." The anonymous editorial was a thorough denunciation of Burns's activities in the Sinclair jury tampering case.

[6] John Dewey (1859–1952) was one of the most important of all American philosophers, and his theories of psychology and social relationships had crucial effects on educational and political

311

reform in the United States. Throughout his long life, Dewey was always able to combine a career of philosophic speculation with an intense concern for social problems.

[7] John Dewey, "Psychology and Justice," *New Republic* 53 (23 November 1927): 9. In the essay, Dewey tried to explore the state of mind of the three members of Governor Fuller's advisory committee in the Sacco and Vanzetti case (see 2 June 1927).

[8] Benjamin Franklin Butler (1818–1893) was the colorful and controversial Massachusetts politician who gained national fame (and Southern hatred) for his career during Reconstruction. He was the prosecutor in the Andrew Johnson impeachment case and, in the 1880s, served a term as governor of Massachusetts.

[9] Louis Russell Glavis (1883–1971) was the man who blew the whistle on the Interior Department, where he was a chief of a field division, thereby starting the controversy that became the Pinchot-Ballinger affair.

[10] Gardner Jackson (1897–1965) was a newspaperman and a sometime public official. The son of wealthy parents, he graduated from Harvard in 1921 and went to work for the *Boston Globe*. He quit his job in order to work full time for Sacco and Vanzetti, and would soon join with Marion Frankfurter in editing the men's letters. During President Franklin Roosevelt's first administration, Jackson accepted a job in the Agricultural Adjustment Administration, but he left after a quarrel over sharecroppers' rights.

[11] Edith Banfield Jackson (1895–1977), a distinguished pediatrician and psychiatrist, was connected with Yale University in various capacities for many years.

[12] "The Wage-Earner and the Common Rule—A Study in the Employer-Employee Relation." The degree was awarded in 1928.

No. 299   December 11, 1927   Washington, D.C.

1. To your good mother you have been a good son, and a never-failing source of happiness. Give her our love. To my mother came the same affliction and at the same age.[1]

2. OWH. closes this sitting in fine form and with practically no work ahead for the next three weeks.

3. Sutherland says he will return to the job Jan 3.[2]

4. When you see No. 559—Hunter v. State of Louisiana in the Journal of cases argued, and decided, bear in mind that it was entered in our Court Oct. 26 & argued last week.[3]

5. I was told by an insider, that his associates, railroad & business men, who were eager to have the Sherman Law liberalized were advised by William [sic] Gordon Merritt[4] to let it alone as it is the only means of curbing labor & that since then they have been quiescent.

[1] Emma Winter Frankfurter would die of cancer on 10 January 1928 at the age of seventy-four.

[2] See 13 November 1927.

[3] *Henry Hunter* v. *State of Louisiana*, 275 U.S. 508. The *per curiam* decision, affirming the Louisiana State Supreme Court because no federal question of substance was raised, was decided the day after this letter was written—thus the entire process from entry to decision had taken only six weeks.

[4] Walter Gordon Merritt (1880–1968), a New York lawyer, specialized in labor relations.

1. I inferred from what Kirstein told me Sunday that it was Choate who exerted the pressure re S.V. on O'Brien.[1]

2. I cannot think of Paul Andrews in the capacity of Research Professor. He is a very nice fellow, with generous instincts & much better fitted for Dean of Syracuse Law School. He is very appreciative of the work of others, but not, I should think, keen in analysis or a student.[2]

3. The Judicial Council reminds of "Not guilty but don't do it again."[3]

4. O.W.H. has just written an opinion (to be declared Jan 3) which is in his best form.[4]

5. Very glad Thompson interview with V. is to appear in the Atlantic.[5]

6. One of the worst fields of fed. jur[isdiction]. is suit on fake fed. questions in D.C. to get construction of State laws. Can't you have your seminar explore this field & then get an article in H.L.R. exposing the frauds etc. practiced?

7. I am glad Sharfman[6] is doing a thorough job.

8. Would it not be well to have some one write an article on the evils of the requirements of evidence in narrative form in the Amer. Bar Assn. L.J., or the Yale Law Review & send a copy to our C.J.?

9. I agree with you that J.W.M. should not take executive office in Z.O.A. What he should do is to make clear to the world that he is not a supporter of the present administration.

[1] See 17 September 1927, n. 5.

[2] Paul Shipman Andrews (1887–1967) was a Syracuse native, a lawyer there, and after 1927, dean of the University of Syracuse Law School. He had worked in the Justice Department under Harlan Fiske Stone.

[3] The Massachusetts Judicial Council, as part of its annual report to the governor, recommended some reforms that seemed clearly inspired by the Sacco and Vanzetti case. It called for greater review of capital cases so that the supreme judicial court would have the power to review all of the acts of a trial judge.

[4] Holmes's opinion on 3 January 1928 was in *Equitable Trust Co. of New York* v. *First National Bank of Trinidad, Colorado*, 275 U.S. 347, a case involving the bankruptcy of a bank engaged in international credit.

[5] William G. Thompson, "Vanzetti's Last Statement," *Atlantic Monthly* 141 (February, 1928): 254. This article, by the attorney for Sacco and Vanzetti, tells of his being summoned to the death cell by Vanzetti and of the conversation that took place only hours before the execution.

[6] Isaiah Leo Sharfman (1886–1969), a Russian-born immigrant and Harvard Law School graduate, taught economics at the University of Michigan from 1916 to 1955; he had just been named chairman of the economics department.

No. 301   December 20, 1927   Washington, D.C.

Your article will give O.W.H. much joy. It is far in advance of its two predecessors.[1] And its luminous quality will make it an effective instrument of education.

When we meet, let me tell you of a talk yesterday with G[eorge].S[utherland]. on conservatism & liberalism in members of the Court—a subject introduced by G.S. who did the talking.

What is the status of the Injunction Article?[2]

Gifford Pinchot has imported Wells[3] to Washington & is full of fight.[4] The North Carolina Senators are true to the Mellon form.[5]

Hamilton has his formal appointment at the Yale L.S.

[1] "Mr. Justice Holmes and the Constitution," *Harvard Law Review* 42 (1927): 121. The "two predecessors" to this twenty-five year commemoration of Holmes's appointment to the Supreme Court, were two earlier articles by FF: "The Constitutional Opinions of Justice Holmes," *Harvard Law Review* 29 (1916): 683, and "Twenty Years of Mr. Justice Holmes' Constitutional Opinions," *Harvard Law Review* 36 (1923): 909.

[2] FF and Nathan Greene, "The Labor Injunction and Federal Legislation," *Harvard Law Review* 42 (1929): 766.

[3] Perhaps Gifford Pinchot's close adviser on conservation matters, Philip P. Wells.

[4] Probably Pinchot's combativeness related to hearings involving the rate-making power of the electric utilities; there were also some rumors about his running for the Senate from Pennsylvania and even a few about his trying to capture the Republican nomination for the presidency.

[5] Senator Furnifold M. Simmons's remarks on taxation policy came during the consideration of the Federal Tax Reduction Bill, and they carried particular weight since he was the ranking Democrat on the Senate Finance Committee. See *New York Times*, 17 and 18 December.

No. 302   December 25, 1927   Washington, D.C.

1. I had Friendly write & telegraph you as requested in your tele-g[ram].

2. I hope you can hold Margold. There seems no chance of your getting Friendly—next year at least. He has not talked with me of his future since his trip to Washington a year ago. But he asked me last week to extend his Xmas absence one day (Tuesday) so as to give him a chance to look into N.Y. offices. And Alice says she thinks he had a letter from Corcoran.

3. R. Walton Moore sent me enclosed copy of bill etc. He has (showed me) a list of some 300 crimes prepared by Dep. of Justice to which it would be applicable.

4. That's an interesting letter from Dr. Park.

5. Also that from Crowder. I didn't know he had settled in Chicago.

6. C.C. did the best of its kind in getting Stimson,[1] but I grow less patient with the kind.

314

7. C.C. is doing quite as badly as Harding in the gradual process of undermining the Federal Courts. High authorities within my ken are very sad about it. Letts, who I see has got R.I., was an uncommonly poor Asst. At. G.[2] Worse is threatened here for J.C. of D.C., & much worse has been done in Tennessee.

In this connection there is talk of Hitz' resigning. He dined with us last week & was very blue about his Court, but said nothing of resigning in the brief private talk we had.

8. As bearing on Brookings.[3] I enclose another note from Miss Bontecou who has doubtless written you fully. Hamilton & others think M. is the villain in the plot. They may be right. But I suspect that Prichett et al may be found "the man behind." My own guess is that the real significance of this event lies in a much broader proposition. The fact that free thought & speech will not be tolerated in the Social Sciences. And that we have here a far intenser & subtler application of the heresy hunt than at Amherst. The Yale offer to Hamilton antedated his knowledge of any danger to his reforms here.

My own belief is that, in America, the evil of the foundations will become terribly manifest. A list of the Trustees of the Brookings Institution should suffice.[4] The American teacher of the Social Sciences (and others who dare express themselves) will experience: "Wretched indeed is that poor man who hangs on princes' favors."[5] If we are to have fine thought here & high spirituality, I fancy the vow of poverty must again be taken.

Miss Bontecou's letter confirms a suspicion I had before that one of our friends lacks courage & suffers from Environment.

9. You seem occupied to overflowing. But the Sleeping Car Porters are among the most deserving applicants.[6]

Eliz & P and Susan, Jack & boy are here. My brother Alfred's grandsons[7] are due tomorrow.

Please give me the full title of that Montaigne translation.[8]

[1] Henry L. Stimson had been appointed on 14 December as governor general of the Philippine Islands; he was confirmed by the Senate on 18 December.

[2] Ira Lloyd Letts (1872–1948), a Rhode Island attorney active in Republican politics, served as assistant attorney general from 1925 to 1927; Coolidge appointed him district judge for Rhode Island in June. In 1935 he returned to private practice.

[3] On 22 December, the newspapers announced the creation of the Brookings Institution. It brought together three independent agencies (including the Brookings School of Economics and Government), and would devote itself to the study of the social sciences.

[4] The trustees of the Institution were mostly presidents of leading universities and well established businessmen. For a complete listing, see *New York Times*, 23 December 1927.

[5] Shakespeare, *Richard III*, iii, 2:366.

[6] Pullman sleeping car porters were locked in a dispute with the Pullman Company, both over union representation and, before the Interstate Commerce Commission, over wages, working conditions, and the tipping practice.

[7] Alfred Brandeis McCreary (b. 1914) and William Bruce McCreary (b. 1918) were the sons of Alfred Brandeis's daughter Amy.

[8] Perhaps the new edition, by Oxford University Press, of the E. J. Trechmann translation of the *Essays* (London, 1927).

No. 303   January 12, 1928   Washington, D.C.

1. Yesterday No. 500, Casey v U.S. (Criminal Case) was argued.[1] Petition for cert. filed Sept 1/27. Certiorari granted Nov 21, 1927. also No. 600 Nigro v U.S. (Criminal)—certificate filed Oct 31/27.[2]

Both, as I recall, had been set for the December sitting & were postponed to Jan. because of the important questions involved (Harrison Act) for which the J.J. wanted time.

2. When S.V. fears subside & the appreciation of Civil Liberty revives, possibly interest can be aroused in our project of speaking on Boston Common without a license.[3] Then, it may be well to bear in mind—for those who fear disturbances—what was said in Beatty v. Gillbanks, 15 Cox's C[riminal].C[ases]. 138, 146:[4]

"The present decision of the justices amounts to this, that a man may be punished for acting legally if he knows that his so doing may induce another man to act unlawfully—a proposition without any authority to support it."

Thank you much for the Montaigne.

[1] *Casey* v. *United States*, 276 U.S. 413 (1928), involved a Seattle attorney convicted of selling narcotics to prisoners who were his clients. The issue of entrapment arose from the use of a federal agent to apprehend the attorney. The case is notable in part because of the revealing difference between Holmes's view and LDB's. Holmes wrote the Court's opinion, upholding the conviction; LDB dissented (at 425), not to protect Casey, but to "protect the Government. To protect it from illegal conduct of its officers. To preserve the purity of its courts."

[2] *Nigro* v. *United States*, 276 U.S. 332 (1928), broadened the interpretation of the Harrison Anti-Narcotic Act of 1914 (38 *U.S. Stat.* 785, ch. 1) by prohibiting "any person," and not merely those listed in Sec. 1 of the law, from selling drugs without a written order.

[3] See 13 May 1925.

[4] This English case of 1882 defined the right of peaceful assembly in connection with an incident involving the Salvation Army.

No. 304   January 27, 1928   Washington, D.C.

DEAR FELIX: 1. It will be good to have another summer with you at Chatham, & we shall hope that Marion can at least be with us for a while at the beginning and at the close of the season, if not throughout.

2. You are doing a good job on the Mellon tax projects.

3. We close our session Monday with plenty of work ahead for the 3 weeks of recess.

No. 305   January 28, 1928   Washington, D.C.

1. Do you recall this from Xenophon's Memorabilia?

"Should I be more serviceable to the State, if I took an employment, where function would be wholly bounded in my person, and take up all my time, than I am by instructing everyone, as I do, and in furnishing the Republic with a great number of citizens who are capable to serve her?" [1]

2. As to Goldsmith. [2] Act as usual on your own good judgment. Of course, other things being equal, it is always preferable to take some one whom there is reason to believe will become a law teacher.

3. By the way, if ever you have a first class man available whom H.L.S. wont take, let me know. I may find him a desirable berth in some other law school.

4. What do you know of Gregory H[*], who is doing the Legal Research Bureau for the press, as to our opinions?

5. Glad to see the Thompson interview is reproduced in N.R. [3]

6. We are very sorry Marion has not been well & glad to know she is well on the mend.

It's rather surprising that the Herald published the Mencken. [4]

[1] Bk. I, ch. 6, par. 15.

[2] Irving Baer Goldsmith (b. 1902) had been selected by FF to serve as LDB's clerk for the October 1928 term. After his year in Washington, Goldsmith went into private practice in Chicago. He also lectured at Northwestern Law School. For LDB's less-than-satisfactory early relations with Goldsmith, see 7, 12, and 15 October 1928.

[3] See 15 December 1927. The *Atlantic Monthly* interview was republished in *New Republic* 53 (1 February 1928): 294.

[4] Henry Louis Mencken (1880–1956), the caustic "sage of Baltimore," was at the height of his popularity and influence as a critic of American life, its false standards, and its tawdry politics and cheap literature. The Bostom *Herald* had published Mencken's "Ghosts of Sacco, Vanzetti Sure to Plague Courts." In the article Mencken asserted that despite the hopes of the "Boston Babbitts," the case would not disappear; indeed "the plain fact is that the Sacco-Vanzetti uproar, in its sweetest and worst forms has yet to begin." That sentiment echoed one expressed privately by LDB to FF in a letter of 17 January 1928. There LDB wrote: "SV. seems destined to continue to plague." And he quoted the lines from *Macbeth* (III, iv: 79): "The time has been that when the brains were out, the man would die and there an end."

No. 306   February 5, 1928   Washington, D.C.

1. As to records & briefs for Law School. It can all be arranged at the proper time, without saying anything to O.W.H. His practice is to send

the records & briefs to the Clerk's office as soon as the decisions or orders are entered. He does not even wait for the period allowed for rehearing petitions to elapse. The matter of sending to Cambridge rests with the Clerk's Office. They defer matters until vacation because they have the leisure then.

Our new Clerk is ideal.[1] Young (33) despite 18 years of experience in the office (and I think as page). Able. Eager. Competent & apparently of a character as fine as his ability. He is very efficient. If he knows why you want the records, I think he will be willing to arrange that during each recess, all the records & briefs of cases disposed of at the preceding sitting will be sent you. Don't apply to him now, as he is to be married tomorrow[2] (I am told), in the West. But I think you might tackle him in a month or two.

Meanwhile, send him (with a letter) a copy of "Business" and also send him every article on jurisdiction & practice hereafter appearing by you or in H.L.R. He is really interested & tries to learn all he can.

2. I am glad the publication of S.V. records has proceeded so far as to have you draft a prefatory note. Who will sign?[3]

3. Ehrmann[4] & wife were here last Tuesday. He seems much developed by his experience.

4. It was good to have Cardozo review "Business."[5]

5. Who is Samuel Grafton who did the "Company" piece in N.R.? Very well done.[6]

6. It is a satisfaction that the unemployment problem is at last receiving attention. I think the N.R. (which has criticized Smith's silence unwisely heretofore) is right in urging him to think & lead on this subject.[7]

7. Learned Hand was in Wednesday. He is enthusiastic about "Business." I was surprised to hear him say that he hoped you would take up the obsolete diversity of citizenship jurisdiction.

8. He had been in Charleston with George & Juliette [Rublee]. George is waiting there for a "call"—an appointment to Mexico which Cal seems slow in giving.

9. O.W.H. is in fine form.

It's good to know Marion is making such progress.

[1] Charles Elmore Cropley (1894–1952) started in the Supreme Court as a page in 1907, and moved through the ranks until he was named Clerk in 1927.

[2] Actually, Cropley was married on the day before this letter was written.

[3] FF lined up a host of distinguished public figures who were willing to sign his "Prefatory Note" to the five-volume published transcript. These included Newton D. Baker, Emory Buckner,

Charles C. Burlingham, John W. Davis, Bernard Flexner, Raymond Fosdick, Charles P. Howland, Victor Morawetz, Charles Nagel, Walter H. Pollak, and Elihu Root.

[4] Herbert Brutus Ehrmann (1891–1970), a Louisville native and Boston attorney, had been actively involved in the defense of Sacco and Vanzetti.

[5] Benjamin Cardozo's praise-filled review appeared in *New Republic* 53 (8 February 1928): 329.

[6] Samuel Grafton, "The Company," *New Republic* 53 (1 February 1928): 299. The article was a light and humorous discussion of the way Americans invest their loyalties, concerns, and lives in "the Company" where they work. Grafton (b. 1907), a writer, journalist, and publishing executive, was connected with the *New York Post* from 1934 to 1949.

[7] "Al Smith's Opportunity," *New Republic* 53 (1 February 1928): 308. The anonymous editorial suggested that the unemployment issue would be the best possible way for Smith to distinguish his approach to national life from that of "an enlightened servant of business like Mr. Hoover."

No. 307   February 9, 1928   Washington, D.C.

1. When I called on O.W.H., on the 5th, he seemed more brilliant—sprudelst[1]—than I have seen him for years—ranging with a perfect memory over wide fields of literature. He keenly enjoys now his recesses, which are in the main vacations.

2. I expect to see J.W.M. tomorrow, en his route to Cincinnati. B.F. was coming here today from Baltimore, but found he [sic] Jonas[2] wanted him there all of today.

3. You have not mentioned what I consider the worst of Hughes' retainers. His effort to set aside the Swift Armour consent decree.[3] Das war gemeins.[4]

4. You spoke last summer of the possibility of getting Evans Clark to write for the N.Y. Times an article on Savings Bank Insurance.[5] With the growing success, Miss Grady is encountering ever more intense opposition in the Legislature, with Henry Lee Shattuck as the devil in chief. If you think you can get Evans Clark to write, you might ask Miss Grady whether she would like that now. King should quickly do his best. Cook[6] gave her a good editorial.

5. Stimson was very grateful (wrote me from France) for what I had done for him there, but I can't recall what it was.

6. What say you to this, re Chicago crime: "Rich men look sad, and ruffians dance and leap; The one in fear to lose what they enjoy, the other to enjoy by rage & war." Richard II. Act II, Sc. 4.

I am glad of what you wrote Merz. We must have official liquidators & receivers.

[1] "bubbling, sparkling."

[2] Jonas Stein Friedenwald (1897–1955), like his father, Harry Friedenwald, was a well-known Baltimore ophthalmologist and a committed Zionist.

[3] In the summer and fall of 1919 the Federal Trade Commission had held hearings over the extent of monopolization in the meat packing industry, and in early 1920 all parties agreed to a consent decree providing that the big companies would divest themselves of many of their operations (cold storage warehouses, retail stores, railroad terminals, market newspapers) not directly related to meat production. Before long, however, the big packers were attempting to set aside some of the provisions of the decree.

[4] "That was common, vulgar."

[5] Evans Clark (1888–1970) had edited several industrial magazines, and between 1925 and 1928 was a feature writer for the *New York Times*, specializing in business and industry. From 1928 until 1953 Clark headed the Twentieth Century Fund. He did not write an article on savings bank insurance for the *Times*.

[6] Waldo Lincoln Cook (1865–1951) was one of FF's favorite editors because of his enthusiastic and consistent support of Sacco and Vanzetti. He had been associated with the *Springfield Republican* since 1888 and was now its chief editorial writer and editor.

No. 308   February 11, 1928   Washington, D.C.

1. The Margold papers are interesting & sad.[1] If M. concludes not to remain at Harvard, dont let him tie himself up with an agreement to return to practice, until I shall have had an opportunity to suggest his name for a teaching job I have in mind. (Not Louisville.)

2. Senator Shipstead[2] was in last evening. His Anti-injunction bill is the result of his intimacy with Andrew Furuseth who almost lives at the Shipsteads. If the injunction bill[3] (which I haven't seen) is not drawn as it should be, you can doubtless get it changed, as you deem wise. For the subcommittee of the judiciary consists of Tom Walsh, Norris and Blaine. Furuseth is also intimate with the La Follettes—breakfasts there every Sunday.

3. Senator Blaine was in the other day. I took occasion to talk to him and Sen La Follette[4] jointly on restricting federal jurisdiction whenever they saw a chance. Blaine seemed entirely in accord. I guess it would be a good idea for you to write him a line accompanying "Business."

4. Learned Hand didn't go into detail on diversity of citizenship jurisdiction.[5] But he left the impression that he thought it ought to [be] restricted wherever possible & that he hoped you would tackle the job.

5. As far as I can foresee, I shall not need Goldsmith before Oct 1. My idea would be to have Friendly come here toward the middle or end of September—if as is usual, there is then some work to be done, & I should like to have him break in Goldsmith for a day or two. G. will have a hard time as the successor to F.[6]

Hope Marion's good progress continues.

6. What do you think of the work (Industrial & political) of the

Federal Council of the Churches of Christ. They have lost their angel &
are appealing for help. Should we send them some money?

[1] LDB refers to the bitter fight to secure a professorship for Nathan Margold at the Harvard Law
School; see 15 December 1926, n. 2.

[2] Henrik Shipstead (1881–1960), a former dentist, represented Minnesota in the United States
Senate from 1923 to 1947. A Farmer-Laborite (and for years the only one in the Senate), he was
aligned with other midwestern progressives, especially the La Follettes.

[3] The Shipstead anti-injunction bill, drawn primarily by the self-taught seaman Andrew Furuseth, had been introduced on 12 December 1927 (S. 1482). On 13 February LDB wrote: "I suppose
it would be best for you and Sayre to write a joint letter to Senator Shipstead & to send copies to
each member of the Subcommittee. Shipstead is thoroughly well meaning, but equally ignorant &
puts his faith in Furuseth who has the same qualities." Many congressmen who were sympathetic
to his aims could not support the bill as written, and finally, in May 1928 the judiciary subcommittee called in FF and other legislative experts to draft a proper bill. That measure was introduced
by George Norris on 29 May 1928, and the new version provided the basis for the legislation that
eventually was enacted.

[4] Robert Marion La Follette, Jr. (1895–1953), the eldest son of the great Wisconsin progressive,
served as his father's secretary, and was elected to fill out his father's term in 1925. He was reelected
three times in his own right, until he was finally defeated by Joseph R. McCarthy, in 1946. His
outstanding work in the Senate was his investigation of how the civil liberties of unionists were
abused by industrialists during the 1930s.

[5] See 5 February and 16 March 1928.

[6] See 7, 12, and 15 October 1928.

No. 309   February 22, 1928   Washington, D.C.

1. Yes, Laughlin did well.[1]

2. Exhibit B. should earn for Powell absolution for all past sins.[2]

3. Was your talk with R.P. before he had received Powell's letter? &
what next?

4. I don't recall the alleged clash with Lowell of fifty years ago. Still
it may have occurred. I recall that Langdell[3] considered that A. L.
L[owell]. & Frank C.J. had committed an unpardonable sin by not
staying for the third year. The clash may have occurred in connection
with the H.L.S. Assn. celebration in 1886,[4] when undoubtedly I had
the say. I have no recollection.

5. Both Harold and the Massies[5] told us of Christie's being with the
Hydroelectric Comn.

6. You will recall your & my vain enquiries to learn something of one
Samuel R. Wachtel[l] who argued so well the Wiener Bank Case against
Hughes.[6] "Tout vient a qui sait attendre."[7] A week ago a Mrs. Wachtel[l] (who had called previously at the Court & found we were not in
session) sent up her name at Florence Court. Having neither Friendly

321

nor Poindexter[8] available, I bade the elevator boy have her come up. A comely youngish woman appeared. The enclosed letter tells the rest. Except the first of my cross-examination. S.R. came to America from Crackow at the age of 13; had a very hard boyhood & youth; got his education at Cooper's Union; intended first to be an engineer; later went into the law; studied law at N.Y. Law School; was admitted 17 years ago; was in the office of Mr. or Judge Mannheim or Manheimer, is now head of the firm of Wachtel, Manheim(er) (son of the judge);[9] & is now 43; has quite a number of foreign clients. Comes home tired after the day's work & loves best music which his wife supplies on the piano. It was quite a sentimental journey episode.

7. An editor of the N.R. ought to know better the needs of this democracy than to say: "Next to being corrupt, complacency & inertia in the face of corrupt[ion] is the unforgivable offence" etc. (Feb. 22 issue p. 4) It is much above being corrupt. Some corruption will happen among fallibles. But complacency is the Seven Deadly Sins heaped into one.

8. This Administration is debauching the judiciary with inexcusable political appointments. The latest is Green of Iowa.[10] A man in his 72d year[11] for the Court of Claims. He has been in Congress since 1911. Before that he was a petty Iowa lawyer; then a petty state district judge until 1911. Alf. A. Wheat had been urged for the place, but he is without political support. This was a most unpardonable offense as there was no need to consider the wishes of local Senators. Some one in Al Smith's interest & that of the law, ought to make a study of Cal's enormities in this line—a long one.[12]

---

[1] James Laurence Laughlin (1850–1933), a well known economist, chaired the Department of Political Economy at the University of Chicago. On 20 February, Laughlin published a letter in the *New York Times* condemning the Carnegie Foundation for abolishing its chair of historical research in Washington (a position held with important results by J. Franklin Jameson for twenty years). What probably appealed to LDB, however, were Laughlin's remarks about the recent shake-up of the Brookings Institution (see 25 December 1927), which had sent Walton H. Hamilton to Yale (see 20 December 1927). A strong indication that LDB or FF may have prompted the Laughlin letter is Laughlin's having quoted, in his piece, the very lines from Xenophon which LDB had shared with FF on 28 January 1928.

[2] Perhaps a reference to the Margold matter at the Law School (see 15 December 1926, n. 2); Powell supported hiring Margold and wrote a letter to Pound to that effect.

[3] Christopher Columbus Langdell (1826–1906), the legendary dean of the Harvard Law School, had been the man most responsible for those reforms which made Harvard into the country's leading center for legal study.

[4] The celebration took place in connection with the 250th anniversary of the founding of Harvard College. From its inception on 23 September 1886, LDB took an active interest in the

affairs of the Law School Association. He was its first secretary, and he served in that capacity for many years.

[5] Perhaps this report on Canadian politics came from Charles Vincent Massey (1887–1967), the first ambassador from Canada (1926–1930) and later governor general of Canada, and his wife, Alice Stuart Massey (d. 1950), an author.

[6] See 9 March 1927.

[7] "Everything comes to one who waits."

[8] Poindexter was LDB's "messenger," provided by the Supreme Court, but characterized by LDB's daughter, Elizabeth, as "a very helpful member of the household."

[9] Wachtell's partner was Louis Manheim.

[10] William Raymond Green (1856–1947) had been a state judge before coming to Congress. His new appointment to the court of claims involved service from 1928 until 1942.

[11] Interestingly, Green was born less than a week before LDB himself.

[12] See 29 February 1928.

No. 310   February 26, 1928   Washington, D.C.

1. In your fight all along the line against Lowell et al, there is the comforting thought that time as well as truth, are running in your favor. "My faith is great in time, and that which shapes it to its perfect end."

2. What will Margold do & what will be done for him? Can't you get him an immediate Asst. Professorship at Yale? [1]

3. As to Sutherland—I have seen too little of him to be entitled to an opinion. But it looks as if R.P.'s striving were rather for gentility than for intellect. [2]

4. I have not seen the Mass. Public Utility (Valuation) Bill. But from what Joe Eastman sent, it looks as if there is need of steering to avoid invalidity under the Equality Clause.

5. There ought to be, in the interest of truth & of Al Smith, a careful study of Hoover preachment during the last 7 years, with an eye on his forgetfulness of labor & the evidence of unemployment. My impression is that, with all his industrial planning, he paid no heed to the obviously resulting lessening of labor employment by the methods of efficiency so pushed by him. Rejoicing in sawing oneself off a limb—or N.Y.'s surprise at congestion resulting from the erection of skyscrapers, is the fair comparison.

6. Reading[3] is now in a class with those Los Angeles patriots.

7. Where was Powell when the Faculty met?

It's good [*] & Green have turned to you.

[1] Margold reentered private practice until 1933 when he joined the New Deal's Department of the Interior.

[2] It is unclear whether LDB is discussing his former clerk, William Sutherland, or someone else by that name. In any case, no one named Sutherland then taught at Harvard Law School.

[3] LDB may be referring, here, to the case of Massachusetts Attorney General Arthur K. Reading. He had helped in the prosecution of Sacco and Vanzetti and defended the trial. Now he was implicated in a shake-down scheme in which he had received $25,000 from a local club. On this date he began preparing for his impeachment fight. On 10 June he was impeached and resigned, and in July was disbarred.

No. 311   February 29, 1928   Washington, D.C.

1. O.W.H's lack of an opinion on Feb 20 was not due to lack of readiness on his part. He also distributed Tuesday opinion assigned to him last Saturday.

2. OWH. has been absent this week, because of a cough (not serious) but his new MD (the old one died) has ordered him to stay indoors. His recuperative powers are as amazing as ever; & the MD. says his arteries are as of a man of 40.

3. The Coolidge debauch of the Judiciary continues apace.[1] You have noticed appointment of Peyton Gordon to S.C. of the District.[2] You will have heard from Hitz how the Court had twice endeavored to prevent Gordon's reappointment as Dist. Atty. The bar wanted Adkins[3] for the J.P. of the District, & he would have accepted at a considerable financial sacrifice. Alfred Wheat would have been glad to get either that judgeship or the one on the Ct of Claims; & would make a good judge.

4. The Senate Comtee is doing a very serious thing in the treatment of Esch.[4] Such action is bound to destroy morale & independence in action. Of course it would have been better not to have appointed Esch originally, but for a very different reason.

5. Alice sends you enclosed passage from Bacon which will interest also Chafee if he doesn't know it.

6. Would Margold prefer Columbia to Yale? Those were good letters from the faculty members.

7. Estelle [Frankfurter], who was in Monday told us of your conquest of Vassar.

Ex A. G. Gregory was in yesterday & is strong for Al Smith.

[1] See 22 February 1928.

[2] Peyton Gordon (1870–1946) had been named district attorney for Washington, D.C., by Harding in 1921 and then was reappointed by Coolidge in 1926. Gordon served as an associate justice of the district's supreme court until 1941.

[3] Jesse Corcoran Adkins (1879–1955), a Washington, D.C., attorney, had been in and out of the Justice Department since 1905, and had been assistant attorney general from 1912 to 1916. In 1930, he would, in fact, receive an appointment as associate justice of the district supreme court.

[4] John Jacob Esch (1861–1941) represented Wisconsin in Congress for more than twenty years; his best known legislation was the Transportation Act of 1920, written with Cummins of Iowa. In 1921 Esch was appointed to the Interstate Commerce Commission, but in 1928 the Senate Committee on Interstate Commerce questioned his judgment, and the full Senate rejected his confirmation for reappointment on 17 March.

No. 312   March 4, 1928   Washington, D.C.

1. R. Walton Moore [1] is an "old Virginian of the best type"—now in his fifth term in Congress—formerly commerce counsel for the Southern carriers. When he dined with us Thursday, he volunteered the suggestion that the diversity of juris citizenship jurisdiction should be abridged. That led to my telling him I would ask you to send him your "Business" & his saying that with a little pushing (which he was ready to give) he thought a bill or bills could be put through, raising the jurisdictional amount & otherwise bringing abridgement. In the course of the talk, it was suggested that you & associates might be willing to draw the desirable bills.

I suggest now that you merely send him "Business" with a letter saying that you do so at my suggestion. I think he will answer, asking you to draw some bills etc. & furnish data. When the time comes for work on your part, Friendly can, I think, be drafted by you. He has become keenly interested in jurisdictional matters.

2. Alice thinks enclosed from William James [2] on teachers will interest you.

3. I hope the opposition press will put to full use the recent oil disclosures. [3] To do so, they must be brought home skillfully to C.C. & his Cabinet. Not only the doctrine of noscitur a sociis; [4] but as an explanation of the persistent silence & attempt at suppression which has gone forward for 4 1/2 years, despite Daugherty & Fall iniquities. The high-ups must have known. And Hoover should not be permitted to escape, because of his personal sanctity, & the immoral acts must be brought home to the leaders of the party of moral ideas by insinuation & more.

4. Experienced Republicans realize that the Scandals, & particularly Will Hays' last disclosure, has [sic] made things very difficult for the party—if the Democrats don't make fools of themselves. One of those experienced Republicans said to me in private: "I am sure Smith will be nominated. And then, if he is, it will be an even bet which party wins."

If the Democrats can find & utilize some men as politically wise and

325

as loyal as Amos Kendall, Frank Blair and Isaac Hill,[5] there should be an extremely good chance of putting Smith into the White House, and now that the prosperity bubble is bursting and unemployment is in the public eye.

5. Your diary entry is a terrible indictment of R.P. It is fine to see Calvert [Magruder] rise to full height & Landis's courage. Redlich talked well.[6]

6. Glad the Judiciary matter is being taken up. Who are the 27 Madison Ave. men?

7. With good men following Reading,[7] I am reminded of Edmund Benedikts "Gott, was hab die Familie aber ungluck."[8]

On regular docket, we reached last week the first of the Certs filed Oct 10/27 & have passed the last day of 1926 term's entries.

[1] Robert Walton Moore (1859–1941), after a career in Virginia politics, came to Congress in 1919 and remained there until 1931. In 1933 he joined the State Department.

[2] William James (1842–1910) was the illustrious Harvard psychologist and philosopher.

[3] The Senate investigating committee, doggedly pursuing the oil scandals of the Harding administration, had discovered what appeared to be more fraudulent sales of the Teapot Dome reserves. While attempting to trace the profits of that sale, it was disclosed that some of the money might have come into the Republican party campaign fund. Two days earlier, Will Hays admitted before the Senate committee that Harry Sinclair had given him $260,000. Hays claimed that he returned $100,000 of that sum.

[4] "He is recognizable from his associates."

[5] Amos Kendall (1789–1864), Francis Preston Blair (1791–1876), and Isaac Hill (1789–1851) were all members of President Andrew Jackson's "kitchen cabinet."

[6] This entry might have had to do with the attempt to give Nathan Margold a professorship (see 15 December 1926, n. 2); all those named here supported Margold.

[7] See 26 February 1928, n. 3.

[8] "God, what does the family have but misfortune."

No. 313   March 10, 1928   Washington, D.C.

1. You were in our thoughts today.

2. O.W.H.'s doctor discharged himself yesterday, and H. expected to be on hand Monday. We shall probably close the present sitting Tuesday to give our jj. time for opinions etc.

3. Florence Kelley was in last Monday before seeing Walsh. She says the Children's Bureau had no money for the work the bill (if enacted) would require & feared there was little chance of them getting any.

4. There is no chance for Sam Warner[1] in the Law School job I had in mind. How are Margold's plans developing?

5. I hope you & Landis are planning an annual, for H.L.R., on "Business of the U.S.S.C. at the last term."[2] For the Oct. Term 1927

326

article I hope the work Friendly will do for my annual survey will be helpful. I have suggested that he make it so, & lay the basis for the work of future secretaries.

These Annual articles will make the Second Edition of "Business" an easier job.

[1] Sam Bass Warner (1889–1979) graduated from Harvard Law School in 1915, and taught there from 1928 until 1945. He was an expert on criminal justice and criminal statistics and advised the Wickersham Commission (see 13 March 1929, n. 2) after 1929.

[2] See 18 July 1927, n. 2.

No. 314   March 16, 1928   Washington, D.C.

1. Isadore Levine [sic] made a most creditable appearance in our Court—well prepared, dignified, tactful.[1] With experience added, he should do much.

2. I hope next year your Seminar will produce an article demonstrating the futility of our Grants of certiorari's in Federal Empl[oyer]. Liability Cases (1916–1927 terms).

3. Hasn't the time come for legislation bringing the RR's under compensation acts? If so this simple device might be suggested to John B. Andrews.[2] Have Congress pass an act making it optional for RRs in any state that has the requisite compensation law, to elect to come under it in respect to its interstate operations; & wherever it does elect, make the state law apply to all accidents happening within the state.

4. R. W. Moore writes me that he has written you asking for draft of bill or bills. (See 7).[3]

5. DeHaas was here Wednesday (with [*] of Chicago Chronicle) & Mrs. Lindheim, Zip[4] & Miss Franklin[5] (of Chicago) were here yesterday. The revolt is growing.[6] If only Mack & Wise were resolute!

6. Your S.V. has done well. What is total number sold to date?

7. I should think limiting diversity of jurisdiction:
   (a) By raising the limit to $10,000—might escape serious opposition.
   (b) By excluding foreign corporations which have a usual place of business within the state (excepting interstate RR, telegraph & telephone companies) might get reasonable support. I make the exceptions only in order not to have the combined opposition of the utilities.

What amendments are prepared, ought to be each by a separate bill & each bill as short as possible.

I assume you will write Friendly.[7] I shall not say anything to him.

8. Alice is much pleased with the Herald review of the Karl Goldmark.[8] Did you have it inserted? And who did it?

9. Alice is sending Elizabeth the Brailsford[9] article.

10. Yes, Charlie Merz has done well.

11. Alice sends you the clipping from Madison, which Elizabeth sent to show that there are some free speakers there.

12. That enquiry into Civil Service is a bit different from Cal's performances.

13. I have seen nothing of moment in the press about the Shipping Board Scandal.[10] (Still, I understand there is another member about as guilty, who it was expected would go before this.) The fact is that Cal. is willing to appoint men to office in reckless disregard of character & despite warnings.

14. The Review of "Business" is a worthy one.

[1] Levin had argued *Hemphill* v. *Orloff*, 277 U.S. 537. The dispute involved the attempt of a "foreign" corporation doing business in Michigan to collect a promisory note although the corporation had not complied with Michigan law.

[2] John Bertram Andrews (1880–1943) was the secretary and executive officer of the American Association for Labor Legislation, an organization dedicated to improving labor conditions.

[3] See 4 March 1928.

[4] Zip Falk Szold (1888–1979) was a social worker and secretary of the National Consumers' League before marrying Robert Szold in 1917. Active in Hadassah for more than five decades, Mrs. Szold was president of the organization from 1929 to 1931, and played an active part in bringing the Brandeis group back to power in 1930.

[5] Pearl Franklin (1885–1958), a lawyer and a lifelong leader of Hadassah, was the president of the Chicago chapter.

[6] See 16 June 1927, n. 3.

[7] See 4 March 1928.

[8] Alice Goldmark Brandeis had just published her translation of *Notes from the Life of a Viennese Composer* (New York: Albert and Charles Boni, 1927), the memoirs of Karl Goldmark (1830–1915).

[9] Henry Noel Brailsford, (1873–1958), a well known English journalist, published numerous books as well as countless articles and editorials.

[10] A federal grand jury was investigating a loan of $15,000 to W. S. Hill, a former member of the Shipping Board. The loan was made by Joseph L. Bley, of the West Coast Shipping interests. Within weeks, Philip S. Teller, another member of the Board, also resigned his position.

No. 315   March 29, 1928   Washington, D.C.

1. OWH is in fine form. Daily, for the last five days he has called me spontaneously—propria persona[1] on the telephone. On four days, to talk opinions. In one case, he read me one on the telephone—a whole

opinion. Yesterday, the call was solely to tell me that he had beat me to it, & has discovered the first dandelion on the wall of Potomac basin.

2. Last year or earlier, you told me E. H. Warren[2] had doubt whether on the whole business corporations had been a blessing or a damage to America—(as distinguished from unincorporated businesses). Has he written anything on the subject, or has any other person? And who has written on the dangers, social, economic & political, incident to our business being absorbed by corporations.[3]

Please let me have as soon as you can any references available.

3. I suppose you saw the Federal Dist. Court jurisdiction bill reported by Senate Judiciary (in U.S. Daily of yesterday or Tuesday).[4]

4. That's good about the Outlook.

5. I do not understand fully the reference to R. L. O'Brien.

6. Those are great stuff in N.Y. World on Republican honesty.[5]

7. I hope the N.Y. World, N.R. & Nation will not fail to make the most of Secy of Labor's report on unemployment & prevent his misleading the public by misinterpreting the facts gathered by Ethelbert Stewart.[6] They are really worse than I supposed. If his guess of near 1,900,000 shrinkage in employment since 1925 is correct, the number of unemployment must be at least 4,000,000—possibly much more. (He assumes N.Y. fairly represents the U.S. and manufacturing & railroading fairly represent all employments). For

  (a) The number employed in N.Y. factories in Jan, 1925 was about the same as in Jan, 1914. Think of (a) growth in population by natural growth & immigration, (b) gain in employables through trek to cities.

The A.F. of L. report their average unemployed at 18 percent—rising to 30 in Phila.

I guess that means about 20 percent skilled & unskilled. 20% of 23,000,000 = 4,600,000.

8. Is John Dickinson going to H.L.S. for the Chair on Legislation?[7]

9. What has happened with Margold's Columbia prospect?

10. That's an interesting report of Columbia L.S.

[1] "in one's own proper person."

[2] Edward Henry Warren (1873–1945) had taught law at Harvard since 1904. In 1916, he had been the only member of the faculty to oppose LDB's confirmation to the Supreme Court.

[3] Edward H. Warren, *Corporate Advantages Without Incorporation* (New York: Baker, Voorhis, and Co., 1929).

[4] Senate bill 3151 was not acted upon during the session.

[5] The *World* had kept up a string of editorials and editorial cartoons on the oil scandals and other

problems of the Republican administrations. It had also featured news stories of Democratic attacks on the administration.

⁶Ethelbert Stewart (1857–1936), a statistician in various governmental agencies, served as commissioner of labor statistics from 1920 to 1932. Secretary James J. Davis reported on national unemployment to the Senate. See *New York Times*, 27 March 1928.

⁷Dickinson never returned to the Harvard Law School in any capacity.

No. 316   April 10, 1928   Washington, D.C.

Holmes's dissent in the Black & White Taxi Cab Case will stand among his notable opinions.¹ It was delivered with fervor.

Galloway did a good job.

¹*Black & White Taxi Co.* v. *Brown & Yellow Taxi Co.*, 276 U.S. 528 (1928). The Brown & Yellow Co. enjoyed a monopoly arrangement with the Louisville & Nashville railroad for servicing the Louisville station. The Black & White, knowing that such an arrangement would be declared illegal under Kentucky law, invaded the business. To evade the anticipated results of a Kentucky state court judgment, the Brown & Yellow had itself rechartered in Tennessee, and then brought suit in a federal court. Under the old rule enunciated by Joseph Story in *Swift* v. *Tyson*, 16 Pet. 1 (1842), the federal court was not bound by the Kentucky state court's monopoly doctrine. The evasion worked, and six members of the Supreme Court supported the contention of the Brown & Yellow Co. Holmes was joined in his dissent by LDB and Stone. The case illustrated perfectly the anomalies of the existing law of "diversity of citizenship jurisdiction." The minority finally secured the reversal of *Swift* in the *Erie Railroad* case, removing one incentive to resort to a federal court; see 3 May 1938, n. 5.

No. 317   April 21, 1928   Washington, D.C.

1. Answering your enquiry: I think it would be an excellent idea to draft a bill to correct the alleged rule acted on as to general law in the Black & White taxi case. The draft bill should go to Sen. Tom Walsh. He sat through the reading of the opinions, seated in a front seat, & seemed much interested.

2. Another bill should be drawn, correcting the court's error in construction of the Fed Statutes as to what is a fraud on its jurisdiction. Such action as was taken in the Black & White Case, ought to be prohibited whether strictly a fraud or not. That bill should go to Judge Moore.

3. Another bill should be drafted to put an end to removals, where there is a several controversy.¹ That provision is being construed as removing the whole cause—an obvious injustice to those defendants who want to remain in the State Court, & to the pl[ainti]ff. That bill also should go to Judge Moore.

4. I was asked by the C.J. to go with him & Van (for obvious reasons)

to Sen. Norris (& T. J. Walsh) to get them to put through the amendment (enclosed) to the ridiculous appeal act (Jan 31/28) which the Amer. Bar Assn had ignorantly put through.[2] I told Walsh that I had heard that his Boston speech was fine. This pleased him.

5. Glad to hear of your talk on unemployment. Yes Beveridge gave Ethelbert Stuart [sic] what was coming to him.[3] Who wrote "Laid Off."[4]

6. If the Atlantic got the real stuff on Lawyer's Ethics it would be helpful. But you cant & others wont give it.

7. Is the Law Quarterly article out?[5]

8. I wont believe the $2,000,000 Filene tale without a certificate of the trustees, duly countersigned.

9. R.P. on this was naive, as to Margold.

10. Perhaps the Donnelley decision was *because* of certain views as to prohibition.[6]

We are due in Boston June 5. Hope you & Marion will reserve that evening. And that we may see you two at Chatham at the weekend & thereafter.

[1] A case which involves several separable and distinct questions, only some of which are federal in nature.

[2] The new law (45 *U.S. Statutes*, ch. 14 [1928]) abolished the writ of error and ordered that all relief heretofore obtainable by a writ of error should now be possible through appeal. The act was approved 31 January 1928. The amendment which LDB, Taft, and Van Devanter urged was passed on 26 April as 45 *U.S. Statutes*, ch. 440 (1928). It permitted the writ of error at the appeal level.

[3] Sir William Henry Beveridge (1879–1963), a political scientist and authority on insurance and unemployment, was director of the London School of Economics. The reference is to his slashing attack on Ethelbert Stewart's unemployment report (see 29 March 1928), which appeared as a communication, "The British Know," *New Republic* 54 (11 April 1928): 247.

[4] The article, *New Republic* 54 (11 April 1928): 236, was signed by Anne W. Armstrong.

[5] See 18 July 1927, n. 3. The first instalment of this three-part work appeared in April.

[6] John Donnelley, the prohibition director of Nevada, had been convicted and fined $500 for ignoring a violation of the Volstead Act. He appealed his conviction on the grounds that enforcement officers have discretion to ignore some cases and prosecute others. The Supreme Court (including LDB) upheld the conviction by a vote of 7–2. See *Donnelley* v. *United States*, 276 U.S. 505 (1928).

No. 318   May 10, 1928   Washington, D.C.

Re the C.J.'s diversity of jurisdiction point.

He speaks feelingly on this subject whenever it came up. I think his point is theoretical, like much of the economists mouthing of the "rational man." Of course, the bankers & still less the investors, do not give the subject of litigation any thought when they make loans. What rate they get depends mainly on the money market, and the credit of the

State or municipality. And we are reminded frequently that it is not the federal courts of the West and South, but those of New York in which the bankers' counsel are mainly interested.

Moreover, they & everybody within every State ought to be made to care whether the State tribunals are worthy & not seek the "easier way."

The Due Process cases teach us that State Courts were the mainstay (until recently) of vested interests.

No. 319   May 14, 1928   Washington, D.C.

1. You will be delighted with O.W.H.'s three dissents delivered today.[1]

2. Your drafting bureau might next fall prepare a series of bills to restore to the States the taxing power of which they have been robbed by extreme government instrumentalities decisions & Interstate Commerce decisions of recent years.

3. Today's grist of decisions reduces materially the volume of undisposed of cases.

4. Norman [Hapgood] is due here on 28th.

[1] The Supreme Court announced twenty-four decisions on Monday, 14 May, and Justice Holmes (besides joining with LDB in two dissents written by the latter), entered three dissents of his own (in all three of which he was joined by LDB). *Long* v. *Rockwood*, 277 U.S. 142, centered on the right of the state to tax income from patents; the majority opinion by McReynolds held such a tax unconstitutional as a tax on the right of patent itself. Holmes argued that patents are used by the patentees for personal profit, and that there was no reason the state should not include the income as long as the tax was not discriminatory. *Springer* v. *Philippine Islands*, 277 U.S. 189, involved the creation, by the Philippine government, of various companies to do business—the stock to be held by the government and voted by government officials. The majority (Sutherland) regarded this as a breach of the separation of powers. Holmes argued that sovereignty required a certain latitude to function and that, in this instance, he was unable to see a separation issue since the corporations did not perform government functions. *Panhandle Oil Co.* v. *Knox*, 277 U.S. 220, centered on a Mississippi law taxing dealers in gasoline, by the gallon, as applied to sales to federal agencies (the Coast Guard or a Veterans Hospital). The majority (Butler) saw it as a standard case of a state attempting to tax the federal government, unconstitutional since the landmark case of *McCulloch* v. *Maryland*, 4 Wheat 316 (1819). Holmes took issue with Marshall and argued that the Courts were well able to forestall Marshall's well-known dictum that "the power to tax involves the power to destroy," by requiring that the tax be no greater on government contractors than on others.

No. 320   May 23, 1928   Washington, D.C.

FF: Miss Grady is to speak in Springfield on Thursday June 7 at 4 : 15 PM. before the Teachers Association on Savings Bank Insurance. I wonder whether you could get your S.V. friend of the [Springfield] Republican[1] to attend in person. I think if he did, and came to understand fully what

S.B.I. has achieved and its potential value for Massachusetts, we should get wholehearted, powerful support from the paper.

The Republican has never expressed hostility. We had friendly notices in our campaign in 1906–7 when we were getting the bill enacted, and occasionally have had notices since. But far less from them than from many a paper of less public virtue. I have suspected that the ramifications of the Massachusetts Mutual Life Ins Co., a Springfield institution, may be the cause.

Miss Grady can tell you about the local situation there if you will telephone her. Possibly it would be desirable for you to do that in any event.

[1] Waldo Cook.

No. 321   June 15, 1928   Chatham, Mass.

It was good to have had the weekend talk.

1. Glad to hear Bullard will see Miss Grady.[1]

2. Al Smith should be able to beat Hoover, depressed by a stock market smash.[2] Vare should help neutralize Tammany.[3]

3. Now that state taxation is becoming confessedly burdensome & the federal taxes growing ever lighter, might it not be possible to get through Congress legislation which permitted equal taxation of intrastate and interstate commerce, & do away with the court-made tax discrimination against intrastate commerce? Isn't there somewhere a lawyer who could draw the bill & with or without economist's aid, present the supporting argument? Powell's articles would furnish a collection of the legal material.[4] It would probably take years to get the legislation, but the idea set agoing would win converts steadily.

4. Elizabeth has a son, Walter,[5] born on the 13th—which seems to be a favorite day in the Brandeis family—my father's, my own, & Louis Wehle's.

I suppose some reviewer of the wire tapping decision will discern that in favor of property the Constitution is liberally construed—in favor of liberty, strictly.[6]

[1] Frederic Lauriston Bullard (1866–1952) was the Boston *Herald* editorial writer whose Sacco and Vanzetti editorial won the Pulitzer Prize for 1926.

[2] In mid-June stock prices on Wall Street fell dramatically in a series of record trading days. The break in prices was temporary, of course, and the "smash" was not a factor in the election of 1928.

[3] William S. Vare was still under a cloud because of his campaign expenses (see 23 May 1926, n. 1) and would be expelled from the Senate in December 1929. But Vare had been a strong Hoover

supporter, endorsed him at the recent Republican convention, and stampeded the Pennsylvania delegation behind him. LDB hoped that this might help balance the taint of Al Smith's long association with Tammany Hall.

[4] Thomas R. Powell published a two-part article on the subject: "Contemporary Commerce Clause Controversies over State Taxation," *University of Pennsylvania Law Review* 76 (1928): 733, 958.

[5] Walter Brandeis Raushenbush (b. 1928) graduated from Harvard in 1950, and from the University of Wisconsin Law School in 1953. After the Air Force and three years of private practice, he joined the law faculty at Wisconsin. His special interest is in real estate law.

[6] *Olmstead* v. *United States*; *McInnis* v. *United States*; *Green* v. *United States*, 277 U.S. 438 (1928). Chief Justice Taft, speaking for a majority of 5 to 4, argued that convictions for prohibition related crimes, even though obtained by wiretap evidence, should be allowed to stand. Taft ruled that wiretap evidence did not constitute "search and seizure" within the meaning of the Fourth Amendment. LDB fired off an eloquent dissent which the *New York Times* called "one of the most sharply worded opinions from the bench in years" (5 June 1928). Calling wiretapping worse than tampering with the mails, LDB warned that "the greatest dangers to liberty lurk in the insidious encroachment by men of zeal, well meaning but without understanding." And, in one of his most often quoted passages, he said: "Our government is the potent, the omnipresent teacher. For good or ill, it teaches the whole people by its example. Crime is contagious. If the government becomes a lawbreaker, it breeds contempt for the law; it invites every man to become a law unto himself; it invites anarchy." Justice Holmes, writing that LDB had summed up his own opinion, added another famous word: "We have to choose, and for my part I think it less evil that some criminals should escape than that the government should play an ignoble part." In 1934, Congress registered agreement with the dissenters and passed a law prohibiting wiretapping without a warrant.

No. 322   July 7, 1928   Chatham, Mass.

1. Your Cornell article is admirable [1]—informing, suggestive, wise. It is so comprehensive that it covers in summary form or by reference most of what I had thought of in connection with "Business of the District Court." But I think that it does not render less desirable the suggested new series. To carry the requisite weight, recommendations must be supported by volume and the arguments must be developed with the copious illustrations which experience affords. If you do start this series, soon, in order to stake out your claim, might it not be well, to begin, after the necessary introductory matter, with the Diversity Jurisdiction that being the most vulnerable etc.? And at or near the end of the series should come a full treatment of the criminal jurisdiction.

What would you think of this for the line of the discussion under each of the several heads?

First the present law—then how it came about,—then what may be conveniently dispensed with.

2. For our No. 252 there was no excuse. [2]

3. I am indeed glad to have J.W.M.'s letter of 5th about deHaas.

4. It is not surprising that JWM. should have a recurrence of his old

trouble after the worry & strain of the last nine months & I hope he will be resolute about vacationing now.

5. Your correspondence with Maguire[3] proves again how much in resolution is lacking even in the best.

6. We shall hope to see Dean & Alice when they come to the Cape.

7. If Strawn was worse now than his address at Cornell some years ago, he must have grown with age.[4]

8. Yes the Boston Globe has some real insight.

9. The Bar Assn. Journal comes out well.

10. We are expecting the Hamiltons for the weekend.

11. Doubtless you will recall in Achad A Ham's [sic] "Moses" what he says of the priests.[5]

[1] FF, "The Distribution of Judicial Power between United States and State Courts," *Cornell Law Quarterly* 13 (1928): 499.

[2] No. 252, *Williams* v. *Great Southern Lumber Co.*, 277 U.S. 19, was decided in April 1928 by a unanimous Court, Justice Sanford delivering the opinion. Williams, the head of a local union, had been shot to death in an incident in his office where a group came to serve warrants on three other men. His widow sued the company for conspiring to kill him, and won a verdict in the lower court. The key question was whether the "group" was a mob acting with the company or a legitimate posse sent by the Chief of Police. The Supreme Court found for the company, on the basis of substantial (and not merely technical) errors, holding that the Appeals Court had correctly reversed the verdict.

[3] Roscoe Pound was trying to establish an Institute on Legislation within the Law School, and wanted to appoint Nathan Shattuck in an "advisory" capacity. The dean had said he would be willing to have the faculty discuss the proposal, but if they could not reach agreement, he would take the matter to the University Corporation for approval. FF had sent a blistering letter to his colleague, John M. Maguire, on 30 June, attacking Pound and defending the rights of the faculty to participate in such important decisions. Maguire agreed with FF's basic points, but tried to calm him down in a letter of 4 July, only to have FF explode on the subject once again the following day.

[4] As president of the American Bar Association, Chicago businessman and lawyer Silas Hardy Strawn (1866–1946) delivered numerous speeches, and it is not known about which one FF complained. For the Cornell speech, see 14 February 1925, n. 8.

[5] In his famous essay on Moses (1904), Achad Ha'am had distinguished the "Prophet" from the "Priest." The Prophet was a man of truth, an absolutist with "justice in his soul." The Priest, on the other hand, "who was the Prophet's trusted spokesman, follows the mob, makes them the sort of 'god' they want, and builds him an altar. . . . expediency is the guiding principle of the Priest." Leon Simon, tr. and ed., *Achad Ha'am: Essays, Letters, Memoirs* (Oxford: Oxford University Press, 1946), 111.

No. 323   July 14, 1928   Chatham, Mass.

1. Unless Max Lowenthal's study is to cover the subject, would it not be profitable to have one of your seminars consider the establishment of official receivers as a means of freeing the Fed Courts of patronage & also of diminishing the duties practically of the judges?[1]

2. Many thanks for the data for Miss Grady. The Boston Herald of today announces the Boston Five Cents Savings agency.[2]

3. Should not Walter L. be reminded of Von Jhering's statement in Der Kampf ums Recht,[3] that it is a greater social crime or sin to suffer silently the doing of wrong than to commit the wrong?

4. Smith has by his appointment of Raskob,[4] achieved assurance of three things: (1) an effective organization of the campaign; (2) adequate funds; (3) silencing of "Business views with alarm." His chore now should be to secure the Progressive vote. For that he should (a) stress his Water power views & efforts[5] (b) make the most of the Federal Trade Comn public utility disclosure.[6] That is not mudslinging. He must not ignore moral indignation. Much of what Norris said in statement (N.Y. Times yesterday) should be met by Smith's action & utterances.[7] And Labor should be reminded soon of his views on unemployment.

5. Cook & Beard should not be dormant too long.

6. Chafee has sent me "The Inquiring Mind"[8] doubtless at your suggestion. I am glad of it.

[1] Max Lowenthal (1888–1971), a New York lawyer, was a disciple of FF's (although he had never been his student) and was close to labor circles. He never published a full study of court patronage, but in his The Investor Pays (New York: A. A. Knopf, 1933), an examination of railroad bankruptcy and subsequent court receivership, he touched upon some questions of court patronage.

[2] The Boston Five Cents Savings Bank was the largest in New England, and its announcement (9 July) of the establishment of a Savings Bank Insurance agency marked an important victory for the system.

[3] Rudolph von Jhering, Der Kampf Ums Recht (Vienna: Manz, 1872).

[4] John Jakob Raskob (1879–1950) had left General Motors in order to become the chairman of the Democratic National Committee.

[5] From the beginning of his political career, Al Smith had opposed turning over New York's waterpower sites to private companies. His view was that a public corporation should be formed that would sell power to the "power barons" who ran the private utilities.

[6] Throughout the spring of 1928, hearings before the Federal Trade Commission revealed a concerted nationwide plan to fight the public ownership movement. Private utilities had raised large sums of money, fought unfavorable legislation in various states, even attempted to influence opinion in schools by spreading propaganda among children.

[7] In a statement issued to reject the presidential nomination by the Farmer-Labor party, George W. Norris, the leading authority on public power in the Senate, condemned both parties for apparently avoiding the public power issue.

[8] (New York, 1928). The book was a collection of essays on judicial, free speech, and industrial problems.

No. 324　　　　August 1, 1928　　　　Chatham, Mass.

1. Glad to have the July Quarterly[1] and the Morris Cohen.

2. You did a good job in getting W.L. started in the July 21 World.[2]

He should be made to keep persistently to his promise to return to the Republican delinquencies of the last 8 years with an—in these H.H. acquiesced.

3. D. D. Knowlton[3] is a fine character, right minded generally—probably better than any one procurable whom Eastman could get accepted—but not adequate as an advocate in our Court, a position of extreme difficulty because of the sharing of time with Esterline,[4] who has grown annually less valuable.

4. W. E. Stephen has eagerness & persistence which should make him a useful citizen despite limitations.

5. The presidential campaign will be a real one, with ever increasing unknown quantities. The greatest danger is that the women will go astray. I hope that no time will be lost in starting to set them right.

6. I should think that our decisions at recent terms would convince the Hand j.j. that either way they or we are not particularly competent to decide questions of "general law."[5]

7. The New Leader gave Croly, on his presidential doubts, a deserved smack.[6]

8. The inability of the Comtee to get a hall for Aug 22,[7] is revealing.

9. Auntie B. was much excited over the Slater case result.

10. Eliz. & Paul have been with us since the 26th & are hoping you & Marion will come over soon.

[1] See 18 July 1927, n. 3.

[2] In an editorial entitled "The World and Mr. Hoover: 1920 and 1928," Lippmann referred to an editorial the paper had run on 21 January 1920, which had called Herbert Hoover the man best qualified to succeed Woodrow Wilson as president. Several newspapers had recently reprinted that editorial, and the *World* still thought Hoover well qualified for the office. But Hoover had to share some of the blame for bad Republican policies in the intervening eight years.

[3] Daniel Waldo Knowlton (1881–1969), a New York attorney, had joined the Interstate Commerce Commission in 1922. He worked up through the ranks to become, in 1928, chief counsel to the Commission, holding that job until his retirement in 1952.

[4] Blackburn Esterline (1877–1928) was assistant to Solicitor General William Mitchell, and appeared in more than a hundred cases before the Supreme Court.

[5] Both Learned and Augustus Hand sat on the circuit Court of Appeals for the Second Circuit. ("General law" refers to the non-federal questions that the federal courts were deciding in their diversity jurisdiction.)

[6] In a front page attack by Norman Thomas, the *New Leader* for 28 July ridiculed "Mr. Croly's very long, involved, rather dull and yet somewhat amusing, rationalization of the essential vagueness, not to say cowardice of what he calls the progressive position." Croly had called a vote for the Socialist party in the upcoming election a wasted vote because the Socialists had failed to exhibit growth; Thomas offered to compare the growth curve of his party with that of *The New Republic's* subscription list.

[7] A group of Bostonians wished to hold a memorial meeting on the anniversary of the execution of Sacco and Vanzetti. They were refused places for the holding of the meeting all over the city. See 2 and 23 September 1928.

No. 325   August 24, 1928   Chatham, Mass.

1. Al Smith's speech[1] is wise and worthy. Boston Herald should be ashamed of itself.[2]

2. Your Hoover power material will doubtless be made good use of.

3. Smith should, in connection with power,[3] bring out clearly its significance to the farmers with his expanding use of electricity.

4. In Winston's Andrew Johnson, you will be interested particularly in the Chapter on the trial of Mrs. Surrat [sic]. Macdonnel [sic] might have included that story in his "Historical Trials."[4]

5. Elizabeth has been reading your July instalment in the Quarterly.[5]

[1]Governor Smith accepted his party's nomination in a spirited speech of 22 August, delivered in Albany. He launched an attack on Republican "reaction" and outlined his own positions on the major domestic and foreign policy issues. The text is in the *New York Times*, 23 August 1928.

[2]In an editorial on this day entitled "Gov. Smith as a Spender," the Boston *Herald* attacked Smith for his allegedly spendthrift policies as governor of New York, policies which the paper claimed disqualified Smith from criticizing the Coolidge administration for its economic policies.

[3]See 14 July 1928.

[4]See 17 September 1927, n. 10. LDB refers here to Robert Watson Winston, *Andrew Johnson, Plebeian and Patriot* (New York: H. Holt and Co., 1928), ch. 8. Mrs. Surratt was executed on flimsy evidence because she was the landlady of several of the conspirators who killed Abraham Lincoln.

[5]See 18 July 1927, n. 3.

No. 326   September 2, 1928   Chatham, Mass.

1. I hope some Democrats will make clear to the Harding-Coolidge-Hoover pseudo-drys how close is the connection between Chicago, Philadelphia bootleggerism & Crime.

2. That's promising fee news from Cardozo.

3. R.P. seems to have his mind on one job.

4. Yes. The Kallen episode is helpful.[1] And should make easier the task of freeing the [Boston] Common.[2] Anderson will help on that if called upon, provided there is anything he can do.

5. I knew you would join in my schadenfreude[3] over A.L.L.'s recent notoriety.[4] The shrewd man of business will begin to question his views on S.V.

6. The N.R. and the Nation on Smith should help dispel the defeatism of our friends. And also such talk as Sen. Blaine's.[5] But the disease of defeatism is widespread. I found it in George Anderson.

7. The recent Worcester Case of mistaken conviction should help.

[1]In a bizarre incident, Horace M. Kallen was charged with blasphemy in Boston under a law dating from 1697. While talking to a Sacco and Vanzetti memorial meeting, he remarked that if the two

men had been anarchists, then so were Jesus, Socrates, and others. Kallen announced that he welcomed a trial, but the charges were quickly and quietly dropped.

[2] See 13 May 1925 and 12 January 1928.

[3] "malicious pleasure."

[4] The newspaper revealed that a federal investigation had uncovered an immense land fraud that cheated many New England investors. Harvard's president, A. Lawrence Lowell (who had headed Governor Fuller's advisory committee in the Sacco and Vanzetti case) had lost a reported $70,000.

[5] Senator John J. Blaine, while campaigning for La Follette in Wisconsin, roundly denounced the Harding-Coolidge record but stopped short of endorsing Smith. Blaine finally bolted his party and endorsed Smith in October.

No. 327   September 6, 1928   Chatham, Mass.

1. Meiklejohn's address is a thing modern of almost unequalled beauty.[1]

2. Dry Republican worshippers of Coolidge should be made to state why there will be less corruption and bootlegging if Hoover is elected.

3. I'll send the 1922–4 Surveys upon my return to Washington.

4. We plan to leave here tomorrow & to be at the Bellevue two or three days. Of course, it would be fine to see you there before we start for Washington, which may be either Sunday or Monday, dependent largely upon date of Miss Grady's return from abroad. But you must not shorten your stay at Win[d]sor, or let Marion travel faster than is best for her—i.a. because it is uncertain.

[1] Undoubtedly LDB refers to Meiklejohn's address, "In Memoriam," delivered in Boston on the anniversary of the execution of Sacco and Vanzetti. In his speech Meiklejohn compared the behavior of Boston with that of Athens during the trial and execution of Socrates. The talk is reprinted in the 5 September 1928 issue of *The New Republic*.

No. 328   September 13, 1928   Washington, D.C.

1. Will the Bar Assn act?[1]

2. I suppose you noticed the copious pictures in the press of John Coolidge, accompanied to & from his new job at the New Haven, by a Secret Service man. The World, N.R. & Nation should explode.

"Can such things be,
And overcome us a summer cloud
Without our special wonder?"[2]

3. Walter L. might have added to Republican Phila & Chicago etc. as crime centers, Republican Washington under Coolidge-appointed

Commissioners & Prosecuting Attorney & under his eyes. Note this editorial from today's Post.[3]

[1] LDB had enclosed a clipping reporting that Max David Steuer (1870–1940), a noted criminal lawyer, had been fined $5,251 for concealing undeclared goods in his luggage when he and his wife returned from Europe. Steuer had defended Harry M. Daugherty on a charge of conspiring to defraud the government.

[2] *Macbeth*, III, 4: 110. John Coolidge, the president's twenty-two-year-old son, had taken a job on 8 September with the New York, New Haven & Hartford Railroad.

[3] The unsigned editorial, "Police Reform Needed," demanded that "the Police Department muddle" be straightened out by a thorough reform of Washington's police department.

No. 329   September 18, 1928[1]   Washington, D.C.

1. Our congratulations to Marion on getting off her S.V. ms.[2]

2. Mrs. Willebrandt may be doing the "Rum, Romanism & Rebellion" soon.[3]

3. Here most Smith sympathizers are defectors. But [*] distinguished Republican ex Senator still thinks that Smith will be elected & that it will not be by a narrow margin.

4. I remember Schuntag well & favorably.

5. More D[istrict of]. C[olumbia]. spy stuff enclosed.

[1] LDB erroneously dated this letter "8/18/28."

[2] Marion D. Frankfurter and Gardner Jackson, eds., *The Letters of Sacco and Vanzetti* (New York: Viking Press, 1928). FF had asked Jackson to let his wife join in the task of editing and publishing these death house letters, hoping that the work would help her to recover from a severe depression she suffered in late 1927 and 1928.

[3] Mabel Walker Willebrandt (1889–1963), a California lawyer and Republican progressive, had been appointed assistant attorney general in 1921, and directed federal prohibition prosecutions. She was a friend of Susan Brandeis and would be a frequent dinner guest at the Brandeis apartment. She had attacked Smith, both for his position on prohibition and for certain alleged deficiencies of "character," in an Ohio speech before a Methodist conference. Her remarks were given wide publicity and called forth angry replies from Democrats. "Rum, Romanism & Rebellion" was the notorious phrase spoken by Rev. Samuel D. Burchard against the Democrats during the election of 1884. The insult was thought to have angered so many New York Irishmen as to have cost James G. Blaine the state and thrown the election to Grover Cleveland.

No. 330   September 23, 1928[1]   Washington, D.C.

1. Poor R.P.

2. Gardner Jackson has pasted the appropriate label on Richard Walden Hale in the Nation.[2]

3. Jos Lee is fine. I guess he would join Zach Chafee in freeing the Common.[3]

4. Lowell Mellet, who is personally for Smith, was in last evening. He was enthusiastic over the Omaha speech, but says Al did a very poor

job in Oklahoma.[4] (He listened to both over the radio). It was the performance he criticized; as he approved of both the subject & the place. I.a. he says Al's evidence as to participation of the Republi[can]. Nat. Comtee in Klu [sic] Klux propaganda was woefully insufficient.

5. Mrs. Burt Wheeler who was also in & has been in Minn., says Dem. chances (Al) there are very good & Shipstead's chances are also.[5]

6. I was amazed to find Leo Rowe (who was in Friday) a Hoover man & a wholly unthinking one. He was for H. because he was "internationally minded" and because he (R.) thinks the gains socially through National Prohibition are large.

7. Jim Landis should write H.J.F.

8. Hoover isn't getting yet all he deserves on labor.

9. Walter did a neat job on Max Steuer—[*] is *collosal*.[6]

[1] LDB erroneously dated this letter "8/23/28."

[2] In "The Way of Boston," *Nation* 127 (26 September 1928): 297, Gardner Jackson recounted the difficulty in getting a place to hold the Sacco and Vanzetti memorial meeting (see 1 August 1928). The first choice of the organizers had been the Old South Church's meeting house. Richard Walden Hale (1871–1943), a Boston attorney and treasurer of the Old South, had declared himself in favor of the meeting, but after checking with the other trustees, denied the use of the facility to the group.

[3] See 13 May 1925 and 12 January and 2 September 1928. Joseph Lee (1862–1937), a Boston social worker, had been very active in municipal affairs and had labored with LDB in several reform efforts.

[4] Smith spoke at Omaha on 18 September, emphasizing farm policy and also fielding some questions on prohibition; his speech in Oklahoma City, on 20 September, was a direct attack on the Ku Klux Klan and an attempt to connect the Klan with Republicanism.

[5] Henrik Shipstead won reelection to the Senate in Minnesota; but Smith suffered a substantial (59% to 41%) defeat there in the November election.

[6] See 13 September 1928, n. 1. Lippmann's comments on the case came in the New York *World*.

No. 331   September 28, 1928[1]   Chatham, Mass.

1. I presume you are familiar with Sen. Walsh's discussion of the 1916 Act (Congr. Rec 2756), in which he insisted that in a case coming from C.C.A. on certiorari, only the Federal Questions should come to our Court. The adoption of that proposition would relieve us of many troubles.

2. Is the recent (small) rise in the price of wheat due to Al Smith's proposals re farm relief?

3. What Villard says about getting Jews is interesting.[2]

4. Al Smith is certainly doing a good job in the North West. Manton C.J. told me today that Norris and Bob La Follette will come out for him at or after the Milwaukee speech.[3] Sed Quaere.[4]

5. Bryan C.J.[5] says he thinks Florida is safe for Al.[6]

6. Bingham C.J.[7] thinks Democrats have a fair chance in N.H. because of Republican split—I.a. that a longtime French Canadian there said to him, with a chuckle, that he was happy over having landed—for "we are all going to work for Al & the Democratic candidate for Gov.[8]

7. Today's figures on growth of religious sects, suggests that Mabel Willebrandt & her allies may be the minority on that issue.[9]

8. We shall be glad to see Mr. Soecar.

9. Wm. Allen White doesn't look very nice with that $500 fee.[10]

10. Hoover's statistics are being pretty well riddled.

11. I guess this campaign will happily put an end to the pernicious era of good feeling.

Good to see Marion's book, in press.[11]

[1] LDB erroneously dated this letter "8/28/28."

[2] On 24 September Villard had written to FF asking for names for the board of directors of *The Nation*. The only two real workers on the board, he claimed, were Morris Ernst and Maurice Wertheim. "I know lots of good Jewish people who would come on and work like tigers," he said, "but we obviously cannot have an all-Jewish board."

[3] Robert M. La Follette, Jr., remained neutral in the presidential campaign, refusing to endorse either candidate. George W. Norris bolted his party and endorsed Smith in late October.

[4] "But inquire." A legal term meaning that the statement is doubted and needs to be examined further.

[5] Nathan Philemon Bryan (1872–1935) was a Florida lawyer, head of the system of higher education in that state, and then its U.S. Senator. He had been appointed to the Circuit Court of Appeals for the 5th Circuit in 1920.

[6] Hoover swamped Smith in Florida, getting almost 60 percent of the vote.

[7] George Hutchins Bingham (1864–1949), from New Hampshire, had been on the First Circuit Court of Appeals since 1913.

[8] Hoover took New Hampshire 59 to 41 percent. The Republican candidate for governor, C. W. Tobey, also won.

[9] See 18 September 1928. On 27 August the Census Bureau revealed figures on the growth of American religion during the decade 1916–1926. Although all major sects enjoyed an increase in membership, the Roman Catholics far outdistanced the Protestant gains. Catholics increased from 15.7 million to 18.6 million members during the ten year period.

[10] Testimony before the Federal Trade Commission on 19 September revealed that the New Jersey utility interests had spent large sums of money in efforts to curry public opinion. Among the revelations was that William Allen White, the Kansas progressive, had accepted a $500 fee, back in 1926, for addressing the National Electric Light Association.

[11] See 18 September 1928, n. 2.

No. 332   October 1, 1928[1]   Washington, D.C.

1. Hoover "in the hands of his friends" verily cuts a pitiable figure. The Caldwell letter,[2] atop Mrs. Willebrand [sic][3] will take a deal more of denials to obliterate the effect.

"Spiele nicht mit Schiessgewahr, etc."[4]

These are severe blows to women in public life.

2. Alice suggests as Philadelphia director of the Nation, Bob Bruere's friend Morris Leeds.[5] Or would Morris L. Cooke do better? Neither is just Oswald V[illard]'s kind. But either, if he accepted, would add much to the Nation and to his own eduction.

3. Too bad about Jane Addams.[6] Will she stomach the bigotry campaign? Couldn't she be headed off?

4. The Keatings were in (& Father Ryan) last evening. All thought Smith would surely be elected if it weren't for anti Catholicism; & all feared his defeat.

5. What will R.P. do about Ruggles?[7] If he comes in our press should holler about the Business School's subsidy from the utilities.

6. It's fine to learn how the students respondent [sic] to yur Fed. Jur. & Adm. Law courses & that you must reject half of the applicants.

The World editorial page is doing a good job.

[1] LDB erroneously dated this letter "9/1/28."

[2] Mrs. Willie W. Caldwell warned in a letter, secured by the *Washington Post* and then given wide publicity, that the election of Smith would result in America's becoming "Romanized and rum ridden." Herbert Hoover quickly and unequivocally repudiated the letter.

[3] See 18 September 1928, n. 3.

[4] "Don't play with fire."

[5] Morris Evans Leeds (1869–1952), a Philadelphia manufacturer and inventor, was involved in a great many civic and social activities.

[6] Jane Addams (1860–1935) was one of the best loved figures of the progressive movement and a leading reformer for more than forty years. She was best known as the founder of Hull House in Chicago in 1889. Apparently, Miss Addams had made it clear that she was about to endorse Hoover. The formal announcement, however, did not come until 18 October in conjunction with an endorsement by twenty-eight other prominent social workers.

[7] Clyde Orval Ruggles (1878–1958) had just left his position as dean of the business college at Ohio State University in order to become professor of public utility management and regulation at Harvard, where he taught for twenty years.

No. 333   October 7, 1928[1]   Washington, D.C.

Re yours of 5th.

1. I don't think there is anything of value which I can suggest for the campaign. Smith is entitled to win the liberals. To do this:

(a) It might be wise to drive home the power issue,[2] & show how much of an element power would be in farm economics and farm comforts; that to the city workers also light, heat & power are as necessary as water; electric light is often the substitute for sunlight; & no more inherent reason why the State should surrender to a private company the control of the water power, than of water for

343

drinking & washing. The power issue ought to help win farmers, laborers, & city white collar employees as well as liberals. And there is nothing Smith understands better.

(b) To make clear his stand & striving for improved labor & social economic conditions.

(c) To strive specifically to win the women voters, for whose social-economic aims he has done so much.

(d) To remind of his constant respect for liberty, and his human sympathy which transcends even tolerance.

(e) Appeal to the young—courageous, affirmative action, to advance human happiness.

Of course all of this is merely reasons why thinking, redblooded men & women should vote for Smith—not suggestions to one who has proved himself one of the wisest of politicians.

On re-reading this I am confirmed in the belief that I have nothing of value to suggest.

2. Mrs. Helm[3] (widow of the admiral), former social secretary for Mrs. Wilson, has just returned from her farm at Grayville, Illinois (about 40 miles from Evansville, Indiana). She says quite a number of farmers, lifelong Republicans, will vote for Smith on the farm issue— and that while travelling to her Tennessee farm (on the Mississippi) (a Democratic region) she heard people talk only politics.

She says Democratic speakers should invade Ill.—the Republican farm areas—and are much needed there.[4]

3. Billy Hitz was in, last evening, in much gloom politically. The prevalence of Democratic defeatists is sickening. "Our doubts are traitors."[5]

4. Mrs. Hitz told us that Frederic has left Harvard L.S. & has entered Yale L.S. Why?

5. Has Walker D. Hines[6] declared hims[elf]. If he is for Smith he should say so. That would help with textile men South & North.

Monte Lemann has a very high opinion of Borah's nephew just appointed D.J., E. Dis. La.[7]

I have not had or seen any statement of Judicial Council's report better than the U.S. Daily furnished.

I can't suggest any way of bringing Ottinger's[8] worthlessness home.

If the U.S.S.C. justices could testify, and Harlan would, no one could doubt.

Billy Hitz said John Lord O'Brien [sic][9] concurs in our view.

[1] LDB erroneously dated this letter "9/7/28."

[2] See 14 July 1928.

[3] Edith Benham Helm (d. 1962) was Mrs. Wilson's social secretary until her marriage to Admiral James Meredith Helm (1855–1927).

[4] Hoover took Illinois in the election by 57 to 42 percent.

[5] Shakespeare, *Measure for Measure*, I, 4: 77.

[6] Walker Downer Hines (1870–1934) was a lawyer who practiced in Louisville until 1906 and then in New York City. He was an expert on transportation and shipping.

[7] Wayne G. Borah (1891–1966) served as district judge for the Eastern District of Louisiana until 1949, when he was elevated to the Court of Appeals of the Fifth Circuit.

[8] Albert Ottinger (1878–1938), a New York lawyer and former state attorney general, was about to be defeated for the governorship by Franklin D. Roosevelt. See 15 October 1928.

[9] John Lord O'Brian (1874–1973) was a Buffalo, New York, lawyer who also practiced in Washington, D.C. He dabbled in politics and compiled, over his long lifetime, a respected record in public service—particularly during both world wars.

No. 334   October 7, 1928[1]   Washington, D.C.

1. It looks at the moment as if Goldsmith would prove himself impossible—and that soon. I spoke to him frankly yesterday after the second grave offense.

The task of introducing him to his work, I left to Friendly's oral instructions and demonstration and his explicit written memo. My supplement was to tell him, with the utmost brevity:

    (a) that he must report at the office each day at 9AM.

    (b) that whatever he sees, hears or infers is to remain confidential as to everyone, now & forever after.

He started work Monday Oct 1. Wednesday he did not appear until noon (after I had left for Conference); could not be reached by telephone at his hotel (Wardman Park[)]. There was specific work for him to do for the Conference—as he knew. When I returned late in the afternoon, he expresseed himself as most sorry & explained his default thus: that he had been poisoned by seafood; had been awake until the early hours, and that the hotel telephone clerk had omitted to wake him at 8 as directed; that he was accustomed at home to be awakened (by a servant); would buy an alarm clock & that this would not happen again.

Saturday, he again did not appear before I left for Conference & sent no word. I left a memo on his desk at 9:15 to see me as soon as he came in. He knew that there was specific work to do for the Conference. On returning from the Conference, I went immediately to my office, before going to the apartment. When I started to talk with him he asked whether I had seen his note on my desk [*]. As I had not we talked at once. He did not claim to have been sick, but said he had been very tired (from hard work during the last few days & perhaps unduly hard work in Chicago to finish up there); and that he had gone to bed at 11P.M. His note, which I found later, was of the same tenor substantially.

I made clear to him the needs of his position as aid. He was explicit in his regrets & that it shouldn't happen again.

His excuses are barely plausible. I suspect his habits are bad—the victim of drink or worse vices. I have a sense of his being untrustworthy; and something of the sense of uncleanness about him.

Do you know of anything which might bear upon the situation?

He appears to have a legal sense & to know the law; and his judgment so far as evidenced in his memos on Certioraris & other motions, seemed good.[2]

Homes J. is in great shape & evidently relieved in having survived Oct 4.[3] He talks now of what he will do on certs. next summer—if he is alive. More soon on other matters.

[1] LDB erroneously dated this letter "9/7/28."
  [2] See next two letters, and 15 October 1928.
  [3] On 4 October 1928, Justice Oliver Wendell Holmes, Jr., passed something of a milestone by becoming the oldest man ever to sit on the United States Supreme Court, surpassing the record set by Chief Justice Roger B. Taney in 1864.

No. 335   October 10, 1928[1]   Washington, D.C.

1. I wrote you sunday re Goldsmith. Since my frank talk the grand fear seems to have entered his soul. He is evidently making a great effort, & the question seems now to be whether he possesses the requisite self-control.[2]

2. Thanks for H.M.'s letter re Knapp.[3]

3. I am glad that Kirstein will have to declare himself.

4. Boyle's memo is interesting & his interest cheering.

5. In Monday's certs. allowed you will find the habitual grants of Fed. Empl[oyer]. Liability cases.

6. When you are considering further Business of Lower Fed. Courts & Appeals to U.S., keep in mind the unnecessary delays all along the line in appeals to C.C.A. & to U.S.S.C. which might be done by changing statutes, rules & practice to speed up the litigation—with result[ing] economies to Courts, litigants & counsel.

[1] LDB erroneously dated this letter "9/10/28."
  [2] See next letter and 15 October 1928.
  [3] George L. Knapp (1872–19[?]), editor of *Labor*, had spoken with LDB, who on 25 September

346

had suggested to FF that Knapp might be enlisted in the Smith campaign. FF had evidently passed this suggestion on to Henry Morgenthau, Sr., an active worker for Smith and, at the moment, heading up the Democratic financial campaign in New York state. Morgenthau (1856–1946), a German immigrant who had made a fortune in the United States, became deeply involved in many reform efforts, and was high in the councils of the Democratic party; Wilson had appointed him ambassador to Turkey. Neither FF nor LDB had much regard for Morgenthau's abilities, and LDB had crossed swords with him over the establishment of a Jewish State in Palestine.

No. 336   October 12, 1928   Washington, D.C.

Yours of 9th re Goldsmith reached me Wednesday P.M. & your telegram abut Shulman yesterday noon.[1] If I had felt free to consult only my own preference, I should have made the switch to Shulman. But making the change would be a severe blow to G. and might impair his future success for an appreciable time, so I concluded to talk further frankly with Goldsmith, to see whether he was, with full knowledge of all the restrictions and burdens involved, prepared to undertake the task of making good. He assured me that he was willing and anxious & felt that he had the will power to carry out the program, which involves total abstinence from drink and generally keeping himself in such training as will give him his maximum working capacity.

I should have kept him under observation a little longer before talking with him on the subject—if an accident had not put him into possession of the contents of your telegram before I saw it; the Marshal opened it & telephoned it to my office, while I was out and Goldsmith there. It seemed necessary, therefore, to take up the matter with G. at once.[2]

[1] See preceding letters. FF, who selected LDB's clerks, wrote back immediately to say that Goldsmith's conduct was intolerable, and that LDB should not have to be bothered by such behavior. On 11 October he telegraphed to say that Harry Shulman, the research fellow at Harvard, was available if LDB cared to make a switch. Shulman (1903–1955) was a Russian immigrant who did, in fact, become LDB's clerk for the 1929 term. Upon leaving Washington, Shulman went to Yale Law School, where he taught until 1954, when he became dean of the school.

[2] See 15 October 1928.

No. 337   October 12, 1928[1]   Washington, D.C.

1. Everett H. Brown Jr. of Philadelphia made a beautiful argument in an admiralty case this week.[2]

2. Samuel R. Wachtel[l] called.[3] He is a native of Galicia; came to America age 12, worked as tailor till age 18; has represented Austrian interests for past 5 years in effort to recover the property in alien custodian hands; and is to be honored next Summer [by] the University of Vienna by a degree in recognition of his services.

347

3. Basil Manly [sic] was in last evening, strong for Smith but doubtful of result. Yet he is quite sure that 4/5 of the La Follette vote of 1924 will be for Smith. He thinks that applies to the whole country except Idaho, which he says will go for Hoover.[4] He seems quite fearful of Virginia where Bishop Cannon's[5] power is said to be very great.[6]

4. The story that Norris will come out for Smith on the 25th persists.[7]

5. Katherine Dodd[8] says A.L.[9] is coming out for Smith. That's pretty good considering his sometime devotion to Cal.

[1] LDB erroneously dated this letter "9/12/28."

[2] Everett H. Brown, Jr. (1888–1951) was a graduate of the University of Pennsylvania Law School and an attorney in Germantown, Pennsylvania. The case (which Brown won, McReynolds delivering the opinion for a unanimous Court) was *Charles Warner Co.* v. *Independent Pier Co.*, 278 U.S. 85; it involved a collision between two ships in the Schuykill River.

[3] See 9 March 1927 and 22 February 1928.

[4] Idaho voted for Hoover by 65 to 35 percent.

[5] Bishop James Cannon, Jr. (1864–1944), a Methodist clergyman in Virginia, devoted most of his life to the battle against alcohol; he was a leading force in the powerful Anti-Saloon League.

[6] Virginia voted for Hoover by 54 to 46 percent.

[7] See 28 September 1928, n. 3.

[8] Katherine Dodd (1892–1965) was a noted pediatrician and professor of pediatrics at various universities. She had been a classmate of Susan Brandeis's at Bryn Mawr.

[9] Abraham Lincoln Filene (1865–1957) and his brother Edward had built up a large department store business in Boston. With advice from LDB, who served as Filene's attorney prior to 1916, the brothers pioneered in progressive industrial relations.

No. 338   October 15, 1928   Washington, D.C.

1. Your power article is of more than temporary significance.[1] Whatever the issue of the campaign, the struggle for government ownership must become widespread and persistent. For the decisions and attitudes of the Supreme Court have made public ownership the only way out;— and banker rapacity has made the fight urgent. The intensity of this campaign should serve to put an end to the pernicious era of good feeling between parties. Americans may again realize that fighting, politically & economically, is the price of liberty & life, and weapons long hanging "in monumental mockery"[2] should be repaired & furbished for use. There are good days ahead for the lawyer, the economist and the political scientist if they can be awakened from lethargy.

2. I suppose you saw Harlan's statement on Ottinger in the N.Y. Times of the 11th (?).[3] Remind me of the incident when we meet.

3. Goldsmith has certainly had the shock and scare of his life and seems determined to make good. Still, it is a comfort to think of Shul-

man as a possible reserve. If he is not permanently attached in N.Y. perhaps you may have him in mind for next year.[4]

4. I am glad at your dig at My Lord.

5. Harold's Bookman article[5] seemed to me less valuable than most of his.

6. The next 3 weeks should show constant gains for Al Smith.

[1] FF, "Mr. Hoover on Power Control," *New Republic* 56 (17 October 1928): 240. The article reviewed the various contradictions in statements on public power that Hoover had issued since 1928: "One thing is clear: instead of Mr. Hoover educating the electrical industry, the power interests have educated Mr. Hoover."

[2] Shakespeare, *Troilus and Cressida*, III, 3: 153. On 21 October LDB wrote to FF: "Al Smith's offensive is refreshingly Napoleonic. He is reminding us what a political opposition is for; and the gain now & hereafter should be great."

[3] See first letter of 7 October 1928, n. 8. The *New York Times* reported that Harlan F. Stone, LDB's colleague, wrote Ottinger a letter congratulating him warmly upon his nomination and wishing him success in the campaign.

[4] See 7, 10, and 12 October 1928. Goldsmith remained as LDB's clerk for the full year; Shulman succeeded him in 1929. See 29 September 1929.

[5] Harold J. Laski, "Crisis in the Modern State," *Bookman* 68 (October 1928): 182.

No. 339   November 1, 1928   Washington, D.C.

Allen heiligen,[1] 1928

(56 years ago today we went
with the Benedickts [sic] to the
Huzzarenburg.)[2]

1. Smith has performed for the country an inestimable service by his campaigning. I am not disturbed by the bitterness exhibited by the people. Their intolerance and meanness merely discloses what is. It is humiliating of course. But intolerance is not nearly as dangerous to the Republic as the seeming somnolent tolerance incident to political indifference. That is what had enveloped us for 8 years. If we don't get a Democratic administration, we are pretty sure of getting a militant opposition. And that achievement will be Smith's, in any event.

My faith in the people &, hence, in the result, abides. But if things go wrong, there will be some satisfaction in it's being Hoover, the Prosperity Maker, who has the period of Zores.[3]

2. Grace Abbot [sic] is back. She is for Hoover and Prohibition.

3. Mrs. Woodrow Wilson has been in—full of fire for Smith, and charmingly entertaining in her tales of the Baltimore meet[ing].

349

4. It's too bad about Newt Baker & Croly.[4] Baker was here, in Court, Oct 1, but merely in attendance. He looked as he usually does.

5. We are glad to have your Atlantic review of Redlich.[5]

6. I suppose you have noted the plentitude of P.C's!!

[1] All Saints Day.

[2] See 6 April 1923, n. 2.

[3] Troubles.

[4] Newton D. Baker, after a strenuous schedule of campaign appearances on behalf of Smith, was prostrated with acute neuritis and chronic fatigue. Herbert Croly, about seven weeks before this letter, suffered a massive paralytic stroke. He never fully recovered and died in May 1930.

[5] FF reviewed Redlich's biography, *Emperor Francis Joseph of Austria* (New York: Macmillan, 1928) in a praise filled notice in *Atlantic Monthly* 142 (November 1928): 18.

No. 340   November 4, 1928   Washington, D.C.

1. About your N.R. article[1] there seems to be widespread unanimous opinion.

2. Tannenbaum, who was in Friday (a man who is constantly growing in intellect & engaging qualities), says the Institute is a unit in favor of Smith—with the possible exception of Hardy.[2] You will recall "Harvard College & the Slums."

3. Thanks for the Outlook—"The time has been that when the brains were out, the man was dead and there an end."[3]

4. The N.R. article was very good—on S.V.[4]

5. Of perhaps greater importance was Hilda Ageloff's on "The Third Degree."[5] Even a civilized people may be guilty of individual gross miscarriages of justice, particularly in periods of hysteria. But our police practices—and the attitude of most prosecutors & the bar thereto carry us back to the age of torture on the continent.

6. If, as I expect, Roosevelt is elected,[6] I should like through you to put in early two requests:

(a) Far reaching attack on "The Third Degree."

(b) Good counsel in N.Y.'s cases before our Court.

We were all surprised the other day to note a really lawyerlike argument from W.H. King, who represented the N.Y.C. tax department.[7]

A. L. Filene's secretary is a son of one of my earliest clients—E. Storey Smith.

[1] FF, in "Why I Am for Smith," *New Republic* 56 (31 October 1928): 292, gave eight reasons for preferring Smith to Hoover in the upcoming election.

[2] An associate of Frank Tannenbaum's at the Brookings Institution, Charles Oscar Hardy (1884–1948), had taught economics at Chicago and Iowa before coming to Washington. He wrote numerous books on economic topics.

[3] Shakespeare, *Macbeth*, III, iv: 79.

[4] Prior to his joint trial with Sacco, Vanzetti had been convicted of an attempted payroll hijacking in Bridgewater. On 31 October 1928, *The Outlook* published four articles on the Bridgewater crime, including a full confession by a professional criminal, sustaining Vanzetti's claim that he had been innocent of the Bridgewater crime. "Vanzetti Was Innocent," *New Republic* 56 (7 November 1928): 317, summarized the disclosures of *The Outlook*'s articles.

[5] Also in the 7 November issue of *The New Republic*, at 321. Hilda Ageloff, a reporter with the Nassau, Long Island, *Daily Star*, gave some accounts of brutal questioning of accused criminals by the police.

[6] In fact, the winner of the 1928 gubernatorial election in New York was Franklin Delano Roosevelt (1882–1945). The scion of a patrician New York family and a cousin of Theodore Roosevelt, he had attended Harvard College and Columbia Law School. After a short career in New York politics, Wilson named him assistant secretary of the Navy. In 1920, he went down as James Cox's vice presidential candidate in the Harding landslide, and the following year was struck with polio which left him crippled for the rest of his life. In 1932 he won the presidency and gained reelection to that office three more times, leading the nation through the worst depression in history and then through its most devastating war.

FF was particularly close to Roosevelt—at one period even living in the White House. Roosevelt consulted regularly with him about appointments to the judiciary and to various New Deal agencies, and he named FF to the Supreme Court in 1939. LDB's influence also rose during the years when Roosevelt was in charge of the government. The president consulted with him occasionally and sought his advice on various matters, generally through intermediaries. LDB also maintained very close contact with dozens of the young men and women who flocked to Washington to help reform the country during the 1930s. The problem of the New Dealers in reconciling the strong Brandeisian view against big business, with the countervailing "New Nationalism" view of many of the old Theodore Roosevelt progressives, is nicely told in Ellis Hawley, *The New Deal and the Problem of Monopoly* (Princeton: Princeton University Press, 1966). For the role of LDB and FF in picking New Deal personnel and shaping policies, see Nelson L. Dawson, *Louis D. Brandeis, Felix Frankfurter, and the New Deal* (Hamden, Conn.: Archon Books, 1980), and Murphy, *The Brandeis/Frankfurter Connection*.

[7] William H. King (1872–1951) was from 1916 to his retirement assistant New York corporation counsel and head of the division of taxes. On 29 October he had argued *Ex parte the Public National Bank of New York*, 278 U.S. 101.

No. 341   November 6, 1928   Washington, D.C.

1. You have earned in the resuscitated Democratic Party a position as thinker, which should enable you to exert much influence hereafter. If this day's voting goes wrong, the urgent task will be to devise ways and means by which Smith may, without loss of the momentum, become the recognized leader of a militant opposition to the Republican rule. If that function can be exercised by him he will be able to render a service politically almost as great as if he were President, and in some ways, may do perhaps more than a President could.

2. Brandt (of the St. Louis Post Dispatch),[1] one of the very best, was in yesterday. I asked him about Borah's $1000 per. He was greatly surprised at the rumor, says he would put the question directly to Borah. I am not surprised. I think I must have written you after he was robbed

of $400 and his secretary of $300 cash the night after his speech at Omaha[2]—that I could conceive of no explanation of his having that amount of cash except (a) that he was paid for his speech; (b) that he had engaged in a successful poker game; or (c) that he was in league with the bootleggers.

3. Hughes does not surprise me either.[3]

Nearly all Washington folk, though Smithites, are defeatists.

[1] Raymond Peter Brandt (1896–1974) returned from Oxford to join the Washington bureau of the *Post Dispatch* in 1923, and was chief of the bureau from 1934 until 1961.

[2] Actually, Senator Borah had spoken, on 29 September, at the University of Nebraska at Lincoln. He and his secretary, Sam Jones, retired to their hotel room, leaving the door unlocked. In the morning, Senator Borah was missing $400 and Mr. Jones was missing $300.

[3] On 1 November Charles Evans Hughes made a speech denouncing Smith's stands on prohibition, water power, and the tariff. He said that Smith had "delusions of grandeur."

No. 342   November 8, 1928   Washington, D.C.

We have nothing to regret but the result.[1] What did it—the women mainly or the great god prosperity?

New York City is the most disturbing. Even more so than the State. Why should Copeland have run so far ahead.[2] One of the unworthy?

The big cities in New York State and elsewhere are generally disappointing.[3] Did labor go wrong? Did foreigners go wrong? What did the Catholics do? And what the bootleggers?

Stocks went up yesterday. Wheat and Cotton down. As for the farmers, I am reminded of Sir Toby:

"God give wisdom to those who haven't, and those that are fools, let them use their talents."[4]

Massachusetts has redeemed herself.[5] Gov. Fuller to the newspaper men was amusing.[6]

[1] Herbert Hoover decisively defeated Alfred E. Smith, 21.4 million (58.8 percent) to 15.0 million (41.2 percent). The electoral vote was 444–87.

[2] Royal Samuel Copeland (1868–1938) had gone to the Senate from New York in 1923. He won reelection in 1928 with a large plurality, leading Smith and the other Democrats in the New York City returns.

[3] Actually Smith did very well in the cities, carrying the twelve largest cities of the nation, all of which had given majorities to Coolidge in 1924.

[4] Sir Toby Belch in Shakespeare's *Twelfth Night*, I, v: 14.

[5] David I. Walsh was reelected to the Senate from Massachusetts; and Frank Gilman Allen (1874–1950), a Republican, was elected governor. Al Smith carried the state narrowly, winning 50.5 percent of the vote.

[6] Massachusetts was one of the few northern states to go for Smith in the 1928 election, and Republicans had put forward a number of reasons why they thought it had happened. Governor

Fuller laughed, said "I told you so," but refused to explain what he meant to reporters. Prior to the balloting Fuller had predicted Hoover would carry the state by 250,000 votes.

No. 343   November 14, 1928   Washington, D.C.

1. Thanks for your birthday best wishes.[1] To the happiness and usefulness you have, throughout long years, contributed very much.

2. If I should chance to see Franklin Roosevelt, I should not hesitate to talk with him about my two requests.[2] But I think it entirely unnecessary that I should see him. If he can be induced to take up these matters, I am sure that the request from you will accomplish what we desire.

3. Would it not be possible, in aid of the militant Democratic opposition, to organize, from Smith's recent aids & others, a sort of general staff & expert body, which would supply thought and research for the men on the firing line, and have them always supplied with ammunition when the opportunities for attack arise?[3] They are sure to be numerous.

I mentioned this project to Ben Flexner. He thought it would be valuable, and said: "There will be no difficulty in getting the money needed." Some will, of course, be needed; but the unpaid thinking & help such as you have given is essential, if the project is to succeed.

3. [sic] The sadness over Smith's defeat is widespread; and encouraging. S. E. Morrison[sic]'s letter is fine.

4. O.W.H. is in fine form. He seemed like one of 67 at last week's conference.

5. We had a delightful evening Sunday with Alfred Cohen.

6. Emma Erving spoke of a joyous visit with you & Marion.

[1] On 13 November, LDB was seventy-two.
[2] See 4 November 1928.
[3] See 1 January 1925.

No. 344   November 23, 1928[1]   Washington, D.C.

1. Your and Landis' "S.C. and the Judiciary Act of 1925"[2] is admirable—perhaps the best in form of the series. It will furnish a model for future years.

2. Our order re Rapid Transit Case reargument, and the comment of the N.Y. papers thereon,[3] may make it much easier to secure from F.D.R. action on the request for good counsel in N.Y. cases. One of my

associates suggested a propos the [New York] World's suggestion in "New Lawyers" to amend by striking out "new."[4]

3. Lockwood[5] reports O.W.H. much better (he had only a cold), that he will probably remain housed today & tomorrow, but hopes to return to the Court Monday.

4. Do you believe, as do some others, that many Catholics (i.a. Poles & Italians) did not vote for Smith, and also many wets in New York, New Jersey & generally did not?

5. Miss Luddington dined with us yesterday.

6. Paul Anderson[6] thinks that it was the Catholic issue, pre-eminently, that defeated Smith, and he & others seem to think that in the West & South he lost heavily by lack of what they deem Presidential Dignity—lack [of] High hat, frock coat etc.

[1] LDB erroneously dated this letter "11/23/24."

[2] *Harvard Law Review* 42 (November 1928): 1.

[3] On 19 November the Supreme Court ordered a reargument of the Interborough Rapid Transit Case—a case centering on a proposed fare increase. The Court's order bluntly rebuked the lawyers on both sides and commanded that the new briefs "shall be compact, logically arranged with proper headings, concise and free from burdensome, irrelevant and immaterial matter." The *New York Times* was particularly harsh in its editorial criticism (20 November), accusing the lawyers of the sin of pride for thinking that they had done a good job in filing such a mass of information—sixteen briefs totalling 7,000 pages or 878,000 words. On the next day the paper continued its attack, condemning their "avalanches of superfluous words and useless documents." *Gilchrist* v. *Interborough Rapid Transit*, 279 U.S. 159 was reargued in mid-January and decided on 8 April 1929. Charles Evans Hughes appeared for the Interborough at the rehearing.

[4] Actually the New York *World's* editorial (21 November) was entitled "Wanted: A New Lawyer" (so that striking the word "new" left "Wanted: A Lawyer"). According to the *World* the lawyers were incompetent, and the paper strongly urged "swapping horses while crossing a stream" and finding new counsel.

[5] John Edwards Lockwood (b. 1904) was Justice Holmes's clerk for the 1928–1929 year, and then moved to New York City and private practice.

[6] Paul Y. Anderson (1893–1938) was with the Washington bureau of the *St. Louis Post Dispatch*. He won the Pulitzer Prize in 1928 in connection with his work on the reopening of the oil scandal investigation.

No. 345   November 29, 1928   Washington, D.C.

1. This may interest you.[1] I guess the S.V. agitation has had its effect on the judge. Surely the S.V. movement is gaining in force.

2. At this moment comes Marion's book—which we were eagerly expecting. As yet we have seen only the outside—& the Committee—both worthy.[2]

3. There will be an opinion on this.[3] These are cases entered before the new rule came into effect. Amidon's friend Guy Corliss[4] suffered a

354

similar ignominious expulsion—after sitting in court 9 days. The new jurisdictional rule is giving the Court much satisfaction. You may have noticed that Monday, the three cases presented were all dismissed.

[1] LDB had enclosed a clipping from the *Washington Post* of 27 November. It told the story of a West Virginia judge who refused to sentence to death a man whom he believed inocent of murder, despite a jury verdict of guilty. The state supreme court named a special judge who set an execution date.

[2] See 18 September 1928, n. 2.

[3] LDB enclosed a second clipping from the *Post*, this one entitled "Supreme Court to Penalize for Appeals Made to Delay." The Court announced that it intended to enforce the rule penalizing (up to 10 percent of the amount involved) those who appealed cases merely to avoid the execution of lower court. In a Nebraska case and in a second one from Kansas, the Court declared that no federal question had been presented and that it reserved the right to impose the penalty.

[4] Guy Carleton Haynes Corliss (1858–1937) had moved to the Dakota Territory in 1886 and in 1889 was elected to the supreme court of the new state. After a career of teaching and practice, he moved from North Dakota to Oregon and practiced law there.

No. 346   December 25, 1928   Washington, D.C.

1. I think it would be helpful to have an article written on the proper conduct of hearings & of the requirements of orders on application for interlocutory injunction, particularly under §266,[1] discussed i.a. in Lawrence v. St. L.-S.F. Ry (274 U.S. 586),[2] including the obligation to write opinions, and also the weight given by us to the decisions of the Dist. Court in such applications. Perhaps the article could more effectively be broadened so as to include the jurisdiction under §266.—and what proceedings in the cause should be heard by a single judge & the effect, if any, of having them heard by 3 instead of 1. In this connection you will be interested in the record in No. 99 (1927 Term),[3] when this case comes back to our Court (heard but not yet decided). Also whether there is in appeals any right, so that appeal could not be dismissed for lack of substantial general question.[4]

2. You doubtless know well this tale, which came to me once removed, through a good source, who claims to have it from Treadway of Berkshire County.[5] Treadway says that Gov. Fuller told him that there came to the Gov's office during the S.V. investigation a man who stated that he was an eyewitness to the shooting, saw Sacco do it with a revolver and that Vanzetti had a shotgun. The man says he didn't testify & (the Gov. didn't make him public) because he knew he would be killed if he did so.

3. The obstinate inquiring mind still longs to know how Borah and secretary happened to have $700 in pocket.[6]

4. That's an interesting excerpt from Strachey.

5. And a beautiful note of Kellogg's on Colvin.

6. The second FF. research fellow should be worked out somehow. A. L[awrence Lowell]. and R.P. are true to form.

7. Witkie is refreshing. How do you account for him?

8. Our congratulations to Marion on the second printing.[7]

9. That was a nice appreciation of Alvin Johnson's of your papers.

10. I guess Hughes will do more harm than good hereafter.

[1] See 31 May 1927, n. 6.

[2] See 31 May 1927, n. 3.

[3] LDB meant the 1928 Term. No. 99 was the continuation of *Lawrence* v. *St. Louis-San Francisco Railway Co.* The first round can be found at 274 U.S. 588; this case, under the same name, can be found at 278 U.S. 228. It had been argued on 3 December 1928, and on 2 January 1929 LDB, for a unanimous Court, affirmed the decision of the district court permanently enjoining the Oklahoma Corporation Commission from preventing the railroad from removing its shops and division point to another place in the state.

[4] Such an article was in fact written. See John E. Lockwood, Carlyle E. Maw, and Samuel L. Rosenberg, "The Use of the Federal Injunction in Constitutional Litigation," *Harvard Law Review* 43 (1930): 426.

[5] Allen Towner Treadway (1867–1947) represented Berkshire County in the House of Representatives from 1913 to 1945; he was a Republican.

[6] See 6 November 1928.

[7] See 18 September 1928, n. 2.

No. 347   January 29, 1929   Washington, D.C.

1. Who wrote the World editorial on P.S.C.?[1] Does this and the Court decisions under Smyth v. Ames[2] spell widespread extension of public ownership in the near future?

2. Bob Benjamin should have more joy in his own firm.

3. Yes, O.W.H. is in fine form, & joyous; to which happy condition Mrs. Holmes' returned health and the extraordinary continuance of sunshine have contributed. He has had quite a number of unimportant cases, but I think it also an element that he minimizes the importance of those he gets. Of course, his determination to finish the job on the Sunday following the assignment leads to this.

4. I had not heard of Bradley's death.

5. McGuire of the Brookings Institution is next in Berlin as you will see from enclosed.

6. My congratulations to Marion on her English edition.[3]

7. The community will lose nothing in R. L. O'Brien's withdrawal.[4] What will he do?

8. Wouldn't official receivers appointed by the whole D.C. have a pretty good chance of being fairly free from politics?

[1] In "The City Club's Appeal to Governor Roosevelt" in this date's issue, the *World* endorsed the City Club's demand that the governor launch an investigation of the state's Public Service Commission for its failure to keep rates down, as well as for alleged misconduct in several areas.

[2] 169 U.S. 466 (1898). In this critically important decision, the Supreme Court had boldly asserted its right to the judicial review of utility rate-fixing by state administrative agencies. The decision laid down a "rule" for determining a fair return, but it was so vague and complex as to leave wide discretion to the courts and, hence, endless bickering and divided decisions. See the discussion in Mason, *Brandeis*, 548–53.

[3] Of *The Letters of Sacco and Vanzetti*.

[4] Robert Lincoln O'Brien had just announced his retirement from the editorship of the Boston *Herald*.

No. 348   February 4, 1929   Washington, D.C.

1. Kent is all wrong.

2. I was much interested in your correspondence re Hughes & agree entirely with all that you say. By an odd coincidence Learned Hand (with Hitz) called on the afternoon of the day your letter arrived. The talk on the N.Y. receivership scandal [1] gave occasion to discuss the ethics of the bar & generally crime. I aired, with perhaps unseemly vehemence, my views on the leaders—saying i.a., that a single one does more harm etc. than a thousand shysters, & there was considerable discussion of Hughes. L.H. (as well [as] I) may have had you in mind as the discussion proceeded, but no mention of you or of the views of any other person was made. The pursuit of the "golden fleece" was the theme.

3. Mark Potter has an interesting mind. There are blind spots which keep him near the interests. But it must always stand to his credit (a) that we probably owe Eastman's appointment to him, and (b) that it was he to whom I recommended Otto Beyer [2] & he who grew so enthusiastic that he opened Beyer's way to Dan. Willard.

4. Miss Grady has new evidence of H.L. Shattuck's short-comings. [3]

5. I guess we shall see a strong trend toward public ownership before long. I understand Hoover fears the P[ublic].U[tilities]. Co's folly is hurrying it on.

[1] New York was in the midst of a scandal involving corruption and bribery in the "bankruptcy business," the grand jury handing down the first indictments on this date. Beginning with the case of David Steinhardt (who had been granted 126 receiverships since 1923), investigations revealed numerous cases of lawyers running bankrupt firms in their own interest or in the interests of their friends—sometimes even in the interest of the bankrupt himself. A good discussion of the legal issues is in a feature article, *New York Times*, 20 January 1929, IX: 10. More and more creditors,

judges, and members of the bar were moving to the position long held by LDB—that professional, full-time public receivers should be appointed and not private attorneys.

[2] Otto Sternhoff Beyer (1886–1948) was a construction engineer who became an expert on labor relations in transportation. He served in several high government positions during the New Deal and World War II.

3 See 9 February 1928.

No. 349   February 4, 1929   Washington, D.C.

Boni[1] should have sent you copies of his letter to me & of my reply. He wrote, "the name which strikes me most favorably (to undertake the task) is Felix Frankfurter. Before approaching anyone regarding the undertaking I should [want] to know whether this would meet with your approval."—I answered in substance: "If the project should ever become desirable no one would be more competent than Prof. Frankfurter. But I know that now he has work on hand of *far greater importance*"—which I affirm again.

[1] Albert Boni (1892–1981) was a publisher, and in later years would be a pioneer in the process of microfilming materials. He had suggested publishing a selection of LDB's legal opinions, and proposed FF as a likely editor for such a volume.

No. 350   February 13, 1929   Washington, D.C.

1. Yours of 12th brings many interesting clippings. Perhaps enclosed about Burlingame[1] of Wan case fame has escaped you.

2. Miss Grady was much cheered by you.

3. Mack (as Redlich may have told you) really wanted some advice on judicial conduct: i.e. whether a D.J. who appointed a receiver should himself pass upon the receiver's compensation. I answered emphatically No, & the[n] took occasion to talk—

   (a) On the impropriety of large receiver's fee (including the $35,000 additional allowed by him in N.E. Oil, "because the parties agreed.") I made it clear to him that the chief party is the Court protecting the judicial reputation etc.

   (b) On the need of official receivers & liquidations.

4. When we meet—much re Cabinet.

5. Eugene Meyer was in yesterday. He should have a post, but is pretty sure that he won't.[2]

6. Perhaps you had in mind my introducing Hoover to the Wilson administration.

7. Young Blau ought to inherit ability & more.[3]

8. I am glad Columbia appreciates the "Injunction" articles.[4]

9. Hamilton is due here for a day Saturday.

Sir Arthur Salter[5] was in last week, and Gardiner's son in law Mallen Monday.

---

[1] For the notorious Wan case, see 31 October 1924, n. 2. Guy E. Burlingame had been one of the brutal detectives on the Washington, D.C., police force and was mentioned by name in LDB's blistering opinion. For the preceding three weeks he had been headline news in the *Washington Post*. A palmist and former lover, Mrs. Helen Blalock, had issued wide ranging charges of corruption against Captain Burlingame. And on 11 February the United States Senate, without a single dissenting vote, withheld his pay as a police officer until these charges could be cleared up.

[2] Meyer did not receive a position in Hoover's cabinet.

[3] Clarence Isaac Blau (b. 1907) would graduate from Harvard Law School in 1931 and go directly into public service, working in many New Deal and wartime agencies. His father, to whom LDB makes reference, was Dr. Joel Blau (1878–1927) a well known rabbi and writer on Jewish topics, who ministered to several New York City congregations before being called to the West London Synagogue in 1925.

[4] See 18 July 1927, n.3.

[5] Sir Arthur Salter (1881–1975), an economist and the holder of so many public offices that he was known as "the civil servant par excellence," specialized in admiralty and shipping questions.

No. 351   February 21, 1929   Washington, D.C.

1. My brother would have said: "That is just like Marshall Bullitt."[1]

2. I hope F.D.R. appreciates what you said of Owen Young.

3. C. C. Burlingham came here Tuesday re N.Y. judicial scandal.[2] After Conference with the C.J. and Harlan & with John Davis, he called on me, being really puzzled as to what to do & much concerned, & seeking advice. I told him:

(a) that they must eliminate possibility of patronage in either bankruptcy or equity receiverships, by appointing official receivers & liquidators, & meanwhile standing resolutely against any large fees to any one in judicial proceedings. The money-changers must be excluded from the Temple.

(b) that they must put an end to the fake diversity of citizenship jurisdiction, particularly in receivership cases.

(c) generally reduce federal jurisdiction, so that there be no increase & eventually a reduction in number of judges, so that the honor of office will revive.

(d) Take the judicial offices out of politics, so that we can get men of proper calibre.

He said he agreed with everything, except as to the possibility of getting official receiverships for all the Circuits & Districts through Congress, & told of (1) their effort (? in 1924) to do this via Congress & (2) via the

D.J.s when all were willing except Winslow[3] & Bondy.[4] I told him to take this up.

You may not have seen the report of the Bar Comtee on present scandalous condition. I enclose copy which please treat as confidential & return after perusal.

C.C.B. told me that the recent appointment of the Circuit judge (from Vt) was the worst yet.[5]

I advised him to stop passage of the present bill for 3 more D.J.s which has passed the House, so as not to let C.C. make another appointment.[6] He said he would see Wagner[7] about that.

4. Apropos our recent orders of reargument. I think there should again be brought prominently before the bar—its inadequate presentations (to which you called attention in your article on the Worcester Labor Case)—This week's batch present striking instances of the bar's failures, in

    (a) Harlan's Danish Treaty case[8]

    (b) The Oklahoma Coop. gin case[9]

    (c) The income tax (B & M-Old Colony & Co. cases)[10]

5. Bickle [sic] made an excellent argument in the Lake Cargo cases.[11]

6. I shall be delighted to see Cuthbert Pound. I hope he can come during a recess when there will be no difficulty in arranging adequate time.

5. [sic] Hope you wrote T. J. Walsh on the Stolen Property Bill.[12] See U.S. Daily Feb 20, p.3.

6. Glad you have satisfied Boni.[13]

7. Did Maston's first wife die? If so when?

---

[1] William Marshall Bullitt (1873–1957), a Louisville attorney, had been solicitor general during the last year of the Taft administration, and later served as counsel to the Shipping Board and the Emergency Fleet Corporation.

[2] See 4 February 1929, n. 1.

[3] Francis Asbury Winslow (1866–1932), appointed by Harding to be a judge for the Southern District of New York, was heavily implicated in the current scandal and was under investigation both in Washington and New York. Bowing to heavy pressure, he resigned in April.

[4] William Bondy (1871–1964) had been appointed to the same court as Winslow in the same year.

[5] Harrie Brigham-Chase Chase (1889–1969), a Battleboro attorney, had been a justice of the superior court and of the Supreme Court of Vermont. Coolidge had just named him judge of the U.S. Court of Appeals for the Second District. He became chief judge in 1953.

[6] The bill was passed by the Senate and signed by Coolidge on 27 February. But most of his judicial appointments were stalled in the Senate and left for President Hoover to make.

[7] Robert Francis Wagner (1877–1953) of New York was one of the powerful members of the Senate, where he served from 1926 to 1949. Born in Germany, Wagner worked his way through

law school and rose rapidly in New York state politics. During the New Deal he drafted and secured passage of several important pieces of legislation. The National Labor Relations Act (1935), known popularly as the Wagner Act, was probably the culmination of his career.

[8] *Nielson* v. *Johnson*, 279 U.S. 47, decided on 18 February, declared that treaties with foreign countries, in this case Denmark, involving tax agreements, took precedence over any conflicting state laws.

[9] Cattle owners in Oklahoma had formed a marketing cooperative to sell their livestock, and found that the commercial dealers declared a boycott against the cooperative. The secretary of agriculture petitioned for an end to the boycott, on the grounds that it restrained trade, and the Court, speaking through Holmes, granted the request. *U.S.* v. *American Livestock Commission Co. et al.*, 279 U.S. 435.

[10] The two cases involved similar issues. In *Old Colony Trust Co. et al.* v. *Commissioner of Internal Revenue*, 279 U.S. 716, the question was whether, when a company paid the income taxes on any of its executives' salaries, the men had to declare the amount of the taxes as additional income. In *U.S.* v. *Boston & Maine*, 279 U.S. 732, a parent company paid the taxes for a subsidiary. Did the subsidiary have to declare that amount as income? In both cases, Chief Justice Taft affirmed the government's contention that the taxes should be considered as additional income.

[11] See 279 U.S. 812. The case had been argued on 19 and 20 February. The Court found that the major points had become moot, and dismissed the original bill of complaints per curiam. Henry Wolf Biklé argued against John W. Davis. Biklé (1877–1942) was general counsel for the Pennsylvania Railroad and also professor of law at the University of Pennsylvania.

[12] The bill, H.R. 10287, prohibited sending or receiving stolen property through interstate and foreign commerce. The measure was reported out, but not acted on during the session.

[13] See 4 February 1929.

No. 352   February 27, 1929   Washington, D.C.

1. The Carnegie outrage [1] should make a good story for the World.

2. No 514 [2] will, when you get the record, suggest:

    (1) What happens under the new attitude on the Equality Clause

    (2) "   "   when a state is so benighted as not to provide for recovery of monies paid on taxes under protest.

    Each subject would justify a H.L.R. article.

3. Another would be justified by cases like Cudahy [3] & its predecessors, where the State power of taxation over foreign corporations was curtailed. Could & should the State protect itself by requiring all foreign corpor[ation]s (so far as permitted by the Commerce Clause) to organize a domestic subsidiary—in analogy to Texas requirement as to RRs? And i.a. how much has Texas gained by that expedient?

4. It looks now as if Miss Grady had handled her situation with consummate wisdom & skill. [4]

5. I told Walton Hamilton when here recently that I thought a serious wrong would be done if you were taken from H.L. School. Yale L.S. should be helped & encouraged in its commendable efforts—but not by weakening the going concern at Cambridge.

361

6. Hamilton said nothing to me of the L.L.D. & I shall remain officially ignorant until called upon to act.[5]

[1] In 1905 Andrew Carnegie had established the Carnegie Foundation for the Advancement of Teaching and gave a $10 million endowment to provide pensions for retired teachers. By 1929, 3,600 teachers were in this program, and in April the trustees announced that it would be necessary to reduce radically the amount of the pensions. Professorial salaries had risen far faster than the endowment, which now stood at $30 million. The Teachers Insurance and Annuity Association, also backed by the Carnegie Corporation, was another operation and unaffected by the announcement.

[2] *Ohio Oil Co.* v. *Conway*, 279 U.S. 813, decided per curiam on 5 March, involved a proceeding in the Louisiana state court system, and came to the federal courts on diversity of citizenship, only because of the amount of money involved. The company was suing for an injunction against the enforcement of an increased severance tax on production of oil. The Supreme Court ruled that an injunction should be granted until the constitutionality of the tax could be decided, provided the company continued to pay the old tax rate and gave bond ensuring its ability and obligation to pay the new tax should it be found valid.

[3] *Cudahy Packing Co.* v. *Henkle*, 278 U.S. 460, had been decided on 18 February. Washington levied a tax on this "foreign" corporation from Maine, in the form of a filing fee and an annual license tax, both determined by its authorized capital stock, with a statutory maximum. McReynolds argued that this tax was, in fact, an unconstitutional burden upon interstate commerce and an attempt to tax property beyond the jurisdiction of the state. LDB dissented and was joined by Holmes. He argued that the charges were very small, that half of the corporation's business within the state was intrastate, that the tax was obviously no more than a fair contribution to the necessary expenses of the state, and no more than was levied upon domestic corporations.

[4] See 4 February 1929.

[5] FF had told LDB that the Yale Law School was contemplating awarding LDB an honorary degree. LDB, however, had an inflexible principle which prohibited his accepting such honors while a judge. When the offer finally came, by a unanimous vote of the faculty, LDB promptly declined; see 20 February 1930, and LDB to Charles E. Clark, 12 March 1930.

No. 353   March 1, 1929   Washington, D.C.

I hope the World, the N.R. & the Nation will not fail to make clear the full significance of Mitchell's appointment as A.G.[1]

It is the most hopeful event in the legal-judicial sphere in half a century; and at no time was there as great a need.

To have attained this post by sheer merit—despite party label,[2] because of (a) his legal ability

(b) high professional standards

(c) absolute courage & independence

with the prospect of thereby cleaning the Department & securing hereafter at least, respectable federal judges, is a matter of supreme public importance. If Hoover will stand by him (I think he intends to do so), there should soon be a marked change in the professional attitude that will pervade even NY City & Chicago.

And a large premium is added to the appointment by the incidental riddance of Donovan[3] from administrative circles. I understand D. has behaved very badly.

I don't think Mitchell is a "liberal"—But he is a gentleman and intelligent & pure minded.

He was as S.G. incomparably better than even John W. Davis.

[1] William D. Mitchell was on Hoover's proposed cabinet slate, and was speedily confirmed by the Senate on 5 March. *The New Republic* applauded the selection in "A Fine Appointment," an editorial in its 13 March issue.

[2] Mitchell described himself as a Democrat in his *Who's Who* article.

[3] William ("Wild Bill") Joseph Donovan (1883–1959), a highly decorated officer during World War I, served as assistant to the attorney general from 1925 to 1929 and was rumored to be in line for the appointment. Hoover, however, declined to appoint him to any cabinet position. During World War II, Donovan served as director of the Office of Strategic Services, and thereby became the virtual architect of the secret intelligence gathering machinery of the United States government.

No. 354   March 6, 1929   Washington, D.C.

1. I am glad you wrote Bob Szold as you did. I had received enclosed from Bob Miller on the same day; and immediately requested Harlan to work against Buchanan's appointment, which he is doing.[1] B. is making a drive a la modern business, determined to overcome sales resistance. He was here Monday & tried to see Mitchell, who declined to see him, sending word that he is still Solicitor General. Urgent appeals to the Chief [Justice] & others are coming in his behalf from different parts of the Union. He is certainly making a bad impression upon members of our Court by his methods.

It is lamentable that men like Bob Szold and Bob Miller haven't a better sense of the public interest.

2. What you say to C.C. [Burlingham] about the judges is true. Neither Woolsey nor Wheat are more than respectable.[2] They are that, and, perhaps, considering what the N.Y. districts have become, that is a good deal.

3. Hoover has made a good start in putting law observance first in his message.[3] I have asked Harlan to get him (a) to give to the foreign embassies the tip that liquor should not be served to Americans, (b) to get his Cabinet to refuse to go to dinners where liquor is served.

3. [sic] I agree with you that it is important that you get out a case book on Federal jurisdiction, and if Turrentine is available to you as aid, I shall be glad to provide for that purpose the Twenty five hundred (2500) Dollars.[4]

4. I suppose H. L. Shattuck's passing into the Treasuryship will deprive the Com[monweal]th of his services as legislator.[5]

[1] John Grier Buchanan (1888–1986), a Pittsburgh attorney, had been mentioned as a possibility to replace William Mitchell as solicitor general; he did not receive the appointment.

[2] Alfred A. Wheat and John Munro Woolsey (1877–1945) had been nominated to federal judgeships by Coolidge, but their nominations had not been acted upon by 4 March 1929, when Coolidge left office. President Hoover resubmitted both names and both were confirmed by the Senate. Wheat went to the Supreme Court for the District of Columbia, and Woolsey to the District Court for the Southern District of New York.

[3] See 13 March 1929, n. 2.

[4] The book, *Cases and Other Authorities on Federal Jurisdiction and Procedure* (Chicago: Callaghan, 1931), was eventually edited by FF and Wilber G. Katz. Lowell Turrentine (b. 1895) had graduated from the Harvard Law School in 1922, and then taught at Stanford.

[5] Henry Lee Shattuck had just been appointed treasurer of Harvard College.

No. 355   March 8, 1929[1]   Washington, D.C.

1. O.W.H. was in the pink of condition on the eve of his birthday.[2]

2. That['s] a good letter from Crane.

3. I hope our press won't fail to comment appreciatively on Mrs. Hoover's rejection of the protection of a secretive service man.[3]

4. Now that J.D.R. Jr. have [sic] won over Harvard,[4] couldn't he be induced to clean up the Col Fuel & Iron Co. situation? Much would be gained if he went no further than to prevent the Co. officials from hampering Miss Roche in her efforts.[5] If there is any chance of getting R. to act, E. P. Costigan could advise definitely what it is that he should be asked to do.

5. I think the C.J. is not being called upon for advice by H. But Harlan has been; doubtless contributed to the Inaugural; & will be called upon for advice often hereafter.

Of course, it would have been much better if general judicial reform could have been divorced from prohibition.[6] But that was impossible. I think Harlan will be glad to have suggestions from you at any time.

[1] LDB erroneously dated this letter "4/8/29."

[2] This date marked Justice Holmes's eighty-eighth birthday.

[3] Mrs. Hoover announced on 5 March, the day after her husband was inaugurated, that she would dispense with the protection of the Secret Service.

[4] Perhaps LDB refers to the fact that the Rockefeller Foundation had announced, one week before, a half million dollar gift to Harvard's Fogg Art Museum. John Davison Rockefeller, Jr. (1874–1960) shared in the huge fortune of his famous father, the founder of Standard Oil, but was best known for his philanthropic activities.

[5] Josephine Aspinwall Roche (1886–1976) was an experienced social worker who would serve the Roosevelt administration as assistant secretary of the treasury. Miss Roche had come into an inheritance which made her chief stockholder in the third largest coal producing mine in Colorado.

She immediately began protesting against the antiunion and, as she saw it, unenlightened and repressive management of the company. Eventually she bought additional stock giving her controlling interest in the mine, the Rocky Mountain Fuel Company. She then recognized the United Mine Workers as bargaining agent for the men, and negotiated a model contract which gave the workers a decent wage scale, and incentives that made them, to some extent, cooperating partners in the firm. From the start, the Rockefeller owned Colorado Fuel and Iron Company, which was strongly antiunion, opposed her policies and did all it could to undermine her work. See Josephine Roche, "Mines and Men," *Survey* 61 (15 December 1928): 61.

[6]LDB refers here to Hoover's announced plan for a national commission to investigate crime. See next letter, n. 2.

No. 356   March 13, 1929   Washington, D.C.

1. Edward P. Costigan, Counselor at Law, Denver. I haven't the street address. He returned to D. immediately on resigning from the Tariff Comn last year & has been Miss Roche's close adviser throughout.[1]

2. Of course Harlan is not a "thorough"—But I see no reason why you shouldn't let him have your view direct at any time. Doubtless he would be glad to hear from you—on any subject; inter alia on the right men for the Commission.[2]

3. The C.J. is urging Mitchell to draft a bill to submit to the extra session on the subsidiary courts without a jury.

4. I read Mrs. Matthew's first article[3] carefully & glanced at the next. They seemed to me unworthy and I think did Eugene M injustice.

5. Hoover made an excellent impression when we called yesterday. It is an immense relief to think that C.C. has passed into the discard.

6. Might it not be well to send Mitchell your Cornell article?[4]

7. O.W.H. is in fine form. I said to him Monday, "By Wednesday you—true spendthrift as you are—will have your cases written & then nothing to do for nearly four weeks." He answered, "I mean to enjoy myself, reading metaphysics."

8. Lowell must be squirming a bit, despite his thick hide.[5]

9. I had not heard of A. A. Young's death.[6]

[1]See preceding letter, n. 5.

[2]The strong interest in law enforcement that Hoover revealed in his inaugural address (see 6 March 1929) bore its first fruit in his announcement on 9 March of the details of a high-level commission to study the problem in all of its aspects. Officially "the National Commission on Law Observance and Enforcement," the group soon became known as the Wickersham Committee after its chairman, George W. Wickersham, LDB's old antagonist from the Pinchot-Ballinger fight. As the next few letters will show, LDB and FF took an active part in helping to choose members of the Commission. During the next two years, the Wickersham Committee undertook a comprehensive study of the whole area of federal jurisprudence and legal administration. See their fourteen-volume *Report of the National Commission on Law Observance and Enforcement* (Washington, D.C.: 1929–1931). Unfortunately, the findings of the Commission were largely overlooked because of the furor

raised by the report on enforcement of prohibition, which implied that prohibition legislation was not enforceable, but that the experiment should not be abandoned—a position calculated to draw fire from both wets and drys. See 17 March 1929.

[3] LDB undoubtedly refers to a three-article series in *The New Republic* by Gertrude Mathews Shelby: "So This is Farm Relief: The Sorry Record of the Farm Loan System" (13 February); "So This is Farm-Relief Finance: How the Politicians Betray the Farmers (20 February); and "Politics in the Farm-Loan System" (27 February). Eugene Meyer was the head of the Farm Loan Board.

[4] See 7 July 1928, n. 1.

[5] "President Lowell and the Sacco Alibi," *New Republic* 58 (13 March 1929): 58, recounted an episode in the advisory committee's deliberations wherein Lowell accused two witnesses for Sacco of lying, but later was forced to apologize when documentation substantiating their testimony was presented.

[6] Young had died on 8 March.

No. 357   March 15, 1929   Washington, D.C.

1. I hope you are writing Harlan [1] your views on
    (a) Bikle [2] & Andrews [3]
    (b) On Monte Leman [sic]. [4] Dean talked to me of him on Sunday—said Covington [5] is for him & suggested C. had better talk to Harlan.

I think it best not to make suggestions to him unless asked.

He did ask me about Ballantyne. [6]

2. Otto Beyer brought in Sir Henry Thornton [7] last evening—a grand fellow. He thinks public ownership is inevitable in a democracy—but that we must not be in a hurry & spoil things. Also that he is getting from the men better service than a private enterprise can. He also fears "bigness" & thinks RR systems can be too big.

Mark Sullivan, [8] who was also in, says Hoover wrote practically every word of his 4 campaign speeches.

[1] At this stage in the effort to staff the newly announced National Commission on Law Observance and Enforcement, FF and LDB were offering their suggestions through Harlan Fiske Stone. But see next letter.

[2] Henry W. Biklé was not chosen for the commission.

[3] Probably William Shankland Andrews (1858–1936), who was judge of the Supreme Court of New York from 1900 to 1917, at which time he went to the court of appeals. He was not chosen for the Commission.

[4] Monte Lemann was chosen a commissioner.

[5] James Harry Covington (1870–1942) resigned his seat as a Maryland congressman in 1914 to accept Wilson's appointment as chief justice of the Washington, D.C., Supreme Court. After notable wartime service, he resigned in 1918 to form Covington & Burling, one of the largest and most prestigious of Washington's law firms. Dean Acheson was a member of that firm.

[6] Possibly Arthur Atwood Ballantine (1883–1960), a friend of FF's from law school days. Ballantine practiced law in Boston until the war. He would work in the Treasury Department as assistant secretary and as under secretary, 1931–1933.

[7] Sir Henry Worth Thornton (1871–1933), an American who had long experience with the

Pennsylvania Railroad, had been in England when the war broke out. The British government commandeered his services in running the railroads in northern France. In 1922 he became president and chairman of the board of directors of the Canadian National Railways.

[8] Mark Sullivan (1874–1952), after a short law career, entered into muckraking journalism and free-lance writing. From 1906 to 1914 he was chief correspondent for *Collier's* (and thereby closely associated with LDB in the Ballinger affair). In 1914 he became editor of the magazine and remained so until 1919. He may be best known for his six-volume chronicle, *Our Times—The United States, 1900–1925* (New York: Scribners, 1926–1935).

No. 358   March 17, 1929   Washington, D.C.

Confidential:

The President sent for me & I had a long talk with him [*] about his Law Commission, which he is taking very much to heart. He discussed with me the human material (only lawyers) and I had a chance to suggest Judge Andrews, Bikle, and Monte Lemon [sic].

What he needs & so far has failed to think of is a man for chairman—someone, who besides other qualities, can dramatize the situation. If you can think of the right man, wire me.

No. 359   March 26, 1929   Washington, D.C.

1. Thanks for Kenyon telegram. I felt too doubtful about him to recommend to H. I mentioned him to Harlan as having been suggested "by someone." He answered "I think Thatcher [sic] would be better than that." [1]

The hunt for the right man continues. I suggested to Harlan Genl. Crowder for a side-man. Harlan was delighted & said he would put him up to Hoover. [2]

2. I remember now having recommended Stimson as counsel. Doubtless, it was to Hoover as you say.

3. I am glad you had so fine a visit to Cincinnati. The city seems to be having a renaissance.

4. Hoover appreciates how meagre the lawyer-list is.

5. I can't believe Hoover would be so innocent as to send Gov. Fuller to France. [3]

6. We called on the President Tuesday, March 12.

7. Saw O.W.H. yesterday. He was in fine form & very happy at having had on Sunday his second drive with Mrs. Holmes after a long interval.

8. That's an interesting letter of Eva Lundberg Christie.

9. Some one with an understanding of sociology, economics, political science & law—perhaps Schlesinger[4]—ought to consider whether the chances for working out the great problems of capital & labor & democracy may not be better in Germany now than in the U.S.A. It is claimed that it is being tackled there by forces dominant in 1848, whereas here the Constitution as interpreted trammels constructive development.

[1] Despite Stone and LDB's view that Judge Thomas D. Thacher would be superior, Hoover eventually did appoint to the Commission William Squire Kenyon (1869–1933), the former senator from Iowa. Since 1922, Kenyon had been judge of the U.S. Circuit Court for the 8th Circuit.
   [2] General Crowder was not appointed.
   [3] There had been some speculation that former Governor Alvan T. Fuller was about to replace Myron T. Herrick as ambassador to France (see *New York Times*, 21 March 1929); but the rumors were false.
   [4] Arthur Meier Schlesinger, Sr. (1888–1965), had been a professor of American history at Harvard since 1924. His many books covered the whole range of United States history and, in several instances, offered striking and provocative new approaches.

No. 360   March 29, 1929   Washington, D.C.

1. That is a fine letter of Judge Kellogg's. [1]
2. Also Newlin's. [2] When I had my talk with Hoover, he made a survey of the States to show their emptiness. When he said: "There is no one in California—even the Courts are wretched there." I said: "I hear there is a good man at Los Angeles, who is now President of the American Bar Assn." He answered with a word indicating that he didn't think so. Newlin's name wasn't mentioned.
3. Yes, Denison[3] is a good man. But Hoover said he wants a man for Chairman who is not over 60; and Denison is in his 68th year. I mentioned Denison to Harlan who thinks well of him for a side position only.
4. Glad to hear your S.V. is still selling. How high have the sales of Marion's letters gone?
5. I am glad to know that Henry T. Hunt is giving a stir to Mooney. [4]
6. I am enclosing letter & paper from Furuseth. Have written "judicial office precludes."
7. It would be good to have Laski in America for a while next year. [5]
8. Prof. W. W. Cook[6] was in yesterday about his Institute for Legal Research. He is making some progress.

[1] The letter came from New York judge Henry Theodore Kellogg (1869–1942). He said he had wanted to write for a long time, to express his thanks to FF for what he was doing at the Harvard Law School (from which Kellogg had graduated in 1892), especially regarding legislation.

368

[2] Gurney Elwood Newlin (1880–1955), a California attorney active in civic affairs, was currently the president of the American Bar Association.

[3] Arthur Carter Denison (1861–1942), currently presiding judge of the U.S. Court of Appeals in Cincinnati, was not appointed to Hoover's Commission on Law Enforcement.

[4] Hunt was about to publish his *The Case of Thomas J. Mooney and Warren K. Billings* (New York: National Mooney–Billings Committee, 1929).

[5] Laski hoped to teach at Yale in March 1930 but was prevented from doing so by Labour party matters. He came in March 1931.

[6] Walter Wheeler Cook (1873–1943), who taught law at several leading institutions, was presently at Johns Hopkins. He was one of the "legal realists," and a founder of the Institute for Legal Research at Hopkins.

No. 361   April 3, 1929   Washington, D.C.

1. Now that the gasoline tax has become universal, it occurs to me that it might be well to provoke a state excise tax on intrastate gross receipts of all street-using (including street crossing) light, power & telephone companies—and that, with adequate knowledge & ingenuity, some tax could be devised which would have a tendency to take some of the swollen earnings out of these companies. My thought is (a) to hitch an able economist with an able young graduate of yours & have them explore factually & legally the situation in each of the states & (b) to have Ben Flexner drawn in for consultation. To be effective the thing must be both comprehensive and intensive.

2. B. F. Goldstein[1] turned up after his visit to you. He is a vigorous person, has shown a fine instinct in his proposal for H.L.S.—and there should come good things from him if duly tended.

3. McAdoo wont do[2]—as Hoover is steering clear of politics & wants no pronounced partisans on the prohibition question. He is thinking most broadly on law enforcement.

[1] Benjamin Franklin Goldstein (1895–1974) graduated from Harvard Law School in 1917, and later practiced in Illinois. He was active in Harvard Law School alumni affairs.

[2] For Hoover's crime commission.

No. 362   April 11, 1929   Washington, D.C.

1. Yes, $2500 appropriation for an aid for your casebook on jurisdiction, is applicable to Katz or any one else whom you may select.[1]

2. In the argument of 667–668 yesterday, an appeal from 2nd C.C.A. to test constitutionality of the N.Y. optometrist law,[2] Seligsberg,[3] counsel for Kresge, admitted in answer to McReynolds' question that he would have had a remedy by injunction in State court. Thereupon

McR. said, "I think the decree dismissing bill should be affirmed on that ground. What justification is there for your coming into a federal court to make us construe the state statute" etc?

3. Guthrie's argument in 226, the Philippine Catholic Church case [4] (on Tuesday) was the best I have ever heard from him—and a very good one.

[1] See 6 March 1929, n. 4. Wilber Griffith Katz (1902–1975) graduated from Harvard Law School in 1926. After a period of private practice, he began a long association with the University of Chicago Law School in 1930, serving as dean from 1939 to 1962. He and FF eventually collaborated on the book. See also 20 September 1929.

[2] The two cases were *Roschen* v. *Ward* and *S. S. Kresge* v. *Ward*, 279 U.S. 337, argued on 10 April and decided on 22 April, Holmes giving the opinion for a unanimous Court. The cases dealt with the New York statute making it unlawful to sell eyeglasses at retail unless a physician or optometrist was in charge of the place of sale. The Court upheld the statute, Holmes saying that the question of the wisdom of the measure was for the legislature, not the courts to decide.

[3] Walter N. Seligsberg (1882–1945), the losing attorney in the Kresge case, had graduated from Columbia Law School in 1904 and then practiced in New York City.

[4] *Gonzales* v. *Roman Catholic Archbishop of Manila*, 280 U.S. 1. In 1820, a bequest provided for a chaplaincy in the Philippines. The holder of the chaplaincy was to be the nearest male relative in line of descent from the founder or her grandson. The last incumbent resigned, and the archbishop denied his son the position for lack of qualifications. The archbishop used the income from the bequest for various educational purposes in the interim, and the disappointed son sued. LDB, for a unanimous Court, upheld the archbishop, arguing that in the absence of fraud, the ecclesiastical question of qualification should be decided by canon law. William D. Guthrie represented the archbishop.

No. 363   April 21, 1929   Washington, D.C.

1. We like your Davison much. Hope he will take the job here if you can spare him. [1]

2. Fosdick is silly about Miss Roche's "persecution complex." [2] I suggest that you write Costigan confidentially & ask him to tell you precisely what the Col. F. & I. Co have done & what he would like to have them do.

3. The C.J. told Thatcher [sic] with much emphasis that he ought to stick to his District Court job. [3] Van and Harlan agree. Those 3 C.C. judges seem to have no conception of the mess they have allowed the Southern District of N.Y. to get into.

4. The Prest's Law Comn seems to make urgent that series on Business of the Federal District Courts for which you have sketched the picture in the Cornell article and this week's N.R. [4]

5. Mrs. Holmes turned seriously ill Tuesday, I judge. [5] O.W.H. was absent from Court that day—has attended since. But yesterday at Conference he seemed crushed, and fully twenty years older than he has been

for months—actually the old man. But he has done this week two opinions which I hope he will deliver tomorrow.

When the time comes, Lockwood should be told to insist on staying with O.W.H. substantially all summer. He is needed as no Secretary ever has been, & is evidently much beloved by O.W.H.[6]

[1] James Forrester Davison (b. 1902), a young Canadian who graduated from Harvard Law School in 1929, did take a job in Washington, D.C.—teaching law at George Washington University for his entire career.

[2] See 8 March 1929, n. 5.

[3] Thomas D. Thacher had been mentioned both in connection with the Law Enforcement Commission and for the Solicitor General's position.

[4] "The Federal Courts," *New Republic* 58 (24 April 1929): 273. For the Cornell article, see 7 July 1928, n. 1.

[5] Fanny Dixwell Holmes was near death, and she finally died on 30 April. To Frederick Pollock, Holmes wrote: "We have had our share. For sixty years she made life poetry for me. . . ."

[6] Holmes's clerk did, in fact, stay with the Justice during the summer of 1929.

No. 364   April 22, 1929   Washington, D.C.

Only a word to tell you that O.W.H. turned up at Court with a smile &, as you saw, delivered his two opinions.[1]

He wrote yesterday his Saturday P.M. assignment.

He is not yet at his normal, but had gone a long way in pulling himself together.

[1] The two opinions Holmes delivered were both short and for a unanimous court, *Weiss* v. *Weiner*, 279 U.S. 333, and *Roschen* v. *Ward*, 279 U.S. 337 (see 11 April 1929, n. 2).

No. 365   April 28, 1929   Washington, D.C.

1. I assume you will not further R.P.'s ambition. It would be a disservice to the President.[1]

2. Yes. Hutchins will be a great loss to Yale L.S. men, but it should give us a good law school at U. of C. & a liberalized University.[2]

3. Richards' death opens the way to improving Wisconsin.[3] I have advised Phil La Follette (an extraordinarily promising man) to consult you about a Dean.

4. Tell Whitehead that "The Aims of Education" I could understand. It is an admirable piece.[4]

5. O.W.H. is making a grand fight. But it is a very hard one.

6. Glad Al Smith is coming to dine with the Harvard 40.[5]

Bill Rice is being considered for Dean at Wisconsin. Despite his mental limitations he may be the best man available for Wisconsin, as

fitting their special needs—whether he has the executive ability, including tact in dealing with men—Phil La F. will know much better than
we. He has proved his courage, liberal attitude and devotion to public
interests; and with Phil behind him might enable the State to make
the most use of the School as an instrument of social & political
development.[6]

Charles Eliot's father-in-law Dodge[7] has just been in. He is a friend
of Ed Costigan & Miss Roche & opened his talk with me by speaking of
his desire to get Rockefeller to take a friendly attitude. I suggested that
he see you when he goes to New England.[8]

[1] Apparently Dean Roscoe Pound had asked for FF's help in gaining a position on the Law Enforcement Commission. Eventually Hoover did appoint Pound.

[2] Robert Maynard Hutchins (1899–1977) had just left his position as dean of the Yale Law
School to assume, at the age of thirty, the presidency of the University of Chicago. His twenty years
at Chicago were notable for dramatic experimentation and the creation of a first-rate liberal
university.

[3] Harry Sanger Richards (1868–1929), the dean of the University of Wisconsin Law School
since 1903, had died on 21 April.

[4] Alfred North Whitehead, "The Aims of Education," New Republic 58 (17 April 1929): 244.

[5] On 15 May, Smith attended a dinner given in his honor by the forty Harvard professors who
had endorsed his candidacy in 1928.

[6] William Rice, a professor at the Wisconsin Law School, did not receive the appointment.

[7] Clarence Phelps Dodge (1877–1939) was a Colorado publisher and at one time a progressive
politician. His daughter Regina had married Charles W. Eliot, II, the son of the former president
of Harvard.

[8] See 8 March 1929, n. 5.

No. 366   May 11, 1929   Washington, D.C.

1. I saw O.W.H. a week ago today. He took the bait—telephoned
me himself Wednesday asking me to come to see him & read me his
piece—which is fine.[1]

Yesterday we had a Conference. I asked the C.J. to give him some
opinions to write, one each week. Instead he gave OWH 3, with a
promise on the donee's part not to write more than one a week. He is in
fine form again, working as of old.

2. Dean Bates[2] was in Thursday. I assume he is remaining at Ann
Arbor. I told him earnestly our views as to what a state Law School & its
Law Journal should do for its Judiciary.

3. Learned Hand, Alfred Bettman[3] and Prof. Beale are looked for
this afternoon.

4. Tomorrow I am to see Josephine Roche. I suppose you take "Labor"

& have seen in the last two numbers the progress they are making with public opinion. Notably the 2 to 1 vote of commend by the State Industrial Commission.[4]

It was good to have had such talks last week. At all events, Thatcher [sic] stays put.[5] But how a well-meaning Bar Comtee could entrust the Bankruptcy Cleansing job to Donovan is beyond comprehension.[6]

[1] Perhaps a part of the memorial service for Mrs. Holmes, held at the justice's home a few weeks after her death.

[2] Henry Moore Bates (1869–1949) was the dean of the University of Michigan Law School from 1910 to 1939.

[3] Alfred Bettman (1873–1945), a Cincinnati attorney, had worked with FF on the Cleveland Survey. He was active throughout his life in numerous civic undertakings.

[4] See 8 March 1929, n. 5. *Labor* had carried articles on the Rocky Mountain Co. in its issues of 4 and 11 May. Workers in other mining companies demanded the same rights as those in Miss Roche's company, and the Colorado State Industrial Commission, by a majority vote, granted their request.

[5] See 21 April 1929.

[6] See 4 February 1929. On 24 April, William J. Donovan was chosen to represent the three New York bar associations in the investigation into the bankruptcy scandals.

No. 367   May 16, 1929   Washington, D.C.

1. Miss Grady sends me the Globe with account of your & Marion's reception of Gov. Smith.[1]

2. With May-June wheat at $1.05, and U.S. having most of the 125,000,000 bushel increase in the North American carry over, the N.R. ought not to let Jardine[2] escape for the (political) advice he gave farmers last fall to hold their wheat. It has not been so low since 1914.[3]

3. I asked Allen Johnson about Bob Valentine.[4] He didn't remember whether he was on his list. Said he would look & thanked me. He will probably write you.

4. O.W.H. said today he wouldn't object to carrying on as judge until he was 90. I told him I wanted him to complete his 50 years as judge.[5] He had a bit of a cough last Monday & has some throat trouble still. But his main trouble is the many odds & ends he is bothering himself with. Still he is calm—for him at this season.

5. Thanks for the L.G. pamphlet. They have certainly done a good job.

6. I hope you calmed Shulman. If he needs more, tell him to rest in blissful ignorance of the article.

7. All my Am. Law Institute callers from N.Y. were strong in praise of Charlie Hughes.[6]

[1] The Frankfurters hosted Smith in connection with the dinner with Harvard professors on 15 May; see 28 April 1929, n. 5.

[2] William M. Jardine (1879–1955) had taught at various agricultural colleges in the Midwest and West. President Coolidge had named him secretary of agriculture, and he served in that position through Coolidge's term.

[3] *The New Republic* attacked Jardine in precisely these terms in its issue of 5 June (p. 56).

[4] Allen Johnson (1870–1931) was a professor of history at Yale until 1926, when he took over the editorship of the monumental *Dictionary of American Biography*. LDB and FF wanted to make certain that their friend, Robert G. Valentine, was to be included in the project. Valentine was, in fact, included (XIX: 142), the sketch of his life written by FF.

[5] Holmes had become a judge in 1882; he resigned his seat on 12 January 1932, two months prior to his ninety-first birthday.

[6] LDB here is not referring to Charles Evans Hughes, but to his son, Charles Evans Hughes, Jr. (1889–1950), a New York attorney who would be appointed, two weeks after this letter, as solicitor general of the United States. He would resign the office in April 1930 when his father was named chief justice.

No. 368   May 20, 1929   Washington, D.C.

1. That's excellent advice you gave W. D. Lewis.[1] Glad Cardozo & Harlan agree.

2. Glad Thatcher [sic] is impressed by your Cornell article & is spreading the gospel.

3. A.L.G. shows that the English know a good thing when they see it.

4. The Whitehead remarks had a double interest for us.

5. The Texas invitation via Shaffer is interesting.

6. Walter Lippmann called last Friday. I suppose he reported to you on Emory Buckner's dinner last week & of the lawyers' view of the S.V. discussions.

7. Miss Roche was here recently.[2] I hope you have heard from Costigan. The enemy has played its old game of shutting down on all local bank credit, long enjoyed, despite an excellent financial statement. They have need of $150,000 for working capital. The Amalgamated Bank has furnished $50,000. Paul Warburg[3] (!) $25,000; $25,000 (I have forgotten whether this is Villard); she hoped Herbert Lehman[4] would furnish $25,000; and I suggested that she apply to Evans Clark, Secy. of the Twentieth Century Foundation for $25,000. All of the loans are secured by part of an issue of outstanding bonds (first mortgage) and are, as I recall, half repayable in 9 months, half in 18 months. I suppose Bruce Bliven will use his influence in favor, if he has any.[5]

8. Hoover has in his omnivorous appetites resemblance to Teddy [Roosevelt]. He has no less political sense; but I am inclined to think, greater seriousness & as much vigor, wider experience; & greater famil-

374

iarity with facts. On the other hand, the "pols" seem to me much weaker than in Teddy's day.

[1] Probably William Draper Lewis (1867–1949), a noted legal scholar and currently director of the American Law Institute.

[2] See 8 March 1929, n. 5.

[3] Paul Moritz Warburg (1868–1932) was a member of the powerful family of German bankers. He came to the United States, married into the Loeb family, and was connected with the New York banking firm of Kuhn, Loeb & Co. In 1914 Wilson appointed him to the Federal Reserve Board. He was active in various public, charitable, and Jewish work throughout his life.

[4] Herbert Henry Lehman (1878–1963), after spending some time in the family's banking firm, had entered politics as a supporter of Al Smith. He was currently serving as Franklin Roosevelt's lieutenant governor, and in 1932, was elected to the first of his five terms as governor.

[5] Bliven was one of the three trustees of E. A. Filene's Twentieth Century Fund.

No. 369   May 24, 1929   Washington, D.C.

1. I am glad you think well of the O'Fallon opinion.[1] I guess no one of the majority knows the RR's plight, but I guess P.B. understands.

2. That's very decent of Lewis.

3. Josephine Roche writes me that "acting Governor Lehman is going to make me a loan of $25,000. You can understand how much his assistance and interest mean. I now have only $15,000 to secure. Both Mr. Villard and Freda Kirchwey[2] felt it would be useless to appeal to Mr. Filene's Foundation. In fact Freda had already discussed with Evans Clark the possibility of my obtaining assistance there."[3]

If Villard and Freda are right, Bruce Bliven ought to resign at once from the Foundation. It won't have a chance in his lifetime of doing as good a job & that without spending anything probably. Couldn't B.B., without indicating any source of information, take the initiative in proposing the loan to the Board, or whatever is the body to act?

4. Jos. Lee is grand.

5. O.W.H. read W.L.—thought it "good," but that he shows he is moving in a field with which he is not as familiar as in the Preface studies.[4]

6. W.L. mentioned the Buckner dinner episode in connection with my denunciation of leaders of the bar "as is"—he didn't mention who was present.

7. I hear Ben Flexner is to return within a few days. Would he be interested in the Josephine Roche proposition?

[1] The case was *St. Louis & O'Fallon Railway Co.* v. *United States*, 279 U.S. 461, decided on 20 May. It turned upon the tremendously difficult question of how to justly fix a railroad's "value"—in this case it was necessary to fix it in order to "recapture" excessive profits and use them to help poorer

railroad companies; but the case had obvious implications for the crucial matter of how the Interstate Commerce Commission fixed rates. The majority of five brushed aside all the technicalities and overturned the I.C.C. opinion (written by LDB's longtime friend, Joseph B. Eastman) on the simple ground that the Commission had not given due weight to the "reproduction cost" after 1914. LDB entered a sixty-page dissent which, once again, laboriously reviewed the difficulties, piled detail upon detail, and tried to show why the Commission had behaved properly. He was joined by Holmes and Stone. Stone also entered a ten-page additional dissent and was joined in that by Holmes and LDB. For a clear statement of the complicated issues involved, perhaps written by FF himself, see "The O'Fallon Decision," *New Republic* 59 (29 May 1929): 30. That article begins: "By a five-to-three decision the Supreme Court has . . . interjected a formidable obstacle to the success of utility regulation. It has almost capriciously upset years of work by the trained experts of the Interstate Commerce Commission, and has disregarded the judgment of the three ablest minds in its own body—Justices Holmes, Brandeis and Stone."

[2] Freda Kirchwey (1893–1976), the daughter of Dean George W. Kirchwey of the Columbia Law School, was an experienced journalist. She joined Villard on *The Nation* and stayed there, in various important capacities, until 1955.

[3] Freda Kirchwey was married to Evans Clark, head of the Twentieth Century Fund.

[4] It is unclear which of Lippmann's books or articles Holmes was commenting upon. By "the Preface studies," Holmes probably meant Lippmann's *A Preface to Politics* (New York: M. Kennerley, 1913) and his newest book, *A Preface to Morals* (New York: Macmillan, 1929).

No. 370   May 29, 1929   Washington, D.C.

1. John T. Vance, Law Librarian of the Congressional [Library] [1] sails on June 1 on the Belgenland, Red Star Line from New York. He plans (after attending Librarians' Congresses in Spain and Italy) to go to Vienna to see the Library there. I think he would appreciate a letter to your uncle. [2] He is a worthy public servant, and your uncle would doubtless enjoy meeting him.

2. It is good to know that your intra mural year has been so satisfactory. The extra-mural has also been very fruitful.

3. I suppose you have arranged to have O.W.H.'s dissent [3] printed in full in the N.R. The Nation should also have wit to do it. [4]

4. Yes McR. played into our hands most finely. More when we meet.

5. Joe Cotton will have now a great opportunity. "What will he do with it?" [5]

[1] John Thomas Vance (1884–1943) practiced law in Kentucky and Washington, D.C., until 1924, when he was named law librarian at the Library of Congress. He was about to leave for the first World Library and Bibliographical Congress in Rome and Venice.

[2] FF's uncle, whom he greatly admired and even idolized as a young boy, was Solomon Friedrich Frankfurter (1856–1941), a famous scholar who wrote books in many fields. He was very active in Jewish affairs in Austria, and from 1919 to 1923, the director of the University of Vienna Library. See 3 May 1938.

[3] This was the landmark case of *U.S.* v. *Schwimmer*, 279 U.S. 644, decided two days earlier. Rosika Schwimmer was a Hungarian-born pacifist, and, by all accounts, a woman of high character and intelligence. Her application for U.S. citizenship had been rejected because she would not swear to "bear arms in defense of her country." Justice Butler contended that it was one of the duties

of citizens to bear arms to defend their homelands and also that her attitude might discourage others from defending America. Justice Holmes wrote a two page dissent (in which LDB joined), and argued with unusual eloquence, even for him, that Schwimmer was being excluded for her views, and while he could not agree with them, he admired her optimism, her sincerity, and her potential usefulness as a citizen of the United States. In a famous passage, Holmes said: "Some of her answers might excite popular prejudice, but if there is any principle of the Constitution that more imperatively calls for attachment than any other it is the principle of free thought—not free thought for those who agree with us, but freedom for the thought that we hate. I think that we should adhere to that principle with regard to admission into, as well as to life within this country." He also pointed out that the Quakers held to her view, that they have done their share to make America the country that it is, and that he was not aware that "we regretted our inability to expel them because they believe more than some of us do in the teachings of the Sermon on the Mount."

[4] *The New Republic* published Holmes's dissent in its issue of 12 June 1929 (pp. 92–93). *The Nation* did not publish the entire dissent, but carried a blistering editorial, "Treason to Conscience," *Nation* 128 (12 June 1929): 689, that quoted the well known passage from Holmes's dissent.

[5] Five days earlier, Hoover had named Joseph P. Cotton as under secretary of state. FF always claimed the credit for Cotton's appointment. He had been charged by his old boss, Henry L. Stimson, now secretary of state, to find an able under secretary. FF not only made the approach to Cotton, but when Senate progressives suspicious of some of Cotton's wealthy clients stalled the nomination, FF reassured them and secured their support. The whole story is told in Phillips, ed., *Felix Frankfurter Reminisces*, ch. 21. Cotton was confirmed on 7 June and sworn in on 20 June.

No. 371   June 7, 1929   [?]

In pursuing the judicial statistics—

I. The chief judge of every State appellate court ought to be made to furnish data showing, for the year 1928, (a) the number of criminal cases (1) on the docket (2) added (3) disposed of—also (4) how long on docket before reached and disposed of. Also, when prosecution instituted in trial court.

II. After that has been done the judge of every trial court hearing criminal cases, ought to be made to furnish similar information.

And each court should report what percentage of whole of the time spent in hearings is devoted to criminal cases.

After the answers are in, each addressee should be asked for his suggestions as to how disposition of cases can be speeded.

If this is persistently pursued, a great speeding up is almost sure to result.[1]

[1] See also 17 June 1929.

No. 372   June 15, 1929   Chatham, Mass.

1. In our talk yesterday we mentioned as subjects of investigation the police methods generally and third degree specifically. I assume you

are making a large head, of the use of detectives & their methods, their effect on crime-making and their efficacy as means of conviction.

2. Also as a more general head the growing tendency to rely upon the police for media of proof. A great war can't be won by an exclusively mercenary array.

3. Also the fundamental enquiry (excluding in this connection liquor) to what extent criminal law has been overworked; that is to what extent court remedies and preventive administration should be substituted in dealing with mala prohibita.[1] Such subjects should tempt able investigators to enter the service. A worthy report on any one of these (or a score of other subjects) would alone justify years of the Commission's efforts.[2]

The thing Wick.[3] should impress upon the President is that "one bad oyster (in appointment of judge or U.S. atty) will spoil the stew."

[1] "Evils prohibited by law" contrasted with offenses evil in themselves. See 2 July 1926.

[2] See 13 March 1929, n. 2.

[3] George W. Wickersham's appointment as head of the Commission had been announced on 20 May.

No. 373   June 17, 1929   Chatham, Mass.

In carry[ing] out the process of "Permeation"—I suggest that after the individual letters have gone to (a) Federal Judges & (b) U.S. Attys and (c) Chiefs of Police[1]

I. Similar letters be sent to all the judges of the appellate courts of the States, but asking them in proposing remedies to differentiate between those of general application & those required because of peculiar conditions existing in their respective States.

II. Then, that appropriate letters go to the Attys General of the several States.

III. Then that letters go [to] the judges of the trial court[s] which hear criminal cases.

IV. Then that letters go to the local prosecuting attorneys

V. Then to the Presidents of Bar Assn[s].

VI. Then to teachers of Criminal Law.

Every letter should be individual, & be addressed by name, care being taken to obtain accurate information as to who is incumbent etc. & his address. And each man should be made to feel: "You are the Man."[2]

And that there is an all seeing eye.

378

[1] See 7 June 1929.

[2] Nathan to King David, 2 *Samuel*, 12:7.

No. 374   July 16, 1929   Chatham, Mass.

1. F. P. Walsh[1] made prompt use of your material. The selection of Donovan is not reassuring.[2] The interests know their friends.

2. Bliven meant well, but didn't do a very good job.[3]

3. If Wick. is tactfully firm, H.H.'s persistent interest can be made to yield only good. Of course W. must not waste his powder or accept any second rate man, and H.H. is too intelligent to attempt to force him.

4. You put it strong to J.W.M., but not more so than needed. I hope that yesterday did not pass without action.

5. Walton Hamilton is in good form & greatly pleased with his Summer course on Constitutional law to the young.

[1] Frank Patrick Walsh (1864–1939) was a Missouri progressive whom President Wilson had named in 1915 to head the Federal Commission on Industrial Relations. Governor Roosevelt had just appointed him a member of the New York Commission on the Revision of Public Utility Laws—a new Commission that had been prompted by a sensational merger of New York electric utility companies. It was in this connection that FF had advised him.

[2] William J. Donovan had been appointed counsel to the same commission.

[3] Probably LDB refers to an anonymous editorial entitled "An Open Letter to Owen D. Young," *New Republic* 59 (17 July 1929): 219. FF had prompted the editorial (on 14 July LDB had written him: "You made the Young situation clear to Bliven"). The letter was an attack on the utilities merger (see n. 1 above) which had been accomplished by men closely associated with Young.

No. 375   July 18, 1929   Chatham, Mass.

1. Wick's letter was inexcusable. But I am not sure its results will not in the end be good. It starts the idea which will not down, I guess. And if he keeps silent now as you advise, and lets others rage, there may in time be a valuable precipitation.[1]

2. Max sent me the Interstate Larceny bill & report (& other papers). I wrote him it would be a very serious mistake & said I assumed he had talked with you or would do so.[2]

[1] On 16 July George Wickersham issued his first statement on prohibition in the form of a letter to be read to the National Conference of Governors in Groton, Connecticut. Wickersham offered the proposal that LDB and FF had favored for years—namely a division of responsibility between state and federal governments with the federal government restricting itself to interstate violations and to the prevention of smuggling, while the states policed their own territories. There was a predictable firestorm of commentary, including calls for Wickersham's resignation and a suggestion that

Congress cut off funding for the Commission. Wickersham did, in fact, remain silent during the ensuing debate.

[2] The chief conduit to the proceedings of the National Law Enforcement Commission for LDB and FF was FF's friend, Max Lowenthal, who had been appointed secretary to the Commission.

No. 376   July 21, 1929   Chatham, Mass.

1. The N.R. might appropriately comment on the I.C.C.'s recent action in ordering that the practice of hauling private cars for the officials of other RR[s] & their families cease. This is one of the abuses uncovered in the Second Advance Rate Case (1913–14). It took 15 years to get the practice stopped. (See U.S. Daily July 19/29) [1]

2. You made the situation clear to Chas. E. Clark.[2] I talked to Hamilton to the same effect when he was here, and had done so earlier. He is entirely of that view now; & agrees that the thing to do is to be keen in discovering & securing the unattached young.

3. Paul, Elizabeth & Walter arrived yesterday in good form. They have already expressed the hope of seeing you here soon.

4. I will hold Richard W. Hale's books awaiting your coming.

5. A. N. Holcombe was here yesterday to see Auntie B. Later I had a talk with him. Does he represent the Political Science Department at Harvard?!!

[1] *The New Republic* carried no such notice.

[2] About Yale's desire to hire FF for their own law school; see 27 February 1929. Charles Edward Clark (1889–1963) was Yale Law School's dean from 1929 to 1939, when Roosevelt named him to the Second Circuit Court of Appeals. From 1954 to 1959 he was chief judge of that circuit.

No. 377   August 14, 1929   Chatham, Mass.

1. Yes, Snowden[1] did well in asserting British right. It should strengthen the Labor Party to have secured the support of all parties in so important a matter.

2. The further comment on the Wick. proposal re Prohibition is promising.[2] It is, at least, a way out.

3. Even deHaas admits that the "respectable receivership" is a decent way out of the mess which the W.Z.O. & Z.O.A. have created.[3] Harry Friedenwald's[4] spirit is always fine.

4. V.D. can act quickly if there is no decision to write. But if this job involves one, the time will doubtless be long. And I fear that, in any event, it will not be over before the Term opens. We can't afford a diversion after Oct 6.

5. We are glad that the Schlesingers came and hope to see them again in early September. [5]

[1] Philip Snowden (1864–1937), a leading socialist writer and polemicist, was chancellor of the exchequer in Ramsay MacDonald's first Labour government. He had just delivered a tough speech to the Hague Conference which was discussing the merits of the Young Plan for reparations repayment. By standing up for British interests, as against the French and, to a lesser degree, the Americans, Snowden allied the Labour party on this issue with the position of the other major British parties.

[2] See 18 July 1929.

[3] In 1929, Lipsky and his supporters were still in control of the American Zionist Organization. But there was growing dissatisfaction with the continual decline in membership, the steady accumulation of a deficit, and the inability to attract contributions from wealthy American Jews. During the next few months, however, talks engineered by Bernard Flexner would begin the process of first reintegrating the Brandeis-Mack faction into the movement, and then of having that faction assume the leadership. The first step would be a meeting in September between LDB and Felix Warburg, followed by LDB's cautious willingness to emerge publicly. See 23 September 1929.

[4] Harry Friedenwald (1864–1950), a Baltimore ophthalmoligist, teacher of medicine, and a pioneering American Zionist had been active in the movement since the 1890s and from 1904 to 1910 he was president of what was then called the Federation of American Zionists. When the Brandeis-Mack faction needed "a personality" to stand as their candidate to defeat Lipsky in the 1928 Convention, Friedenwald was suggested, but declined the offer.

[5] On 6 August LDB had written: "The Schlesingers were here yesterday & we like them much." The feeling was clearly mutual. In his autobiography Arthur M. Schlesinger wrote: "The trait called greatness is an elusive one, but if it comprehends humility, moral majesty, faith in the common folk, deep human compassion, and constancy of purpose—in short, the quality of having made the world better for having lived in it—then Brandeis alone of the men I have known fulfilled the requirements."

No. 378   August 24, 1929   Chatham, Mass.

1. We plan to leave here for Boston on the afternoon of Monday, Sept. 9. Paul and Elizabeth are to leave on Saturday the seventh.

2. W.L.'s editorial was read to the assembled company yesterday. You taught him much. [1]

3. Re Hutcheson's circular letter. [2] The form is less good than I should have expected from him, and to have stated his own view, as he did on page 2, seems to me particularly bad form. I hope he will have long talks with you.

4. J.W.M. may well congratulate himself that he was not at Zurich. [3]

5. Sorry Alfred Cohen is not returning to N.Y. via Chatham.

6. What does your remark on Waldo Cook, and non-forgetting refer to? I guess some enclosure was omitted.

7. We are reading with much satisfaction the Charles Eliot Norton letters, published in 1914. [4] I had valued much his service to art culture, and used semi-occasionally [to] go to Shady Hill. But I had no idea of

the range of his activities and the extent of his important services to the country. He was indeed a most valuable citizen, with rare insight and a full appreciation of the value of courage and of free speech.

[1] "Anniversary," on 23 August, marked the execution of Sacco and Vanzetti two years earlier. Too many questions about the case still remained unanswered, Lippmann argued, and if the men were indeed found innocent, Massachsuetts would have much to answer for.

[2] FF had asked Federal District Judge Joseph Chappell Hutcheson, Jr. (1879–1973) of Texas to take up the job of gathering judicial statistics from his fellow judges. In 1931 Hutcheson would be elevated to the Fifth Circuit Court of Appeals, and served as chief judge from 1948 to 1959.

[3] The Sixteenth Biennial Zionist Congress was held in Zurich for two weeks ending 11 August. The tone of the meeting can be gauged by the fact that the final session lasted for twelve hours, all through the night, and was finally ended by the selection of a coalition administration. The newly formed Jewish Agency began its history at this Congress. But the alliance between the wealthy non-Zionists and the floundering Lipsky administration in America was to be short-lived. See 23 September 1929.

[4] *The Letters of Charles Eliot Norton with Biographical Comment by His Daughter Sara Norton and M. A. deWolfe Howe* (Boston: Houghton Mifflin, 1913). Norton (1827–1908) was the colorful and popular professor of art history at Harvard at the end of the nineteenth century. LDB had known him slightly as a young law student.

No. 379　　　　　August 27, 1929　　　　　Chatham, Mass.

1. Campbell, the N.Y. prohibition Comr, seems to be already acting on the Wick. letters and today comes Washington confirmation. [1]

2. And today comes also Hoover's states rights public land declaration. [2] It looks like fighting all along the line.

3. I fear that Weizmann-Lipsky policies & actions have a large part in the Palestine disaster—indirectly. [3]

4. Snowden's firmness is encouraging. [4]

5. I am glad you were so favorably impressed with Hutcheson. He should prove a great force for good in judicial matters.

6. I had a call from Butzel of Detroit, a newly appointed judge who did not make personally a good impression, & disclosed a pretty low in sphere of state judiciary. [5] He tells me that Isidor Levin [sic] will become practically head of the forum.

7. I understand from your telephone via Elizabeth that Powers [6] of the Globe is to [be] here Saturday noon, Sept. 7.

8. Re Rocky Mt Fuel Co enclosed reports. [7] I suppose the N.R. will already have set up some mention. But it should not fail to discuss fully the significance of this use of organized labor's purchasing power—the most neglected of social forces. Now that the employer-financial world has learned that high wages & the spending of them is essential to their own prosperity, and is voluble on "cooperation," labor should be taught

that the spending must be primarily for the product of those who are friends, & it is easy enough to do so without getting enmeshed with the courts.

[1] On 26 August, Maurice Campbell (1868–1942), the federal prohibition administrator of the Eastern District of New York, issued a statement calling for the transfer to state jurisdiction of cases involving New York speakeasies. Campbell, who had a varied career in many fields, resigned his post in 1930 calling for the repeal of prohibition. He then edited *Repeal*, a monthly magazine advocating prohibition reform on the grounds that the experiment could not be enforced.

[2] Hoover suggested turning over 200,000,000 acres of federal lands to the states.

[3] A series of violent riots by Arab mobs, erupting on 23 August, left more than a hundred Jews dead and many injured. Protests from all over the world (15,000 Jews marched on the British Embassy in New York City on this date) followed, but Weizmann and Lipsky seemed unable to influence the British government to support the Jewish settlements. Their apparent impotence was another factor leading to the downfall of the Lipsky administration.

[4] See 14 August 1929, n. 1.

[5] Henry Magnus Butzel (1871–1963) had just been appointed to fill an unexpired term on the Michigan Supreme Court. He was reelected frequently and served several terms as chief justice. See 10 November 1929.

[6] James H. Powers was a reporter for the *Boston Globe*.

[7] When the Rockefeller interests cut wages 16 to 20 percent at its mines in Colorado, the union members in the Rocky Mountain Company owned by Josephine Roche (see 8 March 1929, n. 5) had voluntarily taken a wage cut, and then went out to sell the company's product to sympathetic consumers in order to help the owner withstand the increased competition from Rockefeller.

No. 380   September 6, 1929   Chatham, Mass.

1. George Young[1] was brought here by Charles Crane[2] this AM—obviously in order that Y. might talk with me, or rather have me talk with him, on the Palestine situation. Crane immediately left us alone, and went into the next room to Alice, Eliz. and Paul. And pretty promptly Young, as adviser of the Labor Party asked me about Palestine etc.—the past and the future. There was no option; but I was not sorry to do so. I told him fully and frankly my view—will tell you the details Monday. I was emphatic in my opposition to Great Britain's relinquishment of the Mandate (which he suggested) and against any material change in the fundamentals of the government;—insisting that there should be merely an avoidance of the British blundering largely responsible; and that we must start over & traverse the ground with a view to avoiding the same mistakes. i.a. that the Zionist Palestine Executive should be abolished etc. I told him that you, Mack & I agreed & why we kept silent. I told him that because of judicial office there were additional reasons governing me. He thought you might at the proper time help much, saying that "our people have confidence in him," and he wondered whether you could get leave from the Law School. He asked who among the English Jews might help in the present situation. I suggested

Sir Herbert Samuel. He then named Reading[3] and I told Y. of my work with R. in 1920. I told him I thought Samuel, who knew the country, could help more. Young leaves America in Oct.

He said, unless something was done, it would not be surprising if in 2 or 3 years Great Britain surrendered her Mandate—that is [if] the views of some I[ndependent]. L[abour]. P[arty]. men might prevail.

I told him what I thought of Gabriel[4] & he left me the impression that he had no better opinion of Gabriel (see p. 2 for addition).

2. Morris Leeds' report to the Friends on unemployment, quotes Whiting Williams[5] on the demoralization incident to irregularity and lack of employment and adds: "It is easy for those who are thus disheartened and embittered to turn to careers of crime."

Dr. Jastrow[6] at Yale spoke of the relation of misery to crime. Before the President's Comn makes its report, it should have made a thorough investigation of this subject.

3. Kenyon's letter is encouraging. I shall of course, be glad to talk with him; and also with Farrand if there is occasion. The letter to the C.J.s should yield interesting [*].

4. And Goldrick's letter shows awakeness.

5. I fear the C.J. is less well than he was when the Term closed & that he is suffering still from his post term-Cincinnati excess. Nothing from him; but this is from one who saw him at Murray Bay.[7]

1. (continued) I put strongly the error of British in making it impossible for Jews to serve in the police & in the civil service and that in the future this should be corrected. Also that now that speech can be had with a few powerful Jewish leaders represented by the [Jewish] Agency, it would be possible to develop means by which Jews could help with men and money, without placing greater burden on the British in their own time of need.

Please have 1. copied and send one copy to Mack to be kept strictly confidential and one to me.

[1] Sir George Young (1872–1952), a Labour party intellectual, was an authority on the Middle East and a frequent lecturer and teacher in the United States.

[2] Charles Richard Crane (1858–1939) was a wealthy Chicago manufacturer, a former client of LDB's, and a progressive, active in numerous civic enterprises. He was a friend of Wilson's, and had helped to bring LDB and Wilson together during the 1912 campaign.

[3] Rufus Daniel Isaacs, first marquess of Reading (1860–1935) was a world famous lawyer, elected to Parliament in 1904 and named lord chief justice in 1913, the first Jew to hold that position. He undertook several diplomatic missions to the United States and in 1920 became viceroy of India, a position he held until 1926. Isaacs was a committed Zionist.

[4] Edmund Vivian Gabriel (1875–1950), then in the United States, had been financial adviser and assistant administrator in Palestine in 1918 and 1919.

[5] Whiting Williams (1878–1975) was a lecturer, author, and consultant on labor problems.

[6] Perhaps Joseph Jastrow (1863–1944), a prolific social psychologist and frequent university lecturer.

[7] Murray Bay, Quebec, where the Tafts had a cottage. The chief justice's health had been failing steadily. By January 1930 he was asking Van Devanter to announce his opinions, and by the end of that month he was convinced that he would be unable to carry on. On 3 February he sent Hoover his resignation. William Howard Taft died on 8 March 1930.

No. 381 September 20, 1929 Washington, D.C.

1. I had not thought it important that I should see MacDonald.[1] But I think it very important that you should. And if it proves that I am to see him, I want you present.

2. The most far reaching demand that we have to make is no discrimination and actual equal opportunity; that means, i.a. equal opportunity in every branch of the government service and under every government contract. Equal with Arabs and equal with British—with a few excepted positions.

I have faith that there are, or will be, in Palestine Jews who can, from the highest to the lowest positions, win out against the Arab in service. We should expect our Jews to do so; and our Jews should understand that no coddling [is] allowed.

For some of the tasks, for which Ashkenazim and Sephardim are not suitable, the Yemenites are. And even for the low-waged positions it should be possible, with aid of workingmen's plots a la Mohl, to get subsidiary family earnings which will, with Jewish intelligence & persistence, enable even Ashkenazim and Sephardim to take jobs at as low wages as Arabs. For the general cultural advantage & social services will be furnished them, in any event, by Jewish philanthropists, in a way not to pauperize, I hope.

Talk over such extension of the housing projects with B.F. when he is with you Wednesday.

3. Jews must not, after the present emergency is over, be denied the opportunity of defending themselves.[2] As against the Bedouins, our pioneers are in a position not unlike the American settlers against the Indians. I saw myself the need of their self-defense in 1919 in Poreah, with our Shomer,[3] on guard mounted on the hill top, and the black-tented Bedouins below who had peaceably but with ever robber purpose, crossed the Jordan. As to other Arabs, the position is not different in essence, of course. Most Arabs will have guns, or at least knives, concealed, if possession is prohibited. Of course, Jews should be adequately

represented in an adequate police force. But under Palestinian conditions, no police force can be adequate if the Jews are kept defenseless.

4. We must make it clear to the British that our demand is for personal safety and opportunity—and try tactfully to have them forget about reparations,[4] or rather to let "reparations" mean reparation by wrongdoing Arabs, not by the Government. Let me have your thoughts on the above & other matters in your mind.

5. B.F. will report fully to you on the [Felix] Warburg interview.[5] W. could not have behaved better. I think Kirstein had no small part in convincing W. he should call on me.

6. Kenyon (Sept 5 letter) learned his lesson well.

7. I had a line from Hutcheson that he expects to call on me here.

8. The Herald roast of Nichols is well done.

9. Likewise your answer to W.L.'s preposterous editorial.

10. As to the Katz fellowship.[6] My thought had been to pay the amount to the Law School to be applied to that specific purpose. If for any reason you think that would be undesirable, I will pay the amount into your special account and have you make the payment to him from time to time as is common on fellowships.

My thoughts had been to make the first payment Oct 1. ($625), and quarterly thereafter—if payment in that way accords with your wishes.

11. As to distributing "Labor Injunctions."[7]

    (a) I do not think of any designation of the donor more clearly innocuous than "a friend of the Harvard Law School." Of course you will send out many personally, and among these the Senators, Representatives and Judges with whom you have had personal relations on the subject. Please send a copy to Jacob H. Gilbert, 42 Broadway. A copy should go to Furuseth and to Dr. George L. Knapp of Labor.

12. I do not think it wise to distribute copies generally to Senators and Representatives. But all legal periodicals should have copies; and so far as you can identify those who act as counsel for labor unions as "desirable citizens" the free instruction might be helpful.

13. AF of L News Sept 14.

14. Enclosed from the C.J. looks pretty bad. Yes, he was more precise than usual about L.M.

[1] Prime Minister Ramsay MacDonald was due to arrive in America (where one of his main intentions was the negotiation of a naval treaty) on 5 October. Naturally, his visit provided an opportunity for American and Canadian Zionists to speak to him about conditions in Palestine under the Mandate,

particularly in view of the recent riots there (see 27 August 1929, n. 3). LDB did eventually meet with MacDonald (see 5 and 10 October 1929).

[2] The British marines, rushed to Palestine from Egypt on 25 August, had disarmed the Jewish population. See *New York Times*, 27 August and 1 September 1929.

[3] *Shomer* is Hebrew for guard or watchman.

[4] On 28 August the World Zionist Organization demanded reparations for loss of life and property in the Palestine riots.

[5] See next letter.

[6] See 6 March and 11 April 1929.

[7] See 20 December 1927, n. 2. FF and Nathan Greene published *The Labor Injunction* in January 1930.

No. 382   September 23, 1929   Washington, D.C.

1. Ben Flexner is to be here Saturday, again. Meanwhile he will submit to you the minutes of the Warburg interview and the draft of a formula of what Warburg may say publicly as to the extent of my participation in his management.[1] I am not sure that Ben realizes fully, as you do, the severe limitations which judicial office and my small vitality impose & I shall rely upon you to thresh this out with him, so that when he comes here Saturday (with others) there will be little to say on that subject.

During the four vacation months there will be ample time at Chatham for conferences and thinking, and that study of current facts on which thinking and judgment must be based if they are to be valuable. But during the eight months of the Term the situation is very different. About half of that, which is devoted to arguments and conferences is practically a closed season. And the recess period may not be heavily invaded by either conferences or study of things Palestinian.

I had hoped that Warburg would be satisfied with my confining my functions strictly to thinking and the exercise of judgment, with the results communicated to him privately without its being publicly known that I was advising. He seems to think that this will not suffice, and that even public knowledge that he had advised with and consulted me would not be enough. I, of course, want to avail, so far as may be, of this opportunity of rescuing the Zionist movement from its aberrations and making prevail the policies which seem to us essential. But the difficulty, in view of my severe limitations, of utilizing not only my thinking and judgment, but such prestige as I have with the Jewish public, presents a problem which may be insoluble. And it may be necessary to very regretfully answer "non possumus"[2] to that.

Needless to say Warburg is entitled to all the help we can give him. And we want to help one who apparently is eager to go our way. I think he does not realize how much he will gain in support if, without any publicity as to my participation, only our small group are with him. For if we are with him, the forces of discontent aroused by deHaas and others will be at least quiescent. And the published participation of the other members of our group will lead to the assumption that I too approve etc.

2. The Bardo disclosures as to the shipbuilders lobbying on the Cruiser bill and the Merchant Marine,[3] should make it possible now to secure Congressional legislation requiring registration of legislative agents, and legislative counsel, with publication of expenses, on the general lines of the Mass. law long in force. The Federal law should be far more comprehensive. It should include all publicity men, require the filing of all contracts, monthly filing of expenditures and also as exhibits filing of all publicity matter etc. The Legislative Drafting Bureau counsel ought to be set to work promptly to draft a model bill and when it is introduced the N.R., Nation, N.Y. World et al. should give heavy support.

Wont you write on this, to the Senator most fit for the job?

3. The Senate's action in requiring the data from the tariff favors applicants and the formation of a women's consumers comtee, show that some progress has been made since my futile effort to secure, as counsel for the Young Men's Democratic Club, leave to cross-examine witnesses.

4. I hear that Bardo, formerly V.P. of the New Haven, was a very bad actor there.

[1] The important "interview" between LDB and Felix Warburg took place on 19 September. Felix Moritz Warburg (1871–1937) was, like his brother Paul, a German-born banker and a partner in Kuhn, Loeb & Co. With the death of Louis Marshall two weeks earlier, Warburg became the head of the new Jewish Agency and the link to those non-Zionist philanthropists willing to contribute to Palestinian projects. Bernard Flexner had approached him about the possibilities of cooperation between the non-Zionists and the Brandeis-Mack wing of the American Zionist movement. Warburg was more than anxious. At their meeting he suggested that LDB leave the Supreme Court and assume the leadership of American Jewry. LDB of course refused, but did agree to come out in the open (see 5 October 1929), promising to say a few words at a meeting that Warburg would arrange on 24 November. That meeting would be a symbol of peace between the Brandeis-Mack faction and the rich non-Zionists. The attitude of the Zionist press toward LDB's reentry into active affairs can be summed up by the title of an article by Louis I. Newman, "The Return of the Pilot." Without the support of Warburg and his friends, the Lipskyites' days were numbered.

[2] "Not possible."

[3] In widely publicized hearings, commented upon even by President Hoover, the Senate Naval Affairs Committee was uncovering another major scandal. A group of large shipbuilders had financed an expensive lobby, headed by William B. Shearer, to destroy the disarmament conference of 1927 in Geneva and to propagandize for the Merchant Marine Act of 1928. Clinton Lloyd Bardo

(1867–1937), formerly a railroad executive, had assumed the presidency of the New York Shipbuilding Company in 1928. He testified before the committee on 21 September, revealing the amounts paid to Shearer but stating that nothing improper had been done.

No. 383   September 26, 1929   Washington, D.C.

1. Re Katz. The $625 check to your special account has been signed (Oct 1) and you should receive notice thereof (as of the $1500 deposit) on October 2.[1] Please call up 161 Devonshire if you do not. I assume from your silence that quarterly payments are o.k.

2. It's fine to know that the students are flocking to the seminar. Not surprising.

3. I rather think MacDonald wont want to see either of us; and perhaps, with his other absorptions, official and social, it will be as well. I had to decline the invitation to luncheon at the British Embassy October 5, i.a. because of my declination of all White House and Canadian minister invites. I shall probably meet MacDonald for a moment when he calls that day on the C.J. at the Capitol.[2]

4. Max [Lowenthal] probably told you of his and Monte [Lemann]'s call Monday.

5. When I wrote you about a bill for lobby registration,[3] I didn't know that Carraway [sic] had gotten something of the sort through as a joint resolution at the last session & that it was stalled in the House.[4] Probably the Carraway resolution was wholly inadequate.

6. Thanks to Schlesinger, Fox[5] and Greene[6] of the Amer. Historical Association were here Tuesday for a Conference with Vance (2 hrs), in which the whole subject of (a) colonial legislation, (b) colonial judicial systems and unwritten law, with a [view] to gathering the source material and editing it and alternately (c) writing American Legal History. The subject was fully & sympathetically discussed.

7. Fox and Greene were eager, and Greene (who impresses me as a person of rare quality) volunteered that he would write you.

Greene said they would try to get together promptly for conference six to twelve of the historians most likely to know & be interested; would then take it up at their Nov. Exec. Comtee meeting, with a view to bringing it up at the Annual Conference (which I think is at Durham, North Carolina Christmas week).

8. I think I made clear to them that what we need is high class scholarship, directed to this field; and that, if the comprehensive plan is well conceived and a worthy sample product can be fashioned and exhib-

389

ited, there will be no obstacle to their getting from some sources, the essential financial aid. Greene, I think, appreciates this fully.

9. Also that they should seek cooperation from the several law schools and the historical societies etc in the several states, but (at least at this stage) should not get entangled with, or look for help from, either the American Bar Assn or the American Law Institute.

I mentioned Cardozo as among the few judges who might be interested—and if interested, help much.

10. If this thing shapes up well, and in time, you may think it wise to say something on the subject at your U.C. talk on Research. But there is so much that we want the Law Schools to do in fields other than early history, that perhaps we had better leave this to the historians, at the present stage.

11. Not knowing the lay of the land, I thought it unwise to mention Notestein to Fox and Greene. But I did speak to Hamilton in July on this subject. He is the kind of historian whose studies should be directed to the colonial law.

12. Gregory (T. W.) was here yesterday. He explained the Texas political flap.[7] Says it is wholly anti-Catholic, and thinks (as the Democrats wont nominate a Catholic again), the State is safely Democratic. He says Colquet [sic] (the only Texan selected by Hoover for high office—i.e. RR. Labor arbitrator) is a very, very bad egg, who should be very closely watched.[8]

[1] See 20 September 1929.
  [2] See 5 and 10 October 1929.
  [3] See preceding letter.
  [4] Thaddeus Horatius Caraway (1871–1931) represented Arkansas in the House from 1913 to 1921. He was elected to the Senate in 1920 and remained there until his death. His resolution on lobbying was S. Res. 197.
  [5] Dixon Ryan Fox (1887–1945), a leading American historian, taught at Columbia from 1912 to 1934, when he accepted the presidency of Union College. He was coeditor (with Schlesinger) of the authoritative thirteen-volume *History of American Life* series.
  [6] Evarts Boutell Greene (1870–1943), another leading colonial and revolutionary historian, taught at the University of Illinois until 1923, when he moved to Columbia.
  [7] The Democratic party in Texas split down the middle during the 1929 gubernatorial race, one candidate running explicitly against Al Smith. See *New York Times*, 1 September 1929.
  [8] Oscar Branch Colquitt (1861–1940), an old time Texas politico and oilman, had served as governor of the state from 1911 to 1915.

No. 384   September 29, 1929   Washington, D.C

1. J.W.M. or B.F. have doubtless told you of the plan agreed upon at yesterday's Palestine conference.[1]

2. If Warburg accedes, it will be just as well not to have any session with MacDonald; or if we have one, to limit its scope.[2]

3. As to you appearing at N.Y. Comn Enquiry:[3]
If the invitation comes in due form, I think
   (a) that it is wise to respond
   (b) that it will be best to talk on the ineffectiveness of regulation of the present sort—the great superiority of regulation by means of a contract, and therefore of the importance of the state's retaining its power etc.
A clear compact argument, inviting cross-examination.

4. Schulman [sic] is here & enters upon the job with the promise of his being both helpful & an enjoyable associate.

5. Goldsmith left yesterday, with, I think, a determination to make good in practice & life.[4]

[1] For the details of the conference, see next letter.
[2] See 10 October 1929.
[3] Perhaps FF was anticipating an invitation to testify before the New York State Commission on the Revision of Public Utility Laws; see 16 July 1929, n. 1.
[4] See 7, 12, and 15 October 1928.

No. 385   October 5, 1929   Washington, D.C.

1. Since writing you yesterday, I have, from Mack, yours of 3rd to J.W.M. & deH with accompanying memo.

As I entered the Conference on Sat. Sept 28,[1] my impression was in accord with your view, although deH. had outlined to me his view the day before. The conference, which was a real one, in which no words were wasted, led me to the conclusion that the decision arrived at was the wisest one.

It was helpful in clearing my mind.
   (a) I am convinced that present situation requires some public action on my part—to satisfy not only American Jewish public opinion, but British officialdom and my own peace of mind. On the British official attitude, deHaas' talk with Passfield[2] & the undersecretary at P's residence was illuminating.
   (b) I was also convinced that a few words spoken at Warburg's meeting would be the least taxing & least embarrassing of any public action suggested; and probably less so than a statement by Warburg of my participation would be.
   (c) The Washington conference Nov. 3. is not within the realm of

the controversial. Warburg is to call it personally. Neither rabbis, nor Jewish poli[ti]cians, nor American dignitaries, are to be present. I shall say literally only a few words—and I think my appearance there will not interfere with my otherwise universal "preclude," [3] just as my limited Zionist appearances prior to 1921 left me otherwise unembarrassed.

Abstinence at this time on my part would naturally be interpreted as loss of faith.

I think if you had been present at the Conference you would have reached the same conclusion.

2. Enclosed re Kelley [sic], seems to close the chapter of the 4 responsible for the Wan case. Two died. Burlinghame [sic] got his show last spring and now Kelley. [4]

Mail may reach me more promptly if addressed to P.O.B. (without number) U. (You) Street Station. Poindexter calls for my mail.

[1] The conference was held to discuss, among other things, the extent of LDB's role in American Zionism during the next months. See 23 September 1929, n. 1.

[2] With the return of the Labour party to power, the old Fabian socialist, Sidney Webb, was created Baron Passfield and appointed secretary of state for the colonies. In that position, he would become a factor in Palestinian affairs and in British policy toward Palestine. The Passfield White Paper of October 1930 proposed restricting Jewish migration to Palestine and was condemned by Zionists (including LDB) as contrary to the Balfour Declaration.

[3] LDB's standard method of avoiding invitations was to state "Judicial office precludes . . ."

[4] For the Wan case, see 31 October 1924, n. 2. For the disgrace of Burlingame, see 13 February 1929. Now Lieutenant Edward Kelly was involved in a scandal of his own. Kelly, one of the detectives responsible for the heartless torture of Wan, was currently chief of the homicide squad of the Washington, D.C., police force. A grand jury had just demanded that he be relieved of that responsibility and transferred because of his bungling of a homicide investigation. See the sensational articles in *The Washington Post* on 1 and 2 October 1929.

No. 386　　　October 5, 1929　　　Washington, D.C.

1. Telephone has come from Mr. Wright? [1] of the British Embassy asking whether I could come to see Mr. MacDonald on Wednesday at 5:30PM. I answered yes.

I suppose this is the result of your cabling.

Let me know what you think I should say if, as I expect, there will be a chance to talk Palestine.

As the invitation was to tea, it may be that others will be there also. [2]

2. H. W. Nevi[n]son, [3] who came here with the MacDonald party to represent the Manchester Guardian called this afternoon. You will recall

he spent a month or two in Palestine some years ago &, as I recall, was pro-Zionist.

He said he thought the situation in the Near East a very serious one as Ibn Saud[4] could at any time he really wanted move on with his Wahabis et al 300,000 strong—that now he was in peace etc. And that the local Arabs were discontented.

I took the occasion to present to him my views on Jewish self-defence etc.[5] & my belief that the recent outbreak would result in a quickening of Jewish development in Palestine etc.

3. Donovan wrote you handsomely.

4. O.W.H. was in fine shape yesterday.

5. Max told you of my talks with Grenv. Clark[6] & Friendly, and with Chafee and Kenyon.

6. You have doubtless heard from deHaas of his visit here Thursday.

[1] Michael Wright was the third secretary at the British Embassy.

[2] See next letter.

[3] Henry Wood Nevinson (1856–1941) was a distinguished liberal journalist with a wealth of American contacts. FF called him "a wonderful creature, the author of my favorite autobiography," and described him as a pacifist capable of passionate outbreaks and one who covered every war for forty years. (Phillips, ed., *Felix Frankfurter Reminisces*, 93.)

[4] Abdul al-Aziz Ibn Saud (c. 1888–1953) was the founder of Saudi Arabia and its first king. His family were the leaders of the Wahabi movement within ultraorthodox Islam.

[5] See 20 September 1929.

[6] Grenville Clark (1882–1967) was a classmate of FF's at Harvard Law School, a lifelong friend, and possibly the person who first introduced FF to Franklin Roosevelt. A lawyer connected over the years with the most influential New York law firms, Clark was very active in numerous civic causes (FF called him "a great citizen").

No. 387   October 10, 1929   Washington, D.C.

1. B.F. will send you copy of my memo to him of the interview with MacDonald, and will also transmit my suggestion that a copy of Feisel's [sic] letter to you be sent through Harold to Passfield.[1]

2. MacDonald was entirely friendly. Said he was glad we had met at last, but I am not sure that much of what I said to him will stick. He tried to listen. We were alone in the front embassy room, seated on the sofa, out of sight even, while we talked, of all others at the tea. And there were none but the Embassy folk there except Borah and Swanson[2] and their wives. MacD. had talked to Borah before he did to me, while he was taking copiously of tea and cakes. (As he came in I had said to him in a low voice that I wanted a little talk with him.)

But MacDonald look[ed] very distracted. Alice thought alarmingly so. She heard at the Ishbel luncheon[3] that he had been up till 4 A.M. with his Secretary after the Tuesday function at the Embassy and that he was up again at 7 A.M. to attend the Breakfast with 18 labor men at Secy Davis'.[4]

All that looks like a repetition of his earlier conduct as P[rime] M[inister]. Mark Sullivan who was in last evening with the O'Briens [sic] & Col. Ritchie, of the British Army[5] (Harold's friend) said MacD. had unquestionably made an excellent impression.

Nevinson says MacD's impromptu N.Y. speech was the best he ever made.[6]

You and Gay will know what it is best to do about promoting Savings Bank Insurance among faculty members.[7] I suppose Schlesinger would be glad to help. If a circular is decided upon, please send me a copy when issued.

[1] One of the crucial documents in the ever-sharpening debate between Jews and Arabs over Palestine was the famous letter written by King Feisal (1885–1933) to FF on 3 March 1919. The two men had met in Paris, had a cordial interview (arranged by T. E. Lawrence), and agreed to put their thoughts in writing. The key passage of the Feisal letter read: "We Arabs, especially the educated among us, look with the deepest sympathy on the Zionist movement. . . . [W]e will wish the Jews a most hearty welcome home."

[2] Claude Augustus Swanson (1862–1939), a former Virginia congressman and governor, served in the Senate from 1910 until he agreed to be Franklin Roosevelt's secretary of the navy in 1933. He was the ranking Democrat on the Senate Foreign Relations Committee (Borah was the chairman of that committee).

[3] Ramsay MacDonald was accompanied to the United States by his daughter Ishbel.

[4] James John Davis (1873–1947) was a Welsh immigrant who began as an ironworker and went on to serve as secretary of labor for Harding, Coolidge, and Hoover. Davis resigned in 1930 to enter the Senate from Pennsylvania, and remained there until 1945.

[5] Perhaps Lt. Col. Thomas Fraser Ritchie (1875–1931).

[6] Probably his remarks upon arriving in the city on 5 October.

[7] Professor Edwin Francis Gay (1867–1942), a professor of economics and former dean of the Harvard Business School, had held several important positions in the government's effort to mobilize the economy during the war. LDB had asked him to head a committee of Harvard professors to publicize the Massachusetts Savings Bank Insurance scheme to other members of the faculty.

No. 388   October 13, 1929   Washington, D.C.

1. The C.J. has abandoned the practice of taking as law clerk a Yale graduate. Instead, he has taken as permanent assistant Robertson, former Ass't Clerk. The man who wrote the book on L[ower].C[ourt]. jurisdiction.[1] In view of the C.J.'s health,[2] this is fortunate & should greatly facilitate his work, on certioraris, statements of jurisdiction & otherwise. (Besides, I guess, the C.J.'s choice last year of Parsons,[3]

against the advice of the faculty, was not a happy one.) The C.J. seemed pretty ragged at Conference yesterday.

2. The C.J. submitted to the Council, at my suggestion, the project of increasing to 5 the number of judges on C.C.A. & District C. of Appeals—the submission being for discussion & consideration now & during the year; & for action next year. Dennison [sic] and Manton are for it. The others reserved their opinions. My suggestion was that the 5 be made up by calling in, where necessary, district judges. The argument in favor: (a) there should be an opinion, & adequate ones, in every case. If C.C.A. decision final, for that reason. If not final, to aid Counsel in determining whether to appeal & to help us. (b) To secure benefit of more minds at argument. (c) To secure benefit of more minds in Conference.

I think it would be well to start discussion of this project in the law reviews. You will recall Anderson and B. Hand are for it.

3. My impression is that Shulman is too good in mind, temper, and aspirations to waste on a New York or other law offices. ("Lass den [*]"). Can't you land him somewhere in a law school next fall? You will recall that Yale needs men; and Hamilton thinks that the right man there would find no opposition on the score of anti-Semitism.[4]

4. It seems to me that a great service could be done generally to American law and to the Jews by placing desirable ones in the law school faculties. There is in the Jew a certain potential spirituality and sense of public service which can be more easily aroused and directed, than at present is discernible in American non-Jews. And the difficulty which the Law Schools now have in getting able men may offer opportunities, not open in other fields of intellectual activity. The satisfaction I had in having Page and Friendly with me is a good deal mitigated by the thought of their present activities.[5] Of course it is possible that they, or at least Friendly, may reform and leave his occupation.[6]

It would have been possible to divert Goldsmith from the private practice, but he lacked the qualities which would have made him desirable in a law school, or in any important public service. He is in the Maslon class.

5. That's an admirable statement by Sheldon Glueck[7] re uniform definition of crimes.

[1] Reynolds Robertson, *Appellate Practice and Procedure in the Supreme Court* . . . (New York: Prentice-Hall, 1928).

[2] See 6 September 1929, n. 7.

[3] John Edward Parsons (1903–1976) had graduated from Yale Law School in 1928. After a year

with Chief Justice Taft, he moved to New York where he practiced law, first in Henry L. Stimson's firm, and then independently after 1936.

[4] Harry Shulman did in fact go to Yale after leaving LDB, and eventually became dean there.

[5] Both Robert Page and Henry J. Friendly were in private practice.

[6] For LDB's personal decision to reject teaching and go into private practice, see LDB to Charles Nagel, 12 July 1879 and to Adolph Brandeis, 30 May 1883.

[7] Sheldon Glueck (1896–1980) taught criminology and criminal law at Harvard until 1963, and was particularly expert in the study of juvenile delinquency.

No. 389   October 19, 1929   Washington, D.C.

1. Has Welch Pogue's article in 41 H.L.R.[1] stirred action by any State authorities? Might not a letter of enquiry to State A.G.'s and/or Commissions stir desirable action?

2. The almost unanimous vote of the Senate in favor of a Consumers' Counsel is interesting—32 years after the Dingley Paine performance.[2]

3. I suppose you have seen the Johns Hopkins Institute of Law proposed questionaire on proposed changes in diversity of citizenship (Yntema).[3] They are addressed to counsel in the recent (3 years) case[s] & resemble in character Prof. Bingham's[4] proposals to the Prest's Law Comn.

4. The Mass. Public Utilities Comn. did well in the Edison case.[5]

5. O.W.H. is in great form. Had George Rublee & Joe Cotton for dinner last evening.

6. There is great consternation in high judicial circles over nomination of Hopkins[6] as Kansas D.J. and Watson[7] in Pa., feeling that there is a bowing to political demands of State Senators; and feeling that the A.G. has not been unbending. Hopkins is said to be the very worst, altho State C.J., and Buffington[8] is said to have written the Senate Comtee a letter saying Watson is totally unfit. It is likely something of this will come out from belligerent Senators.

7. Hutcheson was in for a while yesterday. I think I made him realize better the importance of demonstrating the obvious & the need of mass presentation of facts.[9] Of course, no mention was made of your correspondence returned herewith.

8. You will find from the coming disposition of Certioraris that some obsessions continue—altho' there is a tendency to be sparing in granting.

9. The C.J. seemed much better at yesterday's & today's conferences.

[1] The article, which was originally a paper in FF's course in federal jurisdiction, was "State Determination of State Law and the Judicial Code," *Harvard Law Review* 41 (March 1928): 623. Lloyd

Welch Pogue (b. 1899) had graduated from the University of Michigan Law School and, after a year of graduate work at Harvard, practiced first in New York and then in Washington, D.C.

[2] On 17 October the Senate voted to create a Consumers' Counsel to be attached to the legislative branch, to be paid $10,000 per year, and to represent the concerns of consumers before the Tariff Commission. LDB's remark about the "Dingley Paine performance" refers to his own appearance, on 11 January 1897, before the House Ways and Means Committee to testify on the Dingley tariff bill. LDB announced that he had come "to appear on behalf of the consumer," and his testimony was greeted with ridicule and indifference. See Mason, *Brandeis*, 91–92.

[3] Hessel Edward Yntema (1891–1966) taught law at several law schools. He was currently attached to Johns Hopkins and would remain there until he went into government service in 1933. For LDB's opinion of him, see 21 December 1929.

[4] Probably Professor Joseph Walter Bingham (1878–1973), who taught law at Cornell and, for a long period, at Stanford; his special field was maritime law.

[5] On 11 October the Massachusetts Department of Public Utilities refused to approve the company's plan for a stock split, and a week later, announced an investigation into the company's rates.

[6] Richard J. Hopkins (1873–1943) was a Kansas politician and former lieutenant governor of the state. In 1923 he had been appointed to the Kansas Supreme Court, and President Hoover had just nominated him to the District Court for Kansas. He was confirmed on 19 December.

[7] Albert Leisenring Watson (1876–1960) was confirmed as district judge for the middle district of Pennsylvania early in 1930. He had been active in Republican politics in the state and was the son of a state senator.

[8] The Chief Justice of Pennsylvania was Robert Von Moschzisker (1870–1939); Joseph Buffington (1855–1947) had been a circuit court judge for the third circuit since 1906.

[9] See 24 August 1929, n. 2.

No. 390   October 21, 1929   Washington, D.C.

In connection with the investigation by the Prest's Commission on the Causes of Crime, what enquiry is being made into

(a) Blackmailing by gov't officials & bribery of them

(b) The complementary—racketeering.

Both involving pusillanimous submissions or prudent (?) yielding.

Must not the whole question of the "Struggle for Law" by the Community receive consideration?

No. 391   October 22, 1929   Washington, D.C.

FF: I have J.W.M. of 21st with enclosures & copy of deH's of 21st to you.

1. I agree with JWM absolutely that you would be much the best for the F.P.A. meeting [1]—and if not deH. Miss Szold knows too much & can't talk to such an audience. Bob [Szold] knows very little, can't marshal his knowledge & I am sure would not be effective in what is necessarily a contest.

2. I think it important that B.F. be made to see that he & Warburg must take over deHaas. He is indispensable to them & the Cause at this time.

3. B.F. should also be made to see that Warburg personally must provide the money required to finance an appropriate publicity bureau, including deHaas.

4. DeHaas has the qualities of a most valuable aid. He was to Herzl. He was to me. He has been during the past two years to JWM. I am sure B.F. & Warburg would have a like experience with him, if they secured him as aid.

Won't you take up these things with B.F.?

[1] The Foreign Policy Association, in both Philadelphia and New York, scheduled debates on the question of British policy in Palestine; the Zionists were considering who would make the best presentation. FF declined to undertake the assignment on the grounds that it would take too much time to prepare. The Zionists were represented by Maurice Samuel, a well-known author of books on Jewish topics.

No. 392   November 10, 1929   Washington, D.C.

1. I am not surprised at Joe Warren's having to renounce the Acting Deanship.[1] You, of course, recall his breakdown.

2. I guess I am responsible for Butzel J's determination to take "as much time as necessary in writing his opinions." He talked to me of his cleaning up the docket, & I pitched into him hard. Glad to see he is teachable. He did not impress me favorably,[2] & I guess would be glad now, if he had not rejected my advice to get rid of his stock interests.[3] I think he was heavily in General Motors. He gave generally a pervading sense of a low tone prevailing in the Mich. Court.

3. It's fine that your project of working in the Law Schools into Hutcheson's job,[4] is being accepted. Max will have told you of our talk yesterday.

4. Hope R.P. will be exiled to Canada for a while.

5. B.F. has doubtless told you of his & deH's visit here on Nov 5. They were really chummy.[5]

6. Also that Norman Hapgood is to spend 3 weeks in Palestine for Jewish Telegraphic Agency.[6]

7. Alice has gotten Mrs. Shulman attached to Mrs. La Follette as aid on the Senator's biography.[7]

[1] Joseph Warren (1876–1942) had been a member of the Harvard law faculty since 1909. He had been the acting dean once before, in 1925. This time he was appointed in September, but had to resign on 30 October 1929.

²See 27 August 1929.

³ LDB refers, of course, to the catastrophic stock market crash that occurred at the end of October. Within the week, stock prices would reach their nadir and begin the long and slow climb back.

⁴See 24 August 1929, n. 2.

⁵See preceding letter.

⁶Although not himself a Jew, Norman Hapgood was an ardent Zionist.

⁷Belle Case La Follette had begun work on a massive biography of her late husband; she died before she could finish it, and their daughter Fola (with financial help from the Brandeises) completed the two-volume study.

No. 393   November 15, 1929   Washington, D.C.

1. Many thanks for the birthday greeting.[1] Throughout long years you have done very much to make them useful and joyous.

2. Max has handled the crisis with consumate skill.

3. I notice (U.S. Daily Nov. 15/29, p. 11) that Powell is to speak at the Tax Conference on Nov. 21. Could he not take occasion to give currency to the project of having Congress pass a law, which will (by authorizing state taxation that does not discriminate against interstate commerce etc.) prevent the Commerce Clause from operating to create tax discrimination against intrastate commerce in favor of interstate. It may be that there would be most chance of passing it by a simple bill applying only to the Gasoline tax.

4. Ned McClennen, who is a trustee of the Cambridge Savings Bk, is trying to get his Bank to establish an Insurance Department. If Prof. Gay should (without mentioning Ned or me) go into the Bank & indicate to the Prest. et al his interest in promoting Savings Bank Ins. it might be useful.

5. I suppose you have seen the Vanguard Press vol. of O.W.H.'s dissenting opinions.[2] He seemed a little guilty the other day at not having discouraged the publication, but is undoubtedly glad that it is out—as I am.

6. Who is James J. Robinson,[3] the Research Fellow who wrote me a nice birthday letter?

7. Jewish Daily Bulletin Nov. 14/ quotes from "New Palestine" an article by Sidebotham strongly criticizing the British administration.[4]

¹Two days earlier LDB became seventy-three years old.

²Alfred Lief, ed., *The Dissenting Opinions of Mr. Justice Holmes* (New York: Vanguard Press, 1929).

³James Jacquess Robinson (1893–1980) graduated from Harvard Law School in 1919. After teaching at the University of Indiana, he returned to Harvard in 1929 as a research fellow, after which he again taught law in Bloomington until 1941. During the next thirty years, Robinson

accepted a number of special assignments, many of them outside the United States—from 1954 to 1969 he was a justice on the Supreme Court of Libya.

[4] Herbert Sidebotham (1872–1940) was a British journalist who, throughout a long career, remained consistently pro-Zionist and critical of the British administration in Palestine.

No. 394   November 29, 1929   Washington, D.C.

You know how reluctant I was to come out publicly re Palestine. I am glad you thought well of the talk.[1] Magnes' characteristic performance[2] made plain, confident talk seem desirable. It will be difficult to ward off demands and statements. But it seemed necessary to speak out in view of the emergency. And people seem to think it has done good.

As you were responsible for my seeing MacDonald, I think you ought to know that O.W.H. told me Harold L had written him—that Mac-Donald had said "He had been more impressed by me than anyone he had met in America." That opinion may be of some service hereafter.

O.W.H. is in fine form—joyous & enterprising.

[1] LDB's long-awaited public remarks came at a meeting of Jewish leaders—both Zionists and non-Zionists—on 24 November. He spoke briefly, reaffirming his belief in the viability of a Jewish state in Palestine, praising the settlers for their courage in meeting present difficulties, and urging continued support for the Zionist ideal. His talk is reprinted in full in the *New York Times*, 25 November 1929.

[2] Magnes had issued a series of statements regarding Jewish-Arab relations in Palestine. The "performance" LDB mentions here was probably Magnes's long cablegram to the *New York Day*, a Yiddish daily, urging a spirit of cooperation and conciliation and the creation of a genuinely binational state in Palestine.

No. 395   December 2, 1929   Washington, D.C.

1. I have heard no members of the Court say a word about the Survey of 1928 Term.[1] My guess is that Knaebel's[2] suggestion is the result rather of his own timorousness.

2. Upon receipt of yours re Joe Eastman, I talked again to Harlan & he arranged immediately to see HH this afternoon, & I saw him landed at 1 p.m. at the Executive Office. I made clear to him what refusal to appoint would bring in Western attacks. Also talked to G. W. Anderson who is to call up J. L. Richards[3] this evening to stir up Massachusetts friends. (J.L.R. who was here a few weeks ago thought E. was practically safe.) Tom Woodward[4] was in. He has been busy this past 3 weeks getting signatures for E. from the I.C.C. bar—& told me he had about 160 & had deposited these at the White House today.[5]

3. Drew Pearson[6] was in today with Dick Boekel [sic]. I had a thought of saying something about the Joe Cotton article, but concluded it was wiser not to do so.

4. Dont let Ben F. get tired re Palestine.

5. Senator Shipstead asked me Saturday what to read on Equity Practice. I told him he should waste no time, but get, as soon as you could give it, your book or articles on Injunctions.[7] You may already have heard from him. He has not got his strength back yet.

6. You will be interested in No. 60.[8] which goes under another cover.

7. C.C.B. probably told you he tried for me also.

[1] FF and James M. Landis, "The Business of the Supreme Court at October Term, 1928," *Harvard Law Review* 43 (1929): 33. See 21 December 1929.

[2] Ernest Knaebel (1872–1947) was the Supreme Court reporter from 1916 until his retirement in 1943.

[3] James Lorin Richards (1858–1955), was chairman of the board of the Boston Consolidated Gas Co. In that capacity he and LDB met back in 1905 and were able, between them, to arrive at a compromise solution to the great Boston gas fight, a solution that centered on LDB's espousal of the "sliding scale." After that LDB and Richards maintained a great respect for one another.

[4] Thomas Mullen Woodward (1884–1975), a Washington attorney, specialized in transportation law, and had extensive experience with the Interstate Commerce Commission.

[5] Joseph B. Eastman, LDB's old comrade from the Public Franchise league, was reappointed to the Interstate Commerce Commission on 18 December and confirmed the next day.

[6] Drew (Andrew Russell) Pearson (1897–1969) was a young but already experienced reporter, currently on the staff of the *United States Daily*. He developed into one of the country's most colorful and controversial Washington correspondents, most famous for his exposures of political figures and for his column, "Washington Merry-Go-Round."

[7] See 20 December 1927, n. 2, and 20 September 1929, n. 7.

[8] No. 60 was *Railroad Commission of California et al.* v. *Los Angeles Railroad Corporation*, 280 U.S. 145, decided on this date. The company had bound itself by its franchise contracts to a rate of five cents, and now claimed that it was unable to survive at that fare. But in the appeals process the question of state vs. municipal jurisdiction had been debated, and the majority of the Supreme Court decided the issue on that basis. LDB, joined by Holmes, dissented, arguing that the question was one of the franchise contracts, and that the proper course was to remand the case to the trial court for a decision.

No. 396   December 5, 1929   Washington, D.C.

1. The Nation has again gone ignorantly wrong on Palestine.[1] Couldn't it be arranged that it & the N.R. consult Mack or deHaas before blurting out stuff on Palestine?

2. Note enclosed letter to Zimmern returned. I suppose you have some other address to which it may be sent.

3. Don't be misled by Wick's source for his French quotation. It is Moliere not Louis XIII who said that.

4. We had Judge Grubb & daughter[2] in last evening. I have not heard from Max, but guess things must have gone well.

5. To reduce Federal taxes now seems to me not only inadvisable, but reckless. Moreover, this wholesale process of lending is very dangerous. I don't think they have any watchdog like Eugene Meyer in the outfit.

6. No one on our Court thinks of retiring or dying, but Harlan wisely thinks it's time to ponder over possible men for the Court. We lost in Edwin B. Parker[3] one of the best possibilities. Whom besides Cardozo, whom Harlan is keen for, would you suggest?

7. When your men write up the Certs., couldn't they (or somebody else) take in the 14 years since the 1916 Act as to Fed Empl Liability cases granted, & show that it was all futile—besides being unworthy.

8. I am glad you are sending for the Ceylon stuff. Wouldn't it be well to know about Malta also?

9. I assume you recd back (from me) the Savings Bank Ins. proof.

10. Had you seen the enclosed re So. Dist. N.Y. Bankrupcty rules etc. Please let me know what you think of their recommendation?

[1] Perhaps LDB means the editorial paragraph in the *Nation*'s issue of 27 November (p. 613), which contended that "things seem to be getting worse rather than better in the Near East." It urged the Zionists not to depend on England, but to "work out a method of dealing directly with the Arabs."

[2] District Judge William Irwin Grubb (1862–1935) and his daughter Katharine were from Alabama. He was one of the members of Hoover's Commission on Law Enforcement.

[3] Edwin B. Parker (1868–1929) had died on 30 October. A Texas lawyer, he had come to Washington during World War I as a dollar-a-year man and became a member of the War Industries Board. An expert in international law, he served on several important commissions and was a trustee of the Carnegie Endowment for International Peace.

No. 397　　　December 11, 1929　　　Washington, D.C.

1. Obedient to your telegram I called on O.W.H. Hiss was still there. The Justice was in the best of form, rollicking, playful in spirit & entirely without worry of any kind. I concluded he needed no assurance about Hiss.[1]

2. I had not mentioned to Shulman our plans for his teaching until Saturday last—then after he told me of his meeting with Clark at the banquet on the occasion of the honorary degrees given to Bohlen et al the evening before. Shulman had told me Thursday that Bohlen wanted him to attend & wanted to direct him into teaching. I encouraged him to attend the banquet. Saturday he told me Bohlen wanted him to undertake work for the Am. Law Institute. I discouraged that.

3. I agree with you as to S.D.N.Y. Bankruptcy proposals.

4. Warburg was in town on other matters—called me up & came in for a little talk. He is sorely tried by Weiz[mann]., Us[s]his[ch]kin, Lipsky et al.

5. Greene is evidently a doer.[2]

[1] Justice Holmes's clerk for October 1929 term was Alger Hiss (b. 1904), a bright and attractive young graduate from Harvard Law School later to gain notoriety as an alleged communist spy. Justice Holmes had an informal rule that his clerks should not marry. Hiss did not know about that custom and had become engaged to Priscilla Hobson. When informed of the rule, he rushed over to Holmes to confess and ask for mercy. FF, in a panic, asked LDB to go over and help in the negotiations. See next letter.

[2] See 26 September 1929.

No. 398   December 17, 1929   Washington, D.C.

1. Thanks for your special delivery. I have declined to approve the Geller-Peel project.[1]

2. I hope Buxton[2] is right about Eastman,[3] but here there is still great alarm—e.g. on Bob Wool[l]ey's part, who was in yesterday & said he had been working 3 weeks almost exclusively on this—to get support from different parts of the Country into line. I feel, personally, less confident of H.H., since his performance re judges (where he lacked all personal prejudice). I fear he resembles Taft politically, in his lack of resoluteness and political sense.

3. O.W.H. talked to me about Hiss' marriage the other day. I think you had better exact from his next secretary a vow of one year's celibacy.

4. Kirstein brought David Sarnof [sic][4] in—a man of rare intelligence, perception & engaging qualities. If you have not met him, let K. bring him in. I regret his association with Owen Young.

5. Max seemed really troubled last week.

[1] Max Alter Geller (b. 1899) and Roy Victor Peel (1896–1978) were then assistant professors of government at New York University. They had written LDB asking his permission to edit a book of his dissenting opinions. On 12 December LDB had written to FF asking him if he knew anything about the two men and if there were any objections to the project. FF had evidently suggested that LDB not give his approval.

[2] Frank W. Buxton (1877–1974) was a close friend of FF's, and for twenty years editor of the Boston *Herald*.

[3] See 2 December 1929, n. 5.

[4] David Sarnoff (1891–1971), a Russian immigrant, rose from errand boy and wireless operator to become a powerful corporation executive, most notably with the National Broadcasting Company and as chairman of the board of the Radio Corporation of America. In both concerns he was connected with Owen D. Young.

1. October Term 28 Business is grand.[1] If any of my brethren read it thoughtfully, they will find many problems to be solved. I hope that with your enlarged numbers in the seminar you will be able to have made or started, the comprehensive studies of Per Curs. and of Certs. In connection with the former, consideration should be given to what the form of P.C. should be—obviously more should be said than at present. And consideration should also be given as to whether the reasons for denial of a cert. should not be stated in general terms.

2. Yntema was in Monday. I told him (1) that his enquiry[2] should include question whether the whole of D.Ct. jurisdiction based solely on alleged constitutional questions should not be abolished; (2) that questionaire could serve no purpose save to suggest; (3) that ample source for making up his mind exists in the records, briefs & opinions which are accessible to those sufficiently earnest in the enquiry & they should do the work necessary; (4) also spoke to him of improper fed. criminal jurisdiction. He seems to be a nice fellow, but altogether unfitted for the class of work the Johns Hopkins School is setting out to do.

3. I have not seen the Cotton-FF story[3] to which you refer.

4. Cotton was in last week—agreeable, frank, friendly & able. But he seemed to me, so far as appearance discloses, to have suffered severely from his 20 years of N.Y. practice since the Ballinger days.

5. Sorry to hear that Bliven also has not been well. It looks as if he were not as keen as he should be on Savings Bank Insurance; and to its relation to the whole subject of insurance, which is of consequence far greater than that to which the N.R. is giving much space.

6. The stories of banker ineptitude & recklessness are appalling.[4] If the Federal Reserve & the administration had not come to the relief, a number of the most potent banks would have come to grief, & I guess the Natl. City was one.

7. We shall see now what the Great Medicine Man can do to prevent a slump in business.

8. The Lord Hewart book & the Commission[5] show what is possible in England.

9. Tom Walsh says Charlie Michelson[6] is entitled to the credit for resurrecting & uniting the Democrats.

Fredk. A. Stokes Co. seems to have gotten out a new printing of "Other People's Money"—It has a gorgeous golden jacket.[7]

You handled the Van Devanter situation most skilfully—and justly.

[1] See 2 December 1929, n. 1.

[2] See 19 October 1929.

[3] Perhaps the story of Cotton's appointment as under secretary of state; see 29 May 1929, n. 5.

[4] In the wake of the stock market crash.

[5] Gordon Hewart first Viscount Hewart (1870–1943) was the lord chief justice of England. His important book, *The New Despotism* (London: E. Benn, 1929) was a learned and passionate plea against growing English bureaucracy and its effects on administration and law. Lord Hewart had been proposed for membership on a new commission to investigate the prospects for electoral reform in Great Britain. There was an outcry, however, over the propriety of a judicial officer participating in this legislative function and Hewart, after justifying his participation as a peer of the realm, withdrew his name from consideration.

[6] Charles Michelson (1896–1947), an experienced reporter and editorial writer, was the chief Washington correspondent for the New York *World* between 1927 and 1929. That year he became the director of publicity for the Democratic party and he worked in that capacity until 1940.

[7] This was merely a new printing of the 1914 book by LDB. A new edition, with an introduction by Norman Hapgood, would come from Stokes in 1932. Frederick Abbot Stokes (1857–1939) had been associated, since 1881, with the publishing house that later bore his name.

No. 400   January 9, 1930   Washington, D.C.

1. O.W.H. is indeed "to the manner born"—He is presiding with great firmness, alertness and joy.[1] A marked rejuvenescence has been effected; and he is definitely without worry in those unaccustomed duties incident to his new office. It is several years since we have had so good a C.J.

2. Miss Comstock was in yesterday. She was not definite, but it seems there is pretty bad sledding. R.P.'s alibi was indeed ingenuous.[2] But he is naive to think that you can be fooled.

3. I had 1 1/2 hours with Tom Thatcher [sic] and Knox last Friday, which I fear did not increase their joy.[3] I was emphatic that our Court should not approve their domesticating the money changers in the Temple. Also against our approving their employing so undiscriminating a [*] as a 5 years membership in the State Bar. But if they wished to do so on their own responsibility & think they have the power, I do not object to their doing so to meet a local emergency. That is their hunt.

[1] Chief Justice Taft's health grew steadily worse, and on 6 January he was compelled to announce a temporary suspension of his work on the Court. The next day he entered the hospital for a rest. He never took up his duties again and would resign on 3 February. Mr. Justice Holmes, as the senior associate justice, temporarily assumed the duties of chief justice.

[2] It is unclear what matter is being discussed here, but since both Ada Comstock and Roscoe Pound were commissioners on the Wickersham Commission on Crime and Law Enforcement, it may be assumed that some aspect of its work is involved.

[3] Thomas D. Thacher and John Clark Knox were both judges on the District Court for the Southern District of New York. That court was beginning the process of reexamining its rules of practice and procedures, including the appointment of receivers for insolvent businesses. By mid-

year, Knox would be ready, as senior judge, to appoint a committee of lawyers to make formal recommendations. No doubt the pair had come to see LDB in order to have his views at this early stage of their deliberations.

No. 401   January 11, 1930   Washington, D.C.

O.W.H. presided beautifully & calmly at today's conference. Stone says it was the best conference he has attended since coming onto the Court. I have begged H. not to write an opinion tomorrow & he half assented & I guess will refrain.

Stone says Coolidge objected to appointing Cardoza [sic] (whom S. as Atty [General] proposed) because he didn't want two Jews on the bench, that H.H. would not be swayed by that, but might object to putting on another from N.Y.[1]

Stone was very receptive to the suggestions of Newt Baker and Biklé. Said he thought Pa Senators were committed to Von Moschzisker and might kick at B., or anyone else from Pennsylvania on that account.

[1] Stone himself was from New York.

No. 402   January 16, 1930   Washington, D.C.

1. "The Labor Injunction" is an admirable piece of work—the subject vital. I am glad to have my name associated with it.[1] Thanks also for the special copy which came from Cambridge.[2]

2. Philip Kerr called me up last evening to express his and Genl. Smuts[3] regrets that they were unable to see me. Mrs. Massey had talked to Alice about Philip Kerr's coming a fortnight ago, a possible dinner with him and the Masseys at our apartment had been talked of, and P.K. assumed that the invitation had included Genl. Smuts. It was quite as well that I didn't see Smuts. He was very very worn by the endless festivities and no talk with him could have been of value.

3. I think, however, that it would be desirable for you to send to him also copies of Feisal & your letters and a statement of the data in the Weisgal letter.[4]

4. Hope you will have a good day in N.Y. on the 18th.

5. We have very good days with O.W.H. presiding; and a vaudeville show yesterday of case dealing with Fed[eral]. Empl[oyers]. [Liability] Act, an admiralty invading Compensation Act case and an alleged retroactive tax afforded Harlan and me much amusement.[5]

It has been suggest[ed] that Radcliffe students might profitably take as a thesis Jewish & Arab rights in Palestine, instead of German-Polish rights in Silesia, which appears to have occupied one of them who called recently.

[1] FF and Greene's *The Labor Injunction*, which had just appeared, bore this dedication: "To Mr. Justice Brandeis for whom law is not a system of artificial reason, but the application of ethical ideals, with freedom at the core."

[2] LDB received a copy from FF and Greene and another from Macmillan, the publisher.

[3] Jan Christiaan Smuts (1870–1950), the leading statesman of South Africa, visited the United States and Canada in early 1930, made a number of speeches and received an honorary degree from the University of Toronto. Smuts was sympathetic to Zionism and one of his speeches (given on the day this letter was written) was before the Zionist Organization of America. He attacked the policy of the MacDonald government and warned that they could not retreat from the promises of the Balfour Declaration.

[4] See 10 October 1929.

[5] The employers' liability case was *Baltimore & Ohio Southwestern Railroad Co.* v. *Carroll*, 280 U.S. 491; the admiralty case was *Employers' Liability Assurance Corp.* v. *Cook* et al., 281 U.S. 233; and the retroactive tax case was *Cooper* v. *U.S.*, 280 U.S. 409.

No. 403   January 23, 1930   Washington, D.C.

1. Your correspondence with Nutter is interesting.[1] Courage, persistence and militancy are the qualities with which he is not sufficiently endowed. The lack of them has prevented his forty years of public activities—and good common sense—without anything substantial to show in results.

2. You are entirely right in your letter to Monte.[2] The President is primarily to blame, Wick. to blame for yielding to him, and the others for yielding to Wick. Of course, if Wick had had the stuff to say Non possumus[3] all would have been easy. The President would have yielded & all concerned better off. Max has doubtless told you of my talk on Monday to Harlan.

3. There is great danger of H.H. refusing further to act on Mitchell's advice. The breaking point may come. H.H. may conclude to avoid a scandal & fill the first vacancy on our Court by appointing Mitchell.[4] Harlan again started the talk yesterday about judges for our Court— asked i.a. about Parker[5] and Heckinlooper [sic].[6] What do you know of them & how would they compare with Hutcheson?

4. Yes, Evarts Greene is a very satisfactory party.

5. Shulman is evidently not long on decision. He is going through agonies. Was glad to see that you & I agree fully as to this matter.

6. O.W.H. continues to handle the C.J. duties well.[7] But he said yesterday that he will be glad to have the C.J. resume sway.

407

[1] FF had written to Nutter on 15 January, complimenting him on the report Nutter had prepared on "Training for the Bar" for the Massachusetts Bar Association. He called for testing of character as well as for technical knowledge.

[2] On 20 January, FF told Lemann that he had been trying to get Walter Lippmann's support for the Crime Commission for a long time, but to no avail. He and Learned Hand had met with Lippmann, and had done their best to convert him, but the editor had not budged.

[3] "Not possible."

[4] Attorney General William D. Mitchell was never appointed to the Supreme Court.

[5] John Johnston Parker (1885–1958) was a North Carolina lawyer and Republican politician whom Coolidge had appointed a circuit court judge in October 1925. President Hoover nominated Parker to an associate justiceship on the Supreme Court two months after this letter was written. But after a protracted confirmation fight in the Senate, led by representatives of American labor and blacks, the Senate rejected the appointment by a vote of forty-one to thirty-nine.

[6] Smith Hickenlooper (1880–1933), a Harvard Law graduate who practiced in Cincinnati, had become a federal district judge in 1923, and then a judge of the circuit court of appeals in January 1929. He was not nominated to the Supreme Court.

[7] On 19 January LDB had written: "Our acting C.J. is giving Harlan & me much joy & the others are behaving well, so far as treatment of O.W.H. is concerned."

No. 404   January 28, 1930   Washington, D.C.

Re yours 22d

1. It will no doubt be better for you to talk to Howland Shaw.[1]

2. I am very glad Shulman has buttoned up the Yale instructorship. He seems happy now, but needed to be pushed into the water. Your communications, a telegram of confirmation from Bohlen & a further letter from Clark have given him joy.

Re yours 27th

3. I have reported to Harlan on Heckinlooper [sic].

4. There is a persistently recurrent rumor (repeated by Hitz and others) that there is danger that Calvin Coolidge may be appointed to our Court. I can't believe that there is any danger, but should anything be done about it?

5. I don't think deHaas is spending much time on his archeological researches. I told him early in December other things were more urgent. He loves to wander in these historic-literary field[s] & amidst his grilling work and unwellness.[2] He may have gravel[3] & has been confined to the house. I fancy he has gotten rest from his writing.

6. In the New India (British) of Dec. there was an excellent article by Israel Cohen[4] of the character you suggest is most advisable. I wrote Mack suggesting that he have it published in the International Section of The Nation.

7. Hope you have not suffered unduly from R.P.

[1] Gardiner Howland Shaw (1893–1965), a Harvard educated career diplomat, had served in Turkey before becoming chief of the State Department's Division of Near Eastern Affairs.

[2] Besides studies of Herzl (1927) and of LDB (1929), de Haas wrote a book with Rabbi Stephen S. Wise that appeared later in the year denouncing British policy in Palestine, called *The Great Betrayal*. He also edited *The Encyclopedia of Jewish Knowledge* (New York: Behrman's Jewish Book House, 1934) and wrote a history of Palestine (1934).

[3] Kidney stones.

[4] Israel Cohen (1879–1961) was an English Zionist, a prolific writer and editor, and after 1922, secretary to the Zionist Organization of London. His article in *The New India* was not republished in *The Nation*.

No. 405   January 28, 1930   Washington, D.C.

Since writing you this morning I have your second letter of 27th

1. As bearing on Bonbright's[1] letter, you should know this. Last week Harlan told me that he hears that N.Y. financial interests think that Sutherland, Butler & Sanford are not helping them much by their opinions. H. said he didn't know whether that meant that they objected to their decisions or to their lack of reasoning to support them.

Yesterday H. told me that his former partner, Dulles,[2] had just spent an evening with him & that they were very unhappy over the Baltimore opinion,[3] that they fear it might lead to serious trouble, that they thought the prudent investment rule far better than reproduction value, that as to depreciation, the reproduction value rule was simply unworkable, unless it be for occasional use in a law suit & then there was as much chance of losing by it as winning.

All this falls in well with Pagles remark to you and Owen Young's recent expression of opinion, which he has long held. I think N.Y. doesn't like the Los Angeles decision either.[4]

2. I suppose you saw in U.S. Daily of 25th or 27th the I.C.C. proposal in answer to request of Sen. Howell.[5] Reproduction Cost 1914, with actual expenditures since, less depreciation on same basis.

3. I doubt whether I can add anything to what will readily occur to you re Bonbright's enquiry. It might be well to glance over Gerry Henderson's articles.[6] There may be something there not fresh in mind.

4. I am glad to know that Donovan is true to form. He is a continuing source of danger in many fields.

5. I shall try to find out something about Vandenberg.[7] Some things of his impressed me also with his having streaks of liberal insight.

6. Note enclosed letter from Colver's daughter, Mrs. Mark Harris.[8] I have written her that I am asking you to advise her.

7. I am glad Clark liked Shulman's letter. It was practically dictated by me.[9]

8. You will see from enclosed that O.W.H. is doing finely.

[1] James Cummings Bonbright (1891–1985) taught economics and finance at Columbia University. He had written to FF in connection with his work as a member of the New York State Commission on the Revision of Public Utility Laws (see 16 July 1929, n. 1).

[2] John Foster Dulles (1888–1959) had been a partner of Harlan F. Stone's in the New York firm of Sullivan & Cromwell. He would serve at the highest levels of foreign policy formulation and negotiation and in 1953 was appointed by President Eisenhower to be secretary of state.

[3] *United Railways and Electric Co. of Baltimore* v. *West*, 280 U.S. 234, decided on 6 January 1930, once again entered the thorny thicket of valuation in rate-making. The company contended that the rate ordered by the Maryland Public Service Commission for its Baltimore lines was confiscatory. The majority directly attacked LDB's view that prudent investment ought to determine the issue (see 18 July 1927, n. 4). Just compensation, Sutherland argued, must include more than interest on mere investment and to fix it, the courts must use judgment and knowledge of both facts and law. LDB answered this eight-page decision with a thirty-three page dissent (in which he was joined by Holmes); Stone dissented separately, agreeing with LDB but desiring to add a word of his own on the question of depreciation.

[4] For the Los Angeles decision, see 2 December 1929, n. 8.

[5] Robert Beecher Howell (1864–1933) represented Nebraska in the Senate from 1923 until his death.

[6] In 1919 and 1920, Gerard Henderson had written some articles on this topic for *The New Republic*.

[7] Arthur Hendrick Vandenberg (1884–1951) had been a Michigan journalist until appointed, in 1928, to fill a vacancy in the U.S. Senate. He was elected in his own right later in the year, and served until his death. He helped shape America's bipartisan foreign policy after World War II.

[8] William Byron Colver (1870–1926) had been a member of the Federal Trade Commission from 1917 to 1920; but he was best known as a newspaper and magazine magnate, the editor and general manager of the Scripps-Howard chain and of the Newspaper Enterprise Association. His daughter, Polly Anne, had married Mark Harris.

[9] The letter accepting the offer to teach at Yale; see preceding letter.

No. 406   February 6, 1930   Washington, D.C.

1. That's a fine batch of letters about your book.[1]

2. Jack has sent me clipping (Congr. Record) of your good letter to Vandenberg.[2]

3. I hear confidentially that the A.G. is likely to ask Thatcher [sic] to become S.G.[3] It would be a pity to have him leave N.Y.; & probably John Lord O'Brien [sic] or Seth Richardson[4] would be better as S.G.

4. We had a nice call this A.M. from Miss Van Waters.[5] Alice wanted to consult her about the local Juvenile Court situation which is very bad.

5. Yes, Harlan is disappointed.[6] I.a. he had been a staunch supporter of Cardozo for Associate Justice & wants liberal appointments.

6. The heavy drop in commodity prices is, I think, affecting the views of the public utility men on valuation. If it continues, and John

Lord O'Brien & Mitchell attempt to enforce the antitrust law and bring down prices of copper and steel, the companies may become ardent prudent investment advocates.[7]

7. Hope you will land Katz.[8]

[1] See 20 September 1929, n. 7.

[2] FF had written to Senator Arthur Vandenberg on 29 January, in support of the Senator's bill on contempt of court proceedings. The bill was designed to combat the abuse wherein (as in the Craig contempt case) the accusing judge also heard the contempt case. The letter was inserted into *The Congressional Record* for 3 February 1930 (71st Cong; 2nd Sess., 2905).

[3] This information proved correct. Two weeks later Judge Thomas D. Thacher was nominated to be solicitor general to replace Charles Evans Hughes, Jr., who resigned upon his father's nomination as chief justice. Thacher was unanimously confirmed by the Senate, and took up his new duties on 21 April.

[4] Seth Whitley Richardson (1880–1953) was a veteran North Dakota lawyer named assistant attorney general by Hoover in 1929.

[5] Miriam Van Waters (1887–1974) was an experienced social worker, specializing in juvenile delinquency questions and women prisoners. She was currently a staff member for the Wickersham Commission.

[6] No doubt at the nomination of Charles Evans Hughes to be chief justice of the Supreme Court. Taft had submitted his resignation òn 3 February, and on the same day Hoover sent forward the name of Hughes.

[7] For the background of this issue, see 18 July 1927, n. 4. As prices began to fall as a result of the depression, the "replacement cost" of a utility's property declined and became a less attractive base upon which to gauge a fair rate of return. LDB's point is that if prices continued to fall, more utilities would advocate the "prudent investment" base, which was calculated on the original cost of the properties.

[8] Wilber G. Katz "landed," not at Harvard, as FF wished, but at the University of Chicago Law School later this year.

No. 407   February 18, 1930   Washington, D.C.

1. Borah told Harlan yesterday that but for Brookhart's speech, he (Borah) would have put over C.E.H.'s rejection—that he had four pledged, who withdrew, & that if those 4 had voted with him enough others would have followed.[1]

2. We ought to get out of the foray, quickly, the legislation limiting Federal jurisdiction.

I assume you will do the needed advising of the Senators.

3. Prof. John H. Gray attended the debate, missing only Nye's[2] speech. He thinks it the most signif[ic]ant debate since Jackson's days. Says Sen. George[3] did better than any one else.

4. It looks as if a lot of men were finding out R.P.

[1] Hughes's nomination encountered immediate opposition in the Senate from progressives like Borah, Glass, Norris, La Follette, Nye, Blaine, and others. They objected to the fact that he had resigned from the High Court in order to seek the presidency in 1916, and, echoing a charge often

made by LDB in letters to FF, that he had become a high-priced corporation lawyer devoted to defending business corporations. On 13 February, Hughes was confirmed in the Senate by a vote of fifty-two to twenty-six. And on the next day LDB wrote to FF: "What you say of the effect of self-righteousness is probably true. But the total effect will doubtless be good. And the struggle was a worthy manifestation of reviving manhood." Senator Smith Brookhart spoke against the nomination on 13 February.

[2] Gerald Prentice Nye (1892–1971) was a North Dakota progressive editor, appointed to the Senate in November 1925 to fill a vacancy and subsequently elected three times. He was best known for his investigation of the role of the munitions makers in causing World War I, and for his sponsorship of neutrality legislation before World War II.

[3] Walter Franklin George (1878–1957) had come up through the Georgia judicial system and was an associate justice of the state's supreme court in 1922, when he resigned to run successfully for the Senate. He served there until 1951.

No. 408   February 20, 1930   Washington, D.C.

1. Re yours of 18th. Of course, I appreciate Clark's and Hamilton's willingness to have Yale give me an L.L.D.[1] But actions taken by me in recent years precludes acceptance. U. of Wisconsin made me several tentative offers which, upon consideration, I declined. It seemed—and still seems to me—that a member of our Court had better decline the gift of honor as he would gifts of less valued material things. I hope that when we have a chance to talk over this matter, as we do other things, you will agree with me.

2. The provision in Longshoreman's & Harbor Workers' Act, §21b (44 Stat 1436): "The order of the Court allowing of any such stay" etc. is a better limitation than that of the Clayton Act & might be taken as a model for legislation limiting injunctions in labor cases & under §266 of the Jud. Code.[2]

3. Glad to know Norman Angell[3] will write.

4. C.C.B. seems to agree with you re C.E.H.

[1] See 27 February 1929, n. 5.

[2] See 31 May 1927, n. 6. The act that LDB quotes from was passed in March 1927 and designed to provide workers' compensation for various maritime employees. The passage he cites reads: "The order of the court allowing any such stay shall contain a specific finding, based upon evidence submitted to the court and identified by reference thereto, that such irreparable damage would result to the employer, and specifying the nature of the damage." LDB regarded this provision as more satisfactory than the more general limitation on injunctions in §266 of the Judicial Code.

[3] Norman Angell (1872–1967) was a well known English writer and lecturer with wide experience in the United States, and a frequent contributor to *The New Republic*. LDB and FF were eager to get him to write on Zionism, and Angell obliged with a pro-Zionist article in the 11 April edition of *New Palestine*.

No. 409   February 23, 1930   Washington, D.C.

1. That's excellent advice you gave Max on the 19th.

2. O.W.H. laid down his burdens this noon, after a few happy words of goodbye to the old C.J. & of greeting to the new. He seemed very happy as we went home together.

3. Manton's Sparkhill [sic] Realty decision, which we reversed via Sutherland J, was a monstrous rape of jurisdiction.[1] He should be pilloried.

4. And the N.R. & World should lambast H.H. for his "curbing appropriations" today after his reckless (or worse) cut of the corporation's tax.[2]

[1] The case was *White* v. *Sparkill Realty Corp.*, 280 U.S. 500, decided by a unanimous Court on 24 February. The company owned some land in the jurisdiction of the Southern District of New York which the state appropriated for public and state park purposes. The company sued for an injunction in a federal court. The district court (Judge Manton writing for the two other judges—because Section 266 of the Judicial Code required a three-judge hearing before such an injunction could issue) granted the injunction. The Supreme Court ruled that there was adequate remedy at law by ejectment, and that such an action should be brought in a state court.

[2] President Hoover's call for strict economy came in a message to a conference of treasury and congressional leaders. Unless economy measures were adopted, he threatened, it might be necessary to increase taxes by as much as 40 percent.

No. 410   March 2, 1930   Washington, D.C.

1. Your report on the Research Fellowship is most satisfactory.

2. Tom Thatcher [sic] will have to make a very good S.G. to justify his retiring.[1]

3. C.E.H. Jr. did not make good.

4. The new C.J. made an excellent record in his first week, including the conference.

5. Gov. Roosevelt did a good job in appointing Maltbie,[2] of which Eastman advises me.

6. As to No. 45.[3] I guess it was as O.W.H. reports from the S.J.C. [of Massachusetts]. There were other more objectionable things which attracted attention & were eliminated.

7. If the N.R. has a man competent to do it, there should be a contrast drawn—of H.H. busting the Stevenson plan,[4] and of his quiescence at the Copper Trust bleeding Europe, incidentally keeping up prices with the aid of shutting down domestic mines, while receiving large imports from Chili.

8. Glad to hear that Lehman J. is also on Govt. Lawlessness.[5]

9. I suppose you are noting persistent decline in commodity prices. Probably the fall in silver is the most significant.[6]

10. The Sparkhill [sic] decision was worse than "absurd."[7]

11. We had Judge Healy[8] in & were very favorably impressed.

12. Yes that is a very knowing Kiplinger letter.[9]

[1] See 6 February 1930, n. 3.

[2] Milo Roy Maltbie (1871–19[?]) was one of the country's leading experts on public utility regulation. Franklin Roosevelt had just named him chairman of the New York State Public Service Commission.

[3] No. 45 was *Tagg Bros.* v. *U.S.*, 280 U.S. 420, decided on 24 February with LDB reading the opinion for a unanimous Court. The secretary of agriculture had fixed maximum commissions for those buying and selling cattle in interstate commerce at the Omaha stockyards—in accordance with the Packers and Stockyards Act of 1921. The brokers brought suit to enjoin the order's enforcement, claiming that their commissions were not subject to regulation by the Act, that the Act was in other ways unconstitutional, and that the new rates were confiscatory. LDB and the Court upheld the government on every point.

[4] The Stevenson Plan was a British government measure to support artificially the price of rubber (on behalf of the colonial growers) by rigidly restricting production.

[5] Irving Lehman (1876–1945) had been elected to the state's supreme court in 1908, and served there until 1924 when he was nominated by both parties for the state court of appeals. In 1937 he was again nominated by both parties, and he served as chief justice of the court from 1940 until his death. Three days earlier he had delivered a speech before the New York State Bar Association decrying police methods.

[6] The price of silver plummeted, reaching new lows on 5 January, 7 January, 24 February, and 4 June 1930.

[7] See preceding letter, n. 1.

[8] Perhaps Robert E. Healy (1883–1946), a Vermont lawyer who had been both a judge of the U.S. Court of Customs Appeals and an associate justice of Vermont's Supreme Court until his resignation in 1915. From 1928 to 1934 he was chief counsel of the Federal Trade Commission and then was appointed to the new Securities and Exchange Commission.

[9] Willard Monroe Kiplinger (1891–1967), an Ohio journalist, specialized in business and finance. In 1923 he began to issue the "Kiplinger Letters," highly regarded analyses of current business trends. He also founded the magazine *Changing Times* in 1947.

No. 411   March 8, 1930   Washington, D.C.

1. The S.G. was well prepared in the Patton Case,[1] but he argued that—as he has others—like a law student, without the sure touch of an experienced advocate, the antithesis of Mitchell. His main defect has been in administration. The briefs have not been ready in time; they are not as good as in the Mitchell days; and one lacks the sense that the Court may comfortably lean on the S.G.'s judgment.

2. I have little knowledge of Bond C.J., but the impression given by his performance in the Baltimore case is that he would be distinctly undesirable.[2]

3. You doubtless noticed that Fed. Empl. Liability cert are not in favor with the New Regime.

4. I don't think Harlan knows much about what's in H.H.'s mind judicially or otherwise.

5. O.W.H. is in the pink of condition & spirits.

6. Harlan referred to power being projected as the great coming issue & H.H. not leading & possibly on the wrong side. He evidently thinks that H.H. lacks the political mind.

7. Claude Branch,[3] the S.G.'s chief aid, has done increasingly well. He is thoroughly prepared and his arguments are growing steadily better. They were, at first, heavy & tiresome.

8. It's good to have R.P. frank. Where will you place Katz?[4]

9. Alfred Cohn dined with us Wednesday.

10. Glad to hear of your talk to Yale faculty.[5]

[1] *Patton* v. *U.S.*, 281 U.S. 276, was argued on 25 February. During a trial one of the jurors got sick and could not continue to serve. Both sides agreed to waive their rights to a trial by twelve jurors so that the trial might continue. The defendants were found guilty and promptly appealed on the grounds that they really had no power to waive their constitutional right to a trial by twelve jurors. The Court disagreed. The case was argued by Solicitor General Charles Evans Hughes, Jr., who had already announced his resignation in view of his father's appointment as chief justice. The father had been sworn in the day before the case was heard, but, of course, recused himself.

[2] Chief Justice Carroll Bond of Maryland was not nominated to the Supreme Court.

[3] Claude Raymond Branch (1886–1978) had graduated from Harvard Law in 1911 and set up practice in Providence, Rhode Island. He came to Washington in 1929 to work in the Justice Department, but after 1935 returned to private practice.

[4] See 6 February 1930, n. 8.

[5] In 1930 FF delivered the Dodge Lectures at Yale, subsequently published as *The Public and Its Government* (New Haven: Yale University Press, 1930).

No. 412   March 10, 1930   Washington, D.C.

1. When we were considering the possibility of a new Justice, a successor to Sanford was not in our minds.[1] I suppose H.H. will not be so quick on the trigger this time.[2]

2. I guess Sapiro will not be wanted by anybody for P.

3. O.W.H. had finished by this A.M. answers to all letters received before today,[3] leaving many to Hiss. He has borne the judicial deaths[4] well, performing his part in adjourning the Court, with his usual dignity.

4. Enclosed from the Phil. Tribune (Negro) followed an editorial of a week earlier, reproducing from April 1/29, my unemployment statement.[5] This shows manly enlightenment on the negros' [sic] part.

5. Glad you have Hart for next year.[6]

6. The World under W.L. is acting very differently than it did 25 years ago, when the "What is Equitable" editorials stirred the country.[7]

7. Morris L. Cooke was in yesterday, returning from Fla. He is delighted with Frank Roosevelt & the Malt[b]ie appointment, & Bonbright's for their fitness.[8]

The bill retd. herewith.

Walton Hamilton is coming in today.

[1] Justice Edward T. Sanford died unexpectedly on 8 March 1930. He had served the Court for seven years.

[2] When Taft resigned as chief justice, Hoover announced the nomination of Charles Evans Hughes on the same day. The scalding that Hughes got in the Senate (see 18 February 1930, n. 1) made the president more cautious. This time he would wait two weeks before announcing his choice, John J. Parker. But even the delay did not help and Parker was rejected by the Senate (see 23 January 1930, n. 5).

[3] Holmes's eighty-ninth birthday was on 8 March.

[4] On the same day that word came of Sanford's death, former Chief Justice William Howard Taft also died.

[5] On 1 April 1928, LDB wrote a letter to Clarence Henry Howard, president of the Commonwealth Steel Co. of St. Louis. The letter was an eloquent plea for regularity of employment, something LDB had advocated for more than a quarter of a century. "For the Commonwealther who 'is steady in his work,' there shall be steady work," the statement began. LDB went on to argue that regularity in employment was just as important as regularity in the payment of interest on bonds. No business which fails to provide this security to its workers, he concluded, "is socially solvent." The statement was published on the front page of the April 1929 issue of the *Survey Graphic*, and LDB hoped it would attract more attention as the unemployment rate soared in the early 1930s. See 24 March 1930.

[6] FF had secured Henry Melvin Hart, Jr. (1904–1969) to serve as LDB's clerk for the 1930–1931 year. After his clerkship, he returned to Harvard to teach legal history and law for many years, becoming Dane Professor of Law in 1960. In the late 1930s Hart worked in the Justice Department for a short period.

[7] LDB refers to the dozens of editorials that the crusading New York *World* published in the famous exposure of the Equitable Life Assurance Society in 1905. That exposure had a major effect on LDB, who was drawn to the cause of insurance reform.

[8] See 28 January, n. 1, and 2 March 1930, n. 2.

No. 413   March 12, 1930   Washington, D.C.

As to Howland Shaw: [1]

1. I think he ought to be made to understand the Zionist question. I was told Shaw was bitten with the pro-Arab argument of the self-determination & other "liberal" doctrine.

2. If you have additional names of desirables for U.S.S.C. produce them.

3. The decrease in factory employment figures is worse than the N.R.

figures indicate.[2] They make no allowance for the annual increase in population.

[1]See 28 January 1930.

[2]"Exploiting the Unemployed," *New Republic* 62 (12 March 1930): 85.

No. 414   March 17, 1930   Washington, D.C.

1. I hear that considerable pressure is being brought to secure Parker's nomination for U.S.S.C. & that he is being seriously considered.[1] Would it not be well for you to get to some of insurgents via Max [Lowenthal] or otherwise, the objections to him?

2. Walton R. Moore told us yesterday that Harding had about determined to appoint Henry W. Anderson[2] for the vacancy later filled with Sanford; & was deflected from Anderson only by Glass' emphatic declaration that he would stoutly oppose & that Swanson when communicated with, said he would back Glass in opposing.

3. Walton Moore is much disturbed by the bill for the regulation of interstate busses; thinks it is a railroad measure; that it will throw the motors into R.R. control; thereby greatly increasing federal power; and adding to the burdens of the I.C.C. That means a great deal, coming from him, who so long was counsel for the RRs. He says bill as reported does not follow the Comn's recommendations, which were to leave supervision largely to the State commissions. The opposition to this bill should be stirred up.[3]

The Redlichs are coming in 4 P.M. tomorrow.

[1]See 23 January 1930, n. 5.

[2]Henry Watkins Anderson (1870–1954) was a prominent Richmond, Virginia, attorney and a former candidate for state governor.

[3]After considerable debate and amendment, House Bill 10288 was returned to the Interstate Commerce Committee for further study.

No. 415   March 24, 1930   Washington, D.C.

1. Gus Hand was in yesterday. Says they are much disappointed by selection of Parker—thinks Denison or Dietrich would have been better if C.C. judge to be appointed;[1] and, of course, it should have been Cardozo.

2. Mabel Willebrand[t] was in the day before. Also thought it should have been Cardozo; but thinks well of Parker. She says he is "a liberal

conservative like Justice Stone." She also said that there was real danger of James D.J.[2] being appointed or another as bad. Mrs. Willebrand[t] had urged H.H. originally to appoint Parker Att. Gen. She thinks Mitchell is having an unhappy time and is not doing well as A.G.

She says Wick all wrong about Prohibition enforcement—that situation has worsened because of uncertainty as to who would administer.

3. Glad you had so good a day at Albany.

4. Things look pretty bad at London. I guess Morrow & George have some regrets at having left Mexico—and it looks as if Morrow might lose his primary election.[3]

5. Every one here talks very blue about H.H.'s performances. Surely the Huston episode[4] must be very hurtful. His & Barnes' persistent returning prosperity talk is becoming tiresome. The fact is, the whole world is suffering & the constant decline in commodity prices can't be helped by H.H.'s talks.

I am enclosing the page from April/29 Survey Graphic with my "Right to Work" statement. Couldn't the N.R. be induced to take that position & talk persistently on it? Or if not the N.R., the Nation or The New Freeman?[5] If W.L. really cared, The World might do it.

[1] President Hoover, on 11 March, had announced that he would fill Sanford's seat on the Supreme Court from among the circuit court judges. He passed over both Arthur C. Denison and Frank Sigel Dietrich (1863–1930), a ninth circuit judge since 1926, in order to nominate John J. Parker (see 23 January 1930, n. 5).

[2] William Parry James (1870–1940), a California attorney, had been appointed to the District Court for the Southern District of California in 1923.

[3] Dwight W. Morrow, ambassador to Mexico, and George Rublee, his legal advisor (and LDB and FF's close friend), left their duties in Mexico City to attend the London Naval Conference. Morrow was a delegate and Rublee, an advisor to the delegation. Morrow had also filed for the Republican senatorial nomination from New Jersey. Despite stiff opposition from the drys, Morrow would win the Republican primary handily on 17 June, and the general election in November. He died in October 1931. The London Conference was a sequel to the Washington Conference at the beginning of the decade, designed to further the course of naval reduction. The work of disarmament ended, however, with the Japanese invasion of Manchuria in 1931.

[4] Claudius Hart Huston (1876–1952), the chairman of the Republican National Committee, had been a Tennessee businessman and Hoover's assistant in the Department of Commerce in the early 1920s. While he was president and treasurer of the Tennessee River Improvement Association, he had accepted a donation of $36,000 from the Union Carbide Co., and, it was later revealed, he used the money to speculate on margin buying on the stock exchange. There were insistent and vocal calls for his resignation, but he refused to give in, thereby incurring the ire of the Hoover administration. Finally, Huston succumbed to the pressure and resigned on 7 August. See 26 May 1930.

[5] See 10 March 1930, n. 5. None of these periodicals reprinted the statement.

No. 416   March 26, 1930   Washington, D.C.

If 5 Justices were consulted about the openings [on the Supreme Court] I think it safe to say O.W.H., Harlan & I were not among the number. Harlan has repeated to me what he said to H.H. about Parker—that he had handed him a memo more than a year ago, re P's becoming A.G.; that H.H. spoke recently to him & Harlan answered he didn't know any more than was contained in the memo; that HH asked him what I thought of P. & Harlan answered that I didn't seem to have a very pronounced opinion, but was inclined to think he would not prove liberal; that he (Harlan) had not recommended him. H. never mentioned Mi[t]chell's talking to him on the subject or that he (Harlan) had read P's opinions.

H.H. asked me in March 1929, when he was seeking a head, & others, for the Crime Comn.[1] what I thought of Parker. I told him then he seemed a laboring, conscientious judge, judging from the few opinions that came before us, but I hadn't even the impression of striking qualities.

The slight mention of P. by my brethren at the last conference, did not disclose or indicate that any one of them had been consulted.

I have been reminded of late, in several connections, that "Hell is paved with good intentions."

[1] See 17 March 1929.

No. 417   April 1, 1930   Washington, D.C.

1. It is not true that H.H. spoke to me about the C.J. ship. He never mentioned the subject, nor did he ever mention C.E.H. to me. When I saw him about two months ago, we talked for an hour about possibilities for the Court, but I assumed it was about side judges. Parker was not mentioned then. Our interview closed with his saying: "Well, if I should nominate Cardozo or Owen Roberts, it would not lessen the dignity and efficiency of the Court."

2. Dean Acheson was in yesterday. I think he had something to say about Parker, but other people present prevented. I think you might elicit what he had in mind, if "innocent like"—and without mentioning me in any way—you enquired whether he knows anything about P.

3. Dean told two things about HH which were interesting. (a) His friend Louis [sic] Douglas[1] & wife were at Clemenceau's country place in Sept. about a fortnight, because D's father was an intimate friend &

C. wanted to see the son before he died.[2] D. used to see C. daily about an hour. On one occasion he asked C. what he thought of our President. C answered: "He has one terrible lack—an essential of a good ruler. He lacks courage."

(b) Ned Burling has been campaigning with Ruth McCormick[3] & is just back. He says folk there think H.H. the greatest failure of any President—not excluding Taft.

4. The little that is in the Washington papers concerning Shaw report is very disconcerting.[4]

5. This about HH has disturbed me. Eastman says that when he called on the President shortly after the reappointment, HH said: "There never was any doubt about your renomination."[5]

[1] Lewis Williams Douglas (1894–1974) was the son of a wealthy Arizona copper magnate and banker, James Stuart Douglas (1868–1949). The son inherited the business interest of his father and also developed a political and diplomatic career. He was currently representing Arizona in the House of Representatives. From 1947 to 1950 he would be United States ambassador to Great Britain—while his friend Dean Acheson was secretary of state.

[2] George Clemenceau (1841–1929), the French statesman and wartime premier, died on 24 November 1929.

[3] Ruth Hanna McCormick was the Republican candidate for the Senate from Illinois. She lost by 700,000 votes in the November election.

[4] A British Inquiry Commission, headed by Sir Walter Shaw, had sailed for Palestine in October 1929, in order to investigate the growing conflicts between Arabs and Jews. It issued its findings in March 1930, and LDB and the other Zionists were angered by its report. The majority of the Commission blamed the recent riots on the conflict between Jewish and Arab national aspirations and on confusing British policies. It recommended reduced immigration of Jews and a clear divorce between government in Palestine and the Zionist organization. In general Arabs praised the report, and Zionists regarded it as an exoneration of the rioters. On 3 April LDB wrote to FF: "Yes the Commission's report is very disappointing & it's un-British and defeatist. I trust it will be bracing to our Jews. The last clause of the Tribune editorial embodies the great truth—'But the ultimate answer will be written in the relative vitality and actuality of the two nationalisms now face to face upon the ground.'" See also LDB to Julian W. Mack, 5 April 1930.

[5] See 2 December 1929, n. 5.

No. 418   April 15, 1930   Washington, D.C.

1. Glad you had satisfactory talk with Howland Shaw.[1]

2. Assume you wrote J.W.M. re consulship.[2]

3. There is ample material available to support the Weizmann statements marked in N.P. article retd. herewith.

I suggest you ask B.F. to get the article written & published. It is a thing which should emanate from the Warburg entourage.

4. Harlan said to me today that the day before P[arker]'s nomination

he told H.H., in answer to H.H.'s enquiry as to what I thought, that I believed he might have serious trouble from the labor end & that he (Harlan) advised H.H. to look into the matter thoroughly before acting.

5. I haven't seen Swisher's study.[3] He asked me to look it over, but thought it better I should not do so. He is a fine fellow, I think.

6. Glad to have the H.L.R. with the portrait, L.H.'s piece, et al.[4]

7. It's fine that the Dodge Lectures started in so well.[5]

[1] See 12 March 1930.

[2] Perhaps relating to rumors that the American counsel general to Jerusalem, Paul Knabenshue (1883–1942), was about to resign (see 30 April 1930). Knabenshue was not regarded as sympathetic to Jewish interests in Palestine (and when the riots broke out in 1929 he cabled the State Department that "Moslem attacks were precipitated by provocative acts of the Jews."). He did not leave Palestine until 1932.

[3] Carl Brent Swisher (1897–1968), the noted constitutional historian, was at this time an instructor in government at Columbia University. He had just published *Stephen J. Field, Craftsman of the Law* (Washington: The Brookings Institution, 1930).

[4] The April 1930 issue of the *Harvard Law Review* contained a facsimile of Charles S. Hopkinson's portrait of Oliver Wendell Holmes. The illustration was to accompany the publication of Learned Hand's address, "Mr. Justice Holmes," (at 857) delivered on 20 March at the presentation of the portrait to the School.

[5] See 8 March 1930, n. 5.

No. 419   April 16, 1930   Washington, D.C.

1. Couldn't you get the N.R. and/or The Nation and the Living Age to reprint Norman Angell's article in April 11 New Palestine.[1]

2. The World (& all others available) should make a terrible scream over Director of Census statement in U.S. Daily of today, p. 1, about postponing for a year unemployment figures.[2]

This is a blind to keep these figures out of the 1930 campaign.

3. Gov. Roosevelt should be prepared to pounce upon Hoover at the end of the 60 days (? early May) when H.H. said all unemployment trouble would be over.[3]

4. I suppose you noticed drop in copper from 18 to 14 cents yesterday.

[1] Norman Angell, "A Liberal Interprets Zionism," *New Palestine* 18 (11 April 1930): 238. Angell contended that the Jews had long ties to Palestine, and deserved the opportunity to develop there. None of the magazines LDB suggests here reprinted the article.

[2] Within a week, Secretary of Commerce Lamont issued a clarifying statement: a special bureau would expedite the reporting of national unemployment figures.

[3] The statement, one of President Hoover's attempts to encourage the performance of the American economy by issuing optimistic prophecies, was made on 7 March 1930; see *New York Times*, 8 March 1930.

1. Please send to Lowell Mellett copies of the Feisal correspondence [1] together with your statement as to how it came about, saying you do so at my request.

In view of hostile American liberal press, I thought it advisable to enlighten the Scripps-Howard Press & asked Mellett to come in yesterday. Happily Parker of N.Y., the Scripps Editor in Chief,[2] was in town; so he was present at our talk.

I omitted to mention to them the Feisal correspondence. I gave Mellett a copy of Norman Angell's article and the Manchester Guardian clipping which you had sent me.

2. You seem to have had a field day at New Haven.

3. H.H.'s troubles with our Court seem to grow no less. It would be very unfortunate if Parker appeared before the Comtee.[3]

4. W.L.'s absence seems very fortunate.[4]

5. The C.J. continues to handle himself very well.

6. Wouldn't it be advisable to have one of your seminar make a careful study of Dist. Ct. of Appeals (say during last 10 years) & show the increasing importance of the jurisdictions & its persistent wrongness?

There is an effort to add new judges; highly desirable if good selections are made.

[1] See 10 October 1929, n. 1.
[2] George Bertrand Parker (1886–1949) had worked in Oklahoma and Ohio journalism before assuming, in 1927, the post of editor in chief for the nineteen newspapers in the Scripps-Howard chain. In 1936, Parker won the Pulitzer Prize for editorial writing.
[3] In view of the mounting criticism of his stands on labor and race issues, Judge John Parker offered to testify before the Senate Judiciary Committee. In the end, Parker explained his views in a letter to the Committee, but by that time the Committee had reported adversely by a vote of ten to six.
[4] During this period Walter Lippmann made annual tours to Europe.

1. You seem to have captured New Haven completely.[1] How Lowell et al would rejoice if you yielded to Yale's blandishments.

2. Jewish Daily Bulletin April 29, p. 12 reports that Knabenshue will resign as Consul & is returning to U.S. to establish an American-Palestine Bank.[2]

3. Be on the watch for 454. Corp Com. of Okl. v. Lowe. Sequel to the Frost Case.[3] It will deserve writing up. Counsel for Comn. stated

incidentally that effect of Frost Case (followed by 454) was to paralyze the hopeful co-op movement in gins in Okl.—that 100 which had been started with investment of $3,000,000 were lying idle & deteriorating.

A letter to E. S. Ratliff,[4] who appeared as counsel for the Comn. (& said he had been for 10 years) would elicit the facts.

4. V.D. & others here thinks [sic] chances on Parker are about even.[5]

[1] With FF's Dodge lectures; see 8 March 1930, n. 5.

[2] See 15 April 1930, n. 2.

[3] *Corporation Commission of Oklahoma* v. *Lowe*, 281 U.S. 431, had been argued the day before, and would be decided on 19 May with Chief Justice Hughes speaking for a unanimous Court. William Lowe operated cotton gins in Oklahoma City. When he learned that the state's Corporation Commission was about to license a rival ginning operation, to be operated on a cooperative plan, he sought an injunction, claiming "unfair competition." Cooperatives were required to return a portion of their profits to their customers and therefore could conduct business on a more favorable basis than his own operation. The Court responded that no law or regulation prohibited Lowe from also distributing rebates to his customers; therefore there was no unfair competition, and no injunction should issue.

In *Frost* v. *Corporation Commission of Oklahoma*, 278 U.S. 515 (1929), Sutherland spoke for the majority, and LDB (joined by Holmes and Stone) entered a long dissent. The majority ruled that a license to operate a cotton gin was akin to a public utility franchise, and thus a property right. To get such a license, the applicant had to demonstrate need; but the law allowed a cooperative gin, when supported by 100 signers, to be excused from the needs provision. The majority held that the immunity granted to cooperatives, but not to private individuals, violated the equal protection clause of the Fourteenth Amendment.

[4] Edgar Samuel Ratliff (1880–19[?]) had been born in Tennessee, but came to the Oklahoma Territory in 1904. A minor Democratic politician, he was finishing his term as attorney for the state's Corporation Commission.

[5] See 23 January 1930, n. 5.

No. 422   May 1, 1930   Washington, D.C.

1. Now that the performance of the U.S.S.C. has become a matter of general professional interest, would it not be desirable to establish the precedent of having in the Harvard Law Review, after the retirement of each of the performers from the stage, a worthy estimate of his judicial performance? I suggest beginning in the 1930–31 Review with Taft, following with Sanford & thereafter regularly, as each actor departs.[1] It would educate lawyers & lay foundation for press notices.

2. If you have any men competent for the task, would it not be wise to have them work out prior to the next session of Congress, article & bills for restoring, so far as Congress has powers so to do, to the States the powers to deal, by way of regulation and taxation, with foreign corporations?[2]

3. The World is doing a good job.

[1] No article appeared in the *Harvard Law Review* on either Taft or Sanford.

[2] See Henry Rottschaefer, "State Jurisdiction of Income for Tax Purposes," *Harvard Law Review* 44 (May 1931): 1075. See also, in the same issue, (at 1111), a brief anonymous note: "Compulsory Incorporation and the Power to Tax."

No. 423   May 2, 1930   Washington, D.C.

1. Re Beard's letter of 27th just recd. with yours of 1st.

I have no idea who (if any one) is getting out a collection of my dissenting opinions. I wrote those N.Y. University folk that I couldn't consent to that.[1]

I did give Alfred Lief[2] (and the Vanguard Press) liberty to use extracts from my opinions, in a book Lief is compiling which is to be entitled "The Social and Economic Views of Mr. Justice Brandeis." It is possible that Beard may be referring to that.[3] James Henle[4] offered some time ago to submit the M.S. to me when completed. I told him I did not want to see it.

2. Your "Labor Injunction" is making a deep impression.[5]

3. I think the rumor that Experimental College will close is unfounded, a misinterpretation of a remark of Prest. Frank's made two years ago.[6]

[1] See 17 December 1929.

[2] Alfred Lief (1901–1972) had compiled the dissenting opinions of Justice Holmes (see 15 November 1929). He also wrote other books including a biography of George W. Norris and a full-length study of LDB: *Brandeis: The Personal History of an American Ideal* (New York: Stackpole Sons, 1936).

[3] Vanguard brought the book out in 1930. When it appeared it contained a brief "Foreword" written by Charles Beard.

[4] James Henle (1891–1973), president of Vanguard Press, was a Louisville native, related by marriage to Bernard Flexner. See in connection with the Lief book LDB to Henle, 10 February 1930.

[5] See 20 September 1929, n. 7.

[6] Alexander Meiklejohn's "Experimental College" at the University of Wisconsin was not closed.

No. 424   May 8, 1930   Washington, D.C.

1. In the defeat of Parker[1]—or rather of H.H.—you have played an important part, through The World and otherwise.

2. G. W. Anderson says: "Parker is a victim of the unpopularity of the Supreme Court." The Baltimore case[2] was the last straw. And Taft's death removed the protection afforded by a widely loved personality.

Thanks partly to the new C.J., his former allies are much chastened—in manner, at least.

3. Directly, Organized Labor has doubtless gained most by the encounter. It has, at last, reasserted itself; should be encouraged to activity & wider assertion in its demand; ought now to get rid of the yellow dog contract;[3] and also otherwise make inroads on "Government by Injunction."

4. The Negro also has moved a step forward.[4]

5. And, of course, the Progressives of both parties.

6. Poor H.H. cuts a pitiable figure. It is truly pathetic. And he was hoist by the errors of his guardians—Dixon, Newton, Mitchell.[5]

7. Yes, Mitchell's figure is [a] sad one. And he, himself, must be very unhappy.

8. Hoover's part in furthering the stock boom is understated in the The [sic] World Editorial.[6] The worst boosts came after his inauguration.

9. You will recall my severest count against his social-economics is his silence re unemployment, during the technological advance, 1921–1929.

10. I am glad of Paul Kellogg's[7] reference to me re Swarthmore Institute, because I had a most serious difference of opinion with Paul Douglas (of whom I have a very high opinion) as to what Swarthmore should do.[8] He wants the Institute to cover the whole field of Unemployment, with candles burning in all seven branches of the subject. I think they should concentrate on "Irregularity in Employment," and let other institutions deal with the other branches. I reported our talk to M.L. Cooke,[9] but have not heard what has been decided.

11. Poor Max [Lowenthal] is having a sad time. Monte [Lemann] was in yesterday. I advised his telephoning you, which he said he would do. I told Eleanor today that only this is clear & beyond debate. Max should decide nothing now. He is not in a fit state to do so. He should take her & the children (or she him and them) to the farm immediately and forget about the Commission completely until he is entirely fit.[10]

12. I think C.A. Beard must have misunderstood what the Vanguard book is to be. They doubtless told him that in format it is to be like "The Dissenting Opinions" of O.W.H. But I understood from Lief's letter etc. that "The new book will aim to present those aspects of your Economic (and social) beliefs which are unfolded in opinions, both majority and minority (and otherwise).["] I am sorry to hear that he was

not "accurate or well-balanced in his editorial work on Holmes' "Dissenting Opinions." He merely asked permission "to garner your words from the Reports." That he was, of course, free to do; & I preferred to take a chance of what he would do, than to take the responsiblity of examining his M.S.—I have never seen him.

13. Note from Mellett & clipping enclosed.

14. "Who's Who in the Nation's Capital" gives Frances Scott Key Smith as great grandson of F.S.K., born 1872. Graduate National University Law School. Republican, Major Q[uarter].M[aster]. Reserves, etc.

---

[1] The final Senate vote against Parker (forty-one to thirty-nine) was taken on 7 May.

[2] See the second letter of 28 January 1930, n. 3.

[3] A "yellow dog contract" required prospective workers to promise that they would never join a union. In one of his opinions as a circuit court judge, Parker had upheld the yellow dog contract in a West Virginia mine case.

[4] Negroes had protested that Parker's decisions had undermined their right to vote and had flouted the constitutional guarantees of the Thirteenth, Fourteenth, and Fifteenth Amendments. The NAACP took a particularly active role in the campaign against him.

[5] On 30 April, the Senate had learned of a letter written by Joseph Moore Dixon (1867–1934) to Walter Hughes Newton (1880–1941). Dixon, a native North Carolinian who had moved to Montana, represented that state in both the House and the Senate, and was now serving as first assistant secretary of the interior. Newton, a congressman from Minnesota, had resigned to serve as Hoover's private secretary. In his letter, written on 13 March, only five days after Justice Sanford's death, Dixon urged the nomination of John J. Parker on entirely political grounds. Speaking as one born in North Carolina, Dixon argued that the Parker appointment might help pry that state into the Republican column and urged it as a "master political stroke." On 5 May Attorney General Mitchell denied that President Hoover had ever seen the Dixon letter or that it had influenced him in any way.

[6] On 6 May the New York *World* published an editorial entitled "A Presidential Prophecy." It noted Hoover's recent prediction that the country had passed through the worst of the depression and expressed the hope that, in view of his other failed predictions, he knew this time what he was talking about. The editorial also noted Hoover's expansive statements during his tenure as secretary of commerce.

[7] Paul Underwood Kellogg (1879–1958) edited *The Survey* from 1902 to 1942. He served on numerous charitable and reform boards and headed the famous Pittsburgh Survey of industrial conditions in the steel industry. LDB's high regard for Kellogg and his colleagues led him to leave one-quarter of his estate to the Survey Associates "for the maintenance of civil liberty and the promotion of workers' education in the United States."

[8] At LDB's prodding, Morris L. Cooke persuaded the administration at Swarthmore College to establish the Swarthmore Institute on Unemployment. The Institute had hired as its director Paul Howard Douglas (1892–1976), a professor of economics at the University of Chicago between 1920 and 1948, who later represented Illinois in the Senate from 1949 until 1966.

[9] See LDB to Morris L. Cooke, 18 April 1930.

[10] Max Lowenthal, secretary to the Wickersham Commission, was passing through some kind of a crisis. He and his wife, Eleanor, took LDB's advice and retreated to their farm in New Milford, Connecticut. Then, on 31 July, Lowenthal resigned his position with the Commission. He offered no reasons, but two rumors persisted. According to one, his wife and family were extremely reluctant to spend another winter in Washington, D.C.; and according to another, Lowenthal

found himself in disagreement with certain of the Commission's policies. He declared his intention to devote himself to private research.

No. 425   May 13, 1930   Washington, D.C.

1. Is the Atlantic article [1] your Bar Assn. of the City of N.Y. address, or the New Orleans one revamped?

2. Yes, the Roberts appointment is a fitting sequel to the Parker rejection. [2] I suppose The World will now have a Chapter III.

3. It might be well to have some notice taken of the P.C. (May 5/30) in 674, [3] which, like Yamkill Electrick {sic} case (Jan 20/30), [4] dismissed appeal that challenged the power of the State to authorize municipality to supply electric light & power to adjoining rural region—of course clear as matter of law, but suggestive as matter of policy.

4. McCurdy was in today. The growth is not visible.

5. I am having Harlan read the May '30 Ill. Law Rev. article [5] & he will subject Mark Sullivan to the perusal.

6. Yes, the Bar Assn. may be relied upon as true to form except C.C.B.'s. He is cheering.

7. I have neither seen or heard anything from Max for a week.

[1] FF, "Democracy and the Expert," *Atlantic Monthly* 146 (November 1930): 649.

[2] Owen J. Roberts was nominated to the Supreme Court on 9 May and easily confirmed by the Senate on 20 May.

[3] *Holmes* v. *City of Fayetteville, North Carolina*, 280 U.S. 700. Holmes sued the city to prevent it from extending electricity to customers outside the city limits—which it was specifically allowed to do according to state law. The Supreme Court dismissed the case for want of any federal question. For the lower court's decision, see 197 N.C. 740.

[4] *Yamkill Electric Co.* v. *McMinnville*, 280 U.S. 531, was an Oregon case involving the same issue as *Holmes* v. *Fayetteville*. The lower court decision may be found at 280 Pac. 504; the Supreme Court once again dismissed for want of a substantial federal question.

[5] Charles B. Elder, "The Constitutional Rate of Return for Public Utilities," *Illinois Law Review* 25 (May 1930): 1. The article was continued in the next issue at p. 165.

No. 426   May 18, 1930   Washington, D.C.

1. We are due the Bellevue AM. Tuesday, June 3rd. Hope you and Marion will dine with us at 7 : 30 that evening.

2. Alice Cameron's "In Defense of England," May 14/Nation p. 571 stated what I think is a truth rarely realized in this country. [1]

3. There should be published in the early autumn, say in the October Atlantic, a worthy article discussing "The Engineering Mind" & H.H., showing the engineer's lack of appreciation of the imponderable, his lack

of intuitive knowledge, his lack of broad generalization & of human nature which are of the essence of the statesman.[2]

Much of that passage from Ecclessiasticus (c. 38) which you sent me from Spain is applicable.[3]

[1] Alice M. Cameron's letter to *The Nation* complained about the magazine's treatment of England in recent months, especially its constant focusing on economic decline. The journal should give attention to "the astounding progress in culture, in civilization, and in all that makes for real democracy among our people." She pointed especially to the decrease in crime and drinking, the advances in education, and the high voting rates among the English people. See also 19 September 1930.

[2] No such article appeared in *The Atlantic Monthly*.

[3] In that chapter, Sirach reviewed the work of various craftsmen: "All of these rely upon their hands, and each is skillful in his own work. Without them a city cannot be established. . . . Yet they are not sought out for the council of the people, nor do they attain eminence in the public assembly."

No. 427   May 21, 1930   Washington, D.C.

1. Alice and I were very glad to hear from Laski that you and Marion are planning a trip to England. Nothing could give you so much refreshment after your strenuous year. Now we are doubly glad because you can do much for Palestine by making clear to those in authority what their almost unbelievable action in suspending the immigration permit means—and what the English attitude should be.[1]

2. You know what my doubts were as to MacDonald's adequacy. His shelving the unemployment problem in favor of International Disarmament talk has brought its natural repercussion in Oswald Mosely's [sic][2] resignation and other labor remonstrances.

3. Yes, George [Rublee] brought Morrow in, about 3 weeks ago, for a long talk, and later sent Dean in, before he was called to Englewood to aid in preparing the speech.

4. The confirmation of Roberts[3] closes happily a worthy struggle.

5. I am glad to see the Diversity of Citizen jurisdictional repeal bill launched in the Senate.[4]

6. MacDonald seems to be losing friends almost as rapidly as H.H. He certainly is losing for England the friendship of World Jewry.

7. I shall write Mrs. Croly.[5]

8. The appreciate of Isaac A. Isaacs[6] is good.

Brailsford has an excellent article in the May Menorah.[7]

[1] LDB refers to the continuing investigation of Palestine by the British government. After the Shaw Commission report of March 1930 (see 1 April 1930, n. 4), Zionist outrage led to the appointment of another Commission, this one led by Sir John Hope Simpson (see 22 October 1930, n. 1). No

doubt LDB hoped that FF might influence that investigation. On 15 June, however, Harold Laski wrote to Holmes: "And much energy expended in preventing Felix from coming here to dip his fingers in the Zionist pie and create immense embarrassment. It seems to be one of Brandeis's blind spots not to see that when the British government has a commission of enquiry in Palestine not even Felix can get guarantees about policy until the commission has reported, and that to send him here just now, instead of when there is a document to discuss, would injure his prestige and waste his time." (Howe, ed., *Holmes-Laski Letters*, II, 1261.) FF did not go to England.

[2] Sir Oswald Ernald Mosley (1896–1980) had entered Parliament as a conservative. He joined Labour in 1924 and was a junior minister in the MacDonald government of 1929, but resigned when the cabinet rejected his economic proposals. Mosley then became the leader of English fascism and specialized in anti-Semitic and racist political speeches.

[3] See 13 May 1930, n. 2.

[4] The bill (S. 4357) was introduced by George W. Norris on 5 May. Nothing came of it.

[5] Herbert Croly had died in Santa Barbara, California, on 17 May.

[6] Sir Isaac Alfred Isaacs (1855–1948), a distinguished Australian jurist and statesman, served both as chief justice of Australia and as governor general.

[7] H. N. Brailsford, "Caesar and the Appeal of Massacre," *Menorah Journal* 18 (May 1930): 389, was a biting attack on the Palestine Commission Report, which he described as typical of the British ruling class mentality.

No. 428   May 26, 1930   Washington, D.C.

1. O.W.H. said, as we drove from Court today: "I feel a great relief at having spoken my mind." His dissent to-day was the most emphatic and outspoken of anything that I recall of his. And after what the Senate & the press have done of late, it will be understood.

2. McR. said in delivering his opinion, in substance—"From the rule there (in Farmers L. & T. Co. v. Minnesota) laid down, the result here ought to be clear to an unclouded mind." [1]

3. I am glad you wrote Harold [Laski].

4. What you said to Walter [Lippmann] is true. H.H.'s lack of courage is almost phenomenal. Notably in his failure to remove Claudius Huston. [2] Mabel Willebrandt, who was in yesterday, said he had selected Huston originally for Chairman so as to have in that office one who would agree with him; that he did not say so but proceeded by having friends go about through the States & get local political leaders to write letters urging his appointment; that now H.H. is reversing the process—i.e. having letters sent in urging his retirement. Mabel said: "It is quite embarrassing." She thinks he will retire, but possibly not until after election. [3]

[1] The case which brought forth the spirited dissent of Justice Holmes was *Baldwin* v. *Missouri*, 281 U.S. 586, decided this date, Justice McReynolds reading the opinion of the majority. An Illinois citizen died leaving all her property to her son; some of that property, however, was deposited in Missouri banks, and Missouri tried to collect a tax on it. The majority concluded that being taxed by two states was a violation of the due process clause of the Fourteenth Amendment. Holmes

began his dissent by saying "Although this decision hardly can be called a surprise after *Farmers Loan & Trust Co.* v. *Missouri* . . . and although I stated my views in [that] case, still, as the term is not over, I think it legitimate to add one or two reflections to what I have said before. I have not yet adequately expressed the more than anxiety that I feel at the ever increasing scope given to the Fourteenth Amendment in cutting down what I believe to be the constitutional rights of the States. As the decisions now stand, I see hardly any limit but the sky to the invalidating of those rights if they happen to strike a majority of this Court as for any reason undesirable. I cannot believe that the Amendment was intended to give us *carte blanche* to embody our economic or moral beliefs in its prohibitions." LDB and Stone joined in the dissent. The majority's position had been stated on 6 January 1930 in *Farmers Loan Co.* v. *Minnesota*, 280 U.S. 204, a case involving New York and Minnesota. Holmes and LDB dissented there also.

² See 24 March 1930, n. 4.

³ Huston resigned as Republican national chairman on 7 August.

No. 429   May 27, 1930   Washington, D.C.

1. S.S.W. should not fail to understand Owen Young after your letter.

2. I am glad that Laski will undertake "to straighten out" the difficulty which our American bourgeois are experiencing in getting Palestine visas. But I do not agree at all that this is a relatively unimportant matter for us. I am strongly of opinion that if Laski fails to secure a rectification of the practice that we should endeavor to secure the intervention of our State Department. I know of nothing likely to occur which is of more importance to our ability to aid in advancing our economic program. For us, this is "a major essay."

3. Savings Bank Insurance is becoming so successful & so prominent in the financial press (also in N.Y. Evening Post) that Charles Merz might care to write up the subject.

June 1st. two new insurance banks will open. Our percentage of gain for first four months is very large, while the commercial companies lost over 12 percent as compared with last year. Our small lapse rate in 1930 was even less than in 1929, while the commercial companies' lapse ratio has become huge. See enclosed memo as to lapse of industrial policies.

4. The N.R. would be far more effective in its attacks on the unwisdom of the worldly-wise business leaders, & their Washington representatives, if the editors would particularize.

In a democracy, it is essential that we have responsible government. Ministries—in business & finance as in political government—should fall when they make miserable failures. Our Kings of finance and our Captains of Industry are all in office, and men still listen to them.

Commanders in Chief, Generals & Admirals, who brought such disasters upon the country, or failed to avert them, would be court martialed.

Of course, to make an effective campaign, men must know the facts & use them as a skilled advocate would do.

Note Mellon (U.S. Daily May 27) reduces banks' interest rate on govt. funds to 1/2 percent. He didn't increase the rate during the long high money period.

No. 430   May 30, 1930   [Washington, D.C.]

Memorandum

If Holmes and a few of us live a little while, the Court ought to come out of the trough of recent years. Hughes is mundane but intelligent and the recent events in the Senate and their aftermath [1] ought to have considerable influence. As a matter of fact the tail feathers of Butler and some of them have been completely plucked. The truth is that Taft for some time had really lost his grip and V.D. and Pierce Butler and McReynolds were running him. In addition to his being with them in their desires, they were with him in some of his own independent foolishness.

Hughes has real energy and intelligence. In the conferences, time is not much wasted. Hughes doesn't read long statements, as did Taft, in regard to certioraris. And certioraris on Federal Employers' Liability have stopped. Time isn't wasted in needlessly stating matters and he uses good judgment in selecting writers for opinions. For instance, Butler when a Corporation is to be curbed and himself taking the Texas and New Orleans Case.[2] It is quite amusing to see how Butler has been soft-pedalled.

Hughes' opinions are like his old opinions on the Court—he has no imagination but he is a good artisan. Of course he has a strong feeling for the reputation of the Court and hasn't been wanting to upset recent decisions of the Court like the Farmers Loan and Trust Co. v. Minnesota,[3] as to the taxing power of the state, because he does not want the Court to appear to be a see-saw. But if Roberts is what we expect him to be, I think we may gradually see a decidedly different temper on the Court.

Stone feels very happy—he feels vindicated by all that has happened and he likes the joy of combat. He really does not know how to work, though he likes to be working.

431

[1] LDB probably refers to the rejection of John J. Parker and the bitter debate over the confirmation of Chief Justice Hughes. See 23 January and 18 February 1930.

[2] In *Texas & New Orleans Railroad Co.* v. *Brotherhood of Railway & Steamship Clerks*, 281 U.S. 548, Chief Justice Hughes read a unanimous opinion (with Justice McReynolds abstaining from any part in the case) on 26 May 1930. The union charged that the company had established a "company union" and, after coercing workers to join it, recognized it, rather than the Brotherhood, as the bargaining agent. Two lower courts had found for the Brotherhood and ordered the company to disband its union and to resume negotiations at once with the Brotherhood. The high court accepted the findings of the lower courts and upheld their decrees at every point. LDB here praises Hughes, a former corporation lawyer, for assigning to himself this prolabor opinion.

[3] See 26 May 1930, n. 1.

No. 431   June 24, 1930   Chatham, Mass.

1. Put this up to your labor-economic Statesman:

State old age pensions for wage and salary earners is unfortunately a social necessity. Utilize the institution to counteract the tendency to deny employment to men over forty:

By putting an occupation-tax on the employment of men under forty, from which tax those over would be free.

Consider whether the tax should be a percentage of the wages of those under forty, or be solely on the act of employment.

If the latter, the legislation would tend to discourage also turn over, and to promote regularity of employment.

Consider whether the tax should be a progressive one.

The rate of taxation should be dependent approximately upon the amount required to be raised for the pensions.

2. The November H.L.R. should carry the story of the genesis of the recent equity admiralty rules, with reference to the opinion of Fuller C.J. abrogating the earlier practice; the analogy of the present practice of the Court of Claims; the present practice when there are appeals from jury waived case; & the former practice in writs of error etc. from the Court of territories.

3. I fear H.H. has punished us by the 2 most recent nominations for the S.C. of D.C.[1]

B. Hand carried all hearts.[2]

[1] The Congress had just authorized two new associate justice positions for the Supreme Court of Washington, D.C. On 23 June, President Hoover sent forward the names of Oscar Raymond Luhring (1879–1944), a former Indiana congressman and currently a special assistant to the secretary of labor; and Joseph Winston Cox (1875–1939), a Washington, D.C., attorney and occasional instructor at the George Washington Law School. The Senate confirmed both men.

[2] Learned Hand and his wife had paid the Brandeises a visit at Chatham a few days earlier.

No. 432   September 19, 1930   Washington, D.C.

1. Alice learned from the Shulmans of Mrs. Howit's address and "placed" her with Mrs. La Follette before your letter came, & her work begins on Monday.

2. I agree entirely that we should be very gentle, though firm, with Great Britain. My further studies [1] deepen my sense of the inadequacy of the Palestine Administration. Their dilatoriness in matters vitally affecting business, has been distressingly dilatory, in matters where action means life or death. We must hope that they will do better now. [2]

3. My official copy of the Minutes has come from Geneva. [3] If yours doesn't come soon, I will send you mine.

4. I enclose letter from Wise, and one to him. I guess what he says of J.W.M. is true. Of course, such meetings are distressing at best. But J.W.M. permitted himself, in his dedication to duty, to be worn out. [4]

5. The facts in Alice Cameron's "Is England Played Out" Sept 10 Nation, setting forth human gains despite adversity, could be taken as an effective text by the N.R., pointing the lesson to America—thus doing both England and The Nation a good turn. [5]

6. Could B. F. Goldstein of Chicago be won as a Zionist intellectual? We are greatly in need of strengthening there. [6]

---

[1] LDB devoted the summer of 1930 to an arduous study of all aspects of the Palestine situation—in accord with his letter of 23 September 1929, warning that his age would make day to day management of the Zionist movement impossible, but that he could give his summers to study and thought. In July and August he sent out floods of letters requesting information on Palestine and on Zionist affairs. And in an effort of self-education reminiscent of his search for factual detail before undertaking a reform effort a quarter century before, he sought out minute statistical detail on a large variety of questions: everything from dietary habits of the settlers to the data on fund collection, from patterns of crop rotation to the latest studies of water power and irrigation, from rates of interest charged to Palestinian Arabs to the progress of the school system.

[2] LDB's hopes for the British administration of Palestine would last only another month. See 22 October 1930.

[3] Probably the minutes from the meeting of the League of Nations's Commission on Mandates. The League's Commission issued a report highly critical of the British administration of its Palestine Mandate. See New York Times, 26 August 1930, for the League's report and the British reply.

[4] Julian Mack went to Europe in early August for the meeting of the Jewish Agency's administration committee; and from Europe, he embarked on a tour of Palestine, returning to the United States in November.

[5] The article (Nation 131: 265) reiterated the same points made by Alice Cameron in her letter to The Nation published in the 14 May issue (see 18 May 1930). The New Republic did not pick up the story.

[6] One of LDB's most persistent themes during these months was the need for young Jewish intellectuals—willing to study and master the facts and arguments of Palestine development, and to serve as the movement's "brain trust." See for one example, LDB to Robert Szold, 19 August 1930.

No. 433   September 26, 1930   Washington, D.C.

1. Harlan was in today. Says he has full copy of Parce's speech, so I return clipping.

2. Of course there is no a priori agreement in conference to grant S.G.'s request for cert.—but in practice his recommendations bear great weight because:

    (a) He knows how many cases there are involving same Q[ues-tion]s, & how important it is that we should pass upon questions.

    (b) Our confidence in S.G.s, particularly in Mitchell as S.G., who was both wise, judicial & a lawyer especially careful & well advised.

But you will find instances where we denied emphatically the S.G's requests & recommendations & refused to follow his advice either to grant or to deny, both where Govt is petitioner and where it is respondent. The fact that Mitchell recommended created in practice a presumption.

No. 434   October 22, 1930   Washington, D.C.

1. The Labour Government has dealt us a foul blow.[1] Evidently Passfield compelled Simpson to modify his report. They are taking their revenge. You will recalled [sic] Shiels'[2] remark quoted by London.

2. Warburg did well to defer statement until full report & White Paper received.

3. I had a satisfactory talk with Snell[3] Monday (in presence of de-Haas, Zuckerman[4] & Israel Thurman[5]). I hope you have seen in full his address to the Amer. Congress[6]—it was a difficult task well performed. Evidently, the Govt was particularly incensed at the Zionists' converting the enquiry into a judicial one. The three lawyers on the Comn. considered whether it was advisable to allow evidence as to the broader political questions to come in, as requested by the Arabs; concluded to do so, because there would be a great Arab holler if they did not; and then concluded to make findings on it because they had admitted it.

4. I have some thoughts as to our future policy which I shall communicate later.

5. Goldstein behave[d] well in the Chicago case.[7]

6. If you & Landis say anything in your article on Oct 29 Term, in your Nov. article,[8] please send me a copy now.

7. Monte Leman[n] was in Sunday. He is fine. He says two illusions of his have been dispelled by his service on the Prest's Commission—R.P. and Newton Baker.

8. Miriam Van Waters was in yesterday. She too is fine.

[1] On 21 October 1930 the British issued simultaneously the Hope-Simpson Report and the Passfield White Paper. Following the Shaw Report (see 1 April 1930, n. 4), the government dispatched Sir John Hope-Simpson (1868–1961), a retired civil servant resident in India, to examine Arab complaints against Jewish immigration. Sir John spent only two months in Palestine, and listened primarily to Arab groups—refusing even to consider material submitted by Jewish agricultural experts. His estimate of available arable land was 40 percent below that held by the Jewish Agency, and thus he concluded that Palestine could support no further immigration. He went on to detail many of the Arab charges against the Jewish settlers and reported them as if true. Following his recommendation that all further immigration be suspended, the colonial secretary, Lord Passfield (Sidney Webb), issued a White Paper which restricted further Jewish immigration and redefined the Balfour Declaration primarily in terms of obligations to the Arabs, severely limiting the promise of a Jewish homeland.

Naturally the White Paper caused an immediate uproar among Jews and supporters of a Jewish homeland. The government's failure to consult either with the Zionist Organization or with the Jewish Agency led Chaim Weizmann, Felix Warburg, and Lord Melchett to resign from the Jewish Agency. Prestigious Englishmen from all parties denounced the new policy as the betrayal of a solemn trust, and Zionist organizations in various countries mounted a massive anti-British campaign. Finally, on 13 February 1931, Prime Minister Ramsay MacDonald released a letter to Weizmann in which he sought to clarify the White Paper, but which in effect, repealed it.

[2] Sir Thomas Drummond Shiels (1881–1953), a physician, entered Parliament as a Labour representative in 1924. He was currently an undersecretary in the British Colonial Office.

[3] Henry Snell (1865–1944) was another Labour politician and diplomat, later Baron Snell. In 1929 he served as a member of the Commission of Inquiry sent to investigate the riots in Palestine.

[4] Perhaps William Zuckermann (1885–1961), a prominent Jewish-American journalist and writer, and the New York correspondent of the *London Jewish Chronicle.*

[5] Probably Israel Noah Thurmin (1884–1982), a Harvard graduate, New York attorney, and businessman active in Jewish affairs. Thurmin was a vice president of the American Jewish Congress, and in that connection might have met LDB in Washington.

[6] Snell had delivered the main address at a banquet in his honor, in Washington, D.C., on 19 October, hosted by the American Jewish Congress. Snell urged his Jewish hearers not to lose faith in Britain's intentions for the future Jewish homeland in Palestine.

[7] Benjamin F. Goldstein had argued on behalf of the appellants, who included the city of Chicago, in *Smith* v. *Illinois Bell Telephone Co.*, 282 U.S. 133. The decision, in an opinion by Hughes, established the right of the State to set intrastate telephone rates, and the right of the district court to determine allowable depreciation—and that these powers were not taken away, as the phone company claimed, by the Interstate Commerce Act; also, bypassing the reproduction cost-prudent investment controversy, the court held that the allowable depreciation should be governed by the utility's actual financial experience.

[8] FF and James M. Landis, "The Business of the Supreme Court at the October Term, 1929," *Harvard Law Review* 44 (November 1930): 1.

No. 435   October 23, 1930   Washington, D.C.

1. Five hours after writing you yesterday, I saw the Times with Warburg's amazingly effective statement.[1] Five hours after that came

your letter telling of your day in New York. The statement is so good that it may be more helpful than if he had followed our advice and not resigned—provided of course that he works with us as indicated, i.a. continues to give liberally.

2. You know, from Nathan Kaplan's [2] letter, of the havoc suffered by Arab urban landlords as the result of the massacres and the boycott,[3] and, from K and the J[ewish] D[aily] B[ulletin], of the heavy losses and bankruptcies among leading Arab merchants as the result, to some extent of the boycott, & largely through drop in orange and wheat prices. The British statement will cause a precipitous drop in land values, already in heavy decline; and also otherwise have a very depressing effect economically. It is possible to so conduct affairs that these heavy losses fall mainly upon the Arabs, and serve as a help to our cause; that is, by making the Arabs see the result of the baleful Passfield-Mufti policy, so that they will bring pressure upon the British to abandon their fell purpose; if not now, relatively soon.

(a) We must ensure Jewish employment by an active, widespread, continuous building program. (1) The Jews, for instance, at Haifa, should have the opportunity of living in houses built by Jews on land owned by Jews. (2) The colonist should have the opportunity of employing Jews living in their own houses, as in the Hedera suburb. (3) The 1000 family settlement project should be proceeded with. Settlers' families are now in Palestine awaiting the opportunity.

If we go forward vigorously with this program (which, as you know, I have been urging for a year) any slack there may be in Jewish employment will be taken up; and much business will result to Jewish industries and traders.

This building project needs money from abroad. You will recall that I urged also other building enterprises which social-minded non-Zionist Jews might contribute to, and which even Anti-Zionists need not shrink from. That is, school buildings badly needed in many places; so badly that it was necessary to close schools because of lack of proper buildings. Even a Julius Rosenwald might give for this purpose. Indeed, he has to a slight extent, as I recall.

(b) The Palestine Jews should, [*], become economically self-sufficient. That involves (1) Buying nothing abroad unnecessarily. (You will recall my letter to Hexter which you read at Chatham.)[4] (2) Buying their food from the Jewish colonists. (You may not have seen my letter to Viteles, sent via P.E.C. and my more recent letter to Nathan Kaplan re "[*]") (3) Employing, whenever possible, Jewish labor. (Many letters on this subject to Joshua Bernhardt. [5]) (4) Not buying unnecessarily from non-Jewish shops.

This policy is practically forced upon the Palestinian Jews by the British treatment of even sporadic unemployment as an excuse for stopping immigration. The Simpson-Passfield statement on unemployed in view of what Simpson told Hexter at Athens about the absence of unemployment in May, and in view of the fine employment condition on July 31, reported in [*]'s memo recently sent you by J. C. Hyams, is a shocking example of the Government's [*].

The policy suggested by me above is one which rests for execution with the Palestinians. It obviously is one which cannot be proclaimed from the housetops. And it is essential that the policy of Jewish self-sufficiency, Jewish performance, be not distorted into an Arab boycott.

(3) If these policies are proceeded with, the terrible drain on Jewish resources (which Hoofien [6] and Ruppin [7] estimated [I think over-estimated] at $4,000,000 a year) will be reduced largely.

(4) Moreover, the "Buy goods made in Palestine" policy will cut down government revenues from customs duties, now in large measure paid by Jews.

Let me know what you think of this policy suggested—and how you think it can be put into execution.

Who is responsible for that terrible editorial in yesterday's "Times?" [8]

[1] The statement was issued by Felix M. Warburg in conjunction with his resignation, in protest against the new British policy, as chairman of the administrative committee of the Jewish Agency. See the front page story, *New York Times*, 22 October 1930.

[2] Nathan D. Kaplan (1877–1952) had been a Chicago attorney and one of the leading Zionists in the Midwest. In 1927 he moved to Palestine and became a member of the Tel Aviv municipal council from 1936 to 1941.

[3] In February 1930 the Arabs organized a boycott against Jewish middle men and merchants in Palestine—particularly in Jerusalem. As a result, Jewish tenants left the houses and apartments they were renting from Arab landlords.

[4] See LDB to Maurice B. Hexter, 7 September 1930.

[5] Joshua Bernhardt (b. 1893) was an economist and statistician, the American authority on the economics of the sugar industry. Between 1927 and 1933 he served as secretary of the Palestine Economic Corporation.

[6] Eliezer Siegfried Hoofien (1881–1957) had settled in Palestine in 1912, and served in several managerial positions with the Anglo-Palestine Bank, ultimately becoming general manager in 1924.

[7] Dr. Arthur Ruppin (1876–1943) was a sociologist who pioneered in the collection of data regarding the Jews. Head of the Zionist Organization's Palestine office in Jaffa from 1908 until his death, Ruppin was responsible for the day-by-day development of Jewish settlement in the region. Ruppin placed his highest priority on the purchase of new lands, and under his direction and at his urging much territory was purchased with Zionist funds.

[8] On 22 October the *New York Times* ran an editorial, "The Palestine Report," which can only be described as anti-Zionist. "Great Britain's new policy in Palestine," it began, "is a blow at

437

Zionist aspiration only in the sense that it registers a verdict already pronounced by the facts."
According to the editorial, "the new British policy amounts to an affirmation that there has been
too great haste in the building of the Jewish Homeland."

No. 436   October 29, 1930   Washington, D.C.

When I reached home yesterday, I found that the President had, since
4:55 PM, been trying to reach me & had asked me to call him at 5:30.
I got there shortly before six PM, was asked into his private room in the
East end; & found Mrs. Hoover there with him. She left immediately;
and I had nearly an hour with the President.

He began: I want to talk with you on the Palestine situation. I think
if the Jews press too hard, the British will surrender the Mandate to the
League of Nations. They have so many Moslems among their subjects,
whose ill will they are incurring etc. I told him that I did not think the
British would relinquish the Mandate; that British leaders, the Conservatives, Baldwin,[1] Churchill, Chamberlain,[2] Amery; the Liberal
leaders, Lloyd George[3] and Samuel had declared their opposition to the
Passfield policy, etc.; that I knew a large part of the Labor leaders were
friendly to the Zionist cause; that I thought we might have developments immediately, after the King's Speech;[4] and that I thought the
Rothermere Press[5] and the Morning Post didn't represent predominant
British opinion. But that in any event, the Jews have their backs to the
wall; that they must fight; but that their fight was against the present
government (which I thought would fall soon) and not against the
British people; and that what the American Jews would do was to make
this clear; and to insist that the Mandate be lived up to; that we considered the British people our friends, etc.

Beginning then with his breakfast with us at Paris in June 1919, I
told him of my talks with Balfour on that day and on my return to Paris
in July; of my talks with [*]; of my then complete faith in the Home
Govt, as opposed to the local administrators (a faith which endured until
the appearance of the Shaw report);[6] and that in my only public utterance
in nine years (at Warburg's meeting Nov 24, 1929)[7] I had reiterated my
earlier faith in the Home Government; of the rude shock received then
by the Shaw report, the suspension of immigration, etc; of the Passfield
pernicious enmity; and of the "fool" action, from any point of view, of
which the Cabinet Office had been guilty; the series of mistakes made
by them—spoke of my meeting with MacDonald last year;[8] told him

the state secret of my talk with Lindsay[9] at Henderson's [10] suggestion; of Henderson's statement before the League of Nation's Council etc.

Meanwhile, I had been telling him of Jewish achievements in Palestine, of the benefit accruing to the Arabs generally; of the small body of Arabs leaders responsible for stirring up the enmity—agitation made possible by the local administration's action which enabled the Arab leaders to say: "The Government is with us." Of the ability of the Jews there to handle Jewish-Arab relations if adverse Government influence absent.

Then I showed him that the recent proposals were wholly inadmissible; that Jews had learned to make "bricks without straw"—but to make them without clay also was impossible; that the proposal was not only to suspend immigration and stop land sales; saying that we must be patient and we must not go too fast; but that we couldn't slacken our pace. I explained the rapid increase of Arab population, through betterment of Arab conditions & seepage in from Syria & Transjordania.

Then we discussed causes of local British Anti-Semitism and of mistakes of Home Government; of the failure of local officials to understand (I told him my reference to the Mark Twain remark in converstaion with Waters-Taylor); that we hoped for a clearing out of many of the local officials when we got a friendly govt.

The President then spoke of his great concern over the possible instability of the British Empire; of the serious consequences to America if it should fall to pieces; (I added "to the world"); and that he wanted to avoid doing anything that would make the British task more difficult etc. (He had spoken before of MacDonald's lacks & Henderson's limitations and generally of the lacks in the members of the present Government.) I told him that we should clearly differentiate between the British people and the present government. He asked whether I thought he should do anything now. I answered "not at present"; that U.S. has a special interest under the Treaty, etc; and that the Jews were interested as never before; and that the American Jews, over four millions, might more disturb Anglo-American relations than the Irish had in the past (it was in this connection that I told him of my talks with Lindsay.) But that at present we should assume that the Passfield proposals would be turned down; that they included proposals for aid to Arabs through grants of money which would require action by Parliament; and that I didn't believe Parliament would grant the money etc. (In this connection our heavy contributions to Arabs, in land purchases etc.—the discrimination against us in Govt jobs; when large percentage of taxes paid by us was discussed).

Finally, I said that, with his permission, I would take the liberty of letting him know hereafter in case any matter arose which changed the situation, or the attitude which he should take; and in that event, would make suggestions; but, at present, nothing should be done by him. To this he nodded assent.

He had fully assented to my statements as to the "fool" mistakes made by the Home Government; and had said what we want is to enable them to save their faces and step down gracefully—to this I most heartily assented.

He mentioned Transjordan possibilities for Arabs. I added "also for Jews"; and told him of our complaint that Transjordan had been excluded from the Palestine territory; spoke of its fertility & possibilities; of the exclusion of Jews of the Frontier forces etc.

The President did not say anything about any person having urged him to act; or of any exertion of pressure upon him. And I got no distinct impression as to whether his sending for me was wholly spontaneous or had been prompted.

Except for his remark at the beginning of our interview he said nothing about the danger of Great Britain's relinquishing the Mandate or of American Jews pressing too hard.

I expect Ben [Flexner] this AM; will show him this memo & ask him to tell Warburg, Bob [Szold] and deHaas of it, and to ask them to treat it as confidential.

Please return this memo to me.

Later. Ben would like you to send him a copy of the above. Please send me a copy when you return this.

[1] Stanley Baldwin (1867–1947), the acknowledged leader of the Conservatives, was chosen prime minister three times between the wars.

[2] Arthur Neville Chamberlain (1869–1940) had been elected to Parliament as a Conservative in 1918, and would succeed Stanley Baldwin as prime minister in 1937. Chamberlain is best remembered for his failure to avert the outbreak of World War II and for his policy of "appeasement" toward Hitler.

[3] David Lloyd George (1863–1945) had become prime minister in 1916 and led England through World War I. He was favorably disposed to a Jewish homeland in Palestine and had played a large part in the adoption of the Balfour Declaration. Only five days before this letter, he had issued an angry denunciation of the new British policy for Palestine, calling it a breach of faith.

[4] King George V opened Parliament on 28 October with a brief address; he said nothing about Palestine policy, but Ramsay MacDonald, in opening the House of Commons, responded to a question from Stanley Baldwin by denying that the Passfield White Paper was a reversal of British policy and stating that he was "amazed" at the outpouring of protest in regard to its issuance.

[5] Harold Sidney Harmsworth, first viscount Rothermere (1868–1940) had gone into the newspaper business with his brother in 1894. By the 1920s he was the master of a huge newspaper empire, including such popular papers as the *Evening News*, the *Daily Mail*, and the *Daily Mirror*.

[6] See 1 April 1930, n. 4.

[7] See 23 September and 5 October 1929.

[8] See 10 October 1929.

[9] Sir Ronald Charles Lindsay (1877–1945), an experienced career diplomat, was the British ambassador to the United States from 1930 to 1939. On 19 June 1930 Lindsay and LDB met at the Bellevue Hotel in Boston and discussed British policy in Palestine. After leaving that meeting LDB wrote to Julian W. Mack: "I had my say to Lindsay—two hours and twenty minutes—as frankly as I could discuss the subject with you or anyone else. He listened attentively every minute. . . . Whether I have done any good, I, of course, can't say, but he knows we are in earnest. And—now 3 1/2 hours later—I do not regret anything said or feel that I have omitted anything that it would have been wise to say."

[10] Arthur Henderson (1863–1935), a labor organizer and later a leader of the Labour party, was currently foreign secretary in the MacDonald government. In 1934 he would win the Nobel Peace Prize for his work on behalf of disarmament.

No. 437   November 6, 1930   Washington, D.C.

FF: 1. Warburg sent me copy his telegram to you of yesterday, suggesting that I reenforce his, B.F.'s and Bob [Szold]'s request.[1] I told him (when he called me on telephone today) that I did not, because I felt you were a better judge than I as to what was desirable & possible; & that we needed you here also.

2. The above was said by me after he had reported his telephone from Weizmann of meeting with Prime Minister yesterday & latter's proposal to appoint a Comtee. of 3 of the Cabinet to consider withdrawal of Passf. White Paper; Weizmann's and Warburg's desire to have you go to London; & Warburg's enquiry whether he could give you any message from me. I added that we should strongly insist that Weiz. should not commit the Z.O. to anything; that we must have submitted to us in writing any proposal—

  (a) Because time for calm consideration is essential
  (b) So that this would help Great Britain to understand that we are determined, and that America must be consulted.

"My faith is great in time"—And in insistent aloofness. I think from what we know now, it would be undesirable to have any one at London at present who could be said to represent us; and, as matters stand now, B.F., Ben Cohen etc. should not go either.

3. This afternoon Bob called me re the excitement there in Yiddish Press etc. anent speech said to have been made by Mack to Actions Committee saying we urge refusal to accept Weizmann's resignation

etc;[2] also Hexter's[3] telephone to Warburg about it. I told Bob that he should consult you; tell you the above (1 and 2), and further, that, in my opinion,

    (a) We should insist on a strict preservance by the Actions Committee of the status quo; that is, neither accept nor reject Weizmann's resignation and not appoint a provisional committee to work with Weizmann, but

    (b) That the Actions Committee should direct Weizmann not to assent to anything, or make any suggestions, but merely to listen and report to us, and

    (c) That I think we should not assent to anything (after we get a proposal) until we know what Ruttenburg [sic][4] representing Palestine Yishub[5] thinks. Palestinians are the king pins.

That I thought this course important, both *vis-a-vis* Great Britain and as a matter of internal policy. Bob said that he was being hounded to call a meeting of the Adm. Comtee W[ednes]day. I told him he might say what I think, as above; and that he should say further that we cannot know what Mack did say to the Actions Comtee until we have a radio from him (I fear that Mack has not correctly interpreted the message to him embodying our views.), which Bob is asking for.

4. I enclose papers from Rhoade about Stimson's attitude & the Near East Division.

5. I have written Julius Rosenwald as you suggested.

6. Lowell Mellett was in yesterday with Roy Howard and I talked Zionism with him, as you suggested. He was not wholly convinced; but said he would talk further. He is friendly to Jews; has some personal friends (I suppose quasi intellectuals) knew many in his boyhood; and was in Palestine in 1924. I made some impression & he promised to talk further with me. I guess he will not say anything that is not helpful.

[1] That FF go immediately to London to aid in the negotiations over the Passfield White Paper.

[2] Chaim Weizmann had resigned his position as head of the World Zionist Organization and the Jewish Agency for Palestine in protest over the new British policy. The Actions Committee was the executive organ of the World Zionist Organization.

[3] Maurice Beck Hexter (b. 1891) was a prominent Jewish official in several communal and philanthropic agencies, and a non-Zionist member of the Jewish Agency. After the issuance of the Passfield White Paper, he was one of those appointed to negotiate with the British cabinet.

[4] Pinhas Rutenberg (1879–1942), a colorful Russian-born activist, emigrated to Palestine in 1919 and used his engineering skills to develop the country's water and electrical resources. He founded the Palestine Electric Corporation.

[5] The Yishub or Yishuv refers to the Jewish community in Palestine before the creation of the State of Israel in 1948.

No. 438   November 12, 1930   Washington, D.C.

FF: 1. No. Joe Cotton did not say that he came at Stimson's request.[1] Nor did he say that he would tell Stimson. But he seemed to agree fully with my recommendation that nothing should be said or done by our Government at present. And he appeared to assent fully to my statement that I would take the liberty of letting him know if there was anything that I thought the govt should do or that he should know. I do not recall that Stimson's name was mentioned by either of us.

2. I have finished reading the Shaw report—a most extraordinary document, with recommendations wholly impractical in the main. On the assumptions made, there never would be room for the Jews, and the expense of the operations, if borne by Palestine, would through taxation, place an intolerable burden on the Jews for the benefit of the Arabs.

Moreover, I should suppose it would be gravely resented by the rich Arabs.

(a) The landowners would have their lands taken at a fraction of what they are now getting, or

(b) Would have their rental greatly reduced, and

(c) The Arab moneylenders would lose at least most of their interest.

The simple remedy for the lack of land for the fellaheen,[2] adequate in quantity and quality, is to move the surplus Arab population into Transjordania—a part of Palestine improperly segregated; and to use the excessive money which Jews are paying for land (in western Palestine) to establish the fellaheen in Transjordania.

There was no serious difficulty in moving Greeks from Asia Minor or Turks from the Balkans. And I understand the Italians have recently removed 70,000 or more Arabs from the danger zone of Tripolitania.[3]

If the Arabs are so badly off in P., how does Simpson account for the fact that there Arab population is increasing rapidly, while in Syria, Transjordania and Iraq it is at best, stationary?

What has happened to Gay's circular?[4]

Bob [Szold] was here yesterday.

[1] On 31 October LDB had written: "Joe Cotton was in for hour & a half. Satisfactory talk. I advised our government do nothing & say nothing in order to give the British govt. chance to step down. Meanwhile, it is for the Jews to express themselves fully & act."

[2] Arab peasants or laborers.

[3] Northwestern Libya.

[4] See 10 October 1929.

No. 439   November 13, 1930   Washington, D.C.

FF: Re yours of 12th.

In your letter to Stimson I suggest emphasizing:

(1) That it is not a question of holding scales even, but of performing two disparate obligations.

(2) That the duty to the Jews is not the duty to the Jews of P but to the Jews of the world.

3. That "civil and religious rights" of Arabs are not prejudiced by letting them sell their lands at very high prices.

4. That we have been of great benefit to the Arab. Else how account for the large increase of Arab population since 1922, while the Arab population of Syria and Transjordania are stationary or shrinking.

5. That the difficulties with alleged inadequacy of land are due to British folly in segregating Transjordania from Palestine.

6. Perhaps you may think it wise to send him a copy of Rutenberg's letter of Oct 14 to Malcolm McD[onald]. So I enclose my copy. If you have copies made please send me one when you return this.

Our thanks to you and Marion for the birthday greetings.[1]

[1] This date marked LDB's seventy-fourth birthday.

No. 440   November 15, 1930   Washington, D.C.

FF: 1. I enclose letter from William Yale,[1] Nov [*]. I think [it] best that I should not even acknowledge it, leaving you to write him that it was sent to you, in view of your relations to Prince Feisal,[2] and that you will be glad to talk with him when he comes to Boston.

2. Enclosed also Oct 29 Davar, a ringing number. If American Jews are as determined as the Palestinian, the ultimate outcome will be satisfactory to us.

[1] William Yale (1887–1975) graduated from Yale and worked in the State Department as a middle eastern expert during World War I; he then joined the faculty at the University of New Hampshire.
[2] See 10 October 1929, n. 1.

No. 441   November 29, 1930   Washington, D.C.

1. Roberts says that the Phila. District Judges (Dickinson[1] and Thompson[2]) are dead against what he termed "nursing receiverships"

and commonly, when appointing receivers, (? temporary), make an order requiring them to report in 60 days what should be done with the concern. It would be worthwhile to have one of your graduates at Phila. make a full report on the practice & perhaps write an article.

2. Has anything been heard from the Gay circular?[3] I wonder whether "the interests" are interfering.

3. Ought not some fellow write a comprehensive article showing absurdity of recent extension of tax immunity to alleged U.S. instrumentalities etc.; and prepare a bill for consent by Congress to such taxation? The coming insurgent Congress might pass it, as all States will be eager for all the revenue they can get.

4. If I were editor of the N.R. in these days of depression, there would be no issue without a reminder of impotent, curseful bigness.

5. H.H. is true to form in selecting Doak.[4]

6. W. S. Gifford reminds much of H.H. in his talk.[5] He didn't have "vision" enough to accept Prudent Investment.[6]

[1] Oliver Booth Dickinson (1857–1939), a Philadelphia lawyer and an active Democrat, had been appointed district judge in 1914.

[2] Joseph Whitaker Thompson (1861–1946) had been appointed district judge also for the Eastern District of Pennsylvania in 1912 and he served until 1931, when he was elevated to the circuit court of appeals.

[3] See 10 October 1929.

[4] William Nuckles Doak (1882–1933) had been an official of the Brotherhood of Railroad Trainmen. President Hoover, on 28 November nominated him to be secretary of labor to replace James J. Davis who had been elected to the Senate.

[5] Walter Sherman Gifford (1885–1966) came up through the American Telephone and Telegraph Co. until becoming its president and chairman of the board. In 1950, President Truman appointed him ambassador to Great Britain. Gifford had just made a speech predicting the speedy return of prosperity (see *New York Times*, 25 November 1930).

[6] In fixing rates; see 18 July 1927, n. 4. The New York Telephone Co. had been embroiled throughout 1930 in trying to get a rate increase; but the New York Public Service Commission rejected the proposal after the matter became involved in the political campaign.

No. 442   December 4, 1930   Washington, D.C.

FF: Re your letter of 2d & telegram of 3rd.

1. It would, of course, be desirable if possible (from the point of view of allaying Arab irritation—except an agreement satisfactory to us would irritate them more) to reach an early agreement, as suggested by Kish [sic].[1] But it seems to me that every communication from & to London makes it clearer that it must take a long time—probably many months—before any such agreement can be worked out; and that we must reduce the attempted pace. There is no reason why Jews, distrib-

uted over the five Continents or six, should move more rapidly than the Colonial Office & British Cabinet with their highly concentrated powers.

2. I do not think any conceivable arrangement would be more satisfactory than the unsatisfactory status quo, unless as a part of the arrangement we succeeded in having Transjordania opened up to Jews as well as Arabs. $12,500,000 cash would do wonders, if expended there (including cost of transferring Arabs to Transjordania).[2]

3. In view of the above, and the fact that of the short time between say Dec. 17th and Jan 5th, and much would be lost by the Xmas-New Year diversions, I can't see how you could accomplish much by going to England. On the other hand, the fact of your having been there, and particularly of your coming, might be deemed to have estopped[3] America in some way.

4. As to the wisdom of your going—the possibilities of accomplishment. Your judgment (with superior knowledge) would probably be better than that of any of us. And I think you should state it frankly.

5. I wonder whether you have read Harold Nicholson's [sic] "Lord Carnoch" (Arthur Nicholson [sic])[4]—a most illuminating account of the process of diplomacy—which suggests in method much applicable to our present situation.

6. I think Benj. Goldstein may consider that he has won by getting so far. It will surely give W.S. Gifford pain; & should give all the public-minded hope.[5]

7. Rosenbaum, the grain man, I met during the war days. My brother considered him very able &, in some ways, very engaging, but perhaps too sharp. He could help much on Palestine under Goldstein's tutelage. G. should go to Palestine next summer.

8. You doubtless had letter from Max Rhoade. I suppose you will see Elwood Mead on Dec. 6 at Foreign Policy Assn.

[1] Perhaps Frederick Herman Kisch (1888–1943), who had met Chaim Weizmann during the war and in 1922 joined the Zionist Executive in Jerusalem. After 1929, he was also head of the Palestine Executive of the Jewish Agency. He was a strong believer in better Arab-Jewish relations and learned Arabic in order to negotiate directly with Arab leaders. After Weizmann failed to be reelected head of the World Organization in 1931, Kisch left the movement. He was killed in action, in Tunisia, during World War II.

[2] See 12 November 1930.

[3] To prevent one, by one's own acts, from claiming some right.

[4] Sir Arthur Nicolson (1849–1928) and his son, Sir Harold George Nicolson (1886–1968), both held high positions of trust and responsibility in the British foreign service. Harold was also something of an intellectual and wrote numerous books. He had just completed a biography of his

father which LDB was reading. Harold G. Nicolson, *Portrait of a Diplomatist; Being the Life of Sir Arthur Nicolson, First Lord Carnoch and a Study of the Origins of the Great War* (Boston: Houghton Mifflin, 1930).

[5] On 1 December the High Court handed down its decision in *Smith* v. *Illinois Bell Telephone* (see 22 October 1930, n. 7).

No. 443   December 9, 1930   Washington, D.C.

1. George Roberts[1] ought to know that the utilities' behavior—preeminently their over-capitalization—is leading straight, either to a terrific attack on their rates—very vulnerable because of price decline—or to public ownership. Eastern Republican leaders who know the facts are beginning to say so. (I learn from Harlan.)

2. I can't answer your Bakelite enquiry.

3. You put the situation very forcibly,[2] in your letter and I was relieved today to get Laski's confirmation, which should, just a little, assuage Warburg's distress. Ben [Flexner] wired me Sunday & I confirmed your judgment.

4. Rutenberg also was wise.

5. R. G. Dodge[3] was in Court yesterday & I asked him to Alice's Monday. He came & was very nice. I think he has been prematurely aged by the dourness of his financial association. It's a heavy price men pay for an ungenerous occupation.

[1] Probably the prominent economist and banker, George Evan Roberts (1857–1948), president of the National City Bank of New York.

[2] Probably FF's reasons for deciding not to make the trip to England over the Christmas break in order to negotiate a revision of the Passfield White Paper.

[3] Robert Gray Dodge (1872–1964) was a leading Boston lawyer and a dabbler in Massachusetts Republican politics.

No. 444   December 16, 1930   Washington, D.C.

1. I enclose letter from Hexter, Nov 28. I wrote him yesterday my views on Simpson report.[1] J. C. Hyman[2] may send you copy.

2. The result on rehearing in Broad River Power case may puzzle & will interest you. I am told that the Co. is a part of Ass[ociate]d. Gas & Electric holdings. If so, the ground set forth by V.D. (et al) should be made to bother them. It is a terrific indictment, & I think V.D. et al didn't quite realize what their condemnation means.[3]

3. Dennis' articles in N.R.[4] are knowing and generally fine.

447

4. If there is anybody on N.R. who knows about RRs, he should read Lissner's [sic] articles in Railway Age a few months ago, re steady pace of steel rails etc.[5]

[1] See LDB to Maurice B. Hexter, 15 December 1930.

[2] Joseph C. Hyman (1889–1949) was a member of the council for the Jewish Agency and held a number of important posts in the Joint Distribution Committee.

[3] *Broad River Power Co.* v. *South Carolina*, 281 U.S. 528, was originally argued and decided in May 1930. The company had operated a street railway system in Columbia, South Carolina, and then abandoned it. The Supreme Court of the state ordered that the operation be resumed. Since it was a losing operation, the company argued, they were being deprived of their property without due process in violation of the Fourteenth Amendment. The South Carolina court concluded that although the books showed a loss, the operation could have been profitable if properly managed. That court also ruled that the street railway operation was part and parcel of their franchise as a power company and that they could not abandon part of their franchise contract without the consent of the state. Justice Stone's opinion, in the May decision, dealt with only the second question—did the company have the right to abandon part of its franchise contract? The Court unanimously sustained the South Carolina high court. On the rehearing, which was decided on 15 December (282 U.S. 187), LDB, Hughes, Holmes, and Stone adhered to their earlier views. But Justices Van Devanter, McReynolds, Sutherland, and Butler took up the first question and delivered the "terrific indictment" that LDB mentions here. Quoting the South Carolina court, they pointed out that the company "planned to discontinue it and pursued a course tending to depress the business and make it unremunerative." Thus all eight justices (Roberts took no part in the case) agreed to dismiss the cause, but for differing reasons.

[4] Lawrence Dennis began a five part series of articles in *The New Republic* on 19 November. The articles, which ran to the issue of 17 December, dealt with foreign investment in the United States and how it led to economic difficulties during the depression. The general title was "'Sold' on Foreign Bonds."

[5] LDB probably means a series of articles by F. J. Lisman in *Railway Age*. In the 16 August issue, Lisman, a banker and a close observer of railroading, wrote "A Diagnosis of Railway Ills," *Railway Age* 89: 311. That piece did examine the high price of steel rails (p. 316), and in the issues of 1 and 8 November (*Railway Age* 89: 920, 981), under the title, "Best Defense Is the Offensive," he followed up on the points he had raised in August.

No. 445   December 27, 1930   Washington, D.C.

1. Yours 21st reached me yesterday; yours of 25th today.

2. I hope you have set at rest the matter with Warburg, so that he will cease to bother you.[1] He surely ought not to ask anyone but a slave to go abroad for him without putting at the disposal of his representative at least One Million Dollars new money—for keeps. Perhaps you have seen what I wrote Ben [Flexner], Bob [Szold], and Julius Simon on the subject of Warburg's proper action in the present emergency for which he is in part responsible.[2]

3. Perhaps you have, despite your seclusion, heard some of the Z.O.A. perturbation (incident to ZOA & World Z.O. political situation) about someone answering the London call for an American repre-

sentative. I answered Bob that I knew too little of Zionist political conditions to advise. But I had no objection to the Administrative Comtee. sending Wise and deHaas at its expense.

4. Bob said the group (meeting at 10AM today) was also determined to get a vote on opposing Weizmann. I told Bob I agreed with him that it was not necessary to decide that question now, & I thought decision should be deferred.[3]

5. As to Weizmann's successor or successors, I guess you & I can defer advising for the present. It won't do to have Ussishkin in the presidium, if any.

6. Did you ask Genl [*] for specifications?

7. What Sedgwick and Sidney Hilman say doesn't surprise me. The surprising thing is that men should have really thought "a New Era" had come & acted accordingly.[4]

8. Mack's performance in stocks is a replica of his 1921–2 experience. I didn't expect H. Gans would get caught.

9. Did Alfred Lief send you the arbitration report of Judge Langdon's dissent, with Lief's foreword?[5]

[1] About coming to England to negotiate regarding the future of England's Palestine policy.

[2] LDB took the position that Felix M. Warburg had a direct and personal responsibility to provide needed financial support. See LDB to Robert Szold, 19 December 1930.

[3] Weizmann, of course, had resigned his position as head of the World Zionist Organization in protest over the Passfield White Paper. He was defeated for the position in 1931, and Nahum Sokolow was elected.

[4] Those who celebrated American prosperity in the 1920s boasted that "a new era" had been achieved in which serious economic problems were either overcome or on their way to permanent extinction.

[5] In the summer of 1930 an enthusiastic new effort began to secure the release from prison of Tom Mooney and Warren K. Billings (see 21 January 1922, n. 2). The California Supreme Court held a hearing on the matter and on 1 December, despite evidence of false testimony in the original trial, refused to recommend a pardon. Justice William Henry Langdon (1873–1939) was a lone dissenter in the court's refusal, calling his brethren's decision one motivated by passion. His spirited dissent was distributed with a foreword by Alfred Lief as *Mr. Justice Langdon Dissents: A New Chapter in the Mooney-Billings Case.*

No. 446   January 6, 1931   Washington, D.C.

1. Make sure that Harlan's dissent in the C.M. & St. P. case[1] is duly appreciated by N.R., H.L.R. & other publications.[2]

2. We scored some in the Bunn case,[3] & the O'Gorman & Young[4] following expression in the Duck blind case.[5] Realism may be restored in Constitutional Law.

3. The S.G.[6] was in yesterday. I guess to enquire about Austern[7] for

next year. He seemed weary & I guess may have doubts whether he was not better off as D.J.

¹ *United States* v. *Chicago, Milwaukee & St. Paul Ry. Co.*, 282 U.S. 311 (1931). In reorganizing a bankrupt railroad, the receivers wrote into their contract a priority clause securing certain proceeds to pay their fees. This was a local contract matter, they argued, and thus immune from I.C.C. regulation. The I.C.C. disallowed the clause, the receivers appealed, and the Court, in a five to three decision, held that the I.C.C. had no power to regulate the receivership proceedings since they did not constitute interstate commerce. Justice Stone, joined by LDB and Holmes, wrote a vigorous dissent, attacking the excessive fees, amounting to nearly $2 million, which went to the bankers and lawyers.

² See 26 January 1931, n. 4, and 2 February 1931, n. 2.

³ In *Willcuts* v. *Bunn*, 282 U.S. 216, decided the previous day, Chief Justice Hughes, for a unanimous Court, held that net profits on the sale of county and city bonds were taxable as income. While the interest on such bonds remained exempt from federal taxes, the Court found that the various revenue acts validly encompassed profits from sales.

⁴ *O'Gorman & Young* v. *Hartford Fire Insurance Co.*, 282 U.S. 251 (1931). LDB, for a five to four majority, affirmed a lower court ruling permitting states to regulate commissions paid by fire insurance companies to their agents, since insurance was a business affected with a public interest. Emphasis was placed—both in this case and in the one described in n. 5, below—on the presumption of validity of state statutes.

⁵ *Wampler* v. *Lecompte*, 282 U.S. 172, had been decided on 8 December 1930. Speaking for a unanimous Court, LDB ruled that a Maryland law on the placing of duck blinds, which gave riparian owners preferential treatment, did not violate the equal protection clause of the Fourteenth Amendment.

⁶ The solicitor general was Thomas Day Thacher.

⁷ Herman Thomas Austern (1905–1984) had clerked for Julian Mack for a year before becoming LDB's clerk for the October 1930 term. He later joined a Washington law firm. See 8 January 1931 (second letter).

No. 447   January 8, 1931   Washington, D.C.

When young man writes on Congressional legislation which will restore to the States fields of taxation of which they have been robbed by absurd extensions of the doctrine of immunity of Federal instrumentalities and of interstate commerce, I hope he will:

(a) draw the appropriate legislation
(b) show how the restoration of this taxing power will obviate in large measure the need of ever increasing federal grants in aid of State functions.

No. 448   January 8, 1931   Washington, D.C.

The S.G. talked with me Sunday about getting Austern next year. And since Austern's return from N.Y. I have had considerable talk with him about his future. He mentions a possibility of his going to Bob Szold's firm, which I should think well of if he goes to N.Y. to practice & there is work enough there for him. But are there not chances for him in some of the lesser Law Schools? As is [sic] U. of Chicago impossible? or U. of N.Y.? or Cornell? Paul Andrews was very eager last year for good man for Syracuse? [1]

[1] After finishing his year as LDB's clerk, Austern entered private practice with the prestigious Washington firm of Covington & Burling; he did, however, teach law as an adjunct professor at the New York University Law School.

No. 449   January 26, 1931   Washington, D.C.

1. I enclose letter with enclosures from Hexter.
2. When Bob La F. was in I spoke to him of desirability of legislation to correct CM & St P decision [1] & suggested he see Eastman, which was done. Paul tells me that E's counsel advised nothing could be done, I suppose frightened off by the Constitutional talk of S[tone]. I told Paul to tell Bob the correspondence had better be sent to you. I thought you would get Max [Lowenthal] to tackle this phase also.
3. Harlan was glad to see N.R. on the Film case, as was I. [2]
4. You did well for Monte [Lemann].
5. I think it would be much better for Laski to postpone his visit to OWH until the recess following Mch. 8. We shall be in session then & probably until Mch. 24. You know how busy OWH will be on 8th without engrossing visitor. [3]
6. I hope the law reviews will feature CM & StP decision. Harlan is eager for more recognition. [4]

[1] See 6 January 1931, n. 1.
[2] In *Educational Films Corporation of America* v. *Ward*, 282 U.S. 379, decided 12 January 1931, the Court contrived to distinguish an earlier decision of the Taft Court and allowed states to impose a corporate franchise tax measured partly by income from federal copyright. LDB, Holmes, and Stone had dissented in the earlier case, and the new chief justice, along with Owen Roberts, made the majority, joined now by McReynolds. *The New Republic* applauded the decision in an editorial paragraph in the 28 January 1931 issue.
[3] 8 March would be Justice Holmes's ninetieth birthday. On 20 January, in response to an enquiry from FF, LDB had written: "It seems unwise [for me] to write on OWH. for the March HLR—wholly aside from lack of time and making a precedent. It is best that the C.J. should speak for all of the Court. As to the desirable, as between him and me, he brought up the subject when he was requested (by others) to write for my seventieth & we agreed that it was undesirable."
[4] Nathan L. Jacobs, a student in FF's graduate course in administrative law, undertook the assignment. His work appeared as "The Interstate Commerce Commission and Interstate Railroad Reorganization," *Harvard Law Review* 45 (1932): 855.

No. 450   January 27, 1931   Washington, D.C.

1. I am glad to know from yours of 24th that the requirements of the Wisconsin job have been fully considered.[1]

2. The Treasury prospects for March & later are probably worse than suggested in the editorial. Customs receipts are now running at about 2/3 of last year. It is very important that Congress should be on hand when the full effect of the depression is evidenced by the Mch 15 returns. During the war the President had it ever on hand. This peacetime is more serious for USA than the war.

3. I suppose you saw the Metropolitan Ins. Co. figures on unemployment among its industrial policy holders in 46 cities.

at full work about 55 per cent.

at part work about 21   ″   ″

unemployed about 24 per cent.

4. Harlan learns from Dulles that Swain [sic][2] who, as you supposed, devised the CM & StP formula, did so with the exact thing in view that happened. He has inserted a like provision in the recent Seaboard Ry papers; and is jubilant over the Constitutional talk in the opinion which he assumes will prevent legislation. Max should have no difficulty in undermining Swain by his draft bill.

5. I don't recall ever having seen Russel. He has impressed me as being a dangerous employee, & I think that also, for other reasons, Phil [La Follette] should not have him. I am very doubtful as to the wisdom of his importing foreign talent. He ought, in my opinion, to work with the best that Wisconsin affords. Only a very exceptional person could justify a departure from that rule. Of course, I realize that he and Bob are wise politically & know their people. But I can't help doubting the wisdom of their ventures in this connection.

[1] Governor Philip La Follette had sounded out FF about the possibility of naming James Landis to a position in his administration. Although it is not clear from the documents exactly what position La Follete had in mind, FF, somewhat to LDB's surprise, had indicated that Landis had certain deficiencies which rendered him unsuited to the job.

[2] Robert Taylor Swaine (1886–1949) was a senior partner in a prestigious New York law firm, as well as a director of several major corporations.

No. 451   February 2, 1931   Washington, D.C.

1. Commerce Reports—Jan. 26/31 p. 204—in its article on Germany. After commenting on the spread between raw material prices and

those of (wholesale) manufactured products, and the spread between wholesale and retail prices adds: "The German public confidently expects a further substantial break in retail prices; until this occurs, and until the public modifies the present frame of mind, no sustained revival can be expected in German business."

This is markedly true also of America. N.R. should take note; also the World, if it dares.

2. In CM & StP matter, Max should see the record & brief in No. 88. U.S. v. Atlanta, Birmingham & Coast R.R. argued on Jan 30th,[1] and should familiarize himself with what the ICC has done in endeavor to keep down bankers' charges in connection with both reorganization & issue of securities in ordinary course.

The NR article (Feb 4) is a very poor job of journalism.[2]

3. OWH.'s letter means "nothing in particular." Of course he is conscious that 90 years "ist kein Kinderspiel"[3] and perhaps the extraordinary vigor of the C.J. makes his own tired feeling more prominent. But he is in good shape. And, of course, he won't resign until he feels he must.

4. That's nice about Shulsky and Amberg.

5. I am glad to see Meinertzhagen[4] emerging. I wish he might do more.

6. We are postponing the C. W. Eliot letters[5] to Chatham.

7. Yes, it would be wise to avoid Sampson[6] if possible.

8. Abe Flexner was in Friday. Says Ben is about well again.

9. Alfred Cohen was in Saturday and Morris Cohen yesterday.

10. I shall write Brailsford.

11. The view expressed by Emlyn-Jones[7] of Lord Melchett[8] accords with Eugene Meyer's opinion.

---

[1] *United States* v. *Atlanta, Birmingham and Coast R.R.*, 282 U.S. 522 (1931). In a report, the I.C.C. recommended that only part of the old equipment of a reorganized railroad could be carried as value in the new company, thus providing a lower valuation base for rate-making. The railroad challenged the report in the district court, but the Supreme Court, speaking through LDB, held there was no basis for a court challenge, and drew a distinction between an I.C.C. "report" and an "order." The case related to the earlier Chicago, Milwaukee proceedings (see 6 January 1931, n. 1) in that once again bankers tried to exclude part of the financial dealings from control of the I.C.C.

[2] The unsigned "Bad Omen for Railroad Consolidation," *New Republic* 65 (4 February 1931): 313, disappointed LDB because it focussed almost entirely on minor and technical aspects of the decision and ignored the major issues of banker control and excessive fees. FF had supplied the journal its information on the case.

[3] "is not a light thing"

[4] Richard Henry Meinertzhagen (1878–1967), a British colonel, had played an important part

in the colonial administration of Palestine in the 1920s, and was one of the few British officials sympathetic to Zionist aspirations in the Holy Land.

[5] LDB may be referring to Henry James, Jr., *Charles W. Eliot*, 2 vols. (Boston: Houghton Mifflin, 1930), which contains many of President Eliot's letters.

[6] Possibly Arthur W. Sampson, who would become executive secretary of the Savings Bank Insurance League upon Alice H. Grady's death in 1934.

[7] John Emlyn-Jones (1889–1953), a former Labour member of Parliament, was a director in many British firms.

[8] Henry Melchett, the second Baron Melchett of Landford (1898–1949), was a British industrialist who shared his father's Zionist sympathies. After the rise of Hitler, he formally adopted Judaism as a personal faith and practice, and became active as chairman of the Jewish Agency Council.

No. 452   February 5, 1931   Washington, D.C.

1. Your "Restatement" returned herewith. I am very glad you have done it & hope Foreign Affairs won't cut it. [1]

2. I suggest that you begin with the McDonald [sic] quotation p. 2, followed with Einstein & then quote Mark Twain, beginning with the sentence "Palestine is desolate & unlovely" & then quoting only a part of what precedes it. [2]

3. Landau [3] tells me that McLaren [4] Secy of Williamstown Institute of Politics "is considering advisability of devoting part of the next session to Palestine" and "that Mr. Crane will visit Palestine within the next few months."

A new danger front.

[1] FF, "The Palestine Situation Restated," *Foreign Affairs* 9 (1931): 409, attacked recent British policy in Palestine, especially the Passfield White Paper of 1930 (see 22 October 1930). The article was one of FF's rare public statements on Zionism, and its appearance in an influential journal was one factor in the MacDonald government's decision to abandon the White Paper.

[2] FF reversed this advice and began his article with the uncomplimentary description of Palestine in Twain's *Innocents Abroad*, and followed with Ramsay MacDonald's praise for the work of the Jewish settlers.

[3] Jacob Landau (1892–1952), a Vienna-born journalist, founded and ran the Jewish Telegraphic Agency.

[4] Walter Wallace McLaren (1877–1970), an economist at Williams College headed the Institute on Politics there from 1921 to 1932.

No. 453   February 14, 1931   Washington, D.C.

1. I am glad of progress on Fed. Jur. and Adm. Law case books, [1] and am asking Miss Malloch to deposit $500 to your special account to see you through as suggested.

2. I am just emerging from an influenza week, so have not seen

O.W.H. since Feb 2. But I have no reason to think him other than in good form. Of course the approach of the 90th excites him, but I doubt whether his remark about the Sabbath had the significance you attribute to it. His Sundays are ordinarily too full, so full that I have avoided intrusion on that day.

3. Landau suggested to me that you are the man who should be opposed to Anderson.

4. W.L. is true to form. His best service in recent years was performed by being absent at the crucial period of the Parker fight.[2]

5. I suppose you have heard that there is [a] fight on David Lilienthal as an outsider.[3]

6. At Mack's request I am enclose [sic] correspondence re Hebrew University.

7. Joe Cotton's plight is very sad[4]—for the country, for family and friends. You were right in not recommending Stanley King.

[1] See 6 March 1929 and 17 May 1931.
[2] See 23 January 1930, n. 5.
[3] David Eli Lilienthal (1899–1981), a Harvard Law graduate, was then practicing in Chicago. He was being considered for, and would become, a member of the Wisconsin Public Service Commission. In 1933 President Roosevelt named him a director of the Tennessee Valley Authority, and he served until 1946, when President Truman named him as chairman of the newly created Atomic Energy Commission.
[4] Cotton was then quite ill, and died the following month.

No. 454　　　February 24, 1931　　　Washington, D.C.

1. Make sure that Roberts' dissent in Coolidge v. Long is duly appreciated by the Law Reviews.[1]

2. Yes, Hart's article shows great maturity.[2]

3. Lilienthal was in today. I guess Phil made a good selection.[3]

4. Mrs. Ellis[4] was in yesterday & gave good reports of you & Marion.

5. OWH is in good form.

6. You will enjoy McR's two tax opinions.[5]

Be sure to read Sidney L. Herold in Feb. Tulane Law Review.[6]

In conference room C.J. started a talk of Harvard Law School men going to N.Y. He, Butler and Roberts were strong against it. Said able, well-trained men should go West or to small cities East—and become men—& leaders in their communities.

[1] An irrevocable trust had been established, reserving to the settlor a life income, with the remainder to be divided among his five sons. After the creation of the trust, but prior to the death of the settlor, Massachusetts passed an inheritance tax. The Supreme Court held the tax to be retroactive

insofar as it affected this trust, and therefore unconstitutional. Holmes, Stone, and LDB, joined in Roberts's vigorous dissent, which argued that the tax could legitimately reach any future shifts in income, such as would occur on the death of the settlor. *Coolidge* v. *Long*, 282 U.S. 582 (1931). An unsigned note appeared in the May issue of 44 *Harvard Law Review* at 1103 praising the "most able and exhaustive dissenting opinion" of Justice Roberts.

[2] Hart had reviewed Carl B. Swisher's biography of the great nineteenth-century jurist, Stephen B. Field, at *Harvard Law Review* 44 (1931): 669.

[3] Of Lilienthal for the Wisconsin Public Service Commission.

[4] Perhaps Amy Friedman Ellis, whose husband worked in LDB's law firm from 1896 to 1900.

[5] In *Alward* v. *Johnson*, 282 U.S. 509, and *Denman* v. *Slayton*, 282 U.S. 514, McReynolds had upheld the power of states to establish various classifications for tax purposes.

[6] "French Language and the Louisiana Lawyer," *Tulane Law Review* 5 (1931): 169; Herold was president of the Louisiana Bar Association.

No. 455   March 17, 1931   Washington, D.C.

1. Austern has returned from N.Y. nauseated with the moral tone of the bar etc. I think he would gladly go to a smaller city or to a law school if opportunity offered.[1]

2. I hope you get Marks[2] to make the statement re Savings Bk Insurance promptly. It will lose much in effect if delayed.

[1] See second letter of 8 January 1931.

[2] Perhaps Lionel Simeon Marks (1871–1955), a professor of engineering at Harvard.

No. 456   March [28], 1931   Washington, D.C.

Sloss's[1] letter impresses me as that of a pseudo-learned fool.[2] Perhaps the best treatment is to ignore him.

He fails to see in the steel rail price, the manifestation of Steel Corporation domination. Compare present (& long [*]) price of rails with previous price & with fluctuations in price of pig iron—which in 1913 was $16.31—Feb. '31, $15.70 (March 31 Index N.Y. Trust Co, publication).

I suppose you noticed as to Dep. of Justice enquiry into steel rails, U.S. Daily, March 27, 31, p. 3.

Sloss also fails to see in Equipment Co. prosperity (and supplies) what is perhaps worse than domination, corruption of rail officials, through stock interest & personal affiliation. What illegal combination does, and a little publicity can undo, is indicated by the current prices.

1913 all 90 cents. From 1927 to Nov. 1930 $1.75. Then the noble newspapers talk, followed by some in Congress, etc, brought a weakening. Nov.-Dec. 1.67, Jan. 31 1.61, Feb. 31 1.46. It will go below $1 if the public push persistent. See also March Index.

Compare bituminous coal prices 1913–1925–1931 where competition exists.

I happen to know that within 18 months on a large R.R. they were paying 30 cents a ton more than they should because of a son & nephew in the coal business.

[1] Perhaps Marcus Cauffman Sloss (1869–1958), who had served as an associate justice of the California Supreme Court from 1906–1919, when he resumed private practice in San Francisco.

[2] There is no copy of the Sloss letter in the Frankfurter mss, but it was sent to *The New Republic* as a response to an editorial paragraph (*New Republic* 65 [January 28, 1931]: 284) that complained about the high price of steel rails and hinted at collusion between the railroads and the steel companies.

No. 457   April 27, 1931   Washington, D.C.

1. The Apr. 15 letter from [Lindsay] Rogers shows that you will have an understanding person with whom to discuss Palestine matters. He and Mrs. dined with us last evening and confirmed all you say of his quality. I think he is "on to" Big Business & appreciates the dangers into which our foreign trade & investment have plunged us.

2. Redlich was in yesterday. I hope he won't wholly exhaust OWH with whom he dines this P.M.

3. I am glad Palestine has impressed Estelle.

4. No. 94. P.C. April 27. must have pleased you.[1]

5. My admiration of the C.J.'s performances at conference continues unabated.

[1] In *Ramsey & Gatlin Construction & Aetna Casualty & Surety Co.* v. *Vincennes Bridge Co.*, 283 U.S. 796 (1931), the Court had denied certiorari to an appeal from a Kentucky court because no reason existed for the federal courts to become involved in a matter of state law that raised no federal questions.

No. 458   May 2, 1931   Washington, D.C.

1. Re Friendly. I had been thinking last night of Friendly and that his 3 year trial period would be up soon. I hope he will conclude to go to Harvard now.[1]

2. W. B. Leach[2] (accompanied by Palfrey[3]—silent) made a very good argument, good in manner as well as substance.[4]

3. I am glad Bob [Szold] and JWM had the benefit of your advice. The London reports throw a terrible light on the MacDonald Government.[5]

4. Leach is probably right in his diagnosis, but I don't think it wise

457

for you—or any of our crowd—to make known the facts. At all events, wait until we can talk matters over. I was sorry that Powell's skit appeared in the HLR.[6]

5. We hope to have you & Marion dine with us at the Bellevue, June 2.

6. Austern goes to Dean [Acheson] Sept. 15. I think it would be well for Hart to be here a day or two earlier to have Austern break him in.

7. In April 1 Davar, I hope you noted also "Kiryat Anavim."[7]

8. I was sorry I couldn't see B.V.C. on April 25.

9. See Apr. 20 Day's Orders for 94. Ramsey & Gatlin Construction Co. v. Vincennes Bridge Co.—Per Cur.[8]

[1] Despite constant urging from both LDB and FF to enter teaching, Friendly remained in private practice until his appointment to the circuit court of appeals in 1959. See 28 October and 9 November 1926.

[2] Walter Barton Leach (1900–1971) had served as secretary to Justice Holmes in 1924–1925, and then taught at the Harvard Law School from 1929 to 1969.

[3] John Gorham Palfrey (1875–1945), the scion of a distinguished Boston family, after graduation from Harvard Law, had worked for several years in LDB's firm, and then gone into private practice.

[4] Leach and Palfrey had appeared for the petitioner in *Frank L. Young Co.* v. *McNeal-Edwards Co.*, 283 U.S. 398, argued the preceding week. On 18 May, Holmes, for a unanimous court, sustained their argument in the case, which dealt with the application of state procedure in the federal courts.

[5] Although the MacDonald government had retracted the Passfield White Paper of 1930, the February 1931 statement of policy had done little to clarify His Majesty's government's policy in Palestine as British leaders attempted, unsuccessfully, to placate both Jews and Arabs in their opposing plans for Palestine.

[6] In "An Imaginary Judicial Opinion," *Harvard Law Review* 44 (1931): 889, Powell satirized the Supreme Court's drawing of finespun distinctions (see 26 January 1931, n. 2) in an effort not to overrule precedents.

[7] Kiryat Anavim ("Vineyard City") is a kibbutz eight miles west of Jerusalem founded in 1920. The initiative came from Akiva Ettinger who wished to work out modern methods of hill farming, afforestation, and land reclamation. The settlement had difficult times in its early years, but the pioneers refused to abandon it, and eventually proved the success of the new methods.

[8] See preceding letter, n. 1.

No. 459   May 17, 1931   Washington, D.C.

1. Is "Cases in Administrative Law" really out?[1] It should prove a great help in instilling sound notions.

2. Very glad Mania Shochat [sic][2] impressed you also so much, and that you have written J.W.M. When Bob Szold was here, he had not even seen her.

3. Deborah Kallen was in yesterday, & joins in the general view that Jews could get on well enough with the Arabs but for the British

interference & influence. I fear you & I will have to revise somewhat our favorable judgment of English officials.

4. Yes, delay should be the policy.[3]

5. Our leaders of business are beginning "to get theirs." Did you notice Comm'er of Education Cooper[4] in today's U.S. Daily?[5] I fear H.H. won't like it.

6. Glad your Episcopal friend was impressed.

7. Gardner Jackson (who was in Wednesday) thought Hastings[6] had probably written H.H.'s disarmament address.[7]

Please invite Hermann [Blumgart] to dine with us on June 2.

[1] FF and J. Forrester Davison, *Cases and Other Materials on Administrative Law* (Chicago: Commerce Clearing House, 1931).

[2] Manya Wilbuschewitz-Shohat (1880–1961) was among the founders of the Palestine self-defense movement, first in HaShomer and later in the Haganah. In the 1930s she traveled extensively in the United States on behalf of Histadrut, the general labor organization of the Yishuv.

[3] Regarding British plans in Palestine.

[4] William John Cooper (1882–1935), after extensive teaching and administrative experience in California, served as U.S. commissioner of education during the Hoover administration.

[5] Cooper had announced that the U.S. Office of Education would seek funds from Congress to conduct a nationwide survey of "exceptional children," including a study of adolescent crime and delinquency.

[6] George Aubrey Hastings (1885–1956), a newspaperman and public relations advisor, served as an administrative assistant to President Hoover in 1931 and 1932.

[7] In a speech opening the World Chambers of Commerce conference in Washington, Hoover urged a general disarmament as a means of cutting down overburdened national budgets and as an aid to reviving business activity.

No. 460   May 20, 1931   Washington, D.C.

1. Brodie[1] was in yesterday (with Bob [Szold]) and handed me the enclosed memo by Morris Ruffman on the grave delays interposed by British officialdom to American capitalists seeking Palestine visas. I hope you will take this matter up at once with Brodie (420 Lexington Ave NYC) and the State Department.

Brodie is confident that, if unnecessary obstacles are removed, we can send into Palestine each year, at least, $5,000,000 new capital, by 300 capitalist immigrants.

2. U.S. Daily, May 20, 1931, p. 1, giving living costs in Mass. on April 30, gives "Food and Light" as at 166 percent of 1913.

The price of bituminous coal at the pit mouth is as low as in 1913. The coal efficiency in 1931 is vastly more than (in the best plants several times what it was) in 1913. Lewis Goldberg[2] ought to get busy on this promptly.

[1] Israel Benjamin Brodie (1884–1965) was a Baltimore lawyer and an active Zionist; he was one of the founders and, later, director of the Palestine Economic Corporation.

[2] Lewis Goldberg (1887–1974), a graduate of the Harvard Law School, would be appointed the following year as a justice of the Massachusetts Superior Court, where he would serve for forty-one years. He was active in a number of civic and Jewish organizations in the Boston area.

No. 461   June 11, 1931   Chatham, Mass.

1. Alexander Hamilton Institute Ad, U.S. Daily June 9/ p.5 is a temperate document, & its predictions "when will business recover" probably sound if it read "begin to recover."[1] But it is silent as to the 8 obstacles, which vitally affect the pace and the scope.

The Census (1930) returns appearing on population throw much light on the extent of birth control. Thus figures (U.S. Daily) given on Oregon show population under 5 years, 268,000; 5 to 9 years, 281,000. If the birth rate were stable, these figures would probably be reversed.

2. Note Keynes on loan sharks in clipping enclosed.[2]

3. DeHaas writes that May 6 to June 7 25 "capitalist" applications with over $200,000 capital for Palestine visas.

[1] In an upbeat, full page advertisement entitled "The Making of a Business Revival," the Institute argued against major government programs to deal with the depression. The bottom had probably been reached in December 1930, according to the advertisement, and the best thing that could be done was to rely on the natural workings of the economy to bring about recovery.

[2] In a series of lectures at the New School for Social Research, Keynes addressed a number of depression problems, including the status of the money in banks. He urged deposit in less liquid assets, such as bonds.

No. 462   June 26, 1931   Chatham, Mass.

1. For the declining birthrate in Mass., see U.S. Daily, June 24, p. 2 (Census of Bay State).[1] The Justrium Liberorum was Augustan legislation.[2]

2. I have had from B.F. a further, and more bitter, letter on Mohl.[3] I hope you were able to mollify him a little.

3. The New River College is awake.

4. Some day, somebody ought to talk strongly on "The avoidance of controversial questions" by Amer. Bar Assoc. Journal.

5. The N.R. article on the movies' avoidance of offense to the social workers points to an inevitable evil of bigness & mass production.[4] We can't get liberty in amusements or in more serious things unless the producer may cater to small audiences or bodies of customers. Unlike the Times Sunday editor (who undoubtedly feared to give offense to the

insurance companies) a small free paper would be glad to take up Savings Bank Insurance.

It was a fine little visit we had from you. Our best to you & Marion for the "Westward Ho." [5] We shall expect you back in early September.

[1] The most recent census reported a decline of 13.2 percent in the number of persons under one year old in Massachusetts, and a 9.4 percent decline in number of people less than five years old, compared to the 1920 census. All other age groups showed increases. This was part of a nationwide response to the Depression—fewer new births per thousand of the population.

[2] Under legislation passed during the reign of Augustus, women who had three children (four if they were free women) were relieved of the necessity of having a *tutor*, or guardian, without whose assent they could not engage in major property transactions. The purpose of the law was to encourage child-bearing, especially among the upper classes.

[3] Emanuel N. Mohl (1883–19[?]), an American trained engineer, had headed the Palestine Industrial Survey in 1923. He later held several advisory positions to the Palestine government.

[4] "Sociology, Fate, Form and Films," *New Republic* 67 (3 June 1931): 72. Murray Godwin, a frequent contributor to left-wing journals, accused American critics of ignoring the important Soviet films because they did not like the new social types portrayed in them, in which individualism was played down and social significance emphasized.

[5] The Frankfurters were leaving to spend the summer in Los Angeles, where FF would be working on a survey of the criminal justice system similar to the one he and Roscoe Pound had done in Cleveland. See 12 January 1921, n. 3.

No. 463   July 17, 1931   Chatham, Mass.

1. It is fortunate that the Los Angeles papers are inadequate & that you are cut off from telephone and radio. The current news is now so engrossing that the criminal survey would be much impeded if you were in the midst of things. I hope your work will be largely done before the Fall term.

2. It looks as if H.H. would have a serious slump after his recent exaltation. Like his other projects it was much belated, inadequate & badly handled.

3. Meanwhile, things economic at home are only growing worse still. The N.R. article by Eiteman is an admirable one, but for a part of the last paragraph. [1]

4. Our group has done well at Basle, & apparently has carried out substantially its whole program. [2] The $4,000,000 indebtedness is the sole trouble. If there were no debts there would be fair going despite the depression, the Arabs & the English.

5. Stanley King, Harry Kendall, [3] Davison, Filene & Edwin Smith [4] were here last week on unemployment.

6. The Census figures on N.Y. City population 9 yrs. in N.Y. Times July 16 fully confirms the prediction on population arrest. [5]

7. Wisconsin & Pennsylvania show rich fruits for your labor injunction work & should help the struggle at Washington.

[1] Wilfard J. Eiteman, "Two Decades of Depression: Will the 1930's Parallel the 1870's?" *New Republic* 67 (15 July 1931): 222. Eiteman, an economist at Albion College in Michigan, drew a number of parallels between the depressions of 1873 and 1929, including the insistence of government leaders that the difficulties would not last long. In his conclusion, however, he argued against using the previous experience as a guide toward dealing with contemporary problems.

[2] At the Seventeenth Zionist Congress in Basle earlier in the month, a coalition led by the Brandeis-Mack faction had forced Chaim Weizmann to step down from the presidency, a direct result of WZO impotence in the face of the Passfield White Paper. The new WZO Executive adopted a program emphasizing practical work to build up the Yishuv.

[3] Harry Kendall (1876–1958) was a Louisville insurance company executive.

[4] Edwin Whittier Smith (1857–1937), a Pittsburgh attorney, also served as a director of several insurance companies.

[5] The article detailed a significant drop in population among the younger age groups, with a corresponding percentage increase in the older age brackets.

No. 464   July 22, 1931   Chatham, Mass.

1. That's a nice letter from McCracken.[1] N.C. seems very hard hit financially. 40% of the recent $100,000,000 annual expenditure went for debt service, but the leading men are approaching the situation manfully.[2]

2. Far from manful is the proposal of California to have the United States finance the great state water conservation program.[3] These Californians ought to be ashamed of themselves.

3. The Moores-Castle-Klein misrepresentation continues and the great men take no note of such trifles as the Russell Sage-Yale survey of unemployment in New Haven.[4]

4. Warburg and Adler[5] wanted me to cable Mack re the proposed Congress resolution on Jewish majority, but I declined.

5. Aydelotte[6] replied, saying he would avail of the invitation to see me, if he came to the Cape.

6. The only business that seems to be going well is Savings Bank Life Insurance. June '31 new business was 60% over June '30. (That is about the same percentage as for the eight months). The insurance companies had over 12% loss as compared with 1930. Stanley King has promised to follow your lead & send circular to Amherst faculty; and Harry Kimball[7] to send one to the Mount Holyoke faculty. I enclose new "Brief Survey."

7. I hope your Criminal survey is progressing.

[1] There is no letter from a McCracken in the Frankfurter MSS.

[2] The Supreme Court of North Carolina had ruled that bonds issued by various counties to

compensate for decreasing revenue were not for a "special" purpose, and the counties were therefore subject to constitutional limits on indebtedness.

[3] California wanted Congress to appropriate $160,000,000 to finance a massive water development plan. The state claimed that millions of acres of previously unused land had come under development, including six million in the San Joaquin Valley alone, and that the total cost of the entire program, some $375,000,000, was beyond its resources.

[4] The study, undertaken by the Russell Sage Foundation and Yale University, showed an 18 percent unemployment rate in New Haven, nearly double the figures released by the federal government.

[5] Cyrus Adler (1863–1940), an Arkansas-born scholar, writer, and archivist, was a major figure in American Jewish affairs. The president of both Dropsie College and the Jewish Theological Seminary, he succeeded Louis Marshall as head of the American Jewish Committee.

[6] Frank Aydelotte (1880–1956) served as president of Swarthmore College from 1921 to 1940.

[7] (Harry) Everett Kimball (1873–1948) taught government at Smith College, and directed its social work school from 1921 to 1943.

No. 465   August 19, 1931   Chatham, Mass.

1. Extremely sorry to learn that you are again afflicted by boils. They plagued me intermittently for at least six or seven years, and taught me (a) that the medical profession knows little or nothing about them, (b) that they are the penalty for overdoing.

2. I am indeed sorry also that the work has been so much interfered with. There's so much else ahead of you that I wish it were possible for you to begin soon the long deferred sabattical. Man also is entitled to a moratorium.

3. DeHaas, Neumann [1] and (later) six others were here Friday, Saturday, Sunday last, and today Jacob Landau was here. So I am having ample occasion to consider Zionist-Palestine problems. Mack and Bob [Szold] will probably be here Sunday. Our group is much encouraged, but it has a serious fight ahead to crush a recrudescent Weizmann-Lipsky recovery. [2]

4. H.H. and his Farm Board are becoming imbecile. [3] It is a disgrace. And all economic reports still are disturbing.

5. The British have the great merit of trying to be truthful.

6. The John Graham Brooks were here Monday in fine form.

7. It was fine that Mrs. LaFollette lived to see her two boys in high office, carrying forward their father's work. [4]

[1] Emanuel Neumann (1893–1980) was one of the most active and effective American Zionists of the twentieth century. He held numerous offices in the movement and undertook important diplomatic assignments. He sided with Weizmann during the split of 1921, but by the end of the decade had grown disillusioned with the Lipsky leaders.

[2] The Depression had made it impossible for the new ZOA administration, headed by Robert Szold, to raise funds necessary to eliminate the organization's debt (inherited from Lipsky) or to

embark on new programs. This led to charges by Lipsky and Weizmann that the Brandeis group could not deliver on its promises, but it never developed into a serious threat to the Szold administration. Although Weizmann would be reelected to the WZO presidency in 1933, Lipsky would never again hold an important office in American Zionist affairs.

[3] On 31 July Hoover had proposed that the Federal Farm Board sell substantial amounts of surplus wheat and cotton to Germany on liberal credit terms. Farm organizations immediately attacked the idea, claiming that the market for current crops would be depressed even further by using the stored crops. Germany, then in the midst of its worst depression, embraced Hoover's suggestion, but the Farm Board turned it down. With some glee, LDB termed the fiasco "amusing" on 10 August.

[4] LDB's old friend, Belle Case La Follette, had died the previous day.

No. 466   September 16, 1931   Washington, D.C.

FF. The CJ sends notice that because of docket conditions arguments will not begin until Oct. 12, thus leaving the first week free for disposition of certioraris & jurisdictional statements. This should make the going very easy for OWH, if you can get physician's orders:

(a) that OWH shall not let visitors & letters interfere with leisure

(b) that he will not write opinions except during recess

Hope Alfred Cohen will develop for you immunity from boils.

Note American's editorial on Sav. Bk. Ins. There is another in Sept. 14 issue—very good.

No. 467   September 18, 1931   Washington, D.C.

Re R. and F. letters returned herewith.

1. Napoleon says that he often won his battles years before they were fought.

(a) There is a great difference between formulating and declaring a policy. The adm. should promptly formulate its policy both as to disarmament and as to cancellation [of war debts] & work sedulously to the ends decided upon. As to disarmament, where we can act alone, it should declare our own policy now. Obviously we could disarm if no other country did. Denmark has disarmed, why can't we? Surely we are not afraid of Great Britain now, or of any other country? We should say now, we will do it, whether the rest of the world does it or not. The Borah 5 year Naval & Military Holiday would do for a starter perhaps.[1] American opinion, if fearlessly led, is ripe. As to debt cancellation, there may be good reason for going slow on declarations. There can be none for delaying the decision. (We made dreadful mistakes in our debt settlement program. All should have been on the same basis. If this had

464

been done, we should have had full power to deal with each. Of course, the only wise policy would have been to cancel, at that time, all war debts.)

Be Brave. Be Brave.

And Everywhere be brave.

(Particularly where it can save us from deficits)

(b) F. proposal of "repeal of capital gains & losses clause in income tax" seems to me most unwise.[2] It is in the class with Mellon's program of aiding business by wiping out the super tax on incomes over $100,000 and other reductions of income and corporation taxes "to stimulate business." I am amazed that F. should advocate such a scheme, unless it be because, although the device of very practical men, it is doctrinaire. Having avoided income taxes on gains through stock dividends, and escaped income taxes in recent years by deducting capital losses, Mellonites now want to escape income taxes on the huge gains the moneyed men will make when there comes a reasonable (and unreasonable) rise in stocks and bonds they are now buying at bargain counters.

(c) If I knew who had the Latin American securities (have not been able to ascertain) I might have something to say as to F's (3).

(d) F's (4) as it is ordinarily talked has in it elements of unwisdom.

2. I shall be glad to see Chapman Rose,[3] & if he wants to see me before he goes to OWH, let him come in at 10 A.M. Oct. 2.

3. That's a nice note of Cardozo's. The date of my entry in your book was Sept. 14, & doubtless my letter to you was written that day.

4. Yes, that British Navy action is very serious.[4]

5. I hope you can come to "Charlie's" relief.

6. Hart makes a very good impression.

[1] On 13 September, Senator Borah had proposed a five-year suspension of all naval construction by the great powers, not only for the sake of peace, but to relieve nations of the high cost of military preparedness.

[2] It is possible but not certain that "F" is Herbert Feis, but on 10 September, Senator David A. Reed (R.-Penn.) had suggested three ways to reduce the government's deficit. He called for a general sales tax of one percent, an increase in inheritance taxes, and repeal of the capital gains and losses provisions of the tax code. The bill was considered but never approved; in 1934 the capital gains and losses sections were modified, but not repealed.

[3] Horace Chapman Rose (b. 1907) would serve as Oliver Wendell Holmes's secretary for 1931–1932. He later practiced law in Cleveland, and served first as assistant secretary, then under secretary of the treasury during the Eisenhower administration.

[4] As part of an economy program, Great Britain cut the pay of officers in the British navy by 10 percent and that of enlisted men by 25 percent. This caused great unrest in the navy, and led the government to cancel planned maneuvers; until the issue was resolved, all ships were ordered to return to their home ports.

No. 468   September 23, 1931   Washington, D.C.

1. There is so much to say on the British situation that I defer it until you come to Washington.

2. Then also, my plans for America, which there was no time for in Boston.

3. We have made note to invite Lowndes.[1]

4. I am glad Masters[2] is back in Ala.

5. City Bank stock at $50 is the appropriate mark for our great financial minds.

6. H.H. made a good move in speaking to the Legion against more bonus cash.[3]

7. It's fine to have Myerson take up S.B.I. Have you thought of anyone at Wellesley, Simmons or Clark [colleges].

8. Roosevelt did mighty well with his Extra session.[4]

9. The talk here is that the power interests have switched from Owen Young to Newton Baker.

10. That's a striking record for Jews at H.L.S.

11. Yes, if the Labour Government was fairly represented by Drummond Shields [sic] its fall was natural.[5] His performance was dreadful.

[1] Charles Lucien Barker Lowndes (1903–1967), after graduating from the Harvard Law School in 1926, taught law first at Georgetown, and from 1935 to his death at Duke.

[2] John Volney Masters (1884–1954), another Harvard Law graduate, had taught at the University of Alabama. He had taken a leave to do graduate work, receiving his S.J.D. in 1931, and then returned to Alabama.

[3] In a speech before the American Legion on 21 September, President Hoover had come out against early payment of the bonus voted by Congress to veterans of the world war, since the taxes necessary for the early payment would weigh most heavily upon the poor.

[4] In a move to quiet Republican criticism of his handling of the Walker affair (see 25 August 1932, n. 3), Roosevelt called the New York legislature into special session to pass measures granting immunity to witnesses before the investigating commission. That having been done, he forced the legislature to agree to a relief package despite Republican opposition.

[5] Shiels had served for the last two years as parliamentary under secretary of state for the colonial office. The Labour government had fallen on 26 August because of budgetary problems.

No. 469   September 28, 1931   Washington, D.C.

1. As to OWH, it is essential that the M.D. prescribe in addition to (a) that he write no opinion except in recess; (b) that he rest (preferably take a nap) for an hour from 5 to 6, when the Court is sitting; and (c) that no visitor remain at any time more than 1 1/2 hours.

He has very frequently, at times daily, said to me as we drove home that he wished he could lie down and take a nap, but had an appointment at 5 or 5:15 or 5:30. And he has said often, during the last year, that after 1 1/2 hours a visit becomes burdensome.

2. As to imposts and the tariff, I agree entirely with Keynes, also as to deflation of the pound sterling.[1] Great Britain can't carry the $37,000,000,000 indebtedness. The income from foreign investments of Englishmen must have dropped one-half.

3. Mussey[2] would be the man for Wellesley, but he is spending the year abroad.

4. Harlan remains unhappy about our declaratory judgment decisions.

[1] In commenting upon the economic situation, John Maynard Keynes had called for a general inflation through the issue of two billion dollars in paper money without gold backing.

[2] Henry Raymond Mussey (1875–1940) taught economics at Wellesley from 1922 until his death, and had also put in a brief stint as managing editor of *The Nation*. LDB hoped Mussey would push savings bank insurance at the college.

No. 470   October 2, 1931   Washington, D.C.

1. Wales[1] reported OWH in good form yesterday P.M. I told him I thought it best I should not call until OWH had disposed of his sundry goods & chattels, which customarily take a day or two in unpacking. W. is to let me know when OWH is ready.

2. Rose was in this A.M. & I gave him some directions.[2]

3. I saw the C.J. who will be very ready to cooperate in holding back assignments & giving encouragement.

4. BF was in this A.M. I told him as to your going to England, obviously nothing to be done now except for you not to make any engagements which should prevent your going to England Christmas if that should then appear to be desirable.

5. Gene was in. He is sorely troubled.

6. As to Charles R. Crane. Tell Adler about the Crane-King report;[3] and about CRC's falling in love with the Arabs, that he thinks Ibn Saud the greatest Arab since Mohammed; that this love for Arabs has superseded all others—Russians, Czecho-Slovak, Bulgarian, Albanian; that he thinks only in Asiatics lies now the hope of the world; that CRC has always been a liberal financial supporter of all causes, foreign & domestic, in which he believes; & that it is not improbable that he has helped in Arab activities.

Have just had a call from Wales to come at 5:30.

6:10 Have just seen OWH. He is in pretty good form.

[1] Robert Willett Wales (1906–1983), a 1930 graduate of Harvard Law, had just spent the year as secretary to Holmes. After leaving Holmes, Wales practiced first in Chicago and then in New York, with a short service in the Treasury Department.

[2] About caring for Holmes; see 18 September 1931.

[3] For the King-Crane report of 1919, see Harry N. Howard, "An American Experiment in Peace Making: The King-Crane Commission," *Moslem World* 32 (1942): 124; for the reaction of LDB and American Zionists, see Urofsky, *American Zionism*, 236–37.

No. 471   October 5, 1931   Washington, D.C.

Thanks for your generous greeting which has just come.[1]

1. I have an impression (do not know) that JWM is again calling on Austern for help.[2] This is very wrong, and I hope you can make JWM understand this. Such a course is apt to impair either Austern's work for the firm or his health, or both.

2. Re OWH. Matters are not going too well. A crisis seemed near yesterday. In response to OWH's question, the M.D. had answered that he ought to resign. Mary[3] summoned me & I made OWH see that he should not, at least at present. So he was on hand this A.M., and was enough himself to be eager to make a detour on the way back from Court, to see a new statute [sic] erected in Potomac Park Extension.

But he seems incapable of keeping within bounds. Thursday afternoon, in spite of the fatigue of the journey, he insisted on going to Arlington.[4] Charles says he was very weak then. In good form today A.M. & Saturday. But when I saw him Friday P.M., he was tired out by over an hour's visit from Mrs. Jennings whom he gallantly escorted to the front door.

3. Rose is taking hold admirably. No one could do better. I have made clear to him & Mary the essential limitations.

[1] Perhaps to mark the opening of the 1931 Term.

[2] Austern had clerked for Judge Mack before working for LDB.

[3] Mary Donnellan had served as a maid for Holmes for many years.

[4] After the death of his wife in April 1929, Holmes took near daily rides to place flowers on her grave in Arlington National Cemetery. LDB notes here that he insisted upon visiting the grave on the very day he returned to Washington from his summer recess in Massachusetts.

No. 472   October 10, 1931   Washington, D.C.

1. OWH continues to bear the burden, despite 4 hated I.C.C. cases with huge records, & a Presidential visit, with much standing around Monday, and a dental operation Tuesday.

2. H.H.'s bank manifesto was not merely bad in form.[1] There is probably more to fear than to hope from the banker aggregations, bad as the bank situation is. With our banks, the fundamental defect is the confusion of three functions which should be kept religiously segregated: (a) Commercial banking. It is the duty to take business risks, for merchants & manufacturers, and the bankers should not avoid wise risks but know whom & when to trust: (b) Savings banking. It's the duty of the Savings bank man to take practically no risk. His prime duty is to promote safety. (c) Security banking. Buying and selling. This involves not only knowing fundamental merits but knowledge of markets, etc. Our banking men have by combining these three functions not only dulled & confused their wits, but all too often have confused funds of the three departments & disregarded trust obligations.[2]

We are having Rose in to dine Sunday.

[1] In an effort to support the faltering banking system, Hoover had proposed setting up a private corporation which would loan money to banks outside the regulations of the Federal Reserve System. This, in effect, would have created a private central bank, managed by private bankers, without any governmental supervision.

[2] FF incorporated these ideas into a letter to the New York *Herald-Tribune*, published on 19 October 1931. See 25 October 1931.

No. 473   October 11, 1931   Washington, D.C.

1. OWH was at a four hour conference yesterday, throughout in good form & appeared generally in about the same condition as last year.

2. George Rublee was in yesterday. Of course much saddened by Dwight's death.[1] And gloom was added by his unsuccessful efforts to get loans for the Columbian govt.[2] He says NY bankers told him that "no foreign govt could get a loan now—not even Holland."

[1] Morrow had unexpectedly died on 5 October 1931.

[2] Rublee had been retained by the Columbians as a financial advisor.

No. 474   October 25, 1931   Washington, D.C.

1. Hart handed me clipping from Herald-Tribune of 19th with your letter on banks.[1] It was tellingly put.

2. OWH is bearing up pretty well, but he is undoubtedly older; doesn't catch on as he did at arguments, and is not having a good time.

3. The British delegate to AFL (Beard)[2] was in today. He is a MacDonald man, & evidently doesn't think that Labor will suffer more than

very temporarily from recent occurrences. Seems to think they will gain industrially from being out, politically.

4. It seems clear that our organized RR Labor will not permit wiping out Federal Employers Liability Act. This has occurred to me:

Have Congress pass a voluntary act by which interstate RR employees may get the benefit of the state compensation acts of the state in which they reside and are employed; and provide that assent shall be presumed unless employee and RR file rejection.

If you think well of this, it might be well to put it up to Bikle. The coming Congress would doubtless pass the Act, if desired by the RRs.

5. Borah was true to form.[3]

[1] FF's letter, repeating LDB's views in his letter of 10 October, had pointed out that banks served three distinct functions, savings, commercial transactions, and securities investment, and that these areas should be kept strictly separated, since they involved different values and means of doing business.

[2] Possibly John Beard (1871–1950), general counsel to the Trade Union Congress.

[3] In an interview with a French correspondent, Borah had said he would cancel all inter-Allied debts provided German reparations were also eliminated. Borah also criticized the Versailles Treaty, and proposed that certain parts dealing with Germany be revised.

No. 475   November 8, 1931   Washington, D.C.

1. OWH was cheered a bit by being able to deliver the two opinions last Monday,[1] but he seems definitely older.

2. There has been no "opportunity" of sounding Hart.[2] Of course I can, without occasion, take up the subject with him. But would that be wise? Hadn't he better be asked by Williston to talk with me.

3. The granting of certiorari in No. 477 Boston & Maine RR v. Amberg [sic][3] (from Mass.) affords additional reason for Congressional legislation concerning accidents to RR employees.

3. Norman and George Anderson are in town.

[1] In *United States* v. *Kirby Lumber Co.*, 284 U.S. 1, the Court upheld a broad interpretation of income amenable to federal taxation. *Moore* v. *Bay*, 284 U.S. 4, confirmed the supremacy of federal over state liens, as well as the priority of trustees for the estate in bankruptcy matters. Both cases had been decided on 2 November 1931.

[2] Hart was then serving as LDB's clerk, and was being considered for the Harvard law faculty. He did in fact join the Law School in 1932, and taught there until his death in 1969.

[3] The case was eventually argued on 24–25 February 1932. Justice Stone handed down the Court's opinion on 14 March 1932, holding that a state workmen's compensation law, in this case that of Massachusetts, applied to employees of interstate railroads when they were engaged strictly in intrastate activities. The Court noted that it had not been the intention of Congress to exclude the states from action in those areas under their control through the Federal Employers Liability Act. *Boston & Maine R.R. Co.* v. *Armburg*, 285 U.S. 234 (1932).

No. 476   November 19, 1931   Washington, D.C.

1. I have just finished the Nov. H.L.R.[1] and have written a brief note to Schoene[2]—all that it seemed wise to say.

You and Bikle have made fine presentations.[3] I hope you will write Bikle, Donald Richberg,[4] Hamilton[5] and Max Lerner[6] and also Dr. Balogh.[7] It seems better that I should not.

2. I know Trabue[8] from early days to the present. He is the narrowest thing on earth. That's fine of Bruere.

3. The Marbury news is interesting.

4. Yes, it was a fine birthday party.

5. I am glad Harold [Laski] is not discouraged. But his eagerness for outright socialism is surprising. I don't agree at all with what is apparently his free trade view. In my opinion, a large part of the unemployment of the last 10 years might have been averted if England had had an appropriate tariff on manufactures, dairy products and farm truck.

[1] To mark LDB's seventy-fifth birthday, the *Harvard Law Review, Yale Law Journal*, and *Columbia Law Review* had all dedicated their November 1931 issues to him.

[2] Lester Philip Schoene (1908–1976) was then president of the *Harvard Law Review*. He would stay on at Harvard to do a year of graduate work with FF, and then practiced law in Virginia.

[3] The two leading articles of that issue were Bikle, "Mr. Justice Brandeis and the Regulation of Railroads," *Harvard Law Review* 45 (1931): 4, and FF, "Mr. Justice Brandeis and the Constitution," *id.* at 33.

[4] Richberg had written "The Industrial Liberalism of Justice Brandeis," *Columbia Law Review* 31 (1931): 1094.

[5] Walton Hamilton had also contributed to the *Columbia* issue, with "The Jurist's Art," *id.* at 1073.

[6] Max Lerner (b. 1902), an economist trained at the Brookings Institution, would be an editor of *The Nation*, write a nationally syndicated column, and from 1949 to 1973 serve as professor of American Civilization at Brandeis University. LDB's reference to him here relates to his article, "The Social Thought of Mr. Justice Brandeis," *Yale Law Journal* 41 (1931): 1.

[7] Elemer Balogh, a professor of law at the University of Kaunas in Lithuania and secretary-general of the International Academy of Comparative Law, had contributed an appreciative preface on LDB to the November issue of the *Harvard Law Review*.

[8] Edmund Francis Trabue (1855–1936) was a Louisville lawyer specializing in railroad matters.

No. 477   November 25, 1931   Washington, D.C.

1. You certainly did a thorough job on my Constitutional opinions. It "refreshed the mind" in many respects. OWH likes the article much.

2. OWH is in fine form, and is now enjoying the sessions as well as other things.

3. Permutit Case[1] will doubtless give pain again to our friends in the Second Circuit, and also to Denison, who I see is retiring. I am glad our court is so united in curbing patent excesses.

4. I hope you will write Harlan about his I.C.C. dissent.[2]

5. I judge from carbon rec'd from JWM that you concluded to have him write deH.

6. John Lord O'Brian made today the best argument I have heard from him, in the Whitestone Branch Case.[3]

[1] *Permutit Co.* v. *Graver Co.*, 284 U.S. 52 (1931). In the decision handed down on 23 November, LDB, for a unanimous court, upheld the seventh circuit in limiting the reach of patents. Permutit owned a patent for softening water, and had sued Graver, which marketed another device, for infringement. Permutit had won a similar case in the second circuit, which had given patent protection an extremely broad reach.

[2] In *Chicago, Rock Island & Pacific Ry. Co.* v. *United States*, 284 U.S. 80 (1931), the Court, through Justice Sutherland, upheld one I.C.C. regulation on accounting of car leases by shorter lines from larger carriers, but struck down another rule giving the shorter lines two "free" days for such interchanged cars. Stone, joined by Holmes and LDB, argued in dissent that the rule was neither unreasonable nor arbitrary. On 4 December, FF wrote Stone fulsomely praising the dissent.

[3] In *Transit Commission of New York* v. *United States*, 284 U.S. 360 (1932), the Court, through Justice Roberts, upheld an I.C.C. order permitting the Long Island Railroad to abandon operation on part of its Whitestone branch. The Court ruled that the Commission had correctly balanced the needs of the commuting public against the financial requirements of the line.

No. 478   December 27, 1931   Washington, D.C.

1. Your Dutchman was in this afternoon—a charming fellow.

2. When you come I hope you will arrange to give some time to Bob La Follette on taxation. I saw him a moment the other day, & he said the Drafting Bureau had not been productive.

3. And where is the man for the progressive corporation tax.

4. Rose telephoned me on 25th that OWH had not been well & the M.D. told him to let up on work for a few days.[1]

Our best wishes for 1932.

[1] Ten days earlier, LDB had written: "No need for secretary for OWH for next term."

No. 479   January 10, 1932   Washington, D.C.

Confidential

1. OWH. handed the C.J. his resignation today,[1] dated Jan. 12, so as to let him deliver an opinion tomorrow.[2] How it happened I will tell you at say 9.15 or 9.30 next Saturday. I saw him immediately after the event at 12.45. He was as calm and gallant as ever in his life.

2. Now that a New Yorker has introduced a Savings Bank Ins. bill,[3] considerably noticed in the press, possibly Charles Merz might find the Sunday Times editor receptive. I should prefer that the bill be killed in

N.Y. but an article in the Times would help much in the Massachusetts business.

3. Your and Landis' Dec. article on the Court is particularly interesting & has some suggestions which should move the C.J.[4]

4. Some one has carried off my "Business of the S.C." If you have a spare copy of the book please send me one.

[1] In his letter of resignation to President Hoover, ending his fifty-year career as a jurist, Holmes wrote: "The condition of my health makes it a duty to break off connections that I cannot leave without deep regret after the affectionate relations of many years and the absorbing interests that have filled my life. But the time has come and I bow to the inevitable." On the day of Holmes's actual retirement, LDB penned him a short note quoting from Schiller's "Thehla's Song," "Ich habe gelebt und geliebt"—"I have lived and loved."

[2] Holmes delivered his last opinion on 11 January in *Dunn* v. *United States*, 284 U.S. 390 (1932).

[3] The campaign for savings bank life insurance in New York, closely watched by LDB, would take six more years before it achieved success. See LDB to Charles Goldmark, 17 March 1938, and to Charles Warren, 30 March 1938.

[4] FF and James M. Landis, "The Business of the Supreme Court at the October Term, 1930," *Harvard Law Review* 45 (1931): 271.

No. 480   January 21, 1932   Washington, D.C.

1. Thanks for the copy of "Business etc."

2. Hope you landed Hart[1] and Garrison.[2]

3. Have heard only Neumann's report of Sunday's meeting. He declared it a "success in every respect." I have no doubt other Senators & officials can be procured as members of Com'tee.[3]

4. My throat has kept me from Court. Otherwise, I am O.K.

5. The foreign reaction on Eugene's Reconstruction Corporation[4] is, I guess something of a surprise to him; & he may not be altogether happy about having Dawes (or any one) as President.[5] Illinois, Iowa banks seem to fail despite the progress on this bill, & the existing Credit Corporation.

6. I hear that many of our big fellows, and particularly estates having estate taxes to pay, are badly embarrassed by the fall in the market value of the securities & drop in dividends.

7. It was fine to see you.

8. Your Governor is afraid you couldn't be confirmed, I hear via OWH.[6]

[1] LDB's clerk, Henry M. Hart, began his long service at the Harvard Law School in September 1932.

[2] Lloyd Kirkham Garrison (b. 1897), after graduation from Harvard Law, had practiced in New

York until Hoover appointed him to the solicitor-general's office in 1929. In 1932, he went to the University of Wisconsin Law School as dean, a post he held until 1945, when he returned to private practice.

³ Emanuel Neumann had begun organizing the American Palestine Committee, comprised of prominent non-Jewish citizens who supported a Jewish homeland in Palestine. The initial meeting at the Hotel Mayflower on 17 January was presided over by vice-president Charles Curtis, and featured a number of speakers, including FF.

⁴ A wave of bank failures finally forced President Hoover into seeking some form of federal action to save the faltering system. On 8 December 1931 he had recommended the establishment of a Reconstruction Finance Corporation, with a capital of $500 million and authority to borrow up to $3 billion more, which it could then lend to banks in order to protect the credit structure.

⁵ As president of the RFC, Hoover named former vice-president Charles Dawes, then serving as ambassador to Great Britain. The president of the RFC held little power, and Washington rumor had it that Hoover had created the position to (1) eliminate Dawes politically; (2) open up the ambassadorial post to which he named Secretary of the Treasury Andrew Mellon; thus (3) allowing Hoover to name his own man, Ogden Mills, to head the Treasury.

⁶ There was already considerable speculation about the possibility of FF's being nominated to the Supreme Judicial Court of Massachusetts. In June, Massachusetts governor Joseph Buell Ely (1881–1956) presented the nomination, triggering an outburst of enthusiasm from liberals and denunciations from conservatives. Former Governor Alvan T. Fuller vowed he would sooner cut off his arm than see FF confirmed. LDB argued against FF's going on the Massachusetts court, believing he could do more effective work remaining at Harvard. Faced with a determined opposition from enemies as well as this advice from LDB, FF ultimately declined the nomination, and in a widely publicized letter to Ely on 29 June 1932, claimed that he owed a larger obligation to legal education and the training of an enlightened bench and bar than could be met through service as a judge. Michael Parrish suggests that "by rejecting Ely, an ally of Al Smith who had made a series of bitter attacks on Roosevelt, he signaled loyalty to F.D.R. and a willingness to play a larger role in the [1932 presidential] campaign." *Felix Frankfurter*, p. 210. See also letters of 23 and 26 June 1932.

No. 481   January 26, 1932   Washington, D.C.

1. Harlan, who was in Sunday, said that H.H. was shying away from Cardozo,¹ that H.H. and Mitchell did not seem inclined to Baker;² & that H.H. had territory in mind, & that Phillips³ seemed their favorite.

2. Harlan has certainly grown much in recent years.

3. When Eugene called on Jan. 1 & told me of the Reconstruction Corp. project, he said he told H.H. that he didn't want to have any thing to do with it unless he was the boss; & that H.H. said he should be chairman. There was no suggestion then of any president.

4. What would you say to this for a starter in the taxation of corporate bigness? Amend the Corporation Tax Act by adding to the profits tax that all corporations with gross assets of $1,000,000 or more shall pay an annual franchise tax of one-fourth (1/4) of such assets held at end of preceding year; and providing that no deduction of amount should be

made for holding of, or in, a subsidiary or other corporation. If we got that for now, it would be easy to build up a real curse of bigness tax later.

5. Hope Mrs. Howitt will get onto the Reconstruction Corp.

6. That's fine about Garrison; also of Vodrey. [4]

7. I have about recovered my voice, & hope to see OWH soon.

8. Wise doubtless reported to you on his Sunday visit.

9. I appreciate Cardozo's disinclination to leave his present job. [5]

[1] To replace Holmes on the Supreme Court; see 16 February 1932.

[2] Among those rumored as a replacement for Holmes was Newton D. Baker.

[3] Orie Leon Phillips (1885-[?]), was a New Mexico Republican, named district judge by Harding in 1923, and then to the Tenth Circuit Court of Appeals by Hoover in April, 1929. He was chief judge of that court from 1940 to 1955.

[4] William Henry Vodrey (1873–1954) was an Ohio attorney and general counsel as well as a partner in the Burch-Moore newspaper chain.

[5] As chief judge of the New York Court of Appeals.

No. 482   February 13, 1932   Washington, D.C.

1. Your publisher advised me Feb. 4 that the Administrative Law book is coming, but it has not come yet. [1]

2. Friendly was in. Of course I advised his taking the RFC job. Eugene was in yesterday & I told him not to let F. get away from him. It is evident that the wise men of the firm are repeating what they did about the Harvard offer. [2]

3. Cochran [3] was also in last week. Since then, I have a letter that they (Eugene) turned him down for the coveted job. Eugene didn't mention C. to me, so I was silent on that subject.

4. The Keynes' book interests me much. [4] An extraordinary economic mind that should have been put to work by the British.

5. Had a talk with Herbert Feis last Monday on the lines of his memo sent you, returned herewith. [5] He said of Eugene: "He is a great speculator," referring to his attitude re R.F.C.

6. Eugene is none too cocky, & certainly realizes the seriousness of the situation.

7. It's fine that Garrison is going to Madison.

8. My throat has been kicking up again, but hope to attend Court on resumption of the sittings Monday.

9. OWH was in fine form when I saw him on the 8th.

10. Glad you wrote Stimson about R. [6] R. would be the supreme calamity.

11. That's an interesting article on C. P. Scott.[7]

12. Julius Simon & Bob S[zold] were here Thursday. S happy over Palestine progress. No unemployment there among Jews.

[1] See 17 May 1931 and 19 February 1932.

[2] Friendly did not leave his private practice to work for the RFC; see 2 May 1931, n. 1.

[3] Although LDB persistenty misspells this name in a number of letters, there is little doubt that he meant Thomas G. Corcoran. Eventually, LDB begins to spell it correctly.

[4] LDB is perhaps referring to Quincy Wright, ed., *Unemployment as a World Problem* (Chicago: University of Chicago Press, 1931), which included an essay by Keynes, "An Economic Analysis of Unemployment."

[5] Herbert Feis (1893–1972) had recently become economic advisor to Henry Stimson in the State Department, and would later serve with him in the War Department until 1947. He then began a career as a diplomatic historian, writing ten books and winning a Pulitzer Prize for his account of the Potsdam Conference. He had sent FF a memorandum dated 4 February on "The Drift of the World Economic Situation," which predicted a continued downward trend.

[6] Joseph Taylor Robinson (1872–1937) had served as a representative in Congress from 1903 to 1913, was then elected as governor of Arkansas, and resigned two months later to take his seat as senator from that state, a position he held until his death. Robinson had long wanted to be on the Supreme Court, and in 1937 agreed to lead the floor fight for Roosevelt's court-packing plan. He died in the midst of the fight.

[7] Charles Prestwick Scott (1846–1932), a former Liberal member of Parliament, had been editor of the *Manchester Guardian* from 1912 until his death on 1 January 1932. An obituary article appeared in the *New Republic* on 13 January.

No. 483   February 16, 1932   Washington, D.C.

1. The Cardozo nomination was an unexpected boon.[1] Harlan, who was in yesterday at 10 A.M., had no inkling. Spoke of the R[obinson] peril & of his having talked hard to the A.G. on that subject. I gave him then the second Groner[2] memo & he said: "I think he is the best of present possibilities."

2. I suppose you noticed the fate of the Stratton case (No. 178)[3] & recalled the paper shown you in June 30.

3. I am very glad you have the Harvard Palestinians under your tutelage.

4. Also that Sok[olow] fared so well in Boston.

5. I agree with your doubts re new Glass bill.[4] I guess the only real justification (other than the eternal psychological) is the fact that the Govt is absorbing by its short-term loans, so much of the banks' lending capacity. The stock market seems to be getting over its delight.

6. News about the Insull properties[5] indicates that the family will soon be shorn of its greatness, and may join Otto H. Kahn[6] as Opera Angels only.

[1] Hoover had been under immense pressure from liberals both in the Congress and around the country not to name a conservative to replace Holmes on the Court, and Cardozo had been the name most often mentioned favorably by them. Hoover, however, had reportedly been leery of naming a second Jew to the High Bench, and at one point had suggested to New York Senator Robert F. Wagner that if LDB resigned, it would be easier to name Cardozo. Another consideration in the president's view was that the Court already had two New Yorkers, Hughes and Stone, and that there ought to be some geographical distribution among the members. Stephen Wise, FF, and others lobbied strenuously for Cardozo, and a key factor was Wise's winning over Senator Borah. Borah went to see Hoover, and convinced the president that a religious issue did not exist, and that appointment of the distinguished New York jurist would bring nothing but praise to the beleaguered Hoover for rising above petty partisan and regional considerations. In fact, the nomination was universally acclaimed, and quickly confirmed by the Senate.

[2] Duncan Lawrence Groner (1873–1957) had been a judge of the District Court for the Eastern District of Virginia from 1921 to 1931, and from 1931 until his retirement in 1948 served on the Circuit Court of Appeals for the District of Columbia.

[3] *Stratton* v. *St. Louis Southwestern Ry. Co.*, 284 U.S. 530, decided the day before with an opinion by Justice Stone, held that where a state mechanism existed for the recovery of taxes paid under duress, there was no need for intervention by the federal courts. The case followed LDB's longheld views on maintaining strict adherence to federalist divisions of responsibility, with federal courts abstaining from interference with strictly local matters.

[4] Senator Carter Glass of Virginia had proposed legislation which would require national banks and trust companies to eliminate their securities operations in the stock market. Such a provision was eventually enacted in the Glass-Steagall Act of 1933.

[5] The Insull empire of public utilities holding companies had never been adequately financed, with much of the stock little more than water, and it had collapsed during the Depression. See 23 August 1926, n. 9.

[6] Otto Hermann Kahn (1867–1934), by then a retired partner of Kuhn, Loeb & Co., devoted most of his time and money to various cultural enterprises, especially the Metropolitan Opera Company, of which he was past chairman of the board.

No. 484   February 19, 1932   Washington, D.C.

1. The "Administrative Law Cases" has come. A most alluring volume. And I like the Preface.[1]

2. Hart has recovered the missing "Business."[2] If not needed by you, I will retain for my bedroom study the copy you sent recently.

3. Enclosed from Friendly, discloses his Achilles' heel. He stated to me that before Eugene had summoned him, he had been "dreaming" whether by some happy chance he might not get the job, and was eager to come.[3] Showing more emotion than he had ever disclosed to me. I fancy his superiors are not much given to patriotic endeavor.

4. Mrs. Stimson's concern is not surprising. It's fine to know that Rogers[4] is so treasured.

5. The C.J. hopes that Cardozo will have been confirmed in time to come for the session beginning Mch 14. There will probably be only 4 more weeks of hearings after the present sitting which ends on the 29th.

6. Glad you talked at the Ely dinner to [*].

My throat is slowly mending.

[1] In the preface, the authors set out a brief history of the development of administrative agencies to deal with the complexities of governing a modern society.

[2] See 10 January 1932.

[3] See 13 February 1932.

[4] Probably James Grafton Rogers (1873–1971), the dean of the University of Colorado Law School. From 1931 to 1933 Rogers served in Washington as assistant secretary of state; he then went on to the Yale Law School and a distinguished career in government service.

No. 485   February 25, 1932   Washington, D.C.

1. I doubt whether Cardozo would be helped by having him now set wise about McR. As I wrote you, it is not only McR, but Butler and Van who protested in advance to the A.G. Whether they represented Sutherland also, Harlan did not know.[1] I have no doubt all four will be formally correct in their behavior. Later, Harlan can initiate him C. into the truth, if C. does not discover it for himself.

2. Of course, Cardozo ought to have a good secretary; but I doubt whether even a good man, if unfamiliar with USSC affairs, and without prior close acquaintance with Cardozo, could help much in the 2 1/2 months which will remain of this term.

3. I am more disturbed by the fact that March 14 C. will be injected (by reason of the C.J.'s efficiency & drive) into a large number of deeply controversial cases, assigned for that week & the next. Besides that, I am told, there will be many certioraris; and all this when C. will be handicapped & disturbed by lack of an adequate workshop, and bothered by well-meaning courtesies.

4. Harlan is a good man to talk with C. on these or other matters, but can't you see C. when you go to N.Y. on your Patent bar speech?[2]

5. No. 19, Benson case, is a fine fruit of the Jensen and Ben Avon cases.[3] More about this in June.

6. Also about the New Court House and the Court.[4]

7. Your memo on Baker[5] should illuminate.

8. Pretty much all the New Yorkers we see are pro-Baker, as are the mugwump type of Democrats from elsewhere. Sen. Barkley[6] & other regulars say he is not available.

9. I don't know whether the C.J. was for Cardozo, or knew anything before H.H. decided to nominate C.

10. At least the Benson case afforded opportunity for what, I suspect, was the first citation of F. & D.'s Administrative Law Cases.[7]

478

11. I have promised to talk to Bob La Follette on taxation during the coming recess. Will Max have his tax bill draft & memo by that time?

12. Marshall [Bullitt] should prepare also bill & memo on taking reorganization of RRs out of hands of bankers & putting it into hands of official liquidators. I suppose you noticed U.S. Daily, Feb 23, item on reorganization to realty bond act in N.Y.[8]

[1] The four conservative members of the Court could hardly have been pleased at Cardozo's nomination, but McReynolds, an open anti-Semite, would have been especially chagrined at the prospect of another Jew, and a liberal one at that, among the brethren.

[2] On 2 March, in an address to the New York Patent Law Association, FF expressed his opposition to the recently enacted Federal Kidnapping Law, on the grounds that too many issues were becoming subject to federal regulation.

[3] In *Crowell* v. *Benson*, 285 U.S. 22 (1932), Chief Justice Hughes, speaking for the majority, upheld the power of Congress to revise maritime laws in order to provide workmen's compensation for maritime workers, and also upheld the creation of non-Article III courts to hear these cases. But he also ruled that Congress could not provide for an administrative agency to perform a judicial function, thus denying regular Article III courts jurisdiction to review the administrative findings. LDB, joined by Stone and Roberts, dissented from this last holding, arguing that Article III grants the judicial power to the federal government. Congress may therefore apportion jurisdiction to different courts, even to state courts and administrative bodies. LDB's views have long since gained acceptance, due to the obvious internal contradiction in the majority ruling.

The earlier cases were *Southern Pacific Co.* v. *Jensen*, 244 U.S. 205 (1917), and *Ohio Valley Water Co.* v. *Ben Avon Borough*, 253 U.S. 287 (1920). LDB took no part in the first case, which upheld the validity of a federal workman's compensation law and affirmed the power of federal courts to hear cases under the law. For *Ben Avon* see 31 May 1922, n. 4.

[4] See 23 May 1926, n. 2.

[5] In early February, FF wrote several letters on why he could not support Newton D. Baker for the 1932 Democratic presidential nomination. FF claimed that Baker was a single issue candidate—the League of Nations—and there were many other problems which had to be addressed. In all of these letters, FF indicated that he was going to support Franklin D. Roosevelt for the nomination.

[6] Alben William Barkley (1877–1956) had served as United States senator from Kentucky since 1927, and during the New Deal became majority leader in the upper house. From 1949 to 1953 he was vice-president of the United States, after which he returned to the Senate.

[7] LDB relied on the Frankfurter-Davison book on administrative law in his dissent to argue that the function of the courts is not to review administrative agencies, but to keep them within statutory authority. See 285 U.S. 22, 89, n. 25.

[8] The attorney general of New York reported that an investigation of companies selling realty bonds revealed that more than 500,000 persons had bought bonds with a face value of over a half billion dollars, nearly all of which were now in default.

No. 486   March 17, 1932   Washington, D.C.

1. Cardozo is safely installed & seems to be taking his work calmly.

2. He was in last Sunday (with the C.J.) on his rounds to the JJ., & is coming in next Sunday to dine with us alone at 7.

3. Yes, Kreuger is a prime exhibit for "The Curse of Bigness."[1] Lee,

Higginson & their clients must be heavy sufferers.[2] Have you heard anything?

4. Michelson & the Houston [sic] Thompsons were in last evening, & M. had to bear a strong blast on the behavior of the House Democrats.

5. Rifkind[3] was in Monday. Most enthusiastic over the Pro-Palestine meeting.[4]

6. C.C.B. & Happer dined with us (& the J.G. Rogers & Delanos) Sunday.

7. Let Max urge on Denny also, raising the corporation tax to 20 percent.

8. Yes, Borah did a good job on B.N.C. & I think S.S.W. is entitled to much of the credit.[5]

9. I think it would be unwise to make U.S. income taxes payable otherwise than quarterly. It would be desirable to make all state taxes also payable in quarterly installments.

10. I will ask Eastman about the Alleghany Co. when I see him.

11. We are asking Harold Rosenwald[6] for Monday.

12. Cochrane [sic] was in, critical (of everyone) & doubts whether they will keep him.

[1] On 12 March, Ivar Kreuger (1880–1932), the Swedish match king, had committed suicide in his Paris apartment. Kreuger and his partner, Paul Toll, had originally made a fortune in their native Sweden and been hailed in the 1920s as financial geniuses. It turned out that Kreuger had sold nearly $100 million worth of unsecured bonds, and the financial depression had led to the collapse of the empire.

[2] Millions of the Kreuger bonds had been sold through Lee, Higginson & Co., which had recommended the investments to their customers as extremely sound. Subsequent investigations revealed the almost complete failure of the Boston firm to investigate the financial worthiness of the debentures.

[3] Simon Hirsch Rifkind (b. 1901) served as legal advisor to New York Senator Robert F. Wagner from 1927 to 1933. After setting up an influential law firm in New York, he was named a federal district judge in 1941; he returned to private practice in 1950.

[4] See 21 January 1932, n. 3.

[5] See 16 February 1932, n. 1.

[6] Harold Rosenwald (b. 1907) was then assistant counsel of the RFC; he would serve in several government agencies before entering private practice after the Second World War.

No. 487   March 24, 1932   Washington, D.C.

1. Re 463.[1] I am sending under another cover 5 copies. I have already sent copies to Slichter[2] and to Beard. Shall be glad to have you send to Harold [Laski] & Redlich as you suggested.

Can probably get you additional copies if wanted.

2. Herbert Feis was in yesterday. Talked of plans of the rich now being carried out to put in trust for their property for children etc. to evade coming gift & estate taxes.[3]

Max should draft bill for special income taxes on all gifts in trust for children, or kin, etc. I see no reason why the U.S. shouldn't have power to put a super income tax on any class of income, no matter when the trust was created. Do you?

If lawyers for people can't beat evasion they had better bury themselves.

The Edwin Samuels[4] were in yesterday.

[1] *New State Ice Co.* v. *Liebmann*, 285 U.S. 262, decided three days earlier, contained one of LDB's most famous dissents. An Oklahoma law required anyone entering the ice business to secure a certificate of necessity, and the New State firm, which held such a license, sought to enjoin Liebmann from entering the field without a license. The majority, speaking through Justice Sutherland, held the state statute unconstitutional because it fostered monopoly. The aim of the Oklahoma law, he wrote, "is not to encourage competition, but to prevent it; not to regulate the business, but to preclude persons from engaging in it."

Although one might have expected LDB to side with an opinion which nominally supported competition and sustained small business, he instead saw the Oklahoma law as an attempt, perhaps unwise and ineffectual, to exercise the state's police power to meet unique economic conditions generated by the Depression, which he termed "more serious than war." He could not "believe that the framers of the Fourteenth Amendment, or the States which ratified it, intended to deprive us of the power to correct the evils of technological unemployment and excess productive capacity."

Although LDB's dissents have been praised for their craftsmanship and legal reasoning, they are rarely noted for stylistic grace. In this opinion, however, LDB summed up, with an unusually eloquent statement, his philosophy of judicial restraint and his faith in the federal system.

"Denial of the the right to experiment," he declared, "may be fraught with serious consequences to the Nation. It is one of the happy incidents of the federal system that a single courageous State may, if its citizens choose, serve as a laboratory and try novel social and economic experiments without risk to the rest of the country. The Court has the power to prevent an experiment. We may strike down the statute which embodies it on the ground that, in our opinion, the measure is arbitrary, capricious or unreasonable. . . . But in the exercise of this high power, we must be ever on our guard, lest we erect our prejudices into legal principles. If we would guide by the light of reason, we must let our minds be bold."

On 22 March, FF wrote LDB: "Your Ice opinion is truly monumental, a most impressive guide for decades to come, one of those dissents that render history."

[2] Sumner Huber Slichter (1892–1959) was professor of business economics at Harvard, and the author of a number of books on contemporary economic problems.

[3] Congress was then in the final stages of passing a new estate and gift tax, which reached a maximum rate of 45 percent on estates larger than $10 million, and 33 1/3 percent on gifts in excess of that amount. See 4 April 1932.

[4] Edwin Herbert Samuel, the second Viscount Samuel (1898–1978), was the son of the first British high commissioner of Palestine. He had settled in Palestine in 1920, holding a number of positions in the mandatory administration. In 1954, he joined the faculty of the Hebrew University, where he taught political science until his retirement in 1969.

No. 488   March 30, 1932   Washington, D.C.

1. Yes, money leadership for the Democrats was true to form. It looks now as if we might get a decent revenue bill.

2. The Treasury is, I think, grossly misrepresenting what really high income tax & gift tax & estate tax might yield., i.e., as an emergency measure losses might be deemed deductions from income tax.[1] I think Phil's Wisconsin Act does that. Can't Max help on the whole subject?

3. The blow-up on the Mo-Pac. loan is encouraging.[2] Poor H.H. can't help going wrong.

4. The skepticism among the young which you report is promising.

5. Bonbright sent me his book.[3] Haven't had chance to read it yet.

6. Are you planning to come here with Marion in the Easter vacation as you thought possible?

[1] The Treasury Department, reflecting Secretary Mellon's antipathy toward the estate and gift tax, had projected relatively low figures for anticipated revenues. These in turn had brought forth a barrage of criticism from a number of economists, who argued, as did LDB, that effective enforcement would bring in a fairly large sum.

[2] The Interstate Commerce Commission had reluctantly approved a $12.8 million loan from the RFC to the Missouri-Pacific, which would cover, among other items, repayment of nearly $6 million in loans from the Morgan bank and Kuhn, Loeb. The action had been severely criticized in the Senate two days earlier as little more than a raid on the treasury to support private banks.

[3] James C. Bonbright and Gardner C. Means, *The Holding Company: Its Public Significance and Its Reputation* (New York: McGraw-Hill, 1932), would have a major impact during the New Deal in regard to utilities regulation.

No. 489   April 3, 1932   Washington, D.C.

1. Could Max present in parallel columns the predictions of the Hoover Treasury & the facts during the past 3 years, as to anticipated revenues and surplus or deficits? That might be effectively used by our Senators in coming debates.

2. Isn't there some economist who can now prepare a worthy article making a frontal attack on tax immunities?

This is most opportune time for starting, with the battle-cry: "No more tax exempts. Federal, State or Municipal."

3. As bearing on the Administration yell about balancing the budget. Compare that with W. L. drule [sic].

A year and a half ago when I urged on Gene heavy taxes on the rich to balance the budget, he took the position it was not necessary: that we had over-paid off the war bonds in the past and could afford now to run into debt to meet current needs for a while.

4. The British have done grandly. It's fine to hear them encourage us not to despond.

No. 490   April 4, 1932   Washington, D.C.

The remedy for this [1] & Untermyer's case [2] would be a progressive income tax, in addition to the regular progressive income tax on all income in excess of say $4000 for each beneficiary of any "trusts" created inter vivos [3] at any time since March 1, 1913.

And on all created by will which were immune from the estate tax under our decisions.

Could Max draw this up for LaGuardia, [4] & for our Progressive Senators.

Sen. Black [5] was in Monday & declared himself favorable to taxing wealth fully by income, gift & estate taxes.

[1] LDB had enclosed a clipping from the *Washington Daily News* of this date, reporting a speech on the floor of the House by Fiorello H. LaGuardia of New York. LaGuardia had claimed that the large New York banks were advising their clients to establish trust funds before the new estate tax went into effect in order to shelter their fortunes. See 24 March 1932.

[2] *Untermyer, Executrix, et al.* v. *Anderson*, 276 U.S. 440 (1928), permitted exclusion of certain types of gifts from the Estate and Gift Tax Act of 1924. LDB, together with Stone and Holmes, had dissented, holding that Congress's intent to reach all gifts was both clear and reasonable.

[3] An *inter vivos* trust is one created while the grantor is still alive, as compared to a testamentary trust created through a will.

[4] Fiorello Henry LaGuardia (1882–1947), then a member of Congress, had already earned national fame as an enemy of the corrupt Tammany Hall machine in New York. LaGuardia put together a winning political coalition of ethnic and labor groups and in 1933 began his twelve-year reign as New York's mayor.

[5] Hugo LaFayette Black (1886–1971) was then serving the first of his two terms as United States senator from Alabama. Roosevelt named him to the Supreme Court in 1937, and there was a brief flurry when it was discovered that he had been a member of the Ku Klux Klan as a young man. Black went on to become one of the handful of giants on the bench, arguing for the application of the Bill of Rights to the states through the Fourteenth Amendment and a literalist approach to the First Amendment, which he believed prohibited any form of restriction on any form of speech.

No. 491   April 10, 1932   Washington, D.C.

1. I saw OWH twice during the week just closed. He was in fine form, & in answer to my enquiry as to his reading, said he had taken up with pony [1] the last six books of the Aenied, (the only thing of Virgil he had not read). Monday he sent me a bloodroot blossom "to give me pain," the fruit of his morning's search after hearing we had discovered none among the early spring flowers.

2. Re Cardozo's letter to you.[2] His performance, judicially and in tact, has been 100% good, but he has had, as he shows, shocks at the treatment received. I told him yesterday as he drove with me to the Mayflower, "dass er sich daruber hinwegsetzen muss"[3] i.a., the mastiffs have been inconsiderate.

3. The proposed Emergency Bill to plug for the future the Untermyer hole would help, but we must go further.

4. Yes, don't fail to promptly praise Harlan's performance.[4]

5. Kirstein was in yesterday homeward bound.

6. I understand that Prof. A. T. Mason has an article on my Constitutional decisions in the April U. of P. Law Review.[5] Shall probably receive it tomorrow. Yes, I saw [*] Act.

7. No definite report on Eliz. & Paul. Paul is now helping State Industrial Board on the unemployment act.

[1] A "pony" is a literal translation of a foreign language text, often used by students.

[2] There is no copy of the Cardozo letter in FF's papers.

[3] "that he must ignore it, brush it aside."

[4] See next letter, n. 1.

[5] "Mr. Justice Brandeis and the Constitution," *University of Pennsylvania Law Review* 80 (1932): 799. Mason dealt primarily with LDB's opinions and dissents on labor and industrial matters, and praised him for his use of social and economic materials.

No. 492   May 1, 1932   Washington, D.C.

1. Harlan must like "The Supreme Court & the Balanced Budget."[1] Some others will not, if good friends call it to their attention.

2. Gene was in today. My thought throughout the talk was: "Tu l'a volu George d'Andin."[2] He really looks very badly. I think is not sleeping well and the strain is telling on him.

3. He has had some talk with George Rublee; will probably try to get him as Associate Counsel; & leave the administrative work to the General Counsel to be selected.[3]

[1] "The Supreme Court and the Balanced Budget," *New Republic* 70 (27 April 1932): 287. FF, in an unsigned editorial, argued that the budget had not been balanced because of hostility to taxing the wealthy evidenced by the administration and by the Court, which had struck down as unconstitutional part of the recent estate and gift tax. In that case, *Heiner* v. *Donnan*, 285 U.S. 312 (1932), Stone and LDB had strongly dissented, and the editorial praised Stone's dissent.

[2] "You wanted it, George d'Andin." *George Dandin*, a 1668 play by Moliere, tells the story of a socially ambitious peasant, whose advantageous marriage brings him only unhappiness.

[3] Rublee did not join the RFC in any capacity.

No. 493   May [?], 1932   Washington, D.C.

1. Of course "there was a reason" why the C.J. assigned the George Otis Smith case to me,[1] but from the point of view of the Court, he was justified.

2. About the Packers case there is a story.[2]

3. I understand that RFC would have helped tide over the Exchange Trust Co., if Boston banks had been willing to do their part.

4. I am very sorry that the Brooks family suffers financially through the Kreuger & Toll.[3] I knew they would feel deeply, because of Hallowell's[4] large part in L[ee] H[igginson] & Co.'s participation. JGB[5] showed me letter written by H. last summer when in Europe on that business.

5. Yesterday's performance on Wall St. must give H.H. & Gene added pain.

Hitz was in Sunday, and Geo. Rublee & Hutcheson yesterday. Monday Herbert Feis brought in Morgan[6] (now of Chase Bank, before that 7 years abroad) who spoke warmly of you.

[1] *U.S.* v. *George Otis Smith*, 286 U.S. 6 (1932). The Senate, after confirming Smith's nomination to the Federal Power Commission in 1930, and after he had taken office, voted to rescind the confirmation. Hoover denied that the Senate had this power, and the case came to the Court for adjudication. LDB delivered the opinion of the Court, holding that since the Senate rules themselves did not provide for such a reconsideration, it lacked the power.

[2] *United States* v. *Swift & Co. et al.*, 286 U.S. 106 (1932), decided on 2 May, dealt with an injunction against a cartel of meat packers to stop them from selling non-meat products. The packers had gone into court several times seeking to modify the 1920 ruling, and in his opinion for the Court, Cardozo had used strong language in describing the firms' efforts to evade the decree. Nonetheless, because it was a consent decree, the packers had the right to seek modification. Because of the various practices engaged in by the packers, however, the lower court relief was reversed. Hughes, Sutherland, and Stone did not participate in the decision; Butler and Van Devanter dissented. See unsigned editorial (written by FF), "The Packers vs. The Government," *New Republic* 76 (25 May 1932): 33. See also 9 February 1928.

[3] See 17 March 1932.

[4] Norwood Penrose Hallowell (1875–1961) had been associated with the Boston banking firm of Lee, Higginson since 1905, ultimately becoming president and chairman of the board.

[5] Probably John Graham Brooks.

[6] Shepard Ashman Morgan (1884–1973) had spent most of the 1920s in Berlin as director of the Office of Reparations Payments, after which he became vice-president of foreign services for the Chase National Bank.

No. 494   May 9, 1932   Washington, D.C.

1. H.H. has gone stark mad on economy and balancing the budget; and the shameless stupid stampede of the Democrats makes the situation alarming.[1] It is pretty late to start a counter movement, but could not

something be done, like the 1000 economists protest against the tariff?[2] The economists ought to act to save their honor.

2. Sumner Slichter's N.R. article states the sound view.[3]

There is an extraordinarily knowing article by David Cushman Coyle,[4] consulting engineer, N.Y., "Business vs. Finance" in "Corporate Practice Review." April 1932, p. 6.[5] I suppose this would be just in Virgil Jordan's[6] line.

H.H. is doubtless encouraged by the last few days' rise in the stock market, ignoring the ever weakening commodity prices.

Can B.F. find out about Coyle?

[1] In a message to Congress on 5 May which many saw as the opening gun of his presidential campaign, Hoover called for an immediate balancing of the budget, and blamed the Democratically controlled Congress for the failure to implement his proposals.

[2] On 4 May 1930, more than a thousand economists had presented a protest against the higher rates then being proposed, and which would be enacted in the Hawley-Smoot Tariff.

[3] Slichter, "Should the Budget be Balanced?" *New Republic* 70 (20 April 1932): 262, argued that a federal deficit was not terrible, especially if the funds were used to generate jobs and stimulate the economy.

[4] David Cushman Coyle (1887–1969), a consulting engineer with his own firm in New York, advised the government extensively during the New Deal's building program.

[5] In "Business v. Finance: The Irrepressible Conflict," *Corporate Practice Review* 4 (1932): 6, Coyle cited LDB's *New State Ice* decision to the effect that business had built enough for a while. He also approved heavy taxation of large ventures as a means of cutting back business.

[6] Virgil Jordan (1892–1965), an economist, had been in charge of publications for the National Industrial Conference Board from 1920 to 1929, and was later president of the Board.

No. 495   May 12, 1932   Washington, D.C.

Re yours of 11th.

1. I am glad Slichter will talk bold.

2. The Hoover volte face adopting Sen. Robinson's $2,300,000,000 proposal[1] is interesting. But I dread the proposal of "tax exempt bonds." The cloven foot is ever to be found in the Hoover-Robinson combination.

3. I am sorry Harry Shulman will not get credit for his article, except at home.[2]

4. The disclosure of Fred Lehman's[3] opinion on Nat. Bk. affiliates[4] delights me. I never made a real study of the subject. But when they first appeared I was unable to see how they, or the direct investment in securities, could be held legal.

5. Can't you get one of your jurisdiction men to write an article for the fall exploring the inequity of Fed. Court spending its time on mail

fraud cases, by examples of these largely intra-state fraud?[5] Every time one of those cases comes up on certiorari, I boil over anew in indignation.

[1] The proposal called for a two-stage issuance of government bonds. $300 million would be provided immediately for advances to hard pressed state and municipal governments, and at a later date $2 billion in bonds would be used to finance construction loans to local governments for self-liquidating projects in order to reduce unemployment.

[2] Shulman had sent FF a draft of an article he had written on *Crowell* v. *Benson* (see 25 February 1932), in which he had attacked the majority position and praised LDB's dissent. FF had suggested toning down some of the language, so that Shulman's major argument would not be dismissed because of abusive rhetoric. Shulman evidently remained unhappy with the article, and feared the embarrassment of praising publicly the man for whom he had clerked; in the end he chose to publish it unsigned. See "Judicial Review of Administrative Findings—*Crowell* v. *Benson*," *Yale Law Journal* 41 (May 1932): 1037.

[3] Frederick William Lehman (1853–1931) had served as solicitor general of the United States from 1910 to 1912.

[4] Senator Carter Glass was then waging a campaign against banking affiliates, which he charged violated the National Banking Act. In support of this position, he had produced an opinion written by Lehman twenty-one years earlier.

[5] While there were several articles on jurisdiction, nothing on this particular aspect appeared in either volume 46 (1932–1933) or 47 (1933–1934) of the *Harvard Law Review*.

No. 496   May 15, 1932   Washington, D.C.

1. J.W.M.'s enthusiastic reference to your "book on me" is the first notice to come. In the same mail with his letter this morning came one from the Yale Press, opened later, which tells that the book is being sent at your request. Doubtless tomorrow will bring it. Alice is very eager.[1]

2. About the "Linseed King" case[2] is a story when we meet.

3. Our plan is to leave here Tuesday evening May 31st, and hope you and Marion can dine with us Wednesday at 7 P.M. at the Bellevue, as usual.

4. Your memo on "Third Year Class Work" is most interesting & if your associates heed it should lead to important results.

5. Those are handsome editorials of Desha Breckenridge[3] on civil liberties and Mary & Walter B. Smith.

6. Judge Moorman[4] and Judge Allen,[5] who were here for the Law Institute, expressed regret at the Bell & Harlan county behavior.[6]

7. The W.L. editorial you sent is returned herewith so that it may be preserved for the "Walter Lippmann for President" men. This great internationalist does not mention specifically army & navy appr[opriations]. I assume they are put on a par with Children's Bureau.

8. The President's new construction relief plan[7] (which has properly aroused Garner[8]) embodies a number of suggestions—those concerning

487

loans for public and private new profit earning projects, and easing up on security—which show that in part it is prompted by Gene. He complained to me of these lacks in the present measure.

9. Nathan Amster[9] (who turned up last week) said that it was Storrow who introduced Kreuger & Toll securities to Boston,[10] that Kirstein, Kuffenberg and David Ellis[11] bought through Storrow. (L. E. K[irstein]. didn't let on to me that he had any—if indeed he did.) Austin thought that the L[ee] H[igginson] & Co, firm & partners individually, probably held very little of the stuff, but this he gave as his guess.

10. If I am right in my understanding that no British Government securities (national or municipal) are tax-exempt, it might do some good to give publicity to that fact through N.R. and otherwise.

11. M.R. quietly folded his tent, & sailed for Italy, as I learned yesterday at conference.

12. OWH was in good form when I saw him yesterday, but his memory (particularly for names) is failing badly. He couldn't remember Stone's name, when he wanted to tell me that H. had been in the day before.[12]

[1] FF had edited *Mr. Justice Brandeis*, with an introduction by Oliver Wendell Holmes, and essays by Charles Evans Hughes, Max Lerner, Donald Richberg, Henry W. Biklé, Walton Hamilton as well as one by himself.

[2] *Planters Cotton Oil Co.* v. *Hopkins*, 286 U.S. 332 (1932). H.N. Chapman, the so-called "Linseed Oil King," had shifted his assets from one company into three newly created ones in order to avoid taxes. Speaking for a unanimous Court, Cardozo held that the Internal Revenue Service had been correct in refusing to recognize the transfers, since the new companies were not significantly different from the old one, and therefore the alleged losses were not transferable.

[3] Desha Breckinridge (1867–1935) was editor and publisher of the *Lexington* (Ky.) *Herald*.

[4] Charles Harwood Moorman (1876–1938) had been a judge of the Circuit Court of Appeals for the Sixth Circuit since 1925, and lived in Louisville.

[5] Florence Ellinwood Allen (1884–1966), also a member of the sixth circuit, had written widely on various aspects of the law, including international treaties.

[6] Conditions approximating civil warfare had erupted in Kentucky as union organizers rallied coal miners, and coal operators imported thugs to defeat the drive. Vigilante groups beat up reporters and other "outsiders" who came to investigate events in the two counties, and, to all apparent purpose, law enforcement had either ceased to exist or sheriffs worked openly on the side of the operators.

[7] Hoover had suggested increasing the funding of the RFC by $1.5 billion, of which two-thirds would go for self-liqidating public works projects and to private businesses which would generate jobs.

[8] John Nance Garner (1868–1967) served as a member of the Texas delegation to the House of Representatives from 1898 to 1932, the last term as Speaker of the House. He was a major contender for the 1932 Democratic presidential nomination, but accepted the second spot on the ticket, and served as Roosevelt's vice-president for two terms.

[9] Nathan Leonard Amster (1869–1939), a Rumanian immigrant, developed his knowledge

of mining into a considerable fortune in the West. He then settled first in Boston and later in New York.

[10] See 17 March 1932, n. 1.

[11] David Abram Ellis (1873–1929), a Boston attorney, had worked in the Brandeis office after his graduation from Harvard. He worked closely with, and then succeeded Storrow, as chairman of the Boston School Board.

[12] However, after visiting Holmes on 28 May, LDB wrote to FF the following day: "OWH. was in fine form yesterday, so much so that both Harlan and I thought we discovered a particle of regret at his resignation."

No. 497   May 20, 1932   Washington, D.C.

1. "Theses in Administrative Law, etc"[1] returned herewith, is most interesting, & should prove of great value to other members of the faculty, and other schools privileged to see it.

If there is no objection, I suggest that you let Cardozo see it. He is most enthusiastic about your "Business" & we have several times discussed how it came about, & why it is [*].

2. Your answer to Ballantyne [sic] is excellent in substance and manner. He can hardly let it lie unanswered.[2]

3. The Postal Savings shows what can and should be done to prevent hoarding. The government has foolishly discouraged deposits at the behest of the banks.

4. Hamilton was in, & happy you are taking Nathanson.[3]

5. I encouraged Harlan to express his strongly felt views on the Bradford decision.[4]

6. Poor L[ee] H[igginson] & Co.'s reputation must be entirely shattered.[5] Isn't there here also a bit of "the Curse of Bigness?" They didn't take ordinary precautions. But the fundamental defect is that no one in authority has time to think.

7. The book is finely presented.[6]

It is fine that the Administrative Law case book is to be so widely adopted at once.

[1] There is no article or memorandum by this title in the Frankfurter MSS, but FF may have sent LDB a copy of the introduction he had written for a symposium on administrative law which would be published in *Iowa Law Review* 18 (January 1933): 12.

[2] At this time, FF and Arthur Ballantine exchanged several letters in which FF attacked the economic policies of the government as being unresponsive to the economic hardships of the nation, while Ballantine defended them as reflecting the best wisdom available on the subject.

[3] Nathaniel Louis Nathanson (1908–1984), then a senior in the Yale Law School, would clerk for Julian Mack in 1933–1934, and for LDB the following year. After a brief stint with the Securities and Exchange Commission, he would enter a long teaching career at Northwestern University Law School, where he specialized in administrative law.

[4] *Bradford Electric Co.* v. *Clapper*, 286 U.S. 145 (1932). LDB, speaking for an unanimous Court, held that, in a federal court, a workmen's compensation law of another state is a "public act" under the full faith and credit clause, and thus constrained choice of law on constitutional grounds. Stone concurred, but was reluctant to apply so rigid a rule if there was a compelling state policy in the forum state. Stone's view later gained primacy in choice of law standards.

[5] Following the Kreuger scandals; see 17 March 1932, n. 1.

[6] See preceding letter, n. 1.

No. 498   June 12, 1932   Chatham, Mass.

Despite the assertion of a balanced budget, it is probable that the deficit in the year beginning July 1/32 (if figured as deficits or surpluses have been in the past) will be, under the new Revenue Act, about as large as in the current year, and in the year beginning July 1/33 not much smaller.

Despite increase in the corporation tax, the yield based on the calendar year 1932 profits will probably be less, because of worsening business. And despite the increase in income tax rates, the passing and reduction of dividends in 1932, and other lessened income, may neutralize the higher rates.

The small yield of the increased corporation and income taxes will not be demonstrated before March 15/33; but then or before the need of further revenue will become apparent and, unless Hoover is re-elected, there will be an urgent, perhaps irresistible, demand for an extra session. Before that there should be a careful survey of the existing measure made in the interest of increasing the revenue, and not of protecting the rich. Obviously that must be made by some one not connected with the Treasury, and perhaps best by an entirely fresh mind which has not become accustomed to glaring defects or wrongs in the past legislation made in the interest of the tax payer.

Many of these, which will seem like corrections of detail and do not serve to increase rates, might be put over without a great fight. For instance, those relating to deductions from gross income. As I understand the Act and the practice, deductions logically applicable to the whole of a tax payer's income, are applied wholly to that part of the income which is taxable. Thus the tax payer's expenses incident to taking care of his property (like commissions & expenses of the man of business), although properly applicable to the whole estate or income, are in part deducted from the taxable income before figuring the tax.

Similarly, the 15 percent deductions on account of gifts to charitable purposes are apparently deducted from the taxable part of the income, not apportioned between taxable & non-taxable.

I have no doubt that a careful study of the Act, in connection with past decisions & rulings of the Department & of the Board of Tax Appeals & the tax books would uncover possibilities of stopping revenue leaks, aggregating hundreds of millions of dollars.

It occurs to me that one of your (or Landis') unemployed able students who took up such a study might render an important service to the Country, and do much for his own professional future.

Of course, he should jot down all amendments which should be made to increase income needed to overcome strained interpretations of our Court, some holdings of unconstitutionality.

In this connection all hearings before Ways & Means Com'tee & Finance Com'tee in the past 15 years should be studied.

The absurdity of stopping the increase of rate at 55 percent for incomes of $1,000,000, instead of raising the rate thereafter at least proportionate is too glaring to stand, if there is need of revenue & a determined attack.

No. 499   June 23, 1932   Chatham, Mass.

1. The phraseology of your declination will be a delicate matter.[1]

2. Gov. Ely gave many a bad quarter of an hour. I didn't know that there is a vacancy. When & how did it occur?

3. It is 20 years nearly since, thanks to RR Labor opposition, the Sutherland Com'n's compensation bill was turned down.[2] With the need for economy & efficiency in RRs, the Courts & otherwise, & the chastening of RR labor by the depression etc., it would be a good time to revive the agitation for the law at the next session of Congress. Some good men, who will treat the subject factually in the light of the 20 years experience, should lay the firm foundation for the movement by an article in the Law Review.

4. Many other matters I reserve for discussion when you come. Glad to know that you plan to be here soon.

5. I suppose Hitz refers to the effort to apply the 10% reduction to judicial salaries.[3]

[1] Regarding FF's proposed nomination to the Massachusetts Supreme Judicial Court; see 21 January 1932, and the next letter.
[2] In 1910, Congress had authorized a commission to make a thorough study of employers'

liability and workmen's compensation. The commission recommended a federal plan for workers engaged in interstate commerce, and then-senator George Sutherland, later to be villified as an enemy of labor, led the floor fight which saw final passage of the bill in 1916. Some railway unions opposed the original commission plan as not providing sufficient benefits.

³ Among the various economy moves proposed by the Hoover administration was one to reduce the salaries of federal employees by 10 percent. This would have encountered Art. III, Sec. 1 of the Constitution, which provided that the compensation of federal judges "shall not be diminished during their continuance in office."

No. 500   June 26, 1932   Chatham, Mass.

MY DEAR FELIX Further consideration confirms the opinion that you should decline the appointment.

The honor is great. The office would afford an unusual opportunity for high service to the Commonwealth and to the Nation, in a time of need. But, for the reasons expressed to you orally, I think you will render to the nation, the Commonwealth and the law service more far-reaching and enduring by continuing your activities in the humbler office of teacher at the Law School. [1]

[1] In his letter to Governor Ely, FF wrote: "Your Excellency's nomination of me for the Supreme Judicial Court has presented the most difficult decision of my professional life. . . . You have offered me an opportunity that comes to very few lawyers. To join the bench which can draw upon the spirit of Shaw and Holmes for the creative tasks of judicial administration in our day is a call of high honor and of profound importance to the well-being of the Commonwealth. . . .

"But I have other responsibilities to the law which, after much anguish of mind, I feel I ought not now to sever. As against the opportunities for immediate achievement on the bench, the long-term effects on legal education make their claim.

"The grave problems already upon us and those looming on the horizon require as never before a courageous and learned bar. And from such a bar alone can come an enlightened judiciary. The future direction of bar and bench will be determined by the quality of our law schools. . . .

"This work must go forward, and I cannot bring myself to believe that I should prematurely abandon my share in it, however great and honorable the opportunity you offer me.

"I should have less confidence in the rightness of this position had not the admonition of colleagues made me feel that to leave this school now would be a kind of desertion."

No. 501   July 2, 1932   Chatham, Mass.

Roosevelt's nomination is a comfort. [1]

1. Sorry the publication of your letter is so long delayed. When once your declination is known, there will be a volume of rejoicing, on the lines indicated in the second paragraph of Freund's letter. [2]

2. What a contrast between Great Britain's triumph in debt conversion at 3 1/2 percent, taxable, and U.S. Treas. showing of more and [more] bank failures and hoarding. No explanation now possible of

putting it on the small state banks. The July 1, /32 newspaper is a historical document of great value.

3. Ballantyne [sic] is quite resourceful in excuses, but not very powerful in his reasoning.[3]

4. Nothing could have been more absurd than the anti-hoarding program in which he presumably concurred. The simple thing for the government to do was to open wide the door of the Postal Savings, and then have the RFC (acting under the original Postal Savings provisions) lend the available funds to the banks worthy of credit, and use any surplus for current government purpose. Thus runs on banks could have been neutralized; the U.S. would have taken the risk of solvency, knowing all, instead of asking depositors, knowing nothing, to do so. That obvious choice was tabooed, because it was "socialistic." There is much to say to you when your mind is freed from S.J.C. worries.

[1] As the Democratic candidate for president. LDB shared FF's enthusiasm for Roosevelt, unlike many liberals who considered the New York governor too shallow. Justice Holmes characterized Roosevelt as "a second-class intellect, but a first-rate temperament," while Walter Lippmann had recently pontificated that Roosevelt was "a pleasant man, without any important qualifications for the office, who would very much like to be President." On 11 July 1932, LDB wrote to his nephew, Louis Wehle: "The Chicago convention had made the best available choice. Aunt Alice and I think Franklin Roosevelt is much underrated by the Liberals. The opposition of the vested interests, who have opposed him, indicated that they fear him."

[2] On 26 June Ernst Freund had written to FF: "Whether . . . your shift from academic to judicial work will mean a gain to you and to the law, you have undoubtedly duly considered. Only a few days ago I said to Bigelow that you had no equal in the law schools for inspiring and directing productive work, and I fear there will be in this respect an irreplaceable loss."

[3] See 20 May 1932.

No. 502   July 5, 1932   Chatham, Mass.

1. You have made Witte very happy.[1] The review has been returned to you.

2. As you know from a multitude of cases, it is a (? the) common practice of banks to give surety bonds to secure deposits by states, counties or municipalities, or by officials, state or federal, or persons (like receivers or trustees) appointed under state or federal law. In some states, etc. the public or quasi-public funds have priority in payments by the bank; and where they do, the surety, after payment, usually has by subrogation like priority. The whole practice is wasteful & misleading, and tends to much undesirable litigation.

It is probably desirable that public or quasi-public funds should have

493

priority; that before any deposit is made, some appropriate state (or federal) official (or the court) should have to approve the depository in the particular bank; that when he does so, the state official, etc. making the deposit should not be responsible for the result. But if a bank holds deposits which are preferred, the fact and the amount of preferred deposits should be published at frequent intervals, so that ordinary depositors may know what risk he runs by being a deferred creditor.

The use of surety companies involves a great expense and recent experiences show do not always bring security. The many failures of surety companies & need of economy make this an appropriate & hopeful time for surveying the situation with a view to correction, & the subject would be an admirable one for a competent law school graduate, who would embody his results in article for the Law Review as the basis for a sounder practice.[2]

Incidentally this suggests a great defect in bank statements.

Their deposits consist, i.a.

    (a) of ordinary deposits, i.e. sums which the owner of the money deposits for his own convenience & safe keeping.

    (b) of specially secured deposits made for convenience of the depositor like those of the Government by preference or bonds.

    (c) artificial seeming deposits, i.e. the proceeds of unsecured discounted paper. They are not really deposits. They are in essence the right to deplete actual deposits, like (a).

    (d) artificial secured deposits, i.e. the proceeds of discounted paper collaterally secured.

Unless and until banks distinguish in their statements [and] depositions make such a classification, and also show the nature & market value of securities held as collateral, they will fail to instruct either their officials or stockholders and depositors.

[1] Edwin Emil Witte (1887–1960), a professor of economics at the University of Wisconsin, held a variety of important posts in the Wisconsin state government, including membership on the Planning and Labor Relations Board. Together with Paul and Elizabeth Raushenbush, he played a key role in establishing unemployment compensation insurance. FF had just written a very favorable review of Witte's book, *The Government in Labor Disputes*; see *Columbia Law Review* 32 (1932): 920.

[2] See 7 January 1933.

No. 503   July 7, 1932   Chatham, Mass.

Elizabeth reported your telephone talk of yesterday, among other things, in substance, that the Governor told you he had heard that I told

McClennen that I had advised you to accept. I didn't tell McC. that I had given you any advice or that I had talked with you at all. What took place was this:

When he was here over the Fourth he said to me that Thompson[1] had talked with him about the importance of your accepting, & that he (McC) wanted to talk with me; that he (McC) thought it very important you should etc. I told him, of course, you would make an admirable judge and greatly strengthen the bench and that, if I were practicing at the bar here [in Massachusetts] I should wish much that this should come about; but that as a citizen of the Nation I thought it would be a great misfortune if you accepted; and that, unlike himself and Thompson, your primary duty was to the Nation, through teaching etc. I added that the USSC was a much more important office but that I should not have accepted it, had I not been near 60 and had I not had several warnings that I could not long pursue the strenuous life in which I was then engaged—whereas you were 10 years younger. I added further, the difference between his (McC) case and you; that he knew I thought he (McC) should be on the Mass. SJC and that he had a duty to it which you were not under, he owing his primary allegiance to the Courts of the Com[monweal]th; & moreover that he was seven years older than you; that when you reached 60 a different situation might be presented. But at present you were "the most useful lawyer in the U.S." in the particular activities in which you are engaged.

When we got through, I told McC of the elaborate letters of June 28th received from Thompson and from Ehrman[n] and of the letter E. had written me during the winter; and in connection with the latter, that I had not complied with E.'s suggestion to write the Gov., and that I had never said to him directly or indirectly anything that justified the Gov. in giving the impression that I had recommended you for the S.J.C., though I had said to many persons things from which he knew that I considered you qualified.

Then I told McC. of my embarrassment, and my apparent discourtesy in leaving Thompson's and E.'s letters unacknowledged, and I suggested that he tell Thompson on his return to Boston that in my opinion it would be a mistake for you to accept. I did this because I did not not want to write Thompson anything.

I am sure McC. reported correctly and tactfully my message. He is an admirable witness.

[1] Possibly William Goodrich Thompson.

You have doubtless seen the schedule of RR executive salaries above $10,000.[1] Far more important would be the publication of the executives' salaries of:

(a) other utilities

(b) banks

(c) large industrial and mercantile companies (including in salary agreements for contingent compensation like the Bethlehem [Steel Corporation]).

The salaries are absurdly disproportionate to service performed and even, quite generally, a form of graft.

Andrew Winslow told me Sunday (confidential) of the sad plight of his friend Alexander Smith (associate of Malcolm Chase in the New England Oil Case). He has lost his millions, and, as Winslow told me, is about to lose his $100,000 salary in the Abitibi Paper & Power Co. (see N.Y. stock list) to make way for George C. Lee.

Nothing in the days of princelings could be more absurd than that:

1. Companies like Abitibi should pay such a salary or

2. George C. Lee be the recipient

$25,000 would be ample compensation.

Is there not some person who can write a ripping article on the subject. (The power rate case investigation must furnish considerable material & recent allegations much more), all in preparation for an investigation, under Senate resolution, by Federal Trade Commission or other body, to cover all

1. Banks connected with Federal Reserve System

2. Other banks aided by RFC

3. All public utilities engaged in interstate commerce

4. All private business corporations engaged in interstate commerce with capital or resources over $1,000,000 listed on stock exchanges (including curb)

Possibly the income tax returns now give the information. If so, it should be possible to get the enquiry started privately through some Senator pending the recess. The country needs this exposure before the period of recovery sets in. And it would be a wonderful bit of news to show the huge salaries while stockholders are denied dividends.

Nothing from the Governor yet?

[1] On 27 April, as part of an ongoing investigation into railroad costs, the I.C.C. ordered all Class I lines to report the number of employees paid $10,000 a year or more, and if any of these positions

had been created after 1929. The I.C.C. did not release this part of its report, but no doubt with their contacts in the agency both LDB and FF saw the list.

No. 505   July 25, 1932   Chatham, Mass.

1. Let me tell you of Betty Thomas [1] when we meet.

2. Also of my talk with McClennen Saturday. If you get a chance, find out from Bradford what occurred.

3. When you see Watts, [2] tell him about Miss Grady (who returned Saturday) and see that he has a full talk with her. Watts would think it a great achievement if he could raise Massachusetts wages five (5) percent. He can do that for nearly every wage-earner with a family. For those insured in the industrial companies are spending (on their reduced wages), on the average, 10 percent for insurance. They could get better from the Savings Bank at half the cost. Despite reduced earnings, the wage earners paid in 1930 in Mass. $55,000,000 to the Industrial Ins. Co., and in 1931 considerably more. Let Watts read enclosed leaflet.

4. Now that Bob [Szold] is out of the ZOA management, would it be possible to get through him and Margold completion of the legacy advising project worked out. [3] Jewish lawyers would be more receptive now than ever before to an appropriate letter enclosing the appropriate leaflet. It is 17 years since I asked Bob to get this material ready for use.

5. I fear that there is politics in the Chicago Board of Trade order. [4]

6. The week since you left gives much material for discussion.

[1] Possibly Elizabeth Finlay Thomas (18[?]-1955), who in addition to writing several works of poetry and fiction, worked as a reporter for the New York *Morning Telegram*.

[2] Possibly Sidney S. Watts (1879–1961), a Boston industrialist.

[3] See 7 October 1919.

[4] A special committee composed of the secretaries of commerce and agriculture and the attorney general had suspended the Chicago Board of Trade as the principal grain marketing agency of the government for thirty days because of alleged discrimination against the Farmers' National Grain Corporation.

No. 506   August 4, 1932   Chatham, Mass.

1. That is a very encouraging report on Roosevelt.

2. Tom Cochran's [sic] letter is illuminating.

3. The Hooverites will do an extraordinary stunt if they succeed in making the country believe in November that the Administration's policies have turned the corner. We have 3 months—long ones—ahead of us.

4. To present in dramatic form what H.H. had done to our export trade would be an effective argument for R[oosevelt]., and extremely interesting to the economically minded. General talk is no good. Reproduce in schedule the daily news in tabloid form. It's thrilling. I refer not to threats like those centering in Ottawa,[1] but the actual events showing, from day to day, how in some country or other, by governmental action, or mercantile arrangement, some outlet for American goods has been closed.

5. When you next have opportunity have your devoted Norton call on Miss Grady. He could help her much in introducing Savings Bank Insurance to city and state employees.

6. Kirstein was here yesterday. Very glad Sedgwick is taking his article which is fine.[2] Make sure that K's deeds accompany his words.

[1] At the recent Imperial Economic Conference in Ottawa, Canada, Great Britain had persuaded Commonwealth members to tighten trade restrictions. Canada was requested to divert some $50–60 million of purchases from the United States to the United Kingdom in return for trade preferences on Canadian products.

[2] Louis E. Kirstein, "Mind Your Own Business," *Atlantic Monthly* 150 (October 1932): 403. Too many business leaders, he charged, were deciding governmental issues about which they had no expertise, and he called for an adequately trained and paid public service, akin to the British Civil Service, to run the government.

No. 507   August 25, 1932   Chatham, Mass.

1. Sprague[1] is right in arguing that R[oosevelt]. say nothing further on foreign debts.

2. Did you learn anything from Sprague or elsewhere as to who is buying the bonds and stocks on N.Y. Exchange? I see no justification for the rise except the fact that very many stocks as well as bonds reached ridiculously low levels. The moderate rise in commodities furnishes no basis, because, in the main, it rests upon restriction of supplies, not on expansion of demand. With higher prices, the ability to purchase will be curtailed. Wholesalers may buy from expectations of shortage on increased demand, but until there is a definite trend of increased retail sales, there will be little to justify Wall. St.

3. R. has gained much through the Columbus speech[2] and his handling of the Walker hearings.[3]

4. I suppose H.H. will develop further tomorrow his policy of "To those who have shall be given."

5. Shulman will be glad to hear what Harlan says of his review of Crowell v. Benson.[4]

6. Harlan fears that action cutting down Holmes allowance may affect possible resignations.[5]

7. [*] is interesting as usual.

[1] Oliver Mitchell Wentworth Sprague (1873–1953), a professor of banking and finance at Harvard, would serve as a special assistant to the Treasury Department during the first months of the Roosevelt administration.

[2] In a hard hitting speech on 21 August, Roosevelt had attacked Hoover's economic policy, and had put forward his most detailed set of proposals for dealing with the depression so far. His nine-point program included regulating the stock exchange and the banking system, the separation of investment and banking functions, and forbidding bank use of federal funds for speculation.

[3] The corrupt administration of New York City by Tammany Hall had erupted in a series of spectacular hearings into the affairs of Mayor James J. Walker (1881–1946) and his associates. The revelations had led to demands that Roosevelt remove Walker, a step the governor had feared to take prior to the Chicago convention lest he alienate Tammany and lose its votes. With the nomination secured, Roosevelt realized that he could no longer duck the issue, and opened special hearings to determine what should be done. In the midst of this process, Walker suddenly resigned, thus sparing Roosevelt the need to remove him from office.

[4] See 12 May 1932, n. 2.

[5] See 10 January 1933.

No. 508   September 3, 1932   Chatham, Mass.

1. MacArthur's[1] resignation shows how much the B.E.F. episode and the Bonus worries H.H.[2]

2. The Civil Service ruling on bonus & the Legion is a monstrous application of the non-partisanship doctrine.[3]

3. Making prosperity is not an easy game.

4. F.D.R. is coming out [of] the Walker matter well.

5. B.N.C. will need secretary *and* clerk to occupy one another. As you know, I thought even a secretary alone would place him in the predicament of the Irishman with a trunk.

6. The Commerce Clearing House, Inc.—Lilienthal performance is in keeping with Chicago's code of ethics.

7. We plan to leave here Monday 12th & be at the Bellevue until Wednesday evening the 14th, and glad to have you dine with us any and all of the 3 evenings if you happen to be near. But don't interrupt your vacation by any long trip. You will doubtless be needed in Washington for some call before long.

8. I shall send your enclosures to Cambridge with a "Please hold."

[1] Douglas MacArthur (1880–1964) had just resigned as army chief of staff, and retired to live in the Philippines. Recalled to active service at the outbreak of World War Two, he was commander of the Allied forces in the Pacific, and engineered the victory over Japan. After the war, he supervised the military occupation of Japan, and led the country toward economic recovery and a

democratic government. In 1950, President Truman named him commander of United Nations forces in Korea, but dismissed him for insubordination.

[2] In the spring of 1932 an army of 15,000 to 20,000 unemployed veterans had descended upon Washington to petition Congress for immediate payment of a bonus due in 1945. When the Senate defeated the measure, the "Bonus Expeditionary Force" nonetheless stayed on in their camp at Anacostia Flats. Hoover totally misconceived the peaceful nature of the veterans, and feared they were about to launch a revolution against the government. At the end of July, he ordered the army to evict the BEF, and led by MacArthur, armed forces charged the camp, bayoneted a number of the veterans, and burned over their billets. The incident galvanized public opposition to the administration, and contributed to MacArthur's decision to resign from the army.

[3] The Civil Service Commission, under pressure from the White House, had ruled that federal workers could not discuss the bonus publicly, and had dismissed a postal worker for expressing sympathy with the BEF. Hoover recognized the potential backlash, and ordered the reinstatement of the clerk.

No. 509   September 21, 1932   Washington, D.C.

1. The La Follette defeat [1] is a hard blow, but it may result in Roosevelt carrying Wisconsin. [2]

2. Gene is having a hard time with his commodities' rise. Yesterday the average hog price (which was heralded as the advent of prosperity) was as low as in June; the average of grain is painfully low; and cotton has lost nearly two-thirds of its rise.

3. The outstanding indebtedness of America presents perhaps the most serious of all problems. Some say it is $162 billions; some that it is $203 billions. The value of all property was put in 1929 at $396 Billions. If it was that then, it can't be much, if any, more than our debts now. The land values were largely inflated by the expectation of increased population. Now, with an arrested population, there must be a heavy shrinkage, and our industrial buildings and equipment values, representing in part overcapacity or obsolete stuff, must likewise be heavily shrunk. Debts public and private would have to be cut in half to put us into a comfortable position.

4. Alfred Bettman is coming in this afternoon.

[1] Philip La Follette, after one term as governor of Wisconsin, had been defeated in the Republican primary by Walter J. Kohler, who had been governor from 1929 to 1931. Kohler was defeated at the general election in November, and La Follette would be reelected in 1934 and 1936.

[2] Roosevelt would carry Wisconsin by the overwhelming margin of two to one.

No. 510   September 29, 1932   Washington, D.C.

1. Alice is writing Marion. Happily the Gardner Jacksons came in yesterday and told us "All's well." Within a few hours after a letter from

Auntie B. had brought word of Marion's going to the hospital.[1] Your own letter is a great relief, with its confirmation.

2. WL's letter about Al Smith is a painful confirmation of what I had felt.[2]

3. All of our Washington friends believe H.H. is doomed. Harlan and wife are coming in to dine with us alone this evening and we shall hear doubtless something about official views.

4. What C. E. Clark writes about the bankers is very interesting.[3] I hope we shall get full disclosures in authoritative form. We should have as clear a record on banking practices as we are getting on the public utilities.

5. I don't think Mills will like W.L.'s turn to R[oosevelt]. M. is having troubles galore with government finances. The clamor for return to the 2 cent postage is interesting.

You will remember Edward Benedick's [sic]: "Gott! Was hat die Familie aber Ungluck."[4]

[1] Marion Frankfurter suffered from nervous disorders, and had just been hospitalized for a nervous breakdown.

[2] In a letter of 26 September, Walter Lippmann reported on a meeting he had had recently with Al Smith which greatly distressed him. "I don't think that it's merely that some of the people around him are giving him bad advice. I think his hatred and resentment and personal frustration are almost overwhelming. . . . I am afraid that he had developed what almost amounts to a persecution complex, and that his whole attitude is now governed by fierce resentment at the idea that he, a Catholic, couldn't be elected in 1928 and couldn't be nominated in 1932."

[3] There is no copy of such a letter in the Frankfurter MSS.

[4] "God! What does the family have but bad luck."

No. 511   October 16, 1932   Washington, D.C.

1. Paul was wrestling yesterday all day & evening.[1] Saw him only a few moments, but think he was greatly in need of help, & none too hopeful. Sayre will doubtless report to you.

2. Elizabeth is sad about the Progressive defeat.[2] But her class, which opened, as it happened, on the day after the election, has been cheering. There were 33 in attendance. This is the largest number she has had in the course in all these years.

3. Dorothy Kenyon[3] wrote me about the third degree of gangsters. Of course, I agree with you and Roger Baldwin. If this gets started, Jack Gilbert ought to be called in for trial of cases. He has probably more knowledge of actual practices than any one available, and his experience in criminal cases should make him an effective instrument.

4. I am glad to see from Norman's letter that Young and Traylor,[4] Insul [sic] besmirched, are deemed no longer Cabinet timber.

5. Ben Flexner is to come in this A.M., and the Readings at 5:30. We left our cards, but have not yet seen them. From what Roberts tells one of Mrs. R's report of his talk Friday PM, he still practices the art which Gardiner sets forth in P.P. & K.s

Saw OWH yesterday. He was in fine form.

That was a timely publication of your Manton letter.[5]

We were glad to have Marion's letter.

[1] Wisconsin had enacted a pioneering unemployment compensation measure in January 1932, and Governor La Follette had named Paul Raushenbush, who was one of the architects of the plan, to oversee its implementation.

[2] See 21 September 1932, n. 1.

[3] Dorothy Kenyon (1888–1972) was then a practicing attorney in New York; she would later serve as a justice of the municipal court.

[4] Melvin Alvah Traylor (1878–1934) was president of the First-Union Trust & Savings Bank of Chicago, and together with Young, the author of the Reconstruction Finance Corporation bill. Also with Owen Young, he had arranged much of the financing for Insull's operations in Chicago.

[5] In a letter to the *New York Times* published on 14 October, FF had criticized the conduct of federal judges sitting in New York, especially Martin Manton of the second circuit. In connection with the Interborough receivership case, Manton used his position to require the holding of special district court hearings, and then in his role as circuit judge designated who would hold that sitting.

No. 512   October 21, 1932   Washington, D.C.

1. I shall be glad to have a session with FDR (and you) on Sunday, Nov. 20th, either in the forenoon or the afternoon. Saturday the 19th will be absorbed with Court conference, and Monday 21st we shall resume our sitting.

2. I am glad you telephoned [William] Green. I have heard nothing from him since. When he called a month ago, I was emphatic and specific, and he appeared to agree fully. I guess he is as weak in understanding as in resolution. I advised Paul to follow up the conference by a letter to Green, of which he has doubtless sent copies to you and Sayre.

3. To 424 hangs a tale.[1]

4. From one within the Republican stronghold I learn that they have recovered hope since HH's Des Moines trip, and now expect to win, California, Illinois and Ohio, i.a.[2]

5. I find a lot of the "solide menschen," East and West, are proposing to vote for H.H., despite his lacks.

[1] *Wood* v. *Broom*, 287 U.S. 1 (1932). An act of Congress in 1911 had regulated districting in the states for Congressional elections, requiring that districts be compact, contiguous, and approxi-

mately equal in population. A candidate for Congress in Mississippi sued to compel the state to comply. The Court, through Chief Justice Hughes, held that the requirement had been eliminated by an act of Congress in 1924—a ground not relied on by the parties in the case. LDB, with Stone, Roberts, and Cardozo, concurred in the ruling that the complaint should be dismissed, but on the ground that the case was not within the equitable jurisdiction of the federal courts. Compare the later assumption of jurisdiction in such cases, on constitutional grounds, in *Baker* v. *Carr*, 369 U.S. 186 (1962).

[2] Roosevelt carried all three states by convincing majorities.

No. 513   November 9, 1932   Washington, D.C.

1. The job has been thoroughly done.[1] Now comes FDR's real task. He must think out his policy & put it over Congress as W[oodrow] W[ilson] did, and he must begin the work of educating the Country as soon as possible.

2. You may feel some satisfaction in your part in the campaign.

3. I don't wonder if G[eorge]. R[ublee]. "feels sick of it." He saw things more clearly than he allowed himself to act.

4. Among the real good things done is Youngman's defeat. He is one of the few really bad men I have known in Massachusetts.[2]

Our congratulations to Marion.

5. Chapple's & Kohler's defeats are good,[3] & Col. Donovan's gives added joy.[4]

George Rublee came in last week to tell me of his appointment as arbitrator. You did a good job in telephoning Dean & he in talking to Otto Beyer.

[1] Roosevelt had defeated Hoover in the presidential election by a margin of 22.8 million to 15.8 million in the popular vote, and a resounding 472 to 59 in the Electoral College. The Democrats also swept in commanding majorities in both houses of Congress.

[2] William Sterling Youngman (1872–1934) had at one time been a reform ally of LDB in Boston, but then had split with him after they were on opposite sides in the controversial Warren will case (see LDB to Cornelia Warren, 17 February 1916). During the nomination hearings, Youngman had been one of the chief witnesses against LDB. Youngman had worked his way up through the Republican party structure, and had served as lieutenant governor of Massachusetts from 1928 to 1932, but had just been defeated in a bid for the governorship by 74,000 votes.

[3] In Wisconsin, John B. Chapple and Walter J. Kohler, the Republican candidates for U.S. senator and governor, had both been defeated by 25,000 vote margins.

[4] William Joseph Donovan, the Republican candidate for governor of New York, had lost to Herbert H. Lehman by nearly 850,000 votes.

No. 514   November 11, 1932   Washington, D.C.

1. I agree with you that it would be a very, very serious mistake for F.D.R. to go abroad.

And I hope no foreign potentate will come here. The difficulties in the way of converting Americans soon to the necessary international action are formidable enough as it is.

2. G[eorge]. S[utherland]. dug out his own law, I think.

3. I hope Max's study will be published very soon. It should be available before the short session ends.

No. 515   November 13, 1932   Washington, D.C.

DEAR FELIX: My thanks for your and Marion's greeting.[1]

November fifteenth was my Mother's birthday, and throughout long years it was my custom to write on my birthday the letter for hers.

It is a pleasant thought that you, to whom Alice and I owe so much, share my Mother's day.

We cannot wish you and Marion more for the next twenty-five years than to equal the achievements of the past.[2]

[1] For LDB's seventy-sixth birthday, FF had written: "The only relevant wish for you is the unimpaired exercise of all your rich faculties, the continued employment of your wisdom and resolute devotion to the common good."

[2] To this note Alice Brandeis appended the following: "Dear Felix, I don't feel that I can do more than to echo LDB's warm greetings & good wishes. It is a rare privilege to share, even a little, in such a life as yours. With love to you both."

No. 516   November 24, 1932   Washington, D.C.

1. Yesterday had 15–20 minutes satisfactory interview with F.D.R. at which he did most of the talking.

2. He seems well versed in most fundamental facts of the situation. Declared his administration must be liberal and that he expected to lose part of his conservative supporters. I told him "I hope so," that we must realign part of the forces in each party.

3. He realizes also that remedies must be pursued as experiments, & mentioned specifically the agricultural allotment plan.

4. He states our plight, of more debts than assets, & his figures were more extreme than mine. He said in 1928 we had $200,000,000 in debt and $350,000,000 assets. Now we have $250,000,000 debts & $200,000,000 assets.

5. He is dead against the bankers, international & national. Spoke of their exactions in financing, i.a. in reorganization fees, & their selfishness re foreign indebtedness. Said they were willing to cancel debts of

government to government but insisted on treating as holy all debts due to individuals and corporations. Said he told them these affected only 2,000,000 Americans while the loans of our government affected 128,000,000. And that of each class, there were about 11 billion outstanding. He said Mills thought only about $5,000,000[,000] were due to individuals and corporations, but has no faith in Mills' figures. I guess it will be very difficult for him to see, & get the Democrats to see, the need for America to let up on the war debts.

6. He spoke most warmly of Moley's[1] service as economic adviser & that he wanted me to meet him.

7. I had told him on entering that I realized the difficulties which confronted him & wanted him to know that I was ready to help if, in any way, I can.

8. I spoke of his afforestation plan,[2] for which he said he was ready to issue bonds. I spoke of paying these etc. from special estate taxes, of which the states could get their part etc.

9. He said he thought 10 to 15 million city folk must move into the country, or they will be a permanent pauper population to that extent.

10. He seemed fully to appreciate the effect of a static population & that this makes the present "a new era."

11. I was to have seen Baruch at 3 PM, but FDR wanted him for conference, so the engagement with B. was postponed to some time next week.

[1] Raymond Moley (1886–1975) taught government and public law at Columbia from 1923 to 1954, and was one of the original members of Roosevelt's "Brains trust." In the next few months he would consult frequently with LDB, and serve as an important conduit between the jurist and the White House. Moley served as assistant secretary of state and resigned abruptly when Roosevelt failed to back his position at the London Economic Conference (see 8 July 1933, n. 1). After 1936, Moley became a harsh critic of the New Deal.

[2] See 30 January and 6 February 1933.

No. 517   January 7, 1933   Washington, D.C.

1. I hope the N.R. will support the Ashurst non-tax exemption resolution.[1]

2. You will recall my suggestion (in letter from Chatham) that some one ought to work up Surety Co, subrogation bank priorities and the whole surety co. evil, the substituting of bonds for established character as basis for credit in banks and contracts.[2] The receivership of the Indemnity Co. of La. would give an opportunity for wise discourse on that

subject. It is apt to result not only in bank failures in La (when the state & municipality conclude to withdraw their deposits) but to be followed by failures of other surety cos. It is doubtful whether any of them is really solvent. They have not only suffered a drop in value of their investments and of collateral given them to secure their surety bonds but the liability in their own surety bonds is rising heavily. I understand double the normal.

3. I know nothing of value about Guy Thompson.[3]

4. I delivered your message to Mc[*] and heard from him a full accounting of situation in the Commission (& value of or objections to incumbents) which you should know before there is any action taken.

5. Herbert F[eis] was here with Stimson yesterday before his leaving.

[1] On 22 December 1932, Senator Henry F. Ashurst of Arizona had introduced a constitutional amendment to prohibit the United States or any state from issuing tax exempt securities. It was referred to the Judiciary Committee, where it died. There was no piece on it in *The New Republic*.

[2] See 5 July 1932.

[3] Guy Thompson (1875–1958) was a St. Louis attorney, then serving as president of the American Bar Association.

No. 518   January 8, 1933   Washington, D.C.

1. Judge [Robert] Healy, who has made such a fine record in the Fed. Trade Commission investigations, said to me, some time ago, that he would like to talk to Gov. Roosevelt on public utilities. I think he deserves the opportunity. (Although a Republican, he voted for F.D.R.)

2. Eliz. is doubtful whether Dav. Lilienthal will get the reappointment. I suppose F.D.R. will snatch him if he doesn't, & perhaps if he does.

3. There ought to be a woman Ass. Atty General again. Mabel Willebrandt spoke of Jane Humphreys of California as able. I suppose she is a Democrat. I can't recall ever hearing of her. Annette Adams[1] was not good enough to deserve another appointment.

4. You will recall that Jack Gilbert was much occupied a few years ago with the Senatorial investigation of cotton exchanges. He hears that Prof. Moley is interesting himself in cotton. I wish you would send Jack (295 Madison Ave) a letter of introduction to Moley. I have never met him.

[1] Annette Abbott Adams (1877–1956) had been assistant attorney general of the United States from 1920 to 1922, and LDB had heard her argue several cases before the Supreme Court, including the test case for the Volstead Act. After a decade in private practice, she returned to government

service in the New Deal as a member of the Justice Department handling oil litigation. In 1941 she became a member of the Third District Court of Appeals in the California system.

No. 519   January 10, 1933   Washington, D.C.

Re David A. [sic] Walsh's letter about Holmes J.'s allowance.[1] The bill should also provide:

    (a) For the $20,000 retirement allowance of all present and future justices.

    (b) specifically that justices to be appointed shall receive the full $20,000

It is very important that such a bill be passed at the present session of Congress, and steps should be taken promptly to assure this. (Required because of alleged Comptroller's views)

The annexed suggestion has been made,[2] but I think it would be dangerous, so far as it extends to sitting on our Court, and probably undesirable otherwise. At all events, it would probably lead to disunion & so delay action which is urgent.

[1] Section 106 of the Appropriations Act of 1932 had reduced the pensions of retired judges, and many of Holmes's friends had objected to the diminution of his pension, not on grounds that he needed the money, but because they saw it as an insult to him. FF had raised the issue with Senator Walsh, who had responded on 1 December 1932 that he believed Congress had not intended the provision to apply to Supreme Court retirees, but that had been the interpretation given to it by the comptroller of the treasury. He indicated that he and other senators would be willing to introduce an amendment to the next Appropriations Act specifying this if FF thought that would be the most effective means of remedying the situation. See next letter.

[2] A brief note, not in LDB's handwriting, attached to this letter suggested a statute similar to that for circuit judges, permitting them to retire at a stated percentage of their salary after so many years of service.

No. 520   January 13, 1933   Washington, D.C.

1. Thanks for talking to Moley about Jack.[1]

2. The Senate Com'tee has reported what VD says is "satisfactory" & is in accordance with your letter to Dave Walsh.[2]

3. Sen. Tom Walsh called on me Tuesday to see whether I had any suggestions (no need of an alibi for him) for A.G.

4. Wednesday and Thursday McAdoo called on me to discuss proper persons for Secy of State, Secy of Treas and A.G. He is to see F.D.R. Sunday, & wants to make recommendations. He was fine in his talk & attitude.

507

5. Neither got much light from me; and there certainly is a terrible lack of able & desirable available material. Hope you have found some to recommend.

6. Can you think of any one in the West who would be apt to be able to suggest names worth considering for any of the three key posts?

Isn't there some place where Francis Fisher Kane[3] would fit in. And can't something be done for Norman.

[1] See 8 January 1933.

[2] In response to Walsh's letter regarding Holmes's pension, FF had written on 11 January suggesting that provision be made to guarantee a full $20,000 pension for all present and future appointees to the Supreme Court. Walsh replied on 22 January that while he agreed with the proposal, and had found much support among other members of the Finance Committee, there was such a press of work that he doubted if the issue could be addressed in the current session of Congress.

[3] Francis Fisher Kane (1886–1955) had served as United States attorney for the Eastern District of Pennsylvania during the Wilson administration. He did not receive an appointment from Roosevelt, but spent the remainder of his life in establishing and developing the office of public defender.

No. 521   January 21, 1933   Washington, D.C.

1. I suppose you have impressed upon F.D.R. that if he wants to get the benefit of existing and contemplated new sources of revenue, he must equip not only:

    (a) the Department of Justice (in Washington & in the several states)

    (b) the Treasury Dept., and

as so far as new appointments will permit,

    (c) the Tax Board

    (d) the Federal Courts

with lawyers of ability, training & the right attitude.

It is easy to lose several hundred million a year by mere inefficiency, such as practically all the commercial attys for N.Y. State and City customarily exhibit.[1]

The Dep. of Justice at Washington is now equipped (save for the S.G.) better than at any time during my period on the bench.

2. Referring to banks, and deposits of public funds. I think the priority given to the Gov & States, & to some extent to the municipalities (Cf. historical origin) is wholly unsuited to our times so far as concerns bank deposits, and a great evil, indeed a fraud on the other depositors.

I doubt whether Governments should have any priorities in case of insolvency except for taxes. But it seems clear that the law giving a gov't priority over[2] subjects other depositors to very serious risks and disadvantage. The Govt, which should know all about its banks, ought to take cheerfully all the risks which are involved in using the bank; and other depositors ought to be able to rely upon the confidence reposed by the Gov. in using the bank for the deposit of funds.

Moreover, the Govt. should not on deposit take collateral. If it does, that fact should be published. Otherwise, the other depositors suffer as from giving the Govt. a priority.

3. I like your memo to La Follette & telegram to LaGuardia re railroads.[3]

4. An important provision for saving public revenues would be a severe limitation on attorneys' fees in proceedings (of any kind) for tax refunds or abatements, somewhat as is done in Indian matters, Civil War claims & war bounties. Congressmen make a great fuss about the tax reimbursements made by the Treasury. A large part of these would never have been developed but for outrageously large fees (25 to 50 percent) which have stimulated the activity of claim hunters. It is said that Joe Davies[4] got over a million in a year or two. Folk[5] got several hundred thousand in a like period. Jack Gilbert has recently been in a partnership accounting case in which a young firm got over a million for themselves in a year.

I have urged such a provision for limitation on the A.G. & others for several years. Everbody agreed with me. The lawyers' lobby was too potent. Now, it might be possible to overcome the opposition.

Of course the attendant demoralization of the bar has been severe.

I have your telegram about Billy. Have not heard from him yet.

Interesting enclosures returned herewith.

[1] See 4 and 23 November 1928.

[2] When companies go bankrupt, their remaining assets are distributed according to statutory priorities. LDB is objecting to the government, which ought to be able to bear risks better than individual depositors, having an automatic priority over all other creditors.

[3] Many railroads, hard hit by the Depression, were seeking reorganization, and the Senate was considering a provision for such reorganizations as part of a general bankruptcy bill. FF urged La Follette and LaGuardia to keep railroad matters separate, and to provide not only for effective administration of the measure, but for fairness to the public as well as to stockholders and creditors.

[4] Joseph Edward Davies (1876–1958), the first chairman of the Federal Trade Commission, represented a number of foreign countries in litigation in the United States. During the New Deal he would be ambassador to Russia and later Belgium; when the war broke out he served as a special envoy from Roosevelt to Churchill and Stalin. In the 1920s Davies had been counsel to taxpayers seeking refunds in the *Ford Stock Valuation* case of 1927–1928.

No. 522　　　January 30, 1933　　　Washington, D.C.

Upon receipt of your yesterday's letter, I wired you that I could see Niles[1] & the Senators at 3 PM Friday or Sunday and hope you could arrange to have Moley here also. My close period begins Monday with the Court's reconvening.

I am particularly anxious to see Moley.

I agree with FDR—and think

- (a) the real improvement can come only with his declaring at the opening of the extra session [of Congress] a comprehensive program.
- (b) It must be one of such magnitude that it will (and people can see that it will) effect the needed change.
- (c) The change will come, if he will go in for
  - (1) the wholesale reafforestation plan[2]
  - (2) " control of water plan
    to be paid for at first by loans, then by high estate & income taxes with share to the State, all as explained to you.

That plan, if broadly & quickly entered upon could put two million men to work directly by the U.S. & the states within six months; and another million or two indirectly; and would turn many a wheel now idle. It would help:

- (a) transportation
- (b) the farmers
- (c) many merchants and manufacturers.

First All the money spent will be for permanent investment.

Second The project will greatly reduce the immediate demand for relief.

Third It will so hearten folks everywhere and particularly on the Hill that it will make it possible for FDR to put through his other measures, including international debts.

Fourth Unlike share replacing and allotment bills etc., it will rouse no opposition from concerns whose business or property values are deemed threatened by competition or otherwise.

Fifth No one is "threatened" except the super-rich.

Sixth States would see visions of large revenues.

It is this plan that I am eager to talk to Moley about.
See enclosure as to what Mass. proposes.
Had a fine talk with Pelley.[3]

[1] David K. Niles (1890–1952), a longtime Massachusetts progressive, was close to both Presidents Roosevelt and Truman, serving the latter as a White House assistant. During the New Deal he would work with Harry Hopkins in the Works Progress Administration.

[2] Roosevelt had called for a public works program emphasizing reforestation of 161,000,000 acres of land; ultimately, the plan emerged as the Civilian Conservation Corps.

[3] Perhaps John Jeremiah Pelley (1878–1946), an experienced railroad operator and, since 1929, head of LDB's old nemesis, the New York, New Haven and Hartford Railroad.

No. 523   February 6, 1933   Washington, D.C.

1. Niles has doubtless reported to you fully:
    (1) on the proposed talk with the Senate Com'tee. Bob La F. and Cutting [1] came in later without Niles. C. impressed me much more favorably than he had heretofore.
    (2) as to my views on the Roosevelt afforestation-flood control announcement

2. As to the latter: What he proposes is fine in quality, but difficult in quantity for this exigency; and this is pre-eminently a case where difference in degree is difference in kind. We must have the wholesale proposition to meet the emergency. Perhaps R. intends this, & merely put out a trial baloon [sic].

3. The statement is also objectionable, if it means his policy is to test the success by whether the project is self-liquidating. This is a permanént investment which, if the policy for America is right, will be productive, even if the Gov't never gets a penny of income. (Of course it would ultimately get much.) Perhaps this is also his way, as a good politician, of preparing the public.

4. The statement, if it means policy, is also objectionable in that it does embody the higher brackets tax feature. Perhaps this also is his good politics. My idea is that we should issue notes, not bonds; which in no event could be issued now; that we should treat the early expenditures rather as advances in anticipation of the large tax returns which will come in when our super-rich die.

5. As to Donald Richberg. Doubtless he would make a good S.G. But would that not be a waste of him? His social viewpoint etc. are assets which should be used elsewhere. Another [William] Mitchell could fill the S.G.[2]

No. 524   February 15, 1933   Washington, D.C.

The Michigan Bank Holiday [1] is a striking manifestation of the Curse of Bigness.

Deposit banking rests upon the law of averages. The huge company depositor destroys the basis of banking. It can ruin a relatively weak bank by a withdrawal. And it destroys the usefulness of the strong ones by fear of withdrawal.

The excess liquidity of the larger banks is now due in large measure to the fact that the great corporations may at any moment, withdraw their huge balances, and leave the bank otherwise helpless unless excessively liquid.

[1]A wave of bank "holidays" had spread across the country in the wake of massive bank failures. Nevada had declared the first holiday in late 1932, and by 4 March 1933 thirty-eight states had followed suit, with the holidays ranging from a few days to a few weeks. Michigan had closed its banks the previous day.

No. 525   February 23, 1933   Washington, D.C.

1. Gilbert Montague [1] reports great success of your opening lecture in N.Y.

2. George Rublee was in yesterday about Dean A. for S.G. [2] & said he would telegraph you.

3. The reported Cabinet is, on the whole, promising, & there are some appointments which we may well be happy over. In Frances Perkins [3] we have the best the U.S. affords, & besides it is a distinct advance to have selected a woman for the Cabinet.

4. It would have been great fun to have x-examined Mitchell et al.

5. Financial matter[s] appear to be growing steadily worse. What do you hear of the N.Y. banks? [4]

[1]Gilbert Holland Montague (1880–1961), a New York attorney, was a widely recognized authority on antitrust law.

[2]Acheson was not named solicitor general; instead, he became under secretary of the treasury, but resigned after six months because of differences with the president over monetary policy.

[3]Frances Perkins (Wilson) (1880–1965) had been a prominent industrial reformer in New York (where she had often worked with the Goldmark sisters), and had held high positions in the state

government under both Alfred Smith and Roosevelt. During her twelve-year tenure as secretary of labor, she proved an ardent advocate of union rights.

[4] New York managed to postpone a bank holiday until 3 March 1933.

No. 526   March 3, 1933   Washington, D.C.

1. George R, Hitz, Eastman have accepted for Wednesday 7 PM. Invitation has been sent also to Bob La F.[1]

3. No doubt improvements can be made in the banking system. But the chief evil is banking practices. Until we can get honest, fearless bankers, no improvement of system will avail much.

Of course, state and federal supervising departments are grossly at fault, and Gene is not without sin in his silence. I guess he could have gotten rid of Mitchell and Costigan, if he had been as insistent as on many occasions.

The government has really been helping in the conspiracy & obtaining (or keeping) depositors' money under false pretence. What it should have done was to open wide the Postal Savings & take itself the risk of lending to worthy banks, making them, in effect, its agents to lend to worthy borrowers.

Then there would have been little hoarding.

[1] FF was about to visit Washington, and the Brandeises had asked him for names of people he would like to have at a dinner they would host for him.

No. 527   March 13, 1933   Washington, D.C.

1. Wallace[1] and Tugwell[2] were in. Our talk was diverted by a remark of T's to Bigness, so we didn't get much into other things. But I worked in (innocent-like, the troubles of all high officials except USSC in this respect), & it struck home.

T. asked about counsel. I mentioned Margold, Erwin Griswold,[3] and Paul Miller,[4] & suggested T. ask you.

2. Later, Ickes[5] came in. Said Margold had been here & had consented to take Finney's place; & that he (Ickes) would try to see the Pres. today & get consent to make the change promptly.

3. In view of Margold going to Ickes, would it be well for you to suggest others to Tugwell. What would you think of Whitney North Seymour?[6] (who I didn't happen to think of then). And (if Dean A. does not become S.G.) would it be possible to get him for Agriculture. It

would be a comedown, but that's a branch of public life in which he is interested, and in which his financial affiliations would be less in the way than elsewhere. I think he is a bit sick of the financial connections, and that the public service interests him now.

Tugwell spoke highly of Max Lowenthal, and said: "I guess he would not be interested. The salary is only $8000, and his public interests are in things financial."

[1] Henry Agard Wallace (1888–1965) served as secretary of agriculture from 1933 to 1940, and as vice-president of the United States from 1941 to 1945. Wallace was a sympathizer of the Soviet Union in the forties, and in 1948 led a third party campaign on a platform of peace and understanding with Russia.

[2] Rexford Guy Tugwell (1891–1979) had taught economics at Columbia when he became involved with the "brains trust." During the early part of the New Deal he was under secretary of agriculture, and after 1937 served in a variety of positions, including governor of Puerto Rico. He wrote a number of books on the Roosevelt administration and on Latin American policy. In many ways, Tugwell represented much of what LDB would oppose in the so-called "first" New Deal, with its fascination for bigness and obsession for large scale planning.

[3] Erwin Nathaniel Griswold (b. 1904) had been in the solicitor general's office since 1929, and at FF's urging, Roosevelt kept him and Paul Miller in the new administration. Griswold left in 1934 to go to the Harvard Law School, where he taught until 1967, serving as dean after 1946. In 1967 President Johnson named him solicitor general of the United States, and he continued in that office during President Nixon's first term.

[4] Paul Duryea Miller (1899–1965), a 1925 graduate of Harvard Law, served as assistant to the solicitor general from 1930 until late in 1933, when he entered private practice in New York.

[5] Harold LeClaire Ickes (1874–1952) had been a lawyer and civic reformer in Chicago before Roosevelt named him secretary of the interior, a position he held until 1946. Ickes also headed the powerful public works program created under the National Industrial Recovery Act. In 1940, Ickes would receive the Louis D. Brandeis Freedom Medal, and shortly afterwards published *Not Guilty* (Washington: Government Printing Office, 1940), in which he defended the policies of Richard A. Ballinger. See LDB to Bernard Flexner, 23 May 1940.

[6] Whitney North Seymour (1901–1983) served as assistant solicitor general from 1931 to 1933, after which he taught at Yale Law School until 1945, while also maintaining a private practice in New York.

No. 528   March 17, 1933   Washington, D.C.

1. It's good that the administration desisted from its purpose to support the 2 Detroit banks. Isadore Levin's memo is interesting. But we must not let ourselves be misled by the proposed central bank or all-in-the-reserve system remedies or branch bank talk.[1] The evidence shows that lack of these things was not the real cause of our trouble.

   (a) Detroit shows

   (1) that it was the big banks in the Reserve System which pulled the others down, and shows

514

(2) what branch or group system will do in this country
With them & with our lack of good traditions, we'll have new examples of holding company evils.

2. Bigness has troubled us more than smallness. Aldrich[2] ought not be allowed to get off with mere pious talk and divorcing of affiliates.[3]

The 84 N.P.[4] and [*] facts which BF has happily given us should be played up in the Nation, or N.R. I suppose the New York Times would not print a letter. Would the Herald Tribune?

3. Will Chicago take Freund[5] or Wis. Siegel? If not, could they find temporary berths in the Departments?

There ought to be a challenge of men being directors in many corps. I doubt whether any man can really perform the duties of director of more than one efficiently. By limiting the number of directorships, we should go far also in promoting honesty, i.e. loyalty to the one master.[6]

[1] The collapse of the banking system evoked numerous proposals on how to reform the Federal Reserve System to avoid such failures in the future. The Glass-Steagall Act, providing deposit insurance, passed as part of the Hundred Days in 1933; more extensive reform took place in the Banking Act of 1935.

[2] Winthrop Williams Aldrich (1885–1974) was president of the Chase National Bank, and in 1934 became chairman of its board. From 1953 to 1957 he would serve as American ambassador to the Court of St. James.

[3] Aldrich and other officials of large banks were worried about proposed reforms then being discussed by the administration, and hoped to head off major limitations on their operations by offering minor concessions.

[4] There is no "84 *New Palestine*." LDB may have been referring to a brief article in *New Palestine* 23 (3 March 1933): 1 about the prosperous economic conditions in Palestine and the resulting shortage of Jewish labor.

[5] Paul Abraham Freund (b. 1908) was then completing his year as LDB's law clerk. After serving in the Justice Department in several positions, he joined the Harvard Law School faculty in 1939, and became Carl M. Loeb University Professor in 1958. Freund has long enjoyed a reputation as a leading constitutional authority. See his "Justice Brandeis: A Law Clerk's Remembrance," *American Jewish History* 68 (1978): 7.

[6] This had long been one of LDB's concerns; see his "Serve One Master Only!" (Part IV of "Breaking the Money Trust"), *Harper's Weekly* 58 (13 December 1913): 10, reprinted in *Other People's Money* (New York: Stokes, 1914), 69–91.

No. 529   March 22, 1933   Washington, D.C.

1. Freund would probably prove just the kind of solicitor Frances Perkins says she needs.[1] He is cautious & deliberate, & has the gravity of demeanor needed to impress the outside world.

2. FDR message on relief[2] was what [sic] just what I should have wished him to say, except that it asks for only a trial order. I want about

10 times as much. Perhaps he does also, and this is merely his trial balloon.

3. He certainly has the most extraordinary political sagacity. Putting the whole Farm Relief difficulties on Wallace's back was a master stroke.[3] Likewise, wonderously wise his pressing forward all desired legislation and postponing attending to the demands for patronage.

4. Denman & multitudes of others are still lingering in Washington.

5. I am still troubled by Big Finance (as Max L. seems to be.)

6. And sooner or later, F.D.R. will have to deal with heavier taxes on the right. My respectable wise ones here seem as much afraid of putting an end to the superrich as they are to putting an end to superbig corporations. Their talk of "regulating them" reminds of 1912.

[1] Freund did not go into the Labor Department, but instead joined the Justice Department.

[2] On the preceding day, President Roosevelt, in a brief message to Congress, laid out his proposal for unemployment relief. He asked authorization to put 250,000 idle Americans to work and to make direct relief grants to the fifty states. The army of unemployed would work on conservation, flood control, and on other public works projects that would not compete with private employment. The president requested no new funds, but proposed to use $200,000,000 already appropriated for public works projects.

[3] On 16 March Roosevelt sent an emergency farm relief proposal to Congress, which embodied what became the Agriculture Adjustment Act. The president called for acreage allotments, crop subsidies, and extensive controls by the Agriculture Department in order to reduce surplus production. Nearly all of these powers were to be lodged in the secretary of agriculture.

No. 530   March 25, 1933   Washington, D.C.

I trust my letter approving Freund for Labor reach[ed] you early Thursday.

1. It has been suggested that if Freund is not selected for Labor, possibly Ray Stevens[1] is worthy of consideration.

2. I see Norris is to introduce some sort of a corporation license bill.[2] In that sort of a measure I see only dangers, & hope you will see to it that he doesn't get far with it. It looks to me like infantile faith in regulation to which the Berle,[3] Means et al. associates are addicted.[4]

3. As bank investigations & the like are to be given free rein, I hope the excessive salary enquiry will be allowed to proceed.

4. The Boston experience in group banking (clipping enclosed) is another bit of evidence against tying up units & getting a terrible fall for all, instead of letting weak independents go to the wall.

5. We like much your Yale Review address,[5] & Harlan has renewed joy.

[1] Roosevelt appointed Stevens to the Federal Trade Commission, and later to the U.S. Tariff Commission, of which he was chairman after 1937.

[2] The idea of federal incorporation of interstate corporations had been around since Theodore Roosevelt's time, and was now receiving renewed interest in Congress. Although several bills were introduced in the next few years, none gained passage.

[3] Adolph Augustus Berle, Jr. (1895–1971), after graduating from the Harvard Law School, had worked briefly with LDB's law firm before going on to a career in law, economics, diplomacy, and government service that established him as one of the most influential public policy intellectuals of the twentieth century.

[4] A major theme of the important study by Berle and Gardiner C. Means, *The Modern Corporation and Private Property* (New York: Macmillan, 1932), was that the private corporation had become so large and powerful, that only extensive government regulation could control it.

[5] "Social Issues before the Supreme Court," *Yale Review* 22 (1933): 476. In this article, FF noted that the Depression had required new ideas and led to a rethinking of past assumptions. New programs embodying these ideas would find legislative expression, and thus come before the courts for approval. He urged judges to Holmes's doctrine of judicial self-restraint; their role was not to approve the wisdom of the new policies, but only to see whether the legislative agencies had the constitutional power to enact them.

No. 531   March 28, 1933   Washington, D.C.

1. Re yours 27th. About Glavis[1] Margold talked with me on 26th. Told him all I know—remains favorable, & told him also of Norman's high opinion.

2. Drew Pearson was in. Says Gardner Jackson has lost most of his money; has only a small salary from the Canadian papers, and needs a job. P. asked me whether there was a possibility for him with the Labor Dept. I referred him to Clara Berger. Margold told me he was considering for Ickes Slattery,[2] whom he & all I know consider a very good man; but some men Ickes are [sic] opposing. If Glavis or Slattery are not taken, possibly you may think Gardner the man for Ickes.

3. It's fine Margold is received so well by the Wash. News.

4. You doubtless noticed that Bigness proved fatal to the Globe & Rutgers Fire Ins. Co., once a model company.[3]

[1] Harold Ickes hired Glavis to work once again the Interior Department, perhaps as a symbolic victory for the Progressives who had fought for conservation two decades earlier. However, he soon found it difficult to get along with Glavis. See 28 August 1934.

[2] Harry Slattery (1887–1949) had been secretary to Gifford Pinchot from 1909 to 1912. In 1933 he became personal assistant to Harold Ickes, then undersecretary, and in 1939 assumed the chief administrator's post in the Rural Electrification Agency.

[3] On 24 March the New York superintendent of insurance had filed a petition to take over assets of the Globe and Rutgers Insurance Company for the purpose of rehabilitation. A severe drop in the value of the firm's securities, which had been among the largest in the state, had led to a demand for regulatory action.

1. Had a satisfactory hour with FDR. He began by asking about Dean. Said [Lewis] Douglas had advised strongly taking him. R. had not yet talked with Cummings. Then, after an appreciative reference by him to you, took up mainly Postal Savings, & freeing the Govt from the grip of the bankers, touching, of course, also on need of safety for savings, and need of extensive public works program. He seemed much interested in the P.O. Savings project, and as I was walking out of the room called after me to that effect.

2. He mentioned Prest. Taylor's [1] visit on U.S. Steel, and that he wanted me to see the figures he left with FDR. That gave me a chance for few words on Bigness and Overcapacity.

As he could not lay his hands on the papers at the moment, he sent them after me (before I left the White House) with the oral message "Return them at your leisure." I did so this AM. They were very illuminating, revealing the Co.'s folly.

Since 1929, it has increased capacity about 12 1/2 percent, expending for construction in 1930 $144,000,000, & a larger amount in 1931. The result of this policy & of the payment of unearned dividends & recent losses in operations is that Co. has less than $70,000,000 cash (& I think [*]) with a good chance of having to borrow before 1934 comes in.

3. I saw Moley a moment as I was entering the elevator. He said he hoped I would talk permanent works program. There was little chance for this. R. had engagement with Woodin [2] for 11 AM. Moley said he wanted to come in to me for a long talk.

4. The Liggett Co. bankruptcy in order to get rid of leases is one of the most dishonest of Big Business tricks. The Liggett Co. is a wholly owned subsidiary of what I suppose is a very rich Liggett concern, Drug Co. etc. [3] You will recall the proposed $25,000,000 deal for the British Co.

This performance should be shown up in an effective article which should interest Henry Hart to do.

It seems to me even more disgusting than the City Corn Exchange bank project, & more obvious. [4]

5. Did you get anyone to do the job on closing loopholes in tax laws? Hiss ought to have some exacting legal work to keep him in form. Could he do that?

6. F.D.R. was to see Frances Perkins after Cabinet meeting yester-

day, perhaps about your immigration proposal. There was no chance to talk to FDR about Jews.[5]

Haven't the English behaved finely?

[1] Myron Charles Taylor (1874–1959), then head of the U.S. Steel Corporation, would later be active in refugee relief work. In 1939, Roosevelt named him as the first American ambassador to the Vatican.

[2] William Hartman Woodin (1868–1934), a Republican, had been president of the American Car and Foundry Company since 1899, until Roosevelt named him as secretary of the treasury.

[3] The Liggett Company, which operated over 450 retail drug stores in the country, had filed for bankruptcy on 31 March, claiming it had done everything it could to cut costs, including closing over 200 stores, but that sales were down over 30 percent from 1929. The previous November Liggett, a wholly owned subsidiary of the United Drug Company, had been restrained from filing on petition of a landlord, who claimed the only reason for the company's actions was in order to cancel its leases.

[4] In what LDB considered a similar abuse of the bankruptcy laws, the Corn Exchange bank had recently bought the building and equipment of another bank which had closed, in what some people charged had been a collusive deal.

[5] American Jewish leaders were increasingly concerned over the anti-Semitic measures then being legislated by the Hitler regime to restrict Jewish economic and civil rights in Germany.

No. 533   April 26, 1933   Washington, D.C.

1. I hope F.D.R. will act soon.[1] It is becoming a disgrace to us all that America does not act.

2. I am entirely ready to talk to Wagner, Bob & Costigan jointly, but deem it unwise for me to solicit the interview.

3. I asked Dean to come in a week ago & suggested that he get Douglas to push him for an Ass. Atty. Gen'l position. We shall really need him when the new legislation is attacked. Can't imagine the A.G. will be adequate for that.

4. I am entirely willing that the N.R. shall establish an "Other People's Money column."[2]

5. Gene called Monday, is coming in Sunday for a talk.

6. We had Wyzanski[3] in Monday.

7. And your bill drafters yesterday.

8. Lionberger Davis was in. He seems a banker of the old type & generally sane.

7 [sic]. The evidence of the Curse of Bigness is accumulating.

8. I am calm about going off gold, but don't like the inflation talk.[4] It is Kunststucke[5] projects.

[1] Concerning the plight of German Jews; Roosevelt did not act.

[2] Starting with the 10 May 1933 issue, *The New Republic* ran a weekly column by John T. Flynn

under the title of LDB's 1914 book, "Other People's Money." The column ran until 4 November 1940.

[3] Charles Edward Wyzanski, Jr. (1906–1986), after a brilliant career at Harvard College and Law School, had clerked for both Augustus and Learned Hand before Roosevelt named him solicitor of the Labor Department in 1933. In 1941 the President appointed him to the District Court for Massachusetts, where he soon earned a reputation as an outstanding liberal jurist.

[4] On 19 April, Roosevelt announced that the United States would go off the gold standard to prevent the increasing deflation of American currency. Roosevelt's action won support from much of the business community, who feared that continued adherence to gold would lead to further economic collapse.

[5] "Clever tricks."

No. 534   April 29, 1933   Washington, D.C.

1. In view of Wise's letter to you, I asked Freund to wire you that MacDonald [sic] [1] had telephoned to enquire whether you were in town.

2. Miss Perkins' of 25th (returned herewith) is indeed distressing and your answer fine. [2] F.D. has showed amply that he has no antisemitism and his appointments of Strauss and of Steinhardt [3] (the latter doubtless a sop to Untermyer [4]) are distinctly helpful. But this action, or rather determination that there shall be none, is a disgrace to America & to F.D.'s administration. You could have doubtless decided before this whether it would be wise for you to see F.D. again. If yes, it should be done immediately.

3. Redlich was in, deeply moved, almost in tears about the German situation, and never before approachingly so Jewish.

4. I guess the Jews of Germany had better make up their minds to move on, all of them. Of course, the nation is crazy now, but life there will never be safe, and it has been distinctly degrading to the present generation of Jews.

5. Hitlerism shows that the Allies were right in 1914, in opposing with all available force German aggression. If only they had not been wrong in 1919.

6. Doubtless you heard from Austern. The situation as to the S.G. [5] is also disturbing.

[1] James Grover McDonald (1886–1964), the chairman of the Foreign Policy Association, would soon take up new responsibilities as League of Nations high commissioner for refugees. President Truman would name him as the first American ambassador to Israel.

[2] There is no copy of this correspondence in either the Frankfurter or Perkins Papers.

[3] Laurence A. Steinhardt (1892–1950), a former law partner of Samuel Untermyer's, had been named by Roosevelt as American minister to Sweden; he would later serve as American ambassador, successively, to Peru, Russia, Turkey, Czechoslovakia, and Canada.

[4] Samuel Untermyer (1858–1940) was a successful New York attorney who, on occasion, represented the Morgan and Rockefeller interests, but also defended labor unions. He had been

520

counsel to the Pujo Committee of 1912–1913, upon whose findings LDB's book, *Other People's Money*, had been based.

[5]James Crawford Biggs (1872–1960), a North Carolina lawyer and Democratic politician, served as FDR's first solicitor general from 1933 to 1935. He compiled an extremely poor record in arguing the government's side in major cases, and LDB was not alone in thinking him inadequate to the job.

No. 535   May 14, 1933   Washington, D.C.

1. What was Lowell's final stab at you?[1]

2. Your letter & telegram re Schacht dinner[2] have come but not the Proskauer memo.[3] I hope your representative gave it to him a l'Angleterre. Baruch wanted to consult me before deciding whether or not to attend, said he was "hot" under the collar. He was greatly relieved when I advised he should not, and immediately wired Sarnoff.

3. Baruch is so stirred up by the Jewish situation that we may now get some active help from him. He is to wire me when he next comes to W. for an appointment.

4. I guess that your best answer to Hull's[4] of 6th is to write him in the tone you did Frances Perkins.

5. Hull seems to me particularly unfit for the job, a fine man, without health, vitality, thorough in the use of his little vigor, and without much knowledge outside his narrow economic field. Despite brave words of his, his & F.D.'s, I guess the so-called Tariff truce is (by reason of reservations) = 0.[5]

6. I suppose you told Flynn[6] "Judicial office precludes."

7. What do you think of Conant?[7]

8. I guess O.W.H. would be willing to sign C.C.B.'s protest.[8]

9. You are right in apprehending Industrial Control Bill.[9] Frances P. (who seems to be the wisest member of the Cabinet) feared it greatly & came in last Wednesday to get my advice. She has proper suspicion of Lou Douglas' judgment.

10. Dean came in about 10 days ago. He spoke, among other things, about defects in the Securities Bill,[10] which disturbed Woodin. Didn't mention Parker Gilbert. I suggested that he consult Tom Cochran [sic]. He was silent. I asked whether he knew T.C. He answered Yes, & left on me the impression that he wouldn't care for T.C.'s advice.

11. F.D.'s readiness to experiment is fine. But I am at times reminded of the Uncle from India's answer to the Private Secretary. When asked by his housekeeper "Do you believe in spirits?" "Yes," said he, "in moderation." I guess his inflation program, the refusal to pay interest in

521

gold on our bonds held abroad, and his economy control projects will do much harm. I wish he would experiment instead with banishing the bankers, through opening P.O. Savings postals etc. & putting on heavier estate taxes.

12. Cousens' [sic] remark[11] ought to make him an ardent supporter of your contingent fee bill.[12]

13. The S.G. appeared in Court as evidence last week. He wouldn't be selected on his looks & there is reason for much apprehension.

Angus McLean[13] (who is probably largely responsible for his selection) talked with me recently, somewhat concerned, & said he would bring S.G. in for advice. But they haven't appeared.

14. It is amazing what the Chicago bar did re Woodward.[14] It is hard to believe that with Strawn on deck, they have experienced religion.

[1] A. L. Lowell had just stepped down as president of Harvard University; see n. 7 below.

[2] In the wake of growing public criticism of Nazi measures against German Jews and the fear of economic reprisals, the head of the Reichsbank, Hjalmar Horace Greeley Schacht (1877–1970), had been dispatched to the United States to explain Hitler's policies and to smooth over increasing German-American friction. David Sarnoff agreed to give a dinner for Schacht and to invite leading American Jewish figures. The dinner, on 12 May, was a distinct failure, with many Jewish leaders refusing to attend, and the rest sitting in stony silence while Schacht made his presentation.

[3] Joseph Mayer Proskauer (1877–1971) enjoyed a long and prosperous legal practice in New York, interrupted by seven years as a justice of the appellate division of the New York Supreme Court in the 1920s. He was also the anti-Zionist president of the American Jewish Committee, and throughout the thirties opposed not only Zionist efforts to open Palestine, but also overt acts of opposition to Nazi policy.

[4] Cordell Hull (1871–1955), a longtime member of the House of Representatives from Tennessee, had been elected to the Senate in 1931, but resigned his seat two years later to become Roosevelt's secretary of state, a post he held until 1944. His tenure at State was marked by efforts to improve relations with Latin America through the "Good Neighbor" policy, and by his desire to remain neutral as war clouds lowered on Europe later in the decade. There is no correspondence between the two men around this date in either the FF or Hull MSS.

[5] One point on which Hull, who is not regarded as a stong secretary of state, did hold firm views was the need to lower the tariff, and he worked throughout the New Deal to secure reciprocal trade agreements to that end.

[6] John Thomas Flynn (1882–1964), a widely-published columnist, wrote over a dozen books on various aspects of contemporary American politics. Perhaps he asked LDB for some public message in connection with his new column, "Other People's Money." See 26 April 1933, n. 2.

[7] James Bryant Conant (1893–1978), a professor of chemistry at Harvard since 1919, had just been named president of the university, replacing FF's old foe, A. Lawrence Lowell. Conant became American high commissioner for Germany from 1953 to 1955, and then ambassador to the newly established Federal Republic of Germany. A widely noted author on educational problems, he conducted several studies of American school systems for the Carnegie Corporation.

[8] Burlingham was leading a fight against a bill in the New York legislature which would have given a disbarred attorney an appeal of right to an appellate court, regardless of the issues of law involved. This would have taken direct control of policing the legal profession out of the hands of the bar associations and thrown it into the courts.

[9] The keystone in Roosevelt's efforts to end the Depression was the National Industrial Recovery

Act, with its plan to promote business cooperation through industry-wide codes. These codes would allow firms to work together, even exempting many actions from the antitrust laws, and in return, employers would agree to minimum wage, maximum hours, and other fair labor standards, as well as the right of workers to organize and bargain collectively. LDB, always opposed to bigness, was unrelenting in his criticism of the NRA, which after some initial accomplishments, drew increasing fire from all segments of the society. The NRA, by then already moribund, met its death in a unanimous Supreme Court decision, *Schechter Poultry Corp.* v. *United States*, 295 U.S. 495 (1935).

[10] The Rayburn-Fletcher Securities Act, which would be signed into law on 27 May, was designed to protect the investing public from being misled by fraudulent or incomplete information provided either by the companies or the stock brokers.

[11] Senator James Couzens had attacked the appointment of Dean Acheson to the Treasury Department, and charged that government officials were in cahoots with the big Wall Street bankers and law firms. He also claimed that Treasury officials had collaborated in assessing large fees in tax cases for the lawyers involved, a feeling LDB shared.

[12] See 21 January 1933.

[13] Angus Wilton McLean (1870–1935), a North Carolina lawyer, had been managing director of the War Finance Corporation during the First World War, and in the 1920s had served as governor of his state.

[14] On 27 April, the Chicago Bar Association had publicly criticized Federal Judge Charles Edgar Woodward (1876–1942) for the frequent appointment of his son's law firm to lucrative receiverships in bankruptcy cases.

No. 536   June 13, 1933   Chatham, Mass.

I am writing before seeing the morning paper.

1. We have failed to get much that seems to me essential & have gotten some Kunststucke [1] of questionable value.

2. The action on the gold clause [2] is terrifying in its implications. A declaration of bankruptcy, or composition, [3] is honorable if warranted by existing conditions. But the deliberate repudiation by the Government of its own solemn obligations, entered into freely in contemplation of the contingency which has arisen and for the purpose of dealing with it, involves an alarming application of [*]. If the Government wished to extricate itself from the assumed emergency, taxation would have afforded an honorable way out.

3. Our Court will apparently be confronted, in a time of greatest need of help, with a Department of Justice as incompetent as was that of Mitchell Palmer.

4. Then the Helvering [4] appointment!!

5. The Walter Newton appointment [5] smacked of an oriental potentate.

6. And that civil rights, the protest against Hitler, should have to rely upon Joe Robinson, [6] Hatfield [7] & Hamilton Fish. [8]

7. Departures from the moral law are the main causes of our present discontent. Further departures are not "the way out."

8. Arthur Morgan[9] & Dave Lilienthal have gotten the most alluring job in the govt.

9. I should think John H. Fahey would decline that offered him.[10]

10. Ben F's letter is interesting.

[1] "Clever tricks."

[2] As part of his plan to devalue the currency in order to produce inflation, Roosevelt had secured a joint resolution of Congress on 5 June nullifying the gold clause common to nearly all corporate bonds as well as those of the government itself. The clause, which called for the payment of principal and interest in gold, aimed at protecting the bond holder from the devaluation of his asset through inflation or the disparity of various kinds of circulating money. Ultimately, the matter came before the Supreme Court; see 24 February 1935.

[3] An agreement between a debtor and his creditors, whereby in return for an immediate payment, the latter agree to take less than the whole amount of their claims.

[4] Guy Tresillian Helvering (1878–1946) had served in Congress as a representative from Kansas during the Wilson years, after which he remained active in the state's Democratic party. Roosevelt had just named him as commissioner of internal revenue, a post he held for ten years until appointed federal district judge for Kansas.

[5] To the Home Loan Bank Board.

[6] Robinson had denounced anti-Semitism in Germany in a speech on 10 June.

[7] Possibly Henry Drury Hatfield (1875–1962), a former governor of West Virginia then serving his only term as a United States senator from that state.

[8] Hamilton Fish (b. 1888) served in Congress as a representative from New York for twenty-five years, beginning with the Republican landslide of 1920. Although originally a progressive, Fish became extremely conservative as the years went by, and during the thirties was an outspoken critic of the New Deal, as well as one of the nation's leading isolationists. On 24 May, he had introduced a Senate resolution asking Roosevelt to aid German Jews.

[9] Arthur Ernest Morgan (1878–1975), a civil engineer with vast experience in dam building and flood control, was president of Antioch College when Roosevelt named him as chairman of the Tennessee Valley Authority. Of the three directors, Morgan was nominally most committed to the idea of total planning, and once described the agency as a vast scheme for "a designed and planned social and economic order." Eventually, after repeated clashes with Lilienthal and Harcourt Morgan, Roosevelt removed Arthur Morgan in April 1938.

[10] It is unclear what John H. Fahey (1873–1950), the editor of the *Boston Traveler*, had been offered, but he did not enter government service until November 1933, when Roosevelt named him head of the Home Owners Loan Corporation.

No. 537   July 8, 1933   Chatham, Mass.

It was fine to have you here & to get a glimpse of Marion.

1. Inflation, going-off-gold and stabilizing are matters as to which men may reasonably differ, and as to which the same individual, be he statesman or economist, may change his own mind. But Keynes notwithstanding, the tone and circumstances of F.D.'s July 3 allocution to the World Conference [1] are to all very disquieting as a symptom, & he

may be a manifestation of the disintegrating effect of absolute power on mind and character. And, in that connection, disregard of the "brain trust" may be serious. Remember, we have no Congress until Jan/34.

2. I guess Paul [*] had little joy from his visit. I talked to him mainly of bankers serving two masters & removing the Curse of Bigness. He wanted to talk, i.a. of the Securities bill[2] which he thinks, like other investment bankers, will do more harm than good, & of other administration policies; but these I passed over without discussion.

3. It was a great loss to have T.G. Jones killed at the age of 26.

4. Tom Cochrane [sic] was effective with E.A.F.

[1] At the World Economic Conference then meeting in London, representatives of six European countries called for continuation of the gold standard as the medium of international exchange. In his letter to the Conference dated 3 July, Roosevelt categorically rejected the gold standard, and in effect scuttled any impact the Conference might have had on stabilizing international trade and currency.

[2] See 14 May 1933, n. 10.

No. 538   July 14, 1933   Chatham, Mass.

1. That was a superb order of F.D.'s re Postmasters.[1] I had been specially eager for that since the Myers case.[2] Hope F.D. will act similarly on some offices in the Treas.

2. Yes, Ickes at the head of public works helps much.[3] But he also is getting to be overworked.

3. As to recovery bill, when we meet I will tell you of some talk with one of my former, ablest clients, who has been doing his customary thinking.

4. I am very glad you wrote F.D. re Dep. of Justice.

5. Hope the contingent fee matter will not sleep.[4]

6. Also that John T. Flynn has been started on lawyers' fees.

7. Cutting fees (and executive salaries) to the reasonable will have as by-product getting the able young into the public service.

8. [Al] Smith a director in N.Y. Life Ins. Co.!!
   "When he grew up he was lost totally
   And he married a member of the Corps de ballet."[5]

[1] Two days earlier President Roosevelt, through executive order, had placed all postmasters of first, second, and third class post offices under civil service rules, thus removing some 15,000 patronage positions.

[2] See 27 October 1926, n. 1.

[3] Over the protests of Harry Hopkins, who wanted to tie the public works title of the National

Industrial Recovery Act to his relief program, Roosevelt assigned the responsibility to Secretary of the Interior Ickes.

[4] See 21 January 1933.

[5] Gilbert and Sullivan, *Patience*, Act II.

No. 539   August 3, 1933   Chatham, Mass.

1. Yours with the H[ouse]. of C[ommons]. clipping came shortly after my yesterday's letter was mailed. I am glad you & Marion will have such good company for a year.[1]

2. W.H.'s letter is significant. I recall his history.

3. Howe[2] is indeed a dangerous influence.

4. Hope R[aymond]. M[oley]. will find the new assignment congenial.

5. Amidst our anxieties there is promise in many specific undertakings:

    (a) The Tennessee Valley Project.

    (b) The Civil Conservation Camps.

    (c) The water control, conservation, and development projects which Ickes announces.

    (d) The subsistence farm projects.

    (e) J.B. Eastman's increased influence.

    (f) The Wagner-Perkins Federal Employment projects.

    (g) Getting rid of child-labor.

    (h)   "   "   " the yellow dog contracts & company unions.

    (i) Shortening hours of labor.

    (j) Divorcing bank affiliates.

    (k) Reduced war veteran payments.

6. But the dangers of the N.R.A., of the banking aid, RFC & Treas, repudiation & inflation, and of infallibility, are very real.

[1] FF and his wife were preparing to spend a year in England, with FF accepting an offer to teach at Oxford as the visiting Eastman Professor; they would leave in the autumn of 1933.

[2] Louis McHenry Howe (1871–1936) devoted his entire life to furthering the political fortunes of Franklin D. Roosevelt. The two met in 1911 and Howe served as aide and secretary to Roosevelt until his own death. Many who liked Roosevelt detested the unkempt, abrasive, and politically shrewd Howe.

No. 540   August 5, 1933   Chatham, Mass.

1. Al Smith on need of editorial criticism in a democracy is most timely. Indeed, we should have informative expositions in N.R. or

Nation, etc., showing that the need of hearing both sides is as necessary for statecraft as in the courts.

The public should have compared "His Majesty's Opposition" (subsidized) with the suppression by Soviet, Hitler, and Mussolini of minority views as traitorous, and the American tendency to do the same. Ellery Sedgwick might get Laski to do the piece.[1]

2. I do not believe that 2 billion or any appreciable amount of new securities are needed or are held back by the Securities Act. My own guess is that nothing can be more wholesome in finance than not issuing securities for private enterprises now. What we need is that banks shall lend to business men of ability & trustworthiness.

3. I have not much joy in the thought of the new Vincent Astor weekly[2] and hope it won't come off. Indeed, I think the Vincent Astor friendship a bad influence, without either party being conscious of it. I guess that association is responsible in large part for F.D. disinclination to tackle heavy estate taxes.

4. It would be fine if Moley would, instead, really devote himself to tackling the crime problem. With his social and economic sense, he might do a worthy job, with FD's backing, a job of enduring value and one which would not be thought by the A.G. to trespass on his preserve.

5. W.L.'s insight and free talk on steel prices is cheering. Is this, in part, fruits of Amos P's articles?[3]

6. The U.S. Steel is showing its cloven foot in the H. C. Frick Co.—coal mining performance.[4] What has become of the enquiry into steel rail prices? Ought not N.R. and Nation enquire?

7. Joe Kennedy's views seem to be making themselves felt on the Stock Exchange.[5]

[1] Laski did not write on this subject for the *Atlantic Monthly*.

[2] William Vincent Astor (1891–1959), a member of a fabulously wealthy family, was a financier who tended to back the policies of his friend Franklin Roosevelt, although he believed that "the backward masses would be served best by an enlightened capitalism." In 1933, with Raymond Moley as editor, Astor founded *Today*, which as Moley's views changed, became more critical of the New Deal. *Today* later merged into *Newsweek*.

[3] Amos Pinchot had written a series of articles on Walter Lippmann, beginning in *The Nation* 137 (5 July 1933): 7, in which he criticized the columnist for, among other things, inconsistency and obfuscation.

[4] Immediately after receiving an increase in wages, several thousand miners at the H. C. Frick Coke Company, a subsidiary of U.S. Steel, had gone out on strike to secure recognition of the United Mine Workers as their bargaining agent. The company, which had refused to deal with unions since the bloody Homestead strike, began laying in arms and hiring what amounted to a private army.

[5] Joseph Patrick Kennedy (1888–1969) had made his fortune, first in banking and then as an early producer of motion pictures, and Roosevelt had named him chairman of the newly created

Securities and Exchange Commission. During his tenure he worked to eliminate many of the abuses which had characterized the stock market earlier. In 1938, Roosevelt appointed Kennedy as ambassador to the Court of St. James, and the two soon had a falling out over the extent of American involvement in the European war. Later, Kennedy devoted his contacts, fortune, and skills in helping to elect his son, John F. Kennedy, as president.

No. 541 August 14, 1933 Chatham, Mass.

1. Ray Stevens and Nelson Perkins[1] were here yesterday to discuss the foreign securities problems.

2. I am glad Erwin Griswold will stay for a year with the Dept. of Justice. That should insure adequate argument of the tax cases at least.

3. Yes, W.L. on steel prices is astonishing, Ueberhaupt.[2] U.S. Steel is getting a long delayed airing. I was glad to see the N.R. on "Steel Mill."[3]

4. Hugh Johnson[4] telephoned me. I urged upon him protection of real labor organizations, and told him that when I return to W. in September shall hope to have a long talk with him. He said he would arrange for that as soon as he heard of my return. I want to amplify then what I told him in May, that without regularity of employment, the New Deal is impossible.

5. Sam Rosenman[5] turned up on the 11th. I took occasion to talk comprehensively on regularity of employment, the small unit, smaller executive corporate salaries, and heavy estate taxes. He asked what you thought of my views, and said that he was to see F.D. this week and would talk fully with him on these matters. I made clear to him that these were essentials, not of the present emergency relief, but of the New Deal and democracy, & should be acted on at the January session. He asked whether I thought F.D. should begin the education in advance of the next session. I answered that F.D.'s political sagacity was so much above that of everyone else that he would know when to begin.

6. N.R.A. is having troubles galore. The drop in commodity prices is doubtless in part an incident of curbing the speculation.

7. I suppose you have noticed how the financial interests are playing up the Australian recovery. The articles I have seen were far more skillful and tactful than is usual with those so originating.

8. I had a request from [*] for another interview. Did you see him?

9. Was Oswald in this week's Nation due to your prod?[6]

[1] Thomas Nelson Perkins (1870–1937), a prestigious Boston attorney, had a number of clients with foreign investments.

[2] "In general."

[3] Much of the 16 August 1933 issue of *The New Republic* had been devoted to the National Industrial Recovery Act, and especially to the proposed Steel Code, which the editorial writers condemned as far too favorable to corporate interests. In an article entitled "Steel Mill," the editors drew a devastating portrait of the terrible conditions confronting workers.

[4] Hugh Samuel Johnson (1882–1942), director of the draft during World War I, headed the National Recovery Administration. Johnson's one-year tenure saw a paramilitary spirit converge with the latest techniques in public relations to sweep the nation into a Blue Eagle craze, as dozens of industries signed code agreements. Johnson, who had an alcohol problem, sometimes sought advice from LDB, even though the latter personally opposed the whole philosophy behind the NRA. Later on, when the NRA came under attack, Johnson asserted publicly that he had consulted with LDB, precipitating an uproar over this apparent breach of judicial ethics. See letters after 19 September 1934.

[5] Samuel Irving Rosenman (1896–1973), who had once been in practice with LDB's daughter Susan, had served as counsel to Roosevelt during the latter's tenure as governor of New York. Although a member of the New York Supreme Court during these years, he frequently advised the president, and in 1943 he resigned from the bench to become special White House counsel. Rosenman later compiled an edition of Roosevelt's public addresses and papers.

[6] In his editorial in the 16 August issue of *The Nation*, Oswald Garrison Villard attacked Roosevelt for his duplicity in dealing with the London Economic Conference, and asserted that even while one might support the New Deal in general, this did not require a blind defense of all of the president's actions.

No. 542   August 17, 1933   Chatham, Mass.

1. Re yours of 15th. Saturday evening Ray [Stevens] telephoned from N.Y. asking whether he could see me Sunday, saying that Nelson Perkins would drive him from Boston. They came at 11 AM Sunday & stayed until 12.40. Ray began, setting forth fully the situation as to the Foreign Securities Corporation [1] & his view that it would be a great mistake for F.D. to set the corporation into action; told also of his talk with F.D. et al. as to the proposed committee. I told them, that that [sic] I agreed that it would be a great mistake for F.D. to take any such steps now; and that he should be helped to postpone action. Perkins then told the story of the proposed committee of Hoover days, and later developments in relation thereto. In that connection, P. asked what I thought of Ray for chairman of the Com'tee. I said promptly "I veto that." Ray said he agreed, and Perkins said: "Well, so you will continue on your job at $8500 a year." No further talk was had on that particular branch of the subject. [2]

I advised them that the proposed committee should be an advisory committee merely, for the present formed to gather information & to advise the President etc. & thus to give F.D. an excuse to stave off action until Congress meets; and that the personnel should be untainted and that there should be dropped from the proposed list, i.a., C. F. Adams, [3]

N. D. Baker (whom F.D. had not objected to) and George Rublee (because of his Columbian connection) and all bank or "Preferred List" men. Both Ray and Perkins expressed themselves as satisfied that a way out has been suggested.

2. Ray said there were other matters he would like to talk with me about; that he thought he could get away for a little vacation in a week; and that he could come here then.

3. The Wickham Steed article returned herewith is grand.[4]

4. Redlich's letter[5] is very interesting. His concern about U.S. is not unfounded. I guess Austria will be enabled to pull through.

5. It is difficult to think of Palfrey in connection with "the rough and tumble of practice."

6. 1000 copies of "The Investor Pays,"[6] despite its fine press and the Senate investigation, confirms Laski's views on Americans' book-buying.

7. Raymond Robbins [sic] would be interesting, but as a witness to be taken with discretion.

8. David Lawrence's editorial on the N.R.A. in last week's U.S. News is worth reading.[7]

9. What is Gene doing with the Post?[8]

[1] The *New York Times* had reported on this day that Roosevelt was going to appoint a commission to protect the interests of American holders of foreign securities. Nothing came of the proposal, however, in part because the State Department objected that such a commission would interfere with the conduct of foreign policy in economic matters. A private, nongovernmental Foreign Bondholders' Protective Committee was later organized at the president's suggestion.

[2] Stevens remained at his position with the Federal Trade Commission.

[3] Charles Francis Adams (1886–1954), a Boston banker and businessman, had served as secretary of the navy during the Hoover administration; he was currently chairman of the State Street Trust Company.

[4] In "Making Public Opinion," *Fortnightly Review* 139 (May 1933): 564, the British writer noted the clever use by the Nazis in appealing for "fair play" from Great Britain to undo the Versailles Treaty.

[5] In a letter of 1 August, the Viennese jurist noted his fears that the "mechanistic' economic solutions being proposed by Roosevelt's academic advisers would fail, and plunge the United States into a situation akin to that of Germany, with the subsequent rise of dictatorship. In particular, Redlich worried about the incompatability of goals in the NIRA.

[6] Max Lowenthal's *The Investor Pays* (New York: A.A. Knopf, 1933), was an expose of the financial manipulations behind the reorganization of the Chicago, Milwaukee & St. Paul railroad. See 6 January 1931, n. 1.

[7] Columnist David Lawrence (1888–1973) had founded the *U.S. News* in 1933; he later founded the *World Report*, and merged the two into one magazine in 1947. In "Adventure in Price-Fixing," *United States News* 1 (12 August 1933): 16, Lawrence argued that the NRA was not true price-fixing. Only one element out of many could be controlled, so that real prices would be determined by how the market affected all the other variables.

After resigning from the Reconstruction Finance Agency in May, Meyer had purchased the *Washington Post*.

No. 543   September 10, 1933   Chatham, Mass.

1. There will be much to talk over Tuesday. The industrial interests and the bankers & the Republican chiefs seem to be rallying for the onslaught. F.D. will have to watch his steps.

2. Sam Rosenman was here again. Says he talked to F.D. on the matter I had discussed most of the time from 10:30 PM to 2 AM; that F.D. was much interested & took some notes; and that he (Rosenman) thought I should see some of my suggestions in the next message to Congress; also that F.D. wanted to talk more with me. Perhaps.

3. What say you to this for dealing with the Del. et al. foreign corporations outrage?[1]

Have Congress levy an excise tax on all state corporations which do not have their principal place of business in the state in which organized.

[1] Delaware's extremely liberal incorporation laws had led many major American corporations, no matter where headquartered, to secure corporate charters in that state. By doing so, they were able to evade stricter regulations concerning business and financial operations in other states. "Foreign" corporations here refer to those chartered in another state.

No. 544   September 15, 1933   Washington, D.C.

1. Eastman was in. He is working actively on the RR steel needs data & I endeavored to impress upon him the importance of getting data in shape for the President soon as possible & seeing him.

2. Landis was in. Told him to work out some way of continuing Law School and Commission jobs, and suggested he talk with you as to possibility of wrenching Henry Friendly loose now. Friendly must have regretted many times his decision not to come here.[1] Landis said he would talk with you.

[1] Despite repeated urging by LDB, Friendly remained in private practice until his appointment as court of appeals judge in 1959.

No. 545   September 20, 1933   Washington, D.C.

1. After much effort on Max's part, it seems very doubtful if we get Ascoli[1] here, due apparently to Frank just not acting, saying it is a fine idea but just not doing anything. Max is in despair about it Rhoda says.[2]

2. Moley was in yesterday & I laid before him the principal projects of my "New Deal" scheme, calling for legislation at the January session.[3] He seemed generally interested, particularly in the proposal of a Fed. excise tax to encourage adoption of insurance reserve legislation a la Wisconsin in all the states.

3. Frances Perkins was in alone at dinner last evening. I endeavored to impress on her that anti-securities bill pro[pa]ganda concerning capital issues & the general call on the part of administration men for capital goods expenditure, by private industries was mistaken.

4. We shall not say Goodbye, but "au revoir."[4]

Wyzanski is thinking.

"He leaves his friends to dignify them more."[5]

[1] Max Ascoli (1898–1978) had been a professor of jurisprudence in Italy before emigrating to the United States in 1931. From 1933 to 1950 he taught at the New School for Social Research in New York, after which he became editor of *The Reporter*.

[2] This first paragraph was written by Alice Brandeis.

[3] See 3 August 1933.

[4] See id., n. 1.

[5] *Two Gentlemen of Verona*, I, vi, 4.

No. 546   October 24, 1933   Washington, D.C.

1. Yours of 5th & 10th came late & almost by the same mail. Your memo for the first lecture I shared with Cardozo, Harlan & the C.J. It is fine to think of you and Marion in academic English calm and cheer.

2. Your satellites will have reported amply that things are not going well here. If only F.D. had refrained from Kunststucke[1] which imperil so much that is good. My own doubts and fears expressed before and after the "allocution" are intensified.[2]

3. Our term opens with a super abundance of work assured. Our first 2 weeks of hearing were interesting, with full court in attendance throughout.

4. Saw OWH yesterday. I had insisted the week before that the new secretary[3] must be installed quickly. That was done, with Hiss holding over a bit to smooth the way. I found OWH calm yesterday (He had been much perturbed the week before) and everything running smoothly; & Howe looking forward to a good winter.

5. I know not what has happened to the Moley magazine.[4] It has not appeared, I am told, & no one knows when it will. It had been announced for Oct 1, then for Oct. 10. When he was here about a month

ago he expected to be here 2 days each week & was to see me the next week (and weekly thereafter). Is he "spurlos versinkt?"[5]

6. S[amuel]. R[osenman]. has been in & many of your friends, including the William Denmans. Nothing yet about the California judgeship.[6]

7. The S.G. has not disappointed us. Griswold has made fine arguments, with all the leaders in opposition.

8. Josephine January reports that your Prest. Conant, who did not know Roger Baldwin, sent for him; kept him for 2 hours' talk; and R.B. says Conant & he agreed on most things!!

[1] "Clever tricks."

[2] See 8 July 1933.

[3] The new clerk was Mark DeWolfe Howe (1906–1967), who would later have an illustrious teaching career first at Buffalo and then at the Harvard Law School. He edited the Holmes-Laski and the Holmes-Pollack correspondences, and completed two volumes of a definitive biography of Holmes before his death.

[4] See 5 August 1933.

[5] "sunk without a trace."

[6] William Denman (1872–1959), a California reform activist, was named by Roosevelt to Ninth Circuit Court the following year; he became chief judge in 1948.

No. 547   October 30, 1933   Washington, D.C.

Yours 17th and 20th have come.

1. Things here have not bettered since I wrote you last week. The gold purchasing project, extended now to foreign gold, has augmented the uncertainties. To me the whole scheme is unintelligible.

2. Evidently, the dollar is falling abroad more than prices are rising here. That should give foreigners an opportunity to buy cheap such of our cotton as they want or copper or other desired raw material.

3. The protests against N.R.A. are becoming more general and emphatic; and those hitherto favorable are being alienated.

4. We had Stevens & wife in yesterday, also Siegel,[1] who is very happy in his work.

5. J.W.M. was in today, here in obedience to the President's call (via Phillips)[2] on possible liberation of visas.[3] I assume he has sent you the correspondence.

6. I am glad that in the Palestine riots, Jews are conspicuous by their absence.[4]

7. J. G. MacDonald's [sic] entry into League of Nations Com'tee

scheme is regrettable.[5] Bad bungling. I am glad he has nothing to do with the Palestine end.

[1] Probably Melvin Hirsh Siegel (b. 1909), who graduated from Harvard Law School in 1932. After service with the Tennessee Valley Authority, he practiced law in San Francisco.

[2] William Phillips (1878–1968) had been one of the first career officers in the Foreign Service, and held a number of administrative and ambassadorial posts in the State Department. A close friend of Franklin Roosevelt's since college, he would come out of retirement in 1941 to establish a special services office in England.

[3] The British had, in the wake of disturbances in Palestine, practically frozen visas for Jews who wished to settle in the country.

[4] In October 1933, the Arab Executive Committee called for demonstrations throughout Palestine to protest growing Jewish immigration. The British, against whom the protests were directed, responded quickly in putting down the disturbances. A number of the rioters were killed.

[5] McDonald, despite the reservations of a number of Jewish leaders, proved to be extremely sympathetic to the plight of refugees from Hitler, although he could do little. He served as League of Nations high commissioner for refugees from 1933 to 1945.

No. 548   November 9, 1933   Washington, D.C.

1. To Marion and you my thanks for birthday greetings. You have done much to make the years useful & joyous.[1]

2. Sprague came in on 17th pursuant to your & Harold's message. And I guess he will hold on for a while in peace, hoping that the great experimentalist will recant when experience has made clear his errors. Sprague has had a gruelling time.[2]

3. Did I tell you Pierce Butler's story of the lawyer who after listening to a long, involved argument of his opponent opened his own with: "Your Honor, I don't say that a man must be crazy to under[stand] my brother's argument. But it would help."

4. Ben Cohen was in yesterday about the Russian mission.[3] I agree fully with him. George Rublee, who is the most prosperous man on the horizon, and represents the $50,000,000 and $25,000,000 Czarist bond Committees, wants R.B. Standrett Jr.[4] (as does Stanley King).

5. Ben Cohen seems a bit more stable & happier.

6. We are not happy at the thought of Ray Stevens as Chairman of the Foreign Bondholders Com'tee.

7. LaGuardia's election is a joy[5] & Vare's defeat good.[6]

8. There is some comfort in the thought that each day brings Congress' convening nearer. It was a terrible thing to vest absolute power in one man, and adjourn for so long a period.

[1] 13 November marked LDB's seventy-seventh birthday.

[2] Sprague resigned less than two weeks later, charging that the government's gold policies invited a credit breakdown.

[3] The Roosevelt administration was then in the midst of negotiations to reopen diplomatic relations with Russia, which had been broken off after the Communist Revolution. In December, Roosevelt named William C. Bullitt as ambassador to Moscow.

[4] Richard B. Standrett, Jr. (1891–1969) was a lawyer and counsel to a number of institutions involved in foreign trade.

[5] Fiorello LaGuardia, after a decade of reform opposition to Tammany Hall, had been elected mayor of New York by a comfortable margin.

[6] Vare, who three years earlier had been denied a U.S. Senate seat because of alleged campaign excesses, had seen his Philadelphia Republican machine soundly routed in the municipal elections. See 23 May 1926, n. 1.

No. 549 November 16, 1933 Washington, D.C.

1. Our love to Marion. We are very sorry that your beautiful holiday is being clouded by anxiety, & hope the cloud will lift soon.

2. I am glad you have not been here these past 8 weeks; & are not to be close at hand during the coming months. You could not have averted F.D.'s aberrations & plunges. They were the inescapable penalties paid for conferring absolute power. Next year you may, because you were not in this mess, be effective in helping us out of the mire.

3. I am sad over the blasting of many a fair prospect. The loss will not be merely of personal prestige. Liberalism, and experimentation will have received a severe setback; & the reactionaries will be strengthened in their errors.

4. On Nov. 13, at 9 P.M. OWH (under Mary [Donnellan]'s tutelage) called me on telephone to give [birthday] greetings; & on the 14th roses came from him.

5. I omitted to mention that F.D. did not forget his promise (?) to you to send for me. On Nov. 3d the White House asked Alice & me to lunch with him & Mrs. R. on Sunday the 5th alone. (I suppose he was wiping off his slate in preparation for his leaving for Warm Springs on 17th) It seemed wise to express our regrets. There would have been no fair chance to talk policies with F.D. so I am not sorry we couldn't go.

6. I have heard nothing further from Moley.

No. 550 December 17, 1933 Washington, D.C.

1. Our best wishes to you and Marion for the New Year, and our hope that already the medical consultants have been able to relieve your anxiety.

2. F.D.'s speech to the Federal Council of Churches was a noble utterance.[1]

3. Otherwise, there has been little erfreuliches[2] here.

4. Herbert Feis was in again, and has some fine suggestions re tariff. But to put them through would mean a fight F.D. will be loath to enter upon.

5. Tom C[orcoran]. has been in several times. Doubtless he is keeping you fully informed, as others are doing in spots. The difficulties grow no less.

6. Woodward & Lothrop sold within one week over 1100 copies of the jacket edition of "Other Peoples Money." It should teach a lesson to publishers.

7. William Allen White sends you greetings. He says Kansas is still with F.D.

8. Frank Sayre was in. Says politicians and newspapers were too much for him in Dep. Corrections job. It reminds of Tom Osborne.[3] Frank Tannenbaum's book is very impressive.[4]

[1]On 6 December, Roosevelt lambasted America's "pagan ethics" before the Federal Council of Churches of Christ in a nationally broadcast speech. In hard-hitting language, he condemned lynching as "collective murder," referring to the recent rash of mob actions that had swept the country.

[2]"pleasing, encouraging"

[3]Thomas Mott Osborne (1859–1926), a noted prison reformer, had begun his tenure as chairman of New York State's first prison commission by spending a week as a prisoner in the Auburn penitentiary.

[4]Frank Tannenbaum, *Osborne of Sing Sing* (Chapel Hill: University of North Carolina Press, 1933).

No. 551   January 10, 1934   Washington, D.C.

1. The budget message[1] indicates that F.D. has concluded to follow Roper,[2] instead of averting Huey Long[3] as he (F.D.) has suggested doing.

2. See Lady Duff Gordon's letters from Egypt (McClure Phillips & Co. 1902) p. 54, April 13, 1863, as bearing on the RR's request for higher rates:

"I can't get about under £12, thus do Arabs understand competition; the owner of boats said so few were wanted, times were bad on account of the railway etc., he must have double what he used to charge. In vain Omar argued, that was not the way to get employment. 'Maluk' (never mind), and I must go by rail. Is not that Eastern? Up the river, where there is no railroad, I might have had it at half that rate."

Isn't that good enough to have Hart write a piece for the N.R.?[4]

3. If F.D. wants to go slowly in taxing great fortunes, etc. & yet not seem to be following Huey Long, let him say what a democracy demands is not necessarily "distribution of wealth," but "distributing power"— consumer power, economic power, political power and the power of human creative development which comes only from combining individual power with responsibility, & which produces in the highest degree the wealth to be distributed.

[1] Roosevelt's proposed budget contemplated a planned deficit of seven billion dollars in the war against the Depression. The proposed expenditure of $10.5 billion was the largest peacetime budget in the nation's history, and would raise the government's total indebtedness to a record high of $31 billion.

[2] Daniel Calhoun Roper (1867–1935), after a brief tenure in the South Carolina House of Representatives, had held a variety of government patronage appointments. In 1933 Roosevelt named him secretary of commerce, a post Roper held until his death.

[3] Huey Pierce Long (1893–1935), the dynamic and demagogic political boss of Louisiana, had been elected governor of the state in 1928, and United States senator in 1931. He built a huge public following with his "Share the Wealth" platform, and was a major force in pushing Roosevelt leftward toward a more social democratic program in the so-called "Second New Deal."

[4] Hart did not write such a piece for the journal.

No. 552   January 11, 1934   Washington, D.C.

1. That is grand news about Marion, & brings us great rejoicing.

2. This week's batch of opinions will interest you. About #241[1] there is a story.

3. Morris Cohen, who was here last week, told us that OWH told him that the original Wendell (Wandel) was a Dutch Jew.[2]

4. OWH is in fine form intellectually, at times quite gay in his talk.

5. National affairs are about the same. Congressmen and Senators are afraid to talk out, for the present at least.

Hope the new term [at Oxford] is beginning well.

10,000 copies of "Other People's Money" have gone to Pittsburg.

[1] In *Snyder* v. *Massachusetts*, 291 U.S. 97 (1934), a sharply divided Court upheld a murder conviction in which the defendant had not been permitted to accompany the jury to the place of the crime. Justice Cardozo, speaking for the majority, held that since the accused's counsel had been allowed to accompany the jurors and to comment on the physical layout of the place, the defendant was not deprived of due process. Roberts, joined by LDB, Sutherland, and Butler, dissented. Due process, he argued, is a matter of form as well as substance. An accused is to be present at his trial, and the trip to the crime scene was definitely part of the trial.

[2] The Wendells had come from Holland to America in the seventeenth century, and it is possible that they had some Jewish blood, since there was a large Jewish community in the country at the time.

No. 553   January 25, 1934   Washington, D.C.

1. It's fine to think of you and Marion vacationing in London, relieved from your heavy burden of anxiety.[1]

2. Yes, in the main F.D. is having it all his own way. My own apprehensions have not been allayed.[2]

3. Hopkins,[3] who is now worried by graft charges, did an extraordinary job in getting 4,000,000 folk transferred to C.W.A. work. And incidentally, much helpful work was done. (e.g. Prest. Kent[4] of U. of Lousiville told me that they had 300 CWA men painting & renovating their buildings) But the success is alarming. How can the Administration let go? And it seems most improbable that private business or P.W.A. can provide the jobs within the next 3 months for these men.

4. What did the English say to Garvin's recent rapsody [sic]?[5]

5. Tom Cochrane [sic] is doing grand service and everyone loves him, quite naturally. It looks now as if he would get through my federal excise tax to effect regularity of employment, (5% on payrolls after say 1936) through state action. Elizabeth was here 5 days early in January and Paul a week, leaving here on the 23rd. Both were most effective aids.

6. The unemployment reserve bills in Mass. & New York are still in peril.

7. Business is much better, but it cannot be told how much of this is merely the temporary help due to the expenditure of C.W.A. and A.A.A. & the like money.

8. Einstein and wife were in this A.M., after the night at the White House. They were very nice. And F.D.'s entertaining them may help to magnify the significance of the long delayed visa relaxation.[6]

9. Max told me that Note 2 is giving the "kept" lawyers much pain.

10. I agree with you about Florence Allen.

11. I am returning F.D.'s letter of 22d which is just like him.[7]

[1] About Marion Frankfurter's health.

[2] On 24 November 1933 LDB had written: "My main grief is the loss of F.D. as an instrument of advanced political action. The best of measures, even if advocated by him, will be looked upon with suspicion."

[3] Harry Lloyd Hopkins (1890–1946) was Roosevelt's closest advisor on relief matters. He initially headed the emergency relief program, and then directed the immense Works Progress Administration. From 1938 to 1940 he was secretary of commerce, after which he headed the Lend Lease program. During the war, he served as Roosevelt's confidential emissary on a number of overseas missions, especially to Churchill and Stalin.

[4] Raymond Asa Kent (1883–1943) had been dean of the College of Liberal Arts at Northwestern University from 1923 to 1929, and then became president of the University of Louisville, a post he retained until his death. He worked closely with LDB on many of the projects LDB proposed for the university; see, for example, LDB to Joseph Rauch, 23 September 1929.

[5] James L. Garvin, an English reporter, had evidently commented disparagingly on the proposed American budget.

[6] Albert Einstein had arrived in the United States in October 1933 to work at the Princeton Institute for Advanced Study. He made numerous speeches about the plight of German Jews who needed to flee their native land.

[7] In a letter to FF on 22 December 1933, Roosevelt had taken an extremely optimistic view of how well his administration had been doing in fighting the Depression. He urged FF not to believe all that appeared in the foreign press, since most of those sources reflected the old-fashioned Tory viewpoint.

No. 554   February 11, 1934   Washington, D.C.

1. Tom Thatcher [sic] was here last week (apparently for a dinner given by Pierce Butler to the A.G.) He is dejected about state of the N.Y. Bar, & expressed about those on top about our view.

2. F.D. did well on his message on stock exchange legislation,[1] & Tom C. says Ben Cohen did a superb job in bill-drafting. He is generally most enthusiastic about BVC.

3. We also have heard from many persons great commendations of Harold's article.[2]

4. Alpheus Mason writes me that his book[3] will enter tomorrow on the second printing.

5. It's good to know that you are doing some writing on the Crime Survey, and also the Social Sc. Ency. article.[4]

6. The S.G. and Asst. S.G. are outdoing themselves.

7. We are having some of your boys in this afternoon to meet Andrew Furuseth.

8. Our very best to Marion. These must be joyous days for both of you.

9. After Kirstein spoke to me of Jerome Frank[5] I chanced to have an opportunity of talking matters to J.F. He thought [*] will defer to Proskauer.

10. AAA's abandonment of the milk price fixing & exposure of Distributing Company extortion,[6] may be made an exhibit for "Curse of Bigness."

[1] On 9 February, Roosevelt had asked for legislation to regulate the stock exchanges, and the same day the Fletcher-Rayburn bill was introduced in Congress. The bill would regulate the issue of new securities, require greater disclosure of financial information, raise margin requirements, and make it a criminal offense to manipulate stock prices. To oversee the new rules, the bill created a Securities and Exchange Commission.

[2] Harold Laski had written an extremely appreciative piece, "Mr. Justice Brandeis," which appeared in *Harper's Magazine* 168 (January 1934): 209.

[3] *Brandeis—Lawyer and Judge in the Modern State* (Princeton: Princeton University Press, 1933).

[4]FF wrote the introduction to Sheldon and Eleanor Glueck, *One Thousand Juvenile Delinquents* (Cambridge: Harvard University Press, 1934). In the *Encyclopedia of Social Sciences*, FF, with Nathan Greene, wrote the articles on "Labor Injunctions," 8:653–57, and "The United States Supreme Court," 14:474–481; and with Paul Freund, "Interstate Commerce," 8:22–26.

[5]Jerome New Frank (1889–1957), after private practive in Chicago and New York, worked in various New Deal agencies. In 1937 he became commissioner of the Securities and Exchange Commission and, in 1939, its chairman. He was appointed circuit judge for the second circuit in 1941. He also taught law at several universities and wrote a number of books and articles on legal topics.

[6]In a speech to the Wisconsin College of Agriculture on 31 January, Secretary Wallace conceded that the AAA had not helped dairy farmers as much as it had wheat and cotton growers. The AAA would soon implement a new program, fixing milk prices for producers, but leaving the final price to consumers to be set by market conditions. At the same time, news stories indicated that middlemen had made enormous profits under the AAA plan, ranging as high as 25.3 percent in Chicago and 30.8 percent in Philadelphia.

No. 555   February 21, 1934   Washington, D.C.

1. Estelle was in Monday, in very good form.

2. With her Judge Fay Bentley,[1] on the first day of her duties as Juvenile Court Judge. It was a serious fight to the end.

3. Today's unemployment figures (Feb. 1) show poor performance for N.R.A. 2,000,000 re-employment in private industry, about 4,300,000 in C.W.A., A.A.A. & P.W.A. & other Gov. & State jobs.

That raises a real doubt whether nearly all the jobs are not due directly or indirectly to govt. money. Gen. Johnson and Don Richberg are emphatic to the contrary.

4. That business is markedly better & many corporations are making money is undoubted. But is it due to the Government expenditures? And what will happen when C.W.A. dismisses its 4,000,000? Besides their wages paid by the Govt, we have the larger sum given under A.A.A. and lent (?) by R.F.C. The expenditures of those funds would account for much re-employment in private business.

5. Someone has doubtless sent you the report in yesterday's papers of Gen'l Johnson's terrible onslaught on the Washington Post.[2]

6. I had before receipt of your latest letter asked Fritz Wiener[3] in for a Monday & immediately supplemented that by summoning him for an hour's talk. He is unhappy in PWA, mainly, I guess, on account of Berle, who seems to have a stranglehold on Ickes.

7. Wyzanski I had invited recently for a Sunday, but he was obliged to leave town. Will try again.

8. Tom Corcoran seems to be doing grand testifying on the Stock Exchange bill.[4]

9. Germany's sad tale on OSI and Ascoli's letter returned herewith. I don't find Poletti's[5] which you say you enclosed.

10. Those are sad reports from Austria.[6]

[1] Fay Bentley, a social worker, had earned a law degree at night while working with the U.S. Children's Bureau. Roosevelt named her to the Washington, D.C., Juvenile Court in 1934; she was reappointed in 1940 and 1946.

[2] On 19 February Roosevelt issued an executive order, approving the NRA Newspaper Code. At the same time, he released a letter from NRA chief Hugh Johnson, dated 22 December 1933 which, although not mentioning the *Post* by name, criticized "certain newspapers" for raising the straw man of freedom of the press in their opposition to the Newspaper Code. In particular, he noted the papers' opposition to the child labor provisions, which they claimed would destroy their system of sales and distribution.

[3] Frederick Bernays Wiener was executive assistant to Ickes at the Public Works Administration.

[4] See preceding letter, n. 1.

[5] Charles Poletti (b. 1903), a former student of FF's at Harvard, was then serving as counsel to Governor Lehman of New York. He would later be elected as lieutenant governor and governor of the state, but resigned in 1942 to enter military service.

[6] The previous week Austria had been rocked by riots and massacres when Chancellor Dollfuss joined in an all-out attack on what he termed "the Marxists who have ruined our country." When it was over, the socialists had been smashed, but the ruling Christian Socialists were in disarray.

No. 556 February 27, 1934 Washington, D.C.

1. There seems to be a gathering of opposition to F.D. and prospects of a session ending before June 1. seem to be waning. There was some talk once of F.D. getting off April 1.

2. The evidence begins to indicate that the Kunststucke[1] (including both NRA and AAA) are having the effect of retarding recovery. Surely the showing of jobs made in private business (otherwise than by U.S. Govt money) is extremely slim. With the demobilization of C.W.A. forces, the outlook for employment has become quite menacing. Hopkins reports about 575,000 dropped by Feb. 23.

3. Tom C[orcoran]. is having a grand fight on the Stock Exchange bill.[2] I was glad to see E. A. Goldenweisser come out so well.[3]

4. Paul Freund is being heavily leaned on by Tom C.

5. Dean A says Tommy Austern is making a great hit with the firm's clients.

6. I hope you are getting a chance to talk Palestine to British higherups. E[manuel] Neumann seems very hopeful of support, with money from countries other than USA.

[1] "clever tricks."

[2] See 11 February 1934, n. 1.

[3] Goldenweiser had testified the previous day at the Senate committee hearings on the Stock Exchange bill.

No. 557   March 4, 1934   Washington, D.C.

1. I have sent the Shertok memos to JWM with injunction of strictest secrecy.

2. F.D.'s tariff proposal is a very bold move.[1]

3. I wish he had gone forward long ago with heavy taxation of the rich—reduction of the big corporations power and lessening dependence on banks & bankers. No policy can be safe which leave the big fellows with power they still have. His advisers has [sic] infantile faith in regulation. The only safety lies in disarming the enemy.

4. Tom C[orcoran]. says Jim Landis is now behaving very well.

5. Mrs. Burling reports George Rublee, who attended the Stock Exchange hearings (? professionally) as saying that Tom C. made an amazingly good witness. I hear from others like praise of his performance.

6. I have heard nothing of the Cummings rumor[2] to which you refer.

7. OWH is in good form.

[1] On 2 March, Roosevelt asked for congressional authority to stimulate foreign trade by means of reciprocal trade agreements whereby the United States would lower tariffs if other countries would lower their duties. Conversely, Roosevelt also wanted power to raise tariffs by executive order if other nations blocked out American goods.

[2] Rumors were rife that Attorney General Homer Cummings would soon resign; although such rumors rose periodically, Cummings stayed in his post until 9 July 1939.

No. 558   March 18, 1934   Washington, D.C.

1. You and Marion will, I trust, be on the way to Palestine[1] before this reaches England, and will surely return much strengthened for your talks with the British high-ups there and in England. I trust you will have a chance, on your return, to enlighten "die Moly" (Hamilton). Alice says her comment, on the Webb book,[2] is far from understanding.

2. How do you account for R. W. Child's appointment?[3] It is not creditable.

3. Things have not gone well with the Administration since I wrote. The treaty failure[4] may be serious in showing the opposition that F.D. is not invincible, and many revolts are pending. The N.R.A. sessions[5] have, I judge, satisfied no one, and the doubters have become more vocal. The New Republic criticism,[6] which comes pretty near covering the whole field, you see. But I suppose Bliven et al. will never appreciate what is the matter with our attempts at economic control.

542

4. It's fine to hear from you and Marion how joyously things are going with you. There will be need for all your vigor when you return.

5. How do you account for the overwhelming Labor victory in London?[7]

6. Alice wants me to tell you of Mark Howe's complete devotion to OWH, and of the latter's happy birthday.

[1]The Frankfurters visited Palestine for the first time in April 1934. From Jerusalem, FF wrote to Roosevelt on 14 April: "This is a most exciting land—its beauty is magical and the achievements of the Jewish renaissance almost incredible. Someday I should like to tell you about it all, and when you are through with the White House, in 1941, you must journey to Palestine." Cf. LDB to Alice Goldmark Brandeis, 10 July 1919.

[2]Sidney and Beatrice Webb had published a revised edition of *The History of Trade Unionism* (London: Longmans, Green, 1933).

[3]Child was going to Europe as a special representative of Secretary of State Hull to sound out the economic views of various European governments. Some thought this might be a prelude to an effort to revive the World Monetary and Economic Conference.

[4]On 14 March Roosevelt had sustained his first major loss in Congress, when the Senate refused to ratify a treaty with Canada to build a seaway along the St. Lawrence River.

[5]In response to growing criticism of the NRA, Roosevelt had appointed the National Recovery Review Board on 7 March, and named Clarence Darrow as its head. The Board held hearings over the next few months, and in May and June issued three reports severely criticizing the work of the NRA. In a supplemental report, Darrow urged socialized ownership of industry.

[6]In an unsigned editorial, "Labor and the NRA," *New Republic* 78 (14 March 1934): 131, the journal noted Senator Wagner's private report to the president that the labor provisions of the NRA had failed to protect labor adequately, and criticized the efforts of Hugh Johnson to encourage business at the expense of labor. Two supplemental articles the following week detailed this criticism. Jonathan Mitchell, "The Blue Eagle Looks in the Mirror," and William P. Mangold, "Pocket-Picking Under the Codes."

[7]In a series of local by-elections, Labour won nine seats to two for the Conservatives; the results were thought to reflect popular dissatisfaction with government handling of economic policy.

No. 559   April 11, 1934   Washington, D.C.

1 BF writes that you are due at Oxford April 11.[1] Our greetings to you both. The experience should prove of great value to our cause.

2. About U.S. affairs. Tom C. & many others, besides the public print, will have advised you things have gone very badly for the Administration. I see nothing really good since last I wrote, except that the period of abject, silent acquiescence in F.D.'s orders has apparently passed. We have evidence of an opposition in Congress and out. But unfortunately it is largely of the vested interests who have gotten their second wind.

3. The management of the aircraft situation;[2] of the C.W.A. liquidation;[3] AAA failures & plunging;[4] N.R.A. performances; and perhaps

worst of all, the auto mftrs labor "compromise" (for which C. Kelley as counsel for Chrysler is responsible with F.D.—according to Gilbert Montague);[5] the passage over the veto of the restoration of salaries;[6] the uneasiness over inflation prospects; and the absence of reliable evidence of recovery, have struck a severe blow at F.D.'s prestige. And his absence during this critical period has been very unfortunate.[7]

4. I am confirmed in my belief that all his kunststucke[8] were not only harmful & will breed more trouble; and that he erred fundamentally in failing, as OWH would say, "to strike at the jugular."[9] He has restored to the big boys confidence & power, instead of destroying them when they were at his feet. Strangely enough, I agree with this week's N.R. It really looks like "Not Kerensky, Lloyd George."[10] Of course I believe in F.D.'s sincerity & purposes. The trouble is his confidence in his ability to bring folks to happiness by compromise. And his utter inability to grasp the limits of men's possible achievements.

5. In Court, all goes well. The one commanding argument of the Term was I. K. Lewis, Harvard Law S. 1909, now in Duluth.[11] He came via Beloit College to Harvard, & appears to have lived at Rockland Wis. Do you know anything about him? George Wharton Pepper and Charles Bunn[12] were his adversaries. C.B. writes a good brief but can't argue a case.[13]

6. H.L.S. did well to get Erwin Griswold.

[1] Flexner's information about FF's schedule was incorrect.

[2] Senate hearings conducted by Hugo Black just prior to Roosevelt's inauguration had uncovered collusion among the large airlines which bid for the lucrative air mail contracts, aided by the anticompetitive attitude of Hoover's postmaster general, William F. Brown. When Black made Roosevelt aware of the fraud in early 1934, the president ordered the illegal contracts cancelled in mid-February. Unfortunately, the Army Air Corps, which had assured the administration that it could take over delivery of the mails, proved unable to do so, and within a short time several planes had crashed, a number of pilots had been killed, and air mail service disrupted.

[3] After the Civil Works Administration under Harry Hopkins had put over 4,000,000 unemployed persons on the payroll, the huge costs of the program led to pressure on Roosevelt to cut back or disband the agency. In February Roosevelt had decided to end the program, and transferred some of its smaller operations to the Emergency Work Relief Program of the FERA. This action, while placating conservatives, brought a deluge of criticism on the president from the left, for allegedly abandoning the poor and the unemployed.

[4] Actually, the agricultural cutbacks on winter planting, as well as the dust storms in the midwest, had cut down production and led to a significant rise in farm prices. The wheat surplus was wiped out; corn, which had sold at ten cents a bushel in 1932, rose to seventy cents; and farm income in general rose by over a third from the 1932 level.

[5] Hugh Johnson had enormous difficulties in bringing the auto makers into the NRA, and eventually caved in to them, overruling his own labor board and agreeing to a plan which allowed the auto makers to provide for proportional representation in company sponsored unions. The action led Senator Wagner and other friends of labor to join in the chorus of condemnation of the NRA.

[6] Roosevelt had vetoed a measure to restore a 5 percent salary cut to federal employees; Congress had overridden the veto.

[7] Actually, Roosevelt was still in Washington. LDB may have been referring to the president's planned trip to Hawaii, which took him out of the country from 2 July until 10 August.

[8] "clever tricks."

[9] Holmes often referred to a comment which Ralph Waldo Emerson had made to him as a youth, when Holmes had asked the older man to read an essay criticizing Plato. "If you would strike at a king," Emerson had said, "you must kill him."

[10] *The New Republic* 78 (11 April 1934): 232. Commenting on a charge before a congressional hearing that Roosevelt was the Kerensky of the American revolution to be followed by a Stalin or a Hitler, Bruce Bliven had noted that all of the president's actions were relatively mild, aimed not at destroying capitalism, but at preserving it, much as Lloyd George had done in England before the first war. Moreover, Roosevelt had implemented only two relatively progressive measures, unemployment insurance and financial reform, the same two Lloyd George had secured.

[11] Isaac Kenneth Lewis (1880–1971) practiced in Duluth, where he was active in civic affairs, until his retirement.

[12] Charles Bunn (1893–1964) had graduated Harvard Law School in 1917. After a period of private practice and government service, he taught law at the University of Wisconsin from 1934 to 1961.

[13] The case, *Olson* v. *United States*, 292 U.S. (1934), dealt with just compensation for land purchased by the federal government in order to build dams.

No. 560   May 11, 1934   Washington, D.C.

Re yours of May 1st.

1. In my opinion, you should come home as soon as your duties to Oxford permit. This, I assume from your letter, would see you started not later than July 1st.

2. Things are going very badly for F.D. and Democracy and the party. It is not merely that each of the "Kunststucke" [1] have failed; and, because of this failure, F.D.'s position is greatly weakened. A greater danger is due to the fact that the power of his enemies is greatly strengthened otherwise. They have made money, largely owing to F.D.'s policies, they have gotten their second wind. Measures, which 12 months ago could easily have prevailed & which would have promised help to business conditions, cannot now be resorted to. Big Business and Big Finance are not now the abject, planless lot that they were. And F.D. is no longer unerring in his political sense. Criticism has become vocal and effective. Grave fear is expressed by some of F.D.'s best friends that Republicans may get the next House; and some are recalling what happened to Wilson in 1919.

3. Your statement: "I see no purpose in getting involved in Washington matters during the summer. F.D.R. will in any event be away, etc." rests, I think, on a failure to sense the situation. In the first place, it is by no means sure that F.D. will be away long (and I feel sure he ought

545

not to be). He plans now to sail June 22d.[2] He may do that, if Congress adjourns June 15th as is being talked. But it is very doubtful how long F.D. will deem it wise to remain absent, and there will be much for you to do here, even if you should arrive before he returns to work.

4. The serious fundamental questions will be: (a) What can be done under the powers possessed by the President in the legislation had & in process. (b) What can be and should be the program—the keynotes—of the campaign and the program for the 1935 legislation. To these questions you and other real friends of F.D. should give careful consideration. To reach wise conclusions will require on your part considerable study of the situation before you are in a position to advise. And after you have made that study there should be much calm consideration with F.D.'s friends, like Moley, Baruch, etc. It will be all to the good if you have several weeks for such study and consideration before F.D. returns and the talks with him begin.

5. I think it would be unwise for you to ask F.D. whether he wants to see you "for anything before September." He [would] probably say "no." But he needs you, as does the Country, very much.

Will write you on Palestine & other matters soon.

[1] "clever tricks."
[2] Roosevelt sailed from Annapolis on 2 July for a trip to Hawaii; he returned to Oregon on 3 August.

No. 561 May 13, 1934 Washington, D.C.

Further re yours May 1st

1. Doubtless you have already put in daily licks for the Palestine cause in casual talks with those whom you meet and will do so throughout your stay in England, bringing understanding or awakening an interest; every seed dropped may have important consequences.

2. But I have hopes also that you arrange (before July 1) for a more ambitious "convocation" of some "Auseinandersetzung"[1] with some person or persons in authority and/or of influence with the Government. There is, I think, great need of that, primarily to understand their course of action and purposes.

Their attitude has for a long period been so persistently adverse to Jewish interests, particularly in respect to immigration (but also in other respects unfriendly) that I fail to find explanation merely in the common manifestation of bureaucratic error or failure to understand larger implications; or in a bending backwards in the effort to be fair and upright.

It looks as if these acts and refusals on the part of the Palestinian administration (and the Colonial office) were manifestations of a policy to retard and largely prevent Jewish development.

My faith in the British-Jewish enterprise was based upon a conviction that Great Britain had as much to gain as we have from the Jewish penetration of the Near East. Apparently, they have come to another conclusion as to this; and it is important that we should know what their policy & conviction is.

3. If they really want to cooperate with us, it is important that the Jews have an undivided loyalty in respect to the powers in the Near East. But it is obvious, Jews must have an outlet there, in Palestine and Transjordan now, and later in Iraque. There is a force driving Jews as irresistable as gravitation, the torrent must play itself out somewhere. There are indications of a drive on the part of France to have larger Jewish settlements in Syria, and a belief on part of some of our people that if England block[s] our way, we must seek French territory. We ought to know the British desire. They, of course, know of this French possibility. I hope you can as unofficial ambassador without a portfolio be of much help in this connection as well as others.

[1] "exchange of opinions."

No. 562   May 16, 1934   Washington, D.C.

Further answering yours of May 1st.

1. The above clipping tells more than many a volume on American business.[1] Food is the only expenditure which is strictly current. It is not capable of "deferred maintenance," and we may be sure that if people have the money to buy food they will. Undoubtedly, the higher prices have cut consumption. And, of course, cutting consumption cuts employment.

2. Yes, Miss Grady's death[2] is a serious loss. Happily she was able to carry on some work almost to the last day; and her achievement was great. It was a grand life.

3. The achievement runs so far above anything American in insurance that I think Keynes (as an insurance man) may care to see the enclosed papers, the 25th year Brief survey and the dividend sheet.

4. To these should be added this astounding fact. The perdurance of our insurance as compared with that of the companies is such, that last year our gain in "Insurance in Force" was greater than that in Massachu-

setts of any company. The Metropolitan stood second. I suppose the Metropolitan wrote in mass more than 50 times as much as we (counting both ordinary & industrial). The race is not always to the swift.

[1] The undated clipping noted a report from the A&P Company that although its tonnage figures for food had declined in April by 10.1 percent from the same period a year earlier, its business measured in dollars had risen 2.3 percent.

[2] LDB's longtime personal secretary, who after his appointment to the Supreme Court had taken over management of Savings Bank Life Insurance, had died on 19 April 1934.

No. 563   July 20, 1934   Chatham, Mass.

1. I am glad you are thinking of sending F.D. the "cautionary word." He ought to say something nice about the Wisconsin law if he talks there.[1]

2. Ben Cohen as the directing secretary of the "Social insurance" group would help.

3. Frances Perkins, with her hands full of strikes, should be glad to further a modest program on social insurance.

4. All the reports on business coming in now should make F.D. advisors ready for reconsideration of measures.[2]

5. Hope you will have satisfactory talk with Moley.

In a letter of mine to my brother dated Feb. 6/22 I find this: "Saw Eugene Meyer at the Pinchots last evening. He said 5000 banks would have gone broke but for the War Finance Corp. He sees, however, the danger of long continued operations, and he agrees that American business etc. "has bitten off more than it can chew," i.e. there isn't intelligence enough in existence to grapple with the problems bigness and concentration have created."

[1] See next letter, n. 1.

[2] The National Recovery Administration was coming under increasing fire, with charges ranging from its failure to protect consumers to its being little more than a front behind which big business could ignore the antitrust laws.

No. 564   July 26, 1934   Chatham, Mass.

Re yours 24th

1. You have acted very wisely in regard to handling R[aymond]. M[oley].

2. The draft of proposed letter to F.D. re social insurance seems to me all right (returned herewith).[1]

3. I assume he will understand that "premature commitment" means—before his committee reports.[2]

4. When you see him in early August it will be advisable to re-enforce what I said to him on employers bearing the whole cost, & which seemed to impress him very favorably.

5. It's fine to know that you think Frances Perkins can be led to lead on the right side.

The Austrian affair is pretty distrubing.[3]

[1] In the undated draft, FF warned the president against attempting to impose a nationally uniform system of unemployment insurance, because of the intricacies of the federal system. He suggested a careful study of the problem, looking upon the states not as barriers to reform, but as opportunities to establish different plans as experiments to see which worked best. He also suggested, at LDB's prompting, that when next FDR spoke in Wisconsin, he mention that state's plan as one example of how the states could creatively respond to the problem.

[2] The president had named a committee, headed by Secretary of Labor Perkins, to assess the different plans being put forward for a comprehensive social insurance program, and to come up with a compromise measure. The committee had not yet reported its recommendations.

[3] The preceding day, Austrian Nazis had launched an attempted coup to take over the government, and in their attack on the government, had killed the chancellor, Engelbert Dollfuss. Only the protest of the Italian government prevented Germany from intervening at this time.

No. 565   August 1, 1934   Chatham, Mass.

Re yours 29th.

1. I agree emphatically with your advice that Tom should decline the S.G.'s offer;[1] also that he should remain on the R.F.C. payroll with the free hand hitherto enjoyed; and that it would be fine to have his status such that he would be in fact F.D.'s advisor and carry out policies through "Tom's boys." Doubtless that could be effected by his being Moley's resident representative, since you, with fuller knowledge of the situation, suggest it. But it must be borne in mind that Moley is mercurial; and also that some whom F.D. is consulting are not in harmony with Moley and lack confidence in him.

2. The "subsistence homestead" project is a very alluring one with fair possibilities.[2] But the cost of the individual homestead (about $5,000) is creating a fixed charge which will prevent (in most cases) the families becoming self-supporting units & owners. Shad's[3] attention should be called to what we are doing in Palestine (despite high wages & high cost of land) with our homesteads, by starting men in simple structures of which they are rapidly becoming owners. He can get the figures from P.E.C.

549

3. I hope Nathanson will have familiarized himself with my opinions before the term begins.

4. I thought Lewisohn did a creditable job in the Field book. Surely any friend of Jamy's would wish to have something other than Steiner's appear.

[1] Corcoran did not accept a post in the solicitor general's office.

[2] Roosevelt had long been attracted by the idea of resettling urban dwellers in the country, and had arranged to have an appropriation for subsistence homesteads written into the NRA legislation. Although the New Deal built about one hundred communities, the experiment failed to catch on.

[3] Shad Polier (1906–1976) had been a student of FF's at Harvard, and soon after his graduation had won renown as one of the attorneys in the Scottsboro case. He devoted much of his life to work in civil rights and liberties, especially for blacks and Jews. He was the son-in-law of Rabbi Stephen Wise.

No. 566   August 3, 1934   Chatham, Mass.

I. It is reassuring that you and Marion are convinced of large growth in F.D. during the year. He gave you ample time for observation.

II. I hope that recognizing the "irrepressible conflict" [1] he will set his course resolutely, and say as little as possible about it. There has already been far too much "thundering in the wind."

III. Col. Morgan was here (to see Morris Leeds) the day before he was to see the President. M. is a bit too favorable to the cement manufacturers & I hope the President will be firm. I had talked much with Leeds on cement & talked a little with Morgan.

IV. I think the public works program can be met by:

    1. Making inheritance taxes so persistent and all embracing as to put an end to the super-rich and, indeed, the rich as distinguished from the "well-to-do." Of course, all gift, insurance, trust and other leaks must be ended, & the raids of the tax-ambulance chasers and their respectable allies ended also. (Let his Treas. get to work.)

    2. Bear in mind that all p[ublic]. w[orks]. which I recommend is an investment on which the return in direct and indirect income will come later—permanent improvements. In so far as the improvements affect public lands, it will, in part bring direct returns. Timber will be sold, water power will be let. In part, it will promote prosperity, like improved inland navigation & hence income subject to taxation. All inheritance & gift taxes should be allocated to these public lands,

and all taxes by way of direct income from the improvement. In so far as the improvements affect private lands, the resulting gain (protection from flood damage, soil erosion, the benefit from irrigation) can be reached at the appropriate time by appropriate taxes.

3. A large part of the current cost would be a substitute for relief, and to that extent not involve *additional* current expenditure. And, moreover, as this Government expenditure would result in large private expenditures, partial re-imbursement would come almost current from income & other internal revenue taxes.

4. Of course there must be large borrowings. These should come through borrowing direct from the people, instead of from the banks. This direct borrowing should be made via the Post Offices, that is, by deposits, and by sales through the P.O. of government long time obligations.

5. If the figures of estates of decedents of the last "ten years" are studied, it will be found that a very considerable amount would come in from year to year so as to reduce the borrowings and current interest charges.

6. Note that on the proposed public improvements, unlike most building etc., public & private, there would be no depreciation & obsolescence charges but merely maintenance.

VI. [sic] I hope F.D. will want to see you again before October & that you can re-inforce your views (i.a.) that we should refuse to contemplate permanent unemployment. It would be a disgrace for man who has had inventive faculty to overcome the law of gravitation etc.

V. It is a relief to know that he is against Federal Incorporation.

VI. I didn't see the McReynolds story. What was it?

VII. F.D. is right in having Tom stay at R.F.C.

VIII. It is good to know that you are leaving for Cambridge next Thursday. We are due at the Bellevue next Monday (Sep 10) and hope you and Marion can dine with us that evening at 7 : 30, and that you will have time free on the 11th. We plan, unless detained by Boston affairs, to leave for Washington on Tuesday evening.

IX. Lloyd Garrison and Magruder should know of the Preferential Union Shop. It may help them out in some ugly impasse.

Haven't you got a man who could write a worthy article on the Preferential Union Shop?

[1] As the NRA began to collapse, LDB several times warned Roosevelt, both directly and through FF, that he could not count on cooperation from big business, that there was an "irrepressible conflict" between the aims of a democratic society and the needs of monopoly.

No. 567   August 8, 1934   Chatham, Mass.

Re yours Aug 4

1. I showed Elizabeth and Paul the Witte letter.[1] They think the letter itself does not indicate anything definite as to his views. But:

    (a) He is never a fighter for any view.

    (b) Paul suggests that this congenital quality has probably been accentuated by twelve (?) years occupation as bill drafter, in which his function was to give every applicant what he wanted in advice and information.

    (c) That Witte favored passage of the existing Wisconsin Act, because he thought the bill most likely to get enacted of any plan suggested, and not because of a conviction as to its fundamentals.

2. They say Arthur Altmeyer,[2] also, is not a fighter, and was not vitally interested in the fundamentals of the existing (Grove) act. But that he, as an experienced administrator, is probably convinced that we should have state action, knowing the inherent difficulties of administering an act.

3. I hope you have in Wyzanski one who will understand the fundamentals, who cares and who will fight.

4. The Laski incident[3] shows that even in England & the University of London "Eternal vigilance is the price of liberty."

I hope Conant will not be disappointed. He hasn't even a "scrap of paper," I guess.

[1] In a letter of 27 July, Witte had told FF that he wanted the advice of people familiar with the problems of unemployment insurance to meet with him, so he could have the benefit of their views. Witte had been appointed to a committee within the Federal Emergency Relief Administration to look at the problem, and he intimated that a uniform national system might be preferable.

[2] Arthur Joseph Altmeyer (1891–1972) had worked in the Wisconsin government in the 1920s, and Roosevelt had named him chief of the compliance division of the NRA. After 1935 he worked in the Social Security system, and served as chairman of the board from 1937 to 1946.

[3] On a trip to Moscow, Laski had given a lecture at one of the Soviet universities, in which he allegedly defended communism and called for a similar system in Great Britain. Although Laski said that the Soviet press had misreported his speech, it triggered a vehement five-hour debate in the House of Commons in which one member after another rose to denounce Laski. Several called for a reduction of funds to the University of London, where he taught.

No. 568   August 28, 1934   Chatham, Mass.

1. I am hoping much from your full talk with F.D. His position seems to me to be worsening steadily. The problems grow more difficult; and the failure to recognize by action the irresistable conflict and the human limitations of the man on top must give all his well-wishers concern.

2. Such extravagant statements as Richberg's of N.R.A. performance[1] and Tugwell talk[2] enhances the difficulties. And F.D. himself seems less suave in recent utterances.

3. I am glad you find Ed Witte promising in attitude.

4. [*] was here, vacationing a little with Elizabeth & Paul. From reports of his views, I think him a very dangerous influence because of his combination of ability, fine qualities and thoroughly undemocratic views. He is definitely anti-union; and is an admirer of the Auto Mfgrs' achievements.

5. Yes, Amos [Pinchot] honored me also.

6. Who is Henry Lehman [sic]?[3]

7. I have no definite recollection of the impression I got of H.V.'s report, & have not the corporation's annual report here.

8. As to Glavis,[4] you will recall W[oodrow]. W[ilson].'s: "Some men grow and others swell."

9. It looks as if F.D. had not solved the Hugh Johnson problem.[5]

[1] Two days earlier Richberg, in his capacity as executive secretary of the NRA's Executive Council, had submitted an extremely optimistic report to the president on the first eighteen months of the NRA. He claimed that the problems of the Depression were being solved, and he cited significant gains in reducing unemployment and business failures, as well as noting increased profits and due regard for the rights of labor.

[2] Tugwell had given a series of talks in which he had praised the AAA as the major factor in the improvement of farm conditions and income.

[3] Henry Walter Lehmann (b. 1910) had just graduated from the Harvard Law School; he afterwards practiced law in Chicago.

[4] See 28 March 1933.

[5] See next letter.

No. 569   September 19, 1934   Washington, D.C.

Re yours 17th.

Pound is not the only "pathological case" (that was a fine letter of JWM).

The General seems to be worse. One from the Labor Dept. spoke of him as a "maniac." And one from the NRA shook his head ominously

553

on Saturday when he told me of the General['s] speech in N.Y. of which I had not seen a report or heard.

It must have been more than "liquor." What he said of me was not only an indiscretion but a lie.[1] In the few times I have seen him, from May 1933 to the last in early May 1934, he heard from me frankly that I was ag'in the Experiment. Since early May I have heard and had [*] no word from or with him directly or indirectly.

F. R. Kent item[2] enclosed & the Albert H. Loring letter enclosed Sept. 16 (and one other rec'd) are, of course, somewhat embarrassing, as I must remain silent.[3]

If F.D. does not shut up the Gen'l completely, or at least remove him, he too will feel the embarrassment.[4]

I hope he will, as indicated, see you again before he comes here.

Walton Hamilton was in on 17th. Said, with dismay, that Social Security com'tee are to propose an all-comprehending plan to go in effect 5 years from now.

From Madison [Wisconsin] we hear that Ed. Witte wishes he were back there where "he could accomplish something."

[1] In a speech on 14 September, most of which was devoted to a criticism of organized labor, Hugh Johnson said: "During this whole intense experience [of heading the NRA], I have been in constant touch with that old counselor, Judge Louis Brandeis." Why Johnson made the comment is impossible to determine, since he was certainly aware of the implications involved in publicizing the fact that a sitting justice of the Supreme Court had been consulted on executive department affairs which might come before the Court for adjudication. Some people blamed it on Johnson's growing alcohol problem; others saw it as part of the desperation he felt with the NRA coming apart.

[2] Frank Richardson Kent (1877–1958), had been a longtime reporter and then managing editor of the Baltimore *Sun*, after which he wrote a column syndicated in more than a hundred newspapers. The "item" referred to may have been an editorial in the *Sun* of 16 September, which termed the situation "confusion confounded." There is no copy of a Loring letter in the Frankfurter MSS.

[3] According to Bruce Murphy, LDB relied on his lieutenant, FF, to orchestrate a defense if one proved necessary. *Brandeis/Frankfurter Connection*, 146–48.

[4] See 29 September 1934.

No. 570   September 22, 1934   Washington, D.C.

Re yours of 21st.

Before that, had come the piece in the N.R. which I assume must have been yours;[1] and from Norman came the Springfield Republican's editorial of Sept 19/34.[2] Gardner Jackson was in this A.M.

I agree entirely with you that the General is not a knave, and I do not think he is chargeable with having been a fool. I think he must have been drunk or that his mind has gone astray otherwise. Of course, "the interests" may be playing the "knave." I enclose letter of Walter's with editorial from Chicago Tribune.[3]

I don't see how there is anything which can be done which you are not doing. I shall tell the C.J. the facts.

I think I told you of all my relations to Johnson, but perhaps it may be well to repeat the story in brief:

(1) In May '33, while the NRA bill was being talked about, I had a telephone from an old western acquaintance of the elder La Follette days asking to see me. I fixed an hour. With him came in, unannounced, Johnson. I greeted him saying: "Your picture has become familiar to me within the last few days." He answered: "I am sorry to have you say that, and not to remember that in the War Days, when I was Gen'l Crowder's aid[e], and you saved my life with your advice." He soon began to discuss the proposed legislation; he referred, as you will recall, to Baruch's (expected) part, & I told him frankly that the proposed measure was a bad one & my reasons, including the impossiblity of enforcement, the dangers to the small industries, the inefficiency of the big unit, be it government or private. Johnson's secretary(?) Strauss (? Roger W.) came with him.[4]

(2) The next I heard from him was a telephone in Chatham (in 1933). After the code of the International Ladies' Garment workers was put through, the employers' ass'n and employees (through Morris Hillquit) wrote me that at last what I had desired (in 1910 etc.[5]) was being carried through etc. Johnson telephoned me, I guess at Kirstein's instance, (perhaps the telephone was spontaneous.) his satisfaction & wanted me to know, etc.

(3) In the fall of '33, he came in with Kirstein for a brief call, I guess for no particular purpose. I can't recall whether anything definite was discussed, but have an impression something was said about "price maintenance." My article of 1913 on "Competition that Kills"[6] & whether I had still the same view. Kirstein had been *contra*.

(4) Once in the winter, after he had been in the hospital, he came in.

On these occasions I am sure I told him (as I have many others) that I knew no one who could have done more than he, but that the job was an impossible one, etc.

(5) Finally, he came in in early May '34, a crushed man. I told him again that the task was impossible etc., & that he should liquidate as

soon as possible. I was much touched by the brief talk. I felt that he had showed manliness in coming to me who had predicted failure, instead of avoiding me as most men would have done when the predicted failure was apparent, and I am sure that he felt I was his friend; and this has been in his mind often since when he was being, what he considered, hounded & declared that his associates had been "disloyal." Since then I have heard nothing from him in any way.

[1] The unsigned paragraph in "The Week" section of *New Republic* 80 (26 September 1934): 169 read: "Among the minor mysteries of General Johnson's speech is his attempt to drag in the name of Mr. Justice Brandeis as one of the intellectual fathers of the present variety of what Lewis Corey calls Niraism. To hear the General tell it, the distinguished Justice has been his spiritual mentor all through his stormy recent past. But everyone who has read Justice Brandeis's public utterances knows that he is very far from sharing General Johnson's views. Washington observers, moreover, refuse to credit the idea that the two men have had more than the slightest possible personal contact during the past year. Can it be that the doughty General has been misled by some imposter, misrepresenting himself to be the Justice and then misrepresenting the latter's views?"

[2] The editorial in the 19 September issue of the *Springfield Republican* read: "The general's public reference to Justice Brandeis was irresponsible and outrageous because, aside from any betrayal of confidence that may be involved, Justice Brandeis as a member of the Supreme Court cannot afford to sacrifice his dignity by entering into a public controversy with the general concerning alleged private conversation." The editorial went on to suggest that Johnson had outlived his usefulness as head of the NRA.

[3] The editorial asserted that if Johnson's statement were true, then "it conveys a departure from American custom and from judicial ethics which is as truly revolutionary as any project in the New Deal program." While not attacking LDB directly, the editorial strongly criticized the alleged activity, and implied that it disqualified LDB from sitting on some cases.

[4] Possibly Robert Kenneth Straus (b. 1905), a deputy administrator in the NRA, who later joined the Resettlement Administration, and then became a publisher in California.

[5] LDB refers to his activity in the great garment workers strike and the creation of an industry-wide "protocol."

[6] "Cutthroat Prices: The Competition That Kills," *Harper's Weekly* 58 (15 November 1913): 10–12, reprinted in *Business—A Profession*, 243–61.

No. 571   September 25, 1934   Washington, D.C.

Since I told Paul Freund to say to you that I am strongly of opinion that neither F.D. nor the General should say a word, I have from Freund a memo: "F.F. will transmit your views to Hyde Park. The President returns tomorrow and may be hard pressed, F.F. says, to say something in answer to questions at the Press Conference."

Further thought confirms my conviction that neither of the two should say a word. F.D. must find a gracious way of refusing to say anything.[1]

Anything the General could say now would be sure to do harm.

On the other hand, if the General's resignation which you say will be tendered soon and accepted, were tendered & accepted now, it would help some. The rest must be left to time.

The Herald-Tribune's editorial of today[2] and an attempt to disqualify are not agreeable to contemplate, but the incident must be regarded as a casualty, like that of being run into by a drunken autoist, or shot by a lunatic.

This A.M. I told the C.J. and Van all the facts that I have told you.

[1] Unbeknownst to both LDB and FF, Roosevelt had already decided to fire Johnson, and his ill-advised comment was merely the last straw. In fact, Johnson, made aware of the president's decision, chose to tender his resignation this very day.

[2] Like the Chicago *Tribune*, the New York paper called for LDB to recuse himself in any cases involving the NRA.

No. 572   September 29, 1934   Washington, D.C.

1. Re yours [Sept.] 26/34. I am glad the resignation was so promptly accepted.[1]

2. The NRA general set up should result in early liquidation of nearly all except the labor provisions.

3. I told the facts to Sutherland, Harlan & Cardozo, & plan to tell Roberts when he returns Monday.

4. I am not surprised to hear that the students are flocking to the seminar.

5. Brewster, Ivins & Phillips (the tax lawyers) have just issued a leaflet which shows how ridiculously low are the estate, gift & income taxes under Rev[enue]. Act 1934.

Estate tax on $1,000,000	is	$169,000
$5,000,000		$1,692,000
$10,000,000		$4,387,600
$25,000,000		$13,386,600

Income tax on $1,000,000—$533,000

You can never get the "New Deal" under any such scale.

6. Let us have a list of the men here whom we have not seen (with where employed) and whom I should ask in.

Did you find "Modern Palestine" adequate?[2] We had a letter from the Hon. Mrs. Edgerton from Astor Hotel N.Y. saying they would be here but giving no address. We telegraphed the Astor asking them for tomorrow, Sunday, 5 P.M., which replied they had checked out, but didn't know what their address is. British Embassy knows nothing of them.

[1] Johnson's resignation had been immediately accepted, but he did not leave office until 16 October.

[2] Jessie Sampter, ed., *Modern Palestine: A Symposium* (New York: Hadassah, 1933). This was the third edition of Hadassah's guide to Zionism and its work in Palestine.

No. 573 October 7, 1934 Washington, D.C.

1. The President & Fellows did themselves proud.[1] Is Conant entitled to the main credit? What says your Dean?

2. I saw OWH on the 4th & expect to see him today.

3. Alice says Silcox[2] was in last year & she was favorably impressed. I do not recall him.

4. What you say of Zemurray[3] is promising. Did he come to you via Kirstein? And will he have enough interest in Massachusetts to do something for it? With James L. Richards about 77, we need such an able, comprehending man there.

5. Read Wallace's "New Frontier."[4] He may err in economics, but he is a great, exalted possession for America, intelligent, thinking and, in many respects, well-read.

6. Other papers are evidently determined to support the Herald-Tribune,—Chicago Tribune campaign.[5] Note enclosed from Chicago Herald Examiner. There have been persistent unanswered enquiries here from Hearst folk.

Did you notice that LaGuardia is considering as a means of raising revenue the kind of tax on interest over 4% which I thought F.D. ought to advocate as a means of reducing the debt burden (instead of raising prices)?

The proposal of an annual wage appears to be gaining momentum. When it does, some plan which I suggested in the Lincoln Filene letters (1911–12) should be worked out.[6]

[1] Hitler's press aide, Ernst (Putzi) Hanfstaengl, a 1909 graduate of Harvard, had offered the university a $1,000 travel scholarship to enable a Harvard undergraduate to study abroad. Conant had turned the gift down, declaring: "We are unable to accept a gift from one who has been so closely associated with the leaders of a politicial party which has inflicted damage on the universities of Germany." Hitler said the decision was "antiquated," and the Harvard *Crimson* criticized Conant for mixing politics in academic affairs.

[2] Ferdinand Augustus Silcox (1882–1939) worked for more than twelve years with the Forest Service, but because he had some experience with labor, the Labor Department had utilized his services during the First World War as a mediator. Although appointed chief of the Forest Service in 1933, he continued to be called upon as a labor arbitrator.

[3] Samuel Zemurray (1877–1961), a Russian immigrant who started as a day laborer unloading bananas in Alabama, eventually became the largest stockholder and chief executive officer of the United Fruit Company, headquartered in Boston. He did not become involved in civic affairs as LDB hoped he would, although his various philanthropic activities benefited the city.

[4] Henry A. Wallace, *New Frontiers* (New York: Reynal and Hitchcock, 1934).
[5] See 22 September 1934, n. 3, and 25 September, n. 2.
[6] See LDB to A. Lincoln Filene, June 1911.

No. 574   October 29, 1934   Washington, D.C.

1. To avert a Federal Corporation law it seems to me important now to agitate for & pass an act imposing a prohibitive federal excise tax on corporations organized under the laws of a State other than that in which they have their principal place of business.

2. For many reasons, it is important to enact a like Federal excise tax on transactions between corporations & their officers or directors or concerns in which they have a financial interest.

There ought to be no difficulty in getting support for No. 1 sufficient to overcome the interested opposition.

No. 2 might raise much opposition, but ought not the campaign be started soon?

I enclose at Mack's request the Haleli papers. The London treaty with the Revisionists is encouraging.[1]

[1] After several years of strife between the World Zionist Organization and Jabotinsky's World Union of Zionist Revisionists, which had seceded from the WZO, an agreement providing for a merger and settlement of differences had been signed at a special meeting in London.

No. 575   November 10, 1934   Washington, D.C.

1. "What will he do with it?" It is now that F.D.'s test comes.[1]

2. What has become of the proposal to protect the Treasury by curbing tax-lawyers champerty & maintenance?[2]

3. Kennedy was in for an hour on the 8th. An engaging person. If he proceeds in the bank autopsy which he volunteered we shall have a material gain.

4. I have not seen "The Curse"[3] & didn't know that it was out. We are very glad to hear your good report. I should not myself send the copy to F.D. If you think it worthwhile to send him a copy, of course do so.

Huebsch[4] should send Norman a copy.

Since writing the above I have letter from Huebsch announcing copy of "The Curse" on the way to me.

Friends in Mass. (except E.A.F.) seem pretty sad about the Curley triumph.[5]

[1] In the mid-term elections, the Democrats scored a striking victory. Normally, the party in power loses at least some seats to the opposition, but the Democrats actually increased their margin in the House to 322 to 103 Republicans and ten independents. In the Senate, the Democrats elected nine new members, making their majority sixty-nine to thirty-one.

[2] Champerty is a bargain by a third party to carry on the litigation of the plaintiff at his own cost and risk, in return for receiving, if successful, a portion of the proceeds or damages; maintenance consists of supporting or promoting the litigation of another.

[3] Osmond K. Fraenkel, ed., *The Curse of Bigness: Miscellaneous Papers of Louis D. Brandeis* (New York: Viking Press, 1934), contained various articles, speeches, and opinions by LDB. See LDB to Clarence Martin Lewis, 21 March 1934.

[4] Benjamin W. Huebsch (1876–1964) had published *The Freeman* before establishing the Viking Press.

[5] James Michael Curley (1874–1958), the quintessential Irish politician, was, at various times, a member of the city council, member of the House of Representatives, several times mayor of Boston, and in 1934 won the gubernatorial race, with a plurality of more than 106,000 votes over his nearest rival.

No. 576   November 24, 1934   Washington, D.C.

Lee M. Friedman[1], who called on me the other day, said that 3, and possibly 4, members of S.J.C. would resign before the New Year.[2]

Would it not be possible, and advisable, to renew the suggestion that Ned McClennen be nominated?[3]

[1] Lee Max Friedman (1871–1957), a prominent Boston attorney, was active in local civic affairs, as well as in a variety of Jewish organizations.

[2] Only one member of the Supreme Judicial Court of Massachusetts resigned, William Cushing Wait.

[3] McClennen never received a judicial appointment: instead, the governor named Stanley Elroy Qua (1880–1965), who had been a member of the superior court since 1921.

No. 577   December 31, 1934   Washington, D.C.

1. Yours from the Island has come. F.D. made a vast amount of trouble by that Security message etc. last spring.[1] We ought to come back now to the Wagner-Lewis bill,[2] with only real perfecting amendments. Altmeyer, I hear, had made trouble by a compromise amendment of 1% to be pooled. Tom & Ben ought to try to brush away this compromise & doubtless others which will be trouble makers. We should strive for the simon-pure article.

2. Reisman[3] we were glad to see Saturday.

Our best for 1935.

[1] On 8 June 1934, in an effort to head off growing sentiment in both houses of Congress for some sort of social insurance program, Roosevelt had asked Congress to delay any action until a bill could

be prepared which would combine both unemployment compensation and a sweeping program to provide for "the security of the men, women and children of the nation."

[2] The Wagner-Lewis bill provided for a national unemployment compensation program funded by an ingenious tax system devised by LDB. A payroll tax on employers would be collected by the treasury, but in those states where employers were already contributing to state funds, the amounts involved would be deducted from the federal tax. The Wagner-Lewis bill never passed; instead the administration secured the Social Security Act.

[3] David Riesman (b. 1909) would clerk for LDB in the 1935 term, and then go on to a distinguished teaching career, first at the University of Buffalo Law School (1937–1941), the University of Chicago (1946–1958), and finally as Henry Ford II Professor of Social Sciences at Harvard from 1958 until his retirement in 1980.

No. 578   January 19, 1935   Washington, D.C.

1. I enclose letter of 9th from Redlich.[1] Of course, "judicial office precludes." I have written him saying I would confer with you.

2. Your and Hart's Survey of 1933 Term is receiving favorable comment from members of the Court.[2]

3. The Employment Compensation bill[3] has all the defects of which Elizabeth wrote you. Witte, Altmeyer are somewhat troubled about opposition from employers. Perhaps, for this reason, they summoned Paul who arrived yesterday.

4. Sec. Wallace who was in last Sunday said that he is much concerned over outlook for 1935, which he thinks will be much less good for agriculture than 34–5. I suppose you have noticed drop in cotton exports.

[1] There is no copy of a letter from Redlich at this time in the FF MSS.

[2] "The Business of the Supreme Court at October Term, 1933," *Harvard Law Review* 48 (1934): 238.

[3] LDB had been in frequent consultation with his daughter and son-in-law, Elizabeth and Paul Raushenbush, on how to extend the Wisconsin unemployment plan across the nation (see LDB to Elizabeth Raushenbush, 22 April and 8 June 1934). The basic ideological conflict, as LDB saw it, was between a national system administered from Washington, which would have the admitted benefit of uniformity, and a system of individual state programs, which LDB preferred, since it would have local control. Throughout this period the Raushenbushes, as well as other advocates of the Wisconsin plan, were in Washington frequently to consult with LDB and members of the government. See the Raushenbushes, *Our "U.C." Story*, ch. 8.

No. 579   January 23, 1935   Washington, D.C.

1. Glad to hear of progress with bills. The press is beginning to talk on the P[ublic]. U[tility]. holding company measure in recognizable terms.[1]

2. Paul is here since the 18th, summoned by Altmeyer and Witte ostensibly to help in drafting a model bill for the States. He may [al]so be able to do some in mitigating the objectionable features, & is seeing Bob La Follette.

3. There is much unhappiness among brain-trusters.

What is J. M. Keynes' address?

I have given N[athanson]. your message about opinions.

[1] The Public Utilities Holding Company Act of 1935 is generally recognized as the dividing point between the so-called First and Second New Deals. Whereas in his first two years Roosevelt attempted to establish a partnership with business through programs such as the National Recovery Administration, the Second New Deal attacked large concentrations of business power, attempted some redistribution of wealth, and set in motion the creation of the welfare state. LDB, who had consistently opposed many of Roosevelt's earlier measures, welcomed this new approach, which fit into his general views on the nature of the economy and the evil of big business. The Holding Company Act required the simplification of multilayered financial structures and the divestment of operating companies in noncontiguous states. In addition it required all utilities to secure approval from the Securities and Exchange Commission for new stock issues, and provided for regulation of intercompany transactions.

No. 580   February 24, 1935   Washington, D.C.

1. Rowe [1] probably wrote you about OWH's illness. When I had Poindexter telephone Mary [Donnellan] last Friday whether it would be O.K. for me to call that day, she answered that the Justice had "a slight cold." Rowe telephoned this A.M.. that he was seriously ill yesterday with bronchial pneumonia. But later Mary telephoned that he is much better today & that there is no occasion for anxiety. [2]

2. It is a relief to have the Gold Clause case [3] out of the way; but I feel little satisfaction with the Administration's performance. McReynolds' talk was very different from his opinion, [4] was really impressive; better than anything I have ever heard from him.

3. The excerpt about Samuel Want is painfully interesting. I have destroyed it.

4. Walter Wilbur was in about a month ago, in good form. We had not seen him for many years.

5. The removal of Frank [5] should not have involved the others. It is disappointing. I should be sadder about it even than I am, if I were not convinced that the whole AAA production curtailment policy will prove disastrous. The 2,500,000 dispossessed; [6] and the Arkansas anti-free speech proceedings; [7] the suppression of Mrs. Meyer's reports; the lessening of the traffic of the southern railroads are a few of the by-products.

6. You are right that a general must have troops, but he must lay out a campaign that men may live and die for. And it's the business of a leader to lead.

7. If you can produce a man who can write the story of what the auto has done in U.S.A., and get it published, let me know.[8]

Thanks for letting me know about B.F.'s 70th.[9]

[1] James Henry Rowe, Jr. (1909–1985), then Holmes's secretary, would have a distinguished career in both private and public service, including stints as secretary to Franklin Roosevelt, assistant attorney general, and one of the American counsel at the postwar Nuremburg trials.

[2] Holmes died on 6 March 1935.

[3] See 13 June 1933. The constitutional challenge to FDR's "gold clause" program came before the Court in early 1935. In *Norman* v. *Baltimore* & *Ohio* R.R., 294 U.S. 240, the Court upheld the federal power to cancel the clauses in private contracts, because private interests had to give way to the broader federal policy. But in *Perry* v. *United States*, 294 U.S. 330, the Court ruled that the government could not negate its own word, and thus was not entitled to cancel gold clauses in its own bonds. Recognizing, however, that the decision could not be applied without threatening the financial stability of the country, the Court ruled that bondholders were not entitled to payment in gold or its enhanced value since they had not shown damage through receiving payment in other legal tender.

[4] Reynolds, joined by Van Devanter, Sutherland, and Butler, entered a caustic dissent covering all the gold clause cases, and warned that the entire constitutional framework of the country was being threatened.

[5] On 5 February the Agricultural Adjustment Administration had been rocked by a sweeping reorganization which saw the resignations or demotions of dozens of officials. The crisis resulted from continuous friction between upper level policymakers and the middle managers reluctant to implement certain decisions. A number of people interested in large-scale planning, including chief counsel Jerome Frank and his staff, had been forced to resign as well.

[6] A number of farmers did lose their property during the Depression, but how many of those losses resulted from AAA policies is difficult to determine. Some sources blame the dust storms of 1934 and 1935 for displacing over one million people.

[7] LDB may have been referring to recent disturbances in Arkansas as a result of the formation of the Southern Tenant Farmers' Union.

[8] On 7 February 1935 LDB had written: "The automobile performance [is] sad. The discerning historian of 'our present discontent' will someday show that the automobile is perhaps the most potent cause, economic and socially, civil & criminally. The net debit will mark very large."

[9] Bernard Flexner would be seventy on 24 February.

No. 581   March 12, 1935   Washington, D.C.

1. It was good to see something of Marion as well as much of you.[1]

2. The cotton plunge[2] must give F.D. concern & make Wallace squirm. The decision on the curtailment reminds of the darky preacher who said:

> "There has been a great deal of difference in this here congregation whether the sun revolves around the earth or the earth around the sun. I suggest that we settle the matter by a vote today."

3. On dissents, see the opinions at the last term in the two life insurance accident cases.[3]

4. From what I heard yesterday, it seems that the relations of F.D. to the Progressive Senators will need more nursing.

5. Bruce Bliven in N.R. on Bigness is plain stupid.[4] There is much to be said for Bigness, but his talk makes one wonder whether fatty degeneration has set in.

[1] The Frankfurters had come to Washington for the funeral of former Justice Holmes.

[2] On 11 March, cotton futures dropped as much as $9 a bale before closing at $6 down. The drop reflected growing anxiety about the government's crop regulation plan under the AAA and the possiblility of ending the price support program.

[3] LDB is probably referring to *Landress* v. *Phoenix Mutual Life Insurance* Co., 291 U.S. 491 (1934), and *Travelers' Protective Assn.* v. *Prinson*, 291 U.S. 576 (1934). In the former case, Justice Stone held that an apparently healthy person who succumbed to sunstroke did not meet the policy requirement of death by "accident," and that the beneficiary was not entitled to collect under the accident clause. Cardozo wrote a strong dissent in which he called for a common sense interpretation of accident. In the latter case, Cardozo wrote the majority opinion upholding an insurance company's refusal to pay a claim since the insured had died in an explosion of a dynamite truck he had helped to load, thus coming within one of the policy's waiver provisions. This time Stone wrote the dissent, saying that since the deceased was not a regular passenger, and in fact had accepted the driver's offer of a lift, he was removed from the waiver.

[4] In the 13 March issue of *The New Republic*, Bliven had questioned the notion that bigness necessarily equated to badness, especially in government programs. Bliven named LDB as the spiritual father of this view, and wondered why it would be so terrible to have the national government run the entire unemployment relief program, since unemployment was so obviously a national problem.

No. 582   March 25, 1935   Washington, D.C.

1. The question you raise is really a question. The state of the accident has this in its favor—the witnesses are most likely to be there.[1]

2. It will be a very serious matter for F.D. if he weakens on the Holding Co. bill.[2]

3. Unemployment insurance has been so much bedevilled by refusal to pass the Wagner-Lewis bill of the last session, that I shall not be sorry if it should go over to 1936. Anything passed this year will be unutterably bad, and we can't get state action in any event in most states until 1937.[3] Tom [Corcoran] doubtless told you what Witte said.

4. I knew Theophilus Parsons.[4] It seems pretty long ago.

5. The selection of Richberg to succeed Clay Williams[5] was not an advance.

6. Max Lerner would help Harvard.

7. It's fortunate Gene [Meyer] is being bled by his paper.

8. Tell me about Charles Fairman who wrote the paper on Justice Miller.[6]

9. I saw Senator Schall[7] for the first time today. His father must have been a Jew.

[1] The issue involved conflicts of law theory, which law should apply when citizens of different jurisdictions sue in either state or federal courts. Classic theory held that the *situs* of an accident should govern the choice of law, but about this time critics were pointing out inequities which resulted from this approach. Instead, they advocated what became known as interest analysis, in which the interests of the different jurisdictions would be taken into account, so that the state which had the greater policy interest involved would have its law applied.

[2] See 23 January 1935, n. 1.

[3] See 19 January 1935, n. 3.

[4] Theophilus Parsons (1797–1882) had been Dane Professor of Law at Harvard from 1848 to 1869. He wrote numerous treatises on various aspects of commercial law, including a standard two-volume treatise on contracts.

[5] Samuel Clay Williams (1884–1949), a North Carolina lawyer, was president of the R.J. Reynolds Tobacco Company; he had taken a leave of absence to serve as chairman of the five-member National Industrial Recovery Board following Hugh Johnson's resignation.

[6] Charles S. Fairman (b. 1897) taught at Williams College, Stanford, and Washington University before coming to the Harvard Law School in 1955. The paper he wrote on Justice Samuel Miller appeared in *Political Science Quarterly* 50 (1935): 15.

[7] Thomas David Schall (1878–1935), a blind Minneapolis attorney, represented Minnesota in the House of Representatives from 1915 to 1925 and in the Senate from 1925 until his death in an automobile accident in December of this year.

No. 583　　　April 16, 1935　　　Washington, D.C.

1. Riesman said Powell told Tom Eliot[1] two months ago that Bikle had been offered the Deanship.[2]

2. We expect to see John Fulton[3] on Sunday.

3. I will tell you the occasion for the G. letter when we meet.

4. F.D. seems to be regaining lost ground, and the Republicans' split[4] seems to be widening.

5. I don't know whether Savings Bank Insurance gains are reported to you. We still write a very small percentage of all business in Mass. But of the gain made in primary life insurance in force in Mass. in 1935, S.B.I. shows 44.3 per cent (in dollars). The 46 companies, domestic and foreign, only 55.7 per cent. That's going some. Moreover, we are gaining in writing over last year nearly 33%; and the companies are falling steadily behind last year.

6. When do you expect to be in Washington?

[1] Thomas Hopkinson Eliot (b. 1907) had graduated from Harvard Law in 1932. From 1935 to 1938 he was general counsel of the Social Security Board, and then served as a representative in

565

Congress from Massachusetts from 1941 to 1943. In 1952 he joined the faculty of Washington University in St. Louis, and was chancellor from 1962 to 1971.

[2] Possibly of Harvard law; Biklé did not accept a deanship. See 28 September 1935, n. 2.

[3] Perhaps John Faquhar Fulton (1899–1960), a Harvard trained physician who, after several years in England, had joined the Yale Medical School as professor of physiology and later of the history of medicine.

[4] According to an article in the 6 March *New York Times*, Republican leaders were trying to hush up a split between the progressive and conservative elements within the party. Following the disastrous election results of 1932 and 1934, a group of midwestern Republicans, led by Governor Alfred E. Landon of Kansas, was attempting to transfer control of the national organization to the states, and to the more liberal wing of the party, in order to reflect more accurately the mood of the country. At the same time, the Hoover wing of the party wanted the GOP to take an aggressively anti-New Deal stance.

No. 584   July 4, 1935   Chatham, Mass.

1. Your telegram came thoughtfully before the day's papers had reached us. I have entire confidence in Tom's discretion as well as his character.[1] It will be a trying experience, valuable to the country. After this exhibition, F.D. can be under no illusions about Big Business; and we should have a fight to the finish, with F.D. on top.

2. Shortly after your telegram, came one from Groner telling of Billy Hitz's death. It came mercifully in manner and perhaps, for him, mercifully otherwise. Our country has lost a devoted friend.

3. It would have been Billy's wish that Carroll Todd should succeed him, and I am sure Gregory would have recommended him with eagerness.

5. [sic] Judge Nields[2] of Dist. of Delware did a good job in cutting down receivers' and lawyers' fees.

[1] On 3 July Congressman Owen Brewster, a Maine Republican and former governor, charged on the floor of Congress that Tom Corcoran had attempted to coerce his vote. The issue was the "death sentence" provision of the Public Utilities Holding Company bill, a provision favored by the White House that would have dissolved holding companies immediately. According to Brewster, Corcoran threatened to stop a major power project in Maine if he did not vote for the measure. The explosive story monopolized headlines for a week, and Congress set up a committee to investigate the charge, as well as other charges of improper lobbying for and against the bill.

[2] John P. Nields (1868–1943) had been a U.S. attorney under Theodore Roosevelt and Taft. President Hoover had named him District Judge in 1930, and he served until his retirement in 1941.

No. 585   July 19, 1935   Chatham, Mass.

Re yours of 17th.

1. To me also, it seems that the cause has gained much from the episode.[1] Many besides F.D. will have learned to better discern the

armaments of the enemy, to appreciate his character, and to recognize that the conflict is irrepressible.

2. The usefulness of Tom and Ben [Cohen] will have been much enhanced.

3. Driscoll[2] must be quite a fellow.

4. Palestine contributed much to the G.E.L.'s prosperity, following India and South Africa as chief overseas customers.

[1] Regarding Corcoran's alleged improprieties. By now the thrust of the testimony had turned to accusations of improper activities on the part of the utilities working to defeat the "death sentence." Evidence of Corcoran's vindication would come on 31 August when President Roosevelt presented him the pen with which he signed the bill into law.

[2] Denis J. Driscoll (1871–1958) was serving a single term in the House of Representatives from Pennsylvania; he would later be named to the Federal District Court for the Southern District of New York. He testified that he had received 816 telegrams demanding the defeat of the "death sentence" provision. Driscoll concluded that the telegrams were bogus, investigated the matter, and publicly denounced the fraud.

No. 586   August 4, 1935   Chatham, Mass.

Yours 1st rec'd. The House performance[1] & the attitude of the public show how demoralized our people are, and the terrible need of education in what seems almost the obvious.

In vacation, I see the N.Y. Times daily. It is not refreshing & it proves the "irreconcilable conflict."

[1] On 1 August the House of Representatives, for the second time, voted down the Senate "death sentence" provision in the public utilities bill that eliminated all holding companies. Forced to compromise, Roosevelt nonetheless secured the substance of the proposal. The final version of the Wheeler-Rayburn bill wiped out all holding companies more than twice removed from actual operation of utilities, and empowered the SEC, with whom the companies were required to register, to eliminate holding companies beyond the first degree which the SEC deemed not to be in the public interest.

No. 587   August 22, 1935   Chatham, Mass.

Re yours of 20th.

1. I shall not need Riesman in any event before Sept. 15th. Whether I must have him as early as that will depend upon when Nathanson is needed at S.E.C. He had his vacation in July.

2. Enclosed copy of letter from Iron Mt. Mich. disclosing the hideousness of the Ford irregularity of employment.[1] F.D. may care to see.

I should have liked to read it to those Congressmen who wept so piteously over what would happen under the proposed inheritance tax, to the Ford fortune.

3. As I wrote you yesterday, it would be fine to have you here this weekend.

[1] William Kinsey, a member of the Emergency Relief Administration in Michigan, had written on 14 August to Dorothea Nordholt, an official with the Hapgood family's Indiana company. He noted that while the local Ford plant paid excellent wages, they employed their men only three or four months of the year, and during the rest of the time the laid-off workers had to resort to public welfare programs. Moreover, they accumulated so much debt during their unemployed months that when they returned to work a large part of their wages was garnisheed by their creditors. LDB, of course, had been an advocate of regularized employment for more than three decades.

No. 588　　　September 21, 1935　　Washington, D.C.

Re yours of 18.

1. I am perfectly willing to talk with the C.J. about B.N.C., but there is really only one thing that lies in his power, namely sending out the assignments Sunday A.M. instead of late Saturday.

The oral statement is made not because the C.J. wants it. He does not. Have Harlan tell you about this. B.N.C. could, instead of stating the case say in one minute all that is necessary: "I have No.—, X. v. Y., which is here on —— from ——. It involves mainly the question —— in relation to ——. The lower court held ——. We hold this was error (or correct). The judgment is ——." [1]

Every one would welcome such a short statment by him. McR says no more in 19 cases out of 20, and the little he says is inaudible usually.

I suppose the C.J. would be willing to say to B.N.C. that it would be agreeable to him to have C.'s statement so limited. But wouldn't C. feel embarrassed by his doing so, in view of the circumstances?

I never have heard anyone criticize a Justice because a statement was too short—often that it was too long.

2. I will bear in mind what you say of Zemurray.

3. Hope F.D. will take a real rest. On receipt of yours, I wrote Harlan, not "answering" his letter, but show[ed] my eagerness for his return.

[1] Traditionally, opinions of the Supreme Court were read by the justice writing that opinion, with dissenting members having the choice of whether or not they wished to read their opinions as well. As the workload of the Court increased and complex cases led to longer opinions, some of the justices began giving oral summaries only, reserving a full reading only for the most important cases. Cardozo, whose health was already beginning to fail, found this reading tiresome, but hesitated about giving up the tradition. See 5 October 1935.

No. 589   September 22, 1935   Washington, D.C.

In look[ing] over some old papers, I find enclosed file of letters from my classmate Samuel Warren, Jr.,[1] running from Oct. 21, 1878 to June 18, 1879, which led to my removing from St. Louis to Boston.

Some day, as an adviser of recent graduates, you may care to read all. But read now Warren's prophetic utterance on Holmes marked with blue pencil on p. 12 of the letter of May 5, 1879.[2]

The[re] are less significant references to Holmes in other letters.

[1] Samuel Dennis Warren (1852–1910), a member of a prominent New England family with extensive paper mill holdings, had become LDB's close friend while the two were at the Harvard Law School. After graduation, Warren had coaxed LDB to leave St. Louis and return to Boston (see LDB to Warren, 30 May 1879), and the two formed Warren & Brandeis in 1879. Upon the death of his father in 1888, Warren left the firm to take charge of the family interests, but he remained close to LDB until his death. The two also collaborated on the path-breaking essay on "The Right to Privacy," *Harvard Law Review* 4 (1890): 193.

[2] Warren had written: "I have not spoken of Holmes in this letter, but he deserves mention in this particular. I regard him as the greatest American *thinker* in law & I think if he lives he will prove himself a second Austin, not in principles and beliefs, but in ability and purpose. I regard my intercourse with him as the chief good of this past year to me. I think we will make our discussions triangular with some benefit all around." The Warren letters are now in the Frankfurter MSS in the Library of Congress, Box 26, Folder 400.

No. 590   September 28, 1935   Washington, D.C.

1. Re yours 26th. I have no recollection of ever having heard Huey Long argue any case; and no recollection of ever having seen him but once. That was about 3 years ago, when Van whispered to me that the movant for admission of a Louisiana man was Huey Long.

But I may have heard him in the motions in Cumberland T & T Co. v. La. Public Service Comm, 260 US 212, 698, 750. After receipt of your letter, I asked Riesman to telephone the clerk to enquire whether H.L. had ever argued before us, & R[iesman]. then brought me that opinion. You may get further light by looking at the Journal & the briefs which are not at hand.[1]

2. I have not read any announcements of R.P.'s retirement.[2] You may care to have his of Oct 5/26 about you (enclosed) which I ran across the other day.[3]

3. Hutchins' address is grand.[4] I judge from the Times that Hopkins (at Dartmouth) was also.[5]

4. I am not sure that the Herald Tribune's editorial[6] (returned herewith) is not (following Gay's comment) a subtle attempt to influence

Landis. There came to my mind "Man Fuhlt die Absicht und Man ist verstimmt."[7] Perhaps I am unduly suspicious.

5. E[llery]. S[edgwick]. has a way of returning to his Tom Payne [sic] mood. Is there evidence in the Atlantic that he is translating the mood into action?

6. I was very favorably impressed by Zemurray. He talked wholly of the U.S. problems, mainly of unemployment. He rose at the end of 50 minutes, saying that he would like to come another day to talk Palestine. I told him to telegraph when he was ready to do so & he said he would. Neither Palestine nor things Jewish had been mentioned.

7. This from Gina Lombroso's "The Tragedies of Progress" p. 26.[8] "Tiberias nearly imprisoned the inventor of a malleable glass which would have dispensed with many of the workers needed in glass manufacturing, saying, 'I who must exhaust myself to find employment for citizens, judge dangerous the man who invents a machine which would reduce it.' Vespasian refused to adopt a mechanism suggested to him by an inventor that would have reduced the number of men in transporting the columns for the Capital."

8. I asked Wyzanski to come in yesterday. In answer to my question as how things have been going, he spoke regretfully of their failure to get the security unit and the Labor Board into their Dept, considering that unfortunate, and when I answered, they were to be congratulated, he was willing perhaps to concede it as to Labor Board but was insistent that they ought to have had the Security unit. It led to my talking (perhaps too much) on the subject. But I was surprised at his heterodoxies; also on the wisdom of the Secretary's speech making.

[1] This reminiscence and research was occasioned by the fact that Huey Long had been assassinated in Baton Rouge on 8 September.

[2] Pound retired as dean of the Harvard Law School on 24 September, and notice did appear in major newspapers on 25 and 26 September.

[3] Pound had written: "Professor Frankfurter is certainly doing great things with his Research Fellowships, and I am confident that even greater things are in prospect." Pound also wrote that he was continuing to oppose any limits on Law School enrollments, since that would destroy Harvard's national character.

[4] LDB and FF may have had advance copies of the radio talk Hutchins delivered on 2 October. He told parents who were not willing to have their children "enter the world of ideas" to keep them at home. But even there they would not be safe, for modern communication would inevitably bring new ideas into the home, albeit in garbled or fragmentary form. It would be best, therefore, to expose children to new ideas properly, in a collegiate setting, and to train them how to deal with and evaluate them so as to make best use of them in their own lives.

[5] Ernest Martin Hopkins (1877–1964) was president of Dartmouth College from 1916 to 1945. At the school's convocation on 19 September, Hopkins had charged that the problem with the United States since the First World War was the absence of high aspirations among its people. The

purpose of a liberal arts education, he maintained, was to instil this idealism, and a determination not to accept meekly whatever came one's way.

[6] The 24 September editorial praised Landis, and noted how much he had "grown" in his job at the SEC, so that he now had a better understanding of business operations and needs. Although still an idealist, he was now tempered by knowledge of the real world, and would probably make a fine SEC chairman.

[7] "One perceives the purpose and is annoyed."

[8] Gina Lombroso-Ferrero, *The Tragedies of Progress* (New York: E. P. Dutton and Co., 1931).

No. 591   October 5, 1935   Washington, D.C.

1. Re yours of 3rd. Is Lloyd Garrison being considered for Dean?

2. Jim L[andis]. was in Sunday. I whispered to him the Goethe lines with a word of warning.[1]

3. B.N.C. was in on 30th and Harlan on 3rd. Before seeing BNC (and before the C.J. had seen him) I told the C. J. Lehman's two caveats. He, of course, will be glad to have B.N.C. cut the opinion delivery to the minimum.[2] He felt he could not change the long established custom (though burdensome to him) of circulating the assignments late Saturday, but would be glad to hold back B.N.C.'s, if he would not be pained thereby.

4. Austin Levy[3] was in Monday, very interesting & enlightened. But I have not been sure that he is wholly kosher. Are you?

5. Billikopf[4] writes me that he has sent you my April 1914 testimony before the Industrial Commission,[5] which he discovered this summer. (I had forgotten its import). On reading it, the other day, it occurs to me that the campaign against Bigness might get support from labor folk, if the arguments there used were pressed.

6. Has Nealy had his article in Bulletin 615 (S.B.I). I never see the weekly.[6]

[1] Probably LDB's favorite quote from the German author, "*In der Beschrankung zeight Erst der Meister*"—"It is in details that the master primarily reveals himself"—from *Was Wir Bringen*, Scene 19.

[2] See 21 September 1935.

[3] Austin T. Levy (1880–1951) was president of the Stillwater Worsted Mills in Rhode Island, and the author of various pamphlets on economic and social issues.

[4] Jacob Billikopf (1883–1950) was a major figure in Jewish social work circles, first in Kansas City and later in Philadelphia. During World War Two he was actively engaged in aiding refugees from Europe.

[5] United States Commission on Industrial Relations, Sen. Doc. 415, 64th Cong., 1st Sess. (1914), 19:991–1011, 26:7657–81, excerpted in *The Curse of Bigness*, 70–95.

[6] The article on savings bank insurance which appeared in that bulletin was not by Nealy, but by Edward Berman, a professor of economics at the University of Illinois then serving with the Bureau of Labor Statistics. A summary of Bulletin #615 appeared as "Massachusetts System of

Savings-Bank Insurance," *Monthly Labor Review* 41 (August 1935): 291; the full study appeared later in the year.

No. 592   October 18, 1935   Washington, D.C.

1. Riesman brings good reports of you and Marion.

2. Re yours 15th. The good points of Bikle you know. He is now 58. When I saw him last year, he seemed to me an oppressed man, overburdened with his not too congenial corporate cares and without the resiliency & affirmative assertiveness which would be needed; he has not been entirely well. Of course, he is not too old to recuperate in a thoroughly congenial atmosphere. But I suppose he would be confronted with many "mastiffs," and mere power of resistance would not suffice.[1]

3. I am glad Harvard met gallantly the problem Einstein properly characterized.[2]

4. I wish Borah would understand that "Bigness" is the real thing, and answer all the talk of concentration being inevitable, by declaring as did a wise statesman "Fate is inevitable only if it is not resisted."[3]

5. What has become of Gardner Jackson?[4] Here nobody knows. Is he "spurlos verschwinden?"[5]

[1] Although Henry W. Biklé was rumored as a possible successor to Roscoe Pound, he remained as general counsel to the Pennsylvania Railroad and a lecturer at the University of Pennsylvania Law School.

[2] This may have referred to the Massachusetts loyalty oath, which involved foreign professors who "imported knowledge." There were no enforcement provisions against individuals who refused to sign, but some legislators threatened to take action against Harvard through revocation of its charter. Conant urged individual faculty members, many of whom bitterly opposed the oath, to obey the law while the university assumed the burden of fighting it in the courts and the legislature.

[3] Machiavelli, *The Prince*.

[4] Jackson had announced in July 1935 the formation of a national committee on rural politics, aimed to help farmers exert a greater influence in national affairs. Little resulted from its work, and by the following year Jackson was lecturing and writing on rural issues.

[5] "vanished without a trace."

No. 593   December 3, 1935   Washington, D.C.

1. No doubt the S.G.[1] is doing his best, but his implements are very inadequate; considering the difficulty of the questions, the quality of the tribunal, and the experience of their adversaries.

2. I suppose you have read in the Dec. 2 U.S. News Davis' story of the Minnesota Fire Damages grab, & David Lawrence's editorial.[2] There

is no escape from such & worse performances (if that was possible) than by putting a stop to the contingent fee business in claims against the Government, be they for activity before Congress, the Departments or the Courts.[3]

And certainly there is no escape otherwise from the continuing degradation of the profession.

[1] The solicitor general was Stanley Reed.

[2] James Cox Davis (1857–1937), an Iowa lawyer who had been counsel to the U.S. Railroad Administration during the war, and later director-general, had written "A Locomotive Spark that Cost $29,000,000," *U.S. News* 3 (2 December 1935): 3. Claims for damages in Minnesota from fires started by trains while they were under the operation of the federal government had supposedly been settled out of court in 1922 for $12,000,000. Now Congress had allowed these and other claims to be reopened, with the government facing the prospect of paying out even more money. In an accompanying editorial, "Without Conscience" (p. 18), David Lawrence had attacked the whole scheme as a fraud upon the American people.

[3] See 21 January 1933.

No. 594   December 15, 1935   Washington, D.C.

1. There is a possibility that the Littauer gift[1] will help the country & the Jews. I wish Mack could get him to do the equivalent for the Hebrew University.

2. How do you account for Arthur Krock's appreciative column in Times of Dec. 13th?[2]

3. Did you notice the news article in Times of Dec. 10th: "Public Antipathy to "Bigness" Found."?[3]

4. I hope F.D. will now appreciate the wisdom of the frozen snake legend.

5. On March 10/36 it will be possible to begin to determine the great increase in profits of business during '35. If proper preparation is made, F.D. can have the figures in hand for June 15th. This should afford great ammunition in many ways.

6. Hope you & Marion will have a good holdiay.

7. I think there were some better briefs from N.Y.C., but Paxton Blair[4] didn't make a very good impression.

8. McClennen won from my brethren most encomiums.[5] Pity the administration couldn't pick him for some great causes.

[1] Lucius Nathan Littauer (1859–1944), the heir to a glove fortune, had served in Congress from upstate New York from 1897 to 1907, and was a close friend of his Harvard classmate, Theodore Roosevelt. In his later years, Littauer devoted his energies and fortune to philanthropy. He had just given two million dollars to Harvard to found a school of public administration.

[2] Arthur Krock (1886–1974) had worked his way up to editor-in-chief of the *Louisville Times* before moving to the *New York Times* in 1927 as its Washington correspondent. He later wrote an influential column for that paper, and thrice won the Pulitzer Prize. Krock, who was not always friendly to the New Deal, devoted his 13 December column to the appreciative remarks made by Cardinal Mundelein of Chicago when Roosevelt visited Notre Dame. Krock not only endorsed the Cardinal's statement, but then went on to praise the New Deal for the good it had done.

[3] The *Times*, at page 37, reported the results of a survey conducted by the General Foods Corporation. The 8,000 respondents evidenced a widespread suspicion of big corporations, and believed they were not good for the country.

[4] Paxton Blair (1892–1974) was a Harvard graduate and a New York lawyer. From 1934 to 1943, he served as head of the appeals division of the Corporation Counsel of New York City.

[5] LDB's former law partner had appeared as counsel for the Raytheon Corporation in its suit for triple damages under the antitrust law against the Radio Corporation of America. *RCA* v. *Raytheon Mfg. Co.*, 296 U.S. 459 (1935).

No. 595   January 18, 1936   Washington, D.C.

1. That's an encouraging report of your talk with F.D. We shall hope Johnson's characterization of you proves true.[1]

2. There is a further story of No. 49,[2] unless Harlan told it.

3. In view of the apprehension expressed by you of the H.U. Hon. degree, I have written Wise that I cannot accept it. To me, American degrees (and the applicable reason for refusing them) seem to make them differ *toto coelo* from one from Palestine, and I thought no one here could fail to see the difference, if he cared enough to think at all about it. But the fact of your apprehension is enough to make me decline. My only reason for willingness to accept was a possibility of a little aid to Palestine development, & you think it might do harm; we must run no risks.[3]

4. Say to Willard Hurst,[4] that he will be expected to be familiar with all my opinions by Sept. 15th and that the pass mark is 99 1/4 percent. The Shulman digest (if it has been kept up to date) may be of aid to him. Also say that he should otherwise familiarize himself with the tools of the trade. One secretary, whom I asked to give me all the cases on a federal jurisdictional statute, spent about a week in the byways, because he did not know that Shepard's Citations[5] contained cases on the statutes. Nor did he know the Shepard pamphlet on popular names of statutes.

5. Asst. A.G. Goldon [sic] Bell[6] had evoked favorable mention from my brethren.

6. England's action on Italian-Ethiop. peace[7] makes me increasingly uneasy about its wisdom in Palestine affairs. The omnia praesumumtur[8] has been rudely shaken.

[1] Probably Hugh Johnson's remark that FF was "the most influential single individual in the United States." See Parrish, *Felix Frankfurter*, 220–21.

[2] *Moor* v. *Texas & New Orlean R.R. Co.*, 297 U.S. 101 (1936) was a *per curiam* decision that avoided a ruling on the Bankhead Cotton Control Act by relying on procedural grounds for dismissal.

[3] LDB had consistently turned down offers of honorary degrees from American universities, but upon the urging of Stephen Wise, had agreed to accept one from the Hebrew University in Jerusalem. In his letter of 16 January, FF argued that acceptance of the Hebrew University degree would insult LDB's many admirers who had worked so hard, often in opposition to the conservative boards of trustees at places such as Yale, in order to secure an offer to LDB only to have him turn them down. The Latin phrase *"toto coelo"* means "by the whole heavens"—directly opposite.

[4] James Willard Hurst (b. 1910) had graduated from Harvard Law in 1935, and then stayed on for a year as a research fellow. He clerked for LDB in the 1936–1937 term, and then began his long and illustrious career at the University of Wisconsin Law School. On 18 March, LDB again wrote regarding Hurst: "Before Hurst makes his plans for the summer, please impress upon him the importance of being "arbeitsfahig" ["fit for work"] when he enters upon his job, and keeping himself fit until the end of the term & that to this job the general 30 day government sick leave does not apply."

[5] Shepard's is one of the most useful legal research tools. Available for all state and federal reporters, it gives the postdecisional history and citations for a case. Shepard tools are also available for legislative histories and legal writings.

[6] Golden Woolfolk Bell (1886–1966), a California attorney, was on the solicitor general's staff from 1933 to 1939; he held other positions in the Roosevelt administration before returning to private practice in 1946.

[7] Unwilling to go to war to back League of Nations sanctions against Italy for its aggression in Ethiopia, Great Britain and France submitted a proposal to Mussolini which included major concessions to Italy. Negotiated by Sir Samuel Hoare and Pierre Laval on 8 December 1935, the English public condemnation was so strong that the Baldwin government barely survived; Hoare was forced to resign as Foreign Minister, to be replaced by Anthony Eden.

[8] "all things presumed [to be done rightly]"

No. 596   February 9, 1936   Washington, D.C.

1. I assume that you have sent F.D. a copy of Wilson's letter to Mrs. Toy.[1]

2. I hope Tom [Corcoran] and Ben [Cohen] have been able to arrange their much needed vacation.[2]

3. I had Tom in last week, and told him, as campaign material

   (a) To get list & total of Al Smith's salaries

   (b) To get copy of the report on business corruption etc. made by the Youth Commission, with Newton D. Baker & Owen Young at its head.

   (c) To note the Metropolitan's report that it now has $4,234,802,511 of assets—gain $203,694,300 in 1935 had $945,087,418 income 1935

4. When, based on the curve to date, I urged Oct. 26, 1915, limi-

tation of the size of insurance companies, the Metropolitan had less than $300,000,000 assets. And the 90 legal reserve companies, in the aggregate, only $2,573,186,639 assets.

5. Whom did you recommend to Conant for Dean?[3]

[1] Not only FF, but several others, including Norman Hapgood, sent the president a copy of the letter Woodrow Wilson had written to Nancy Saunders Toy (Mrs. Crawford Howell Toy) following his 1915 Jackson Day speech. In that talk, Wilson had given full vent to his emotions, and in an unusual occurrence for him, had lit into the Republicans in an angry and partisan manner. In his letter to Mrs. Toy, an old friend whom he had known for more than twenty years, Wilson indicated that he had no regrets; that there was a real fight on, and that at such times it was better to take the gloves off even if some of the usual proprieties were overstepped. FF no doubt saw the letter in Ray Stannard Baker, *Woodrow Wilson: Life and Letters*, 8 vols. (Garden City, N.Y.: Doubleday, Page, and Co., 1927–1939), 5:126–128.

[2] On 17 February, LDB wrote: "Tom and Ben were in yesterday. Both are sorely in need of a prolonged vacation, if they are to serve well the cause. I have rarely seen a man in good health who needed one more than Tom."

[3] Of the Harvard Law School; see 16 July 1936.

No. 597   February 16, 1936   Washington, D.C.

1. You are having deserved & unexpected success with the Public Adm. Committee.

2. F.D.'s letter to C.C. is sound.[1] If he only would not appoint poor judges and lawyers.

3. Wideman[2] is a loss, but Robert Jackson[3] should be very good.

4. Frank Schechter[4] has much ability.

5. The great movement against Federal Courts, high & low, should be diverted from its present objectives and Kunststucke[5] & canalized on reducing the jurisdiction of the District Courts. Not only should the diversity jurisdiction be abolished (except where there is real prejudice which prevents justice in the state courts) but most of other jurisdiction added in 1875 & later should be abrogated and in no case practically should the appellate federal courts have to pass on the construction of state statutes.[6]

[1] C.C. Burlingham had written to the president complaining of the poor quality of men appointed to the federal bench. Roosevelt replied on 6 February agreeing in part with the charge, but also noting how much the established bar influenced these appointments. He promised to appoint better men if people like Burlingham would find worthy nominees. "They must be liberal from belief and not by lip service. They must have an inherent contempt both for the John W. Davises and the Max Steuers. They must know what life in a tenement means. They must have no social ambitions. There is a job for you!"

[2] LDB thought quite highly of Francis James Wideman (1891–1952), a Florida attorney who had served as an assistant attorney general from 1933 to 1936. Later in this year, Wideman would leave the Justice Department to open a practice in Washington.

[3] Robert Houghwout Jackson (1892–1954) had been a special advisor to Roosevelt when the latter was governor of New York. In 1934 he joined the Internal Revenue Service, and in 1938 would become solicitor genral of the United States. In June 1941 Jackson was named to the Supreme Court, filling the vacancy created by the elevation of Harlan Fiske Stone to the chief justiceship. While on the Court Jackson earned a reputation as a thorough-going liberal, but most people probably remember him for his role as chief American prosecutor at the Nuremberg War Crimes trial.

[4] Frank Schechter (1890–1937) was a lawyer who had already written one treatise on trademarks, and was also respected for his knowledge of international law.

[5] "clever tricks."

[6] The 1875 Act had increased significantly the jurisdiction of the federal courts, and the 1914 revision had helped only insofar as it gave the Supreme Court some permissive controls over its docket. LDB and FF both believed that too many suits were in federal courts which properly belonged in state fora.

No. 598   February 26, 1936   Washington, D.C.

1. Here's another forgotten snake.[1] I will send you soon comparative statement of return on investment 1934 (latest year for which figures available) showing comparison of leading companies with S.B.I., and Equitable at the bottom of that short list.

2. I supposed you noticed in yesterday's Times that the 483 James Butler stores will be sold to the individual managers.[2]

3. The Senate did badly in voting to exempt the preferred bank stock held by R.F.C.[3]

Since writing the above, I have yours re contingent fees. Grand.

Did Tom get this?[4]

[1] LDB enclosed a clipping from the *New York Times* of 21 February regarding the annual meeting of the Equitable Life Assurance Society. The company had enjoyed a prosperous 1935, and now had over $6.2 billion of insurance in force. But the president, Thomas I. Parkinson, denounced the federal government for its increased taxation of assets owned by the company, which in turn reduced profits to the shareholders.

[2] The Butler Company had decided upon this way out of bankruptcy. The company would continue to assist the new owners in marketing, wholesale purchasing, and other activities.

[3] Following the Supreme Court's decision that Maryland could tax preferred bank stock held as security by the RFC, legislation was introduced to exempt such stock from taxation. It passed the Senate, but was later rejected by the House.

[4] The clipping in note 1 above.

No. 599   March 31, 1936   Washington, D.C.

1. It will be fine to see you in April.

2. I am glad you could do something for Copey.[1]

3. Your letter to James E. King was wise.[2] Is he able to do any good through the Transcript?

577

4. [*] will find difficulty in answering your second letter. He is of a type that I came to know well in Boston. Intelligent, refined, with a desire to be just, and lack of moral indignation, qualities which, by reason of desired prestige make them the doers of more injustice than fanatics at times.

5. Do you think, as intimated in Ruppurt's letter that the High Commissioner has been acting under orders from home?

6. The Mandatory's attitude and acts since last spring, & events, lead me to think that you and I were wrong in the opinions expressed to Ben Gurion about the Council; and that the Congress opinion was sound.[3] As you know, the Hoare-Laval[4] episode greatly shook my confidence in the Government's wisdom and virtue.

7. Walter Pollak's decision is very regrettable.

8. I am glad jurisdictional limitation is getting attention.[5]

9. It is fine to see the rising on teachers' oaths.[6]

[1] Charles Townsend Copeland (1860–1952) was one of Harvard's greatest teachers. After a brief career as a drama critic, "Copey" joined the English department and taught generations of men how to write well and appreciate literature. There is no evidence of what FF "did" for Copeland.

[2] There is no copy of this letter in the Frankfurter MSS.

[3] The World Jewish Congress, which Stephen S. Wise had organized, had taken a strong stand insisting that Great Britain live up to its obligations.

[4] See 18 January 1936, n. 7.

[5] Nearly a dozen articles appeared in law reviews on problems of federal jurisdiction during 1936, including two in the *Harvard Law Review* and one coauthored by Harry Shulman in *Yale Law Journal* 45 (1936): 393.

[6] New York State, in the Ives Act, required all school teachers in the state to swear an oath of loyalty to the country. Organizations representing both high school and college teachers were then agitating for a bill to repeal the loyalty oath.

No. 600   April 5, 1936   Washington, D.C.

1. I do not recall specific discussion from the brethren of special quality of JWM opinion in the Sugar Case,[1] but his general standing is very good with the Court, particularly so with the C.J.

2. I guess Graustein[2] is not only "mad America," but also otherwise not kosher. I heard 3 years ago that he owed the Chase $3,000,000 & that his loan was grossly undermargined.

3. I am glad to see that Freund & others recognize the dangers in the tax bill.[3] Couldn't it be gently shelved for further study & as a "compromise" get increase of corporate rates in the higher brackets & big companies & high estate taxes—"temporarily?"

4. Charles S. Fairman should be serviceable.

5. Tom [Corcoran] & Ben [Cohen] were in—in good form.

[1] In an antitrust suit against the Sugar Institute, the trade association of the major sugar refiners, Judge Mack, in district court, ruled the Institute guilty of practices violating the Clayton and Sherman laws. But, since the Institute served a useful purpose, it need not be dissolved providing it abandoned those practices found illegal. 15 F. Supp. 817 (1934). The case was appealed, and on 30 March 1936, the Supreme Court, by a seven to zero vote (Sutherland and Stone not participating) affirmed most of Mack's ruling, while modifying a few sections. *Sugar Institute, Inc.* v. *United States*, 297 U.S. 553 (1936).

[2] Perhaps Archibald Robertson Graustein (1885–1969), who had been at Harvard with FF. A lawyer with offices in both Boston and New York, he also had far-flung business interests, and was president of the International Paper Company.

[3] Congress was then debating a tax on corporate undistributed profits, and eventually would pass the bill, which Roosevelt signed into law on 23 June. Opponents of the bill were concerned that it would be too easy for big companies to shift these funds into other categories to escape the tax.

No. 601   May 13, 1936   Washington, D.C.

1. I hope Ed. Berman[1] arranged to have sent you his "Life Insurance—A Critical Examination," which Harpers issues on May 20.[2] It is admirable, & wide circulation would help immensely. Do what you can to get reviews.

2. Would it not be well to have Hurst read, before the Autumn, "Business of USSC," and Charles Warren's "S.C. in U.S. History" so as to get in the background?

3. J.W.M. was in fine shape & did an exceedingly good job on Juvenile Court bill.[3]

[1] Edward Berman (1897–1938) was a professor of economics at the University of Illinois, then serving with the Bureau of Labor Statistics.

[2] Possibly at LDB's suggestion, Berman had expanded the material he had originally published as Bulletin #615, "Massachusetts System of Savings-Bank Insurance," into book form.

[3] New York State had just extended the jurisdiction of domestic relations courts to include all crimes, other than felonies, committed by juveniles.

No. 602   May 23, 1936   Washington, D.C.

1. The N.O. verdict in the lynching case[1] and the Tampa flogging verdict[2] are among America's most encouraging events of recent years. The South should receive honorable mention from Northern publications.

2. That was a fine review of Gannett's.[3] Would your Boston friends dare to say anything?

In April 1936, S.B.I. gained more than 30% writing of ordinary insurance over April 1935; the [private insurance] companies lost in Mass. 17 percent as compared with April 1935.

Couldn't Fortune gain fame by an article on Life Insurance.

[1] A federal jury in New Orleans awarded $2,500 to parents of a lynched Negro boy who had been accused of murdering a white girl. The boy's parents presented evidence that two of the sheriff's deputies were involved and actively assisted the mob.

[2] A jury in Tampa convicted five former policemen of kidnapping three men from a reform Democrat meeting, and turning them over to others for the purpose of flogging.

[3] Frank Ernest Gannett (1876–1957) was the owner of the New York based Gannett newspaper chain; it is impossible to tell to which review LDB was referring.

No. 603   May 26, 1936   Washington, D.C.

Re yours of 25th.

1. An "Acting Dean" [1] is the thing.

2. I am glad you liked 312. [2]

3. And am eager for your comment on McR. on Municipal Bankruptcy. [3]

4. Couldn't your friend on the Springfield Republican be induced to do a piece on the Berman book? [4] It would help much now where we are working to get a [policy] writing bank in the Springfield territory.

The Mass. Mutual Ins. Co., with their principal place of business there, is working hard to prevent our doing so. They are being hard pressed to hold their own in the Commonwealth. At the end of '35 they had $3,362,863 less insurance in force in Mass. than at the beginning.

5. The 47 companies wrote 17 p.c. less ordinary insurance in April '36 in Mass. than in April '35.

Judd Dewey's [5] article in May Harv. Business School Ass'n Bullet. is given 13 pages. [6]

[1] See 16 July 1936.

[2] B. & O. Railroad et al. v. United States, 298 U.S. 349 (1936). The Court, through Justice Butler, held that the I.C.C. had the power to establish geographic divisions and to set discretionary portions of joint rates to be paid to each carrier, but that if the lines thought the rates confiscatory, they could challenge them by judicial proceedings. LDB, joined by Stone, Roberts, and Cardozo, concurred in the result, but objected to the dicta that the lines could challenge duly enacted regulations by going into federal court. Issues of confiscation had to be timely and properly raised before the I.C.C. in its rate hearings, and not elsewhere, in order to ensure the integrity of the administrative rule and rate-making process.

[3] In Ashton v. Cameron County Water Improvement Dist. No. One, 298 U.S. 513, decided the preceding day, McReynolds, speaking for a five-man majority, ruled that federal bankruptcy rules did not apply to counties, since they were no more than administrative agencies of a state, and that federal power could not be extended that far. Cardozo, joined by LDB, Hughes, and Stone, wrote

a strong dissent. The decision was viewed as one more example of the Court's "war" against the New Deal, since the provision had been designed to give relief to localities hard hit by loss of tax revenues in the depression.

[4] See 13 May 1936, n. 2.

[5] Judd Ellsworth Dewey (1884–1961), a Harvard and Harvard Law graduate, had become counsel to Savings Bank Life Insurance after World War One. An active and effective prosletyzer for SBLI, he eventually became deputy commissioner.

[6] "Savings Bank Life Insurance in Massachusetts," *Harvard Business School Bulletin* 12 (May 1936): 160.

No. 604   June 3, 1936   Washington, D.C.

1. Yes, W.L. is clearly aiming at you. I suppose he thinks he is disinterested.[1]

2. I hope Harlan will not wholly suppress apologia pro sua vita on the occasion.[2]

3. That's interesting correspondence with Stimson.[3]

4. I am glad Francis Shea is taking up the Buffalo job.[4] I have seen Louis Jaffe[5] recently & think he has found himself, and will be much better at teaching than he was as secretary. I.a., his health seems good now.

5. Ormsby-Gore ought to exhibit all the wisdom that has recently been lacking.[6] Ben Gurion[7] and Shertok[8] are fine.

Hope to see you tomorrow & Saturday P.M.

[1] Lippmann had chaired a committee of Harvard alumni appointed to investigate problems in the economics department. The committee defended the academic freedom of the faculty, declaring that economists did not have to hue to a conservative or accepted mode of analysis. But, in what LDB and FF took as a swipe at FF, the committee also urged that only persons committed to teaching should be appointed to the faculty, and not those who spend most of their time on "outside activities."

[2] Stone had agreed to take part in a discussion of the future of the common law with jurists from Great Britain, Canada, and Australia as part of Harvard's tercentenary celebration. FF advised Stone not to bother with details or even prognoses, but, drawing upon his forty years' experience, to give a "powerful and philosophic stream of reflection regarding the underlying attitudes and procedures . . . in formulating and adopting" the law for a dynamic society. The speech was published as "The Common Law in the United States," *Harvard Law Review* 50 (1936): 4.

[3] Stimson had written a book on the Japan-Manchuria issue, and had asked FF to read and comment on the manuscript. FF had been full of praise, and suggested that Stimson publish it as soon as possible. It appeared as *The Far Eastern Crisis: Recollections and Observations* (New York: Harper and Bros., 1936).

[4] Francis Michael Shea (b. 1905), a former student of FF's, had entered government service with the AAA in 1933, after which he went to the Securities and Exchange Commission. In 1936 he became dean of the University of Buffalo Law School, but reentered government work as an assistant attorney general in 1941.

[5] Louis Levinthal Jaffe (b. 1905) had clerked for LDB during the 1933 term. In 1936 he accepted a professorship at the University of Buffalo Law School, where he taught until 1950, when he went to Harvard law as professor of administrative law.

[6] A few days earlier, Ormsby-Gore had been named by Stanley Baldwin to be secretary of state for the colonies. On 19 June, speaking to Commons on the recent riots in Palestine which left 84 dead and 611 injured, he declared that lawlessness must cease and Arab-Jewish understanding promoted; but he also insisted that the government would enforce the law and maintain order.

[7] David Ben-Gurion (1886–1973) had emigrated from Russia to Palestine while a youth, and during his lifetime built up the Histadrut (the general labor federation), the Labor Zionist party, and became one of the chief architects of the State of Israel, of which he served as the first prime minister. Ben-Gurion was one of LDB's favorite Palestinians, not only because he had emerged as the chief opponent of Chaim Weizmann within the Zionist Organization, but because his philosophy of building up the *Yishuv* fit in with LDB's own practical plans. On several occasions, LDB helped finance some of Ben-Gurion's plans, including the secret purchase of arms for the Haganah as well as the purchase of land in the southern Negev which ultimately became the site of the port city of Eilat.

[8] Moshe Shertok (later Sharett) (1894–1965), an editor of *Davar* and a leader of the Palestinian Labor party, was by 1936 the second most influential Jew in Palestine and Ben-Gurion's chief associate. He served as Israel's first foreign minister from 1948 to 1956, and from 1953 to 1955 also was the nation's prime minister.

No. 605 July 16, 1936 Chatham, Mass.

Only a word to say how relieved I was by yours of 7th and Wise's of 9th enclosing copy of O.G. of 6th.[1]

I am still awaiting SSW's which he expected to send on the 8th.

Every postponement by the Government of unwise action is a gain. Fears may be allayed & we have time to educate the unknowing.[2]

Yes, Eddie Morgan[3] was a happy solution. And Conant's slap at the Lippmann Com'tee (what a com'tee) report good.

[1] Wise had met with Ormsby-Gore in London on 8 July to discuss British policy toward Palestine, and had been assured that Britain would retain an open mind in the matter, and would be sensitive to world opinion in any policy which might adversely affect the *Yishuv*. Wise, while noting that the colonial secretary was open and friendly, felt he was nonetheless totally "under the dominance of underlings, relentlessly pursuing their [pro-Arab] policy."

[2] See next letter.

[3] Following Roscoe Pound's resignation as dean of the Harvard Law School, President Conant named Edmund M. Morgan as acting dean until a permanent appointment could be made. Morgan would again serve as acting dean during World War Two when James Landis went to Washington on government service.

No. 606 July 19, 1936 Chatham, Mass.

1. The persistent suggestion in the British press that immigration should be suspended is disturbing,[1] despite O.-G.'s letter of 6th.

2. Much of which we complain may be explained by the prevalence of fear and the resultant policy of "scuttle." But even fear does not explain the pecuniary unfairness toward the Palestinian Jews.

(a) Surely the Mandatory which undertook to preserve order and prohibited Jews from defending themselves ought to have been quick in providing compensation for property of Jews destroyed and also compensation for death and injuries to person. Moreover, to have done so would have tended to suppress the ardor of rioting Arabs.

(b) The Mandatory should not hold back in paying for the keep of refugees from violence, particularly when they left their homes under order of evacuation.

(c) The Mandatory should not exact from the Jews any part of the cost of the Jewish constable or police force made necessary by the Arab rioters.

When it is considered that the greater part of all taxes paid, and, indeed, the whole of the large surplus are due to the Jews, such action on the part of the Mandatory is very unworthy—is, indeed, "schmutzig."[2] Certainly the Govt must know that the Jews who have peopled Palestine are not "rich."

2. [sic] This unfairness is not a new manifestation. It is a continuation & accentuation of a past policy of unfairness manifested in many ways (and involving i.a. departure from the duties prescribed by the Mandate). It was manifested throughout long years:

(a) In not letting the Jews have the State lands (e.g. [*]).

(b) In denying to Jews their fair share of allowances for schools and for public health services.

(c) In denying to Jews their fair share of employment in the many government services and construction jobs.

(d) In denying to Jews their fair share in the Transjordan and police.

Now that we have O.-G. as Colonial Secretary, can't something be done, to secure fair treatment hereafter, and to inaugurate change before the hearings of the Royal Commission begin?

Such a policy of fairness inaugurated in London might go some way in overcoming the hostility of attitude exhibited by local subordinate officials.

Read Ben Gurion's address at convention of Palestine Labor Party in 1931 ("Planning Zionist Policy") reprinted in "Jews & Arabs in Palestine" issued by Hechalutz Press N.Y.C. 1936.

[1] The rumors had solid basis in fact, since the British government was planning to limit immigration following the Arab riots. Alert to the danger, Stephen Wise journeyed to Hyde Park to plead

with Roosevelt to intercede on behalf of the Zionists, and the president informed the British that he hoped they would not close Palestine to further Jewish settlement. For a variety of reasons, the British decided to heed the American request, and no further limitations were placed on Jewish immigration until the 1939 White Paper.

    [2] "dirty."

No. 607   August 20, 1936   Chatham, Mass.

1. It was good to see you, although the more detailed news increased my disquietude about the British. You clearly did all that was possible by talks to officials in England.

2. I wrote Bob [Szold] yesterday that in view of your advice, the project of presenting the American case before the Commission [1] must be abandoned, but that preparation of the case for other purposes should go forward for use in America under your advice. [2] I assume you will, in due time, prepare & send such communication as you think should go to Ormsby Gore, and give directions as to publicity in America.

3. After my letter to Bob was mailed I received one from Brodie enclosing memo & cable from the Tel Aviv office of Am. Econ. Com'tee which indicates that the Weizmann(-Wise) request for its & Brodie's cooperation was sent without communication with Weizmann's Palestine associates; that they do not want our help in preparation; & resented the proposal. Brodie has cabled the Tel Aviv office to do nothing except compile data as to American investments, which I interpret as limiting the work in Palestine to intra-office work, so as not excite Palestinian jealousies etc. [3]

4. Dwight MacDonald [sic] [4] did an excellent job on Part IV proposed. [5] I don't wonder that U.S. Steel kicked. How much of it was printed? What do you know of him?

5. Lilienthal's report is saddening. I am not surprised at what he says of A. E. M[organ].'s condition. [6]
As I told you in Washington, there was something not normal in his look.

6. The Steel and T.V.A. papers go to you under another cover.

7. I suppose you have read, since I saw you, the recent Palcor reports. That received yesterday shows that none of the atrocities has aroused Jews and British as much as the killing of the nurses; [7] and that Government is taking some resolute action. Particularly comforting is the grant of additional Jewish Guards, complying with the request made long ago that their number be 2500 in addition to the 400 in the service prior to

the outbreak.[8] And, apparently, there is an assurance that the Tel Aviv harbor may be fully developed.

8. Of course, I should be glad to see Lilienthal & should suppose that amidst the plenitude of autos, one could be put at his service. Have seen Morris Leeds twice. No mention was made of A. E. M[organ].

[1] Following the Arab riots, His Majesty's government appointed the Peel Commission to look into causes of the disturbances, and to recommend future policy in Palestine.

[2] The various American Zionist bodies prepared a *Memorandum Submitted to the Palestine Royal Commission on American Interests in the Administration of the Palestine Mandate*. The ability of all the competing organizations to work together was an indication that they recognized the seriousness of the situation in Palestine.

[3] The Zionist movement remained plagued by the internecine tensions between the various factions, with the Weizmann group still in control of the WZO, fearful of both the American leadership as well as the militant Palestinians led by Ben-Gurion and Shertok.

[4] Dwight Macdonald (1906–1982), a staff member on *Fortune*, wrote widely for a number of liberal journals. He would later be a visiting professor at a number of colleges, and wrote several books on history, popular culture, and literature.

[5] Macdonald had written a series of articles on "Steelmasters: The Big Four." The last, dealing with the U.S. Steel Corporation, appeared in the 29 August 1936 issue of *The Nation*.

[6] Arthur E. Morgan had become increasingly alienated from the more moderate philosophy advocated by his codirectors on the TVA. He had also come under public criticism for his urging what amounted to a loyalty oath on TVA employees.

[7] On 17 August, two Hadassah nurses had been killed by snipers in Jaffa; the following day, over 50,000 Jewish residents of Tel Aviv attended their funeral. Later in the day, violence erupted, despite a British curfew, in which several Arabs were killed and wounded.

[8] Despite the Zionists' concern that the British would close Palestine, they did applaud England's firm stand regarding the maintenance of law and order in Palestine. More than 20,000 troops were sent in to quell the disturbances, and to head off a threatened Arab general strike. Moreover, recognizing that the Jews had acted only in self-defense, the Mandatory permitted an enlargement of Jewish police units to help defend the settlements.

No. 608   September 20, 1936   Washington, D.C.

1. Yes, it must be a great relief to have the celebration[1] over, and the distinguished visitors leaving, with a returning opportunity of tending to one's knitting.

2. We like much your Sir Horace.

3. It's fine that the German universities were unrepresented. Is there anything more to the story?

4. This came to me from a trustworthy source: A salaried employee of the Crane Co. found $10 deducted from his salary check, with a notation that the company is sure every employee will be glad to contribute to the Landon[2] fund. I should think that action would make F.D. votes, largely with silent acquiescence. The Co. must have branches in nearly every state.

5. Enclosed on union action may interest you.

6. Such newpaper friends as I have seen think that it looks strongly F.D., but I have found some officials with doubts.

7. J.W.M. must have been very sorry to miss the show.

8. I have been reading with much interest Ambassador Dodd's Woodrow Wilson, writing [sic] in 1920, slightly revised in 1932.[3]

[1] Of Harvard University's 300th anniversary.

[2] Alfred Mossman Landon (1887–1987), a Kansas businessman, had served as governor of that state from 1933 to 1937, and compiled a respectable, moderately progressive record, leading the Republicans to name him as their presidential candidate in 1936.

[3] William E. Dodd, ed., *Woodrow Wilson and His Work* (Garden City: Doubleday, Page, and Co., 1920, rev. ed. 1932).

No. 609   September 29, 1936   Washington, D.C.

1. Thanks for the Times which has been returned.

2. I am glad Zemurray is spreading the faith.

3. Hartley's paper shows an extraordinary wide sweep of "rationalization."[1] I guess it will act as a sort of composition in bankruptcy, unless there is socialism, i.e., Government ownership of these businesses. We shall see "ritornare al segne."[2]

4. Life should be easier with R.P. retired. C.C.B. says that Conant is for reducing numbers.

5. The turn of the [St. Louis] Post-Dispatch to Landon must give our friends on the paper pain. I was not surprised as I had heard of Pulitzer's[3] regrets at reports he got of F.D.'s chances being very, very good.

6. Yes, the French money situation was handled finely.[4] Who did it? I hope Blum[5] will not be shaken off.

7. What was Bikle doing in Cambridge?

8. We were very glad to hear of your visit to Auntie B.

9. Voters are so far from the homo sapiens of which men tell that one cannot help having anxiety.

[1] Sir Harold Hartley was then in Washington at a meeting called to discuss the economic and social problems involved in the production, distribution, and utilization of power. In his talk, Hartley stressed that the mechanical aspects of power production and distribution had far outrun man's efforts to deal with the social issues involved.

[2] "A return to the mark."

[3] Joseph Pulitzer (1885–1955) headed the Pulitzer newspaper chain, which his father had founded. The *St. Louis Post-Dispatch* was the flagship of the group.

[4] The French financial crisis resulted from a large national debt and massive budget deficits caused by rearmament, loans to Poland, and other expenditures. That week the French had devalued the franc, but had included provisions to protect holders of particular securities from being adversely affected.

[5] Leon Blum (1872–1950), French author and socialist politician, had recently been named premier, a position he would hold again in 1938.

No. 610   October 4, 1936   Washington, D.C.

Re yours 30th.

1. I do not feel sure of G.H.M.[1] But I should be disposed to take a chance in an appropriate case or matter. He has much to contribute, considerable ability, knowledge arising from acting for important industrialists and he sees. He is not prepared to cut the life line, but he could, as he has an ample fortune and no child. He thinks he can achieve more by not doing so. If he takes the plunge and finds he cannot, he may be prepared to go the whole way. "Only the event will teach us in its hour."[2] It might be well to get him an occasion where he will be called upon to speak out clearly & see whether he is willing to commit himself.

2. I suppose you noticed the clear-headed talk of Hecht (former president of Banks Ass'n?).[3] He had none too good a record. I guess his seeing must be due to his being a Jew & having lived abroad before he came here.

3. I don't wonder at Lothian's concern. Britain's performance continues to be amazingly bad. Most disturbing to me is the trend of leaders to Facism [sic]. Nothing could be worse than their allowing Portugal to be a tool of the fascists. I suppose you saw Dodd Jr's testimony.[4] For two centuries Portugal has obeyed British behest.

4. Conant talked well on freedom of speech & research politically & economical.[5] The interesting enclosed on [*] I return.

5. It is good to have the reports from Shea and Jaffe.

6. How do you explain Wauchope's gift of land to the Effendi?[6] (Palestine Sept. 22)

The birth control discussions particularly interesting.

[1] Perhaps Gilbert Holland Montague.

[2] A variation of Erasmus, *Adagia* (1523), "The event itself will show."

[3] Rudolph S. Hecht (1885–1956) had emigrated from Germany in 1903, and worked his way up to become head of the Hiberian National Bank in New Orleans, as well as running his own investment banking firm. In 1934–1935 he had served as president of the American Bankers Association. In a speech to that group on 21 September, Hecht had urged businessmen to accept moderate change so as to avoid the revolutionary upheavals then shaking Europe.

[4] William E. Dodd, Jr., son of the American ambassador to Germany, had testified on 1 October before an unofficial Labour party commission as to the extent the dictatorships were interfering in the Spanish Civil War. Much of the activity, he asserted, consisted of arms to the Franco forces being openly funnelled through Portugal.

[5] In a speech at the Harvard tercentenary celebration, Conant called for "a spirit of tolerance which allows the expression of all opinions, however heretical they may appear." Without specifi-

cally mentioning Nazi Germany, he decried the anti-intellectualism and anarchy sweeping the world. The text is in the *New York Times*, 19 May 1936.

[6] Sir Arthur Grenfell Wauchope (1874–1947), a career soldier, served as British high commissioner for Palestine from 1931 to 1938. During his term, the *Yishuv* increased in population and prospered thanks to his liberal interpretation of the immigration rules. He tried to reconcile Arab and Jewish interests, and his gift of land to some Arab chieftains was part of his policy of encouraging economic development.

No. 611　　　　　　October 25, 1936　　　　Washington, D.C.

Confidential

1. You may not have heard (because Mrs. Stone has striven to silence the press) that Harlan has been seriously ill for over 10 days with (? acute vascular) dysentary, with high fever, day & night nurses, etc. There is little prospect of his resuming his court work before December; and we shall be fortunate if we get him as early as that. We miss him very, very much.

2. Senator Copeland was in Tuesday to tell me about Palestine. On leaving he said: "I think Landon will be elected."!

3. I wired you yesterday to tell Agronsky[1] that I could see him Tuesday at 3 P.M. What comes to me from New York, recounting his & others' statements is very disquieting. I feel strongly that we must be resolute and yield nothing.[2] Whatever limitations are imposed upon us must be without our consent. I am deeply impressed with the errors made in 1920–1922 in acquiescing then in the curtailment of rights promised by the Balfour Declaration.[3]

4. Sharfman was in today with Morris Cohen.

5. That's a nice letter of John Gans.[4]

[1] Gershon Argonsky (later Agron) (1894–1959) had moved to Palestine after the First World War. In 1932 he founded the *Palestine Post* (later the *Jerusalem Post*), which as the only English-language daily, became a major and influential source of news about Palestine and later Israel to the western world. He served as mayor of Jerusalem from 1955 until his death.

[2] Rumors were already flying that the Peel Commission would recommend partition of Palestine, as well as severe limits on Jewish immigration. Some Zionists were willing to accept a partitioned Palestine, believing that even a truncated Palestine could serve as the core of a Jewish state. LDB, and American Zionists in general, were firmly opposed to giving up anything, and demanded that Great Britain live up to the full terms of the mandate.

[3] In an effort to appease Arab clients, the British government, acting through Colonial Secretary Winston Churchill, had issued a White Paper in 1922 explaining that the Balfour Declaration had never meant the imposition of Jewish nationalism upon Palestine as a whole. In addition, all that part of Palestine east of the Jordan River was detached, and a provisional government under Emir Abdullah, the head of the Hashemite clan, took control.

[4] Possibly John Gans (1892–1974), head of the Gans Steamship Lines; there is no letter from Gans in the FF Papers.

No. 612   November 4, 1936   Washington, D.C.

1. The job was thoroughly done.[1] Tom [Corcoran] and Ben [Cohen] must be happy.[2] We may hardly expect that the Republicans will learn anything. Our task must be to make sure that F.D. does not forget.

2. Harlan seems a little better, but appears to be in for a long pull. We shall miss him very much.

3. F.D. should be of much help re Palestine, i.a.

4. Is there any likelihood of his summoning you soon?

I am eager for the details on Mass. election.

[1] In the presidential election the preceding day, Roosevelt had buried Landon, 27.8 million votes to 16.7 million, and had carried all but two states in the most sweeping victory since that of James Monroe. In addition, the Democrats easily won complete control of both houses of Congress.

[2] However, see next letter.

No. 613   November 5, 1936   Washington, D.C.

1. Tom & Ben were in yesterday, not exultant. The Driscoll defeat they deemed ominous.[1] And they were much concerned lest evil influences exerted on F.D. would rob us of the fruits of victory. The [*] adventure Tom thought particularly dangerous.

2. That's a beaut of letter from William Allen White.[2] He should be promptly secured for the Progressive wing. He belongs with the Norris [and] La Follettes. Can't David Niles bring him in now.

3. Dilliard[3] is always to be relied upon. I should think the attacks on you would now be dropped by the vested interests, as not being good policy, in view of the election. But I guess all of us must expect intensified anti-Semitic attacks as long as Hitler is in power, and for some time after his fall.

4. That Star-Times paper must have given added pain to our friends on Post-Dispatch. Perhaps Pulitzer will quietly repent.

5. The Evarts letter is interesting.[4] Ernest Hopkins was once a hope. He really ought to know better.

6. Tell me about Harris Steinberg.[5] Is he a man we ought to ask in.

7. Curley's defeat must be a great relief to our Mass. friends, but what a fall to be represented by a name, a mockery of past "greatness."[6] I hope F.D. won't be led into rehabilitating Curley.

8. Indeed, I read the Shertok application for visas. It is difficult to believe that the grant of 1800 is an honest estimate of the absorptive capacity.[7] But it gives the Arab chiefs "pain," and it is something to

have that overt evidence that there will be no suspension pending the Commission enquiry.

The determination of "absorptive capacity" is one of fact, not of policy. Aren't the British slipping as much in moral judgments as in intellectual statesmanship?

9. Harlan has been somewhat better for the last 3 days, with normal temperature today.[8]

10. Both Chandler[9] and Coudert[10] made fair arguments.

11. Brien McMahon[11] (a nice looking fellow) did not do the Department credit in the Wood case.[12]

12. Arnold[13] did pretty well in his first (and only) case.[14] Tell me about him.

13. Yes, to get Norris again is an important achievement.[15]

---

[1] Denis J. Driscoll, who had opposed the power companies in the debate over the death sentence clause (see 19 July 1935), had been defeated for reelection from his Pennsylvania House district.

[2] White had written an affectionate letter to FF on 31 October, enclosing a copy of *What It's All About: A Reporter's Story of the Early Campaign of 1936* (New York, 1936). Although Landon had invited him to be in the campaign, he had refused, because he saw that the real powers in the party were still the old guard conservatives. He ended with: "This is all confidential between two American citizens who, if they had been nearer each other during the years, would have been dear friends, I think."

[3] Irving Dilliard (b. 1904) was a longtime reporter and editorial writer for the *St. Louis Post-Dispatch*. He edited *Mr. Justice Brandeis, Great American* (St. Louis: Modern View Press, 1941), as well as books on Hugo Black and Learned Hand.

[4] Jeremiah M. Evarts, a lawyer with the city of New York, had written FF on 30 October that nothing in Landon's campaign had convinced him to change his support for Roosevelt.

[5] Harris B. Steinberg (1912–1969) had just graduated from Harvard law, and had become a special assistant to Thomas E. Dewey, who was then beginning his investigation of crime and racketeering in New York. Steinberg later gained renown as a defense attorney as well as an ardent advocate of civil liberties.

[6] In a race for the United States Senate, Governor James M. Curley had been defeated by the scion of one of Massachusetts' first families, Henry Cabot Lodge, Jr., (1902–1985) by a margin of more than 142,000 votes. Lodge remained in the Senate until 1952, was ambassador to the United Nations in the 1950s, and ran for vice president in 1960.

[7] The term "absorptive capacity" became a focus of much strife between the Zionists and the mandatory government in the late 1930s. The term had first been used in the Hope-Simpson Report of 1930, which claimed that all of the useful arable land in Palestine was now filled, and therefore Palestine could no longer absorb new settlers. The Zionists bitterly attacked the report, because Hope-Simpson had completely ignored the *Yishuv's* record in taking allegedly waste land and converting it to agriculture. The British attempted to manipulate the phrase, as LDB suggests, as a policy strategem to limit immigration, while the Zionists tried to convince the mandatory that so long as reclaimable land remained, more settlers could be absorbed.

[8] See 25 October 1936.

[9] Porter Ralph Chandler (1899–1979) practiced law in New York; he was a member of the city's Board of Education from 1952 to 1970, and president from 1966 to 1969.

[10] Frederic Rene Coudert (1871–1955), a New York attorney, was a specialist in international law, and wrote a number of volumes on the subject. Together with Chandler, he had argued

successfully in *Valentine* v. *United States ex rel. Neidecker*, 299 U.S. 5 (1936). Neidecker was fighting extradition from the United States to France, and the Court sustained his argument that extradition can only take place as a result of congressional approval of a treaty, and not through administrative discretion. Since the extradition treaty with France of 1909 exempted citizens of each other's countries, no extradition could take place.

[11] James O'Brien McMahon (1903–1952), then a special assistant to the attorney general, was a U.S. senator from Connecticut from 1945 to his death, and the author of the McMahon Act for the control of atomic energy.

[12] Despite McMahon's argument, the Court, by vote of five to three, with LDB in the majority, sustained the government's contention that the mere fact of being a current or former employee of the government did not disqualify jurors from sitting in a criminal case involving the theft of government property. *United States* v. *Wood*, 299 U.S. 123 (1936).

[13] Thurman Wesley Arnold (1891–1969) was typical of many young lawyers who went to Washington during the New Deal to "do good" and stayed on to "do well." After teaching at Yale Law School, he took over the antitrust division of the Justice Department, and revivified it in a number of major cases against large corporations. Much of his philosophy during this period (with which LDB agreed) can be found in his important book, *The Folklore of Capitalism* (New Haven: Yale University Press, 1937). From 1943 to 1945 he sat on the U.S. Circuit Court of Appeals for the District of Columbia, and then opened one of Washington's most infuential law firms, Arnold, Fortas & Porter.

[14] Arnold had argued *Helvering* v. *Illinois Life Insurance* Co., 299 U.S. 88 (1936) on 16 October. The Court upheld a seventh circuit ruling that certain reserves of the company were not subject to income taxation.

[15] In the election, veteran liberal George W. Norris of Nebraska had survived the Roosevelt landslide, even though he was a Republican, and was returned for an unprecedented fifth term in the Senate. Norris, now seventy-five, had actively campaigned for Roosevelt.

No. 614   December 12, 1936   Washington, D.C.

1. The abdication is a great relief. And the internment was a good British job. The gent will soon be sorry.[1]

2. Hurst will send you the journal slips.[2] Let him know in what batches you want them sent.

3. Harlan is making good progress. Sat up 1 1/2 hours yesterday.

4. Can't your friends do something now to limit diverse citizenship litigation?

5. Surely the jurisdictional amount should be raised.

6. And can't something be done to curb—cut down—the immunity from federal and state taxation resulting from Fed. & state instrumentalities; with growing Governmental functions, these exemptions are monstrous.

7. Wyzanski did an excellent job in the Seminole case.[3]

8. And the S.G. made a very good argument in the Holyoke W. P. Co.[4] case, much his best performance.

Carl Wheat did well.

[1] On 10 December, Edward Albert Christian George Andrew Patrick David, King Edward VIII (1894–1972), later the Duke of Windsor, abdicated the throne of England so he could marry the woman he loved, an American divorcee, Wallis Warfield Spencer Simpson (1896–1987).

[2] The journal slips were the daily calendar of the Court, and included notations not only of published opinions, but of the memorandum and *per curiam* decisions, as well as a listing of which petitions for error and *certiorari* had been accepted or denied by the Court.

[3] *United States* v. *The Seminole Nation*, 299 U.S. 417 (1937), had been argued before the Court on 10 December 1936. An act of 1924 had given the court of claims all jurisdiction for suits between the government and the Seminole Indians, and had also placed a five-year limit, later extended, on the bringing of certain types of suits. The Seminoles brought suit and sought to include additional claims by amending their complaint. The Court held that these claims were barred.

[4] *Holyoke Water Power Co.* v. *American Writing Paper Co.*, 300 U.S. 324 (1937), had been argued the previous day. A contract between the two companies had called for an annual payment in gold, which was now forbidden by the New Deal's monetary legislation. Over dissent by the four conservatives, the Court held that the contract could be discharged by payment in dollars of the nominal amount. Solicitor General Reed appeared for the Government as amicus.

No. 615   January 19, 1937   Washington, D.C.

1. I suppose Tom [Corcoran] told you what Landis told him about my advice as to Deanship, and Landis' comment.[1]

2. I note from N.Y. Times H.L.S. efforts to reduce numbers. That should help applications to the smaller schools. I trust you will find an appropriate berth for Willard Hurst, lest he be deflected from teaching.[2]

3. Yes Max appears to be doing an excellent job.

4. I hope you will find, someday, a man with the necessary literary talent, i.a., to tell the New Haven story, as well as Max did "The Investor Pays."[3] Mahaffie's[4] data & the reorganization will furnish the necessary material for "Thirty Years After."[5]

5. Who was the man (Steinfelt of ?) whose letter you sent me (about his being lodged here) & who you thought we should invite in on Sunday?

6. Your avenues of publicity should take note of J.F. McElwain's statement. Enclosed is from Wall St. Journal.

7. I enclose latest reports of Wisconsin Act, which also should receive publicity.

[1] FF had written to Landis on 5 January: "Dear Jim: You are aware of my strong belief in candor between friends, and so I have to tell you that I was not one of those who urged your appointment as Dean. . . . I told Conant [that], but the wisdom of others overruled me. . . . But you also know what the School means to me, and how deeply I care for your welfare. No one can possibly wish more eagerly for the School and for you the kind of Deanship which James Barr Ames gave the School. A greater wish my heart could hold for no one." A few days later Landis replied, thanking FF for the note, and informing him that he had also told Conant that he thought himself unqualified.

[2] After completing his year as LDB's clerk, Hurst began his long and distinguished career at the University of Wisconsin Law School.

[3] See 14 July 1928, n. 1.

[4] Charles Delahunt Mahaffie (1884–1969) had served as director of finance for the I.C.C. in the twenties; he was appointed to the Commission in 1930, and remained there until his retirement in 1954, when he entered private practice.

[5] The New Haven story, from a Brandeisian view, was ultimately told by Alpheus T. Mason and Henry Lee Staples, *The Fall of a Railroad Empire: Brandeis and the New Haven Merger Battle* (Syracuse: Syracuse University Press, 1947); for a different point of view, see Richard M. Abrams, "Brandeis and the New Haven-Boston & Maine Merger Battle Revisited," *Business History Review* 36 (1962): 408.

No. 616   February 5, 1937   Washington, D.C.

1. Nathan Claytor sounds promising. L.H.'s letter ret'd herewith. Is he a son of D.C. Municipal judge? [1]

2. Whom did F.D. rely on for his Judiciary Message & bill? [2] Has he consulted you on any of his matters of late? [3]

3. It looks as if he were inviting some pretty radical splits in the Democratic Party & allies.

4. I hope you got from Elizabeth Bob Leach's [4] letter of Jan. 30th which shows a fine record of what can be done under the Wisconsin law for regularization [of employment].

[1] LDB probably meant William Graham Claytor, Jr. (b. 1912), who was clerking that year with Learned Hand, and who would be LDB's secretary for the October 1937 term. Claytor later joined the Washington law firm of Covington & Burling. He was the son of an electrical engineer.

[2] FDR had grown increasingly frustrated over the Supreme Court's invalidation of one New Deal law after another. Following his landslide election in 1936, Roosevelt believed that he had a mandate from the people to act, and that some way would have to be found to circumvent, or at least neutralize, the Cout's opposition.

On this day, Roosevelt sent a message to Congress ostensibly dealing with alleged delays in the federal courts, which he blamed on infirmity among the judges caused by old age. For each federal judge over 70 who had been on the bench for ten or more years, and who did not elect to retire, the president, according to the proposal, would appoint a new judge to aid in the work. He could appoint no more than six new justices to the Supreme Court, and forty-four judges to lower federal courts. The president's claim that he was only acting in the interest of efficiency fooled no one, and immediate opposition developed in both parties against "packing" the Court. The debate, often bitter, dragged on in Congress for 168 days until Roosevelt finally admitted defeat. Roosevelt's message can be found in his *Public Papers*, 6:51–66.

[3] Roosevelt, aware of FF's close ties to LDB, had not consulted him, but on 15 January had written to him: "Very confidentially, I may give you an awful shock in about two weeks. Even if you do not agree, suspend final judgment and I will tell you the story." FF, torn between loyalties to both men, walked a tightrope for the next five months. One result appears to have been a definite cooling of relations between LDB and FF.

[4] Robert Franklin Leach, after graduating from Harvard Law in 1934, practiced law in Minneapolis.

No. 617   March 15, 1937   Washington, D.C.

1. "The American Dream." I am convinced that a worthy democracy is impossible unless we (a) break up the big concerns. (b) secure regularization of employment, and (3) [sic] develop a cooperative enterprise.

2. Yes, Ben Gurion is fine in his presentation, & he appears to have in E. Kaplan [1] a worthy finance aid.

3. I am very glad you sent Loring Christie's letter, [2] which is really significant, & shows him a much abler thinker than I had realized.

[1] Eliezer Kaplan (1891–1952), a Russian–born and trained engineer, had settled in Palestine in 1923, where he soon became a leader of the Histadrut. In 1948 he became the first minister of finance for the new State of Israel.

[2] Christie had written on 7 March to FF, and among other things, noted that he was drafting an "address by Parliament to the King to be read by the P.M. at the Coronation. The problem is to imbed in the bilge a few words to show that Parliament has its own ideas about the meaning of the public oath George VI is going to mumble to the Archbishop—i.e., meaty enough but not too raw to upset tender stomachs."

No. 618   March 29, 1937   Washington, D.C.

Overruling Adkins' Case must give you some satisfaction. [1]
It was Dec. 16–17/14 that I argued Stettler-O'Hara. [2]

[1] On this day, the Supreme Court, by a five-to-four vote, had sustained the constitutionality of Washington's minimum wage law in *West Coast Hotel* v. *Parrish*, 300 U.S. 379, specifically overruling *Adkins* v. *Childrens' Hospital*, 261 U.S. 525 (1923), in which FF had been counsel for the Consumers' League in defense of a similar federal statute. Two days later FF responded: "It is characteristically kind of you to think of the aspects of the Washington minimum wage case that would give me some satisfaction, but, unhappily, it is one of life's bitter-sweets and the bitter far outweighs the sweet."

[2] *Stettler* v. *O'Hara*, 243 U.S. 629 (1917) had tested an Oregon minimum wage law. LDB had been retained as counsel, but had then been nominated to the Court, and FF took over the role. Because of his previous connection with the case, LDB had recused himself, and a divided Court had allowed the favorable lower court ruling to stand, a decision which did not settle the constitutional issue. Six years later the Court handed down *Adkins*. LDB's chronology is correct; he did argue the case in December 1914; the unusually long time the Court took to hand down a decision indicates that its members could not resolve the issue, finally consenting to let the lower court ruling stand.

No. 619   April 5, 1937   Washington, D.C.

1. Ethel Moors was in and told Alice that Marion was much worn by her stay West. We hope she has regained her calm and strength.

2. Yes, deHaas had a record of absolute devotion to the cause. No one can know that better than I. In the early years, I was utterly ignorant of men & things. He had had many experiences of many matters. I

cannot recall a single instance in which he allowed his personal views to affect his advice to me on Zionist matters—an extraordinary record for a teacher. I was much pained by his defection to Jabo & our inability to work out a plan for cooperation with him.[1]

3. Harold [Laski] had a rare triumph here. Hague, the manager and Mrs. Kellogg (Mrs. Cutting's close friend) chanced to be in the Sunday after; & reported details.[2] I judge Mrs. K. thought that the initial lecture by LaGuardia et al. had not been worthy.

4. The fight for minimum wage really began 30 years ago with Muller v. Oregon. I reserve comments on what you say until there is chance for a talk, saying now only that you are laboring under some misapprehensions.[3]

5. Ben and Mims [Flexner] are due here tomorrow on their return from the reduced University of Louisville Centennial celebration.

6. The victories are an amazing manifestation of Spring after a long winter.

8. [sic] I have told Joshua Leibner[4] when he goes to Boston to make sure of seeing you and Marion. He is here for the American kibbutz,[5] a most engaging young fellow.

[1] Jacob deHaas had died of cancer on 21 March. To the chargrin of LDB, deHaas had, at the end, cast his lot with Jabotinsky, whom he had extolled in the same terms he had once reserved for Herzl and LDB.

[2] Laski had delivered the Bronson Cutting Memorial Lecture in Washington, D.C.

[3] On April 1, FF had written deploring the battle then being waged against the Court, but noted that many of the Court's reactionary decisions had provoked the fight. He tried to excuse Roosevelt's own role in the affair, blaming the plan on poor advice from his counselors. See previous letter, n. 1.

[4] Joshua Leibner (b. 1910) had emigrated to Palestine from New York in 1934 to help found Ein Ha-Shofet (see next note). He traveled often, both in America and elsewhere, to raise money for the *Yishuv*.

[5] Beginning around this time, LDB quietly donated $50,000 to establish a kibbutz in Samaria which would be populated primarily by Americans. Ultimately named Ein HaShofet (Spring of the Judge) after LDB, it was affiliated with the federation HaShomer HaTza'ir. Leibner was in America seeking support for the project.

No. 620   May 7, 1937   Washington, D.C.

1. I sent you today by express at request of A. Saphir a copy of documents submitted by them to the Royal Commission.[1] Please send them to Mack. Ask him to show them to Bob Szold (and to S.S.W. if he cares to see them), & then return them to me.

2. Yes, Norman's death is a grievous loss.[2]

3. Bob La Follette's performance, i.a. on Harlan County (which I

traversed on horseback with my brother in 1906, before there was a railroad, a wagon road or an operating coal mine there) should result in ending the industrial spy system.[3]

4. I am glad you are answering Gribben.[4]

5. Some press notices indicate that Conant is not happy over his Gottingen performance.[5]

6. Arthur Hill[6] was in & reported favorably on you and Marion, and Auntie B.

7. Glad to hear your Fed. Jur[isdiction]. seminar so satisfactory. Towey bill[7] & your letter are interesting.

[1] Memoranda submitted by various Zionist organizations to the Peel Commission.

[2] LDB's old friend and colleague in many reform battles, Norman Hapgood, had died on 29 April 1937.

[3] Industrial strife had broken out again in Harlan County, Kentucky, and other coal mining areas as operators tried a variety of means, many illegal, to break the organizing drive of the United Mine Workers. This led to a Senate investigation chaired by La Follette. For the important work of that committee, see Jerold S. Auerbach, "The La Follette Committee: Labor and Civil Liberties in the New Deal," *Journal of American History* 51 (1964): 435.

[4] Col. W. H. Gribben, who claimed to be at work on a biography of Aaron Aaronsohn, had written to FF on 22 August 1936 requesting information. Aaronsohn, according to FF, had played an important role in exciting American Jews about the possibilities of Palestine, but, contrary to Gribben's view, had not enlisted the aid of Woodrow Wilson in the Zionist cause. There is no record that Gribben ever published his study.

[5] In response to an invitation to attend ceremonies marking the 200th anniversary of the University of Goettingen, Harvard sent formal greetings, and expressed regret that it could not send a delegate. In its message it referred to the problem of academic freedom within German universities caused by the Hitler regime. Yale, Princeton, Dartmouth, and other universities in the United States also declined to send representatives.

[6] Arthur Dehon Hill (1869–1947), a prominent Boston attorney and Harvard Law School graduate, had been chief counsel for Sacco and Vanzetti.

[7] Frank William Towey, Jr. (b. 1895), a representative from New Jersey, had introduced a bill to provide better protection from lynching; it died in committee.

No. 621   May 14, 1937   Washington, D.C.

1. The British have behaved shamefully in giving only 770 visas.[1] Fear seems to have obliterated conscience and paralyzed judgment. Nothing can be said in extenuation, except that the other "great nations" would probably have done worse.

2. Littauer's gift to the University in Exile is fine.[2] I guess Mack is entitled to some of the credit.

3. Conant must feel a bit cheap about Gottingen.

4. You must be thrilled by the Roscoe Pound Professorship[3] pamphlet. Robert Grant is active in the canvassing.

5. Bruening's appointment should prove enlightening.[4]

596

6. Today's Naval news [5] will again give Great Britain an uneasy quarter of an hour.

[1] Pending the Peel Commission report, Great Britain had practically closed Palestine to further Jewish immigration, despite the increased number of Jews attempting to flee Germany. The 770 visas barely made a dent in the demand. LDB's reference to other countries included the United States, which continued to enforce its quota system to keep immigration low.

[2] The New School for Social Research in New York had embarked upon a fund raising campaign to support its graduate faculty in political and social sciences, staffed mainly by exiles from Germany fleeing Hitler. The Littauer Foundation had just given $100,000 to the school.

[3] To honor Pound on his retirement as dean, Harvard planned to endow a chair in the law school in his name. The fund-raising was interrupted by the war, and was not completed until the late 1940s. The first occupant, Sheldon Glueck, was named to the chair in 1950.

[4] Harvard had named Dr. Heinrich Bruening (1885–1970), who had been the last chancellor of Germany in the Weimar Republic, to a permanent faculty position. Bruening, who had fled Germany after Hitler's rise, had been at Harvard on a visiting basis since 1934. He returned to Germany in 1951 to teach at the University of Cologne.

[5] A measure had been introduced in the House calling upon the secretary of the navy to proceed with the construction of public works, including some warships.

No. 622   May 26, 1937   Washington, D.C.

1. Qualitatively, your estimate of Van D. seems to me correct. But quantitatively no one could fully appreciate his value who has not observed his work in conferences, particularly in the days of White and of Taft, and who has not watched his performance in Court. [1]

2. Jim Landis' agreement to remain at work [2] until called to Cambridge in September, as reported in the press, seems very unwise. He certainly needs a vacation & time for meditation.

3. His explanation as to the change in the Gold technique is clear, but it doesn't explain the value to the country of the continued purchases.

4. Your friend Jos. Kennedy was in yesterday, a charming Siegfried & most attractive. He is a pessimist as to business future now in store. He certainly has to tackle now the worst of all our messes.

5. It is fine to hear of Grenville Clark's exploits.

[1] Justice Van Devanter was coming to the end of his service on the Supreme Court; he would leave the bench at the end of the session, 2 June 1937.

[2] At the Securities and Exchange Commission.

No. 623   June 19, 1937   Chatham, Mass.

1. F.D. could help much by making the Douglas appointment promptly, [1] letting Robert Jackson plunge unreservedly into the tax enquiry & letting Jim Landis get time for rest and meditation.

2. I am glad you were able to give much time to S.S.W.'s problem.[2] He will need much of your assistance in the near future.

3. The London Statesman's observation is significantly true and very sad.

4. Poletti's success may mean much.[3] The success democratically of the Italian element in our population should have wide implications.

5. When you come here make sure of your transportation. The New Haven has given notice that it will not only discontinue all freight service on the Chatham branch, but also the bus service from Hyannis; and no substitute service has yet been arranged, I am told.

6. A letter from Dean Acheson tells with much joy of Jane's[4] performance at the School & that she is going to Bennington after the summer in France.

[1] William Orville Douglas (1898–1980), after graduating from Columbia, taught at Yale Law School and headed the Securities and Exchange Commission investigation into protective committees before Roosevelt named him to the SEC in 1934. Roosevelt was about to name him SEC chairman to succeed Landis. Douglas's lasting fame, however, would come from his thirty-six years on the Supreme Court, a tenure he began in 1939 when he was named to replace LDB.

[2] Wise was then embroiled in a number of projects aiming to help more Jews escape Germany.

[3] Poletti had just been named to the New York Supreme Court for the City of New York.

[4] Jane Acheson, later Mrs. Dudley B. W. Brown, was the eldest child of the Achesons.

No. 624   July 26, 1937   Chatham, Mass.

1. I am very glad [you] gave Lenharg so much time.

2. Also, that you gave Rabbi Wohl[1] the advice and encouragement which he told me of when here on the 19th.

3. Lewis & Florence Dembitz, who have just returned from Palestine & London, report a fine spirit among our Palestinians and: "We saw Colonel Wedgwood[2] and he told us that Weizmann was selling us for a mess of porridge and that at a dinner held not many days before several Christian members of Parliament had told him so in unmistakable language." From what he said, there can be no doubt that Weizmann OK['d] the partition.[3] Brodetsky[4] admitted that it had been planned to "accept the Report, but only [in] the last minutes had they changed their minds."

4. W[ise]'s letter to Gore was fine.[5] I wish W[eizmann]. had testified to like effect.

5. [*] has carried Lloyd George's blast,[6] which will help despite the defects.

6. I am much relieved that Bob [Szold] and Brodie are accompanying Wise.[7]

7. Messersmith[8] should be helpful in Washington.

[1] Samuel Wohl (1895–1972) was rabbi at the Reading Road Temple in Cincinnati for nearly forty years. He was active in a number of Zionist groups, as well as in leadership of the Reform movement.

[2] Josiah Clement Wedgwood (1872–1943), a radical English politician, was a strong supporter of Zionism, and urged His Majesty's government to fulfill the Balfour promise, turning Palestine into a Jewish state which could then become a self-governing dominion within the Commonwealth. In 1942 he would be elevated to the House of Lords as Baron Wedgwood.

[3] The Peel Commission (see 20 August 1936) had recommended partitioning Palestine, and Chaim Weizmann, adopting the attitude that a "half loaf" was better than nothing, favored the plan. Nearly all of the American Zionists, including LDB, opposed it.

[4] Selig Brodetsky (1888–1954) was a mathematician at the University of Leeds and a leader of the English Jewry. In 1949 he moved to Israel to become president of the Hebrew University.

[5] See 16 July 1936, n. 1.

[6] In the debate over Palestine, Lloyd George condemned the government's attempt to impart a new meaning to the Balfour Declaration. It was a plain and straightforward promise to the Jews, he said, and it was immoral for the Government to go back on its word.

[7] To negotiate, along with the European and Palestinian Zionists, on what British policy would be after the Peel Report.

[8] George Strausser Messersmith (1883–1960) was a career foreign service official reputedly sympathetic to Zionism. From 1937 to 1940 he served in Washington as an assistant secretary of state.

No. 625   July 30, 1937   Chatham, Mass.

1. Re yours 27th. A delay, indeed a rather long one in the decision to partition, should prove helpful, despite the ordinary advantages of having problems settled. The recommendation is so unjust to the Jews, and so unwise for both the British and the Arabs, that time for consideration and for invention is likely to bring a proper adjustment between Jew and Arab. I expect to receive the Report today. From what many say, it must contain findings which may help us to get reversal and relief through the appellate court.

2. Keynes' article and the enclosed are illuminating. It is a satisfaction to find full admission of the egregious error in the Abyssinian affair.[1] Eden's[2] task is, of course, a difficult one; but I can't feel any confidence in his performance.

3. What has become of the project of sending Eustace Percy to us as Ambassador.[3]

4. I hope F.D. won't delay his appointment to U.S.S.C.[4]

5. Is Jim Landis still in Washington? And has Douglas been definitely named for Chairman?[5]

6. Judge Lehman was here yesterday. I gathered from him that he expects a visit at Cotuit from Cardozo in August.

Shall hope to see you here soon. Paul is expected today.

[1] See 18 January 1936, n. 7.

[2] Robert Anthony Eden (1897–1977), later first Earl of Avon, had become an increasingly important figure in English politics, and had recently been named secretary of state for foreign affairs. He would be foreign secretary during the war, and in 1955 became prime minister.

[3] Percy did not become ambassador to Washington, but later in the year was named rector of the Newcastle Division of the University of Durham.

[4] Roosevelt named Hugo Black to succeed Willis Van Devanter on 12 August 1937.

[5] Of the Securities and Exchange Commission.

No. 626   August 21, 1937   Chatham, Mass.

1. I don't wonder that Joshua Leibner's letter impressed you.[1] Alice and I had much joy in seeing him; and Marion and you would. He is young and engaging.

2. Croly's article is very knowing. But he misplaced the responsibility. Taft is the culprit.[2]

3. I am glad you and Marion brought Ethel Moors. She proved to be all that you said of her and very enjoyable. I can't recall having seen her in thirty years. She has grown distinctly younger.

4. Messersmith should prove helpful.

5. You and we will doubtless see Cardozo within the week. He was due to arrive last night at Cotuit.

6. I trust Congress will adjourn today. I expect there will be much to regret in the legislation of the last fortnight. F.D. was well justified in his scoring of the Tydings[3] rider,[4] but wrong earlier in injecting his opposition to the original Tydings Price Maintenance bill (if properly drawn). If there ever was a measure fully considered by Congress & its adjuncts, it was that one, which has been actively fought over for nearly 24 years.[5]

7. Alice sends clippings enclosed and asks what you think of it and Hurd.

8. The discussion of your appointment by W.Z.O.[6] had better await Wise's return.

[1] There is no copy of Leibner's letter in the Frankfurter MSS.

[2] Herbert Croly, of course, had been dead for seven years. FF may have sent LDB a copy of Croly's "Democratic Factions and Insurgent Republicans," *North American Review* 191 (May 1910): 626, which dealt in part with conservation policies.

³Millard Evelyn Tydings (1890–1961), a Maryland lawyer, had been elected to Congress in 1922, and to the Senate in 1926. Despite his position as chairman of the powerful Armed Services Committee, he lost his reelection bid in 1950 because of smears from Joseph McCarthy that he was soft on communism.

⁴The rider, attached to the District of Columbia Tax bill, would permit manufacturers to control the retail price of their articles in those states which permitted price maintenance contracts. Tydings had originally introduced a bill to this effect, but no action had been taken because Roosevelt believed it would modify antitrust laws. After growing tired of waiting for the administration to act, Tydings attached it to the tax bill, and when the president signed the bill on 18 August, he scolded Congress for the tactic, and said he hoped it would not inflate prices too much.

⁵LDB had long been a supporter of price maintenance; see "On Maintaining Makers' Prices," *Harper's Weekly* 57 (14 June 1913): 6, reprinted in *The Curse of Bigness*, 125–28.

⁶FF did not accept any position in the World Zionist Organization.

No. 627   September 6, 1937   Chatham, Mass.

1. I hope you are making progress re health.

2. The Sacco-Vanzetti In Memoriam,[1] in its various manifestations, can not fail to do good. The Unity number is fine. Who is the editor[2] of Unity? Paper returned herewith.

3. Gardner Jackson was here yesterday, with much of interest to report. He is a very useful citizen & happily is looking much better than when I saw him about June 1.

4. Morris Ernst[3] has been here today, also with many tales of interest, including his observations on Italy, where he drove about 1000 miles, largely in places not usually visited. He says, save in the North, conditions of the people make even the share-cropping lot seem endurable.

5. Billikopf also here. Both he and Morris Ernst (and Gardner Jackson) feel much disturbed by the Lewis—F.D. estrangement.[4]

6. Ben Gurion's talk led me to think that he had not been thinking as carefully and as independently as I had expected from him.

We plan to leave Wednesday for Boston & to reach Washington on Saturday. We shall miss not seeing you and Marion.

¹The 16 August 1937 issue of *Unity* was devoted to "In Memoriam, Sacco and Vanzetti, 1927–1937." FF's role in the affair was described in an article by Herbert Ehrmann, "Three Men—Thompson, Frankfurter and Vanzetti," at 223.

² *Unity*'s editor was the noted social activist, Rev. John Haynes Holmes.

³Morris Leopold Ernst (1888–1976), a New York attorney, was involved in many reform activities, and wrote several books on law and social policy.

⁴The labor leader and the president had split over Lewis's dissatisfaction with Roosevelt's behind the scenes help in settling the impending steel strike. Lewis thought that Roosevelt, in gratitude for labor's support in the 1936 election, should have openly sided with the union. In 1940 Lewis would oppose Roosevelt's reelection bid.

No. 628   October 4, 1937   Washington, D.C.

Cazalet [1] was in, 9.15 AM to 10.5, a charming person. After about 15 minutes talk on northern Canada, Russia and Siberia, he introduced Palestine. As to our discussion on that, I am writing via JWM.

Has Cazalet any occupation or profession other than M.P.

Did you have part in selecting Cooper [2] for Black's secretary.

The morning session went off in best possible form, and apparently also the meeting of the Justices with Black, before & after the session.

I gave Cazalet a pass for one of our seats.

[1] Victor Alexander Cazalet (1896–1943), after service in the British army during the war, had entered Parliament in 1923; he later served as parliamentary secretary to the Board of Trade.

[2] Jerome Alfred Cooper (b. 1913) had graduated from Harvard law in 1936, and then clerked for Justice Black from 1937 to 1940. After serving in the navy during the war, he began practice in Birmingham, Alabama.

No. 629   October 8, 1937   Washington, D.C.

1. My thanks for your good wishes for the October Term.

2. Our Junior Justice [1] attending silently this week's conference involving about 300 cases will get some idea of the labor which awaits him.

3. My thanks to you and Shulman for the revised edition, [2] which should help much in educating the bar. It is surprising that as much as half of the cases are new material.

4. Thanks to you also for the minutes of the Mandate & the Parliamentary Report.

5. The British seem determined to enter upon a "New Deal" in foreign affairs, including Palestine.

6. Harold [Laski]'s election to the Labor party executive is fine. The party certainly needs strengthening.

7. I hope to see [William O.] Douglas Sunday, and to find that he got an adequate vacation.

8. F.D. might have answered Judge John H. Clark [sic] by telling him that if he had not quit his job, many cases would have been decided differently. [3]

Elizabeth also, has large classes.

[1] Hugo Black.

[2] Felix Frankfurter and Harry Shulman, *Cases and Other Authorities on Federal Jurisdiction and Procedure* (rev. ed., Chicago: Callaghan and Co., 1937).

The liberal Clarke had resigned from the bench in 1922 to work in the peace movement, and his place had been taken by George Sutherland, who provided a key vote in many of the conservative decisions of the 1920s and 1930s.

No. 630   November 14, 1937   Washington, D.C.

1. To you and Marion our thanks for the birthday greeting.[1]

2. Ben [Cohen], Tom [Corcoran] and Rosenman were in yesterday. Ben reports you in good form. We hope Marion is making sure that you observe the "not too much."

3. Oswald Ryan[2] made a notable half-hour argument—courageous, tactful, well reasoned, excellent in manner and tone.[3]

4. I assume you have read Prof. Julius Lips' "The Savage hits back."[4] What he tells of his own story in the preface, pp. xxi–xxx, ought to be reprinted in some publication which university teachers and scientists read.

5. I get little encouragement from the announcement that Borah will work on anti-trust with F.D. 47 years of the Sherman Law futility ought to be as convincing as the 39 years of Symth v. Ames rule failure.[5] I hope F.D. will not forget that not Monopoly but Bigness is the Curse,[6] and that through taxation the evil may be averted.

6. If States will use their power over foreign corporations as widely as they are our decisions on chain store taxes,[7] much can be accomplished as a result of No. 1.[8] Some writing should be done on this.

7. Labor did a good job on the Duke and her Highness.[9]

[1] The day before, LDB had turned eighty-one.

[2] Oswald Ryan (1888–1982) was then general counsel to the Federal Power Commission; he would later serve for nearly seventeen years as member and chairman of the Civil Aeronautics and Space Authority.

[3] Ryan appeared by leave of the Court in *Railroad Commission of California et al.* v. *Pacific Gas & Electric Company*, 302 U.S. 388 (1938).

[4] Julius E. Lips (1895–1950) had resigned from the University of Cologne in 1933 in protest against Nazi policies. He came to the United States and taught anthropology first at Columbia and then at Howard University. After the war he returned to Germany to become rector of the University of Leipzig. His book, *The Savage Hits Back* (New Haven: Yale University Press, 1937), was an attack on the myth of racial supremacy.

[5] In *Smyth* v. *Ames*, 169 U.S. 466 (1898), the Court took upon itself the right to review all rate decisions to determine whether or not the rate set provided a reasonable return to the regulated utility or railroad.

[6] In an interview with Ray Stannard Baker while the latter was writing his biography of Wilson, LDB had said something quite similar, namely, that Wilson had never understood that the real evil was not monopoly but bigness.

[7] In *Liggett* v. *Lee*, 288 U.S. 517 (1933), the Supreme Court by a bare five to four vote had struck down in part a Florida tax on chain stores as violating due process and equal protection. LDB had filed a massive dissent analyzing the reasons for Florida taxing chain stores more heavily than other enterprises.

[8] A week earlier, in a unanimous opinion delivered by LDB, the Court upheld a Virginia "entrance fee" on foreign corporations seeking to do intrastate business in the Commonwealth, measured by their total authorized capital stock; the Court found no interference by such a tax with interstate commerce. *Atlantic Refining Co.* v. *Virginia*, 302 U.S. 22 (1937).

[9] After abdicating and marrying Mrs. Simpson on 3 June 1937, the Duke of Windsor and his new wife traveled in Austria and then Germany, where they made many approving comments on the Nazi administration of the country. Herbert Morrison, in the 13 November 1937 issue of the Labour magazine *Forward*, had severely criticized the Windsors for their apparent approbation of the Nazis. "The choice before ex-Kings is either to fade out of the public eye or to be a nuisance. It is a hard choice, perhaps . . . but the Duke will be wise to fade." Although *Forward* had a relatively small circulation, the *New York Times* picked up the piece and quoted extensively from it.

No. 631   November 28, 1937   Washington, D.C.

1. Wheeler we have not seen. He has not been here unless it be since Thanksgiving. Mrs. Wheeler was in the day before. There was considerable talk, but no expressions of hate towards F.D.

2. F.D. appears to have done an uncommonly good job on the D.C. Court of Appeals. Groner is clearly the best man for C.J., and I hear good things of Vinson.[1] I know nothing of Edgerton,[2] but gladly take my chances, as Clark[3] has thereby been eliminated.

3. Glad so good a man for next year is in prospect.[4]

4. The enclosures I am sending J.W.M.

5. We had a fine visit from Ben Flexner & Mims on the 26th.

[1] Frederic Moore Vinson (1890–1953) had been a member of Congress from Kentucky for three terms before Roosevelt appointed him to the Court of Appeals for the District of Columbia in 1938. He resigned in 1943 to take on several appointments in the war administration, and in 1945 was named secretary of the treasury. The following year, Truman named him chief justice of the United States after Harlan Stone died.

[2] Henry White Edgerton (1888–1970), a Harvard law graduate, had taught at the George Washington Law School since 1921. In 1938 he began thirty years of service on the United States Circuit Court of Appeals for the District of Columbia.

[3] William Clark (1891–1957) served on the U.S. District Court for New Jersey from 1925 to 1938, when he was named to the Third Circuit Court of Appeals. After World War Two he became part of the American military government in Germany, and was appointed chief justice of the military commission courts in 1949.

[4] LDB's law clerk for the October 1938 term would be Adrian Sanford Fisher (1914–1983); he would later also clerk for FF. After the war, Fisher was a member of the American prosecution team at the Nuremberg trials. He joined the Georgetown Law School where he taught international law and was dean from 1969 to 1975. From 1966 to 1969 he was deputy director of the U.S. Arms Control and Disarmament Agency.

No. 632   December 7, 1937   Washington, D.C.

1. It is fine that you wrote the letter to the Times.[1]

2. You doubtless heard from Tom [Corcoran] (as came to us from other sources) that it is the conversations over colonies, not teeth, which shortened F.D.'s vacation. Couldn't you do something now to get F.D. to say (and thus do) something against partition & in favor of increased immigration to Palestine?[2]

3. I suppose you saw J.W.M. in New York. Hope he is getting on well.

[1] On 28 November FF had written a letter to the *New York Times* opposing the British decision to allow the Grand Mufti of Jerusalem to return to Palestine. Haj Amin el Hussaini had been one of the chief instigators of the 1936 Arab riots, and had openly endorsed Hitler's anti-Semitic policies.

[2] Roosevelt did nothing about either subject.

No. 633   December 12, 1937   Washington, D.C.

I hope you will arrange for a full talk on Palestine with Jos. Kennedy before he sails.[1] Knowledge on his part & sympathy with our views may be of very great service to our cause.

[1] Kennedy was about to take up his new duties as ambassador to the Court of St. James's.

No. 634   December 15, 1937   Washington, D.C.

1. Re yours 12th rec'd today. My hope was (& is) that you will have the full talk with Jos. Kennedy. He cares very much for your opinion.

2. As to Harlan's of Dec. 8,[1] I know of nothing especially depressing. But even Mark Tapley would have a hard time being cheerful, except over your Survey speech.[2] Perhaps I should add S.B.I. which is going finely, and University of Louisville, thanks to Ben Flexner.

3. Very good report comes from Cardozo this A.M. But it is a serious loss to have him absent even for a few days.

Yes, Auntie B's was a great life.[3]

[1] Stone had written that he was upset about recent tax cases and how the Court had disposed of them. Instead of setting out clear rules, Stone said, "We have missed a great opportunity. . . . The net result of what we have done this week is merely to put all the opinions in a pot and stir them up, and insist that the soup is clear."

[2] "Rigid Outlook in a Dynamic World," *Survey Graphic* 27 (1938): 5. The journal's editors had arranged a symposium to discuss the prospects for the next quarter-century. FF had urged people to have open minds, since in a world which changed so rapidly, set views could only lead to disaster.

[3] LDB's close friend and longtime colleague in reform work, Elizabeth Glendower Evans, had died on 12 December. See 5 January 1938.

No. 635   December 28, 1937   Washington, D.C.

1. Yours of 24th from N.Y. reaches me today. Many other letters have been similarly delayed.

2. your report on Judge Mack's eyes is deeply distressing,[1] and the other indications which you mention only less so. Because of his eyes (which I had supposed were only temporary troublesome), I had not written him. I sent him a greeting via Bob [Szold]. Should I do anything more?

3. As you know doubtless, our Court will send (or has) to the A.G. "The Rules of Civil Procedure" adopted pursuant to Act of July 19, 1934, ch. 651.

I asked the C.J. to advise A.G. that I do not approve of their adoption. I am sure several others feel as I do, but thought they must be silent as the Court was committed.

Will anything be done in Congress to prevent them becoming operative?[2]

4. Enclosed letter of Katznelson[3] & copy of letter of Weizmann to Wise should be returned to Wise as soon as read.

[1] Mack had long suffered from diabetes, which, together with advancing age, temporarily threatened his eyesight. Although he recovered his vision, his health in general began to deteriorate.

[2] Pressure had been building for several decades to reform the federal rules of civil procedure and eliminate numerous inconsistencies not only in the federal practice, but between state and federal rules. In 1934 Congress had passed the Rules Enabling Act, and a year later the Supreme Court appointed a highly distinguished Advisory Committee to assist in drafting new rules. The Committee submitted its third draft to the Court in November 1937, and the Court promulgated it with minor changes the following month. Congress had no objections, and the Federal Rules of Civil Procedure became effective on 16 September 1938. The Court upheld the constitutionality of the new rules in *Sibbach* v. *Wilson & Co.*, 312 U.S. 1 (1941).

[3] Berl Katznelson (1887–1944) was the leading ideologue of labor Zionism, and a close colleague of Ben-Gurion in Palestine.

No. 636   January 5, 1938   Washington, D.C.

1. Re yours of 4th. Please say to your associates that as Auntie B. was throughout the long years so much a member of our family, that we deem it appropriate that what is to be said of her should be said by others.

2. Sutherland's resignation, at this time, was like all his other acts,

animated solely by sense of patriotic duty. He felt that he would soon be unable to do the work which he thinks he should (In fact, he has done more than his share) and he felt that there should be ample time for F.D. & the Senate to consider his successor & get him worked in before the end of the Term.

3. The Court needs very much a good lawyer—or judge—of experience and legal knowledge & judgment. I hope you will protect the Court & the Country from the infliction of some inadequate person.

4. Enclosed from Judge Anderson shows him in better shape than I feared he was.

No. 637   January 17, 1938   Washington, D.C.

1. The Court will welcome Stanley Reed.[1]

2. I also urged Willard Hurst to remain at M[adison].[2]

3. The Spanish Ambassador was in yesterday & insists that things are going well in the field.[3]

4. I am glad that F.D. came out against all holding companies,[4] & that Norris is reported to have said: "Do it by taxation."

5. Gus Hand was in yesterday.

6. No, we have not read "Goliath"[5] & assume we should.

7. We have read with much interest Buchan's "Augustus."[6]

8. We remain much concerned about Cardozo.[7]

[1] Stanley Forman Reed (1884–1980), the Solicitor General of the United States, had been nominated to take Sutherland's place. He would serve on the Court nearly two decades, and would occupy a moderating position between the activist and conservative wings.

[2] Hurst was then considering an offer to join the Yale Law School faculty; see next letter.

[3] The ambassador, Fernando de los Rios, was mistaken; the Republican troops were soon to be defeated by Franco's fascists.

[4] At a press conference on 15 January, Roosevelt had called for an end to holding companies, and insisted that the administration would not lift the "death sentence clause" of the Public Utilities Holding Company Act. In the next few days the president sent additional signals that he would not retreat on this issue.

[5] Guiseppe Antonio Borgese, *Goliath: The March of Fascism* (New York: Viking Press, 1937).

[6] John Buchan, *Augustus* (Boston: Houghton Mifflin, 1937).

[7] Cardozo, by now quite ill, would die on 9 July 1938; see 18 July 1938.

No. 638   January 31, 1938   Washington, D.C.

1. Our thanks for "Goliath,"[1] thanks in which Emma Erving joins. She has been with us since Thursday.

2. We enjoyed, as you assumed, Francis Hackett's letter.[2]

3. F.D. asked Alice & me to see him Tuesday, & we had a pleasant social call with only Miss LeHand[3] present. He talked as if Big Business had made no impression on him.

4. Nothing from Kennedy.

5. We expect much help from Reed.

6. He seems to have had a joyous time at Cambridge.

7. Secy Ickes talk last Sunday gave the Jews much satisfaction.[4]

8. Read Buchan's "Augustus."[5]

9. Make sure that Kennedy sees S.S.W.

10. It is good to know that Hurst has declined the Yale offer.[6]

[1] See preceding letter, n. 5.

[2] Hackett wrote FF on 10 December raving about Denmark, which was small but clean and creative in spirit. LDB and his wife had long considered the Danish model an ideal embodiment of their views on small-scale society.

[3] Marguerite Alice "Missy" LeHand (1898–1944) was Roosevelt's confidential secretary. For the Brandeises visit, see next letter.

[4] In a speech to the National Conference of the United Palestine Appeal in Washington on 23 January, Secretary of the Interior Harold Ickes had not only conveyed the president's warm regards to the Zionist movement, but called upon American Jews to align themselves forcefully with the forces of democracy against the growing fascist evil. His talk included a strong denunciation of the European dictators.

[5] See preceding letter, n. 6.

[6] See id., n. 2.

No. 639   February 11, 1938   Washington, D.C.

1. You do Harlan grave injustice. Every member of the Court has been uniformly friendly & some surprisingly fraternal. No one has been so considerate & helpful as Harlan & he has gone out of his way to give much of his time, when there was occasion; and has by this means prevented some utterances which would have been regrettable. H. has done this of his own motion.

2. Who wrote the London Times editorial against Partition reported in Feb. 7 "Palcor" & how & why did they do it?

3. You must have been glad to see reference to Meinertzhagen's letter[1] to the Times a day or two later.

4. As to our visit at the White House, Louis Wehle was the occasion. About 3 weeks earlier F.D. had invited him. F.D. asked about me, said in substance that he would like to see me. Louis said, of course I would come if summoned. F.D. said he didn't want to "summon" me. Louis said, he was sure I would come if invited, & later (after talking to Alice

& me), suggested through McIntyre[2] that during a recess in the late afternoon would be the time. My guess is that F.D.'s mind had turned to me because shortly before there had been much talk of the "Brandeis prudent investment view."[3]

Ben C[ohen]. talked well in the Bond & Share case.[4] Robert Jackson is an advocate, T[om] C[orcoran]'s!!!

Emma Erving had become quite gay before she left.

[1] In a letter to *The Times* (London), published on 7 February, Meinertzhagen defended Zionist policy in Palestine and called upon Great Britain to live up to its responsibilities.

[2] Marvin Hunter McIntyre (1878–1943) was a member of Roosevelt's personal staff.

[3] LDB had long argued that the basis for determining public utility valuation, for rate-making purposes, should be shifted from present plant replacement value to that of historic cost or prudent investment. See 18 July 1927, n. 4, and his dissent in St. *Louis and O'Fallon Ry. Co.* v. *United States*, 279 U.S. 461, 488 (1929).

[4] In *Electric Bond and Share Co.* v. *Securities Exchange Commission*, 303 U.S. 419 (1938), the Supreme Court upheld the provisions of the 1935 Public Utilities Holding Company Act requiring utilities to register security issues with the SEC.

No. 640   February 27, 1938   Washington, D.C.

1. Nothing was heard from Kennedy.

2. That Fortune editorial, returned herewith, is of great interest.[1] Will it be followed up? It is very cautious, but knowing.

3. Austria & Czechoslovakia are apparently behaving much better than Great Britain.[2]

4. I am not despondent about Palestine. The Labor folk are vocal & the net result may in time be good for us.

5. I wonder whether you formed a better opinion of Bernard Joseph[3] than I did.

6. It was fine to see Ben Flexner in such good form. He is doing fine things.

You have made your "Business" article very interesting.[4]

[1] In "The New Deal: Second Time Around," *Fortune* 17 (February 1938): 59, the editors noted that once again Roosevelt was trying to pull the country out of depression, this one the recession of 1937. But unlike the New Deal of 1933, his latest efforts had a much more liberal, some would say leftist, tinge. The overall tone of the piece was not unfavorable to the administration.

[2] In the light of Nazi Germany's professed intention to expand the Third Reich, editorials had begun appearing in Viennese newspapers calling for an alliance between Austria and Czechoslovakia against the fascist union between Germany and Italy. But within two weeks the *Anschluss*, uniting Austria to Germany, occurred, and Hitler triumphantly entered Vienna on 14 March.

[3] Bernard (Dov) Joseph (1899–1980), had emigrated from Canada to Palestine, where he practiced law until 1948. He would be military governor of Jerusalem during the War of Independence, and later served in the Knesset and various government positions.

[4] FF and Adrian Fisher, "The Business of the Supreme Court at the October Terms, 1935 and 1936," *Harvard Law Review* 51 (1938): 577.

No. 641   March 18, 1938   Washington, D.C.

1. Albert Hirst,[1] whose letter of 17th to me is enclosed, is the grandson of a sister of Louis Wehle's father, and a competent fine person in the forties. He came to America more than 20 years ago, while making his living studied law and seems now to have a good practice. He is, I think, counsel to the National Board of Underwriters, i.a.

In acknowledging his letter, I wrote him that I am sending it to you, as you may wish to send some message.

2. Re Boskey's[2] letter ret'd herewith. Our Court has not taken any stand on the administration bill.[3] But individually, I think, most of the men are opposed, & Roberts & I very much so. I have talked with members of the Senate Jud. Committee and with Hatton Summers[4] emphatically against our Court or any one on it having anything to do under the project. We have chores enough.

3. Stanley Reed has had much approval. His doubts are due to innate modesty, I guess.

4. Yes, "Speaking or reading" of opinions are largely ended & I hope will be wholly so.[5]

5. Tell me about the Whitney family. Were not they among "our best people."

6. I have written J.W.M. quite a number of letters.

7. The [New York] World's performance is unspeakably bad.

8. I am glad you had so satisfactory a time in Cincinnati.

9. Gov. Lehman did a good job on S.B.I.[6] But, of course, the chief work lies ahead. The act is merely an opportunity for work which must be efficient.[7] And there is great need of honesty in those who will be connected with it.

[1] Probably Albert Hirst (1887–1974), now a New York attorney specializing in insurance law. He was active in the American Civil Liberties Union, and an opponent of capital punishment.

[2] Probably Bennett Boskey (b. 1916), then a Harvard Law student. After clerking for Learned Hand, Stanley Reed, and Chief Justice Stone, Boskey practiced law in New York City.

[3] Probably the proposal for the Administrative Office of U.S. Courts.

[4] Hatton William Sumners (1875–1962) represented Dallas in Congress from 1913 to 1947, when he retired.

[5] See 21 September and 5 October 1935.

[6] After a short but bitter fight led by the insurance companies against the scheme, the New York legislature had accepted Governor Lehman's proposal and established a savings bank insurance plan, with a limit of $5,000 per policy.

[7] See LDB to Henry Morgenthau, Sr., 20 November 1906, in which he wrote: "If we should get tomorrow the necessary legislation, without having achieved that process of education, we could not make a practical working of the [SBLI] plan."

No. 642   April 7, 1938   Washington, D.C.

1. Geoffrey Parsons did well.[1] Pity Hull was 5 years late in seeing this duty of America.

2. Couldn't Parsons, economists and statesmen see that the only chance of U.S. ending unemployment is to increase population. If we would return to our long course of 2 percent annual increase in population (say over 1,000,000 from immigration) & the others from lessened birth control, there would be demand enough for capital goods as well as others. The idea that an immigrant necessarily displaces a resident worker is unsound. Our vice was in preventing labor organizations & depressing labor standards by organized immigration by the interests.

3. I didn't see the N.Y. Times Black editorial. Presume it was like the ridiculous one your friend Gene published.[2] Black's spirit will not suffer.

4. I did not sanction A. H. Sakier writing you, so far as I recall, & I told him I could have nothing to do with his capitalistic project. But that I am, and long have been, interested in the Yemenites. And have contributed (through Jessie Sampter) for the Yemenite school. Indeed my first gift for Palestine was (in 1911) for helping to build some huts for them in one of the colonies.

Sakier came in to see me (partly as interpreter) for Gluska,[3] the Palestinian Yemenite leader, who impressed me favorably. I think Ben Flexner is right about Sakier & his project.

5. We have seen nothing of Harold [Laski]. He seems to be very much engaged.

6. I should be glad to have your view on the merits of the Dietrick case[4] *after* you have read the record & briefs.

7. Glad to hear Reisman [sic] and Howe (as well as Jaffe) are doing well at Buffalo. Their Dean[5] seemed happy & fine when here.

[1] Geoffrey Parsons (1879–1956) was the chief editorial writer for the New York *Tribune* from 1924 to 1952; in 1942 he won a Pulitzer Prize for his work. The preceding day the *Tribune* had urged support for the Joint Distribution Committee in its work to help oppressed Jews overseas. "All who do not believe a defenseless minority should be crushed to serve the purposes of a dictator will do well if they help to relieve the victims, and thus lessen a reproach to humanity."

[2] Since no editorial on Justice Black appeared in either the *New York Times* or the *Washington Post* around this time, LDB may have been referring to editorial attacks published at the time of Black's

nomination to the Supreme Court. The *Times*, on 18 August 1937, had noted "his almost complete lack of judicial experience and his failure to show thus far any trace of a genuinely judicial temperament." Eugene Meyer's *Post*, on 13 August 1937, had lamented the extreme partisanship of the appointment, a political reward to a man totally unfit for the office. He may also have been thinking of the newspaper attacks which appeared a month later after it was revealed that Black had once been a member of the Ku Klux Klan.

[3] Zekharyah Gluska (1895–1960) was the longtime leader of the Yemenite Jewish community in Palestine.

[4] *Dietrick, Receiver*, v. *Standard Surety & Casualty Co.*, 303 U.S. 471 (1938). A Boston bank had gone into receivership, and among its assets were four "Note-Guaranty" bonds, allegedly guaranteed by the respondent, which denied liability. The Court, by a six to two vote with LDB in the majority, upheld a special master's finding that the surety had been obtained through fraud, and was therefore not binding.

[5] Francis M. Shea.

No. 643   April 14, 1938   Washington, D.C.

1. Yours of 12th comes today. Yesterday Baruch was in. His project,[1] which he detailed to me, seemed to me so unwise and discreditable, that it is almost inconceivable that a man of his ability could have evolved it.

It proves conclusively i.a.

(1) That he has no knowledge of the Jewish question
(2) That he has the American-German-Jewish fears of anti-Semitism in America
(3) That these are greatly augmented by the fears inherent in the rich
(4) That "Wenn Gott nur uns gesund erhalt"[2] is his prayer.

I told him emphatically of my disapproval. Whether he said anything at either of yesterday's meetings I do not know. But I think you should use your private means of reaching F.D. to assure yourself that if B. attempts to reach him on Jewish matters he should be disregarded.

I had some information within the year on his tax dodging which was discreditable.[3]

[1] Baruch was then proposing a "United States of Africa," which would take in refugees from Europe, and which would help Great Britain maintain hegemony in East Africa. By saying "all refugees," Baruch hoped to avoid making this a "Jewish" issue.

[2] "If God will simply preserve our health."

[3] There is nothing concrete about this charge, but Baruch's biographer, Jordan Schwarz, believes it may have something to do with the so-called "Baruch bill" of 1938. The 1936 tax law enacted higher rates on undistributed profits and capital gains; Baruch lobbied successfully to have these rates reduced.

No. 644   May 3, 1938   Washington, D.C.

1. I am very glad you wrote Lady Astor[1] and to Sulzberger[2] frankly. The most serious feature of the serious present is that people ordinarily

612

right minded do not feel any compulsion as of the laws of morality and of honor. Tom Lamont's performance is a terrible example.[3] J. P. M[organ]. & Co.'s lack of action ought to eliminate them.

2. I have not seen the Harper article.[4] Do you *know* that Harlan has talked to Krock et al. as you intimate? Stone's relations to Black have been eminently friendly.

3. Harold doubtless told you of his talk to F.D. about partition, and F.D.'s making note to write to Kennedy to speak to Chamberlain etc. Has F.D. done so?

4. One would think that even Chamberlain might be affected by the increasing terrorism in Palestine and the manifestations in neighboring countries.

5. It would be fine to see you and Marion May 12th.

6. With Swift v. Tyson removed,[5] won't it be possible now to go further in limiting diversity citizenship jurisdiction?

7. I am glad you like the Hinderliter opinion.[6]

8. Harry Mattock acted handsome on your suggestion. The manipulators vs. S.B.I. in the legislature makes one feel decadence in Mass.

[1] Following the *Anschluss*, FF's uncle, Dr. Solomon Frankfurter, had been arrested and put in a concentration camp because of his protests against Nazi restrictions on free speech. Although FF could have asked the American government to intervene (and when President Roosevelt later found out about the matter he berated FF for not coming to him), on principle FF refused to ask Roosevelt for a personal favor of this kind. Instead, he wrote to the American-born Nancy Witcher Langhorne, Viscountess Astor (1879–1964), a leading British activist who, like other members of the Clivedon set, then sympathized with the Nazis. FF had first met Lady Astor during the Paris Peace Conference, and he renewed the acquaintanceship during his year at Oxford. Lady Astor immediately contacted the German ambassador to Great Britain, and threatened to go to Vienna herself unless the Nazis released Dr. Frankfurter. The aged librarian was soon released, but the maltreatment he endured during his imprisonment led to his death shortly afterward.

[2] Arthur Hays Sulzberger (1891–1968) was president and then chairman of the board of the New York Times Company, which he took over in 1935 from his father-in-law, Adolph S. Ochs. On 22 April FF had written criticizing the paper's editorial handling of malfeasance by stock manipulators as compared to the hard line it preached when it came to wrongdoing by labor leaders, such as John L. Lewis.

[3] At this time Lamont was defending himself before the SEC on charges that he had been aware of a friend's illegal stock transactions, and had done nothing about it. He responded that he had no responsibility if a crime was committed by someone else, and that since it was an isolated incident, he had helped the man make good the loss out of friendship.

[4] LDB may have been referring to Marquis W. Childs, "The Supreme Court Today," *Harper's Magazine* 176 (May 1938): 581, which predicted a number of changes would take place within a few years, both in personnel and doctrine. Childs also noted the need for high quality judges, men better than Hugo Black who, he claimed, embarrassed his colleagues by his lack of judicial experience.

[5] In one of the most important decisions of his career, LDB had just handed down the Court's opinion in *Erie Railroad Co.* v. *Tompkins*, 340 U.S. 64 (1938). LDB, and earlier Holmes, had for years been attempting to overrule the holding of *Swift* v. *Tyson*, 16 Pet. 1 (1842) that federal courts

were not bound by state common law, but could promulgate their own decisional doctrine. As a result, many litigants manipulated their business arrangements in order to utilize federal rather than state courts to avoid local law. See, for example, *Black and White Taxicab & Transfer Co.* v. *Brown and Yellow Taxicab & Transfer Co.*, 276 U.S. 518 (1928) (see 10 April 1928). In *Erie*, LDB ruled that federal courts in each state would be bound by the decisional rules of the highest state court on all issues involving state law. The Court thus held that there was no federal common law, and that its predecessor court had acted unconstitutionally in *Swift*.

⁶In a companion decision handed down the same day, *Hinderliter* v. *LaPlata Water Co.*, 304 U.S. 92 (1938), involving an interstate compact, LDB held that there was a federal common law in those cases in which only federal issues were involved, and in which state decisional rules would be inappropriate.

No. 645   June 22, 1938   Chatham, Mass.

1. The Parliamentary Report ¹ goes back to you under another cover. That is, indeed, a noble speech of the Bishop of Durham ² and it is fine that it comes from one of the clericals. Perhaps present Englishmen will soon overcome their degrading fear, and resume their place in the world. Those "18 months" for preparation, which you told of 2 years ago, have long passed.

2. Enclosed letter of May 10th of Wedgwood's (which please return to S.S.W.) speaks a very different language than Chamberlain.

3. Isn't there some paper or periodical that can be induced to write the story of the recent futile attempts of the insurance lobby in Mass? Happily the ignominious action of the Senate in passing the bill for the $5000 limitation was defeated by the House. The resolution for an enquiry makes appropriate a discussion of the subject.

4. What do you hear from Washington?

¹The Peel Commission Report.

²Herbert Hensley Henson (1863–1947), bishop successively of Hereford and Durham, was one of the more eloquent speakers in both the Anglican Church and in the House of Lords. On 18 May, he had attacked the League of Nations' failure to take strong action against Italy for its invasion of Ethiopia as sounding the "funeral oration" for the League.

No. 646   June 30, 1938   Chatham, Mass.

1. The Fireside Talk was an admirable performance, and if persevered in as a platform for action without deviation should bring important results. ¹

2. The Civil Service order was fine. ² Does that put into the Civil Service all the employees not subject to confirmation, except unskilled laborers or casuals? And what are the possibilities of using the unskilled & casuals for political purposes? You will recall our legislation when we

tried to prevent Public Utility bribery by means of employment given at request of Aldermen & the like.[3]

3. Are you following Dick Boeckel's Editorial Research Reports? He has done by them an important public service for which he ought to have recognition by an honorary degree. Let me talk with you of this when we meet.

4. Burton Heath,[4] of the World Telegram, who wrote its S.B.I. articles, would be a man who could do the article I referred to with little labor.

5. I hope what your friend reported on Hitler is true.

6. Kirstein told of the great help you gave him at his meeting or "conference."

7. Al Smith ought to be ashamed of his attitude on wire-tapping etc.[5] Macauley[6] talked well.

Mrs. Lehman reported in a letter dated June 21 to Susan of the "marvellous" improvement of Cardozo. Have you seen or heard from any person who has seen him recently how he appeared?[7]

[1] On 24 June, Roosevelt announced that he would take part in the 1938 congressional election not as president but as head of the Democratic party. He hoped to fashion a Democratic party committed to liberalism, which would forward the goals of the New Deal. Although he was able to influence a few elections, Roosevelt's effort to "purge" the party proved a disaster, especially in the South.

[2] On the previous day Roosevelt had issued an executive order extending the merit system to all federal employees except those at the highest policy-making level. He also forbade political activity by government employees, or the use of political influence to secure jobs, and ordered the Civil Service Commission to enforce the order. The move added 100,000 positions to the civil service system.

[3] See LDB to William H. Gove, 1 April 1903, and letters immediately following.

[4] S. Burton Heath (1898–1949) was then a reporter with the New York World-Telegram; he won a Pulitzer Prize for an exposé resulting in the resignation and later conviction of Judge Manton for taking bribes.

[5] Smith, who was then chairing New York's convention to revise its constitution, had successfully fought off attempts to write a ban against wire-tapping or the use of illegally seized evidence into the document. New York's district attorney, Thomas E. Dewey, had argued the need for having such weapons in order to fight crime. For LDB's attitude toward wire-tapping, see 15 June 1928, n. 6.

[6] Frederick Robertson Macauley (1882–1970), although originally trained as a lawyer, made his reputation as an economist. He was with the National Bureau of Economic Research from 1920 to 1938.

[7] Cardozo's improvement was only temporary; he died on 9 July.

No. 647   July 18, 1938   Chatham, Mass.

1. The "British Foreign Policy" memo, returned herewith, is instructive. When oh when will wisdom prevail?

2.   What C.C.B. writes is fine.[1] It was rare good fortune to have had Cardozo for over six years and that his illness did not come while Stone was sick. Cardozo seemed more nearly robust last summer when he was visiting the Lehmans on the Cape than at any time during his terms on the Court.

3.   Do you know why Black was not at the funeral?

5.   [sic] I do not recall that Dana Malone[2] was helpful in the New Haven fight. Is it claimed that he was, and if so, how?

6.   I am re-reading Meredith Townsend's "Asia and Europe" published (and read by me) in 1901. You should know it.

7.   I suppose the Evian Conference[3] will do some good. At least it helps to make the world understand the inequities, and F.D.'s attitude must prove helpful.

[1] In a letter to FF on 12 July, Charles Burlingham had reported on a visit he had made to see Cardozo on 23 May, at which the dying jurist had repeated over and over, "I'll never get back." Although Burlingham knew Cardozo liked to be contradicted, "I couldn't—I knew that death was waiting."

[2] Dana Malone (1857–1917) had been attorney general of Massachusetts during the New Haven merger battle. Malone did file a brief on behalf of the state against the railroad, but it is difficult to determine how much direct help, if any, he gave to LDB.

[3] In response to the growing problem of refugees attempting to flee Nazi Germany, and the lack of any place for them to go, Roosevelt called for an international conference on the issue which met at Evian-les-Bains in France in the summer of 1938. The conference accomplished nothing, since the United States refused to change its quota laws, and Britain managed to keep consideration of Palestine as a potential refuge off the agenda. Of all the nations present, only tiny Santo Domingo offered to take in any refugees.

No. 648   August 10, 1938   Chatham, Mass.

1.   I hope you have written, or will write, George Rublee what you fear will be the mistaken line of effort.[1] I share your fears.

2.   S.S.W. doubtless told you of our talk as to him on the 8th.

3.   Learned Hand's piece on Cardozo is a beautiful production.[2] Wouldn't he like to write the life?

4.   I am rereading Sam Morrison's [sic] "Maritime History"[3] and can recall no book on American History which is as good. Have you any notion how many copies have been sold?

5.   My Kentucky folk were confident of Barkley's victory, and had estimated his majority at about 50,000.[4] There were several reasons why Chandler[5] should not have run.

6.   The Joseph Lee editorial is fine—as he was. I am glad his son is trying to follow in his footsteps.

7. The Colonial Secretary was well-advised in going to Palestine. The British failure there must be very humiliating to him & to others.

[1] Zionists feared that the Intergovernmental Commission on Refugees, established at the Evian Conference, would not consider Palestine a viable refuge because of British objections, and therefore seek other places. They wanted Rublee, the Commission's head, to pressure His Majesty's government into opening up Palestine to further Jewish immigration. There is no copy of a letter from FF to Rublee on this subject in the FF MSS.

[2] Learned Hand, "Justice Cardozo's Work as a Judge," *United States Law Review* 72 (1938): 496. The piece was reprinted in the Harvard, Yale, and Columbia law journals in January 1939.

[3] Morison had written *The Maritime History of Massachusetts, 1783–1860* in 1921.

[4] One of the few candidates to benefit from Roosevelt's campaign efforts, Alben Barkley had easily defeated Governor Chandler (see next note) in the Democratic primary. Chandler, however, had admitted to using the state's old age pension program in an effort to win votes.

[5] Albert Benjamin "Happy" Chandler (b. 1898) was a Kentucky lawyer who served first as lieutenant governor (1931–1935), then governor of the state (1935–1939), and from 1939 to 1945 as one of its U.S. senators. He then became commissioner of baseball, and was reelected to another term as Kentucky governor in 1955.

No. 649   August 24, 1938   Chatham, Mass.

Re yours of 22d.

1. Claytor came to me Sept. 15th. I suggest that Fisher[1] come for that day, unless upon his enquiry of Claytor, C. wants him to come earlier. C. is now vacationing at Porto Rico and is due back on Labor Day. His best address is probably care of the Marshal [of the Supreme Court].

2. Substantially for the reasons indicated by you, I agree that you should accept the judgeship, if offered.[2]

3. If F.D. insists upon a westerner, would not Bratten[3] be the best?

4. I am extremely sorry to hear of the back.

5. Are you returning to Cambridge as early as Sept. 7th or 8th. We expect to leave for Boston on Wednesday PM (the 7th), to spend the night and Thursday at the Bellevue; and to leave for Washington on the Federal Ex[press]. Thursday. We should be glad to have you and Marion dine with us Wednesday evening, at say 7:40, if that is wise for you; and in any event you and I could have a talk on Thursday.

6. You wrote Paul Kellogg wisely.[4]

7. Newman's letter is interesting.[5] What is he and what was he before he went to the Chadbourne firm?

8. And what has become of Levy?[6]

9. The July 15 "Week" is significant, if it represents a good fraction of English opinion.

10. Lowell Snellet did an excellent job with "Economic Condition of the South."[7]

11. Judge Lehman was here on the 22d. He says that Cardozo was deeply interested in the Tompkins decision,[8] and happy that he had had something to do with the case earlier.

[1] Adrian Fisher would clerk for LDB during the October 1938 term.

[2] After the death of Justice Cardozo the previous month, FF's name began to be mentioned as a successor to the so-called "scholar's seat" on the Supreme Court. According to FF's memoirs, Roosevelt told him that political reasons made it impossible to give him the appointment, much as the president wanted to do so, and in fact FF supplied names of potential candidates to the White House. When Roosevelt called FF on 4 January 1939 to inform him that he was sending his name in to the Senate the following day, FF, standing in his B.V.D.'s, claimed to have been totally surprised. As Michael Parrish notes: "This image of Frankfurter, clad only in undershorts, struck dumb by Roosevelt's change of heart, has a certain romantic appeal—but it is wholly false." *Felix Frankfurter*, 275. In fact, FF set about shortly after Cardozo's death carefully orchestrating a growing campaign to put pressure on Roosevelt to name him to the Court. Tom Corcoran called FF every night to report on progress, and his many former pupils and contacts in the profession, the law schools, and government flooded the president with letters in his behalf. Key administration officials, such as Solicitor General Robert Jackson and Secretary of the Interior Harold Ickes warned Roosevelt that no one knew when another appointment might come, and with everybody expecting Roosevelt to leave office at the end of his second term, he might not have another opportunity to put his friend on the bench. Roosevelt undoubtedly had fun teasing FF that he could not appoint him, but there is little question that for several years he had been hoping to make this appointment.

[3] Sam Gilbert Bratton (1888–1963) had been a judge of the New Mexico Supreme Court for two years before being elected to a single term as United States senator from that state. In 1933, Roosevelt had appointed him to the 10th Circuit Court of Appeals.

[4] Kellogg, in a letter of 27 July, had enclosed an outline prepared by Raymond Gram Swing for a special issue of *Survey Graphic* on the problem of minorities in the world, especially political refugees. FF had responded that this was too broad a topic; the issue should focus on the refugees, especially Jews. The broader topic would take at least a book to cover, while the special issue should have a narrow focus and be hard-hitting.

[5] James Roy Newman (1907–1966) was one of the great, multifaceted geniuses of his generation. A chess prodigy and a mathematical hobbyist whose five-volume *World of Mathematics* sold thousands of copies, Newman had graduated from Columbia Law School in 1929, and then practiced in New York until 1941. There is no copy of a letter from a Newman in the FF Papers.

[6] Louis Levy was a partner in the Chadbourn firm.

[7] Snellet had written in *Commonweal* 28 (1938): 417 that Roosevelt was planning a major campaign to improve economic conditions in the South, including a large increase in WPA projects, as well as added funds for farmers.

[8] See 3 May 1938, n. 5.

No. 650 August 30, 1938 Chatham, Mass.

1. Re yours 24th. The letter to George Rublee may prove to have helped much.

2. Cazalet talked well.

---

3. Since writing the above, today's mail has come with J.T.A. report that Hitler has refused to entertain George's advances,[1] and yours of 28th reporting that Ben Cohen is leaving today for London. Fine.

4. I have not heard yet what London has done today.

5. I know of Bratton only the few opinions which came on certiorari or appeals. They impressed me favorably, as did comments on his character as Senator. But I should agree with you that Hutcheson is safer & better equipped. If F.D. does not wish to go further west than Texas H. has certainly done very good work.[2]

6. Your report on Dave Lilienthal is cheering. I can think of Arthur Morgan's performance, so far as he is concerned, only as a tragedy of one public spirited and with high purpose who is not wholly sane.[3]

7. Thanks for the report on Meredith Townsend & others.

8. I guess your meeting with Lothian will involve "a good wrangle" as he predicts.

9. It will be fine to see you & Marion on the 7th.

[1] On behalf of the Inter-Governmental Committee on Refugees, Rublee had, over British objections, tried in vain to negotiate with Germany to allow emigrating Jews to take material possessions with them.

[2] These were names FF had submitted to the president for consideration as appointees to the Supreme Court seat that eventually went to himself.

[3] On 28 July, LDB had written: "I agree that Arthur Morgan is pathological, and doesn't know when he is telling the truth."

No. 651   September 30, 1938   Washington, D.C.

1. I've wired you that I shall be glad to see Lord Wright[1] Wednesday at 6 P.M.

2. The European news is terrible & not only military action. I fear it means that the British are crumbling. It is not merely that they are unmanly, dishonorable, unwise, misled by pacifism.[2]

3. The most striking evidence of British decay I find in the report on shipping to Palestine, disclosed in the August issue of "Palestine & the Middle East."[3] Don't fail to read it promptly.

4. The Gallup poll gives a good report on you.[4]

5. Fisher is doing well, & I have succeeded in keeping him occupied.

[1] Robert Alderson Wright, Baron Wright (1869–1964) was a highly regarded jurist; he was then on a two-month visit to the United States.

[2] At the Munich conference, concluded the previous day, Great Britain and France renounced their treaty obligations to protect the territorial integrity of Czechoslovakia, and thus gave Hitler a free hand to take over the Czech Sudetenland.

[3] Wellesley Aron, "Founding a Merchant Marine," *Palestine & Middle East Economic Review* 10 (August 1938): 321, proposed developing a joint shipping venture between Great Britain and Palestine. The article noted the huge increase in tonnage entering Palestinian ports, from 982,811 in 1922 to 4,862,120 in 1937.

[4] In a public opinion poll conducted by George Gallup's American Institute of Public Opinion, FF was listed as the clear choice of lawyers to receive the next appointment to the Supreme Court. FF was the favorite of 27 percent of those polled; the next two names, Learned Hand and John W. Davis, received 5 percent each. Interestingly, FF was the favorite among both those who favored Roosevelt and those who opposed the New Deal.

No. 652   October 16, 1938   Washington, D.C.

1. Your book of Holmes lectures is a ray of light in a dark, irrational world. It is fine that the Atlantic assured a wide reading for the first, and I hope it will follow with the second in the November issue.[1]

2. F.D. went very far, in our talk, in his appreciation of the significance of Palestine, the need of keeping it whole and of making it Jewish. He was tremendously interested, and wholly surprised, on learning of the great increase in Arab population since the war, and on hearing of the plenitude of land for Arabs in Arab countries, about which he made specific enquiries. Possible refuges for Jews elsewhere, he spoke of as "satellites," and there was no specific talk of them.

3. Fisher is doing good work, and no one has been more eager than he to do his duty fully.

4. We have had two very much occupied weeks for all since the term began. McR made his first appearance on the 10th.

5. We have not seen your Dean[2] & have heard of him only in the press.

[1] FF had delivered a series of lectures on Holmes in April 1938, now published as *Mr. Justice Holmes and the Supreme Court* (Cambridge: Harvard University Press, 1938). Part of the book was published as "Justice Holmes Defines the Constitution," *Atlantic* 162 (October 1938): 484, but there was no second installment in the November issue.

[2] James Landis.

No. 653   October 17, 1938[1]   Washington, D.C.

1. Calvert Magruder's appointment as counsel[2] gives much joy to some, but, I am told, Frances [Perkins] is much displeased with the selection & the whole outfit, and that it has been "ordered out of the Labor Dept."

2. Who will take Magruder's courses?

620

3. Chamberlain's visit to H[itler] seems about his worst. Before this reaches you, war may have begun.

4. The outcome of the primary elections will not lessen the difficulties of the next Congress.[3]

5. Bikle's letter of May 23 is interesting.[4] Have you "picked out" the student as suggested?

6. I have seen none of the Justices except Black. He and she were in last Saturday in good form. The Harlans have had a most dreary time on Isle au Haut. Weather terribly bad, & no children or grandchildren to cheer them. They are not due here until the 29th.

7. Fisher is installed & hard at work.

8. What do you think of Pecora's performance?[5]

I hope you & Marion are having some good days.

[1] It is possible that this letter was actually written on 17 September 1938 and misdated by LDB.

[2] Magruder had been appointed as special counsel for the Wages and Hours Division of the Labor Department; he would be there less than a year before being appointed U.S. circuit judge.

[3] See 30 June 1938, n. 1.

[4] Biklé had suggested that FF assign one of his students to do a study of how the Fourteenth Amendment's due process clause had come to be applied to other than procedural matters. He also reported that he had taken note of FF's earlier criticism of railroads taking appeals to the Supreme Court whether or not real issues of interstate commerce were involved. Since he had taken over as general counsel for the Pennsylvania Railroad, he had put a stop to such appeals except where there was a clear case of jurisdiction.

[5] Ferdinand Pecora (1882–1971) had won fame as counsel to the Senate Committee on Banking and Finance in its 1933–1934 investigation of banking and stock market practices. At this time he was presiding over the sensational trial of former Tammany leader J. J. Hines, accused of running an illegal lottery.

No. 654   October 24, 1938   Washington, D.C.

1. We had the Evatts[1] in yesterday. They are attractive folk. I was glad the C.J. happened to come in & they had considerable talk.

2. I know nothing of Healy[2] or of Stephen;[3] Schwenbach[4] we know slightly. He has been in two or three times on a Sunday. He did not impress me as being of the caliber needed. But I know very little of him legally, or, indeed, otherwise. What is the reason why Bratton seems unavailable to F.D.?[5]

3. The American protest seems to be helpful on Palestine.[6] But the British are doing such unaccountable stupid & dishonorable things that one can't feel less troubled.

4. Calvert Magruder is having a serious time of it. He looked overworked when in yesterday.

[1] Herbert V. Evatt (1894–1965) was an Australian lawyer, and from 1930 to 1940, a member of the High Court of Australia.

[2] William Healy (1881–1962), an Idaho attorney, had been appointed the year before to the Ninth Circuit Court of Appeals.

[3] Albert Lee Stephens (1874–1965) had had a successful career in public service and on state courts in California before receiving an appointment, also in 1937, to the ninth circuit, of which he ultimately became chief judge.

[4] LDB may have meant Lewis Baxter Schwellenbach (1894–1948), another prominent westerner whom Roosevelt had been considering for a judicial appointment. He was a Seattle attorney until elected to the Senate in 1935; he later became a federal district court judge, and in 1945 President Truman named him secretary of labor.

[5] For the Supreme Court.

[6] Zionists had organized rallies all over the country protesting the British proposal to limit immigration to Palestine. Secretary of State Hull had announced that the United States must be consulted before there could be any changes in the Palestine mandate.

No. 655   November 11, 1938   Washington, D.C.

1. Yes, the result in N.Y. is good,[1] and some Democratic defeats, as in Mass., are not regrettable.[2] But Minnesota is quite serious in its Republican victory, for there the party used not an anti-Semitic whispering campaign, but the most extensive and blatant publicity.[3]

2. C.C.B. helped in New York materially. His letter to Fiorello [LaGuardia] is fine.

3. The British have again done a cravenly foolish thing, inviting representatives of the Arab kingdoms.[4] It is almost inconceivable that men of a nation which had been decent & proved itself reasonably possessed of common sense, should fall down so completely.

4. And the Germans are outdoing themselves in brutality.[5] What will the world do!?

5. It is reassuring to have Messersmith say that the State Dept. will not be lured into German economic relations.

[1] Herbert H. Lehman was elected to his fourth term as governor of New York, defeating Republican Thomas E. Dewey by 67,506 votes.

[2] Democrat James M. Curley, whom LDB had long detested, lost his bid for the governorship to Republican Leverett Saltonstall by over 100,000 votes.

[3] Republican Harold E. Stassen defeated both the Democratic candidate, Thomas Gallagher, and the incumbent, Farmer-Labor candidate Elmer Benson, to become governor of Minnesota. The campaign had been viciously fought, and the Republicans engineered a hearing before Martin Dies's House Un-American Activities Committee in October, where several witnesses claimed that the Minnesota Farmer-Labor party was dominated by Communists and taking its orders directly from Moscow.

[4] In still another effort to resolve the Palestinian problem, His Majesty's government had called for a "Round Table" conference of Jews, Arabs, and British officials to meet at St. James's palace in February 1939. The conference, as everyone expected, was a failure.

[5] In response to the shooting of a minor German official in Paris by a Jew, the Nazis unleashed

the worst attack on Jews in Germany up until that time. On 9–10 November, *Kristallnacht*, "The Night of Broken Glass," saw rampaging Nazi gangs destroy Jewish homes, businesses, and synagogues in every city in Germany.

No. 656   November 23, 1938   Washington, D.C.

1. Yes, the Sulzberger report is illuminating, but only one of many instances of the rich Jews' folly.

2. James McDonald was in, and very frank & decided about Joe Kennedy. (He thinks Myron Taylor has, despite his persistent tolerance, come to realize Joe Kennedy as well as Chamberlain.) I wrote Bob Szold fully as to this.

3. You, Armstrong [1] & Tom [Corcoran] did a good job with F.D.

4. My call on F.D. on 19th was at his request. Apparently he merely wanted to tell me what had occurred since our earlier talk & to say I should communicate with him at Warm Springs, if necessary (through Early [2] or Ben Cohen). Ben, to whom I reported that day, has doubtless reported to you. And today Ben & I concluded that he should telephone Miss LeHand that an expression of satisfaction over Palestine's readiness to take 100,000 refugees within 12 months would be desirable. [3]

5. When I saw F.D. on the 19th, he showed full appreciation of the absurdity of the British Guiana proposition [4] & the value of Palestine.

6. I hope you are keeping Tom strong on Palestine.

7. A few days ago, I read (after 20 odd years) my Faneuil Hall oration enclosed. [5] I think what is there said is the note which should be widely struck throughout America. If you agree, can you get some of your non-Jewish friends to talk or write on that subject? [6]

8. James G. McDonald thought attack on church property might come within a fortnight. [7]

9. I think he realizes the value of Palestine; he mentioned that Sulzberger can't see it.

10. Perhaps Max Warburg sees a little since his brother's imprisonment. [8]

I am glad you are obeying Hermann. [9]

[1] Hamilton Fish Armstrong (1893–1973) was the longtime editor of the prestigious journal, *Foreign Affairs*.

[2] Stephen Early (1889–1951), a former newsman, served as assistant secretary, then secretary and special assistant to Roosevelt.

[3] Roosevelt did not issue such a statement.

[4] In an effort to divert attention from Palestine, British officials had suggested that Jewish refugees might be resettled in British Guiana, a proposal condemned by all Zionist leaders.

[5] "True Americanism," delivered at Faneuil Hall on 4 July 1915, published in Harper's *Weekly* 61 (10 July 1915): 31, reprinted in *Business—A Profession*, 364–74. For details, see LDB to Norman Hapgood, 23 June 1915.

[6] No articles on the subject appeared in the popular press at this time.

[7] McDonald was incorrectly projecting the events of *Kristallnacht*, believing the Nazis would soon spread their attack against Jewish property to other religions. No wholesale confiscation of church property ever took place during the Third Reich, although from time to time specific and isolated instances did occur.

[8] Fritz Warburg (1879–1962), a banker and philanthropist, had been arrested by the Nazis, but was soon released after vociferous protests by his Christian friends.

[9] Herman Blumgart, FF's physician, had evidently given him some medical advice.

No. 657   December 14, 1938   Washington, D.C.

Re yours of 12th.

1. I am very glad you were able to have the few words with F.D. and hope it led him to mention the subject to Eden. Also, that you spoke to Rosenman.

2. You will recall my writing you last term that I think we cannot get rid of unemployment except by large increase of immigration. You have doubtless noticed press reports of Isidor Lubin on that subject before monopoly commission,[1] & of some remarks by Leon Henderson.[2] Also, that N.Y. Daily News has had 3 editorials advocating allowing 13,000,000 immigrants & that Hearst papers & Scripps-Howard have dealt with the subject. I know only papers reported. Have not seen the articles etc.

Couldn't the Times, Herald-Tribune, Fortune and others be induced to take up the subject, wholly on economic-employment lines?

[1] On 1 December, in hearings before the Temporary National Economic Committee, Lubin testified that prior to 1929, the growth of population had been a significant spur to the economy. Since natural population increase was slowing as a result of birth control and economic depression, future growth might be retarded. Henderson also supported the idea that population increase added to economic growth. For LDB's views, see 7 April 1938.

[2] Leon Henderson (1895–1986) had taught economics before entering government service as an aide to Governor Pinchot of Pennsylvania. In 1934 he joined the NRA, and later succeeded William O. Douglas at the SEC. During the war he was a division director in the Office of Price Administration.

No. 658   February 22, 1939   Washington, D.C.

1. It was good to get your first opinion—a good one.[1]

2. The Mitchell-Inness[2] letter is interesting (returned herewith). His is a fine spirit.

3. Beulah wrote me. As yet I have found only 1 letter from the Judge.[3]

4. I am sending you some copies of "True Americanism,"[4] found in our clean up, & some other papers.

That clean up required more of Fisher's time than I had expected.[5] Thanks.

We shall hope to see you soon.

[1] FF's nomination had gone through the Senate easily, and he was sworn in as associate justice on 30 January 1939. He had sent LDB the proofsheets of his first opinion, which would be handed down on 27 February. In *Hale* v. *Bimco Trading, Inc.*, 306 U.S. 375 (1939), the Court struck down a Florida statute imposing an inspection fee on cement imported from out of state sixty times greater than the fee on locally produced cement. The fee, FF declared, was clearly invalid under the commerce clause.

[2] Alfred Mitchell-Inness (1864–1950) had entered the British diplomatic service in 1890; during the First World War he had been assigned as counsel to the British Embassy in Washington, where he had come to know FF.

[3] Beulah Amidon Ratliffe (1895–1958) was writing an article on her father, who had been a friend of both FF and LDB. See "Charles Fremont Amidon, 1856–1937," *North Dakota Historical Quarterly* 8 (1941): 83; the article made no mention of letters to LDB. Beulah Amidon was an associate editor of *The Survey* for twenty-five years.

[4] See 23 November 1938, n. 5.

[5] Fisher had been selected as LDB's clerk for the October 1938 term, but on 13 February 1939, LDB sent in his resignation from the Court. His health had been deteriorating, and a severe bout of grippe incapacitated him for several weeks. On the day of LDB's retirement, FF wrote to him: "Your retirement has its poignant aspect. . . . But its dominant significance is that of triumphal accomplishment, the uttermost exertion of extraordinary powers to great ends, and unflagging serenity in fair weather and foul. The work is done, in so far as one man can do it, and others must carry on where you leave off, inspired by your example and energized by the driving force of your vast achievement." LDB's daughter Elizabeth wrote: "All the things I want to say sound mawkish—or presumptuous from me to you. I cannot bear to use any words at this time that do not ring true. . . . Measuring my words, I do not see how any one person could have done more than you have done." FF took over Fisher as his clerk for the balance of the term, but told him to devote whatever time would be necessary to help LDB clear up his papers.

No. 659   September 1, 1939   Chatham, Mass.

1. Yes, the inevitable war has come.[1] I find myself assuming that victory must come to the Democracies and wondering what kind of peace they should impose. The Versailles Treaty was, of course, a bad one, but I can't believe that it caused this war.

2. It is good to have Solomon Goldman[2] back. He should be able to do much here, and through American influence, much toward wise action on the part of Jews in Palestine. It looks as if the British would realize that the Jews are their friends and act rationally.

3. Emma Erving and Selma were here last week. Selma looking and acting as one in health, and Emma, of course, reasonably joyous.

625

4. We are planning to leave for Washington next Sunday evening (direct) on the Cape Codder.

5. Paul Freund was here recently, and mentioned casually that Magruder is to give the course on torts. Why and how was this brought about. It seems to me very regrettable.

6. And why did Francis Shea accept the Assistant Attorney General's office? Also very regrettable.

We trust all goes well with you and Marion.

Our greetings to Dr. Cohen.

[1] On this day, Hitler invaded Poland, beginning the Second World War.

[2] Solomon Goldman (1893–1953), a conservative rabbi from Chicago, served as president of the Zionist Organization of America from 1938 to 1940. LDB, according to several sources, held a very high opinion of Goldman's ability.

No. 660   September 16, 1939   Washington, D.C.

1. It will be fine to see you on the 25th.

2. You must have found here, outside the White House, much discouragement developed since you left for England.[1]

3. Have not seen Goldman yet. Expect to see him on the 18th. I suppose you read his article in the Palestine Review, which was properly frank in criticism.[2]

4. Shall be glad to have you send, or bring, the Mandates Commission report.[3] No copy has reached me.

5. There may be very few cases in the First C.C.A., but there is very much to be done to make that a worthy court, and to make Magruder a reputation as a judge. And what will he do with the salary paid by the [Harvard Law] School?

Douglas[4] is the only member of the Court whom I have seen, and have heard nothing from the others.

[1] FF had been in England earlier in the summer to accept an honorary degree from Oxford University.

[2] In "The Yishuv Stands Firm," *Palestine Review* 4 (11 August 1939): 266, Goldman criticized people who boasted of the Zionist economic growth in Palestine, and suggested that there was much to be treasured in modest growth and a simple standard of living.

[3] Following the White Paper, the League of Nations Mandate Commission held hearings on whether the new British policy squared with its mandate. On 17 August, the Commission unanimously condemned the White Paper as conflicting with the traditional interpretation of British mandatory responsibilities for Palestine.

[4] Much to LDB's satisfaction, Roosevelt had named the chairman of the Securities and Exchange Commission, William O. Douglas, to succeed him on the Court.

No. 661   February 21, 1940   Washington, D.C.

FF. Mason's letter returned herewith.[1] I have a much better opinion of him than you have, and, at Ben Flexner's suggestion, gave him leave to examine all the papers & other materials sent to Louisville. But I see no requirement that you should give him any definite answer at present. The papers on the Court cases you would, in no event, let him see; and you would not wish anyone to see those of my letters with comments on Court matters, or on any of the justices. And you would have to look over the letters to see which of them should be withheld.[2]

Joe's letter returned herewith.

[1] Alpheus T. Mason had written FF on 19 February: "With his consent and approval I am now beginning work on what may perhaps be a definitive life of Mr. Justice Brandeis. Mr. Bernard Flexner . . . tells me that you have many documents of prime value for my purpose. I should therefore like an opportunity to confer with you as to these in order to make whatever arrangements may be most suitable and convenient to you for examining them." FF wrote at the bottom of this letter: "L.D.B. I shall of course, and gladly, carry out whatever wishes you may have concerning this inquiry. But candor makes me say that my experience with Mason and the quality of his work would not lead me to select him for such a delicate and creative and art-demanding enterprise. Nor do I feel easy in turning over to him your letters during S.C. period." In the end, FF gave Mason little help, and Mason did not gain access to the Court papers.

[2] LDB had determined several years earlier to deposit his papers in the University of Louisville Law Library, and had begun shipping small amounts there. After his retirement he sent the balance, with the major exception of his Court papers which he consigned to the Harvard Law School, where they could only be used with the permission of FF, and later of Paul Freund. According to Pearl von Allmen, the late curator of the Brandeis Papers at Louisville, after LDB's death FF went to Louisville and removed many of his letters to LDB.

No. 662   July 3, 1940   Chatham, Mass.

1. Yours of the 1st comes today. I had longed to hear from you. The news national and international is indeed disturbing.[1] Harold's letter strengthens the hope that the British will not yield.[2]

2. For the Jews, the victory of our party at Pittsburgh is encouraging, and really significant.[3] It should enable us to build a worthy Z.O.A. The high merits of Dr. Solomon [Goldman] made victory possible; and Bob Szold achieved it. He exhibited his fine qualities in a great manner. But the most cheering factor is the spirit manifested by the Zionists themselves, for Bob reports that we had "80 percent of the delegates." He is sad that Stephen Wise should have gone astray, a consequence in part, at least, of his condition which we discussed.[4] Lipsky's campaign was very clever.

3. I had no doubt that the Stimson selection was your work.[5]

4. Doubtless you will feel it desirable to see F.D. at least as often as once a fortnight, as originally suggested. He will need all the comfort as well as aid possible.[6]

5. I wrote F.D. a line on leaving Washington, and he answered promptly and affectionately.[7]

[1] After a winter of stagnation on the battle lines, Germany had launched a major offensive in the spring which soon overran nearly all of western Europe, forcing Great Britain to evacuate its troops at Dunkirk.

[2] Although there is no copy of the Laski letter in the FF Papers, a letter from FF on 28 June refers to Laski's letter of the 10th, which dealt with the determination of the British people not to succumb to Hitler.

[3] At the Pittsburgh ZOA convention, Robert Szold engineered the election of an Executive Committee fully committed to a militant policy designed to achieve a Jewish state in Palestine after the war.

[4] Wise believed that with the war, unity among all Zionist groups was essential, and he became more closely allied with Chaim Weizmann, in the belief that only Weizmann retained sufficient prestige to deal with Great Britain. The militancy and anti-British sentiment of the Goldman-Szold faction disturbed him, and he withdrew for a while from active involvement in ZOA affairs.

[5] President Roosevelt had nominated Henry L. Stimson, FF's first boss and lifelong mentor, to be secretary of war. Despite his being a Republican and seventy-three years old, he had been easily approved by the Senate Military Affairs Committee on 2 July. For FF's involvement in arranging the appointment, see Max Freedman, ed., *Roosevelt and Frankfurter: Their Correspondence, 1928–1945* (Boston: Little, Brown, 1967), 523–30.

[6] FF continued to meet regularly with Roosevelt throughout the war, and to advise him on a number of issues.

[7] See LDB to Roosevelt, 14 June 1940.

No. 663   July 16, 1940   Chatham, Mass.

1. I am glad you were called to Washington, and went; & that you found F.D. "in fine shape, composed & serene." He must have had a most trying & painful period.

You predicted when I last saw you that he would have to yield.[1]

2. What you say of Willkie[2] is very disturbing. Max Lerner in his June 22 article in The Nation did well in predicting Willkie's nomination with such certainty, and also F.D.'s.[3]

3. A letter from Douglas of the 11th from Oregon says: "I am leaving in a few days for an extended fishing trip in the mountains."

4. Word came from Mrs. Stone that they are due at Isle au Haut July 25th or 28th.

5. If the British morale holds, Hitler can't overcome them by October 1st, and everything that he is doing to France and in the "neutral" countries must make the British determined to die or win. It is difficult

to see how any Britisher should want to live unless he resists Hitler successfully.

6. Knox[4] is a good friend of the Jews, and notably of Zionists. Editorially he did for us everything that Dr. Goldman asked.

[1] After the outbreak of war, pressure rose within the Democratic party for Roosevelt to seek a third term. Although the president initially claimed he was not interested, he carefully orchestrated events so that he received the nomination practically by acclamation.

[2] Wendell Lewis Willkie (1892–1944), the 1940 Republican nominee, was an extremely attractive candidate, and Roosevelt feared him. After the election, Willkie went to Europe on a fact-finding mission, and returned to become a strong supporter of Lend-Lease and other Roosevelt measures. Roosevelt wanted to bring the Willkie wing of the Republican party into a union with Democratic liberals to form a new political organization, plans cut off by the death of both men.

[3] In "F.D.R.—Next President," *The Nation* 150 (22 June 1940): 752, Lerner had predicted that the war crisis would generate a demand that Roosevelt remain in the White House. The article was part of a series on men who would be president, and Lerner also identified Willkie as the Republican candidate.

[4] Publisher William Franklin Knox (1874–1944), the Republican vice-presidential candidate in 1936, had just entered the Roosevelt cabinet as secretary of the Navy.

No. 664   July 25, 1940   Chatham, Mass.

1. F.D.'s address to the convention is noble, and convincing.[1]

2. What Walter Lippmann says is very interesting, particularly as coming from him.[2]

3. These will be three serious months. I am still convinced that the British can resist Hitler, and, if they are resolute, better days will be in sight.

4. I can't believe that the Italians will be a deciding factor.[3]

5. Wallace as a human being is fine, the best of all in sight. I don't wonder that F.D. turned to him.[4]

6. How do you explain McNutt[5] & the enthusiasm for him?

7. How do you explain Farley.?[6] Honesty has been his striking characteristic in the past long period.

With us personally all has gone well. The only interruption has been measles for Walter and Elizabeth's anxiety while it lasted. Happily he seems fully recovered.

[1] In a radio message to the Democratic National Convention on 19 July, Roosevelt had accepted the party's nomination, stating he had done so not out of political motives, but because the country demanded everyone serve as best they could. He avoided partisanship through most of the talk, emphasizing the need of all Americans to rally to the common defense. In what many characterized as a courageous move, he used the speech to announce that he would ask Congress to authorize a peacetime draft to build up the nation's military strength.

[2] Lippmann devoted his columns on 23 and 25 July to issues of national defense. In his earlier

piece, he noted that the country had finally swung its attention from details of the many domestic agencies and their politics to the importance of building up national defense. In the 25 July column he urged both candidates to eschew the usual campaign rhetoric, and instead to tell the American people the truth about world issues and the need to build up the nation's defense.

[3] Just before France fell to the German onslaught, Italy declared war on 10 June, although it would be another ten days before the Italian armies entered combat.

[4] Roosevelt had chosen his secretary of agriculture, Henry A. Wallace, to be his running mate in 1940.

[5] Paul Vories McNutt (1891–1955), an Indiana law professor, had been governor of that state from 1933 to 1937, and then held a number of federal assignments. From 1939 to 1945 he headed the Federal Security Administration.

[6] James Aloysius Farley (1888–1976) had been secretary of the New York Democratic party, and helped engineer Roosevelt's political success, especially his capture of the 1932 nomination. He was postmaster general, in charge of patronage, from 1933 to 1940. Farley opposed Roosevelt's decision to run a third time, and had hoped to capture the nomination himself.

No. 665   August 1, 1940   Chatham, Mass.

1. Your Amherst June 15 talk is uncommonly good.[1] (I like your [*] of judges' attachment to freedom of speech).

2. We are glad you did not let us miss Tawney's July 5 letter in the Times.[2] It is very fine.

3. Had Stimson any news justifying his statement (reported in Boston Herald) that England may be overcome within a month?[3] And even if he had, was it wise to give utterance to that view?

4. My faith in British ability to prevent conquest by Germany persists.

I suppose you have heard of Jonathan Goldmark's[4] astonishing achievement in his second year.

[1] FF's speech at the Amherst commencement on 14 June was printed in *Amherst Alumni Council News* 13 (July 1940): 133. FF praised the quality of American higher education, especially that available in good small colleges such as Amherst. The main theme of his talk was an appeal for reason in a world gone mad.

[2] Professor R. H. Tawney's long and eloquent letter of 5 July was published in the *New York Times* on 21 July. The letter explained to American readers exactly why Englishmen, whose hatred of war was so vehement between 1919 and 1939, now felt compelled to fight against Hitler. The war, Tawney argued, was for a life of freedom and democracy and against a twisted and evil dictatorship.

[3] In the debate over the draft bill, Stimson had told the House Military Affairs Committee that Great Britain could be overrun within thirty days, and her fleet might pass into German control, so the United States needed to beef up its defenses. The report in the *Boston Herald* of 1 August may not have been accurate, since it appears that Stimson was not making a prediction, but only describing possible scenarios in order to urge the Committee to pass the controversial peacetime draft measure.

[4] Jonathan Edwards Goldmark (d. 1979), the son of Charles Goldmark, would graduate *magna cum laude* from Harvard Law in 1941. He later settled in the State of Washington where he practiced law and engaged in ranching.

No. 666   August 18, 1940   Chatham, Mass.

1. If the reports are trustworthy, the British are doing grand fighting.[1]

2. What do you say to Willkie's acceptance speech,[2] and what will be done about it?

3. That memo on the first six in the Second Year of H.L.S. is most interesting. Friends to whom I have shown it want to know what Conant and others of Harvard, Yale and Columbia say about it; how the eastern colleges fared in earlier years; & the percentage of their students.

4. Do you happen to know why Peyton Randolph Evans[3] came to be General Counsel of the Farm Loan Bank? I was told that it was because of a difference as to policy with the President. He impressed me as a not very able, but unusually conscientious person.

5. The new Z.O.A. Executive did itself credit at the first meeting of the Committee on the 16th, and I was favorably impressed with a bunch of the "Young Turks" who were here yesterday.

[1] After the fall of France in June, Hitler turned his might on Great Britain, and the Luftwaffe began a sustained air attack to pound the British into submission. But in what has been called the Battle of Britain, the Royal Air Force managed not only to stave off the attack, but inflicted nearly twice as many casualties upon the Germans as it suffered, over 1100 Luftwaffe planes to 650 RAF fighters.

[2] Willkie accepted the Republican presidential nomination on 17 August in his home town of Elwood, Indiana. Although he endorsed the peacetime draft and material support for Great Britain, he attacked both Roosevelt's domestic and foreign policies. The New Deal had failed to bring recovery; overseas events had not elicited an appropriate response from America; and Roosevelt had failed to prepare the country's defenses should it have to meet foreign aggression.

[3] Peyton Randolph Evans (1892–1972) was a Virginia lawyer associated with numerous federal agencies; at this time he was general counsel to the Farm Credit Association.

No. 667   August 30, 1940   Chatham, Mass.

1. The Wallace speech[1] is very fine, a platform, comprehensive, direct, noble. His campaigning ought to make votes. Elizabeth read the speech to us and Paul. None of us would have changed, or omitted, a word, or have added anything.

2. That was a happy reference to Wallace in "the widening of economic opportunity through T.V.A."

3. It is good to have C.C.B.'s active support in hostile New York.

4. H.L.S. of 20th returned herewith.

5. No, I didn't give an interview in the Boston Globe. Clement Norton brought in [a] young friend, Harold Putnam, because he had been writing some articles on S.B.I. in the Hyde Park paper. We talked

generally on current matters, including Palestine; and I told them a story from a recent pro-Palestine campaign. Norton asked whether it might be repeated; and I told him Yes. It was not in the Globe. Putnam, under a misapprehension, supposed he had been authorized to talk generally.

6. I have not seen W.L.'s piece on the Willkie campaign[2] or Willkie's book;[3] haven't heard of either.

7. Elizabeth & Paul leave us on the 4th & we plan to leave for Washington direct on the 8th.

[1] The day before, Henry A. Wallace had accepted the Democratic vice-presidential nomination at Des Moines, Iowa. Entitled "The New Fight for Freedom," his speech was a thoroughgoing defense of the New Deal at home and Roosevelt's emerging policy of aid to Great Britain abroad.

[2] In his column in the *Herald-Tribune* of 27 August, Lippmann had noted that the Republican leadership in Congress thoroughly opposed Roosevelt's efforts to aid Great Britain, although Willkie, in his acceptance speech had pledged that if elected, he would help the English in their struggle. Until Willkie gained control of his party, Lippmann wrote, he could not be considered an effective leader who would then make an effective president.

[3] *This is Wendell Willkie* (New York: Dodd, Mead, and Co., 1940), consisted of a biography of the candidate by Stanley Walker, as well as a number of Willkie's speeches.

No. 668   September 8, 1940   Chatham, Mass.

1. The enclosures returned herewith are encouraging.

2. Indeed, practically all reports on the war and on F.D.-Willkie situation are so. The destroyer action went over remarkably well.[1] Willkie's protests seem very feeble.

3. But in Massachusetts the hatred for F.D. persists, and I find otherwise reasonable men who think Willkie will be elected.

4. It is fine that Magruder is doing so well.

We still plan to leave for Washing[ton] this evening.

[1] Anticipating a cross-channel invasion by the Germans, Prime Minister Winston Churchill pleaded with Roosevelt for some old World War One destroyers to police the English Channel. Fearing a straight gift would never get through Congress, Roosevelt and Churchill worked out a deal whereby the United States traded fifty destroyers in return for leases on British bases in the western Atlantic and the Caribbean. Roosevelt announced the plan on 3 September.

No. 669   August 17, 1941   Chatham, Mass.

1. The F.D.R.-Churchill meeting was skillfully arranged.[1] I am glad you think it was "all to the good." What was the real justification of the risks involved?

632

2. Monet's [sic] report is all to the good.[2] The great destruction of German U boats, captains and crews is cheering, and the continued Russian fighting hopeful.

3. We are delighted with what you report of and from C.C.B. He is performing grandly.

4. Yes, we have read Francis Hackett's book,[3] which should help much.

5. Very sorry to hear report on Ben Cohen.[4]

[1] President Roosevelt and British Prime Minister Winston Churchill had met secretly off the coast of Newfoundland during the preceding week. There they formulated the so-called Atlantic Charter setting out the goals of the peace they would seek after the war. The Charter included the famous Four Freedoms, as well as pledges that neither country sought any territorial aggrandizement.

[2] Jean Omer Marie Gabriel Monnet (1888–1979), a French political economist, was a good friend of FF, and was often consulted by Roosevelt; Monnet is credited with devising the phrase "arsenal of democracy." After the war, Monnet was the chief architect in building a European economic community, with his greatest triumph the Common Market.

[3] *What Mein Kampf Means to America* (New York: Reynal and Hitchcock, 1941).

[4] See 24 August 1941.

No. 670   August 21, 1941   Chatham, Mass.

1. The thoroughly British letter of the M.R., returned herewith, is markedly fine.

2. Harriman's[1] opinion that the Nazis are "bogged down in Russia for the winter" is encouraging. If they are, the Russians should make it a very troublesome winter, and the British a period of effective preparation and troublemaking elsewhere.

3. It would be fine to have Ben Cohen go back to England, and, if Harriman wants him much, Ben should take much satisfaction in going.

4. The months in Washington since we left it must have been very trying ones for all concerned, judging from all the comment that has come direct to us.

5. How have Wheeler et al. taken the F.D.R.-Churchill meeting.[2]

[1] William Averill Harriman (1891–1986) had headed the Union Pacific Railroad which his father had founded until he entered government service in the NRA. During the war, he was sent by Roosevelt on several missions as his representative to Britain and then to Russia, and was ambassador to both countries. He later served as Truman's secretary of commerce, director of the Mutual Security Agency, governor of New York, and personal representative of President Johnson to the Vietnam peace talks in 1968 and 1969.

[2] Following their meeting, Churchill reported to Parliament that he had offered Roosevelt aid in protecting American interests in the Far East. Senator Wheeler, who had grown into a leading and increasingly vocal isolationist, had attacked the prime minister for trying to ensnare the United States into a war with Hitler.

1. F.D.'s good judgment in resisting the appeals for Tom is most heartening.

2. Isn't Ben's unwisdom in large part the fruit of Tom's advice. [1]

3. The good reports on F.D.'s health are indeed a comfort. To have carried the burdens throughout these months is an amazing exhibition of strength. [2]

[1] There had been a growing estrangement between FF and Thomas Corcoran and, to a lesser degree, with Ben Cohen. The two men, who had enjoyed enormous success in the New Deal, began to resent FF's continued treatment of them as former students and continuing disciples. Cohen once complained to a friend: "Felix is incapable of having adult relationships!" In early 1941, it appears that Corcoran had lost some of Roosevelt's confidence, and might be forced out of the government. Cohen remained loyal to his friend, and FF worried that Cohen's services might be lost to the president.

[2] This is the last extant letter from LDB to FF. After LDB returned to Washington in the fall, the two men probably communicated in person. LDB's health, however, began to deteriorate. On 1 October, after taking a drive through Rock Creek Park, he suffered a second heart attack (the first in the late fall of 1938, had been one of the factors leading him to retire from the bench). Three days later he sank into a coma, and died at 7:15 P.M. on 5 October 1941. The following day, about fifty of his close associates and friends gathered in the family's apartment. A string quartet played selections from Beethoven, and Dean Acheson delivered a eulogy (reprinted as "Mr. Justice Brandeis," *Harvard Law Review* 55 [1941]: 191). FF concluded the service with brief remarks in which he compared LDB to Bunyan's Mr. Valiant-for-Truth and quoted: "My sword I give to him that shall succeed me in my pilgrimage, and my courage and skill to him that can get it. My marks and scars I carry with me, to be a witness for me that I have fought his battles who will now be my rewarder." At a similar service following FF's death on 22 February 1965, Paul Freund, LDB's law clerk and FF's pupil and friend, read the same passage.

Index

References are to letter numbers, not pages.
Asterisks indicate letters in which a note identifies the person named.

635

641

Philippine Islands: 7
Phillips, Herbert S.: 481*
Phillips, William: 547*
Philosophy, LDB on: 257
Phleger, Herman H.: 186*
Pinchot, Amos, articles critical of Walter
  Lippmann: 540
Pinchot, Gifford: 259*, 301
Pinchot-Ballinger Affair: 1, 147
Pinkerton v. *Wengert* (1927): 271
Pitney, Mahlon: 82*; death 173
Planters Cotton Oil Co. v. *Hopkins* (1932): 496
Podell, David Louis: 79*
Pogue, Lloyd Welch: 389*
Poland, disorder in: 225
Poletti, Charles: 555*, 623
Police activity, illegal: 230
Police power, federal invasion of state: 237
Polier, Shad: 565*
Pollak, Walter Heilprin: 176*, 221, 599
Pomerene, Atlee: 114*
Poole, Ernest: 113*
Portsmouth Harbor . . . Co. v. *U.S.* (1920):
  127
Posner, Louis Samuel: 21*
Potter, Mark Winslow: 88*, 348
Pound, Cuthbert Winfred: 118*, 211, 351
Pound, Roscoe: 5*, 29, 33, 76, 133, 158,
  173, 208, 261, 272, 277, 309, 312, 404;
  on legal education, 75; and anti-Bolshe-
  vism, 97; and criminal law professorship,
  109; plans for HLS, 165, 205, 207; rumors
  of accepting presidency of University of
  Wisconsin, 179, 207; addresses, 199, 245;
  tries to create Institute on Legislation, 322;
  seeks appointment to Crime Commission,
  365; on FF, 590; retires as dean of HLS, 590
Powell, Thomas Reed: 152*, 192, 210, 393,
  583; on minimum wage cases, 152; review
  of Beck book, 181; supports Margold ap-
  pointment, 309; articles on Commerce
  Clause, 321; satirizes Supreme Court opin-
  ions, 458
Powers, James H.: 379
Pratt, George Dwight, Jr.: 223*
Preferential union shop: 36
Prescott, William Hickling: 268*
Price maintenance: 626
Price vs. *U.S.* (1926): 214
Prince, Morton: 246*
Pritchett, Henry Smith: 140*, 250, 261
Progressive Party (1912): 4
Progressives, problems confronting: 6

Prohibition: 181; FF views on, 133; and rela-
  tion to crime, 326
Proskauer, Joseph Mayer: 535*
Prudent investment rule: 405, 441, 639
Public Institutions Hearings (1894): 262
Public service, LDB on need for ideals in: 34
Public utility holding company bill: 579, 582,
  584, 585, 586
Public works, LDB advice on: 566
Pulitzer, Joseph, endorses Landon: 609*
Pulitzer Prize, *Boston Herald* receives: 275
Pusey & Jones Co. v. *Hanssen* (1923): 126

Q
Qua, Stanley Elroy: 576*

R
Rack-renting: 211, 212, 220
R.R. Comm. of Cal. v. *L.A. R.R. Corp.* (1929):
  395
R.R. Comm. of Cal. v. *Pac. Gas & Elec. Co.*
  (1938): 630
Railroads, Hoovers plans for consolidation of:
  141; and compensation act, 314; LDB on,
  474, 504; FF on, 521
Rail strike of 1922: 99
Ramsey & Gatlin Const. Co. v. *Vincennes Bridge
  Co.* (1931): 457
Raskob, John Jacob: 323*
Ratliff, Edgar Samuel: 421*
Ratliffe, Beulah Amidon: 658*
Raushenbush, Elizabeth Brandeis: 16*, 144,
  195, 198, 220, 503, 511; ill, 123; en-
  gaged, 190; earns doctorate, 298; has son,
  321
Raushenbush, Paul Arthur: 190*, 195, 196,
  198; and Wisconsin unemployment plan,
  511; working on Wagner-Lewis bill, 579
Raushenbush, Walter Brandeis: 321*
Rayburn-Fletcher Securities Act: 535, 537
RCA v. *Raytheon Mfg. Co.* (1935): 594
Reading, Arthur K.: 310
Receivership scandal in New York: 348, 350,
  441; *World* series on, 146
Reconstruction Finance Corporation: 480;
  LDB's suggestions on, 501
Red Cross Line v. *Atl. Fruit Line* (1923): 147
Redlich, Josef: 54*, 87, 256, 312, 457, 534,
  542, 578; book reviewed by FF, 339
Reed, David Aiken: 263*, 467
Reed, James Alexander: 218*
Reed, Stanley Forman, named to Supreme
  Court: 637*, 641

654

Vare, William Scott: 226*, 321; defeated, 548
Vico, Giambattista: 193*
Vienna Bankrott (1973): 125
Villard, Oswald Garrison: 76*, 279, 369, 541; and Jews on board of *Nation,* 331
Vinson, Frederic Moore: 631*
Virginia Ry. Co. v. *U.S.* (1926): 253, 281
Vodrey, William Henry: 481*
Volstead Act: 133
Vrooman, Carl Schurz: 211*

W

Wachtell, Samuel Robert: 264*, 309, 337
Wadsworth, James Wolcott, Jr.: 169*
Waggoner Estate v. *Wichita County* (1927): 262
Wagner, Robert Francis: 351*, 532
Wagner-Lewis bill: 577, 578, 582
Wait, William Cushing: 270*
Wales, Robert Willett: 470* '
Walker, James J.: 507*
Wallace, Henry Agard: 527*, 573, 578; FDR's running mate, 664; acceptance speech, 667
Wallace, Henry Cantwell: 134*
Wallas, Graham: 23*, 239, 263, 273
Walsh, David A.: 519
Walsh, David Ignatius: 169*, 243, 259; on court jurisdiction, 331; reelected, 342
Walsh, Frank Patrick: 374*
Walsh, Thomas James: 113*, 178, 216, 218, 231, 297, 399, 520
Wambaugh, Eugene: 219*
Wampler v. *Lecompte* (1930): 446
Wan v. *U.S.* (1924): 167, 231, 385
Warburg, Felix: 381, 382*, 437, 445, 464; and Palestine cooperation, 384, 385; resigns Jewish Agency in protest against British policy, 435
Warburg, Fritz: 656*
Warburg, Paul Moritz: 368*
War Finance Corporation Act: 92
Warner, Sam Bass: 313*
Warren, Bentley Wirt: 278*
Warren, Charles: 97*, 118, 135, 182, 234; and narcotics cases, 186
Warren, Charles Beecher: 186*
Warren, Edward Henry: 315*
Warren, Joseph: 393*
Warren, Samuel Dennis: 589*
Warren will case, and LDB confirmation: 11
Washington Naval Conference: 80, 82
Washington-Southern Nav. Co. v. *Balt. & Phila. St. Co.* (1923): 144
Washington v. *Dawson* (1923): 147

Watson, Albert Leisenring: 389*
Watson v. *State Comptroller of N.Y.* (1920): 120
Watts, Sidney S.: 505*
Wauchope, Arthur Grenfell: 610*
Webb, Beatrice Potter: 172*
Webb-Kenyon Act: 130, 264
Webb, Nathan: 149*
Webb, S. and B., *Decay of Capitalist Civilization:* 125
Webb, Sidney (Lord Passfield): 172*
Webb v. *O'Brien* (1923): 135
Wedgwood, Josiah Clement: 624*
Wehle, Louis Brandeis: 113*, 639
Weiss v. *Weiner* (1929): 364
Weizmann, Chaim: 25*, 256, 256, 297, 624, 635; tension with LDB, 31, 42; LDB on, 53, 261; breaks off negotiations with ZOA, 62; meets with LDB, 250; meeting with Prime Minister, 437; resigns World Zionist Organization position in protest, 445
Weizmann-Lipsky policies, LDB on: 379
Welliver, Judson Churchill: 204*
Wells, Herbert George: 72*, 79
Wells, Philip Patterson: 209*, 301
West Coast Hotel v. *Parrish* (1937): 618
Western Union Tel. Co. v. *Esteve Bros.* (1921): 191
West Virginia, labor strife in: 38, 47, 66
Wetting, Frank B.: 182
Wheat, Alfred Adams: 176*, 309, 311, 354
Wheat, Carl Irving: 202*
Wheeler, Burton Kendall: 119*, 152, 217, 297, 631, 670; indictment, 157, visits with LDB, 158; prosecutions against dropped, 211
White, Edward Douglass, illness of: 46; death, 66
White, Sir Alfred Frederick: 226
White, William Allen: 115, 121, 331, 550; letter to FF, 613
Whitehead, Alfred North: 267*, 271; on education, 365
White Paper, postponed: 605
White v. *Sparkill Realty Co.* (1930): 409, 410
Whitney, Anita, pardoned: 286
Whitney, Edward Baldwin: 110*
Whitney v. *California* (1927): 221, 279
Wickersham, George W., named head of Crime Commission: 372; first statement as head of Commission, 375; on prohibition, 377, 415; and problems of Commission, 403
Wickersham Commission: 356
Wideman, Francis James: 597*

657

tion of, 21; and need for counsel, 21; conference (1920), 30, 32, 37; contributions to WZO, 52; growing rift with World Zionist Organization, 58; Cleveland convention (1921), 67, 68; situation at end of 1930, 445; new leadership, 662, 666

Zucht v. *King* (1922): 114, 174

Zuckermann, William: 434*